RAWSON'S

Dictionary of

Euphemisms

and Other

Doubletalk

Also by Hugh Rawson
Devious Derivations
Wicked Words
The New International Dictionary of Quotations
(with Margaret Miner)
A Dictionary of Quotations from Shakespeare
(with Margaret Miner)
A Dictionary of Quotations from the Bible
(with Margaret Miner)
An Investment in Knowledge
(with Hillier Krieghbaum)

RAWSON'S

Dictionary of

Euphemisms

and Other

Being a Compilation of Linguistic
Fig Leaves and Verbal Flourishes for
Artful Users of the English Language

Doubletalk

REVISED EDITION

HUGH RAWSON

Crown Publishers, Inc.

New York

Published by Crown Publishers, Inc., 201 East 50th Street, New York, New York 10022. Member of the Crown Publishing Group.

Random House, Inc. New York, Toronto, London, Sydney, Auckland

CROWN is a trademark of Crown Publishers, Inc.

Manufactured in the United States of America

Library of Congress Cataloging-in-Publication Data
Rawson, Hugh.
    Rawson's dictionary of euphemisms and other doubletalk: being a compilation of linguistic fig leaves and verbal flourishes for artful users of the English language/ Hugh Rawson.
        p. cm.
    1. English language—Euphemism—Dictionaries.   2. English language—Synonyms and antonyms.   3. English language—Jargon—Dictionaries.   4. English language—Slang—Dictionaries.
5. English language—Terms and phrases.   I. Title.
PE1449.R34   1995
423'.1—dc20   95-30759
                                                            CIP

ISBN 0-517-70201-0

10   9   8   7   6   5   4   3   2   1

First Revised Edition

For Margaret

Acknowledgments
and a Request

Most sources are given in the text, but the influence of a few is so pervasive as to require special acknowledgment. First is *The Oxford English Dictionary*, edited by Sir James Murray, which I have used in the compact (micrographically reproduced) edition, published by Oxford University Press in 1971. *The Oxford English Dictionary* is a monument to the English language and it is hard to imagine any other dictionary—or compilation of euphemisms—being made without continually consulting it, as well as its four-volume supplement (1972–86), edited by R. W. Burchfield. Nearly as well thumbed were *A Dictionary of American English on Historical Principles* (Sir William A. Cragie and James R. Hurlburt, eds., University of Chicago Press, 1938–44, four volumes) and *A Dictionary of Americanisms* (Mitford M. Mathews, University of Chicago Press, 1951, two volumes).

Also of great use were various works on slang: *The American Thesaurus of Slang* (Lester V. Berrey and Melvin Van den Bark, Thomas Y. Crowell, 1953), *New Dictionary of American Slang* (Robert L. Chapman, ed., Harper & Row, 1986), *College Slang 101* (Connie Eble, Spectacle Lane Press, 1989), *A Dictionary of Soldier Talk* (Col. John R. Elting, Sgt. Mjr. Dan Cragg, and Sgt. First Class Ernest L. Deal, Charles Scribner's Sons, 1984), *Slang and Its Analogues* (J. S. Farmer and W. E. Henley, 1890–1904, Arno Press,

1970), *A Classical Dictionary of the Vulgar Tongue* (Capt. Francis Grose, ed., and annotated by Eric Partridge, Barnes & Noble, 1963), *The Underground Dictionary* (Eugene E. Landy, Simon and Schuster, 1971), *Random House Historical Dictionary of American Slang* (J. E. Lighter, ed., Random House, volume I, 1994), *A Dictionary of Slang and Unconventional English* (Eric Partridge, Macmillan, 1970), *Slang and Euphemism* (Richard A. Spears, Penguin Books, 1991), *Dictionary of American Slang* (Harold Wentworth and Stuart Berg Flexner, Thomas Y. Crowell, 1975), and *Playboy's Book of Forbidden Words* (Robert A. Wilson, ed., Playboy Press, 1972).

Other books that were kept close at hand include the *Third Barnhart Dictionary of New English* (Robert K. Barnhart and Sol Steinmetz, eds., with Clarence L. Barnhart, H. W. Wilson, 1990), *The Barnhart Dictionary of Etymology* (Robert K. Barnhart, ed., H. W. Wilson, 1988), the *Dictionary of American Regional English,* Frederick G. Cassidy, ed., Harvard University Press, volumes I and II, 1985 and 1991), *I Hear America Talking* (Stuart Berg Flexner, Van Nostrand Reinhold, 1976), *Listening to America* (Stuart Berg Flexner, Simon and Schuster, 1982), *Language of the Underworld* (David W. Maurer, University Press of Kentucky, 1981), *The American Language* (H. L. Mencken, Alfred A. Knopf, 1936, plus its supplements of 1945 and 1948, and the one-volume abridged edition, Raven I. McDavid, Jr., ed., with David W. Maurer, 1963), *The Joys of Yiddish* (Leo Rosten, Washington Square Press, 1970), and *Safire's Political Dictionary* (William Safire, Random House, 1978).

Books that provided useful background include *Mrs Grundy* (Peter Fryer, Corgi Books, 1963), *Personalities of Language* (Gary Jennings, Thomas Y. Crowell, 1965), *Doublespeak* (William Lutz, HarperPerennial, 1990), *You English Words* (John Moore, J. B. Lippincott, 1962), *Dr. Bowdler's Legacy* (Noel Perrin, David R. Godine, 1992), *Down in the Holler* (Vance Randolph and George P. Wilson, University of Oklahoma Press, 1953), *The Anatomy of Dirty Words* (Edward Sagarin, Lyle Stuart, 1962), and *In Praise of English* (Joseph T. Shipley, Times Books, 1977).

Periodicals of especial value included *American Speech* (University of Alabama Press for the American Dialect Society), *Quarterly Review of Doublespeak* (National Council of Teachers of English), and *Maledicta* (Maledicta Press).

All quotations from the Bible come from the Authorized or King James Version of 1611. Dates for earliest uses of words come from *The Oxford English Dictionary* unless otherwise specified. Dates for quotations from films come from the annually published *Leonard Maltin's Movie & Video Guide.*

I am indebted to many people: to Patrick Barrett and Margaret Miner for having read manuscript versions of this book; to Gladys Garrastegui, Irene Goodman, Cynthia Kirk, and Karen Trachtman, for typing the manuscript of the first edition in the pre–personal computer age; to Julie Hansen and Julia Moskin for suggestions on updating the first edition; to Tim Beard and the staff of Minor Memorial Library in Roxbury, Connecticut, for help in tracking quotes to sources; to Bar-

bara Livesey, for keeping an eye out for books she knew would be useful to me, and to Brandt Aymar, senior editor, and Kim Hertlein, senior production editor, at Crown Publishers, for shepherding the manuscript of both editions through to publication.

Many individuals have contributed euphemisms, complete with dated citations, or made suggestions that led to entries that are now tied to written sources. I am most grateful to all. Notes on some suggestions were made in the field, so to speak, on the backs of envelopes or other scraps of paper, and it is too much to hope that my records are complete. I apologize to anyone whose name has been left off the following list: Susan Arensberg, Bernard Arkules, Roger Ashling-Treadwell, Betty Bennett, Herman Bogarty, Rebecca L. Brite, Tom Burnam, Joseph Burtell, Ann Close, Robert W. Creamer, Steve Curtin, John Creighton, John L. Cutler, Ronald V. Dahlquist, Philip E. Devine, Douglas M. Dick, David S. Evans, John D. Fitzgerald, William Fuller, Lucille B. Gaignault, Jonathon Green, Hamilton Gregory, Richard Gross, Keith Haight, Maureen Haight, George Haessler, Henry M. Heide, Paul Heacock, Paul Hoffman, George Johnson, Irwin H. Kaiser, Charlotte Koskoff, David Koskoff, Isa Lang, Janet Levoff, Howard E. McCormick, Bob Nadder, Mary Beth A. Otto, William E. Overall, Thomas M. Paikeday, Max C. Peterson, Judith Preble, A. Reader, Christian Robertson, Richard Rubenstein, Elizabeth Rutledge, Mary Sagarin, Lee Sheppard, Richard D. Silberman, Kenneth Silverman, Sidney Sisk, Muriel Smith, A. A. Stone, Matthew Tallmer, Darlene Townsend, Roy Wilder, Jr., Gene Wolfe, and Mark Zollar.

In the hope that this book will go into yet another edition, readers are invited to send new examples of euphemisms, circumlocutions, and doubletalk to me, care of Crown Publishers, Inc., 201 East 50th Street, New York, New York 10022. All contributions will be valued, but those that include complete citations, with author, title, date of publication, and page number, will be especially appreciated.

Hugh Rawson
Roxbury, Connecticut
May 1995

The tongue of man is a twisty thing,
   there are plenty of words there
of every kind, the range of words is wide,
   and their variance.
       —*The Iliad of Homer,* ca. 750 B.C.
       Richmond Lattimore, trans., 1951

There is nothing unclean of itself:
but to him that esteemth any thing
to be unclean, to him it is unclean.
       —*Romans,* 14:14, ca. A.D. 56
       King James Version, 1611

R A W S O N ' S
Dictionary of
Euphemisms
and Other
Doubletalk

Introduction

On the FOP Index & Other Rules of Life
in the Land of Euphemism

Mr. Milquetoast gets up from the table, explaining that he has to go to the *little boys' room* or *see a man about a dog*; a woman announces that she is *expecting*. A secretary complains that her boss is a pain in the *derrière*; an undertaker (or *mortician*) asks delicately where to ship the *loved one*. These are euphemisms—mild, agreeable, or roundabout words used in place of coarse, painful, or offensive ones. The term comes from the Greek *eu*, meaning "well" or "sounding good," and *phēmē*, "speech."

Many euphemisms are so delightfully ridiculous that everyone laughs at them. (Well, almost everyone: The people who call themselves the National Selected Morticians usually manage to keep straight faces.) Yet euphemisms have very serious reasons for existing. They conceal the things people fear the most—death, the dead, the supernatural. They cover up the facts of life —of sex and reproduction and excretion— which inevitably remind even the most refined people that they are made of clay, or worse. They are beloved by individuals and institutions (governments, especially) who are anxious to present only the handsomest possible images of themselves to the world. And they are embedded so deeply in our language that few of us, even those who pride themselves on being plain-spoken, ever get through a day without using them.

The same sophisticates who look down their noses at *little boys' room* and other euphemisms of that ilk will nevertheless say that they are going to the *bathroom* when no bath is intended; that Mary has been *sleeping around* even though she has been getting precious little shut-eye; that John has *passed away* or even *departed* (as if he'd just made the last train to Darien); and that Sam and Janet are *friends*, which sounds a lot better than "unmarried lovers" or, as people used to say, "living in sin."

Thus, euphemisms are society's basic *lingua non franca.* As such, they are outward and visible signs of our inward anxieties, conflicts, fears, and shames. They are like radioactive isotopes. By tracing them, it is possible to see what has been (and is) going on in our language, our minds, and our culture.

Euphemisms can be divided into two general types—positive and negative. The positive ones inflate and magnify, making the euphemized items seem altogether grander and more important than they really are. The negative euphemisms deflate and diminish. They are defensive in nature, offsetting the power of tabooed terms and otherwise eradicating from language everything that people prefer not to deal with directly.

Positive euphemisms include the many fancy occupational titles, which salve the egos of workers by elevating their job status: *access controller* for doorman, *associate* for salesclerk, *custodian* for *janitor* (itself a euphemism for caretaker), the many kinds of *engineer* (*exterminating engineer, mattress engineer, publicity engineer,* ad infinitum), *help* for *servant* (itself an old euphemism for slave), *working girl* for whore, *vice president* for a middle manager (an especially vacuous title when, as often happens, a company lists a couple hundred *vice presidents* on its roster), and so on. A common approach is to try to turn one's trade into a profession, usually in imitation of the medical profession. *Beautician* and the aforementioned *mortician* are the classic examples, but the same imitative instinct is responsible for social workers calling welfare recipients *clients,* for football coaches conducting *clinics,* and for undertakers referring to corpses as *cases* or even *patients.*

Other kinds of positive euphemisms include personal honorifics such as *colonel, doctor, the honorable,* and *major,* as well as the many institutional euphemisms, which convert madhouses into *mental hospitals,* hospitals into *medical centers,* colleges into *universities,* and small business establishments into *emporiums, parlors, salons, shoppes,* and *studios.* The desire to improve one's surroundings is evident, too, in geographical place names, most prominently in the case of the distinctly nongreen *Greenland* (attributed to an early real estate developer named Eric the Red), but also in the designation of many small burgs as *cities;* in the names of some cities, such as *Troy,* New York (originally Vanderheyden's Ferry, its name change in 1789 started a fad for adopting classical place names in the United States); and in the advertising of housing tracts as *enclaves* and *plantations.*

Negative, defensive euphemisms are extremely ancient. It was the Greeks, for example, who transformed the Furies into the *Eumenides* (the Kindly Ones). In many cultures, it is forbidden to pronounce the name of God (hence, pious Jews say *Adonai*) or of Satan (giving rise to *the deuce, the good man, the great fellow,* the generalized *Devil,* and many other roundabouts). The names of the dead, and of animals that are hunted or feared, may also be euphemized this way. The bear is called *grandfather* by many peoples and the tiger is alluded to as the *striped one.* The common motivation seems to be a confusion between the names of things and the things themselves: The name is viewed as an extension of the thing. Thus, to know the name is to give one power over the thing (as in the Rumpelstiltskin story). But such power may be dangerous: "Speak of the Devil and he appears." For mere mortals, then, the safest policy is to use another name, usually a flattering, euphemistic one, in place of the supernatural being's true name.

As strong as—or stronger than—the taboos against names are the taboos against particular words, especially the infamous *four-letter words.* (According to a 1978 Supreme Court decision, the set of *four-letter words* actually contains some words with as few as three and as many as twelve letters, but the logic of Supreme Court decisions is not always immediately apparent.) These words form part of the vocabulary of practically everyone above the age of six or seven. They are not slang terms, but legitimate Standard English of the oldest stock, and they are euphemized in many ways, typically by conversion into pseudo-Latin (e.g., *copulation, defecation, urination*), into slang (*make love, number two, pee*), or into socially acceptable dashes (*f – – –, p – – –, s – – –*). In the electronic media, the function of the dash is fulfilled by the *bleep* (sometimes pronounced *blip*), which has completed the circle and found its way into print.

The taboo against words frequently degenerates into mere prudery. At least—though the defensive principle is the same—the primitive (or *preliterate*) hunter's use of *grandfather* seems to operate on a more elemental level than the excessive modesty that has produced *abdomen* for belly, *afterpart* for ass, *bosom* for breast, *limb* for leg, *white meat* for breast (of a fowl), and so on.

When carried too far, which is what always seems to happen, positive and negative euphemisms tend to coalesce into an unappetizing mush of elegancies and genteelisms, in which the underlying terms are hardly worth the trouble of euphemizing, e.g., *ablutions* for washing, *bender* for knee, *dentures* for false teeth, *expectorate* for spit, *home* for house, *honorarium* for fee, *ill* for sick, *libation* for drink, *perspire* for sweat, *position* for job, *unmentionables* for trousers and underwear, etc.

Many euphemisms, whether positive or negative, are used unconsciously, without intent to evade or deceive. This is because they developed so long ago that hardly anyone remembers the original motivation. Examples include such now-standard terms as *cemetery* (from the Greek word for "sleeping place," it replaced the more deathly "graveyard"), and the names of various barnyard animals, including the *donkey* (the erstwhile ass), the *sire* (or studhorse), and the *rooster* (for cock, and one of many similar evasions, such as *haystack* for haycock, *weather vane* for weathercock, and Louisa May *Alcott*, whose father changed the family name from the nasty-sounding Alcox). Similarly, *cripes, Jiminy Cricket, gee, gosh,* and other watered-down swear words are commonly used, particularly by youngsters and by those who fill in the balloons in comic strips, without much awareness that they were created to replace sacred names. Then there are the terms for which no honest *Anglo-Saxon* (often a euphemism for "dirty") equivalents exist, such as *brassiere,* which has hardly anything to do with the French *bras* (arm) from which it derives, and *toilet,* from the diminutive of *toile* (cloth). These words are unavoidable in daily discourse.

Other euphemisms are employed consciously, and they constitute a much more complex category—hardly surprising, given the ingenuity, not to say the deviousness, of the human mind. Which is not to imply that euphemisms cannot be employed more or less honestly as well as knowingly. For example, garbagemen are upgraded routinely into *sanitation* men, but to say "Here come the sanitation men" is a comparatively venial sin. The meaning does come across intelligibly, and the listener understands that it is time to get out the garbage cans (or *waste management bags,* if you prefer). By the same token, it is honest enough to offer a woman condolences upon "the loss of her husband," where *loss* stands for death. Not only are amenities preserved, by avoiding the troublesome term, the euphemism actually facilitates communication at a difficult time.

Conscious euphemisms also lead to double-thinking, however. They form a kind of code. The euphemism stands for something else, and everyone pretends that the "something else" doesn't exist. The intention may seem to be noble; for example, to use language to turn people's thoughts into politically correct channels—to eliminate sexism by replacing freshmen with *freshpeople* and waiters with *waitrons,* to downplay the hardships of being *physically challenged,* or to rewrite history as *herstory.* As commendable as some of these goals may be, it is this characteristic of euphemisms—their ability to soften the world's hard edges—that also makes them attractive to people and institutions who have something to hide, who don't want to say what they are thinking, and who wish to lie about what they are doing.

It is at this point, where speakers and writers seek not so much to avoid offense as to deceive, that we pass into the universe of dishonest euphemisms, where the conscious elements of circumlocution and doubletalk loom large. Here are the murky worlds of the CIA, the FBI, and the military, where murder is translated into *executive action,* an illegal break-in into a *black bag job,* napalm into *soft* or *selective ordnance,* and bombers into *weapons systems* that *visit a site* or *service a target.* Here are the Wonderlands in which Alice would feel so much at home: advertising, where small becomes *medium* if not *large;* big business, where workers are *dehired* as corporations *rightsize* themselves; small business, where corner laundries brag of being *world-class* outfits; and politics, where gross errors are passed off as *misspeaking,* where lies are *inoperative* statements, where candidates practice *comparative* (not "negative") *campaigning,* and where tax increases are presented to the public as *revenue enhancements* or *user fees.* (Not a new phenomenon: Plutarch credited Solon, an Athenian of the sixth century B.C., with sugarcoating taxes by describing them as *contributions.*)

Here, too, are our great industries: the prison business, where solitary confinement cells are disguised as *adjustment centers, quiet cells,* or *seclusion;* the atomic power business, where smallish accidents are *abnormal occurrences* or simple *events,* while worse ones are *core rearrangements* or *energetic disassemblies;*

the airline business, where planes that crash are said to make *hard landings,* while those that ditch make *water landings;* and, finally, of murder on its largest scale, where people are put into *protective custody* (imprisonment) in *concentration camps* (prison camps) as a first step toward achieving the *Final Solution* (genocide).

George Orwell wrote in a famous essay ("Politics and the English Language," 1946) that "political language . . . is designed to make lies sound truthful and murder respectable, and to give an appearance of solidity to pure wind." His dictum applies equally through the full range of dishonest euphemisms. Nearly 2,400 years before Orwell, the Greek historian Thucydides noted the same effect in equally corrosive terms. Political stresses, he pointed out in the *History of the Peloponnesian War,* distorted the language:

> To fit in with the change of events, words, too, had to change their usual meanings. What used to be described as a thoughtless act of aggression was now regarded as the courage one would expect to find in a party member; to think of the future and wait was merely another way of saying one was a coward; any idea of moderation was just an attempt to disguise one's unmanly character; ability to understand a question from all sides meant that one was totally unfitted for action. Fanatical enthusiasm was the mark of a real man, and to plot against an enemy behind his back was perfectly legitimate self-defense. Anyone who held violent opinions could always be trusted, and anyone who objected to them became a suspect. [tr. Rex Warner.]

Dishonest doubletalk is doubly danger-ous: Besides deceiving those on the receiv-ing end, it helps the users—as Thucydides implied—fool themselves into justifying their actions, no matter what. In our own time, this effect was noted by President Nixon's erstwhile *counsel* (read: "lawyer") John W. Dean III: "If . . . Richard Nixon had said to me, 'John, I want you to do a little crime for me. I want you to obstruct justice,' I would have told him he was crazy and disappeared from sight. No one thought about the Watergate cover-up in those terms—at first, anyway. Rather, it was 'containing' Watergate or keeping the defendants 'on the reservation' or coming up with the right public relations 'sce-nario' and the like" (*New York Times*, 4/6/75). And as the Senate Intelligence Committee observed in 1975, after wading through a morass of euphemisms and circumlocutions in its investigation of American plots to kill foreign leaders: "'Assassinate,' 'murder,' and 'kill' are words many people do not want to speak or hear. They describe acts which should not even be proposed, let alone plotted. Failing to call dirty business by its rightful name may have increased the risk of dirty business being done."

Imprecise language may have other, unintended consequences. For example, the Senate Intelligence Committee learned that CIA records contained numerous ref-erences to "disposing of Castro" or "doing something about Castro." Depending on context, the meanings of these elliptical phrases could be interpreted either in the narrow sense of killing Castro or in the broader sense of dislodging his govern-ment. The vagueness of the language led the agency's own inspector general to con-clude that "in a situation wherein those

speaking may not have actually meant what they seemed to say or may not have said what they actually meant, they should not be surprised if their oral short-hand is interpreted differently than it was intended."

The parallel is hard to escape: Henry II may not have meant that Thomas à Becket, Archbishop of Canterbury, should be killed when he exclaimed, according to the tradi-tional account, "Will no one rid me of this turbulent priest?" Four of his knights thought this was what he wanted, however, and they proceeded to murder the arch-bishop in his cathedral.

Euphemisms are in a constant state of flux. New ones are created almost daily. Many of them prove to be nonce terms—one-day wonders that are never repeated. Of those that are ratified through reuse as true euphemisms, some may last for genera-tions, even centuries, while others fade away or become unconscious euphemisms, still used, but reflexively, without thought of their checkered origins. The ebb and flow of euphemisms is governed to a large extent by two basic rules: Gresham's Law of Language and the Law of Succession.

In monetary theory, where it originated, Gresham's Law can be summarized as "bad money drives out good," meaning that debased or underweight coins will drive good, full-weight coins out of circulation because people will tend to hoard the latter. (By the by: Though Sir Thomas Gresham, 1519–1579, has gotten all the credit, the effect was noticed and explained by earlier monetary experts, including Nicolaus Kop-pernick, 1473–1543, who doubled as an astronomer and who is better known as Copernicus.) In the field of language, it is the "bad" meanings or associations of words that tend to drive competing "good" meanings out of circulation. Thus, *coition, copulation,* and *intercourse* once were general terms for, respectively, coming together, coupling, and communication, but after the words were drawn into service as euphemisms, their sexual meanings became dominant, so that the other senses are hardly ever encountered nowadays. The same thing happened to *crap* (once a general term for chaff, residue, or dregs), *feces* (also dregs, as of wine or salad oil), and *manure* (literally "to work with the hands").

Gresham's Law remains very much in force, of course. Witness what has happened within recent times to *gay,* where the meaning "homosexual" has preempted all others. The law is by no means limited to euphemisms, and its application to other words helps explain why some euphemisms are formed. Thus, the incorrect and pejorative uses of "Jew" as a verb and adjective caused many people, Jews as well as Gentiles, to shift to *Hebrew* even though that term should, in theory, be reserved for the Jews of ancient times or their language. A similar example is "girl," whose pejorative meanings have come to the fore as women have become liberated, with the result that anxiety-ridden men sometimes fall into the worse error of referring to their *lady* friends.

Gresham's Law is the engine that powers the second of the two great euphemistic principles: the Law of Succession. After a euphemism becomes tainted by association with its underlying "bad" word, people will tend to shun it. For example, the seemingly innocent *occupy* was virtually banned by polite society for most of the seventeenth and eighteenth centuries because of its use as a euphemism for engaging in sex. (A man might be said to *occupy* his wife or

to go to an *occupying* house.) Once people begin to shun a term, it usually is necessary to develop a new euphemism to replace the one that has failed. Then the second term will become tainted and a third will appear. In this way, chains of euphemisms evolve. Thus, "mad'" has been euphemized successively as *crazy, insane, lunatic, mentally deranged,* and just plain *mental,* while "dull" has turned into *retarded* and then *exceptional.* Then there are the poor and backward nations that have progressed, so to speak, from *underdeveloped* to *developing* to *emergent.* (*Fledgling* nations never really took hold despite the imprimatur of Eleanor Roosevelt.) This rule also applies to racial designations. Thus, successive generations of black Americans have preferred to be known as *colored people, Negroes, blacks,* and *African-Americans,* the rising generations asserting themselves by casting off the terms associated with their parents.

Extraordinary collections of euphemisms have formed around some topics over the years as a result of the continual creation of new terms, and it seems safe to say that the size of any collection reflects the strength of the underlying taboo. Nowhere is this more evident than in the case of the *private parts,* male and female, whose Anglo-Saxon names are rarely used in mixed company, except by those who are on intimate terms. Thus, the monumental *Slang and Its Analogues* (J. S. Farmer and W. E. Henley, 1890–1904) lists some 650 synonyms for *vagina,* most of them euphemistic, and about half that number for *penis.* (These are just the English synonyms; for *vagina,* for example, Farmer and Henley include perhaps another 900 synonyms in other languages.) Other anatomical parts that have inspired more than their share of euphemisms include the *bosom, bottom, limb,* and *testicles.* All forms of sexual *intercourse* and the subjects of *defecation, urination,* and the *toilet* also are richly euphemistic, as are *menstruation* (well over 100 terms have been noted), all aspects of death and dying (or *passing away*), and disease. It used to be *TB;* the sexual and *social diseases;* and cancer, a.k.a. *the big C,* or a *long illness,* that were euphemized; today, in discussions of AIDS, troublesome words tend to be avoided with references to exchanges of *bodily fluids,* to *people with AIDS* ("victim" is not politically correct), and to the risks of being *sexually active* ("promiscuous" is too "judgmental").

The incidence of euphemisms may also reflect society's ambivalent feelings on certain subjects. Alcohol, for example, is responsible for a great many euphemisms. The appendix to the *Dictionary of American Slang* (1976) includes more synonyms for "drunk"—a total of 356—than for any other term. The practice of punishing criminals with death (*capital punishment*) also makes many people uncomfortable, judging from the number of linguistic evasions for it, both in the United States, where the electric chair may be humorously downplayed as *Ol' Sparky* or the *hot seat,* as well as in other countries, such as France, where the condemned are introduced to *Madame, la guillotine.* Meanwhile, the so-called victimless crime of prostitution has inspired an inordinate number of euphemisms. This book lists well over 100 under *prostitute,* a sixteenth-century Latinate euphemism for "whore," which itself may have begun life as a euphemism for some now-forgotten word, the Old English *hōre* being cognate with the Latin *cara,* darling. The precarious position of *people of color,* a.k.a. *minorities,* and other oft-oppressed groups, such as homosexuals, servants, and women, also is revealed by the variety of terms that have been devised to characterize them.

Just as the clustering of euphemisms around a given term or topic appears to reflect the strength of a particular taboo, so the unusual accumulation of euphemisms around an institution is strongly indicative of interior rot. Thus, the Spanish Inquisition featured an extensive vocabulary of words with double meanings (e.g., *auto-da-fé* for act of faith, and *the question* for torture). In our own time, the number of euphemisms that have collected around the CIA and its *capers* (plots to overthrow foreign governments), the prison business and its noncorrectional *correctional facilities,* the educational industry and its *learning facilitators* (teachers), the medical establishment with its diagnostic *misadventures* (mistakes), and the *Defense* (not War) *Department,* all tend to confirm one's darker suspicions.

The usual assumption is that most of our standard euphemisms for sex, death, reproduction, and other physical functions come from the Victorian era. But this is not so. A great many of the euphemisms that are associated most closely with Victorianism —*bosom, limb,* and *unmentionables,* for instance—actually were popularized prior to the start of Victoria's reign in 1837.

The beginning of the period of pre-Victorian prudery is hard to date—as are most developments in language. Normally, it is only possible to say, on the basis of a quotation from a book, play, poem, letter, journal, newspaper, or other piece of writing that such-and-such word or phrase was being used in such-and-such way when that particular work was composed. But there is no guarantee that the dictionary-maker—or compiler of euphemisms—has found the earliest example. Also, many words, especially slang words, may be used informally for a long time, perhaps centuries, before they are committed to writing of any kind, let alone the sort of document that is likely to be preserved for future generations. As a result, one can only say that fastidiousness in language became increasingly common from about 1750, and that this trend accelerated around the turn of that century, almost as if the incipient Victorians were preparing with ever greater urgency for Her ascent to the throne.

One of the first indications of the new niceness of the eighteenth century is the increasing use of dashes in printed matter. For example, in the early 1700s, Sir Richard Steele could print "damn" in *The Tatler*, but by mid-century the oath was being rendered as *d – – –* or *d – – n* in the works of Henry Fielding, Tobias Smollett, and others. Then there were the high jinks toward the start of the century at Queen Anne's court, where maids of honor thought it great fun to trick someone into asking a question to which they could give a particularly rude answer. (Example: Woman runs into a room, crying in fright, "It is white and follows me," and if asked by some dunderhead what "it" is, replies "Mine arse!" This was called "selling a bargain.") But when the original Joe Miller's joke book was published in 1739, the low word came out as "A – – – " or "a – se" (and "breast" as "– – – – –").

The increase in prudery also is revealed by the coining of new words and the application of older words in new, euphemistic ways. The earliest known use of *drumstick*, in the sense of a leg or *limb*, comes from 1764; the first *rooster* (to avoid "cock") from 1772, and the original *donkey*

(to avoid "arse," pronounced "ass") from 1785. New Englanders had begun converting "damn" into *darn* by the 1770s, while the water pepper plant, formerly known as arsemart or ass-smart, blossomed into *smart weed* by 1787. During the 1790s, women improved their figures with false *bosoms* and men donned *inexpressibles* instead of breeches. By 1813, polite farmers were speaking of the *bosom* of the plow, meaning the forward part of the moldboard, formerly called the "breast." And at about this time, too, begins the nineteenth-century sentimentalization of death, as witnessed on tombstones of the period, which begin recording that people, instead of dying, have *fallen asleep, gone to meet their Maker, passed over the river,* and so on.

The cleaning up of language took place over several generations, but was apparent to people who lived during the period. For example, Dr. Johnson's friend, Mrs. Hester Thrale, referred in her diary in 1782 to "the great change" that had taken place in "female manners" within the previous few years—the comment being occasioned by the reaction of her young daughters when she read them a *Spectator* piece from 1711 in which a woman complained of a "stomach ache." The girls thought it extremely odd for a "*Lady*" to speak these words. And Sir Walter Scott reported in a letter his great-aunt's surprise at revisiting a rakish novel by Aphra Behn and finding that she felt ashamed in the early 1790s to peruse in private what she had heard read aloud in polite society sixty years before. Not long afterward, about 1810, William Hickey, a nabob back from India, paused while recollecting his adventures as a flaming youth in London of the 1760s to note that "In these days of wonderful propriety and general morality, it will scarcely be credited that Mother Cocksedge's house [of *ill fame*] was actually next, of course under the very nose of that vigilant and upright magistrate, Sir John Fielding." Considering the "riotous proceedings" next door, Hickey suspected that Sir John, who had succeeded his novelist half brother as Bow Street magistrate, "must have been deaf as well as blind [which he was, in fact], or at least, well paid for affecting to be so."

In the United States, the new gentility was noted by many observers and decried by some. Nathaniel Ames, a sailor, partly educated at Harvard (expelled in 1814 for setting fire to a brew house in Harvard Yard), observed in *A Mariner's Sketches* (1830):

> I am not the oldest person in the world, but have lived long enough in it to have witnessed a good many alterations. But of all the variations of fashions, manners, religious and political creeds and opinions, nothing has struck me so forcibly as the change which the signification of many English words and phrases, and the manner of using them has undergone. . . . Some years ago folks used to be hanged now and then; now they are uniformly "launched into eternity" . . . "Optical indecision" has replaced squinting; editors of newspapers have left off publishing lists of marriages and deaths, but refer their readers to the "hymeneal register" for an account of the pairs that are daily "yoked to the matrimonial wagon," while the continual retirements of the members of "Adam's lost race," are comprehended under "obituary notices." . . .

> Drinking stoutly before dinner is "taking some refreshment," being as drunk as David's sow, is "considerably excited," a man who makes a swindling failure is "considerably embarrassed"; a lady who flirts shamelessly with every young fellow, is "very free in her manners."

> Besides these and many more alterations, our mother tongue is fast assuming a dress like that of a state's prison convict, one leg of its inexpressibles being made of Greek, and the other of French, while the waistbands are formed of Latin. Fashionable intemperates are no longer afflicted with indigestion, it is "dyspepsy"; the asthma has ceased its ravages and given up the field to "dyspnoes." Good penmanship is "calligraphy," and any kind of writing is "chirography." . . .

> In short, the English language will soon become "neither fish, flesh, nor red herring."

The two great landmarks in the development of pre-Victorian thought are the expurgations of the Bard and the Bible, with *The Family Shakespeare*, by the Bowdlers, appearing in 1807, and Noah Webster's version of the word of God ("with Amendments of the language") coming out in 1833. The objective of the Bowdlers, as stated in the preface to the enlarged second edition of 1818, was to omit "those words and expressions . . . which cannot with propriety be read aloud in a family." (Note that "family" here has essentially the same conventionally sexless connotations as in television's *family time* and the recurrent calls for *family values*.) Though Dr. Thomas Bowdler usually has been given all the credit, the expurgation was primarily the work of his sister, Henrietta Maria (known to familiars as Harriet). She has only herself to blame, however, for the lack of recognition: She didn't sign her name to the book probably because, as a maiden lady, she didn't want to admit publicly to understanding all the things she was censoring.

As for Noah Webster, he carefully took out of the Bible every "whore," every "piss," and even every "stink," while making a great many other curious changes, such as *idolatries* for whoredom, *lewd deeds* for "fornication" (itself a Latinate evasion for an Anglo-Saxon word), and *nurse* for the apparently too animalistic "suck." In his introduction, Webster justified his rewrite of the King James Version of 1611, saying "Purity of mind is a Christian virtue that ought to be carefully guarded; and purity of language is one of the guards which protect this virtue."

The precise causes of this pre-Victorian linguistic revolution, whose legacy remains with us, are difficult to pinpoint, involving as they do a combination of religious revival, industrialization, an emerging middle class, increasing literacy, and an improvement in the status of women. Benchmarks of change include the first conviction for obscenity in the English-speaking world (Edmund Curll, 1727, for reissuing a book that had been previously printed without prosecution as far back as 1683); the Great Awakening, the religious revival that shook New England in the late 1730s and soon spread to the rest of the colonies; the near-simultaneous development of Methodism in England; the British Marriage Act of 1753, outlawing premarital sex; George III's Proclamation against Vice and Immorality of 1787, bidding his sub-

jects to "suppress all loose and licentious prints, books, and publications" (this resulted in the formation in 1802 of the Society for the Suppression of Vice, which initiated prosecutions for printing sexually explicit material); the beginnings of the factory system (Samuel Slater brought most of the secrets of the English textile industry to America under his hat when he left home in 1789); the invention of the steam-powered press (*The Times* of London installed two in 1814 that made 1,100 impressions per hour, a great technological advance); and, especially in the United States, a spirit of egalitarianism that extended to women and affected the language that men used in front of them. As Alexis de Tocqueville noted: "It has often been remarked that in Europe a certain degree of contempt lurks even in the flattery which men lavish upon women; although a European frequently affects to be the slave of a woman, it may be seen that he never sincerely thinks her his equal. In the United States men seldom compliment women, but they ... constantly display an entire confidence in the understanding of a wife and a profound respect for her freedom. . . . Their conduct to women always implies that they suppose them to be virtuous and refined; and such is the respect entertained for the moral freedom of the sex that in the presence of a woman the most guarded language is used lest her ear should be offended by an expression" (*Democracy in America,* 1835, 1840).

The ancient Egyptians called the deadhouse, where bodies were turned into mummies, the *beautiful house,* and the ways of expunging offensive expressions from language have not changed since. Simplest is to make a straight substitution, using a word that has happier connotations than the term one wishes to avoid. Frequently, a legitimate synonym will do. Thus, *agent, speculator,* and *thrifty* have better vibes than "spy," "gambler," and "stingy," although the literal meanings, or denotations, of each pair of words are the same. On this level, all the euphemist has to do is select words with care. Other principles may be applied, however, a half dozen of which are basic to creating—and deciphering—euphemisms. They are:

Foreign languages sound finer. It is permissible for speakers and writers of English to express almost any thought they wish, as long as the more risqué parts of the discussion are rendered in another language, usually French or Latin. The versatility of French (and the influence of French culture) is evident in such diverse fields as love (*affair, amour, liaison*), war (*personnel, sortie, triage*), women's underwear (*brassiere, chemise, lingerie*), and dining (goat, cow, deer, and other animals with English names when they are alive and kicking are served up on the dinner table as the more palatable *chevon, filet mignon,* and *venison*). *French* itself is a euphemistic prefix word for a variety of "wrong" and/or "sexy" things, such as the *French disease* (syphilis) and one of the methods of guarding against it, the *French letter* (condom).

Latin is almost equally popular as a source of euphemisms, especially for the body's sexual and other functions. Thus, such words as *copulation, fellatio, masturbation, pudendum,* and *urination* are regarded as printable and even broadcastable by people (including United States Supreme Court justices) who become exercised at the sight and sound of their English counterparts. ("My English text is chaste, and all licentious passages are left in the decent obscurity of a learned language," Edward Gibbon, *Memoirs,* 1796.) Contributions from other languages include the Dutch *boss* (master), the Spanish *cojones* (balls), and the Yiddish *tushie* (ass). Potty talk, while not a foreign language, strictly speaking, is a distinct idiom that has furnished many euphemisms, for example, *number one, number two, pee, piddle,* and other relics of the nursery, often used by adults when speaking to one another as well as when addressing children.

Bad words are not so bad when abbreviated. Words that otherwise would create consternation if used in mixed company or in public are acceptable when reduced to their initial letters. Essentially, such abbreviations as *BS* and *SOB* work the same way as the dashes in *a – –* and *f – – –* : Everyone knows what letters have been deleted, but no one is seriously offended because the taboo word has not been paraded in all its glory. Dean Acheson even got away with *snafu* when he was secretary of state, though the acronym did cause some comment among the British, not all of whom felt this to be a very diplomatic way of apologizing for an American—er—*foulup.* This acronym also is noteworthy for spawning a host of picturesque albeit short-lived descendants, including *fubar* (where *bar* stands for Beyond All Recognition), *janfu* (Joint Army-Navy), *tarfu* (Things Are Really), and *tuifu* (The Ultimate In). Abbreviations function as euphemisms in many fields, for example, the child's *BM,* the advertiser's *BO,* the hypochondriac's *Big C,* and the various shortenings for offbeat sex, such as *AC/DC* for those who swing both ways, *BD* for bondage and discipline, and *S & M* in honor of Messrs. de Sade and Sacher-Masoch.

Abstractions are not objectionable. The strength of particular taboos may be dissipated by casting ideas in the most general possible terms; also, abstractions, being quite opaque to the uninformed eye (and meaningless to the untrained ear), make ideal cover-up words. Often, it is only a matter of finding the lowest common denominator. Thus, *it, problem, situation,* and *thing* may refer to anything under the sun: the child who keeps playing with *it* and the girl who is said to be doing *it; problem* days and *problem* drinking; the *situation* at the Three Mile Island, Pennsylvania, nuclear power plant; an economic *thing* (slump, recession, or depression), *our thing* (that is, the Cosa Nostra), or the Watergate *thing* (elaborated by the president himself into the *pre-thing* and the *post-thing*). The American tendency toward abstraction was noted early on by de Tocqueville, who believed that democratic nations as a class were "addicted to generic terms and abstract expressions because these modes of speech enlarge thought and assist the operation of the mind by enabling it to include many objects in a small compass." The dark side of this is that abstractions are inherently fuzzy. As de Tocqueville also noted in *Democracy in America*: "An abstract term is like a box with a false bottom; you may put in what ideas you please, and take them out again without being observed." Bureaucrats, engineers, scientists, and those who like to be regarded as scientists, are particularly good at generalizing details out of existence. They have produced such expressions as *aerodynamic personnel decelerator* for parachute, *energy release* for radiation release (as from a nuclear reactor), *episode* and *event* for disasters of different sorts and sizes, *impact attenuation device* for a crash

cushion, *wood interdental stimulator* for a toothpick, and *entrenching tool* for a shovel.

Indirection is better than direction. Topics and terms that are too touchy to be dealt with openly may be alluded to in a variety of ways, most often by mentioning one aspect of the subject, a circumstance involving it, a related subject, or even by saying what it is not. Thus, people really do come together in an *assembly center* and soldiers do stop fighting when they *break off contact with the enemy*, but these are indirect euphemisms for "prison" and "retreat," respectively. *Bite the dust* is a classic of this kind, and the adjective is used advisedly, since the expression appears in Homer's *Iliad*, circa 750 B.C. Many of the common anatomical euphemisms also depend on indirection— the general, locational, it's-somewhere-back-there allusions to the *behind*, the *bottom*, and the *rear*, for example. A special category of anatomical euphemisms are those that conform to the Rule of the Displaced Referent, whereby "unmentionable" parts of the human body are euphemized by referring to nearby "mentionable" parts, for example, *chest* or *neck* for breasts, and *thigh*, a biblical euphemism for the balls. Quaintest of the indirect euphemisms are those that are prefaced with a negative adjective, telling us what they are not, such as *unnatural, unthinkable*, and *unmentionable*. (The latter also appears as a noun in the plural; some women wear *upper unmentionables* and *lower unmentionables*.) An especially famous negative euphemism is the dread *love that dare not speak its name*, but the phrase was not totally dishonest in the beginning, since it dates to 1894 (from a poem by Oscar Wilde's young *friend*, Alfred, Lord Douglas), when "homosexual" was still so new a word as not to be known to many people, regardless of their *sexual orientation.*

Understatement reduces risks. Since a euphemism is, by definition, a mild, agreeable, or roundabout word or phrase, it follows logically that its real meaning is always worse than its apparent meaning. But this is not always obvious to the uninitiated, especially in constructions that acknowledge part of the truth while concealing the extent of its grimness. Thus, a nuclear reactor that is said to be *above critical* is actually out of control, an *active defense* is an attack, *area bombing* amounts to terror bombing, *collateral damage* is civilian damage (as from bombs and rockets), and so on. When an individual confesses to being *economical with the truth,* you can bet that truth is in very short supply, and when a government admits to an *abuse of authority*, the authorities almost certainly have done something very ugly indeed. The soft sell also is basic to such euphemisms as *companion, partner,* and *roommate,* all of which downplay "lover"; to *pro-choice* for pro-abortion, and to *senior citizen* for old person. The danger with understatement is that it may hide the true meaning completely. As a result, euphemists often erect signposts in front of the basic term, for example, *close personal friend, constant companion, criminal conversation* (a legalism for adultery), *meaningful relationship,* etc. The signposts ensure that even dullards will get the message.

The longer the euphemism the better. As a rule, to which there are very few exceptions (*hit* for murder, for instance), euphemisms are longer than the words they replace. They have more letters, they have more syllables, and frequently, two or more words will be deployed in place of a single one. This is partly because the tabooed Anglo-Saxon words tend to be short and partly because it almost always takes more words to evade an idea than to state it directly and honestly. The effect is seen in euphemisms of every type. For instance, *Middle Eastern dancing* is what better "belly" dancers do; advertisers agree that *medication* gives faster relief than "medicine"; writers of financial reports eschew "drop" in favor of *adjustment downward,* and those poor souls who are required to give testimony under oath prefer *at this point in time* to "now." The list is practically endless. For the student of euphemisms, however, a key question is *how much* better are the longer expressions. Precise answers are now available, thanks to the development of the Fog or Pomposity Index (FOP Index, for short).

The FOP Index compares the length of the euphemism or circumlocution to the word or phrase for which it stands, with an additional point being awarded for each additional letter, syllable, or word in the substitute expression. Thus, "medicine" has 8 letters and 3 syllables, while *medication* has 10 letters and an extra, fourth syllable, giving it a point count of 11. Dividing 8 into 11 produces a FOP Index of 1.4. By the same token, *adjustment downward* has a FOP Index of 5.75 compared to "drop" (18 letters, plus 4 extra syllables, plus 1 extra word, for a total of 23, divided by the 4 letters of the euphemized term).

Like most breakthroughs in the social (or soft) sciences, the FOP Index doesn't really tell you anything you didn't already know or, at least, suspect. Everyone (well, almost everyone) has always sensed that *medication* is on the pretentious side. The index, however, arms users with a number to back up their intuition, thus enabling them to crush opponents in debate. It can now be said authoritatively that *lower extremity* (FOP Index of 6.6) outdoes *limb* (1.3) as a euphemism for "leg." In much the same way, *prostitute* (2.4) improves upon *harlot* (1.4) for "whore." And so it goes. *Active defense* has a FOP Index of 2.5 for "attack"; *benign neglect* rates 2.3 for "neglect" (the "benign" being an example of a Meaningless Modifier); *intestinal fortitude* is 6.5 for "guts"; *categorical inaccuracy* is a whopping 10.3 compared to "lie," and *international wildlife conservation park* practically goes off the chart at 17.0 for "zoo."

With quantification, the study of euphemisms has been put on a firm scientific footing. FOP Indexes have been included for a number of the entries in this dictionary and it is hoped that readers will enjoy working out indexes for themselves in other instances. As they proceed, given the nature of the terms for which euphemisms stand, they may also wish to keep in mind Shakespeare's advice (*Henry IV, Part II,* 1596–97):

Tis needful that the most immodest word
Be looked upon and learned.

Euphemisms, circumlocutions, and doubletalk are printed in *italic* type except when discussed in a generic sense, in which case the terms are enclosed in quotation marks, or when used illustratively, in which case the style of the original source is followed. Thus, the first *abattoirs* were constructed in France, "abattoir" entered the English language as a euphemism, and "abattoirs have recently been erected in London." SMALL CAPS indicate a separate entry for that term; for example, see LINGERIE.

A

a – –. Ass. The practice of dashing out part of the A-word dates to at least to the first half of the eighteenth century and remains common in FAMILY newspapers of today. "The precise passage in 'The Alfred Summer' that some parents find objectionable is: 'I would kiss a pig's a – – if I thought it would bring us luck. I would even pray'" (*Waterbury*, Conn., *Republican-American*, 1/9/92). Sometimes the blanks are dropped, leaving just the initial of the terrible three-letter word, e.g., from one of Garry Trudeau's "Doonesbury" strips: "I wish we could just get it over with! Go in, kick A, and get the hell home!" (*Litchfield County*, Conn., *Times*, 12/28/90). See also ARSE, BA, BAM, BLANK, and T AND A.

The preceding quotations shed light on attitudes toward the sacred as well as the profane. In the first case, at least one mother objected to the book because she interpreted the particular passage to mean that "Kissing a pig's (behind) is better than praying." (Parentheses in the original; see also BEHIND.) Meanwhile, the use of "hell" in Trudeau's widely syndicated strip indicates the declining power of blasphemy.

Many newspapers declined to print this word in full up until the mid twentieth century. See also EXPLETIVE DELETED, HECK, and H – – L.

abattoir. A slaughterhouse. One of the great laws governing the formation (and detection) of euphemisms is that the unseemly is more palatable when couched in a foreign language, preferably Latin or its Romantic, fair-sounding descendant, French.

The first *abattoirs* were constructed in France, the word coming from *abattre*, to strike down. English writers reported their existence at least by 1820, according to *The Oxford English Dictionary*, and by 1866, the word had been taken into the language with the *Cyclopedia of Useful Arts* (I, 2) noting: "Abattoirs have recently been erected in London." See also MARKET, GO TO, and PACKING HOUSE.

abdomen. The stomach, belly, or gut. Some people are so refined that they can't stomach "stomach," let alone its lower synonyms. Thus, *The Family Shakespeare*, produced by Harriet and Thomas Bowdler, rendered King Lear's challenge to the storm, "Rumble thy bellyful!" as "Rumble thy fill!" (See also FAMILY.) It would be easier to sniff at such pre-Victorian primness if it weren't for recent history. For example, when the Rodgers and Hammerstein musical *Carousel* was presented before the British Royal Family in 1962, the line "Our hearts are warm, our bellies full" was changed to "Our hearts are warm, and we are full." And the good gray *New York Times* once changed a description by Molly Ivins of a fellow with "a beergut that belongs in the Smithsonian" to "a man with a protuberant abdomen" (*Molly Ivins Can't Say That, Can She?*, 1991). See also MIDDLE EASTERN DANCING, INTESTINAL FORTITUDE, STOMACHACHE, and TUMMY.

aberration. A departure from routine. The long-winded term frequently serves as a smoke screen to obscure the extent of the deviation from normality. Thus, when a rotor blade snapped off a helicopter on the landing pad atop the Pan Am Building in New York City, killing four people on the roof and another on the street, fifty-nine stories below, New York Airways spokesman Daniel Kocivar characterized the accident as a "sort of aberration" (*New York Times*, 5/17/77). Or again: After four hundred whites bombarded a small group of immigrant blacks in Montreal with bricks and bottles, John Kousik, chief of police in the city's East End, explained that "It wasn't a riot at all. It was a melee. No, melee isn't right either. It was not a racial incident. What happened here was an aberration of the social system" (*Ottawa Citizen*, Canada, 7/20/91). See also ABNORMAL OCCURRENCE, ANOMALY, and DISTURBANCE.

ablutions, perform one's. To wash, ceremonially. The phrase dates to the middle of the eighteenth century, when the seeds of Victorianism already were beginning to sprout.

abnormal occurrence. A departure from normality; the principle of obfuscation here is the same as with ABERRATION. The phrase is associated especially with the nuclear power business. For example, following a 1,000-gallon spill of radioactive water from a plant in Waterford, Conn., William Counsil, the facility's supervisor, denied that this had been an "emergency situation," even though 1,200 workers had to be evacuated. He conceded, however, that it was an "abnormal occurrence" (*New York Times*, 3/29/75). See also EVENT and INCIDENT.

above critical. Out of control; running away; melting down; in danger of blowing up. "The reactor began to run out of control—'above critical' in the parlance of the nuclear engineer" (John G. Fuller, *We Almost Lost Detroit*, 1975). A meltdown of the fuel in a nuclear reactor may also be characterized—again in the parlance of the nuclear engineer—as a *superprompt critical power excursion* (where "excursion" equals "runaway") or *prompt critical*, for short. See also BLIP, CORE REARRANGEMENT, ENERGY RELEASE, EVENT, INCIDENT, and SUNSHINE.

abuse of authority. Murder, torture, and the like. When a government goes so far as to admit to an *abuse of authority*, it is a safe bet that something truly terrible has happened. Thus, President Jose Napoleon Duarte of El Salvador won the Foreign Award of the Committee on Public Doublespeak of the National Council of Teachers in 1981 with his understated response to allegations that U.S.-trained government troops had killed thousands of civilians that year. "We will not deny that there may have been certain abuses of authority by the security forces," said *el presidente*. It took more than a decade—partly because the United States government was not anxious to confirm reports of the *abuses of authority*—but their nature became clear in October 1992, when a team of forensic anthropologists began excavating some eight hundred skeletons from around a demolished church in the northeastern town of El Mozote. The victims, mostly women and children, had been mutilated, burned, and shot. See also CASUALTY (for more about U.S. Salvadoran policy in this period) and UNLAWFUL OR ARBITRARY DEPRIVATION OF LIFE.

access controller. A doorman—or *doorkeeper,* to be politically correct and gender-neutral. "Access controller" is part of the continuing trend to inflate job titles, no matter how menial the task. By the same token, bill collectors have metamorphosed into *portfolio administrators* and the even more highfalutin *experts in the management of the accounts receivable asset*; nightclub bouncers into *entertainment coordinators* and SECURITY; casting directors into *artistic administrators*; dormitory housemothers into *residential advisers*; manicurists into *nail technicians*; and so on. See also ENGINEER, TECHNICIAN, and TRAFFIC EXPEDITER.

accident. An omnibus term for any of a variety of unspeakable happenings, ranging from the MESS that Fido makes on the Persian carpet to murder or ASSASSINATION. For example, the Senate Intelligence Committee reported in 1975 that the CIA had once offered $10,000 (in vain) to a Cuban agent for "arranging an accident" for Fidel Castro's brother, Raul. Other kinds of "accident" include "stroke," sometimes referred to as "an accident in the brain," and "pregnancy," a notoriously DELICATE subject, e.g.:

"But, accidents do happen. So, could Midnight take her to one of those nice clinics where these accidents can be taken care of?" (New York *Village Voice,* 1/2/78). See also ANKLE, TO SPRAIN AN; CASUALTY; EVENT; and THERAPEUTIC ACCIDENT.

accouchement. Lying in; childbirth; parturition (as the doctors say). "Meanwhile the skill and patience of the physician had brought about a happy accouchement" (James Joyce, *Ulysses,* 1922). The Frenchification (from *accoucher,* to put to bed) dates to around 1800 in Britain and became popular in the United States after the Civil War. Prior to *accouchement,* a woman is said (assuming one is speaking consistently) to be ENCEINTE. See also PREGNANT.

account for. To kill. When soldiers are being awarded medals for doing a lot of killing, the citations tend to be phrased blandly rather than baldly. As John Keegan notes, "Citation writers, flinching from 'kill', deal largely in 'account for', 'dispatch', 'dispose of'" (*The Face of Battle,* 1976). A typical citation, according to Keegan, might tell how Corporal So-and-so "worked his way round the flank of the machine-gun which was holding up the advance and then charged it, firing his carbine from the hip, so accounting for six of the enemy." See also BITE THE DUST, DISPATCH, DISPOSE, HIT, and the basic military CASUALTY.

AC/DC. Bisexual; a play on Alternating Current/Direct Current. See also AMBIDEXTROUS and BISEXUAL.

achieve a deficiency. To fail; educationese. See also DEFICIENT and UNDERACHIEVER.

act, the. A discreet abbreviation of "sexual act" or "act of generation." The term has been used euphemistically since at least the early seventeenth century. Shakespeare referred to "the act of darkness" in *King Lear* (1605–06). The construction has withstood the test of time, e.g., "One miracle of love that remains to us in this age of uncensored print is that we need not designate with words what we are doing or having done in the act—that is, when we are actually doing it and not writing about it" (*New York Times*, 3/11/77). See also DO, DEED, GENERATION, and IT.

action. A euphemism for violence (or JEOPARDY) on television and for sex in real life. In the first case, the euphemism partakes of the term's military sense ("action" as an engagement with the enemy) and its literary sense (the "action" or series of events that form the plot of a story or drama). The euphemistic meaning is dominant, however, when vice-presidents in charge of PROGRAM PRACTICES consider *action-oriented* scripts. As Joseph Wambaugh, the writer, said on a 1977 NBC-TV news special, "Violence in America": "We never use the word 'violence' in this industry—it's called action." As for sexual *action*: "I therefore denounced the idea of conjugal visits as inherently unfair; single prisoners needed and deserved action just as much as married prisoners did" (Eldridge Cleaver, *Soul on Ice*, 1968). For other examples of the unfortunately common association between violence and sex, see BANG, BUCK, DIE, DO, F – – –, GUN, HIT, JUMP, OFF, POP, SCORE, SWINGING, and ZAP. For other kinds of "action," continue with ACTION FIGURE, EXECUTIVE ACTION, JOB ACTION, POLICE ACTION, and SPECIAL ACTION.

action figure. A doll for boys. Hasbro Industries popularized its GI Joe toy (b. 1964) as an "action figure," but the U.S. Customs Service classified the Hong Kong–made Joe as a doll, subject to a 12 percent import duty. (Imported toy soldiers are not taxed.) Hasbro protested, but the U.S. Court of Appeals for the District of Columbia upheld the Customs Service in 1989, saying that GI Joe is "a representation of a human being used as a child's plaything"—that is, a doll. Don't try to tell this to the next ten-year-old general you meet, however, unless you are anxious to start a fight. See also ACTION.

act of God. A disaster—but not necessarily one that is beyond human power to prevent, despite the effort to dump the blame on the Deity. "It is an odd thing that even the most scientifically sophisticated society known to history insists on building on faults, flood-plains, and evanescent beach fronts, and calls the inevitable disasters that occur 'acts of God'" (James K. Page, Jr., *Smithsonian*, 7/78). Note that "act of God" presumes an awe-ful deity in the Old Testament sense, a god known more by his punishments than his blessings, who is best approached gingerly and indirectly because of his quickness to dish out death and destruction to those who fail him. See also ADONAI.

adjective/adjectival. Either term allows the reader to insert mentally the modifier of his or her choice into the prepared text. They are literary counterparts of the electronic BLEEP and BLIP. Thus, reporting on a tour of the London underworld, Charles Dickens sanitized the words of a notorious fence named Bark, who probably included "bloody" when he yelled: "If the adjective coves [rogues] in the kitchen was men, they'd come up now and do for you!" ("On Duty with Inspector Field," *Household Words*, 6/14/1851). And in our own time, that best-of-all-sportswriters, Red "Walter" Smith, produced "adjectival" and similar gems while fielding unprintable quotes from professional athletes. Recalling a conversation with Babe Ruth, for instance: "He remembered, he said in the husk of voice he had left, how he'd really got his *adjectival* shoulders into a swing and had knocked the *indelicacy* ball against the *Anglo-Saxon* hotel out there" (*New York Herald Tribune*, 8/19/48). The Babe usually described his homers in these terms. More than a dozen years later, Smith sanitized Ruth's words for family consumption in this manner: "'The *naughty-word* day I hit that *naughty-word* ball into that *naughty-word* street over there'" (*New York Herald Tribune*, 4/2/61). See also ANGLO-SAXON, BLANK, F-WORD, *the Shavian adjective* in RUDDY, UNPRINTABLE, and VERNACULAR.

adjust/adjustment/readjustment. To change, a change—almost invariably in a negative or downward direction. "The stock market, for example, rarely 'falls' in the words of Wall Street analysis. Instead it is discovered to be 'easing' or found to have made a 'technical correction' or 'adjustment.' As one financial writer notes, it never seems to 'technically adjust' upwards" (*Time*, 9/19/69). Then there was the ominous reply to the question posed to Patrick Peyton, acting CEO of Grove Weidenfeld, in the wake of his announcement that the publisher would cut back its list of new books by 50 percent: "Asked what effect the reduction will have on staff, Pey-

ton said there would be 'adjustments'" (*Publishers Weekly*, 5/18/90). If all this sounds Orwellian, that is because it is: "For the time being, certainly, it had been found necessary to make a readjustment of rations. (Squealer always spoke of it as a 'readjustment,' never as a 'reduction')" (*Animal Farm*, 1946). See also RECESSION and TECHNICAL ADJUSTMENT.

adjustment center. A solitary confinement cell in the psychologically disturbed language of prison administrators. "Some prisons are now called 'therapeutic correctional communities,' convicts are 'clients of the correctional system,' solitary confinement and punishment cells have become 'adjustment centers,' 'seclusion,' or, in Virginia, 'meditation'" (Jessica Mitford, *Kind and Usual Punishment: The Prison Business*, 1974).

Other forms of solitary that have been recorded in recent years include *administrative detention* (where a prisoner in El Reno, Okla., was put in 1988 after calling a news conference at which he planned to say that he had once sold marijuana to vice presidential candidate Dan Quayle), *behavior adjustment unit* (Camp Hill, Pa., prison), the *quiet cell* (Essex, N.J., County Jail), and the *special housing unit* (at the Attica, New York, Correctional Facility), plus such jawbreakers as *administrative confinement, administrative segregation,* and *therapeutic segregation.* See also SECLUSION, QUIET ROOM, and the basic CORRECTIONAL FACILITY.

adjustment of the front. American troops never "retreat"; see STRATEGIC MOVEMENT TO THE REAR.

administrative assistant. A secretary, a.k.a. *executive assistant, personal assistant,* and *office automation specialist.* Though some *administrative assistants* actually do some administrating, ads for such jobs in the help-wanted pages frequently are cast in terms of dictation, typing, and word processing skills. See also ENGINEER and GAL/GUY FRIDAY.

Adonai. The Hebrew circumlocution for God's real name, YHWH, i.e., Yahweh or, to Christians, Jehovah. The name of God is so highly tabooed that pious Jews say "Adonai" when reading aloud from the Torah (the first five books of the Old Testament). As further protection from the dangers of uttering the sacred name, the euphemism itself may be mumbled. Meanwhile, print ads for such groups as the Committee for the Maintenance of Jewish Standards and the Friends of Jerusalem employ *L – d* and *G'd* when quoting the Torah.

Christians also have been known to avoid "God" in many circumstances. For example, Lady Mary Wortley Montagu blanked out part of the word in an account, though in a private letter, of an early feminist uprising—the attempt (ultimately successful) of a group of women headed by the Duchess of Queensbury to gain admission to the gallery of the House of Lords: "After some modest refusals he [a Sir William Saunderson, who was blocking the door] swore by G – – he would not let them come in. Her Grace with a noble warmth, answered by G – – they would come in, in spite of the Chancellor and the whole House" (to Lady Pomfret, 3/1739).

The taboo against mentioning the name of God—or any other supernatural being, for that matter—is common to many cultures. In most instances, the underlying fear seems to be that saying the being's

name will cause it to appear. As a result, there are many circumlocutions to avoid saying the names of dead people (the ghosts might hear), evil spirits, feared animals, the angel of death, and so forth. See also, for example, DEPARTED ONE, THE; DEVIL, THE; GD; GOOD PEOPLE, THE; GOSH; GRANDFATHER; HIERONYMOUS; LAND; LAW; MAN; SUPREME BEING, and WEALTHY ONE, THE.

adorable. Commonly encountered in classified ads for houses, it translates as "small."

adult. A capacious closet of a word from whose roomy interior different meanings may be plucked, depending on need and circumstance. Technically meaning anyone who has matured—in civil law, fourteen for males and twelve for females—"adult" is used most often to make old people seem younger and to characterize, without describing, certain pleasures that older people prefer to reserve for themselves.

When applied to a home (e.g., the Moncie Home for Adults), the implication is that the residents are rather elderly, "home for adults" actually being a double euphemism, akin to NURSING HOME (see HOME and RESIDENT). Then there are the *adult communities,* whose citizens are old, but not as old as those in *adult homes,* since *adult communities* are merely "retirement villages." Typical age minimums for residence in *adult communities* are forty-eight or fifty-two. An *adult congregate living facility,* meanwhile, is a hotel for retirees.

"Adult" takes on an entirely different coloration when used to modify such words as "book," "entertainment," "film," "novelty," or "theater." Then "adult" means "sex" (just as FAMILY signals the absence of same). Thus, the city of Boston, also known as the Athens of America, boasts an *adult entertainment zone,* also known as "the combat zone," where almost anything goes. (A Bicentennial attempt to upgrade the district's name to *Liberty Tree Neighborhood* didn't take.) On occasion, though, the code can be difficult to decipher. For example, what is one to make of the sign for "Mini-Adult Books," spotted along a highway in Florida by Robert Craft some years ago: Short sex books? Sex books for short people? Simplified porn? The mind boggles. See also EROTICA and SEXUALLY EXPLICIT (or ORIENTED).

advance. Invasion, Japanese-style. Revisionist historians in Japan, who feel their nation was more sinned against than sinning in World War II, have been trying since the early 1980s to have school texts rewritten to characterize that nation's invasion of China in the 1930s as an "advance." Their allies in the conservative Education Ministry have gone so far as to ban "war of aggression" and to require that references to "anti-Japanese resistance" in Korea be rephrased in terms of difficulties in obtaining "the Korean people's cooperation." The soft-pedaling of Japan's role in World War II extends to other media. Thus, a Japanese-made film, *The Tokyo Trial* (1985), passes off the sneak attack on Pearl Harbor in 1941 as "a triumph of tactical surprise." See also COMFORT WOMAN, INCIDENT, and INCURSION.

advanced life-support unit. A paramedic ambulance in New York City. In California, meanwhile, the State Department of Transportation has replaced its emergency vehicles with *major incident-response vehicles.* See also ENTRENCHING TOOL.

advisement, take under. To shelve, usually for good. "I'll take that under advisement" is a typical bureaucratic dodge for deferring action in the hope (not infrequently fulfilled) that the problem will go away of its own accord.

adviser. A soldier in educational guise; for example, one of the 15,000 Cuban *advisers* sent to Angola in 1975–76, or one of 3,000 Russian *advisers* discovered to be in Cuba in 1979. Or were they combat troops? It all depended on whose terminology was being used—just as it did in the world's most famous advisory operation, which began in 1954 when 200 American soldiers were sent to South Vietnam. As President John F. Kennedy said in a TV interview in September 1963: "We can send our men out there as advisers, but they have to win it, the people of Vietnam" (quoted in Theodore C. Sorensen, *Kennedy,* 1965). But the war concluded so badly that "adviser" has been dropped from the American political and military lexicons. When the Reagan administration increased military aid to El Salvador in the spring of 1983, everyone from the president on down steered clear of the word "adviser." Mr. Reagan himself said that "The numbers of trainers [to be sent] will depend on the resources" (WNBC-TV news, 3/10/83). Meanwhile, the official U.S. *Department of Defense Dictionary of Military Terms* (1979) has more than six thousand definitions, but lacks an entry for "adviser." To paraphrase an old saying, one omission is worth a thousand words. See also VIETNAM ERA.

advisory. Warning, usually about dangerous weather conditions, as in "traveler's advisory."

aerodynamic personnel decelerator. A parachute, with a FOP Index of 4.8. See also ENTRENCHING TOOL and VERTICAL INSERTION.

affair. An essentially neutral word that can be used to cover dirty work of various kinds. For example, there is the illicit *affair,* meaning a love affair or intrigue (sometimes described as an EXTRAMARITAL or *premarital affair,* or further fancied up as an *affaire de coeur);* the *affair of honor,* which is a duel or MEETING; the man of *affairs,* or businessman, and the man with an *affair.* The last is the most euphemistic, being one of the blander terms for the PENIS, as in "Her gallant . . . drew out his affair ready erected" (John Cleland, *Memoirs of a Woman of Pleasure,* 1749).

The ordinary, everyday love *affair* or *affaire* (people also have been known to conduct Frenchified *office affaires*) is of some venerability, with the oldest example in *The Oxford English Dictionary* dating from 1702. It took a distinguished British philosopher, Bishop George Berkeley, to sort out the euphemism: "In pure Dialect a vicious Man is a Man of Pleasure . . . a Lady is said to have an affair, a Gentleman to be a gallant, a Rogue in business to be one that knows the world" (*Alciphron, or the Minute Philosopher,* 1732).

Today, "affair" seems to be holding its own, in face of stiff competition from semi-psychological claptrap, such as INVOLVED WITH and RELATIONSHIP, e.g., from a nonliterary ad in the *New York Review of Books* (1/26/78):

KENT STATE PROFESSOR/AUTHOR will respond enthusiastically to all applications received for a discreet and sincere affair to be arranged in Northeast Ohio or surrounding areas.

See also AMOUR, LIAISON, MATINEE, and SEXUAL VARIETY.

affirmative. Yes. "He answered in the affirmative," has a mush-mouth FOP Index of 3.8, compared to the straightforward, "He said yes." See also NEGATIVE and SIGN OFF.

affordable housing. Low-income housing. "It used to be called 'low income housing,' but the name has been changed to 'affordable housing,' presumably to make the thought more palatable to the occupants of the houses in the community that sell for $400,000, $500,000 and more" (*New York Times,* 10/21/90). See also LOW-INCOME and PUBLIC HOUSING DEVELOPMENT.

age, of a certain. Old enough to be circumlocutory about it. The span of years covered by the phrase is imprecise, varying according to who is using it. As good a working definition as any comes from a book on the subject, *Women of a Certain Age* (1979), by Lillian B. Rubin, a sociologist in her "mid-years." The book discusses women aged thirty-five to fifty-four. George Gordon, Lord Byron implied that "a certain age" might start even earlier, however, noting in *Don Juan* (1819–24):

A lady of a 'certain age,' which means
Certainly aged—what her years might be
I know not, never counting past their
   teens.

See also MATURE.

agent. A spy who is on your side. "You mean spies and all that—only we call them agents" (*Charade,* film, 1963).

In current CIA lingo, an *agent* usually is a foreigner. American counterparts of *agents* generally are known as *case officers* and *intelligence* (or *operations*) *officers.* Variant job titles include *intelligence specialist* and *covert human collection source,* as opposed to a *technical means of verification* (a reconnaissance, or spy, satellite) or a *technical collection source,* which is a satellite, wiretap, bug, or other inanimate device used in TECHNICAL SURVEILLANCE. (Broadly, the methods are classified in spy-speak into *humint,* or human intelligence, *elint,* or electronic intelligence, and *imint,* or image intelligence.) See also COMPANY, COMMUNITY, OPERATIVE, and SOURCE OF INFORMATION.

National origin aside, the similarity of *agents* and *spies* has been recognized for at least a couple of centuries. Thus, James Fenimore Cooper reported in the introduction to the 1831 edition of his novel *The Spy* that the story had been inspired by John Jay's reminiscence of having employed during the American Revolution "an agent whose services differed but little from those of a common spy." (The novel apparently was based on Enoch Crosby, a traveling shoemaker who penetrated Loyalist circles in Westchester and nearby New York counties.) As indicated by the title of his book, Cooper himself apparently did not appreciate Jay's fine distinction between "agent" and "spy."

The desirable attributes of modern *agents* were summarized in a CIA cable, when plans were being made in 1960 to assassinate the first prime minister of the Congo (now Zaire), Patrice Lumumba. (Lumumba was killed the following year but apparently not by the agency or its hirelings.) The cable commended a particular *agent* in these terms:

He is indeed aware of the precepts of right and wrong, but if he is given an assignment which may be morally wrong in the eyes of the world, but necessary because his case officer ordered him to carry it out, then it is right, and he will dutifully undertake appropriate action for its execution without pangs of conscience. In a word, he can rationalize all actions. (Senate Intelligence Committee report on American assassination plots against foreign leaders, 11/75)

When suitably qualified, "agent" may have other meanings. For example, meter maids and meter men in New York City are described officially as *parking enforcement agents* or *traffic agents*—another example of the near-universal movement to upgrade job titles and to avoid typing them by sex. (For more about the meter readers, see PRODUCTIVITY TARGET.) The FBI, meanwhile, has *special agents* (in effect, making each and every one of them into something "special"), a ploy that J. Edgar Hoover may have picked up from the post office, which had long employed "special agents" for particular or special purposes. Around the turn of the century, "agent" also was short for "road agent," or highwayman, while today the term may be used to confer legitimacy upon underworld informers, or snitches. As the United States Supreme Court put it in a 1972 decision: "He did not know that Chin Poy was what the Government calls an 'underworld agent' and what [the] petitioner calls a 'stool pigeon' for the Bureau of Narcotics." See also ASSOCIATE, INFORMANT, and INVESTIGATOR.

air support. The official military term for what everyone else calls bombing.

The official position was stated succinctly and dramatically in 1973 by Col. David H. E. Opfer, air attaché at the United

States embassy in Phnom Penh, Cambodia, when he complained to newsmen: "You always write it's bombing, bombing, bombing. It's not bombing. It's air support." For this contribution to semantic clarity, Col. Opfer was honored the following year with one of the first Doublespeak Awards, presented by the Committee on Public Doublespeak of the National Council of Teachers of English. Striding along in Col. Opfer's footsteps was Israel's foreign minister, Yitzhak Shamir, who said in an interview shortly after Israeli jets bombed Palestinian positions near Beirut: "You can't call it bombing. From time to time there are some defensive actions against terrorist bases, against terrorist attempts against the population of Israel" (*New York Times,* 9/24/86). This was the tenth such Israeli *defensive action* of the year. See also ARMED RECONNAISSANCE; DEFENSE, DEPARTMENT OF; ORDNANCE; and PROTECTIVE REACTION.

Alaska sable. Skunk fur; a nineteenth-century euphemism, designed to make skunk more attractive to ladies of fashion.

Alaska strawberries. (1) dried beans, (2) dried prunes. The first, from the same era as ALASKA SABLE, was for the benefit of local digestive tracts, while the second was popularized, so to speak, by American soldiers in World War I. Other forms of *strawberries* include *army strawberries,* which are prunes, *Boston strawberries,* baked beans (what else?), (*coal*) *miner's strawberries,* more beans, and *Mexican strawberries,* red Mexican beans. See also CAPE COD TURKEY.

All-American. White. An investigation by New York City and New York State in 1990–91 revealed that Cosmopolitan Care Corp., one of the city's largest employment agencies, regularly let employers know which job applicants were black or Hispanic by noting on their applications that they did not fulfill the client's request for "All-American" employees. While asserting that it had done nothing wrong, Cosmopolitan agreed at the end of 1991 to pay $1.75 million to settle lawsuits charging it with discrimination. Other code terms for "white" included *blond, natural blond,* and *blue eyes.* See also CAUCASIAN.

all the way. In a sexual sense, *all the way* is too far, the allusion being to what is also called COITION, INTERCOURSE, or a SCREW, depending on the circle in which one happens to be traveling. Note that the usually good connotations of the phrase in nonsexual contexts, where "all the way" indicates complete or unqualified support or agreement, are reversed in the sexual sense, which is in keeping with traditional attitudes on that subject. "The limits to acceptable female sexual behavior varied from family to family and from community to community, but one rule remained constant [until comparatively recently]: Unmarried women were not supposed to 'go all the way.' They were expected to remain virgins until they married" (Barry McCarthy, *What You* Still *Don't Know About Male Sexuality,* 1977). To go *all the way* is the same as to go *the whole route* or the LIMIT. See also GO.

alter. To castrate or spay, as in, from the records of a Florida plantation, "I have sheared the sheep and altered the Lambs" (1852, *A Dictionary of Americanisms*). Farmers and hillfolk, especially in the southeast, have said they were going to *alter* an animal, as well as *change* or *arrange* the poor beast, even while whetting their knives for the operation. In time, of course, "alter" picked up the overly sexy connotations of the word it was designed to replace, with the result that people began steering away from it, too. Castrating a bull might be described as *taking his commission from him.* And speaking of speech in the Ozarks: "The innocent verb alter is not used in the presence of strange women. . . . In mixed company the hillman often says de-horn when he means castrate; I have heard men threaten to *de-horn* a sex-mad evangelist who had been annoying their womenfolk" (Vance Randolph and George P. Wilson, *Down in the Holler,* 1953). "Horn," in this instance, is an example of the anatomical displacement, referring not to the testicles but to the penis (hence the sexually excited "horny"). See also BILATERAL ORCHIDECTOMY and DOCTOR.

alternate sexual preference. Perversion. "The last pervert died in 1957. . . . Nowadays we have sexual minorities and sexual variations, some of them involving sexual aids and sexual toys, and all of them indulged in by folks with alternate sexual preferences. Perversion is a nasty, judgmental word that is likely to hurt the feelings of variants everywhere" (*Time,* 12/27/82). People with *alternate sexual preferences* sometimes are said to follow an *alternative lifestyle* or to be *differently pleasured.* Uneasiness about "perversion" also was evidenced by the brouhaha when David Mamet's 1974 play, *Sexual Perversity in Chicago,* was made into a movie in 1986; so many newspapers refused to accept ads for the film that the title was changed at the last minute to the rather blander *About Last Night . . .* See also PARAPHILIA and SEXUALLY OTHERWISE.

altogether. Naked; in one's BIRTHDAY SUIT. "Altogether" is an example of Reverse Eng-

lish, its euphemistic meaning, "without clothes," being almost precisely opposite its formal dictionary definition, "Completely . . . with everything included; all told." The euphemistic sense was popularized by George Du Maurier's *Trilby* (1894), whose heroine posed for artists in Paris in "the altogether." References to the posing sessions were cut when the novel initially appeared in the United States in serial form in *Harper's Magazine,* apparently on the theory that the mere thought of a woman in *the altogether* would inflame the masses. The House of Harper restored the references when the novel was published in hardcover for the smaller, presumably more sophisticated audience of book buyers, but they apparently were inflamed, too. Witness the long life of the euphemism. See also NUDE.

ambidextrous. The dexterity is sexual, both hetero- and homo-. To say that "Charlie is ambidextrous" is the same as saying "Charlie is AC/DC." Women are rarely described as *ambidextrous,* though they are sometimes said (as are men) to be *versatile.* See also AC/DC and BISEXUAL.

amenities. Agreeable or pleasurable places or features, technically, but frequently a euphemism for the so-called smallest room, or BATHROOM. The term is so discreet that it may have to be explained to those not already in on the secret. From John Cheever's "Playing Fields" (*Playboy,* 7/68):

> "Could I use the amenities?" asked
> Mrs. Hubbard.
> "The what?" said Maryellen.
> "The john," said Mrs. Hubbard.

See also JOHN and TOILET.

amour. Illicit love; an AFFAIR, LIAISON, or RELATIONSHIP. "Intrigue, Philotis, that's an old phrase; I have laid that word by: amour sounds better" (John Dryden, *Marriage à la Mode*, 1673). A petty or passing affair was at one time an *amourette*. The modern counterpart is *AWOL*, from the military acronym, but standing for Amour With Out Love in the dialect of the denizens of singles bars. See also PARAMOUR.

ample. Fat. "She was already more ample than a woman of thirty-eight need be in active life" ("Sarah Grand," *Babs, the Impossible*, 1900). See also PORTLY.

Anglo-Saxon. Dirty, as in "Harry used an Anglo-Saxon word." *Anglo-Saxon* is the only language in the world whose vocabulary consists entirely of FOUR-LETTER WORDS. See also EARTHY and VERNACULAR.

animal companion. A politically correct pet. "Spot, Puff, and Trigger are no longer pets; they are 'animal companions,' who may make life happier and healthier for their human friends. That, at least, is one of the major premises that form the basis for a new interdisciplinary endeavor, the study of relationships between animals and people" (*Science*, 10/23/81). It follows from this that *animal companions* do not have "masters" or "owners." Instead, they are blessed with *guardians, stewards,* and *human companions.* The 1993 *Who's Who of Animals: Biographies of Great Animal Companions* (the biographies of the animals were written by their *human companions*) was published by —what else?—Companion Books, of Durham, N.C. All this may seem like a laughing matter, but it is not. When Professor Roderick Nash of the University of California at Santa Barbara suggested in 1991 that

the centerfold "*Penthouse* Pets," displayed in the men's magazine of that name, might better be called *animal companions,* he was bombarded with sexual harassment charges by fifteen women who didn't get the joke (though they eventually dropped the charges). See also INTERNATIONAL WILDLIFE CONSERVATION PARK.

animated series. Cartoons on TV. *Animated series* are to kids as DAYTIME DRAMAS are to adults.

ankle, to sprain an. To be pregnant but unmarried; an old circumlocution for an exceedingly DELICATE condition, recorded by Capt. Francis Grose, aptly named compiler of *A Classical Dictionary of the Vulgar Tongue* (1796). Variations, working upward, include *stub* (or *stump*) *a toe, break a toe, cut a foot, break an ankle, break a leg, to be broken-kneed* or *broken-legged,* and, most daringly, *to break a leg above the knee.* Eric Partridge dates "break a leg" to circa 1670 in *A Dictionary of Slang and Unconventional English* (1970), and he notes that the French have a similar expression, e.g., *Elle a mal aux genoux* (She has a pain in her knees). Old-timers in the southern part of the United States still use some of these expressions, along with *break her neck* (or *his neck* or *their neck*), which is another way of saying that she, he, or they have gotten married. See also ACCIDENT, PREGNANT, and, for *stubbing one's toe* in yet another way, MENSTRUATION.

anomaly. Disaster. Following the explosion of the space shuttle *Challenger* on January 28, 1985, in which six astronauts and a schoolteacher passenger were killed, a NASA spokesperson explained that flight simulators were being used by experts "working in the anomaly investigation." This helped win the agency a share (along with Morton Thiokol and Rockwell International) of the 1986 Doublespeak Award given by the Committee on Public Doublespeak of the National Council of Teachers of English. See also ABERRATION and CREW TRANSFER CONTAINER.

anticipating. Anticipating birth; PREGNANT. As a rule, women who are *anticipating* do not actually have babies; rather, they bring forth *vital statistics* or BLESSED EVENTS. The gossip columnists, meanwhile, have given us the fatherly *anticipatering, heir conditioned,* and *infanticipating.* By the same treacly token, a newborn bastard is a *sinfant.* See also LOVE CHILD.

antipersonnel weapon. A people-killer—"personnel" being the military way of eliminating figuratively what the weapon eliminates literally. See also PERSONNEL.

Antipersonnel weapons, so named, began showing up in World War II, e.g.: "The antipersonnel mine . . . was dramatically introduced by the Germans in the fall of 1939. . . . Its chief feature was an arrangement whereby the mine, on being tripped, was boosted out of the ground to about the height of a man's waist before exploding. It was really a bomb, which sprayed a wide area with shrapnel" (*Reader's Digest,* 12/42). Loving sobriquets for *antipersonnel weapons* of this sort include *Bouncing Betty, Hopping Sam,* and *Leaping Lena.* An innovation of the Vietnam period was the *Firecracker,* an artillery shell loaded with bomblets (Controlled Fragmentation Munition, officially). See also DAISY-CUTTER, ENHANCED RADIATION WEAPON, FLYING FORTRESS, PEACEKEEPER, SELECTIVE ORDNANCE, SOFT, and the basic military CASUALTY.

antiperspirant. Antisweating. It is very doubtful that the horrid word "sweat" has ever appeared in any of the ads that promise relief from it. See also PERSPIRE.

anti-Semitic. Anti-Jewish. The euphemism was sanctioned by Israeli Prime Minister Menachem Begin, e.g., "One-third of Mr. Begin's prepared text was devoted to what he termed anti-Semitic remarks in the Egyptian press, although Arabs, too, are Semites" (*New York Times,* 1/24/78). "Anti-Semitic" is preferred to "anti-Jewish" because "Jew" is a loaded word. See also ARAB and HEBREW.

antique. Secondhand; see COLLECTIBLE.

anus. Asshole. The polite, medical term comes from the Latin *anus,* ring, circular form, which was a Roman euphemism long before the English adopted the term back around 1400. Thus, Marcellus Tullius Cicero (106–43 B.C.) asserted in one of his letters: "When you speak of the anus, you call it by a name that is not its own; why not rather call it by its own? [He probably was referring to *culus.*] If it is indecent, do not use even the substitute name; if not, you had better call it by its own." See also ARSE, CUL-DE-SAC, and OSSHOLE.

apparatus. The male sexual organs; the GENITALS. Thus, reviewing *Conundrum,* by Jan (née James) Morris: "After eight years of hormone treatment, which made him female in everything but his 'apparatus,' he underwent surgery and had the last vestiges of his masculinity removed" (*New York Times,* 4/9/74). See also SEX REASSIGNMENT.

applesauce. Nonsense or stronger stuff, shit, especially horseshit, a.k.a. *horseapples* and *road apples*. "'I'm about to draw up a budget for the coming year,' Cheshire Superintendent John Barnes said. 'If the state doesn't come through with its promises [of aid for schoolteachers' salaries], we're in deep applesauce'" (Waterbury, Conn., *Republican-American*, 1/22/89). See also BS, DOO-DOO, and FULL OF APPLESAUCE, ETC.

apprehend. To arrest, to nab; police-ese.

appropriate. To steal. With a FOP Index of 2.8, "appropriate" may be further embellished to cover particular kinds of thefts by particular thieves, e.g., bank tellers who *misappropriate* and nations that *expropriate*. The similarity between *appropriating* and stealing was noted in 1864 by a correspondent for the *New York Herald*, William Conyngham, while marching through Georgia with the Union army of Gen. William Tecumseh Sherman: "To draw a line between stealing, and taking and appropriating . . . would puzzle the nicest casuist. Such little freaks as taking the last chicken, the last pound of meal, the last bit of bacon . . . from a poor woman and her flock of children, black or white not considered, came under the order of legitimate business" (Conyngham, *Sherman's March Through the South*, 1865).

For other ways of downplaying theft, see BORROW, CONVEY, EXPROPRIATION, FILCH, FIVE-FINGER DISCOUNT, HOOK, LIBERATE, MOONLIGHT (or MIDNIGHT) REQUISITION, SALVAGE, SAMPLING, SCIENTIFIC AND LITERARY INVESTIGATION, SHRINKAGE, SOCIAL ENGINEERING, and SWIPE.

Arab. Strange as it may seem, an old euphemism for "Jew." Thus, speaking of an engagement in South Haven, across the lake from Chicago, in the summer of 1925: "The Pavilion catered mostly to Gentiles, and when the manager found out that the three of us musicians were Broadway arabs from the tribe of Israel he wouldn't even let us blow note one" (Mezz Mezzrow and Bernard Wolfe, *Really the Blues*, 1946).

Credit for devising this euphemism is given by H. L. Mencken to Jack Conway (d. 1928), a *Variety* staffer, who enriched the language with *palooka, bellylaugh,* SA (for "sex appeal"), *high-hat, pushover,* baloney, *headache* (in the sense of "wife"), and the verbs *to click* (to succeed), *to scram* (Conway's claim to this one has been disputed), and *to laugh that off.* The Arab-for-Jew substitution was popular enough that by 1929 "Arab" was formally banned from the Keith vaudeville circuit. (For other censored terms, see FANNY.) "Arab" is only one of a number of similar euphemisms for "Jew." Among the others: *Joosh* (a Walter Winchell–ism), *Mexican,* and, oddest of all, HEBREW. Of course, Arabs and Jews are still conjoined in another term; see ANTI-SEMITIC.

area bombing. City bombing; also called "saturation bombing" or, more precisely, "terror bombing." "From 1942 to 1944 . . . the British carried on a sustained area bombing campaign with cities and their people candidly its primary targets" (Russell F. Weigley, *The American Way of War*, 1973).

Area bombing was pioneered during World War II by the British, who preferred to fly bombing missions during the night, when the enemy couldn't see them (and when they couldn't see their targets); the Americans, by contrast, flying daytime missions, popularized PRECISION BOMBING. Highlights of the *area bombing* campaign include Hamburg, firebombed at the end of July 1943 (42,000 dead), and Dresden, another firebombing, on the night of February 13–14, 1944 (no one knows how many dead; estimates of the total killed and wounded range from 250,000 to 400,000). See also SPECIFIED STRIKE ZONE.

Arkansas caviar. Long-snouted paddlefish eggs. See also CAPE COD TURKEY.

armed reconnaissance. Bombing; the airborne equivalent of *reconnaissance in force* (search and destroy). Thus, speaking of air operations over North Vietnam, circa 1965: "Attacks were also permitted against certain broad categories of targets, such as vehicles, locomotives and barges, which were defined in Washington. In this type of attack, known as armed reconnaissance, the final selection of a specific target was left to the pilot" (*New York Times* edition of *The Pentagon Papers,* 1971). "Armed reconnaissance" is one of a series of evasions for "bombing" that flourished during the VIETNAM ERA. See also AIR SUPPORT and PROTECTIVE REACTION.

arse. The ass. Some people say "arse" instead of "ass," thinking they are being cute and talking Cockney, but they are really speaking Standard English, since "ass," now commonly thought to be a bad word, began as a mispronunciation of "arse." In effect, the original term has become a euphemism for itself.

"Arse," traced back to about the year 1000 in *The Oxford English Dictionary,* was used without a great deal of shame by many writers for many years, e.g., from Geoffrey Chaucer's *The Miller's Tale* (ca. 1387–1400), in which a young man bestows a dreadfully misplaced kiss—in the dark:

With his mouth he kiste hir naked ers
Ful savourly, er he were war of this

Toward the end of the seventeenth century, polite people began to avoid the word. Samuel Johnson was bold enough to include it in full in his *Dictionary of the English Language* (1755), but other writers of the period frequently felt they had to shield readers from the full force of the expression with dashes or asterisks, as in the following exchange between a master and a serving girl: "I have a great mind to kick your a – –. You, kiss – – – says I" (Henry Fielding, *Shamela,* 1741). This practice has continued into our own century, e.g., "I'm going to whip his – – –," which was how *The New York Times* reported President Jimmy Carter's response to a possible challenge by Massachusetts senator Edward M. Kennedy for the Democratic party's presidential nomination (6/14/79).

"Arse" was changed to "ass" as part of a general dropping of "r" before "s," also evidenced in such pairs as burst/bust, curse/cuss, horse/hoss, and so on. Just when the four-letter "arse" began to be pronounced "ahss" is impossible to say. Shakespeare probably knew the *r*-less pronunciation, playing upon it when he chose Bottom as the name of the weaver who is transformed into an ass in *A Midsummer Night's Dream* (1594). Two hundred years later, Alexander Pope certainly dropped his *r*s. Witness his attack (one of many) on Colley Cibber, ca. 1742:

Cibber! Write all thy Verses upon
  Glasses,
The only way to sav'em from our Arses.

The change in the pronunciation of the four-letter term had reverberations in the countryside. Pre-Victorians became nervous about calling the barnyard critter, the ass, by its rightful name, because the three-letter word sounded like the "bad" four-letter one when the *r* was dropped. This is why we now call this animal a DONKEY.

The loss of the *r* when pronouncing "arse" gradually led to a change in the spelling of the anatomical term, so that it now looks like—as well as sounds like—the donkey's original name. The three-letter spelling, more common in the United States than England, is dated in *The Oxford English Dictionary* to 1860, but most certainly was employed well before then. Thus, a spoof by the young Abraham Lincoln depended in part on such variations of the three-letter word as "bass-ackwards" and "jass-ack." And the original Joe Miller's joke book (1739), which renders the four-letter term variously as "A – –" and "A – se," also includes a jest about an ostler, who managed to prove to a smarty-pants Oxford student that his "saddle" was really a "mule" because it was "something between a *Horse* and an *Ass.*" It seems but a short canter from this to spelling "arse" pronounced "ahss" as "ass."

In other circumstances, of course, "ass" itself may be a euphemism, e.g., such phrases as "get some ass" or "piece of ass," where the true reference is not to the posterior but, depending on exact contest, to the female genitals (an anatomical displacement, parallel to FANNY and TAIL); to an entire woman (considered as a sex object); or, by extension, to the act of sexual intercourse.

As with other topics that are surrounded by especially strong taboos (see MENSTRUATE, PROSTITUTE, TOILET, and VAGINA, for example), there are a great many other euphemisms for the otherwise lowly ass. Among them:

afterpart, ankle (as in "Joe's a pain in the ankle")

back, backseat, BACKSIDE, *beam ends,* BEHIND, *body, boody, bosom of the pants* (see BOSOM), BOTTOM, *breech, bum* (more highly charged in the United Kingdom than the United States; see TRAMP), BUNS, BUTT/BUTTOCKS

caboose, cakes, can, cheeks, crapper (see CRAP)

DERRIÈRE, DUFF

eye (see PIG'S EYE, IN A)

face, FANNY, FUNDAMENT

GLUTEUS MAXIMUS

hams (or *pressed ham* when placed against an automobile window while mooning), *hereafter,* HIERONYMOUS, *hind end, hinderparts,* HINEY, *home base, hunkers* (or *hunkies*)

kazoo, keel, KEISTER

labonza, latter end

neck (typically as *pain in the neck*), *nock* (see KNOCK UP)

PARSON'S- (or POPE'S-) NOSE (the rump of a fowl), *part that went over the fence last, patellas, patoot(ie),* POOP, POOPER, POSTERIOR(S), PRAT

REAR, *rumble seat, rump, rumpus*

saddle (see SADDLEBLOCK ANESTHESIA), SEAT, *setdown,* SIT-ME-DOWN-UPON, *sit-upon* ("sit-upons," by this token, are trousers, or UNMENTIONABLES), *south side, southern exposure, squat* (see also "diddly-squat" in DIDDLY-POO and "hot squat" in HOT SEAT), *squatter, stern, Sunday face*

TAIL, THIGH, TUSHIE

van

whatsis, and WHAT-YOU-MAY-CALL'EM

And this is a mere sampling of the many, often ingenious terms given to this piece of anatomy. Thus, there is a famous prehistoric sculpture known as the Callipygian Venus, with a prominent YOU-KNOW-WHAT (from the Greek *kallipýg(os),* meaning "with beautiful buttocks," originally referring to a statue of Aphrodite). Then there are the various proper names that have been bestowed on the improper part. For example: "Once they're on my payroll, they don't sit around on their old Aristotles" (*Flickers,* WNET-TV, N.Y., 5/23/82); "He'd pull the chair out from under some dignified dowager and catch her just before she went to fall on her daniel" (Mezz Mezzrow and Bernard Wolfe, *Really the Blues,* 1946); and, a nonce term that really deserves to have a long life, "Can't you see [Pete Rose] licking his chops and daring 80-year-old Bob Gibson to groove one? For that matter, can't you see Gibson knocking Rose flat on the Steinbrenner [meaning the inimitable George]?" (*New York Times,* 1/6/91).

See also A – – and OSSHOLE.

artificial. Man-made. Categorizing "man-made" as sexist, the *Random House Webster's College Dictionary* (1991) suggests that speakers and writers replace it with "artificial" or "synthetic." See also PERSON.

Asian. Oriental. "The term *Asian* is to be preferred when describing individuals [from the Orient]" (Frederick S. Holley, comp., *Los Angeles Times Stylebook,* 1981). The trouble with "Oriental," of course, is that Western prejudices against people from the East have affected—one might also say "infected"—the meaning of the traditional word for them. The politically correct "Asian" involves a certain amount of doublethink, however. For example, the *New Dictionary of American Slang* (Robert L.

Chapman, ed., 1986) defines "slant-eye" as "an Asian person or person of Asian descent," which turns a blind eye, so to speak, to millions of Russians, Turks, Saudi Arabians, and other non-Oriental inhabitants of Asia. Similar problems arise with such geographically based terms as "Asian-American," "African-American," "Native American," and "Native Australian," all of which exclude white inhabitants of those territories, no matter of how many generations descent. In point of fact—and political correctness to the contrary—many *Asians* prefer to be described more specifically as "Chinese," "Thai," "Vietnamese," etc. See also CAUCASIAN, NATIVE, and NEGRO.

assassination. A murder or upper-class HIT; the five-syllable word rationalizes the deed while sliding around it with soft-sounding sibilants.

"Yet, the evidence mounts in obscene detail that the murder—a word for which 'assassination' is only a euphemism—of Fidel Castro was a subject of frequent, pointed and practical discussion in the Kennedy Administration—and sometimes by the President himself" (Tom Wicker, *New York Times,* 6/3/75). The United States later renounced *assassination* as an instrument of foreign policy. An executive order issued by President Ronald Reagan on December 4, 1981, stated that "no person employed by or acting on behalf of the U.S. shall engage in or conspire to engage in assassinations." As explicit as this order appears, lower-ranking officials—those on the firing line, so to speak, such as Dewey Claridge, one-time overseer of CIA clandestine operations in Latin America—managed to misread it. When asked by House Intelligence Committee investigators how he reconciled the presidential directive with the killings in Nicaragua by agency-supported Contras of "civilians and Sandinista officials in the provinces, as well as heads of cooperatives, nurses, doctors, and judges," Mr. Claridge replied that "these events don't constitute assassinations because as far as we are concerned assassinations are only those of heads of state. I leave definitions to the politicians" (*Philadelphia Inquirer*, 10/20/84). For this improvement upon standard dictionaries, which define "assassination" as the act of murdering a prominent person, not necessarily a head of state, Mr. Claridge received a Doublespeak Award in 1985 from the Committee on Public Doublespeak of the National Council of Teachers of English.

See also ACCIDENT, DISPOSE, ELIMINATE/ELIMINATION, EXECUTIVE ACTION, and REMOVE. For the quieter, natural way to die, see PASS AWAY.

assault. A common journalistic euphemism for "rape"—a word that was barred for many years from newspapers in Britain and the United States. "Delicacy becomes absurdity when it produces such an anticlimax as is contained in *Pathological tests suggest that she had two blows on the head, was strangled and probably assaulted*" (H. W. Fowler, *A Dictionary of Modern English Usage*, rev. and ed. by Sir Ernest Gowers, 1965). Other forms of "assault," all with the same meaning and all more or less obsolete now that "rape" has become printable, include *brutal assault, criminal assault, felonious assault, improper assault,* and *indecent assault.* See also INTERFERE WITH, MOLEST, RAVAGE, RAVISH, and STATUTORY OFFENSE.

assembly center. A prison camp, American style, also known as a RELOCATION CEN-TER; specifically, one of the camps in which some 100,000 Japanese-Americans were held during World War II on the dubious assumption (not one was ever found guilty of sabotage) that they were more loyal to their country of origin than to the country in which they made their homes. From a firsthand account: "There behind the barbed wire of a hastily built concentration camp, we were assigned temporary quarters. This was one of many such places constructed by the government that spring [of 1942] and euphemistically called assembly centers" (*New York Times*, 7/4/74). See also CONCENTRATION CAMP and PREVENTIVE DETENTION.

assessment. A test; educationese, with a FOP Index of 3.0, also called an *assessment tool* (FOP 4.5) or *evaluation instrument* (FOP 7.0). See also INSTRUMENT and NEEDS ASSESSMENT.

assignation. A meeting between lovers. The fancy "assignation" may come from "assignation house," a nineteenth-century establishment in which rooms were let for short periods. Some hostelries still operate in much the same manner. An eye-opener for commuters to New York City (ca. 1990) was the sign on the York Motel, near the New Jersey end of the Lincoln Tunnel, which advertised the availability of "Color TV, Mirror Rooms, Low Day Rates." All for business conferences presumably. See also HOUSE, MATINEE, and MOTEL.

Assistant to the President for Public Events and Initiatives. Handler, image-maker; the person in charge of shaping presidential messages, schedules, and appearances for maximum political effect. Formally established in the Bush administration (though the techniques were developed into an art form in the Reagan years by Michael Deaver, deputy chief of staff from 1981 to 1985), the position was continued in the Clinton White House. Depending on whether the job is defined as "handler" or "image-maker," the position has a FOP Index of 11 or 7.5. Both pale in comparison, however, to the *Personal Assistant to the Secretary (Special Activities),* who worked as a cook for Joseph A. Califano, secretary of Health, Education and Welfare in the Carter administration. With a FOP Index of 17.8, one of the highest in captivity, "Personal Assistant to the . . ." also demonstrates in spades the general bureaucratic rule that the longer the title, the more menial the position. See also ENGINEER.

associate. A classy term for anyone in a subservient position. For example, salesclerks in the K mart and Wal-Mart chains have been elevated into *associates* (see FRATERNIZATION) and supermarket checkout clerks have been promoted into *part-time career associate scanning professionals.* The Honda plant in Marysville, Ohio, employs *associates,* not workers; an *associate director* in the wasteland of TV is a director's assistant, and an *associate editor* in magazine and book publishing is a junior editor or writer. In the academic world, an *associate in arts* is a student who has not completed the full course of studies, while an *associate professor* must stand aside when a plain, unadorned "professor" walks into the room. The term may also help blur the stigma attached to some occupational specialties, as in police work, where a shoofly —an officer assigned to spy upon fellow officers—is known technically as a *field associate.* See also ENGINEER.

associated with. The executive form of "employed by," sometimes shortened to "with," as in "I used to be with IBM." In general, top dogs are *associated with* firms in particular CAPACITIES or POSITIONS for which they receive REMUNERATION, and when they leave, they RESIGN. Lower-ranking PERSONNEL work at jobs for pay, and they are LET GO. See also HELP.

asylum. A madhouse. Originally a place of refuge, or sanctuary, from which debtors and criminals could not be removed without sacrilege, the meaning of "asylum" gradually was broadened, starting in the eighteenth century, to include institutions for the deaf, the dumb, the blind, the orphaned, and the mad, or lunatic (in effect, the "moonstruck," from Luna, Roman goddess of the moon). "Asylums" for the demented appeared on both sides of the Atlantic practically simultaneously. In 1828, Sir A. Halliday prepared a report, entitled *A General View of the Present State of Lunatics, and Lunatic Asylums, in Great Britain and Ireland.* Two years earlier, in the American hinterland, a petition was prepared for "the addition of a Lunatic Asylum" (Benjamin Drake and E. D. Mansfield, *Cincinnati in 1826,* 1827). In time, of course, "asylum" was tainted by its associations with madness. In New York City, the name of West Fourth Street in Greenwich Village used to be Asylum Street. See also MENTAL HOSPITAL.

athletic supporter. Not an ardent sports fan but a jockstrap; also called a "supporter" for short, as in a furious letter from a famous father to a music critic who had panned his daughter's singing recital: "Some day I hope to meet you. When that happens you'll need a new nose, a lot of beefsteak for black eyes, and perhaps a supporter below!" (President Harry S Truman to Paul Hume, of the *Washington Post,* 12/6/50).

The "jock" in the underlying "jockstrap" is a quintessentially male term, deriving from *jockum,* an old slang term for the penis, almost certainly based, in turn, on the personal name, "Jock," which comes from "John." This makes the phrase "female jock," for a woman athlete, something of a contradiction in terms. See also JOHN and JOHN THOMAS.

at liberty. Out of work; the free-sounding euphemism makes it seem as though one is on vacation. See also BETWEEN ASSIGNMENTS; FURLOUGH; the *gentleman at large* in GENTLEMAN; TRANSITION, IN; and the basic LET GO.

attendance teacher. A truant officer, new style. For some reason, truants who are nabbed by the *attendance teacher* are not called *attendance pupils,* although it would be entirely consistent to do so. See also TEACHER PRESENCE.

at this/that point in time. Now/then. The circumlocutions, known technically as periphrases, have relatively high FOP Indexes of 8.3 and 6.25, respectively. They were used so often by erstwhile presidential COUNSEL John W. Dean III when testifying before the Senate Watergate Committee in 1973 that they came to sum up the tenor of those sessions much as "point of order" did for the Army-McCarthy hearings of 1954. Dean did not invent them, of course. They are standard bureaucratese. For example, Arthur M. Schlesinger, Jr., noted in *A Thousand Days* (1965) that State Department functionaries "never talked about a 'paper' but always 'a piece of paper,' never

said 'at this point' but always 'at this point in time.'" As laughable as they may seem, the stock phrases do have a serious purpose. In conversation generally—and in cross-examination particularly—they enable the speaker to fill the air with words while the mind races ahead to frame the substance of the reply. In this respect, "at this point in time" is merely a more articulate version of the humdrum *er, huh, uh, um, well,* and YOU KNOW. English teachers may frown upon these monosyllabic exhalations, but their utility was noted as long ago as 1839 by Capt. Frederick Marryat in *A Diary of America:*

> There are two syllables—*um, hu* [i.e., huh]—which are very generally used by the Americans as a sort of reply, intimating that they are attentive, and that the party may proceed with his narrative, but by inflection and intonation are made to express dissent or assent, surprise, disdain. I myself found them very convenient at times, and gradually got into the habit of using them.

For more testimonial talk, see INDICATE, NO RECALL (or MEMORY or RECOLLECTION) OF, and THIGH.

attorney. Lawyer. They study law at law school rather than attorneying at attorney school, but most lawyers prefer to be called "attorney" even though this term, which actually refers to a legal agent—to someone who is authorized to act for another—is not as accurate as "lawyer," meaning someone who is entitled to practice law. Evidently, lawyers wish to escape the negative associations connected with the correct name of their profession. (When did you ever hear of a Philadelphia *attorney*?) See also COUNCILOR, COUNSEL, and ENGINEER.

au naturel. Naked, undressed. Pressed into service in English as a euphemism (1905, *OED*), the French culinary term for food that is presented plain, without sauce, has gained thereby a mildly saucy meaning. A charming Frenchified synonym is *à la September morn*, "used by my mother, a native of the Irish ghetto of St. John, New Brunswick, and very much the R.C. (another euphemism!) lace-curtain Irish sort" (Ronald Dahlquist, letter, 12/6/82). See also NUDE.

authentic reproduction. A reproduction, the "authentic" being pure doubletalk, signifying nothing. If something is "authentic," in the legitimate sense of that word, it isn't a "reproduction," and if it is a "reproduction," it isn't "authentic." The phrase is much used by reproducers of furniture and art works. "The Bombay Company offers 'an authentic reproduction of a fine old English antique.' An authentic reproduction strikes me as not far removed from a genuine sham" (John Simon, *Esquire*, 12/5/78). See also RIGHT, NOT; SIMULATED; and UNIQUE REPLICA.

author. Writer; "author" sounds classier because of the ear's uncanny preference for Latinate words with "or" endings. Thus, books are produced by "authors," while lesser works, such as screenplays and magazine articles, are turned out by "writers." The division is echoed in association names, e.g., The Authors Guild, composed mainly of book writers, and the Writers Union, made up mainly of authors of shorter works. See also EDUCATOR and REALTOR.

auto-da-fé. Literally, "act of faith," but in reality, a pious circumlocution for carrying out a sentence of the Holy Office of the Inquisition, most spectacularly by burning at the stake. In English, the Portuguese spelling is more common than the Spanish *auto-de-fé*, but it was in Spain that the Inquisition achieved its greatest notoriety. "Act of faith," which compares well in opacity with the modern FINAL SOLUTION, is merely one of a cluster of words and expressions that were given special meanings by the Inquisitors in their zeal to root out heresy. The bending of the meanings of words is symptomatic of a diseased institution, with the angle of linguistic deflection indicating the seriousness of the cancer within. The Spanish Inquisition represented an advanced case. Consider:

The Inquisitors depended on torture (from the Latin *torquere*, to twist; the name of the inquisitor general, Tomás de Torquemada, being merely a happy coincidence), as few people would confess without torture, or the threat of it, to sins for which they could lose their lives. The Inquisitors did not speak of "torture," however. Rather, they referred to this stage of their inquiry as *the question.*

The Inquisitors were forbidden from repeating tortures, a seemingly enlightened prohibition, which they broke regularly, particularly when victims stopped feeling pain because they had lost consciousness. The Inquisitors got around the prohibition by pretending they had never stopped the torture. Thus, they talked of *continuing to put the question* or of *suspending* it for a time.

The Inquisitors conducted their operations in the *Casa Santa*. The name was the same wherever the building was located. It translates as "Holy House" or "Holy Office."

The Inquisitors were forbidden from committing murder or from shedding blood (priest-torturers gave one another immediate absolution when accidents occurred) and they could not even ask the state to execute the people they had condemned. Accordingly, one of the high points of the *auto-da-fé* came when the Church formally *abandoned* its victims to secular authority, *beseeching* the state to deal moderately with the poor souls, neither taking their lives nor shedding their blood. This pious entreaty was honored in the sense that burning or strangulation do not involve bloodletting, but everyone realized that the request for moderation was for God's ears only. Any secular official who heeded the letter of the Inquisitors' words, rather than their spirit, was likely to face *the question* himself.

The ultimate "act of faith," the public burning, was reserved for those who had committed the greatest crimes in the eyes of the Inquisitors and who also remained *obstinate*, i.e., they had refused to repent despite prolonged *questioning.* People who had fled to other countries were burned in effigy and the bodies of those who had had the good luck to die before being judged were disinterred and burned also. In the case of an especially grievous sinner, the faggots might be dampened in order to roast the victim slowly. Of course, repentance could be made at any time—even as the fire was being lit—and to those who repented, the Church offered *mercy* . . . in the form of strangulation before burning.

In a belated attempt to improve its public image, the Church changed the name of the Holy Office of the Inquisition in 1965 to the Congregation for the Doctrine of Faith.

See also CAPITAL PUNISHMENT and INTERROGATION.

automotive dismantler and recycler. A junkyard operator. "Pennsylvania's state legislators have voted to beautify an eyesore—at least on the books. Henceforth under a newly passed law, the operator of an auto junkyard will be officially known as an 'automotive dismantler and recycler'" (*New Age*, 9/77). The euphemism has even been adopted in Motor City itself, as indicated by the headline in *The Detroit News* (8/18/82):

Junkyards heading for scrapheap
Auto recycling centers help create new image

The *automotive dismantlers and recyclers* deal in "predismantled previously owned parts" (*Time*, 5/11/83). See also PREOWNED and RECYCLER.

automotive internist. The mechanic who cares for cars before they finally die and go to the AUTOMOTIVE DISMANTLER AND RECYCLER. See also ENGINEER.

aversion therapy. The use of pain and/or fear to persuade a person to change his or her behavior; also called *behavior modification.* Typically, *aversion therapy* involves electric shock, forced vomiting, or other painful procedures. The idea is that the "patient" will associate the pain with the undesirable behavior, come to regard that behavior pattern as repugnant, and then change it. The technique has been applied in many up-to-date CORRECTIONAL FACILITIES and MENTAL HOSPITALS. From the standpoint of a person who is forced to undergo it, *aversion therapy* is difficult to distinguish from punishment or torture. And it doesn't always work. For example, from the summary of a 1964 British case: "Aversion therapy was conducted with a male homosexual who had a heart condition. The particular form of aversion therapy involved creation of nausea, by means of an emetic, accompanied by talking about his homosexuality. The second part of the therapy involved recovery from the nausea and talking about pleasant ideas and heterosexual fantasies, which was sometimes aided by lysergic acid. In this case, the patient died as a result of a heart attack brought on by the use of the emetic" (Martin S. Weinberg and Alan P. Bell, *Homosexuality, An Annotated Bibliography*, 1972, in Jonathan Katz, *Gay American History*, 1976). See also ADJUSTMENT CENTER, BRAINWASH, *negative reinforcement* in NEGATIVE, and STRESS-PRODUCING STIMULUS.

B

BA. (1) Bullshit artist; see BS. (2) Bare-ass, completely naked, as in "We went swimming BA." A *bab*, pronounced "bee-ay-bee," is a *bare-ass beach.* See also A – – and CLOTHING OPTIONAL.

backside. The ass; a general reference to the entire back of the body when, in truth, a single portion is meant, e.g., a 1977 Los Angeles KNBC-TV review of *The Act*: "After three hours, not only does the show need a new book, you need a new backside." The oldest example of the word's anatomical sense in *The Oxford English Dictionary* comes from a version of the story of Robin Hood, composed about 1500: "With an arrowe so broad, He shott him into the backe-syde." As commonly happens, the euphemism became tainted by the thought of the word for which it stood. Thus, "backside" was cited as a bawdy term by prim U.S. postal authorities in a 1943–44 proceeding against that primeval playboy, *Esquire.* Even unto the late twentieth century, fastidious people may acknowledge the word's power by omitting the "side" part, e.g., "We can't sit on our backs indefinitely and let them get too far ahead" (CBS-TV, newscast, 6/25/82), or, a common construction, "The Los Angeles Rams have long been a pain in the back for the Giants" (*New York Times*, 10/17/94). See also ARSE.

baksheesh. A bribe. The word for a small present a tip (from the Persian *bakhshish*, gift), becomes a euphemism when applied to large sums transferred beneath the table instead of over it. Thus, Lt. Col. Oliver North testified at the Iran-Contra congressional hearings in July 1987 that he had not bothered to report the offer of a bribe to him by the Iranian arms dealer Manucher Ghorbanifar because "everyone involved in it knew what baksheesh is. And it was expected." The proffered *baksheesh* in this instance was $1 million. See also COMMISSION, CUMSHAW, GRATUITY, and IMPROPER.

ball. A happy-sounding FOUR-LETTER WORD substitutes for a rather coarser one, as in, from *What Really Happened to the Class of '65*: "'In the summers I'd go to the beach. Maybe I'd ball two or three fellows a day'" (Michael Medved and David Wallechinsky, 1977). The copulatory "ball" may simply be a spin-off of "ball" in the good-time sense of "I had a ball last night." The word's sexual sense, however, is reinforced by the proximity of the anatomical ball, or TESTICLE. Thus, predating the antics of the class of '65 by some seventy-five years: "I ballocked that little girl" (anon., *My Secret Life*, ca. 1890). See also BOLLIXED UP, F – – –, and INTERCOURSE.

ball game, end of the. Death. In the words of astronaut Maj. Alfred M. Worden: "When you are out there 200,000 miles from earth, if something goes wrong, you know that's the end of the ball game" (*New York Times*, 8/14/71).

Life frequently is conceived of as a game (see GAME), so it is only natural that death should often be euphemized in game-playing terms, including:

cash in [*one's*] *chips* (or *checks* or *hand* or
    last stack of blues)
drop the cue (billiards)
go to the races
is knocked out (or *KO'd*)

jump the last hurdle
out of the game (or *running)*
pass (or *hand) in one's checks* (or *chips)*
peg out (cribbage)
race is run (or *ran the good race)*
shot the works (from craps, betting all that
    one has on a single roll of the dice)
shuffled (*clean) out of the deck*
struck out
take the last (or *long) count*
throw for a loss
throw in the sponge
throw sixes
throw up the cards
trumped
went to the races

See also PASS AWAY.

balmy. Mad, idiotic. The pleasant word for that which is refreshing or soothing (from "balm," a fragrant resin used in medicine and perfumery) surfaced in mid-nineteenth-century English slang as a mild term for those who are soft-minded. Usually an adjective, the word also has seen service as a noun, e.g., "These are officially classed as 'W.M.'—that is weak-minded—but are invariably known colloquially as 'balmies'" (Lord W. Nevill, *Penal Servitude,* 1903). See also MENTAL.

balneology. "Balneology is, according to *New Scientist* (Volume 67, Number 966), the science of swimming pools" (*Smithsonian,* 1/76). A practitioner of *balneology* is a *balneologist.* See also SWIMMING ENVIRONMENT.

baloney/boloney. A byword for "nonsense" or "rubbish" as well as a euphemism for the decidedly stronger "bull (or horse) shit." For example, speaking of Federal Judge John J. Sirica's refusal to require Richard M. Nixon to testify at the Watergate COVER-UP trial, for fear that such a stand-up performance would kill the (then-ailing) former president, one of the principal defendants, John D. Ehrlichman, asserted that the judge's reasoning was "Just pure—if you'll pardon the expression—baloney" (speech, Dutch Treat Club, New York City, 5/1/79).

On the face of it, "baloney" seems to derive from the bologna sausage, but the connection has never been proved, and attempts have been made to link it to other sources. Perhaps because the English eat *polony* instead of baloney, Eric Partridge, whose opinion is not to be dismissed lightly in these matters, suggested the gypsy *peloni,* testicles, as the source (*A Dictionary of Slang and Unconventional English,* 1970). If this is so, the true euphemistic meaning of "That's a lot of baloney" actually is "That's all balls."

Credit for popularizing baloney-as-rubbish in the United States usually is given to Governor Al Smith, of New York, who talked of the "baloney dollar" after the 1934 devaluation. Smith, in turn, probably picked up the term from Jack Conway, a remarkably fecund wordsmith (see ARAB) and longtime *Variety* staffer. What inspired Conway is unknown. Perhaps "baloney" sprang full-blown from his Zeus-like brow. Or perhaps he got it from the lingo of prizefighting, where a "baloney" used to be a clumsy, unskilled fighter (a "palooka"), or from the Chicago stockyards, where an old bull, fit for making nothing else, was called a "bologna." See also BS; FULL OF APPLESAUCE, ETC.; HOOEY; NUTS; and SHUCKS.

BAM. A female marine, i.e., a Broad-Assed Marine; service slang dating to World War II. See also A – –.

bang. To engage in sexual intercourse and, as a noun, the person *banged* (the *bangee*?) or the act thereof ("to do it standing up," according to an informant who came of age in the Pittsburgh area); a *gang bang* if more than two people are engaged, also called an orgy, if by mutual consent, and gang rape if not. (See also *gang shack* in SHACK UP WITH.) The sexual "bang" may derive from "bang" in the sense of a thrill or excitement, as in "I get a bang out of surfing," but a likelier source is the "bang" that is a loud hit or blow, somewhat in the sense of "Wham, bam, thank you ma'am." This latter sense of "bang" parallels *hammer, nail,* and *pound,* also used with reference to INTERCOURSE. The association between violence and sex is strong. It also is old: "He . . . kist her bonny Mow, Sir;/ . . . and bang'd her side Weam too Sir" (where "Mow" is Scots for "mouth" and "Weam" is a variant of "womb"; Thomas D'Urfey, *Wit and Mirth: Or Pills to Purge Melancholy, Being a Collection . . . of Ballads and Songs,* 1698–1720). See also ACTION, BOINK, and the etymology of F – – –.

barnyard epithet. Bullshit—the most memorable euphemistic circumlocution coined by *The New York Times.*

"Barnyard epithet" arose this way: On February 4, 1970, during the course of the trial of the Chicago Eight for conspiracy to disrupt the Democratic National Convention of 1968, one of the defendants, David Dellinger, exclaimed "Oh, bullshit!" upon hearing Chicago Deputy Police Chief James Riordan's version of Dellinger's actions some seventeen months before. The exclamation became news because Judge Julius Hoffman reprimanded Dellinger for using "that kind of language" and revoked his bail. Covering for the *Times* was Pulitzer

Prize–winner J. Anthony Lukas, who recalled subsequent events this way:

> Knowing the *Times'* sensitivity about such language, I called the National Desk and asked how they wanted to handle Mr. Dellinger's phrase. The editor on duty said he didn't think we could use it and suggested I just say "an obscenity." I objected, arguing that it wasn't, strictly speaking, an obscenity; that if we called it that most people would assume it was something much worse; and that since it was central to the day's events we ought to tell our readers just what Mr. Dellinger had said. The editor thought for a minute and said, "Why don't we call it a barnyard epithet?" Everything considered, that seemed like the best solution, and that was the way it appeared in the *Times* the next morning. (Hillier Krieghbaum, *Pressures on the Press,* 1972)

The *Times* has continued to employ "barnyard epithet" ("Metro Matters," 10/13/94), as well as different variations on the theme, including *barnyard vulgarity* (3/23/77), *henhouse epithet* (1/2/79), *cow-pasture vulgarism* (8/20/80), and *barnyard expression* (9/14/87). So "barnyard epithet" is fertile, to say the least. See also BM and BS.

bastard. It's an epithet now, and has been one for many centuries, but its etymology suggests that it started life as a euphemism. The word comes from the Old French *fils de bast,* packsaddle child, where the *bast,* or packsaddle, often was used as a bed by mule drivers. Its synonym, "bantling," seems to have a parallel etymology, being rooted in the German *bank,* bench, with the implication that the child was begotten on a bench rather than in a bed.

Though somewhat less heavily tabooed than formerly, "bastard" is not yet entirely out of the linguistic woods. It is sometimes euphemized as *B* and *B* – – – – – –, and when a miniseries called "The Bastard" was prepared by a consortium of television stations in 1978, ten of the ninety-three broadcasters diffidently dropped that title in favor of "The Kent Family Chronicles," the subtitle of the John Jakes novel from which the series was adapted. See also BLANKET, BORN ON THE WRONG SIDE OF THE; LOVE CHILD; MIX (or MIXED BREED); and SOB.

bathroom. A generalization for "toilet," most obviously in connection with bathless bathrooms in public buildings. Thus, advising visitors to New York's Metropolitan Museum of Art: "Be prepared not to have to go to the bathroom, since once you leave the exhibit you can't get back in" (Brooklyn, N.Y., *Phoenix*, 1/11/79). See also TOILET.

bathroom tissue. Toilet paper. "Does your husband care about bathroom tissue?" (commercial, WOR-TV, N.Y., 8/8/78). *Bathroom tissue* comes in a variety of grades, the finest of which is said to be—incongruously—"of facial quality." More picturesque are the American *bung-fodder* (the comparison is to the bunghole of a barrel) and the older British *bum-fodder* (from 1653, *OED*). The latter often is abbreviated to *bumf*, in which form it also refers to another kind of paper—that is, the DOCUMENTS that bureaucrats love to shuffle about. For more about the British "bum," see TRAMP.

baton. A billyclub, a nightstick. Police officers who carry *batons* are promoting themselves, in effect, as this sense of the term stems from the *baton* that is a staff of office, carried by a military marshal or other high-ranking official. The term's associations with the conductor's slender *baton* and the *baton* that is twirled by miniskirted majorettes also help obscure the uses to which the billyclub may be put, e.g., "Two police officers beat a blind man with their batons after mistaking his collapsible cane for an illegal martial arts weapon, the authorities said" (AP, 5/16/89). Police have employed *batons* since the nineteenth century. Now they also have *baton rounds* and *anti-riot batons,* which are plastic bullets. At the ranges for which they are designed, 70 to 150 yards, *baton rounds* produce severe bruises; if fired at close range, they can kill. See also OFFICER.

BD (also **b&d, b/d, bd).** Bondage and discipline in ads of a very personal nature. See also SM and, for *BD* in use, the classified ad in FRENCH.

beau. A fop or, more to the point, a dandy. "Dandy has been voted vulgar, and Beau is now the word" (Benjamin Disraeli, *The Young Duke*, 1829).

beautician. A person who works in a beauty parlor; especially a hairdresser. "Beautician" is kissing cousin to MORTICIAN, both descending from "physician." (The prestige of medicine has led some *beauticians* to metamorphose yet again into *beauty therapists.*) The earliest known example of "beautician" comes from a Cleveland, Ohio, telephone directory of 1924. The sonorous appellation seems to have caught on quickly, since, by 1926, newspapers from as far away as Scotland were commenting upon it, e.g., "The immense growth of 'beauty parlors' in the United

States has added to the American language the word 'beautician'" (*Glasgow Herald*, 6/12/26). The establishment in which the *beautician* works also is something of a euphemism: Before *beauty parlors* and *beauty shoppes* appeared on the scene, there were *hairdressing parlors, rooms,* and *salons.* All these euphemisms, however, pale before the seventeenth-century English dressers of female coiffures who called themselves *woman-surgeons.* See also COLOR, COSMETICIAN/COSMETOLOGIST, PARLOR, SALON, and SHOPPE.

bed. The place for repose frequently serves as a euphemism for sexual activity that occurs there. "Those girls were always competing with each other: one would come up, switching her hips like a young duck and whisper in your year, 'Want to go to bed, dear, I'll show you a good time, I'm French'" (Mezz Mezzrow and Bernard Wolfe, *Really the Blues,* 1946).

The euphemistic sense is equally apparent when the noun is converted into a verb, as in "Woo her, wed her, and bed her" (William Shakespeare, *The Taming of the Shrew,* 1593). This is true, too, of such regrettably obsolete terms as *bed-presser,* a fornicator or womanizer; *bed-sister,* a married man's mistress in relation to his wife; and *bed-swerver,* one who is unfaithful to the marriage bed. See also FRENCH, SLEEP WITH, and WANNA GO OUT?.

begad. By God, usually an exclamation. "'Begad! madame,' answered he, ''tis the very same I met'" (Henry Fielding, *Joseph Andrews,* 1742). See also EGAD.

beggar. Bugger, a British euphemism for a pederast, as in "You stupid beggar," or the practice of pederasty, as in "I'll be beggared if I let you do such and such!" See also LADYBIRD.

begorra(h). An Anglo-Irish euphemism for "by God." It is the functional equivalent of *bejeebers* or *bejab(b)ers,* i.e., "By Jesus." See also GOLLY and GOSH.

behind. The ass; the general, locational, it's-somewhere-back-there reference is what is known technically as a topographical euphemism.

In 1882–88, when volume B of *The Oxford English Dictionary* was being prepared, "behind" was considered colloquial and vulgar, and was so labeled. And as recently as 1943–44, "behind" was cited (along with such other filth as BACKSIDE and "bawdy-house") in a post office suit to prevent *Esquire* from sullying the nation's mails. Today, however, "behind" has been overtaken by other words, and it is regarded as such a mild term (comparable to FANNY or TUSHIE) that even the *New York Times,* justly famed for avoiding anything OBSCENE, DEROGATORY, AND SCATOLOGICAL, has found it fit to print—and on its front page yet. Thus, quoting an assistant New York City police chief: "The feeling right now is, 'Cover your behind and forget about taking chances'" (10/27/76).

The oldest anatomical "behind" in *The Oxford English Dictionary* comes from 1786 and actually refers to an article of clothing: "Two young ladies . . . with new Hats on their heads, new Bosoms [see BOSOM], and new Behinds in a band-box" (*Lounger,* no. 54). More typical is King George IV's utterance, from about 1830: "Go and do my bidding—tell him he lies, and kick his behind in my name!" (*Saturday Review,* 2/18/1862). Up to mid-century, however, the anatomical meaning was not necessarily the first one that came to mind, e.g., "The first nine of the Gotham Club are: Burns, behind; T. G. Van Cott, pitcher" (*Porter's Spirit of the Times*, 1857). It probably will be some time, however, before the Baseball Hall of Fame at Cooperstown mounts an exhibition in honor of Yogi Berra, Johnny Bench, and other "Immortal Behinds." Accepted variations on the "behind" theme include *hind end, hind part, hinder part(s), hindhead,* and *hiney*. See also ARSE and CYA.

Bell Telephone Hour. Torture time, circa VIETNAM ERA. The euphemism comes from the field telephones, whose wiring was used to deliver shocks to the GENITALS or breasts of suspected Viet Cong. Domestically, telephones also have been used this way. At the Tucker State Farm (i.e., prison) in Arkansas, the arrangement was known as *the Tucker telephone* up to 1967 when a new warden forbade its use. Suspects in police stations formerly (?) received *telephone calls,* too, but these messages were delivered by placing a phone book on top of the person's head, then hitting it with a hammer. This method of questioning elicits answers without leaving bruises. See also INTERROGATION, STATE FARM/HOSPITAL/TRAINING SCHOOL, and TALK MAN.

bench, the. Judge, the; a topographical euphemism that elevates the incumbent by identifying him (or her) in terms of physical position. "As for magistrates acquiescing in or relishing the term *the bench*—surely language is too important a matter to be left in the hands of magistrates" (John Simon, *Esquire,* 4/25/78). See also OVAL OFFICE.

bender. A drunken spree, perhaps from "bender," a hard drinker (? one who bends his elbow a lot, lifting mug to lips); also, a nineteenth-century evasion for the human "knee," particularly a female one, and particularly in Boston, home of the bean, the cod, and the bluenose. "Young ladies are not allowed to cross their benders in school" (Henry Wadsworth Longfellow, *Kavanagh,* 1849). See also HIGH and LIMB.

benign neglect. Neglect; the "benign," which is just so much eyewash, gives the expression a FOP Index of 2.3. The most famous "benign neglect" of our time occurred in a memo that Senator Daniel Patrick Moynihan (D., N.Y.) wrote on March 2, 1970, in a prior incarnation as urban affairs adviser to President Richard M. Nixon: "The time may have come when the issue of race could benefit from a period of 'benign neglect.'" He took the phrase from the earl of Durham, who had recommended to Queen Victoria in 1839 that Canada be given the right to govern herself, since she had done so well on her own "through a period of benign neglect."

For another form of not-so-benign neglect, see TRIAGE.

bereavement fare. A discount for death in the airline business, also called a *compassionate fare.* "BEREAVEMENT FARES ARE BACK" (headline, *U.S. News & World Report,* 11/30/92). *Bereavement discounts* (usually 15 percent to 20 percent off the most expensive tickets) are offered to passengers whose lateness in making reservations is due to the sudden death or serious illness of a relative. Of course, the bereaved one has to have the presence of mind to come to the ticket office with documentary evidence in hand of the nature of the emergency and of the relationship involved. See also EX GRATIA, PASS AWAY, and WATER LANDING.

betray. To seduce—a word that was deemed for many years to be too sexy to appear in the popular press. Quotation marks around the term are a dead give-away to its conscious use as a euphemism, e.g., "A conviction not so entirely unknown to the 'betrayed' as some amiable theorists would have us believe" (Thomas Hardy, *Tess of the D'Urbervilles,* 1891). This sense of "betray" arose during the period of pre-Victorian prudery (1766, *OED*). The hearts of unreconstructed male chauvinists will be gladdened to know that in traditional English common law an unmarried woman could not sue the person who had *betrayed* her. The legal theory was that she had suffered no harm, even though she might have lost her virginity. If she had the misfortune to become PREGNANT, however, an action could be brought, not by the woman *betrayed,* but by her parents or her master on the grounds that *they* had been damaged through loss of her services.

between assignments. Unemployed. "I was 'between assignments'—Hollywood's euphemism for out of work" (Richard Walter, *Screenwriting: The Art, Craft, and Business of Film and Television Writing,* 1988). See also AT LIBERTY.

beverage host. A bartender at Florida's Walt Disney World. "Thus a bartender, rare species that he is in these precincts, is a 'Beverage Host'" (Robert Craft, *New York Review of Books,* 5/16/74). "Beverage host" is only the latest of many efforts to replace the blunt "bartender." Among them: *bar clerk, bartarian, mixer,* MIXOLOGIST, *server,* and *tapster.* Consistent with this, cocktail wait-resses are sometimes known as *beverage attendants.* See also HIGH, REFRESHMENT, and SALOON.

BF. Bloody fool. "You really are a BF, Arthur" (C. D. Lewis, *Child of Misfortune,* 1939). This is one of many British evasions for "bloody"; see RUDDY.

B-girl. A floozie or part-time prostitute, especially one who works in a bar, receiving a commission on the drinks she persuades customers to buy. "I seem to meet nothing but B-girls out here" (Budd Schulberg, *What Makes Sammy Run?,* 1941). The exact meaning of the "B" in "B-girl" has yet to be pinned down by lexicographers. Some say that it stands for "bar" or "brandy" or for "putting the bee" on a customer to buy a drink. Others theorize that it means "bad," perhaps with reinforcement from "Grade B." Or it may be that "beer" is involved, since "B-girl" (from 1936, *OED*) was preceded by "beer-jerker" (from ca. 1865). For example, concert-saloons (forerunners of the modern night-club), which became popular in New Orleans in the years just after the Civil War, employed "waiter girls, popularly known as 'beer-jerkers,' who sometimes doubled as singers and dancers" (Herbert Asbury, *The French Quarter,* 1936). The *beer-jerker,* like the *B-girl,* did not receive a salary but was allowed to keep any tips, got a 10 percent commission on liquor sales, and usually supplemented this income with prostitution. See also PROSTITUTE and the *B-girl's* cousin, the *V-girl,* or VICTORY GIRL.

bilateral orchidectomy. From the root, "orchid," one might easily suppose this to be a horticultural expression, perhaps having something to do with pruning—and, as it happens, pruning is involved, this being the proper surgeon's way of alluding to an operation otherwise known as "castration." See also ALTER, FIX, MUTILATE, and TESTICLES.

The orchid plant is so called on account of the bulbous shape of its roots, the Latin *orchis* coming from the Greek word for "testicle." It was because of this "sexy" etymology that the eminent Victorian critic and writer John Ruskin (1819–1900) campaigned to have the plant's name changed to "Wreathewort." The failure of Ruskin's noble effort may reflect declining educational standards, his objections to "orchid" not being immediately apparent to those with little Latin and less Greek. See also PARSON-IN-THE-PULPIT.

binocular deprivation. Blinding, the scientific way. "But for a truly gruesome euphemism, try 'binocular deprivation.' That was a description in a Wisconsin journal for a procedure in which a cat's eyes were sewn shut" (Toronto *Globe and Mail,* 2/2/92). See also SACRIFICE.

biosolids. Treated sewage; sludge. The executive committee of the Water Pollution Control Federation adopted "biosolids" as the new name for treated human wastes, according to the *Quarterly Review of Doublespeak* (4/92). The WPCA opted for *biosolids* in preference to such other perfumed possibilities as *bioslurp, prenutri, humanure, black gold,* and *brown gold.* See also FERTILIZER, NIGHT SOIL, and WASTE.

"Biosolids" is just one of many "bio-" compounds that were popularized during the 1960s and 1970s as a result of the space program (*bioexperiment, biosatellite, biosensor*) and the environmental movement (*biodegradable, biodiversity,* and *biotoxic).* It

did not take long for the scientific prefix to be adopted in nonscientific contexts, e.g., *biobeer, biohome, biomorphic* (body-fitting, as a chair) and *bioparent* (see BIRTHPARENT). British breakthroughs include *biobottom,* a biodegradable diaper, and *biosurgery,* the use of maggots to clean wounds.

bipolar disorder. Manic depression. "Bipolar disorder (as manic depressive disease is now called) is a clearly separate disease from schizophrenia" (letter, *New York Times Magazine,* 10/9/88).

birthday suit. Without a suit or other clothes, naked, NUDE.

When Alan Chapin, first selectman of Washington, Conn., spotted someone trying to steal the stereo system from his daughter's car early one morning, he sprang into action, telling the *Litchfield County,* Conn., *Times*: "I ran outside in my birthday suit and was screaming and yelling to my wife to call 911" (7/29/94). People have been going about in invisible *birthday suits* at least since 1771, when Winifred Jenkins told Mrs. Mary Jones how she and a housemaid had been surprised by Sir George Coon while they "bathed in our birth-day soot" (Tobias Smollett, *Humphry Clinker).* Variations of Smollett's era included *birthday attire, birthday clothes, birthday finery,* and *birthday gear.*

birthparent. In theory, anyone who has conceived or sired a child, but in practice an unwed mother or father who has given up a child for adoption; also called a *biological parent, bioparent, genetic parent,* or *natural parent.* An organization in the field is Concerned United Birthparents—CUB, for short. See also LOVE CHILD, NATURAL, NON-MARITAL BIRTH.

bisexual. Homosexual to some degree; sometimes used in self-reference by people who have not come fully to grips with their SEXUAL ORIENTATION. For example, from the account of a National Football League player, who later came all the way out of the closet: "'Bisexual' is a term Stiles and I would use about ourselves at that time. . . . That is a way of putting it, I guess, that's intended to make it more acceptable, maybe even to other football players. The word 'bisexual' also fits the swinger's image—and most everybody can go along with that" (David Kopay and Perry Deane Young, *The David Kopay Story,* 1977).

This usage is not at all new. In *Autobiography of an Androgyne* (1918), the pseudonymous Earl Lind had this to say of New York City's "Paresis Hall," a favorite gathering place in the 1890s of male transvestites ("avocational female-impersonators," in Lind's words): "The Hall's distinctive clientele were bitterly hated, and finally scattered by the police, merely because of their cogenital bisexuality. The sexually full-fledged were crying for blood. . . . Bisexuals must be crushed—right or wrong!" (in Jonathan Katz, *Gay American History,* 1976).

One reason for using "bisexual" in the nineteenth century was that "homosexual" was still a very new word; see LOVE THAT DARE NOT SPEAK ITS NAME, THE. And for other modern forms of bisexuality, continue with AC/DC, AMBIDEXTROUS, and GREEK ARTS.

bite the dust. To die in combat; the phrase sounds trite only because it has been used so many times over so many centuries.

The great Achilles speaks: "Not all these too many Achaians would have bitten the dust, by enemy hands, when I was away in my anger" (*The Iliad of Homer,* ca. 750 B.C., trans. Richmond Lattimore, 1951). Variations include *bite the ground, bite the sand,* and the modern, slangy *kiss the dust.* See also DUST. Homer himself also could be more vivid. Again, from Lattimore's very faithful translation: ". . . Let many companions about him go down headlong into the dust, teeth gripping the ground soil."

For other military deaths, see ACCOUNT FOR, BUY THE FARM, CASUALTY, EXPENDABLE, FALL/FALLEN, GO WEST, and WASTE. For dying in general, continue with PASS AWAY.

black. More a state of mind than a color, "black" applies to any of an infinite variety of skin hues, ranging from an off-white that is whiter than the skin of many so-called whites, to a black that is, indeed, magnificently black. Previously a pejorative term, "black" was adopted as the preferred term of self-reference among younger African-Americans, starting in the second half of the 1960s, e.g., the Black Panthers (1965), "black power" (1966), and "black is beautiful" (1967).

Ethnic designations are in an almost continual state of flux, however, as rising generations disassociate themselves from the labels and attitudes of their parents. "Black" has had a fairly short run, as these things go, and some older people never really got comfortable with it. Thus, in an aside in a Supreme Court opinion, eighty-one-year-old Justice Thurgood Marshall noted that "I spent most of my life fighting to get Negro spelled with a capital 'N.' Then people started saying black and I never liked it" (*New York Times,* 10/17/89). Justice Marshall's preference was for "Afro-American," but by this time, both this and "black" were in the process of being superseded by "African-American," popularized by the Reverend Jesse Jackson in a speech on Martin Luther King Day in 1988: "To be called African-Americans has cultural integrity. It puts us in our proper historical context. Every ethnic group in this country has reference to some land base, some historical cultural base. African-Americans have hit that level of cultural maturity" (AP, 12/21/88).

Now, if one believes the minions of political correctness, "black" is to be avoided in all contexts. Thus, Rosemary Maggio recommended a variety of euphemisms for black-related terms in *The Bias-Free Word Finder* (1992), including "denounce" for "blacklist," "farrier" for "blacksmith," "ostracize" for "blackball," and "outcast" for "blacksheep." Will the nursery rhyme now be changed to "Baa, baa, outcast"?

And what in the world is to be done about General John J. "Black Jack" Pershing (1860–1948), whose nickname originally was "Nigger Jack"? He got this moniker because of his associations with the 10th (Negro) Cavalry. His first command was of Troop H of the 10th in the Montana Territory; he served with the regiment when it charged, along with the regular 1st Cavalry and the better-publicized volunteer Rough Riders, up San Juan Hill in 1898, and he remained an ardent supporter of black units throughout his career. Maybe he can be rebaptized in the history books as "Buffalo Jack" (the black cavalrymen were called "buffalo soldiers" by the Indians on account of their woolly hair) or "Brunette Jack" (picking up the term used by white soldiers in the American west for their black counterparts).

See also CAUCASIAN, NEGRO, and URBAN CONTEMPORARY.

black bag job. An illegal entry by a government employee, typically a member of the FBI or CIA, in order to gain information or to install a HIGHLY CONFIDENTIAL SOURCE (a bug). Obsolete?

The first *black bag jobs,* also known as *bag jobs,* are thought to have been conducted by the FBI in 1942. The phrase probably refers to the small bag, similar to a doctor's bag, in which the AGENT carried a kit of burglar's tools. Supposedly discontinued in 1966 (except at foreign embassies), on the orders of FBI director J. Edgar Hoover, congressional investigators discovered that *black bag jobs* were still being committed in 1973 and perhaps later, albeit under different names, such as "uncontested physical search" (*Wall Street Journal,* 1/18/80). An FBI field supervisor in the post-1966 period might also request approval of an investigation employing an "unorthodox" or "unusual" technique, and promising "full security" (*Time,* 7/5/76). Quoting an unnamed Bureau official, *Time* reported that the okay from headquarters usually would be phrased in the form of "As long as full security is assured, go ahead." Translated, this meant: "Go ahead, but if you're caught, it's your ass."

See also COVERT ACTION (or OPERATION) and SURREPTITIOUS ENTRY.

blame. Damn; alone and in such phrases as *blame my buttons!* and *blame my cats!* "He's my tick and I'll do what I blame please with him or die" (Mark Twain, *The Adventures of Tom Sawyer,* 1876). See also DAD.

blank. An all-purpose substitute for profanity or other tabooed terminology, this written or spoken representation of a dash is the counterpart of the electronically generated BLEEP or BLIP. Credit for introducing the spelled-out word usually is given to Edward Bradley (1827–1889), who wrote under the name "Cuthbert Bede." He used it this way in *The Further Adventures of Verdant Green* (1854): "I wouldn't give a blank for such a blank blank. I'm blank if he doesn't look like he'd swallowed a blank codfish." The intensive form of "blank" is "blankety-blank."

The dash itself, printed variously as – – – – and – – – –, depending on the whims of editors, writers, and printers, appeared long before Bradley was born, of course. For example, from *Joe Miller's Jests: or the Wits Vade-Mecum* (1739):

> *George Ch – – – – n.* who was always accounted a very blunt Speaker, asking a young Lady one Day, what it was o'Clock, and she telling him that her Watch *stood*, I don't wonder at that, Madame, said he, when it is so near your – – – – – –.

Close cousin to the blank is the asterisk, which also is of some antiquity. Thus, Capt. Francis Grose included an entry on "C**t" in the second (1788) edition of the *Classical Dictionary of the Vulgar Tongue.* Similar typographic evasions include the ellipsis (. . .) and random combinations of dingbats (*%&$#!). The latter, which probably came in with invention of the typewriter, are not confined just to comic books, e.g., a contemporary magazine headline, "#¢!@* YOU, TOO" (*Columbia Journalism Review,* 7–8/91).

One trouble with blanking out expressions is that readers may easily assume that the avoided terms are worse than is actually the case. In the aforementioned article on "#¢!@*," for instance, *CJR* reported the ways in which the nation's newspapers covered a shouting match between Barry Bonds, the baseball player, then a member of the Pittsburgh Pirates, and Jim Leyland, his manager. According to the *Milwaukee Journal,* Mr. Leyland went so far as to tell Mr. Bonds that he could "get the . . . out of here." Which sounds like pretty strong stuff. Is it possible that Mr. Leyland used the F-WORD? What a disappointment to learn that newspapers in Chicago, New York, Washington, and elsewhere agreed that the provocative ". . ." stood merely for "hell."

Then there was Mr. Bonds's perception of the way in which he was regarded by others: "They've been saying for four years that I'm a – – –" (*Des Moines Register*). The press rendered this one in a variety of ways, i.e., as "(jerk)," in the Minneapolis *Star Tribune*; as "[problem]" in the *Atlanta Journal-Constitution*; as ". . ." in the *Omaha World-Herald*; as "– –" in *The Denver Post*; and as "– – – –" in the Quad City, Ia., *Times*. No one seems to have quoted Mr. Bonds exactly, so the meaning of the *Register*'s dashes remains a mystery.

And so it goes, and not only on the sports pages, e.g., Texas Representative Sam Rayburn's 1956 appraisal of a fellow Democrat and future president: "Well, if we have to take a Catholic, I hope we don't have to take that little – – – – – Kennedy" (Arthur M. Schlesinger, Jr., *A Thousand Days*, 1965).

See also A – –, ADJECTIVE/ADJECTIVAL, DASH, EXPLETIVE DELETED, F – – –, F-WORD, and OBSCENE, DEROGATORY, AND SCATOLOGICAL.

blanket, born on the wrong side of the. Bastardy. "'Frank Kennedy,' he said, 'was a gentleman, though on the wrong side of the blanket'" (Sir Walter Scott, *Guy Mannering, or The Astrologer,* 1815). By the same token, "blanket love" also was a euphemism for what *The Oxford English Dictionary* terms "illicit amours." See also AMOUR, BASTARD, and LOVE CHILD.

blast. Damn. "Blast," and the adjectival "blasted," dating from the first half of the nineteenth century, continue to see service. For example, President Ronald Reagan expressed his determination to revise the tax code by declaring at a White House gathering on May 29, 1985, "Blast the torpedoes. Full speed ahead," thus watering down ("paraphrasing," as Reagan admitted) the famous remark by Admiral David Farragut, as he led a Union fleet through minefields in Mobile Bay on August 5, 1864. See also DARN.

blazes. A euphemistic expletive for "hell," as in "What in blazes is going wrong?" (*Best of Saturday Night Live,* WNBC-TV, 11/14/79). "Blazes" was especially popular in the nineteenth century when it appeared regularly in such combinations as *hot as blazes, cool as blazes, blue as blazes, black as blazes,* and *by blazes.* See also HECK.

bleeder. British for "a superlative," or "bloody" fool. For more about the British fear of blood, see RUDDY.

bleep. Shit, whether alone or in such combinations as *bullbleep, chickenbleep, horsebleep, scared bleepless;* also a general term for any so-called unspeakable, unprintable expression.

In the first, narrower sense: John Robert Starr, managing editor of *The Arkansas Democrat* and a frequent critic of Bill Clinton when he was governor of that state, recalled Clinton's telling him that "One reason I might run [for president] is so I don't have to wake up to that load of bleep y'all dump on me in The Democrat every morning" (*New York Times,* 12/20/91).

In its wider application, meanwhile, "bleep" is a common rendering in print of the electronic sound made when a censor erases a supposedly unbroadcastable word from a television tape, e.g, the purported comment of the late Billy Martin, following his ejection from a baseball game: "You know what the ironic part of this bleeping game is? . . . I'll get fined $250 and the bleeping umpire blows five calls at second base" (*New York Post,* 7/2/76). See also BLANK, BLIP, EXPLETIVE DELETED, and F-WORD.

blessed event. The birth of a babe (also called a *bundle from heaven*). The euphemistic twist to the expression seems to have been the inspiration of radio and newspaper journalist Walter Winchell, who also used it as a verb, as in "Stop the presses: So-and-so is going to blessed event." Progeny of "blessed event" include *blessed he-vent, blessed she-vent,* and sometimes, alas, *blasted event.* All these and many other coy evasions, such as *little newcomer* and *little stranger,* reflect a reluctance to talk plainly about pregnancy and birth that once was nearly as strong as the refusal to discuss dying and death. In the case of pregnancy, the taboo began to fade in the years following World War II, when the men returned home and the baby boom began, with so many women becoming pregnant at once that the subject became mentionable. See also ANTICIPATING and EXPECTANT.

blessing. A severe rebuke, a sharp scolding, or tongue-lashing. The expression comes from the American South. The earliest example in the *Dictionary of American Regional English* is from a Civil War diary: "The major gave the steamboat man a regular blessing" (1863). The verbal form, "to bless out," parallels "to curse out." See also CUSS.

blip. (1) A dirty word; (2) an explosion, specifically, one at a nuclear power plant.

In the first case, "blip" is an alternate pronunciation of BLEEP. For example: "The blips you hear are four-letter words which our broadcasting code forbids us to use" (WCBS-TV, "60 Minutes," 10/7/78). See also FOUR-LETTER WORD.

In the second, explosive case, when the members of the Nuclear Regulatory Commission gathered to discuss the SITUATION at the Three Mile Island nuclear power plant: "The commissioners were concerned about a percentage problem: if three percent of the bubble was oxygen, what percent oxygen would have to accumulate for it to combine with the hydrogen to cause a 'blip'—an explosion that might, at worst, make a small part of Pennsylvania uninhabitable because of radioactivity for decades" (*Smithsonian,* 7/79). See also ABOVE CRITICAL and, for more about the NRC and Three Mile Island, EVENT.

blow. To engage in oral-genital sex, or the act thereof, as in *a blow, blow job,* or, oh-so-discreetly, *BJ.* "I, anticipating even more pleasure, wouldn't allow her to blow me on the bus, instead we played, as they say, with each other" (letter, Neal Cassady to Jack Kerouac, 3/7/47, in Cassady: *The First Third,* 1971).

Generally regarded as a strong, more-or-less taboo term, the essentially euphemistic origin of the word's sexual sense is evident from the common witticism, dating at least to the 1960s, "Suck—don't blow." It is not at all clear when and how "blow" acquired its sexual meaning, however—a common situation in the case of slang words, which tend to be used for many years before they are written down in documents of the sort that are likely to be preserved and perused by lexicographers. (Both "blow" and "blow job" are missing from the 1972 supplement to *The Oxford English Dictionary* and the oldest sexual "blow" in the *Random House Historical Dictionary of American Slang* comes only from ca. 1930.) Most likely, the sexual sense dates to the early part of the twentieth century. It may derive from "blowoff," meaning the ending, finish, or climax of something (as in "blow off steam") or "blower," a term for a prostitute or thief's mistress, current from the seventeenth to nineteenth centuries, deriving in turn from the Gypsy *blowen,* with the same meaning. The "blow" metaphor might also have been influenced, however, by such old (from the seventeenth century, at least) slang terms for the penis as *flute,* also called *the living* (or *one-holed* or *silent*) *flute* and *whore pipe.* See also CUNNILINGUS, FELLATIO, and MOUTH MUSIC.

blow away. To kill; to get rid of. Thus, speaking of murder: "'We're mystified completely,' said Lt. William Crumm Friday night. 'I don't know why this guy got blown away'" (White Plains, N.Y., *Reporter-Dispatch,* 1/2/82). And speaking of a lesser form of death, i.e., losing a job, an investment banker told the *New York Times:* "As Dutt started to blow some of his senior people away I thought that . . . the company was going to be leaderless soon" (9/6/87). The second sense here is a spin-off from the first, with "blow away" having been dated to the eighteenth century with reference to the execution of spies, traitors, and mutineers by tying them to the mouths of cannons, then firing. See also HIT and LET GO.

BM. A second-order euphemism, the abbreviation standing for *bowel movement*, itself a euphemism though often avoided. Thus, detailing President Dwight D. Eisenhower's recovery from a heart attack on September 24, 1955, Russell Baker felt that he secured a place in journalistic history by becoming "the first reporter in history to report a presidential bowel movement in the *New York Times*" (*The Good Times*, 1989). Baker managed this coup by carefully burying the bowel movement—a "good" one—in the fifty-third paragraph of his story. See also BARNYARD EPITHET and DEFECATE/DEFECATION.

BO. Along Broadway, the initials stand for "box office," but along Madison Avenue, this is the soap huckster's abbreviation for "body odor," itself a euphemism for "bad smell" or "stink." A dread condition that was first revealed to the public in the 1930s, *BO* is to the carcass as HALITOSIS is to the mouth. "Do you ever ask yourself about Body-Odour?" (Dorothy Sayers, *Murder Must Advertise*, 1933). Descendants of *BO* include *CO* (canine odor) and *DO* (dog odor). See also FRAGRANCE and PERSPIRE.

bodily fluids. Semen and vaginal secretions, mainly the former. "The most-used circumlocution in AIDSpeak was 'bodily fluids,' an expression that avoided troublesome words like 'semen'" (Randy Shilts, *And the Band Played On,* 1988). "In the frankest of language, Zamora told the youths about . . . 'outercourse,' sexual practices that prevent the exchange of bodily fluids'" (Des Moines, Ia., *Register,* 5/12/92).

The circumlocution predates the AIDS plague by some years. For example, in the immortal words of Gen. Jack D. Ripper: "I can no longer sit back and allow Communist infiltration, Communist indoctrination, Communist subversion, and the international Communist conspiracy to sap and impurify all of our precious bodily fluids" (*Dr. Strangelove or: How I Learned to Stop Worrying and Love the Bomb,* film, 1964). See also OUTERCOURSE and PEOPLE WITH AIDS.

body briefer. A chic corset with a built-in brassiere; a corselet.

Most women today would die before purchasing a girdle, which is merely a sawed-off corset. Instead, the new woman who wishes to make herself seem slimmer than she really is buys a *body briefer* (also called a *body hugger, body molder,* or *body shaper*). But names aside—and there are plenty more, such as *body garment, control slip, de-emphasizer, form persuader, foundation garment, outerwear enhancer,* and *bustier* (when the underwear is worn as outerwear)—resemblance to a corset is strong, as advertising copy makes clear, e.g., "body briefer with soft contour cups, firm control panty to whittle away inches even before you lose pounds" (Macy's flyer, rec'd 1/9/79). Men also wear corsets, but they are known, less euphemistically, in the trade as *potholders.* See also BRASSIERE, BUST, and LINGERIE.

body count. Dead and wounded enemy count. "Body" has served as euphemistic shorthand for "dead body" since at least the thirteenth century, but it took the Vietnam War to elevate the *body count* into a deceptively precise index of military progress. "Weekly casualty stories reported the number of Americans killed, wounded, or missing, and the number of South Vietnamese killed, but the casualties on the other side were impersonally described as 'the Communist death toll' or the 'body count'" (*Columbia Journalism Review*, 1–2/79).

In the bitter aftermath of the Vietnam War, however, "body count" became a tabooed term. The official *Department of Defense Dictionary of Military and Associated Terms* (1979) does not include an entry on "body count" and American military briefers went to the other extreme during the Gulf War in 1991, insisting that they could not give even rough estimates of how many Iraqis were killed or wounded. See also CASUALTY and NEUTRALIZE/NEUTRALIZATION.

boink. To copulate (with a woman). Thus, reviewing *Exposing Myself*, the no-holds-barred memoir of TV personality Geraldo Rivera: "Despite the many immodest pages devoted to his scoops, his community work, his personality interviews that 'reinvented the genre,' he should have subtitled this opus *Babes I Have Boinked*" (*Gentlemen's Quarterly*, 11/91). Of apparently recent origin, "boink" may be an Americanization of the British "bonk," e.g., "The important thing is that there is no one class represented here; it is a group of people who share the same materialist ambitions, relaxing between getting, spending and bonking (yuppie for sex)" (London *Sunday Times*, 10/12/86). Both B-words suggest a violent act in which a blow is delivered, a metaphor whose all-too-frequent use indicates the oft unloving nature of sexual relationships. See also BANG.

bollixed up. Balled up. "You're getting your cues all bollixed up" (Jerome Weidman, *I Can Get It For You Wholesale!*, 1937). "Bollix," also spelled "bolax" and "bolex," is a variant of "bollock" (or "ballock"), which means "little ball," and which is an extremely old word for "testicle," recorded

in the plural form, "beallucas," as early as ca. 1000. "Ballock" descends from "ball" in the same way that "buttock" comes from BUTT. The sense of "little," though, is not consistently included. Remember the song that innocent schoolchildren sing about "Barnacle Bill the Sailor"? His real name is "Bollocky Bill" and the tradition is that he had big ones. "Balled up," meanwhile, is by today's standards merely a euphemism for "fucked up." See also BALL and TESTICLES.

bone. The only part of the body without a bone, i.e., the penis, especially when erect, in which case the priapic party also may be said to have a *boner, bone-on,* or *ham-bone.* The penile sense of "bone" has been dated to the opening decades of the twentieth century (though not admitted to the 1972 supplement to *The Oxford English Dictionary*). The association is much older, however, with modern usage foreshadowed by the nineteenth-century British *marrow-bone* as slang for the penis, where "marrow" equals "semen." (Shakespeare referred to syphilis in *Troilus and Cressida*, 1601–02, as the "Neapolitan bone-ache" and the "incurable bone-ache," but probably meant by this the painful inflammation of the bones caused by the disease.) The term may also be employed to describe the activity and the act, e.g., *to bone (someone), to give the dog a bone,* and *boning.* To do a *bone dance* or *to jump on (someone's) bones* is to perform the same act, but the allusion then is to movements of the entire skeleton, not to the one boneless part.

A nonce usage, but of interest for anticipating the modern sense as well as for conveying the flavor of nineteenth-century American political oratory, comes from a pro-Calhoun speech by New York City newspaperman Mike Walsh, ca. 1842:

"Workingmen don't want milk and water men to represent them—men who are a mere connecting link between the animal and vegetable kingdom . . . that won't whistle 'We won't go home till morning,' because they don't have wind enough; and that are not lascivious, because they have not got the stamina to keep their back-bone straight" (from Arthur M. Schlesinger, Jr., *The Age of Jackson*, 1945).

See also ENOB, JUMP, and PENIS.

boo-boo. A blunder or foolish error; the baby talk is supposed to mitigate the mistake. "Defense Secretary Wilson, whose recent boo-boo . . . threatens to become historic" (*Los Angeles Times*, 10/17/54). The term may be a reduplication of "boob," used occasionally as a verb as well as a noun to refer to a stupid person, a dolt, in turn from the *booby* that is a dumb bird.

The "historic boo-boo," by the way, was one of Charles E. Wilson's many impolitic remarks, this one made in Detroit, where he suggested that workers should move away from depressed areas rather than wait for military contracts to revive local industry. In the secretary's words: "I've always liked bird dogs better than kennel-fed dogs myself—you know, one who will get out and hunt for food rather than sit on his fanny and yell" (*New York Times*, 10/13/54). See also FANNY.

booked for investigation. Held for interrogation. "Under California law, 'booked for investigation' means that he can be held for questioning for seventy-two hours without being taken before a magistrate" (AP, 12/26/77). The British equivalent of "booked for investigation" is "helping with inquiries." See also DETAIN and FIELD INTERVIEW.

bordello. Literally, a little house, such as a cabin or hut, but in practice a fancy name for a whorehouse. See also HOUSE.

borrow. Steal. "Finally he said that he and some friends had tried unsuccessfully to 'borrow' a car on the Champs-Élysées and that while running away he had been shot" (*New York Times*, 3/27/94). See also APPROPRIATE and PERMANENT BORROWING

bosom, a.k.a. **bazoom.** The breasts. "The balconies and windows were filled with women, well dressed, with bright eyes and bounding bosoms, waving handkerchiefs, exhibiting flags and garlands, and casting bouquets of flowers upon us" (Whig parade in Boston, 9/8/1840, *The Diary of Philip Hone*, Allan Nevins, ed., 1936).

Technically, only the singular form is required: "Bosom I saw, both full, throat warbling" (James Joyce, *Ulysses*, 1922). Modern euphemizers, however, perhaps less certain than Joyce of what they are doing, sometimes double their bets with the plural, as in: "What you react to, first, are the artsy drawings, in color, of a man (well-hung) and a woman (slender but with bosoms) going through a thirty-page sexual exhibition" (review of *The Joy of Sex*, *New York Times*, 2/22/74).

An extremely old word of uncertain origin (perhaps related to the Sanskrit *bhasman*, blowing), "bosom" has signified "breast" since at least the year 1000. Originally, the term was androgynous. Thus, "wife of his bosom" was a more common expression than "husband of her bosom," though both are used in the King James Version of Bible. (Note the masculine examples of "bosom" in HAPPY HUNTING GROUNDS, GONE TO THE.) "Bosom" seems to have taken hold as a euphemism for female breasts during the late eighteenth and early nineteenth centuries, when incipient Victorians were cleaning up their language in preparation for Her ascent to the throne in 1837. For example, this was Samuel Johnson's word of choice when he explained to David Garrick why he had decided to stop paying visits to Drury Lane's "green room" (then, as well as now, the term for the lounge where actors wait before going on stage): "I'll come no more behind your scenes, David; for the silk stockings and white bosoms of your actresses excite my amorous propensities" (from 1749, in Boswell's *Life of Johnson,* 1791).

Frederick Marryat, an unusually sensitive recorder of language (see LIMB), captured the flavor of the pre-Victorian period in *Peter Simple* (1834), with the reproof given to the midshipman hero of the novel for mentioning the "sexy" word while dining with a Miss Minerva on the island of Barbados. In bumbling Simple's words:

> It was my fate to sit opposite to a fine turkey, and I asked my partner if I should have the pleasure of helping her to a piece of the breast. She looked at me very indigantly, and said, "Curse your impudence, sar, I wonder where you larn your manners. Sar, I take a lily turkey *bosom,* if you please. Talk of *breast* to a lady, sar! — really quite *horrid.*"

Meanwhile, women took to wearing *bosom friends* and *false bosoms.* The so-called *friends* were pads for keeping the breasts warm. Originally designed for warding off chest colds, they doubled as falsies, judging from an article in a Philadelphia periodical in 1796 that characterized such coverings for women's "virgin zones" as "scandalous" and "suspicious in appearance" (in Anita Schorsch, *Images of Childhood, An Illustrated Social History,* 1979). As for *false bosoms,* their purpose is apparent from their name. The London *Times* managed to find some virtue in the deception, however, noting in 1799 that "the fashion of *false bosoms* has at least this utility, that it compels our fashionable fair to wear *something*" (in C. Willet and Phyllis Cunnington, *The History of Underclothes,* 1951). In the next century, women padded themselves with *lemon bosoms* and *palpitating bosoms.* Thus, *The Handbook of the Toilet* (1841) lamented the use of "lemon bosoms and many other means of creating fictitious charms in improving the work of Nature." See also PALPITATORS and note *bosom of the pants* in ARSE.

"Bosom" also replaced "breast" in strictly nonanatomical contexts. Thus, the forward part of the moldboard of a plow originally was called the "breast," but as early as 1813, some fastidious farmers had adopted the new terminology, e.g., "This degree of roundness and fulness in the bosom [of the plow] is necessary on heavy ground" (Arthur Young, *General View of the Agriculture of the County of Essex).* By the same token, "breast knots" became *bosom knots,* "breastpins" turned into *bosom pins,* the "bubby blossom" (or "flower") became the *bosom blossom.* It seems likely, too, that the reluctance to say "breast" explains why Congreve's line "Music has charms to soothe a savage breast" is so often misquoted as "savage beast" (*The Mourning Bride,* 1697).

"Breast" was not entirely eliminated, however. It still was preferred when the choice was between it and something even "worse." Thus, Noah Webster euphemized *teat* as *breast* when he bowdlerized the Bible in 1833. In the Bible, according to Webster, such passages as "They shall lament for the teats" (Isaiah 32:12) became "They shall lament for the breasts." (See PECULIAR MEMBERS for more about the pre-Victorian period generally and for Webster in particular.)

"Bosom" remains the politest of the many terms that have been used over the years to describe women's breasts. Most of the words relate to form, function, or size. Among them:

apples

babaloos, bags, balcony, balloons, bazongas (especially those that are large and shapely, and one of many variants on "bosom"), *bazooms, berks* (British, and not to be confused with *berk,* singular, an abbreviation of "Berkeley Hunt," where the "Hunt" is rhyming slang for "cunt"; see RASPBERRY for other rhymes), *beausome* (a beautiful bosom), *(big) brown eyes, big dinners, boobs* (not from "bosom," but from the Elizabethan "bubbies," by way of "boobies"), *Bristols* (short for "Bristol Cities," which is rhyming slang, with "cities" being a play on "titties"), *bubbles, buckets, bumps,* BUST, BUXOM

cans, cantaloupes, charlies (or *charleys*), CHEST, *cream-jugs, cupcakes*

dairies, DEVELOP/DEVELOPMENT, *diddies* (an eighteenth-century corruption of "titties"), *droopers* (or *super-droopers*), DUCKYS, *dumplings*

ENDOWED/ENDOWMENT

FIGURE, *frontal development, fronts, fun bags*

gazangas (also *gazungas,* meaning well-shaped ones), *globes, grapefruits, grapes, growths*

headlights (after automobiles of the 1940s), *hemispheres, hooters* (see also HOOTER)

Jersey Cities (more rhyming slang), *jugs* (from "jugs of milk" and not to be confused with "double-jugs," old and now obsolete British slang for the BUTTOCKS)

kajoobies, kettledrums (or Cupid's kettledrums, eighteenth and nineteenth centuries), *knobs, knockers* (perhaps from the height and shape of old-fashioned door knockers; see also KNOCK UP)

lactatious fountains (obsolete but very hard to beat, as from the *Scientific American* of October 1893: "Japanese children are suckled until their sixth year, and in language unmistakable may be heard asking for the lactatious fountain"), *lemons, lungs, lung warts*

Mae Wests (with the "West-breast" rhyme reinforcing the mental image of the curvaceous actress, whose name also was bestowed upon inflatable life jackets in World War II (learning about this honor, she is said to have exclaimed: "I've been in *Who's Who* and I know what's what, but it's the first time I ever made the dictionary"), *mamas,* MAMMARY GLANDS, *maracas, marshmallows, melons, milk bottles, milkers, molehills, mosob* ("bosom" spelled backward; see also ENOB), *muffins, murphies* (an allusion to potatoes, also called "murphies")

NECK (an anatomical displacement of the eighteenth and nineteenth centuries), *ninnies* (from "ninny" in the sense of "child"?), *ninny jugs, norks* (Australianese, also known as *norgies, norgs,* and *norkers,* all from the picture of a cow's udder on Norco, a popular brand of butter), *nubbies* (also Australian, perhaps from "bubbies"), *nuggies, nugs* (the last two are both American, probably from "jugs," with *fresh nugs* being well-developed ones)

oranges, orbs

PHYSIQUE, *pointers, pumps* (in soda-jerk jargon, dating to at least 1930, "Fix the pumps" means "Look at the girl with big breasts")

raisins (invariably in a disparaging sense: "She is as flat as two raisins on a board"), RISING BEAUTIES

snorbs, spheres ("I only touched her alabaster spheres so much as was absolutely necessary," Casanova, *Memoirs*, ca. 1785–98)

T as in T AND A, TATAS, *teacups, titties* (see TITTIE), *tonsils, TNT* (Two Nifty Tits), *torpedoes* (what they may look like, coming at you), *twins*

warts, watermelons, and, on a fowl, WHITE MEAT

See also FULL-FIGURED and STATUESQUE.

boss. Master. "Boss" comes from the Dutch *baas*, meaning "master," but American servants of the early nineteenth century found it possible to say the foreign word, whereas the English one stuck in their throats, e.g.: "No one, in this republican country, will use the term master or mistress; 'employers,' and the Dutch word 'boss,' are used instead" (Isaac Holmes, *An Account of the United States of America, Derived from Actual Observation,* 1823). Those egalitarian servants, meanwhile, didn't like to be called "servants" either; for more on that topic, see DOMESTIC, HELP, and SERVANT itself.

Though not popularized as a substitute for "master" until after the Revolution, "boss" was used in the colonies from as early as 1645. In the related adjectival senses of best, first-class, or excellent, "boss" also is older than most hipsters probably suspect. Thus, in *The Adventures of Huckleberry Finn* (Mark Twain, 1884), the king congratulates his fellow con man in

these terms: "Good land, duke, lemme hug you! It's the most dazzling idea 'at ever a man struck. Oh, this is the boss dodge, ther' ain't no mistake 'bout it." See also PRINCIPAL (or LARGEST) BEDROOM.

botheration. Damnation; similar alternatives include *tarnation* and *thunderation*. See also DARN and THUNDER.

bottom. The ass; as with BACKSIDE, BEHIND, and REAR, the general directional reference has a specific euphemistic meaning. Consider Commodore Cornelius Vanderbilt (1794–1877): "He was a bellowing rube partial to pinching housemaids' bottoms, yet more than once he burst into tears and sobbed, 'Oh, Goddamnit! I've been a-swearing again!'" (David E. Koskoff, *Saturday Review,* 7/22/78).

"Bottom," from the Indo-European *bhund,* to place solidly, seems to have acquired its anatomical meaning within the last several centuries. (The lack of earlier examples is one reason for thinking that the British "bum" is not a mere contraction of "bottom," since "bum" itself goes back at least to the fourteenth century; see TRAMP.) The anatomical "bottom," meanwhile, probably dates to Elizabethan times. As Joseph Shipley points out in *In Praise of English* (1977), it hardly seems coincidental that the weaver who is transformed into an ass in Shakespeare's *A Midsummer Night's Dream* (1594) is named Nick Bottom.

The Oxford English Dictionary's oldest example of the word in the sense of "The sitting part of a man" (N.B.: not "woman") comes from *Zoönomia* (1794), by Erasmus Darwin, grandfather of Charles. By this time, the word already had acquired sufficient anatomical taint to make it dangerous to use in fastidious company. For example, when Dr. Samuel Johnson referred to a female printer's devil who "had a bottom of good sense," the Bishop of Killaloe managed to keep a straight face, but most of the others present "could not forbear tittering and laughing" (4/20/1781, in Boswell, *Life of Johnson*, 1791). Not having intended to make a joke, Johnson took umbrage at the laughter. Bowsell continues:

> [He] glanced sternly around and called out in a strong tone, 'Where's the merriment?' Then collecting himself, and looking aweful, to make us feel how he could impose restraint, and as it were searching his mind for a still more ludicrous word, he slowly pronounced, 'I say the *woman* was *fundamentally* sensible;' as if he had said, hear this now, and laugh if you dare. We all sat composed as if at a funeral. [And see FUNDAMENT]

During the eighteenth and nineteenth centuries, before the anatomical meaning became dominant, "bottom" was popularized as a synonym for "endurance" or "grit" by sportsmen who used it to describe the spirit of their racehorses and pugilists ("bruisers," as they were often called). The British of this period also liked to think that the men in their army had a great deal of "bottom," e.g.: "For solidity, bottom, and a courage that never wavers, they [British troops] are incomparable" (Robert H. Patterson, *Essays in History and Art*, 1862). "Bottom" in this sense was replaced by yet another euphemism—PLUCK.

Naturally, "bottom" itself has been euphemized. Thus, England is populated by *Higginbothams, Longbothams,* and *Sidebothams* (pronounced "Siddybotaams"), etc. It also has been abbreviated for delicacy as

BTM, BT emptem, and *beetoteetom,* the last of which caused Gerty MacDowell to turn crimson when madcap Cissy Caffrey said it aloud—especially as a gentleman named Bloom happened to be nearby (James Joyce, *Ulysses,* 1922).

bounce. To knock around; to beat up. "Mr. Steiniger . . . maintained that he had shot Mr. Gardiner accidentally and that he had been hired to 'bounce,' or intimidate, Mr. Gardiner" (*New York Times,* 11/2/89). In theory, a *bounce* is less severe than a *hit,* but in this instance the bouncee died. He had been handcuffed, shot in the thigh, and bled to death. As with other terms for violent actions, this one also may refer to sexual INTERCOURSE, as in *to bounce (someone), to bounce refrigerators,* or *to play bouncy-bouncy,* though the sexual sense is reinforced by, if it does not actually derive from, the springiness of mattresses. See also HIT.

boutique. A Frenchified store or other small business establishment, such as The Nail Boutique (Danbury, Conn., Yellow Pages, 1994–95). See also PARLOR.

boy. Now usually a fighting word, except among self-acknowledged "good old boys," the term is revived periodically as a euphemism during time of war or the immediate threat thereof. Then, "boys" or "American boys" may be employed in place of "fighting men" in order to build up sympathy on the home front for the troops in the field. Typically, the call is to "get the boys home by Christmas." However, the palm in this category goes to Sen. Burton K. Wheeler (D., Mont.), a Progressive gone Isolationist, who opposed the Lend-Lease program to aid Britain, asserting in January 1941 that it "will plow under every fourth

American boy." See also GARÇON, LADY, and MAN.

boyfriend. Lover; a double euphemism since the object typically is a man, not a boy, and the friendship often is exceedingly close. "They wouldn't let me say 'lover' on a sketch. I had to say boyfriend. But what's the difference?" (Cher, interview with Dick Cavett, WNET-TV, 3/23/82). See also FRIEND and GIRLFRIEND.

brainwash. The popular term softens the sometimes nasty business of dramatically changing a person's beliefs and behavior. In its most extreme form, when practiced upon captive audiences, *brainwashing* involves breaking down the victim's self-image, precipitating an identity crisis, and substituting a new set of values for the old. A translation from the Chinese—the original has been rendered variously as "thought reform," "ideological reprogramming," and "brain remolding"—"brainwash" dawned upon the Western consciousness after the Chinese Communists began consolidating their victory of 1949 by using the technique to "re-educate" first their fellow citizens and then prisoners taken during the Korean War. See also AVERSION THERAPY, CONSCIOUSNESS-RAISING, INTERROGATION, and REEDUCATION.

brassiere. The garment for supporting the breasts has noticeably little to do with the *bras* (French for "arm") from which its name is derived. In Old French, a *bracière* was an arm protector, and in modern French, *brassière* has carried such non-bust-like meanings as "shoulder strap" (as of a knapsack), "vest" (as worn by a baby), and, as *brassière de sauvetage,* a cork life jacket—all of which are far cries from what are

known informally in the garment district as *boobytraps* or *bust-buckets*. Of course, the full "brassiere" is hardly ever seen anymore, not even in advertisements, which almost always clip it to "bra," e.g., Wonderbra, Miracle Bra, Super-Uplift Bra, and Rudi Gernreich's contradiction in terms—the "No Bra Bra." The reason (linguistically) for this is that the full "brassiere" has been around long enough to have acquired overly sexy connotations. "Bra," which seems to have come in about 1930, is light, airy, and acceptable, as in the popular ditty circa 1940:

> Now you ought to see Ma —
> In her peek-a-boo bra.
> She looks only sweet sixteen.

As for the basic "brassiere": Women have been wearing this garment, or similar items, for some thousands of years. Roman mosaics depict women in outfits that could pass for bikinis on the Riviera today. The first "brassiere" by that name, however, did not appear until the twentieth century. Otto Titzling is reported to have designed one in 1912 as supports for Swanhilda Olafsen, a very large opera singer. Clearly, though, the *brassiere* was an idea whose time had come, as the great change in women's fashions, usually associated with World War I, to freer, looser clothing already was beginning. In fact, the garment also seems to have been invented independently by Mary Phelps Jacob (1892–1970), an American heiress, later better known as Caresse Crosby. As a young debutante, Caresse rebelled against being encased in an armored corset. She made her first *brassiere* one night, just before going to a dance, with the aid of two pocket handkerchiefs, some ribbon, some thread, and a French maid named Marie. She also did something that

Titzling failed to do: She filed a patent application for a "brassiere" on February 12, 1914, and the patent was granted to her on November 3 of that year. As a descendant of Robert Fulton, of steamboat fame, Caresse certainly had inventive genes. Still, one can't help wondering in her case, not to speak of Titzling's, about the extent to which people's lives may be influenced by their names. See also BOSOM, BUST, FIGURE, GAY DECEIVERS, LINGERIE, and PALPITATORS.

break off contact with the enemy. To run away from the fight, to retreat. See also STRATEGIC MOVEMENT TO THE REAR.

break wind. The polite form of "fart," which is a FOUR-LETTER WORD. The phrase dates to at least the sixteenth century. Thus, from a translation by Sir John Harington (1561–1612) of a Latin verse by Sir (or "Saint," depending on one's persuasion) Thomas More: "To break a little wind, sometimes ones life doth save/For want of vent behind, some folke their ruine have."

Where Chaucer and other early English writers used "fart" unashamedly, as in, from *The Miller's Tale* (ca. 1387–1400), "This Nicholas anon leet fle a fart/As greet as it had been a thonder-dent," later generations were more reticent, e.g., "Now they are always in a sweat, and never speak, but they f – – t" (Thomas Gray, *Works in Prose and Verse*, 1740 [1884]). The most recent example of "fart" in *The Oxford English Dictionary* is from 1825, shortly before the official onset of the Victorian era. The rest is silence, or nearly so, as people began to have doubts even about the propriety of "breaking wind." Thus, H. Montgomery Hyde reports in *A History of Pornography* (1966) that "the great English Greek scholar Dr. Gilbert Murray always insisted upon

translating the verb 'to break wind' as 'to blow one's nose.'" Of course, Dr. Murray had plenty of company, including the anonymous editor who rewrote one of the classic nursery rhymes, so that it reads:

> Little Robin Redbreast,
> Sat upon a rail;
> Niddle noddle went his head,
> Wiggle waggle went his tail.

But according to the earliest known version of this verse, as it appears in the first collection of Mother Goose rhymes, *Tom Thumb's Pretty Song Book* (1744):

> Little Robin red breast,
> Sitting on a pole,
> Niddle, Noddle,
> Went his head,
> And Poop went his Hole.

Where "poop," as defined in Nathan Bailey's *English Dictionary* (1721), means "to break Wind backwards softly." See also CREPITATION, FLATULENCE, MADE A TRUMPET OF HIS ASS, POOP, the *petard* in PETER, and RASPBERRY.

brief (or short) illness. Death for socially unacceptable reasons. "The daily faithful know what it means when they see, instead of 'suicide,' death due to a 'brief illness'" (Rinker Buck, *MORE*, 9/77).

Mr. Buck was referring to the veiled language that he himself had employed when writing obituaries for the *Berkshire Eagle*, in Pittsfield, Mass. The custom is widespread. Surveying other publications, *MORE* found that the *Dallas Morning News* did not mention "suicide" without permission from the family of the DECEASED, while the *Philadelphia Inquirer* did not run any obits at all on people who committed suicide unless required to by the prominence of the individuals. By these standards, *Time* magazine's famed circumlocution, "died by his own hand," is relatively explicit.

Mr. Buck also told of being asked to cite "short illness" as the cause of death of an acute alcoholic. Upon reflection, he decided it would be fairer to handle the story in the same way as in the case of a much more prominent drunk, blaming the death instead on "an apparent heart attack." Such evasions are by no means limited to newspapers in the United States. For example, in a report on the Ivory Coast, V. S. Naipaul noted: "On that [necrology] page there was a coded way of referring to certain kinds of death. A death by poisoning was said to have occurred 'after a short illness'—*'après une courte maladie'*" (*New Yorker*, 5/14/84). See also FELO DE SE, ILL/ILLNESS, and OBITUARY.

broad-beamed. Fat-assed. "Captain Morton is . . . bowlegged and broad-beamed (for which the crew would substitute 'lard-assed')" (Thomas Heggen, *Mr. Roberts*, 1946). See also ARSE and PORTLY.

Broken Arrow. A serious accident involving a nuclear weapon. "The Department of Defense has admitted at least eleven of what it calls 'Broken Arrows,' or major nuclear accidents" (Center for Defense Information, *Defense Monitor*, 2/75).

By official definition, a "Broken Arrow" could include a nuclear explosion, a nonnuclear explosion that threatens to cause a nuclear detonation, the theft or loss of a nuclear weapon, radioactive contamination, or any other hazard to the public stemming from a nuclear weapons accident. Thus, the loss of the submarine *Scor-*

pion, apparently hit by one of its own torpedoes while traversing the Atlantic in 1968, constituted a *Broken Arrow,* presumably because it had nuclear weapons aboard. Another, domestic example of a *Broken Arrow* is the jettisoning by a B-52 bomber in 1961 of a 24-megaton bomb at Goldsboro, N.C. This bomb had six interlocking safety catches, five of which were set off by the fall. If the sixth had also gone off, Goldsboro would have witnessed—briefly—an explosion 1,800 times as powerful as that which devastated Hiroshima in 1945.

Lesser accidents with nuclear weapons are classified as *Bent Spears* (damage to a nuclear weapon or component of same) and *Dull Swords* (minor mishaps that could set off a weapon's arming sequence, reduce its yield, or—horrors—turn it into a dud). See also INCIDENT.

BS. The abbreviation helps clean up "bullshit," also euphemized as *bull, bullbleep, bullpeep, bullish,* and BUSHWA, and all also having the general meaning of bunk, nonsense, hot air, rubbish, or BALONEY. Related abbreviations include *CS* (where "C" stands for CHICKEN), *TS* (where "S" sometimes means "situation"), *SOL* (where "OL" means "out of luck"), and *SOS* (depending on context, either "same old shit" or, if in an army mess hall when chipped beef is served on toast, "shit on a shingle"). A *BS artist,* meanwhile, is an expert at throwing it (see also BA).

"BS" may also be described euphemistically as *bullshoot,* in which case the act is *bullshooting,* and the person is a *bullshipper* or *bullshooter* (see SHOOT). Nor does this exhaust the euphemistic riches of the term, as demonstrated by the following: "At one time, oilfield workers vulgarly referred to the sludge that befouls the bottoms of oil tanks as 'bullshit.' This was gradually abbreviated to 'B.S.,' which the industry's trade journal primly translated into 'basic sediment'" (Gary Jennings, *Personalities Of Language*, 1965). Similar prettified translations are *bottom settlings* and *bottom sludge.*

The oldest "bullshit" in *The Random House Historical Dictionary of American Slang* (J. E. Lighter, 1994) comes in the form of a reference to the actual stuff, slightly sanitized with dashes by the original writer: "It would amuse and . . . amaze an Eastern person to hear our first cry when we corrall. It is for fuel, and thus spoken—'Bull sh–t, Bull sh–t' in stentorian tones. Since leaving [Fort] Kearny . . . we have not been able to secure . . . wood . . . for cooking purposes. The universal substitute . . . in dry weather is the manure of oxen . . . which ignites & burns readily" (W. H. Jackson, *Diaries*, 1866). The phrase must have been in use many years before, however, as the short form, *bull,* has been dated to 1850 in the extended sense of talking nonsense.

Judging from early examples, the abbreviated *BS* was popularized among young people. By 1900, it was employed both as noun and verb at the United States Military Academy at West Point, and it was described in 1915 as college slang by Robert Bolwell, who carefully defined the meaning of the initials as *"bovine excrescence,* nonsense, 'hot air'" (*Dialect Notes,* vol. IV, Part III). Echoing Bolwell some seventy-five years later was Gen. Norman Schwartzkopf, who is said to have dismissed an unreliable news report as *bovine scatology* (*American Speech,* Winter 1991).

Besides the basic *S* that comes from the *B,* there are many other euphemisms for the produce of other animals. For example, sheep excrete *buttons* and *dumplings;* horses produce *biscuits, horse apples,* and *road apples;*

geese and other animals leave CALLING CARDS, and buffalo, camels, and cows shit *chips*. Most prolific of all are cows, which turn out *clods, cowslip, flops, heifer dust, meadow dressing, meadow muffins, pasture pies, pats, pies, prairie pancakes,* and *rich dirt.*

The profusion of euphemisms here reflects the omnipresence of animal excrement in the nineteenth-century landscape as well as the usefulness of *buffalo chips* and *buffalo wood,* a.k.a. *bois de vache* (cow wood) for fuel on treeless western plains. As the so-called Pathfinder reported, two decades prior to W. H. Jackson's account: "Our fires were partially made of the *bois de vache . . .* a very good substitute for wood, burning like turf" (John C. Frémont, *Report of the Exploring Expeditions to the Rocky Mountains,* 1843).

Chips come in two basic forms: *round browns,* which do not make very good fuel, and *white flats,* which burn quickly and evenly, producing little smoke and no odor. Children used to spend a lot of time collecting them. Nebraska girls, it was said, could be identified by their toes, which had become overdeveloped from turning over *chips* to see if they were fully cured. *Chips* also loomed large in western song and story. Thus, from a Mormon ballad, cited in "No Fuel Like an Old Fuel" (*Natural History,* 11/80):

> There's a pretty little girl in the
>   outfit ahead,
> Whoa, Ha, Buck and Jerry Boy!
> I wish she was by my side instead,
> Whoa, Ha, Buck and Jerry Boy!
> Look at her now with a pout on her
>   lips
> As daintily with her finger tips
> She picks for the fire some buffalo
>   chips,
> Whoa, Ha, Buck and Jerry Boy!

See also BULLFEATHERS; DEFECATE/DEFECATION; DOG DIRT/DO/LITTER/WASTE; DOO-DOO; FULL OF APPLESAUCE, ETC.; HOOEY; and POPPYCOCK.

buck. To kill by gunshot; also, to copulate. "The prosecution witness . . . said the men decided 'to go to the cab stand late at night and buck them in the head'" (*New York Times,* 6/9/88). Asked by an assistant district attorney just what "buck" meant, the witness replied, "To shoot'em." The lethal "buck" probably comes from "buck" in the sense of "to butt" (with the head), as in "a bucking match." This seems to be an Americanism. "*To Buck.* Used instead of *butt,* applied to animals pushing with their head and horns, and metaphorically of players at football and such games, pugilists, etc." (J. R. Bartlett, *The Dictionary of Americanisms,* 1859). Meanwhile, the copulatory sense appears to be older (1530, *OED*). Originally applied to the doings of rabbits and other critters, this meaning probably derives from the "buck" that is a male animal. In human contexts, the word's euphemistic power is enhanced greatly by its sound, as in the anonymous, early-nineteenth-century rhyme:

Tom and Tim on mischief bent,
Went to the plains of Timbuctoo,
They saw three maidens in a tent,
Tom bucked one, and Tim-bucked-two.

See also ACTION and HIT.

buff. Naked. "Buff," the color, comes from "buffalo," the animal, whose hide, a dull, whitish yellow, is not dissimilar in appearance to human hide. As a byword for lack of clothes, "buff" surfaced circa 1600, and it

has remained popular to the present day. See also NUDE.

bullfeathers. Bullshit. Thus, Evva Gore, owner of the 77 Lounge (a euphemism for "bar"; see SALOON) in Gehring, Neb., objected to the high cost of trucking liquor across the state: "When I saw that [a freight bill] I said 'bullfeathers'" (*Wall Street Journal,* 10/5/87). See also BS and HORSEFEATHERS.

buns. The ass; an obvious allusion to the shape of the BUTTOCKS. "I take an aerobics class three times a week at my health club. In a class of 25, our instructor knows perhaps two of us by name. Still, we are on intimate terms. 'Squeeze those buns!' she hollers to us all" (Woodbury, Conn., *Voices,* 10/24/90). The term also is employed frequently in a generalized, singular sense, as in "Get your buns over here" (overheard conversation, New York City subway, 1981). See also ARSE.

burleycue. An aural euphemism for "burlesque"; the cutesy mispronunciation supposedly softens the sounds of the bumps in the night. It has even been used in a book title: *Burleycue,* by Bernard Sobel (1931). See also ECDYSIAST, EXOTIC DANCER, and, for more about aural euphemisms, HOOR and the cony in RABBIT.

burn. To kill by shooting. Speaking of a plot to overthrow the Panamanian leader General Manuel Antonio Noriega, prior to his removal by U.S. troops at the end of 1989: "We would have seized him, arrested him, maybe burned him" (Eduardo Herrera Hassan, a Panamanian exile in the United States, *New York Times,* 10/29/89).

This sense of "burn" almost certainly derives from the "burn" of the electric chair, a.k.a. HOT SEAT. See also HIT.

burp. Belch. "Belch" is an extremely old word, dating to ca. 1000, but the term has been considered as impolite as the action since Victorian times. *The Oxford English Dictionary* labeled "belch" as "now *vulgar*" (vol. B., 1882–88) and the Hays office, which administered the Hollywood Production Code, still frowned upon the word in the 1940s (H. L. Mencken, *The American Language: Supplement I*, 1945). In deference to the desire to be refined, babies have been *burped*, not *belched*, since the 1930s.

bushwa; also **bushwah, booshwa, booshwah, boushwa,** or **boushwah.** They all add up to the same thing: bullshit. "Looks to me like it's all bushwa" (John Dos Passos, *Three Soldiers*, 1922). Though probably just a mispronunciation of the word for which it stands, imaginative etymologies have been proposed for "bushwa," i.e., that it comes from the French *bourgeois* or even *bois de vache* (cow's wood), the euphemistic name for the buffalo chips, or bits of dried dung, used by the pioneers on the prairies for their fires.

Similar to "bushwa" is "bushlips," a nonce term but redolent with history, alluding to President George Bush's emphatic "Read my lips" promise (later broken) not to raise taxes. This was typically encountered, ca. 1990, in such phrases as "Don't give me any of that bushlips" or "I know pure, unadulterated bushlips when I hear it." See also BS.

business. An omnibus term: In American slang, "business" may refer to the PENIS, the VAGINA, or to sexual INTERCOURSE. A *business girl*, meanwhile, is the British counterpart of the American WORKING GIRL, or whore. Most commonly, "business" is a euphemism for what children and other small animals do when they RELIEVE themselves. "There they were. Drake with his arm around little Nelson's shoulder, leading him down the path to keep him company while he did his 'business'" (John Le Carré, *The Honorable Schoolboy*, 1977). See also IT.

bust. The breasts; the general term for the upper, front part of the body—the head, shoulders, and breast, if one is talking about a statue—has a rather narrower meaning if one is speaking about a real, live woman, e.g., "I do not approve of any dress which shows the bust" (Miss Cleveland, *Pall Mall Gazette*, 3/13/1886). "Bust" also was the term of choice in the United States for many years, as evidenced by the following note on coming of age in the 1930s: "Our sex-related vocabulary was meager. Even if we knew the correct word for anything, we would not utter it. We said 'bust' for breast and wouldn't say 'bra' in mixed company" (Nardi Reed Campion, *New York Times*, 6/27/91). Back in the busty years of the nineteenth and early twentieth centuries, women also wore *bust bodices* and *bust improvers*, which functioned somewhat like BRASSIERES; *bust extenders*, which obscured the shapes of *bustlines* with ruffles, and *bustforms*, which made busts seem larger and/or shapelier. Today's woman accomplishes many of these objectives by donning a *bustier*, a relatively new word (ca. 1980) for a corselet that is so chic it is worn as outerwear. Form and function are apparent from a Saks Fifth Avenue ad, which discloses that "the bustier," stocked in the store's Enhancements [sic] Boutique, "signals the start of a great evening" (*New York Times*, 10/13/94). See also BODY BRIEFER, BOSOM, and BRASSIERE.

butt/buttocks. The ass. The four-letter "butt" is printable and otherwise usable where the three-letter word might offend, e.g., "kiss my royal Irish butt" (Edwin O'Connor, *Last Hurrah*, TV movie version, 1977). The rule also applies to the term's figurative use, as in "Beavis and Butt-Head" (MTV series, 1993).

"Butt," meaning the thicker end of something, was once considered Standard English for "ass." The earliest example in *The Oxford English Dictionary* comes from the fifteenth century, but the word seems to be much older, since "buttock," which is probably a diminutive of it, can be traced back to the thirteenth century. By Victorian times, the human "butt" (as contrasted with the tree butt, the butter butt, and so forth) was regarded, according to the *OED*, as chiefly dialectal and colloquial in the United States, e.g., "The buttocks. The word is used in the West in such phrases as 'I fell on my butt,' 'He kick'd my butt'" (J. R. Bartlett, *The Dictionary of Americanisms*, 1859). The inevitable next step was for polite people to begin to avoid the colloquial term. In Roxbury, Conn., the wife of Col. George Hurlbut, whose store, established in 1850, made him one of the town's richer (and meaner, it is said) citizens, insisted that their sons insert a second *r* into the family name, thus setting mercantile Hurlbu*r*ts apart from those Hurlbuts who remained farmers. This created a certain amount of ill feeling among members of the extended Hurlbut-Hurlburt clan, which only took several generations to evaporate.

The full "buttocks," meanwhile, may also be used euphemistically, as in "That Texas oil worker who was charged in Federal court with having repeatedly slapped some airline attendants [see FLIGHT ATTENDANT] on the buttocks pleaded guilty in Miami" (*New York Times*, 2/24/77). In this case, the euphemistic effect was enhanced by an FBI AGENT who testified discreetly about "the rear anatomy" (see REAR) that was slapped. As if this were not enough, the culprit's name—*mirable dictu*—was Bombard. See also ARSE and, for the lowdown on "bum," BOTTOM.

buxom. Overweight; especially, having large breasts. "When we call a girl buxom we mean that she is fat" (Wilfred Funk, *Word Origins and Their Romantic Stories*, 1950). See also BOSOM and PLUMP.

buy the farm. To die. Explaining to his colonel why a medical evacuation helicopter had to be sent to his position after it was hit by FRIENDLY FIRE in the early-morning hours of February 18, 1970, an American army lieutenant in Vietnam pleaded by radio: "Sir, the only thing I can tell you is that two of my people have bought the farm, and if I don't get it, two more will" (C. D. B. Bryan, *Friendly Fire*, 1976).

"Buy the farm" was popularized by pilots during World War II. Opinion is divided as to the original reference. The most common theory is that the oft-expressed wish of many air force pilots was to buy a farm after the fighting was over; hence, an aviator who ended his war by dying in a crash was said to have "bought the [or "a"] farm." Another belief, favored by jet pilots in the 1950s, was that when a plane crashed on a farm, the farmer would sue the government for damages, and generally receive a large enough sum to retire the mortgage; hence, the pilot was said "to have bought the farm" because he had paid for it with his life.

Whatever the origin, "buy the farm" and, a later variant, "buy the ranch," may have been reinforced by "to buy" and "buy it" in the sense of "to die" (from 1825, *OED*). "Buy the farm" also fits well such metaphors for the grave as *future home, long home, narrow home,* and, for burial, *becoming a landowner.* See also BITE THE DUST, INCAPAC-ITATION, and SPACE.

C

C, The Big. Cancer, a disease so dreaded that many people are reluctant to name it. "Parry's title refers to a cure for 'the Big C,' cancer" (*Publishers Weekly*, review of James Parry's *The Discovery*, 7/17/78). The taboo has faded appreciably in recent years in the United States, but it remains strong in other countries and cultures. For example, the Japanese still avoid their word for cancer, which is *gan*. It took a year for Japanese newspapers to break the news that the Emperor Hirohito had cancer, and when they did, one of the chief dailies, *The Yomiuri Shimbun*, attributed his ill health instead to "bad-natured peritonitis" (9/24/88). See also the *C-word* in F-WORD, HIGH-RISK GROUP, LONG ILLNESS, MOON CHILDREN, ONCOLOGY, TB, TUMOR, and ZEPHYR.

caca (kaka, kahkah). Shit; usually used when speaking to children. "All of us have had a bad early toilet training. . . . All of us at the same time got two zingers—one for the police department and one for the toilet. 'All right, he made a kahkah, call a policeman'" (Lenny Bruce, *How to Talk Dirty and Influence People*, 1972). And on a theoretically more elevated plane, inhabited by the divine Sarah Bernhard and Gabriele d'Annunzio: "Bernhard was one of the few women to refuse him, maliciously describing the poet's liquid brown eyes as petits cacas" (Anatole Broyard, *FMR*, 7/81).

The euphemism seems to date from the nineteenth century. Variants of the period included *ta*, *ta-ta*, and *taw*, all also used (ca. 1870) in the sense of "to ease oneself," according to one of John Russell Bartlett's contributors, the Rev. R. Manning Chipman (*American Speech*, 10/50). The basic term is of ancient stock, however, deriving from the British *cack*, to void excrement; the Latin *cacare*, with same meaning, and ultimately the Indo-European root, *kakka-* (or *kaka-*), also meaning the same. Other descendants of this root include *cacography*, bad handwriting or incorrect spelling; *cacodemon*, an evil spirit; *cacophonous*, referring to harsh, discordant sounds; and POPPYCOCK. See also DEFECATE/DEFECATION and WEE WEE.

Cain. A minced oath, more-or-less translatable as "God" or "hell" in such expressions as *by Cain*, *to raise Cain*, and *what in Cain*. "By Cain, I got lost this morning, or I should have been in to see you" (Joseph Stevens Jones, *The People's Lawyer*, 1839). *To raise Cain* (or *Ned*) also is to cause a commotion, to make a disturbance, which leads to the following specimen of frontier American wit: "Why have we every reason to believe that Adam and Eve were both rowdies? Because . . . they both raised Cain" (*St. Louis Pennant*, 5/2/1840). These expressions are not quite obsolete, e.g., "We can get cantankerous. We can raise Ned" (Rep. Robert H. Michel, R., Ill., C-SPAN, 12/2/93). See also GOSH and HECK.

call girl. A whore; specifically, one who makes connections with her customers by phone; a COURTESAN. Compared to the ordinary WORKING GIRL of the street, the *call girl* generally leads a better, safer life, while catering to a better-heeled clientele, e.g.: "John, these are the finest call girls in the country. . . . They are not dumb broads, but girls who can be trained and programmed.

I have spoken with the madam in Baltimore, and we have been assured their services at the convention" (John W. Dean III, *Blind Ambition,* 1976, quoting G. Gordon Liddy, on the occasion of his presentation to U.S. Attorney General John N. Mitchell, on January 27, 1972, of a million-dollar intelligence-gathering plan—a sawed-off version of which led to the Watergate CAPER).

It is commonly assumed that "call" here represents Alexander Graham Bell's contribution to the world's oldest profession, but this probably isn't so. The telephone, invented in 1876, does predate the oldest known written examples of "call girl" and "call house," meaning the brothel, or HOUSE, in which such a woman formerly lived or to which she was called. The "girl" and the "house" are recorded from the opening decades of the twentieth century; "call boy," in the sexual sense, is a more recent development, linguistically, dating to the 1940s. But women worked on call long before Bell was born. For example, in eighteenth-century London, whores of the better sort—as opposed to streetwalkers—waited in their lodgings until called to the taverns that retained them. Casanova, visiting London in the early 1760s, said he didn't like any of the twelve women who were called, one after another, to the Star tavern where he was staying; he sent each away with a shilling for her trouble. They certainly were *call girls* in fact if not in name. This also is the lifestyle depicted by Hogarth in *A Harlot's Progress* (1731–32). See also PROSTITUTE.

calling card(s). Animal excrement; almost always encountered in the plural. Speaking of geese: "They have left their calling cards all over the ground where people like to stroll" (Gloria Donen Sosin, letter, *New York Times,* 5/14/86). See also DEFECATE/DEFECATION.

calls (or needs) of nature. The periodic requirement that the body discharge waste materials. "The calls of Nature are permitted and Clerical Staff may use the garden below the second gate" (*Tailor & Cutter,* 1852). In our own informal age, the expression "I have to pay a call" is another way of announcing that one has to go to the POWDER ROOM.

cameo performance (appearance, part, role). A bit part on the silver screen. The term was popularized by producer Mike Todd, who wangled brief, low-paying appearances out of more than forty famous actors for his film *Around the World in 80 Days* (1956). Previously, going back to the mid-nineteenth-century, "cameo" had been used to describe short, finely etched literary or theatrical efforts.

camisole. In normal life, a loose-fitting garment, a jacket for men or a short negligee for women, but in MENTAL and other hospitals, a straitjacket; sometimes glorified as an *ambulatory camisole.* "The use of the straitjacket, called the 'camisole,' is now permitted only on written permission of a physician" (*New York Times,* 5/28/73).

canola. Rapeseed. The healthy-sounding term (modeled after "granola"?) was adopted in the late 1970s by Canadian processors. They apparently were squeamish about their product's true name even though it derives from the innocent Latin *rapum* (turnip), not *rapere* (to seize). *Canola* was approved for human consumption in the United States in 1985, perhaps in part because of the change in nomenclature. See also MOLEST and PARSON-IN-THE-PULPIT.

capability. Ability, with a FOP Index of 1.6. "Capability" is favored by bureaucrats and other artful dodgers, especially when acquiring new powers, because of its over-tones of contingency, which suggest to innocent bystanders that the new potential may never be used. Unfortunately, this is not always so. For example: "Late in the fall of 1971 . . . the coordinates for Watergate were fixed even if no brain as yet had made the calculation. The White House retained the Plumbers' 'capability'" (*New York Review of Books*, 4/4/74). And on the inter-national scene: "In early 1961, McGeorge Bundy [National Security Adviser to the president] was informed of a CIA project described as the development of a capa-bility to assassinate. Bundy raised no ob-jection and . . . may have been more affirmative" (report on assassination plots against foreign leaders, Senate Intelligence Committee, 11/75). See also AFFIRMATIVE, EXECUTIVE ACTION, and PLUMBER.

capacity. A voluminous synonym for a high-class job. No manager with a proper sense of his or her own importance would ever be caught saying, "As senior vice pres-ident I supervised such and such." Rather, the proper boardroom style is: "In my capacity as senior vice president, I super-vised . . ." The *capacity*, then, is strictly excess, except for the purpose of emphasiz-ing the highness of the muck-a-muck. See also POSITION.

Cape Cod turkey. Dried salt codfish, some-times further disguised with a sauce. "Factories have been established [in New-foundland] for the production of Cape Cod

turkey; i.e., salted cod fish" (*New York Her-ald*, 6/3/1890). This is one of a large set of tongue-in-cheek euphemisms that have been used over the years to portray fish as flesh. For example:

Alaska turkey. Salmon
Albany beef. Sturgeon, back in the nine-teenth century when poor people couldn't afford much meat and the Hudson River was cleaner than today
Billingsgate pheasant. Red herring or mackerel, dried and salted, British-style
Block Island turkey. Codfish, served and preserved in the same manner as *Cape Cod turkey*
Connecticut River pork. Shad
Cornish duck. Red herring
deep-sea turkey. Salmon, to servicemen in World War I
Digby chicken. Herring again
Gourock ham. More herring
Marblehead turkey. The port of Marble-head is north of Boston, not far from Cape Cod
Norfolk capon. Red herring. Capt. Francis Grose included this one in the 1785 edition of *A Classical Dictionary of the Vulgar Tongue*
submarine chicken (or *turkey*). Salmon, from World War I
Taunton turkey. Herring; the reference is to Taunton, on the river Tone in England, not its namesake in Massachusetts
two-eyed steak. The sheer variety of terms for herring shows that this fish once was as important to British cuisine as *turkey* was to Americans. (Beware: In the southwest, to dine on *Texas turkey* is to partake of armadillo.)
Yarmouth capon. Herring yet again, and dating at least to the seventeenth cen-

tury. Thus, from Thomas Fuller's *History of the Worthies of England* (pre-1661): "A Yarmouth Capon. That is, a Red-herring. I believe few Capons (save what have more fins than feathers) are bred in Yarmouth. But, to countenance this expression, I understand that the Italian friers (when disposed to eat the flesh on Fridays) call Capon *piscem e corte,* a fish out of the coop."

See also ALASKA STRAWBERRIES, ARKANSAS CAVIAR, FILET MIGNON, HOOVER HOG, MINCEMEAT, PRAIRIE OYSTERS, ROCK LOBSTER, SEA SQUAB, and WELSH RAREBIT.

caper. A lighthearted euphemism for dirty business, ranging from the overthrow of a foreign government to a domestic burglary; a COVERT ACTION (OR OPERATION).

Trying to clean up some of the dirty linen in the CIA's closet, Ray S. Cline, a former deputy director of the agency, said of CIA-aided coups in Iran in 1953 and Guatemala in 1954: "The tragedy is that the concept of what CIA was intended to be eventually became gravely distorted as a result of the Iranian and Guatemalan capers" (*Secrets, Spies, and Scholars: Blueprint of the Essential CIA,* 1978). On the home front, meanwhile, President Nixon's men often passed off the Watergate burglary as a *caper.* For instance, H. R. Haldeman, the president's chief of staff, warned his boss on June 30, 1972, just thirteen days after the break-in at the offices of the Democratic National Committee: "You run the risk of more stuff, valid or invalid, surfacing on the Watergate-caper type of thing" (White House tape). See the related HANKY-PANKY and, for more about the Watergate *caper,* continue with CONTAIN, COVER-UP, PLUMBER, and SIGN OFF.

capital punishment. The death penalty. The phrase sounds rather innocuous. The "capital" comes from the Latin *caput,* head, while "punishment" ordinarily implies a chastisement that one survives. If taken literally, "capital punishment" could mean nothing more than a box on the ears, which, of course, is not the case—despite Nancy (Mrs. Ronald) Reagan, who explained in a 1976 TV interview that she favored *capital punishment* "because it saves lives." See also see AUTO-DA-FÉ, EXECUTE, EXECUTION TECHNICIAN, HOT SEAT, MADAME, NECKTIE PARTY (or SOCIABLE), SHOT, and SMOKE.

cardinal. A slow learner. "Teachers routinely assign [grade-school students] to reading and math groups, designating them as robins, bluebirds, and cardinals—euphemisms for smart, average, and not-so-swift" (*New York Times,* 1/3/90). Only the slowest of the *cardinals* are fooled. See also EXCEPTIONAL.

cards and letters. Contributions in the televangelist business. "A ranting TV evangelist (whose pleas for cards and letters are really code words for checks and money orders)" (Clayton E. Carlson, remarks to Harper & Row board of directors, 9/78).

career. A job, as in the help-wanted sign, "Career opportunities available," at the Electronics Boutique (i.e., "electronics store") at the Danbury, Conn., Fair Mall (6/13/92). This usage is in keeping with, and probably flows from, the development in schools of courses in *career education* and *career guidance.* Meanwhile, Apple Computer ran workshops in 1993 at its "career resource center" for laid-off workers. People who need *career guidance* because of lost *career opportunities* may get help from *career* *transition consultants*. See also CONSULTANT, EXPERIENCE, and OUTPLACEMENT.

caregiver. An unpaid nurse, typically a woman and typically serving the very old, the very young, or the very sick. The emphasis is on the "give" part, since the care is provided for free. "The question of who cares for Mom or Dad rarely comes down to who should, who can, or who wants to. It is almost always a female—a daughter or daughter-in-law, a sister, a niece. The word caregiver, as one expert put it, is a euphemism for unpaid female relative" (*Modern Maturity*, 8–9/87). See also HEALTH.

care of, take. To kill, to HIT; a classic example of Reverse English, in which the figurative meaning of the phrase has been twisted 180 degrees from the actual meaning, with its connotations of affection, benevolence, and concern.

For example: At the murder trial of W. A. (Tony) Boyle, former head of the United Mine Workers of America, "the state's key witness testified that he had heard Mr. Boyle give the order in 1969 to 'take care of' Joseph A. Yablonski" (*New York Times*, 4/9/74). Mr. Yablonski, an insurgent candidate for the union presidency, was *taken care of* by being shot to death, along with his wife and daughter.

For other specimens of Reverse English, see FAIR TRADE and JOB ACTION.

carnal knowledge. Sexual intercourse. "Carnal," from the Latin word for "flesh," is a signpost word, erected so that even dullards will understand that "knowledge" in this instance is being used in the good, old-fashioned biblical sense; see KNOW. It should surprise no one to discover that the

branch, or body, of learning called *carnal knowledge* has been pursued studiously, even avidly, for some centuries. For example, speaking of the early New Englanders, who were not always as Puritanical in deed as word, John Josselyn reported in *An Account of Two Voyages to New England* (1674) that the figure of an Indian, cut from red cloth, was used to shame a woman for "suffering an Indian to have carnal knowledge of her." ("Suffer" here is something of a euphemism, too. Even in the word's older, pre-painful sense of merely "allowing" or "enduring," it implies more patient passivity than the woman who earned the Indian badge probably had.)

As typically happens with euphemisms, "carnal knowledge" has worn thin, with the result that some people have begun to steer away from it. For example, the film *Carnal Knowledge* ran into trouble on account of its name. "*Variety* reports that newspapers in 14 cities have balked at carrying ads for the Nichols-Feiffer film. . . . There was no objection to the artwork . . . or to the copy . . . the papers just didn't like the title" (*New Republic*, 9/18/71).

A variant is "carnal relations," as in "On more than one occasion Dewey [New York Governor Thomas E.] had been heard to say that the Ohio senator [Robert A. Taft] should have carnal relations with himself" (David McCullough, *Truman*, 1992).

See also F – – –, INTERCOURSE, KNOCK UP, and RELATIONS.

carry on. To engage in (carefully) unspecified sexual activity outside the bonds of matrimony. The meaning of the generalized "carry on" changes drastically according to context. "The Nurse is carrying on" may mean that she (or he) is working diligently, regardless of interruptions or difficult conditions. Or the implication may be that the nurse's mind is not on her (or his) job. In the second instance, the addition of "with (someone)" can be the giveaway. Thus, quoting a letter from an unnamed Colorado scholar: "Four years ago there was an engineering student here [Denver] who was carrying on with boys in the YMCA building; he was arrested and taken to the police station, where he killed himself with a revolver" (Magnus Hirschfeld, *Homosexuality in Men and Women*, 1914, in Jonathan Katz, *Gay American History*, 1976).

cash advance. A debt; especially, a small loan with a high rate of interest to a bank credit-card customer. "Cash advance" has a nicer jingle to it. By the same token, "cash flow agency" is soft-sell for "debt collection agency." See also NONPERFORMING ASSET, REGISTERED WARRANT, and REVOLVING CREDIT.

casket. The bronze-handled word for coffin. From the standpoint of the undertakers (FUNERAL DIRECTORS), who push the word and the object, "casket" has several advantages over the plainer "coffin": (1) the mere mention of "coffin" inevitably conjures up grim thoughts, while "casket," being also "a small box, or chest, as for jewels," seems one step further removed from the final, fatal condition; (2) "casket" makes the happy suggestion that its contents (the REMAINS) are at least as valuable as the container itself, and (3) the undertaker enjoys a higher markup on the more opulent *casket*.

The funereal men prefer to pass silently by point number three, but the first two have been articulated by the *casket* makers themselves, e.g., "Don't put your bones in any old basket, Lay them neatly in an Acme casket" (televangelist Jim Bakker's uncle used this when selling coffins in Chicago)

and "'Tis but the Casket which lies here, The Gem that filled it Sparkles yet" (Holyoke Marble Works in *American Speech*, 4/26).

"Casket" seems to have been an American invention, made about the middle of the nineteenth century, probably through a discreet shortening of *burial casket*. Almost from the time the euphemism was introduced, some people protested it. As early as 1863, for instance, Nathaniel Hawthorne railed: "'Caskets!' —a vile modern phrase which compels a person of sense and good taste to shrink more disgustedly than ever before from the idea of being buried at all" (*Our Old Home*).

All this was in vain, of course, as undertakers (and, to be fair, most of their customers) have continued to call coffins anything but. Other terms include the understated, nondescriptive *box*, the hopeful *eternity box*, the airtight (all the better to preserve the body) *burial case*, the gentle *slumber cot* (see SLUMBER COT/ROBE/ROOM), *alternative container* (a cardboard coffin), and the space-age CREW TRANSFER CONTAINER. Slang terms tend to be funnier, but the humor is of the gallows variety, e.g., *bone box, cold meat box, crate, pine overcoat, six-foot bungalow, wooden kimono, wooden overcoat,* and *wooden suit*. (The modern "wooden" terms replace the *wooden doublets* and *wooden surtouts* of yore.)

In another field, but illustrative of the same bronze-handled thinking, the people who bring us atomic power have spent a great deal of time figuring out ways to store their precious radioactive wastes in *caskets*.

See also FUNERAL HOME/PARLOR, INTERMENT, PASS AWAY, and SELECTION ROOM.

casualty. Victim. Until a century or so ago, "casualties" were accidents or losses (e.g., "casualty insurance"), but now they are people: dead ones, wounded ones, and, in the military, also missing ones and captives.

The oldest "casualty" in the military sense in *The Oxford English Dictionary* comes from as recently as 1898. An early user was Winston Spencer Churchill: "In spite of more than a hundred casualties, the advance never checked for an instant" (*London to Ladysmith,* 1900). As the Churchillian example implies, "casualty" is ideal for reducing the results of war to dry statistics. For instance: There were 33,769 American *casualties* in the Revolutionary War and 210,291 in the Vietnam CONFLICT.

On etymological grounds, "casualty" may seem at first glance to be appropriate enough. It comes from the Latin *casus,* accident, and violence often does seem to occur in an accidental, random manner, even on battlefields where it is better organized than in civilian life. The opacity of the generalized "casualty"—the way it conceals the horrors of death and disfigurement—is what makes it so appealing to professional soldiers, who almost invariably downplay the bloodiness of their work. This appears to be partly a self-protective reflex to minimize personal responsibility for one's acts, and partly a superstitious avoidance of blunt terms: it is as unlucky for a warrior to mention "death" as it is for the civilian to speak of the DEVIL, who, hearing his name, may appear. See also ACCOUNT FOR, ORDNANCE, and PERSONNEL in this connection. Hospital workers feel much the same way; see EXPIRE.

The military term becomes especially deceptive when employed off the battlefield, e.g., Secretary of State Alexander M. Haig, Jr., told congressional committees inquiring into the murder of three American nuns and a lay worker in El Salvador that national guardsmen of the U.S.-backed government had "inflicted the casualties" (3/18/81). Having thus distanced the United States government from responsibility for the ABUSE OF AUTHORITY, the secretary went on to imply that the women might have been responsible for their own deaths. In HaigSpeak:

> I would like to suggest to you that some of the investigations would lead one to believe that perhaps the vehicle the nuns were riding in may have tried to run a roadblock or may have accidentally been perceived to have been doing so, and there had been an exchange of fire, and perhaps those who inflicted the casualties sought to cover it up, and this could have been at a very low level of both competence and motivation in the context of the issue itself.

In actuality—as Haig knew, or should have known at the time—FBI investigators had already determined that the women had been raped, blindfolded, and killed, execution style, each with a shot in the back of the head. No bullet holes or shell casings were discovered in their van. Thus, there was no evidence to support the allegation about an "exchange of fire." A 1993 State Department report concluded that Mr. Haig's "statement was a clear mistake, which should have been corrected at the time." The women definitely were victims, not *casualties.*

See also ACCIDENT, BITE THE DUST, COLLATERAL DAMAGE, and POSTTRAUMATIC NEUROSIS.

categorical inaccuracy. A lie; usually used when making denials. For example, following his nomination for the vice presidency, Gerald R. Ford spiked rumors that he had been a patient of a New York City psychotherapist by declaring: "That's a categorical inaccuracy" (*New York Times*, 10/17/73). A longer-winded variant, attributed to a lawyer for Yankee owner George Steinbrenner, is "Not in strict conformance with objective reality" (Red Smith, *New York Times*, 5/17/78). See also TERMINOLOGICAL INEXACTITUDE.

cathedral. A secular building with religious pretensions. Thus, the Woolworth Building in New York City was dubbed a *Cathedral of Commerce* when built in 1913. The Roxy Theatre, opened in the same city in 1927, was billed as "the Cathedral of the Motion Pictures." Up the Hudson River in Poughkeepsie, a *News-Cathedral* was opened in 1941; it housed three local newspapers. In modern-day Sweden, meanwhile, the large, luxurious hospitals that grace the world's first postindustrial state have been termed *cathedrals of care.* Then there is the *Cathedral of Learning* at the University of Pittsburgh, informally known, after John Bowman, chancellor of the school when the skyscraper was constructed, as "Bowman's Erection." (For this last, I am indebted to David E. Koskoff's *The Mellons,* 1978.) See also PALACE and PARLOR.

cat house. A brothel, especially a cheap one. "Cat house" comes from "cat," a very old word for "whore," e.g., from a poem of 1401: "Be ware of Cristis curse, and of cattis tailis." See also HOUSE, PUSSY, and, for more about the "tailis" of the "cattis," refer to TAIL.

Caucasian. White. The euphemism enjoyed widespread use during the era of SEPAPATE-BUT-EQUAL facilities, as in "Members of the Caucasian race only served here," but is now restricted mainly to police blotters, e.g., "He had no breakdown of field interviews by race, but Major McCormack said that of the people arrested in New Milford in that period, 96 percent were Caucasian" (Elizabeth Maker, *Litchfield County,* Conn., *Times,* 5/13/94). The Caucasian-white equation was established in 1781 by Johann Friedrich Blumenbach, who divided all humanity into five races on the basis of skull measurements, with one skull from the South Caucasus giving its name to the type because of its supposedly typical white measurements. See also ALL-AMERICAN, FIELD INTERVIEW, and OTHER.

caught or **caught out.** To be made pregnant. "The pride of giving life to an immortal soul is very fine . . . perfectly furious as I was to be caught" (Queen Victoria, letter, 6/15/1858, in *Dearest Child,* 1964). See also PREGNANT.

caught (or **taken) short.** To be in difficult straits on account of the need to empty the bladder or bowels at an awkward time. "I was caught a bit short . . . had the trots" (*Pennies from Heaven,* WNET-TV, 3/15/79). By extension, "taken short" may also refer to the soiling of one's underwear. See also DEFECATE/DEFECATION and PEE.

cemetery. A graveyard; the euphemism is betrayed by its origin, the original Greek *koimeterion,* referring to a "dormitory" or "sleeping place." See SLEEP.

"Cemetery" was applied first by early Christian writers to the Roman catacombs, later to consecrated churchyards, and still later to non-church-related burying grounds. If "cemetery" seems to be a relatively honest, straightforward word today, that is just because we have grown used to it—and it looks good in comparison to some of the newer terms that have been floated by graveyard developers. Among the floaters: *burial-abbey* and *burial-cloister; garden of honor* (for veterans and their wives); *garden of memories* (in the great Forest Lawn Memorial Park of Southern California, the most expensive section, open only to property-holders who possess a Golden Key, is called the *Gardens of Memory); love glade,* MEMORIAL PARK, *mausoleum* (an old word for a fancy tomb that is having something of a revival as rising land prices make it more profitable for graveyard developers to build up instead of digging down); *mortarium,* and *necropolis* (from the Greek for "city of the dead"). Another special kind of graveyard is the *columbarium* or *cinerarium,* which is not a place to see a special kind of 3-D movie, but a site for INURNMENT of CREMAINS (ashes). In the language of slang, too, there are many circumlocutions for "graveyard" (whistling past it, in effect). For example: *bone orchard, boneyard, future home, God's acre* (or *field), Hell's half-acre, last home* (or *abode), marble city* (or *orchard), permanent rest camp, skeleton park, Stiffville,* and *underground jungle.*

For more about the graveyard business today, see (in addition to the aforementioned MEMORIAL PARK), INURNMENT, PERPETUAL CARE, PRENEED, and SPACE. For the great, pre-Victorian shift in graveyard styles, see PASS AWAY.

challenge. A problem; the daring call to battle glosses over the difficulties, which may be insolvable. The term is much used in the education business. " 'Let it be a challenge to you' means you're stuck with it" (Bel Kaufman, *Up the Down Staircase,* 1964).

See also COGNITIVELY CHALLENGED, PHYSICALLY CHALLENGED, VERTICALLY CHALLENGED, and VISUALLY CHALLENGED.

chamber. A discreet shortening of "chamber pot," as from a discussion of the conditions in which slaves lived on Southern plantations, "There are seldom or never any conveniences in the way of chambers" (J. Hume Simons, *The Planter's Guide and Daily Book of Medicine,* 1849). See also CONVENIENCE and UTENSIL.

chapel. An undertaker's establishment; long forms include *funeral chapel, memorial chapel,* and *mortuary chapel.*

The death business, like so many other businesses, seems to be consolidating as it expands. Thus, many *chapels* are parts of the same organization, forming what might be called "chapelchains." For example, in the New York area, Frank E. Campbell, "The Funeral Chapel," Inc.; Riverside Memorial Chapel, Inc. (five *chapels,* plus the affiliated Boulevard-Riverside Chapels, Riverside-Gramercy Chapels, and Riverside-Nassau North Chapels); Schwartz Brothers–Jeffer Memorial Chapel; and Hellman Memorial Chapel, are all owned—along with various FUNERAL HOMES—by anonymously named Service Corporation International, of Houston, Texas. SCI is a billion-dollar corporation that at last count offered its particular services at 662—er—locations in thirty-nine states. Its holdings in 1993 included forty-four flower shops, sixty-two crematories, and 174 cemeteries. Thus, it is a vertically integrated company in more ways than one. See also CEMETERY, FUNERAL DIRECTOR, and MORTUARY.

character line. A wrinkle, as in "Matilda is starting to get character lines." The euphemism is unusually apt, since "character" derives from a Greek verb meaning "to engrave" or "make furrows in."

charms. Parts of the human anatomy that are considered sexually attractive. The term usually is used in connection with a feminine object, as in Lady Mary Wortley Montagu's carefully phrased report on the doings of the notorious Lady Frances Vane: "I am told that though she does not pique herself upon fidelity to any one man (which is but a narrow way of thinking), she boasts that she has always been true to her nation, and, notwithstanding foreign attacks, has always reserved her charms for the use of her countrymen" (letter to Lady Pomfret, 1/1739). Women of today still have their *charms.* For example:

SWEET YOUNG MODEL WITH HOT SUCCULENT BODY 38-22-34 needs love of her charms. $3 brings appreciation of her charms. Sandy Wilson POB 82753 (personal ad, *Ace,* undated, ca. 1976).

There is ample precedent for employing "charms" in a masculine context, too. Thus, from *The Merry Wives of Windsor* (1597):

MISTRESS QUICKLY: ". . . I never knew a woman so dote upon a man. Surely, I think you have charms, la! Yes, in truth.
FALSTAFF: Not I, I assure thee. Setting the attraction of my good parts aside, I have no other charms.

See also FAVORS and PRIVATE PARTS.

chauffeur. A hired driver. The job title began to be Frenchified shortly after the invention of the automobile. "As to the driver, 'chauffeur' seems at present to hold the field" (*Westminster Gazette,* 8/5/02). See also ENGINEER.

check out. To die, especially in hospitals, where live patients are "discharged," while dead ones are said to have "checked out." See also CODE (OUT).

chemical dependency. Addiction. "Captain Pursch . . . gave me the book *Alcoholics Anonymous,* and told me to read it, substituting the words 'chemically dependent' for 'alcoholic'" (Betty Ford, *The Times of My Life,* 1978). "This is the golden age of full disclosure. Actresses, authors, athletes begin comebacks with front-page confessions about their 'chemical dependencies' (isn't anyone embarrassed to be a drug addict?), followed by television coverage when they check into the Betty Ford clinic" (Mayo Kaufman, "Hers," *New York Times,* 2/4/88).

While people with *chemical dependencies* may become *chemically inconvenienced* (i.e., stoned, zonked), it is heartening to know that they do not suffer terribly from "withdrawal." We have this on the authority of Dr. Dennis O'Leary, of George Washington Medical Center. After the disclosure that Supreme Court Justice William Rehnquist was having difficulty dealing with diminished doses of a sleeping pill that had been prescribed for him as a painkiller, Dr. O'Leary went out of his way to deny that Mr. Rehnquist had been addicted. Contending that "addiction is a buzzword" with "negative connotations," the doctor explained that the drug had merely "established an interrelationship with the [Justice's] body, such that if the drug is removed precipitously, there is a reaction" (*Philadephia Inquirer,* 1/6/82). The "reaction" was reported to have included perceptual distortions and hallucinations. Symptoms of actual "withdrawal" would have been much more severe, no doubt. See also DEPENDENCE.

chemise. A slip—and yet another Frenchified undergarment; see LINGERIE for details.

In olden times, "chemise" was applied in English (as it still is in French) to the linen underthings of men as well as women. During the nineteenth century, as "lingerie" itself was coming into fashion, "chemise" gradually became restricted as to feminine garments, replacing "smock" and "shift." From Leigh Hunt's *Autobiography* (1850): "That harmless expression [shift] . . . has been set aside in favour of the French word 'chemise.'" (But it was not all that harmless in some benighted parts of the world: as late as 1907 the use of "shift" in John Millington Synge's *Playboy of the Western World* was one of the lightning rods that led to the "Playboy Riots" in Dublin the following year. The rioters were, presumably, all male and shiftless.)

From *chemise*, in turn, we get *shimmy*, which is used corruptly in place of *chemise* and (also corruptly, some would say) to describe what the *chemise* does during a dance known as the *shimmy shake*. Automobiles, too, are said to *shimmy* when they wobble, but that is another, far less fascinating matter.

See also HANDKERCHIEF; SLIP; and SNOWING DOWN SOUTH, IT'S.

chest. The breasts. "She was so angry at her swinging breasts that she wanted to cry; no matter how nice he was he couldn't fail to notice her 'chest'" (John O'Hara, *Appointment in Samarra*, 1934). Then there's the old joke (a chestnut, so to speak):

JOE: My father has a wooden leg.
MOE: That's nothing; my sister has a cedar chest.

Persons with large *chests* are said to be *chesty* or, more formally, to have *amply* (or *well-*) *endowed chests*. See also BOSOM and ENDOW/ENDOWMENT.

Chevalene. Horse meat. "Chevalene" is the brand name for table-quality horse meat prepared by the M & R Packing Co., of Hartford, Connecticut. You can get Chevalene steaks as well as patties. See also CHEVON, FILET MIGNON, and PACKING HOUSE.

chevon. Goat meat; the U.S. Department of Agriculture has allowed meat-packers to use the French label since 1971. See also FRAGRANT MEAT.

chicken. Chicken shit; also euphemized as *chicken – – – –*, *chicken stuffing*, and *CS* (which is to "chicken" as *BS* is to "bull"). In the military, for instance, a unit in which the commander insists on small-minded attention to unnecessary details may be described as "a chicken outfit." Or a recruit may complain: "Having to polish the back of your belt buckle is a lot of CS." Civilians also have been known to use such expressions. "Cut the chicken and let's get through with it" (*My Six Convicts*, film, 1952). See also CRAP, DEFECATE/DEFECATION, ROOSTER, and STUFF.

children of god. The untouchables in India, from the Sanskrit *Hari*, Vishnu, and *jana*, person. Popularized by Mohandas K. Gandhi in the 1930s, some *children of god* have come to regard the label as insulting. In affirmative-action programs to reserve places for them in medical and engineering schools, the *children of god* are referred to opaquely as *scheduled castes*. See also SPECIAL VILLAGE PEOPLE.

chrissake. Christ's sake. Speaking of the inimitable Cher and her former husband Sonny Bono: "As of 1968, she knew, for chrissake, that she towered over him" (Lawrence J. Quirk, *Totally Uninhibited: The Life and Wild Times of Cher,* 1991). This and other holy names commonly are euphemized by means of deformed spellings. See also CRIPES; CRYING OUT LOUD, FOR; and JIMINY CRICKET.

chronic organic brain syndrome. Senility, with a FOP Index of 3.5.

circular curbside construction. A public urinal. "In the first theater review he submitted to the magazine, [Kenneth] Tynan used the term *'pissoir,'* a word [*New Yorker* editor William] Shawn could not bring himself to put into print. After a long and amiable discussion, it was agreed that *'pissoir'* would be changed to read *'a circular curbside construction'"* (*New Republic,* 2/26/90). The handling of "pissoir" was cited here as an example of *The New Yorker*'s "longstanding resistance to vulgarity," which has since been overcome. See also TOILET.

circumorbital hematoma. A black eye; doctor-talk.

city. Town. European cities usually are important, populous places, but when Americans began naming their towns, they were much more liberal with the "city" designation. Occasionally, this may simply have been the result of overoptimism, but the root cause seems to be the human desire to make one's surroundings appear as grand as possible. "It is strange that the name of city should be given to an unfinished log-house, but such is the case in Texas: every individual possessing three hundred acres of land, calls his lot a city" (Capt. Frederick Marryat, *Narrative of the Travels and Adventures of Monsieur Violet in California,* etc., 1843). "They snipped the ribbon in 1915, they popped the cork, Miami Beach was born. A modest burg they called a city" (Norman Mailer, *Miami and the Siege of Chicago,* 1968). Back in the Old World, the "cities of the plain" also were relatively small, at least by today's standards, but the reference then was to homosexuality, the cities in question being Sodom and Gomorrah, which the Lord destroyed with fire and brimstone on account of the sinfulness of their inhabitants (Genesis 19:24–29). See also GREENLAND and UNIVERSITY.

clarify. To eat one's words, typically by issuing a *clarification* that qualifies, and sometimes flatly contradicts, a previous position or statement. See also MISSPEAK.

Class Four Highway. The official designation in the People's Republic of China for a dirt road.

classic. More than ten years old. "Other premium [cable TV] services, including Encore, which will ask viewers to pay a fee to see classic movies, more than a decade old, will be introduced" (*New York Times,* 5/9/91). Then there is the Women's Tennis Classic, a series of tournaments started by Billie Jean King and Rosie Casals in 1983. In this case, *classic* players had to be at least thirty years of age—older than *classic* movies but not exactly superannuated. See also MASTER.

clean. To rid an area of people, by killing them if need be; a common term for white-washing dirty work. Thus, speaking of the massacre of Palestinians in refugee camps in west Beirut: "After the P.L.O. withdrew . . . the door was opened for the Phalangists to 'clean' the area, in the jargon of the Israeli military" (*New York Times*, 9/20/82). Americans relied on the same mind-numbing metaphor in Vietnam. "According to the official rhetoric, the Viet Cong did not live in places, they 'infested areas'; to 'clean them out' the American forces went on 'sweep and clear' operations or moved all the villagers into refugee camps in order to 'sanitize the area'" (Frances FitzGerald, *Fire in the Lake*, 1972). See also CLEANSE, PURIFY, RECONNAISSANCE IN FORCE, and SANITIZE.

clean air. Anti–clean air. The Clean Air Working Group, representing the aluminum, automobile, oil, paper, and steel industries, distinguished itself for lobbying against tougher amendments to the Clean Air Act. CAWG was one of a number of such deceptively named lobbying groups noted by *Spy* (5/89). Among the others: Citizens for Sensible Control of Acid Rain (see SENSIBLE); Ducks Unlimited, which supports preservation of waterfowl habitats so that its members will have unlimited ducks to kill; and the Washington Forest Protection Association, composed of the largest timber companies in the state of Washington, which fights restrictions on logging. See also ENVIRONMENTAL.

clean bomb. A neutron bomb, whose dirty radioactivity is concentrated in a relatively small area. The bomb is *clean* in the sense that its killing zone is measured in thousands of square yards rather than thousands of square miles. See also ENHANCED RADIATION WEAPON and TACTICAL NUCLEAR WEAPON.

clean harbor. Dirty harbor. The port of New York used to be known as a *clean harbor* because the water was so polluted that it killed the marine organisms that ordinarily attach themselves to the hulls of ships. Now that pollution levels are down, the mollusks and crustaceans are back, hundreds of millions of dollars have to be spent to keep them from devouring wooden piers and bulkheads (an unforeseen consequence of pollution control), and sailors no longer call the cleaner harbor a *clean harbor*. See also EFFLUENT.

cleaning person. A cleaning woman; formerly a cleaning lady, DOMESTIC, HELP, MAID, or SERVANT. "Then there was the white radical feminist, about to meet with the black female militant about a strike of hospital workers; the radical feminist gave her black female cleaning person the day off" (John Leonard, *New York Times*, 8/18/76). See also PERSON.

cleanse. To remove unwanted people from a particular region by killing them or forcing them to move away; essentially synonymous with CLEAN and just as widely employed. "A man who identified himself only as Pioro said he was warned last week that the Serbian irregulars were about to 'cleanse' Vocin, using a euphemism of the Nazis to describe ethnically motivated massacres of civilians" (*New York Times*, 12/19/91). And quoting Abba Eban, Israeli diplomat and former former minister, on his nation's policy following its invasion of Lebanon in 1982: "There is a new vocabulary with special verbs . . . 'to cleanse,' 'to fumigate,' 'to solve by other means,' 'not to put up with,' 'to mean business,' 'to wipe out'" (*New Yorker*, 10/15/82). See also ETHNIC CLEANSING and PURIFY.

client. A catchall term for covering up a variety of less-speakable relationships. Thus, speaking of a JOB ACTION at the Southbury (Conn.) Training School for the retarded: "No clients, however, were left unattended while staff members marched during each shift" (Woodbury, Conn., *Voices*, 10/11/89). Meanwhile, welfare recipients have metamorphosed into the *clients* of social workers, convicts into the *clients* of prison administrators, and patients into the *clients* of psychoanalysts. In each instance, "client" has an important rub-off effect: By dignifying the recipients of services, it elevates proportionately the status of the providers, lifting social workers, prison administrators, et al. onto the same lofty plane as lawyers, who have long had "clients" instead of "customers." See also PATRON.

clinic. Workshop. Shamelessly imitating the medical profession, practitioners in a host of other fields have latched on to "clinic" to describe their own operations. Speaking of a local dialect: "Floridian is now euphemistically and compulsively alliterative. Thus a garage is a 'Collision Clinic,' a furniture store a 'Gallery' selling not tables and chairs but 'Concepts' (though without explaining how one sits on a concept)" (Robert Craft, *New York Review of Books*, 5/16/74). Other kinds of "clinics" include *auto clinic, baseball clinic, beauty clinic* (or *clinque*), *car clinic, coaches clinic, decorator clinic, football clinic, home remodeling clinic, legal clinic, marriage clinic, tax clinic, teachers clinic,* and *writers clinic.* See also CONSULTANT and PARLOR.

cloakroom or **cloaks.** A common British euphemism for (euphemisms all) a LAVATORY, REST ROOM, or TOILET; not to be confused with a "checkroom," which is where Americans actually put their cloaks, overcoats, and parcels. "Cloakrooms" with running water seem to be a relatively recent invention, but the general idea is old: When our medieval ancestors went to the castle *garderobe,* they did not—as the name of the place implies—merely hang up their robes. It is possible, too, that "cloakroom" has been influenced by "closet" (see EASE and WC), and perhaps even by *cloaca,* the Latin word for sewer, which did time as a euphemism for PRIVY. "Cloaca," in turn, comes from Cloacina, Roman goddess of disposal. In the nineteenth century, an especially fancy privy might be hailed as a "Temple of Cloacina," but the short form was more common, e.g., "To every house . . . a cloaca" (Capt. Frederick Marryat, *Olla Podrida,* 1840).

clothes doctor. A launderer. "There are diplomas for everything. (There is even one for ironing, and launderers now call themselves clothes doctors)" (review of Theodore Zeldin's *The French,* in *The New Yorker,* 10/3/83). "Clothes doctor" represents a considerable advance over "clothing refresher," favored by Irish washerwomen in San Francisco about the time of the 1849 gold rush (*American Speech,* 10/46). See also ENGINEER.

clothing optional. Nakedness permitted. Discreetly averting its eyes from its own policies, the Federal Park Service has tolerated what it calls a "clothing-optional lifestyle" since 1992 on the southern part of Gunnison Beach at Sandy Hook, just across New York Harbor from Manhattan. (A large sign on the beach is more explicit, warning those who approach the "clothing-optional" zone that "Beyond This Point You May Encounter Nude Sunbathers.") Much the same terminology is used by sun-loving Californians, where a 900-foot-long strip of Black's Beach in La Jolla was declared, by city ordinance, to be an "optional swimsuit area" as long ago as 1974. See also BA and NUDE.

club. A bar, dressed up as a fraternal organization in order to evade local liquor laws. Thus, Calvin Trillin reported that thirsty guests of the Ramada Inn in Topeka, Kansas, had to become "members" of Le Flambeau Club before they could get a drink at the hostelry's Le Flambeau Bar (*New Yorker*, 8/7/78). See also DONATION and TEMPERANCE.

coach. No one in the egalitarian United States likes to travel "second class," which is what this is in the airline business. See also FIRST CLASS.

code (out). To die; hospital talk, as in "The old man in Ward B is coding out." After dying, he may be said to have *coded*. The term comes from the emergency announcement, *Code Blue*, or one of its variants, such as *Code 9*, *Code 14*, and *Code 99* (*Dr. Heart* also has been reported), used on hospital public address systems to summon doctors and nurses in cases of cardiac arrest or respiratory failure. *No code*, when written on the chart at the foot of a patient's bed, means "Do not use heroic measures to revive this person." See also CHECK OUT, CRUMP, EXPIRE, and PASS AWAY.

coercive diplomacy. Saber rattling, up to and including an occasional swipe with the saber. "The American Bombing of Libya: A Success for Coercive Diplomacy?" (article title, *Survival*, 5–6/87). Then there was Haiti, where the launching of an air attack while American envoys were still negotiating with local military leaders, was hailed as a "textbook example of coercive diplomacy" (Secretary of Defense William Perry, "MacNeil-Lehrer NewsHour," WNET-TV, 9/19/94). The doctrine of "coercive diplomacy" was formulated by Alexander L. George, of the Stanford Center for International Security and Arms Control, and popularized by him in *The Limits of Coercive Diplomacy: Laos, Cuba, and Vietnam* (1971). See also DEFENSE, DEPARTMENT OF and PEACE OFFENSIVE.

cognitively challenged. Slow to learn, retarded, a.k.a. *cerebrally challenged*. See also EXCEPTIONAL, PHYSICALLY CHALLENGED, and SLOW.

cohabitor. Legalistic Latin for a person who is living with another person, also called a *cohabitant* or *cohabitee*. The term presumes a sexual relationship, not necessarily between opposite sexes. The relevant noun, *cohabitation*, once carried the specific meaning of INTERCOURSE, e.g., "The death of Galeas happened by immoderate cohabitacion" (Sir Geoffrey Fentron, *The Historie of Guicciardini*, trans. 1579). Alas, poor Galeas. His death is known to the French as *la morte douce* and by those with sufficiently long memories as *The Rockefeller Syndrome*. See also COMPANION, PARTNER, and POSSLQ.

coin telephone enclosure. A phone booth, with a FOP Index of 2.8. "Enclosure" itself is a euphemism here, in that the newer, abbreviated models do not come close to enclosing the user of the phone—as anyone who has ever tried to speak over the rumble of a passing bus or train can testify. See also ENTRENCHING TOOL and DIRECTORY ASSISTANCE.

coition or **coitus.** Sexual intercourse; a safe, scientific, Latinate retreat, as in the anonymous Roman observation, *Post coitum omne animal triste*—every creature is sad after coitus. Even in the original tongue, the actual meaning is appropriately, and euphemistically, vague. Both "coition" and "coitus" derive from *coire,* where *co* equals "together" and *ire* is "to go." They may be translated as "going together" or, with greater felicity perhaps, as "coming together."

Of the two, "coition" is the older in English, dating to the sixteenth century. "Coitus," meanwhile, is an early-eighteenth-century coinage. Before it became a euphemism, the basic "coition" had other, nonsexual meanings. For instance, back in the sixteenth and seventeenth centuries, people spoke of the "coition" (or "coming together") of magnets, and of the "coition" (or "conjunction") of planets. The word's sexual sense seems to date from the first half of the seventeenth century. Thus, Sir Thomas Browne, despite having a wife, children, and an apparently happy family life, could write: "I would be content . . . that there were any way to perpetuate the world without this trivial and vulgar way of coition" (*Religio Medici,* 1643). In conformance with Gresham's Law (bad meanings drive out good), the sexual sense eventually took over, making the other, older meanings of "coition" obsolete.

The technical, extremely discreet *coitus interruptus* and *coitus reservatus* are simply new names (1900 and 1903, respectively) for ancient methods of birth control. The Bible refers to the first (Onan died because he practiced it; see MASTURBATION) and Hindu and Sanskrit texts to the latter, a.k.a. *karezza.* Members of the Oneida Community, established in central New York State in 1848, also practiced "*coitus reservatus*; or, more colloquially, everything but" (*American Heritage,* 2/69). The Oneidans didn't have a Latin term for the technique at this date, however, so one of their number, H. J. Seymour, retreated into flowery language, explaining the local custom in terms of "checking the flow of amative passion before it reaches the point of exposing the man to the loss of virile energy, or the woman to the danger of undesired childbearing."

For other Latinate words with similar linguistic trajectories, see COPULATE and INTERCOURSE; for more about the quaint customs of the Oneidans, continue with OPEN MARRIAGE.

cojones. The balls, a.k.a. TESTICLES; from the Spanish *cojon,* for the same item in the singular. "Cojones," like "balls," also may be used figuratively for "guts," a.k.a. INTESTINAL FORTITUDE. For instance: "It takes more cojones to be a sportsman where death is a closer party to the game" (Ernest Hemingway, *Death in the Afternoon,* 1932). A very similar, though obsolete, term is "cullion," a French cousin of "cojones." (Both go back to the Latin *culleus,* bag.) Thus, referring to a method of taking oaths that was used before people began to swear upon Bibles: "I wolde I had thy coillons in myn hond/In stede of relikes or seintuarie [holy objects]" (Geoffrey Chaucer, *The Pardoner's Tale,* ca. 1387–1400). For more testimonial talk, see THIGH.

cold, have a. Job, lose one's—Chinese-style. "If a high official is said to have a cold he's likely been fired; if he is 'convalescing,' he has been exiled; and if he is 'extremely ill,' he is about to be murdered" (Paul Theroux, *Riding the Iron Rooster,* 1988). See also LET GO.

collateral damage. Damage to civilians and their property as a result of military action. "In any military operation, you have to consider collateral damage" (Walter Slocombe, C-SPAN, 2/10/94). Curiously, the expression was not included in the 1979 edition of the *Department of Defense Dictionary of Military Terms* even though it was in common use at the time that work was published, e.g., "A primary factor that would influence thinking in governments and among the people in Western Europe is 'collateral damage,' a euphemism for civilian casualties and destruction of nonmilitary structures and facilities" (*New York Times,* 12/6/79). See also CASUALTY, EXCHANGE, and SURGICAL STRIKE.

collectible. Junk, typically encountered in flea markets and elsewhere in the plural form, *collectibles* (or *collectables*). The beauty, desirability, and price of *collectibles* resides entirely in the mind of the beholder since the objects, by definition, have little intrinsic value. "One finds . . . shops with secondhand clothes (now called 'antiques' and viewed as high fashion), and shops filled with less-than-antiques that used to be called 'junk' and are now called 'collectibles'" (*New Yorker,* 11/22/76). See also RESALE SHOP.

collective indiscipline. Mutiny, especially in the First World War. "A point was reached in every army at which either a majority or a disabling minority refused to go on. This point was reached by the French army in May 1917, when 'collective indiscipline' occurred in 54 of the 110 divisions on the Western Front" (John Keegan, *The Face of Battle,* 1976). "The phrase 'collective indiscipline' was carefully used by the generals, but they knew what they faced was far more frightening. It was mutiny" (Gene Smith, *The Ends of Power,* 1990).

collective obsessional behavior. Mass hysteria. Modern social psychologists shun "hysteria" because of its sexist origin. It comes from the Greek word for the uterus, the condition having been associated from ancient times with disturbances of that organ. From the wisdom of Hippocrates: "For hysterial maidens, I prescribe marriage, for they are cured by pregnancy."

colonel. Lacking inherited titles to distinguish themselves from their fellow citizens—and indeed barred from accepting them under the Constitution—Americans have had to make do with a variety of euphemistic honorifics, of which "colonel" is perhaps the most common after HONORABLE itself.

As a title of esteem rather than an actual military rank, "colonel" goes back at least to the eighteenth century. In 1744, reflecting upon the prevalence of *colonels* in the Hudson Valley, Alexander Hamilton (an Annapolis physician, not the other one, who wasn't born yet) explained: "It is a common saying here that a man has no title to that dignity unless he has killed a rattlesnake" (Albert Bushnell Hart, ed., *Hamilton's Itinerarium. . . . From May to September, 1744,* 1907).

The American predilection for titles was noted by many foreign visitors: "Whenever you travel in Maryland (as also in Virginia and Carolina) your ears are constantly astonished by the number of *colonels, majors,* and *captains* that you hear mentioned; in short, the whole country seems at first to you a retreat of heroes" (Edward Kimber, *London Magazine,* 7/1746). "In travelling these dreary roads, a stranger is amazed at the number of *cidevant* military officers and infatuated emigrants he meets with. The miserable places of entertainment, which they call taverns, are generally kept by a colonel or a major; and I have known even waggoners who had formerly been field-officers. They are extremely tenacious of their titles, and . . . rigidly adhere to the vulgar adage, 'once a captain always a captain'" (Charles Janson, *The Stranger in America, 1793–1806,* 1807). A century later, Mark Twain independently reached the same conclusion: "Titles of honor and dignity once acquired in a democracy, even by accident and properly usable for only forty-eight hours, are as pemanent here as eternity is in heaven. You can never take away those titles. Once a justice of peace for a week, always 'judge' afterward. Once a major of militia for a campaign on the Fourth of July, always a major. To be called colonel, purely by mistake and without intention, confers that dignity upon a man for the rest of his life" (4/11/06 in *Mark Twain's Autobiography,* 1924).

No one bemoaned this tendency more than that ardent republican, John Adams, who complained in a letter in 1807: "There is not a country under heaven in which titles and precedency are more eagerly coveted than in this country. The title of Excellency and Honor, and Worship, of Councillor, Senator, Speaker, Major-General, Brigadier-General, Colonel, Lieutenant, Ensign, Sergeant, Corporal, and even Drummer and Fifer, is sought with as furious a zeal as that of Earl, Marquis, or Duke in any other country; and as many intrigues and as much corruption in many cases, are used to obtain them" (quoted by Allen Walker Read in *Notes of the American Dialect Society,* 9/85).

"Major" became an especially popular rank in the South, and was the title usually awarded to those who served as railroad conductors, back in the days when trains regularly carried people as well as freight. The sheer profusion of *colonels,* though, stemmed from the practice of state governors, north and south, of bestowing this rank upon all comers. In 1942, a legislator in Virginia even introduced a bill to enable any citizen of the state to purchase an official colonel's commission for the sum of one dollar (provided that the citizen was adult, male, and white). Of the hordes of state *colonels,* those from Kentucky have long been the most famous. As early as 1825, according to H. L. Mencken's *The American Language, Supplement One* (1945), the Chief Justice of the United States, John Marshall, penned the following:

> In the blue grass region
> > A paradox was born:
> The corn was full of kernels
> > And the colonels full of corn.

color. Dye, in the beauty business. As Robin Weir, operator of a beauty parlor in Washington, D.C., told William Safire: "Used to say *dye.* Then it was *tint.* Now it's *color*" (*New York Times,* 6/10/90). Other forms of non-dyeing include *frosting, highlighting, naturalizing, rinsing,* and *streaking.* The various operations often involve bleaching, now called *prelightening.* The person who does all this is not a hair dyer but a *colorist.* See also BEAUTICIAN and WASH.

P.S. A *suicide blonde* is one who has "dyed by her own hand."

colored. Nonwhite, especially black. "Colored" was the preferred designation for and by African-Americans, as opposed to "Negro" in the North and "nigger" or NIGRA in the South, for about a century, starting in the 1840s. Thus, Booker T. Washington recorded the speech of an old woman who answered his appeal for help to establish Tuskegee Institute in 1881 with a gift that touched him deeply:

> Mr. Washin'ton, God knows I spent de bes' days of my life in slavery. God knows I's is ignorant an' poor, but I knows . . . you is tryin' to make better men an' women for de colored race. I ain't got no money but I want you to take dese six eggs what I's been savin' up, and I wants you to put dese six eggs into de eddication of dese boys an' gals. (*Up From Slavery*, 1901)

The dominance of "colored" during the post–Civil War period also is apparent from the name of the NAACP, the National Association for the Advancement of Colored People, founded in 1909. As late as 1946, for a revival of *Show Boat*, Oscar Hammerstein opted for "colored folks" when replacing "niggers" in the lyrics of "Ol' Man River." (The *N-word* was not yet totally banned when the original production of *Show Boat* opened in the 1927. Just the year before Carl Van Vechten had used *Nigger Heaven,* the slang term for a theater's upper balcony, where blacks once were required to sit, as the title for his novel—a perceptive and sympathetic one

—of life in Harlem.) The original *Show Boat* lyric was true to the way the dock hands who sing the show's opening song would have spoken as they toted bales of cotton, and the politically correct revision took some of the edge off the bitterness of their lament. After World War II, however, it was not possible to use "nigger" without affronting audiences, no matter what the context or how good one's intentions. Thus, the published version of "Ol' Man River" now reads:

> Colored folks work on de Mississippi
> Colored folks work while de white
>   folks play.

By the time of Hammerstein's rewrite, "colored" itself was well on the way to being cast aside by the folk themselves in favor of the previously avoided "Negro," as a new generation distanced itself from the preceding one by adopting another label. Of course, older people—black and white—continued to use the older term for many years afterward, and it would not be at all surprising, given the continual recycling of ethnic labels, if "colored" were restored to favor someday. As Henry Louis Gates said in a letter to his daughters that served as the preface to his memoir, *Colored People* (1994): "In your lifetimes, I suspect, you will go from being African Americans to 'people of color,' to being, once again, 'colored people.' (The linguistic trend toward condensation is strong.) I don't mind any of the names myself. But I have to confess that I like 'colored' best, maybe because when I hear the word, I hear it in my mother's voice and in the sepia tones of my childhood." Mr. Gates, born in 1950, headed the Department of

Afro-American Studies at Harvard when he wrote this.

See also NEGRO and PEOPLE OF COLOR.

come. To experience sexual orgasm, as in the remarkable word palindrome (word by word, it reads the same backward as forward) created by Gerard Benson in *The New Statesman* and included by Willard R. Espy in *An Almanac of Words at Play* (1975):

> "Come, shall I stroke your 'whatever' darling? I am so randy."
> "So am I darling. Whatever your stroke, I shall come."

Now the most common nonclinical term, "come" started out as a euphemism, being essentially a bland, generalized allusion to a specific, intense event. Thus, a reference from pre-1650 to a timeless problem: "Then off he came, & blusht for shame soe soone that he had endit" (*Walking in Meadow Green* in *Bishop Percy's Loose Songs*).

As with most slang words, especially those that are sexually charged, this one was used for many years prior to its inclusion in the "loose song" collected by the learned Thomas Percy (1729–1811), Bishop of Dromore in Ireland. The sexual sense is dated to ca. 1600 in *The Random House Historical Dictionary of American Slang* (1994) and Shakespeare appears to have known it though he did not use it explicitly. Consider the double, double entendre in *Troilus and Cressida* (1601–02), when Troilus re-enters the room in which he and Cressida have just spent the night:

CRESSIDA: My lord, come you again
  into my chamber. [Pause.] You smile
  and mock me, as if I meant
  naughtily.
TROILUS: Ha, ha!

"Come" did not become the word of choice until fairly recently, however. Prior to the twentieth century, people more often were said "to die" or "to spend." Thus, Fanny Hill overheard Polly say (ellipses in the original): "Oh! . . . oh! . . . I can't bear it . . . It is too much . . . I die I am going . . ." (John Cleland, *Memoirs of a Woman of Pleasure*, 1749). Meanwhile, Capt. Francis Grose explained that "to make a coffeehouse of a woman's **** [his asterisks]" was "to go in and out and spend nothing" (*A Classical Dictionary of the Vulgar Tongue*, 1796). This sense of "spend" also goes back several centuries, e.g., from *All's Well That Ends Well* (1602–03): "He wears his honor in a box [sic] unseen . . . Spending his manly marrow [semen] in her arms." See also DIE and O.

During most of the nineteenth century, the dominant term was "spend." Thus, the index of *My Secret Life* (anon., ca. 1890) includes "spending," but not "coming," even though the latter occasionally crops up in the text, and in virtually the same breathless breath as the other, e.g., " 'I'm coming love, are you?' 'Aha-yes . . . I'm spending!' " Probably, "spend" isn't entirely extinct. In the mid-1950s (not entirely beyond the reach of living human memory), Springmaid used the term in an off-color ad showing an American Indian male in a sheet-hammock, obviously in a state of postcoital bliss, and with a BUXOM squaw nearby. The caption: "A buck well-spent on a Springmaid sheet." (Times do change: Such an ad would never be produced today, but for fear of offending an ethnic group rather than because of its sexual innuendo.)

There is no doubt, however, that "come" comes quicker to most people's minds today, and the shift away from "spend" seems to be psychologically significant. Certainly, "come" appears to be a healthier, more positive term than "spend," with its suggestion that precious BODILY FLUIDS are being depleted. The change in orgasmic nomenclature may also have helped relax society's attitudes toward MASTURBATION, as reflected in the slow trend away from *self-abuse* and *self-pollution* to today's liberated SELF- (or MUTUAL-) PLEASURING. See also COITION, INTERCOURSE, and PREORGASMIC.

comfort station. A public toilet. "Comfort station" (and "comfort room") have been with us since circa 1900. The oldest example of a FACILITY of this kind in *A Dictionary of American English* comes from a report in the *New York Evening Post* of June 30, 1904, of "The excavation for the public comfort station in Chatham Square." During World War II, the Japanese also built *comfort stations* for their troops in Asia, but these served an entirely different purpose. See COMFORT WOMAN below.

comfort woman. A girl or woman forced to provide sex for Japanese soldiers, 1932–1945. "An independent historian . . . found incriminating documents in a Defense Agency library after several former 'comfort women,' as the Japanese euphemistically refer to the sex slaves, sued for compensation" (*Portland*, Maine, *Press Herald*, 7/2/92). Perhaps 200,000 women, mainly Koreans, were conscripted for work in *comfort stations*, or brothels, which were established in the wake of Japan's conquering armies (see ADVANCE). When the first *comfort women* came forward to claim reparations in 1991 on the fiftieth anniversary of Pearl Harbor, the Japanese government first denied the existence of the brothels, then sought to shift the blame for running them from the government to private entrepreneurs. Official apologies finally were offered in 1993 and $1 billion was committed as a symbolic payment in 1994, not as compensation to the surviving women (for fear of creating precedents for other victims of Japanese aggression), but in the form of an international "Peace, Friendship and Exchange Initiative." See also EX GRATIA and PROSTITUTE.

P.S. A similar, comforting phrase crops up in the diary of Admiral Robert Peary, the Arctic explorer (who apparently never reached the North Pole, as he claimed in 1909). Peary's expeditions included Inuit women who sewed specialized arctic clothing and, as he put it, served "to render the men contented" (*Natural History*, 11/89).

Cominch. Commander in Chief (U.S. Naval Forces). Admiral Ernest J. King, who held the position, changed the abbreviation for it from "CinCUS" to "Cominch" on March 12, 1942, some three months after Pearl Harbor. The reason for the change will be apparent if you say "CinCUS" aloud.

commerce. A mercantile metaphor for sex —what *The Oxford English Dictionary* primly defines as "Intercourse of the sexes: *esp.* in a bad sense." Current from at least the seventeenth through the nineteenth centuries, the expression seems dated now, though based on the same principle as INTERCOURSE itself. Herewith, a report on divorce Italian-style by Lady Mary Wortley Montagu in a letter to her daughter, Lady Bute (12/8/1751):

> The constant pretext is impotency, to which the man often pleads guilty. . . . However, as this method is not without inconvenience (it being impracticable where there is children) they have taken another here [Genoa]: the husband deposes upon oath that he has had a commerce with his mother-in-law, on which the marriage is declared incestuous and nullified, though the children remain legitimate. You will think this hard on the old lady who is scandalized, but it is no scandal at all, nobody supposing it to be true, without circumstances to confirm.

commission. Technically, a legitimate payment for making a sale, but in international business, frequently a bribe of a public official or private influence-peddler. Some of the influence-peddlers have quite good credentials. Prince Bernhard of the Netherlands, for example. He was required to resign virtually all his official and business posts following a government investigation into his dealings with Lockheed Aircraft Corp., which wanted badly to sell planes to the Dutch Air Force. "The report [of the government commission] charged that Bernhard 'showed himself open to dishonorable requests and offers.' As recently as two years ago, it said, Bernhard asked Lockheed to pay him 'sales commissions' of between $4 million and $6 million" (*Time*, 9/6/76).

The euphemistic meaning of *commission* is not limited strictly to bribery. In Arab countries, where Muslim law forbids interest on loans, lenders instead receive *commissions* on their loans—at the going interest rate, of course.

See also BAKSHEESH, CONTRIBUTION, CUMSHAW, DONATION, KICKBACK, PAY DOWN, and QUESTIONABLE.

commode. A somewhat old-fashioned term for a toilet, still occasionally encountered, as in "She [Jane Fonda] plays one scene on the commode" (*New Yorker*, 2/28/77). In the nineteenth century, before flush toilets were in widespread use, a *commode* was the small cabinet or chair that enclosed a chamber pot, or CHAMBER, and in the eighteenth century, a *commode* was a bawd, or procuress. Thus, *commode*, the French word for "convenient," acquired virtually the same complex of euphemistic meanings as CONVENIENCE. See also TOILET.

communications director. A grandiloquent press agent. "Corporate press agents are now 'communications directors'" (*Quarterly Review of Doublespeak*, 10/87). See also PUBLIC RELATIONS and PUBLICITOR.

community. Establishment, as in the intelligence *community* or the defense *community*. "The intelligence community is made up by and large of people who lie under oath, who plan assassinations" (Frank Mankiewicz to Dick Cavett, WNET-TV, 12/21/78). See also AGENT.

companion. A person who is not married to the person with whom she or he is living; from Latin *com*, together, and *panis*, bread, meaning that the *companions* share the same table (along with other articles of furniture, presumably). Essentially an androgynous term, *companion* used to be applied euphemistically to women more often than to men, and commonly was preceded by such signpost terms as *constant, devoted, frequent, intimate, longtime,* and *traveling,* just to make sure that everyone understood the RELATIONSHIP. Today, in the age of AIDS, *companion* is the standard term in obituaries for surviving male lovers and explanations no longer are considered necessary. See also COHABITOR, PARTNER, ROOMMATE, and SIGNIFICANT OTHER.

companion animal. See ANIMAL COMPANION.

company. In the intelligence COMMUNITY, the informal name for the Central Intelligence Agency. This follows the example of the older British Secret Intelligence Service, known fondly to its employees as "The Firm," or "The Old Firm," while trading on the organizational acronym, "Cia" being the abbreviation for "company" in Spanish. See also AGENT.

Outside the so-called intelligence community, "company" has many of the overtones of COMPANION, as in, "One of his main company functions is . . . to provide company. The company is preferably blond, and under 25 . . . and will be paid $500 apiece for their services" (*New York,* 5/26/75). See also SERVICE.

The sexual use of "company" goes back some ways, e.g., from William Caxton's *Geffroi de la Tour* (1483): "Thamar that had company with her husbondes fader." The similar "Accompany," meantime, is labeled specifically as a euphemism in the monumental *Slang and Its Analogues* (J. S. Farmer and W. E. Henley, 1890–1904), which includes, among other examples, this, from Roger Coke's *Elements of Power and Subjection* (1660): "We teach that upon Festival

and Fasting times, every man forbear to accompany his wife." See also INTERCOURSE.

comparative campaigning. Negative campaigning, itself a euphemism for deceiving the public, smearing an opponent, and, on occasion, sabotaging the other person's campaign. A leading exponent of *comparative campaigning* was Lee Atwater, manager of George Bush's 1988 presidential campaign. "Mr. Atwater . . . a specialist in the political attack, has said this about negative (or, as he prefers it, comparative) campaigning: 'There's no danger as long as it's not too harsh, as long as it's not too shrill, as long as it's factual and as long as it's believable'" (*New York Times,* 8/29/88). The prime example of *negative campaigning* in the 1988 election was the portrayal in TV ads of Mr. Bush's Democratic opponent, Michael Dukakis, as being soft on killer-rapists.

Mr. Atwater, who quantified his campaign formula as "50 percent positive and 50 percent comparative," borrowed from Madison Avenue. Starting in the mid-1970s, some advertisers broke with the conventional wisdom that competing products should never be mentioned and began bashing their rivals by name in *comparative advertising* campaigns. (The British are more explicit about this kind of advertising; they call it "knocking copy.")

The original "negative campaigning" surfaced (by that name) in the wake of Watergate, e.g., "The judge explained that [former presidential appointments secretary Dwight L.] Chapin was not being tried for his part in what the White House likes to call 'negative campaigning,' only for alleged lies to the grand jury about his dealings with Donald Segretti" (*New York Post,* 4/2/74). To put this in context, it should be remembered that Mr. Segretti (whose name in Italian means "secrets"), went to jail for distributing "illegal campaign literature." His finest coup on behalf of the Nixon campaign was sending a letter on Senator Edmund Muskie's stationery that falsely accused Senators Hubert Humphrey and Henry Jackson of sexual misconduct, thus wounding three leading Democrats at once.

See also NEGATIVE.

complete production. Discontinue. IBM did not throw in the towel and discontinue its PCjr in April 1985; rather, in the words of a corporate announcement, it merely "completed production" of that particular product line. IBM's explanation was lucid, however, compared to the General Motors announcement in 1987 that a "volume-related production schedule adjustment" had occurred at one of its assembly plants. By this, GM meant that it was shutting its Chevrolet-Pontiac-Canada Group factory in Framingham, Massachusetts. Then there was the objection of Jack Romanos, president of Paramount Publishing's consumer group, to a reporter's characterization of the demise of the firm's Atheneum operation: "I think 'closing it down' is the wrong phrase," he said. " 'Not continuing to use the imprint's name' would be how I'd phrase it" (*New York Times*, 2/28/94). See also CONSOLIDATE.

compliance assistance personnel. Enforcers. The Environmental Protection Agency converted its enforcement OFFICERS into *compliance assistance personnel* in 1981 as part of the Reagan administration's effort to avoid making life too terribly difficult for polluters. See also EMERGENCY AND REMEDIAL RESPONSE.

concentration camp. A prison camp. Although now popularly associated with Nazi Germany, the institution of the "concentration camp" dates to at least 1901 when Lord Kitchner began putting women and children into such camps during the Boer War in South Africa. His plan was to lay waste to the entire countryside outside the camps, but it didn't work. Instead, he just relieved the Boers of the burden of taking care of their families.

At about the same time, the United States was pursuing a similar policy, which it called "reconcentration," in the Philippines. There, the idea was to separate the populace from the nationalist guerrillas led by Emilio Aguinaldo. With noncombatants "reconcentrated" into certain localities and kept under guard, anyone found outside the designated areas was assumed to be a guerrilla and could be shot on sight. The United States seems to have learned this tactic from the Spanish, who had adopted a policy of *reconcentrado* in an effort to repress the rebellion in Cuba, starting in 1895, that American JINGOS blew up into the Spanish-American War of 1898. *Reconcentrado* involved removing peasants and agricultural workers from farms and confining them to camps, with results that should have surprised no one, i.e., "starvation of thousands of non-combatants through reconcentration" was reported (*Westminster Gazette*, 4/6/1898). The United States used essentially the same tactic in Vietnam, where peasants were forced to leave their homes in the countryside and resettled in New Life Hamlets. In officialese, the idea was to "generate refugees" in order to "attrit" the Viet Cong's population base, thus enlarging the military's SPECIFIED STRIKE ZONES

See also ASSEMBLY CENTER, CORRECTIONAL FACILITY, DETENTION, PROTECTIVE CUSTODY,

PURIFY, REEDUCATION, RELOCATION CENTER, SHELTER, and WATER CURE.

concourse. Sexual intercourse. "This being public broadcasting, the scenes of concourse are accompanied by informative tidbits" (review of "The Nature of Sex," *New York Times,* 11/22/93). The euphemism was formed in much the same way as CONGRESS, the sexual meaning stemming from the term's general sense of an act or instance of meeting, running, or coming together, in turn from the Latin *concursus,* assembly. See also INTERCOURSE.

condition. Disease, affliction. "Prisons have become 'rehabilitative correctional facilities,' housewives are 'homemakers,' deaf people are 'hearing impaired,' a cerebral palsy society tells journalists never to use the word 'suffer' about those with that 'disease' (forbidden), 'affliction' (forbidden), condition (allowed)" (*Economist,* 7/28/90). See also CORRECTIONAL FACILITY, HEARING IMPAIRED, and HOMEMAKER.

confidant. Technically, only a person entrusted with private affairs, commonly love affairs, but euphemistically, a lover; the feminine form is *confidante,* as in the *New York Times* headline: "Kay Summersby Morgan Dies; Eisenhower Confidante in War" (1/21/75). Ms. Morgan's posthumously published memoirs were entitled *Past Forgetting: My Love Affair with Dwight D. Eisenhower.* See also AFFAIR, FRIEND, and RELATIONSHIP.

confidence course. What the U.S. Army used to call an "obstacle course."

confidential informant or **source.** A spy or other means of obtaining information. Thus,

the FBI kept tabs on Leonard Bernstein during the 1970s partly through *confidential informants,* also called *trash covers,* i.e., analyses of garbage discarded by people who knew him. The FBI also has been helped by friendly journalists who thus become *confidential sources.* The "confidential" is especially deceptive; it implies that the spy's identity will be kept secret. But this is not so. All a judge has to do is ask, and the minions of the law will name names. Journalists, by contrast, tend to be more protective of their HIGHLY (or USUALLY RELIABLE SOURCES, and judges have been known to send journalists to jail on this account. See also HIGHLY CONFIDENTIAL (or SENSITIVE) SOURCE, INFORMANT, and SOURCE OF INFORMATION.

confirmed bachelor. A homosexual, also *perennial bachelor*; obsolete except in historic contexts, now that so many *confirmed bachelors* have come out of the closet. Thus, speaking of Ludwig II, of Bavaria (1845–86): "Ludwig, who in his day would have been described as a confirmed bachelor, sent [the actor Josef] Kainz admiring letters and a watch encrusted with diamonds" (*New York Times,* 2/11/93). See also GAY.

conflict. War, as in the Korean *conflict,* which seemed like a war to most people, lasting three years and causing 157,530 American CASUALTIES. Since the war was never officially declared to be one, however, the Veterans Administration now counts 4,931,165 veterans of the "Korean Conflict" (*The World Almanac and Book of Facts,* 1993). As an extension of "war" by other means, "conflict" has a FOP Index of 3.0. See also LIMITED WAR, POLICE ACTION, and VIETNAM ERA.

confound. Damn; a somewhat old-fashioned euphemism in a free-speaking age, occasionally encountered in the present tense, as in "Confound you!" but more often in the past, e.g., "Sir, you are a confounded liar and a cheat." Similar (though it stems from "concern") and even more antique is "consarn," as in "I've always heard tell that there were two kinds of old maids—old maids an' consarned old maids" (Mary E. Wilkins, *A Humble Romance and Other Stories*, 1887). See also DARN.

congress. Sexual intercourse; the general term for an assembly or gathering of persons served as a euphemism for the more intimate kind of meeting from the sixteenth through the nineteenth centuries, e.g., "I picked up a fresh, agreeable young girl called Alice Gibbs and had a very agreeable congress" (Frederick A. Pottle, ed., [James] *Boswell's London Journal, 1762–1763*, 1950). Occasionally, the term was dolled up as *amorous congress* or even *sexual congress,* a construction that has borne the test of time, e.g., "I found only one abrupt verb for sexually congressing a woman" (Kurt Vonnegut, Jr., reviewing the *Random House Dictionary*, 1967, in *Welcome to the Monkey House*, 1970). Note that the term *congressional relations* is a euphemism for lobbying Congress not for sex, despite the occasional overlap of the two activities. See also CONCOURSE and INTERCOURSE.

conjugal. Sexual. The vacuous dictionary definition of the term—"pertaining to marriage or the relation of husband and wife; connubial"—was given body by United States District Judge Vincent P. Biunno, when ruling against a suit by two New Jersey convicts, who asserted that the state's refusal to allow them to go home for *conjugal* visits amounted to unconstitutionally

cruel and unusual punishment. Said the judge: "The term conjugal visits is to be taken as a euphemism for sexual intercourse" (*New York Post,* 7/24/74). See also ACTION and INTERCOURSE.

connection. A somewhat old-fashioned form of sexual intercourse; a RELATIONSHIP. For example, James Boswell, distressed by the unexpected visit of "Signor Gonorrhoea," confronted the source of his infection, an actress known to history only as Mrs. Lewis (and to his journals as Louisa) in these terms: "Madam, I have had no connection with any woman but you these two months" (1/20/1763, Frederick A. Pottle, ed., *Boswell's London Journal, 1762–1763,* 1950). Technically, Boswell's encounter classed as *criminal connection* because it took place outside the bonds of matrimony. As he himself said of Samuel Johnson: "His juvenile attachments to the fair sex were, however, very transient; and it is certain that he formed no criminal connection whatsoever" (*Life of Johnson,* 1791).

The euphemistic *connection* is by no means limited to the so-called civilized nations. Just as prudish are the Nupe, of West Africa: "Nupe lacks any native word for sexual intercourse; instead, its speakers use a word of Arabic derivation that means 'to connect'" (Peter Farb, *Word Play: What Happens When People Talk,* 1974). See also CRIMINAL CONVERSATION, INTERCOURSE, and Noah Webster's use of *carnal connection* in PECULIAR MEMBERS.

consciousness-raising. The process of changing a person's opinions and personality; brainwashing or "remolding."

"Consciousness-raising" was popularized in the late 1960s and early 1970s by the women's movement with regard to developing greater awareness of women's needs, motives, plight, and potential. It is purely a coincidence, no doubt, that the term resembles that devised by the Chinese Communists to characterize their system of group indoctrination. Thus, telling of a visit to Yenan in October 1944, where a Politburo member, P'eng Chen, had established a "university" for cadre members, Theodore H. White reported in *In Search of History* (1978):

He [P'eng] explained his fundamental problem in a phrase: "brain remolding." The men who came in from the field, he said, whether semiliterate battalion commanders or college-trained intellectuals, had to have their minds washed out [see BRAINWASH], had to be remolded in ideology. At first he had thought this could be done in only three months; he had now learned that a full year was necessary to "remold the brain. . . ." His interpreter and I searched for a word better than "brain remolding" and finally the interpreter came up with the phrase "raising their level of consciousness." This was the first time I heard that phrase, which, over the years, moved out of China and into the streets and fashions of America in the 1960s.

consensual nonmonogamy. Mate swapping (the emphasis is on the "sensual" part). "Mary Lou said she and her husband attend conventions around the country of people interested in swapping sex partners, which participants refer to as 'consensual nonmonogamy'" (*New York Times,* 3/22/91). See also EXTRAMARITAL, OPEN MARRIAGE, and SWINGING.

consolidate. Close. When branches of the San Francisco library were being shut for lack of funding, Kent Sims, director of the Mayor's Office of Planning and Economic Development, admonished a reporter never to say "closed." Said Mr. Sims: "Use the word 'consolidate'" (*San Francisco Sunday Chronicle and Examiner,* 4/2/92). See also COMPLETE PRODUCTION, RESTRUCTURE, and RIGHTSIZE.

consultant. An adviser; often a person who "advises" you to buy something. Originally—going back to the seventeenth century—a *consultant* was the person who asked a question of an oracle rather than the person who posed as one. During the nineteenth century, however, consulting physicians began to appear as *consultants,* and since then, trading on the prestige of the medical profession, practically everyone under the sun has adopted the term. See also CLINIC and SPECIALIST in this regard.

Private detectives (also called INVESTIGATORS) were among the first to adopt the medical term. As it happens, the oldest example in *The Oxford English Dictionary* of a detective-consultant refers to the greatest of them all, and it comes from the pen of an author who was himself a medical man: "I must say that I am rather disappointed in our London consultant" (Colonel Ross, owner of Silver Blaze, in Sir Arthur Conan Doyle, *Memoirs of Sherlock Holmes,* 1893).

Then there are the ubiquitous business and management *consultants,* the engineering *consultants,* the teachers who spend more time as *consultants* than as teachers, the *financial consultants* (as at Merrill Lynch) who sell stocks and bonds, and the *sales consultants* who sell Saturn cars. And this only scratches the surface. Others include *career transition consultant,* an employment agency employee (see also CAREER); *chimney consultant,* a glorified chimney sweep; *cremation consultant* (as in Cremation Consultants, of Brooklyn, N.Y.), *educational toy consultant,* a seller of toys; *faculty consultant,* a teacher who grades exams for the Educational Testing Service; *international business consultant,* an influence-peddler (Lockheed Aircraft Corp's principal *consultant* in Japan in the early 1970s was Mr. Yoshio Kodama, who was recognized unofficially as that nation's most important *kurumaku,* or wire-puller, a term that comes from the Kabuki theater, where its literal meaning, "black curtain," suggests the way in which Mr. Kodama manipulated events from behind the scenes); *leasing consultant,* a leasing agent; *mortuary consultant,* an undertaker; *moving consultant,* an estimator for a furniture mover; *political consultant* (formerly known as a "handler"); *sales consultant,* a salesperson; *transportation investment consultant,* a person who sells automobiles; and *White House consultant,* the official position of E. Howard Hunt, Jr., the Watergate PLUMBER.

The proliferation of *consultants* suggests that this title soon will supersede ENGINEER as the most favored title for upgrading one's occupation and oneself.

consumer. A sick person; a patient—in the clutches of the medical establishment. "Patients are called 'consumers,' patients who pay with private insurance are called 'retail customers,' and getting patients is called 'patient accrual'" (William Lutz, *Doublespeak,* 1989). Sometimes the *consumer's* skin may have to be cut or other-

wise penetrated, in which case he or she is said to have undergone a PROCEDURE.

consumer unit. A household to a government statistician.

contact. To beat up, perhaps to kill. For example, Peter Rosner, a New York City PR man, asked two young toughs in 1983 to "contact" a young actor who didn't go away after his daughter tried to end her relationship with him. They *contacted* the spurned suitor by bashing him over the head with a baseball bat on August 25 of that year and he died of his injuries shortly thereafter. One of the *contact* men was convicted of first-degree manslaughter. Mr. Rosner also was convicted, but merely for perjury, having denied to a grand injury that he had asked the killer to *contact* the actor. See also HIT.

contain. To obstruct justice; specifically and historically, the White House conspiracy to COVER-UP the Watergate scandal. The psychology of the terminology is typical of official euphemism and doubletalk generally. As John W. Dean III, erstwhile COUNSEL to President Nixon, explained:

> If Bob Haldeman or John Ehrlichman or even Richard Nixon had said to me, "John, I want you to do a little crime for me. I want you to obstruct justice," I would have told him he was crazy and disappeared from sight. No one thought about the Watergate coverup in those terms—at first, anyway. Rather it was "containing" Watergate or keeping the defendants "on the reservation" or coming up with the right public relations "scenario" and

the like. No one was motivated to get involved in a criminal conspiracy to obstruct justice—but under the law that is what occurred. (*New York Times*, 4/6/75)

Nixon himself never admitted to seeing things Dean's way. As he insisted in a televised interview with David Frost on May 4, 1977: "I was trying to contain it politically. And that's a very different motive from the motive of attempting to cover up criminal activities of an individual." For another notable Nixonian legal opinion, see ILLEGAL.

continental. A curse; short for "continental damn." Memories of the worthlessness of money issued by the Continental Congresses during the Revolution lasted for many years, with the term becoming both a disparagement in its own right and a euphemism for something worse. "He didn't give a continental for anybody. Beg your pardon, friend, for coming so near saying a cuss-word" (Mark Twain, *Roughing It*, 1872). See also CUSS.

contingent worker. A disposable employee; a low-paid worker with few if any benefits and no job protection. "Employment agencies call them contingent workers, flexible workers or assignment workers. Some labor economists, by contrast, call them disposable and throwaway workers" (*New York Times*, 3/15/93). Perhaps a third of the nation's labor force is composed of *contingent workers.*

continuing (or adult) drama. A primetime, nighttime soap opera, as distinguished from a DAYTIME DRAMA. "He has three 'sophisticated adult dramas' this fall. That's

the CBS term for a nighttime soap opera about sex and money" (*Boston Globe*, 7/22/80). See also ANIMATED SERIES.

contract. An offer to pay for a murder or the murder itself. " 'There's one thing I haven't told you, . . . 'I've done some hits—you know, a contract' " (*Harper's*, 11/74). See also HIT.

contribution. An illegal payment, typically a bribe, payoff, or ransom. For example, Cardinal Jamie Sin, of Manila, denied that the Mitsui had paid $3 million to ransom a kidnapped employee. "I am now saying," said the Cardinal, "that maybe a contribution was made" (New York *Daily News*, 4/5/87). The *contribution,* according to His Eminence, was intended to cover expenses of the abduction. And if this explanation fudged the truth, it could be described as a venial sin of Cardinal Sin. See also COMMISSION, DONATION, KICKBACK, and REWARD.

controlled circulation. Circulation for free in the newspaper and magazine business. The circulation is "controlled" by distributing copies to everyone who has a mailbox.

convalescent hospital. An old-age home. "Many of the 'rest homes' of the 1950s, with their broad verandas sporting rows of rocking chairs, have been replaced by 'convalescent hospitals'—air-conditioned, cinderblock edifices whose windows are sealed shut. The word *convalescent* implies recovery, yet few who enter leave by the same door" (*New Age*, 11/77). See also HOME, NURSING HOME, and REST HOUSE.

convenience. A toilet—sometimes, especially in Britain, a "public convenience" or, humorously dismissing someone else's attempt at humor, "Henny Youngman would have thrown that one down the porcelain convenience" (B. C., *New York Post*, 8/8/75).

Before the advent of indoor plumbing, "convenience" and "convenient" also were used with reference to chamber pots (see CHAMBER). The allusive language contrasts starkly with the openness of the article's use, which shocked at least one French visitor to Britain:

> Drinking much and long leads to unavoidable consequences. Will it be credited that, in a corner of the very dining-room, there is a certain convenient piece of furniture, to be used by anybody who wants it? The operation is performed very deliberately and undisguisedly, as a matter of course, and occasions no interruption of the conversation. (Louis Simond, *A Journal of Tour in Great Britain*, 3/5/1810)

The euphemistic uses of "convenience" in the seventeenth, eighteenth, and early nineteenth centuries parallel those of COMMODE. A "convenience" in this era might also be a spittoon (or CUSPIDOR), a wife, a mistress, or a harlot (also known as a *convenient*). Thus, with this versatile term, it was not impossible for a *convenience* to make use of a *convenience*, e.g., "A convenience to spit in appeared on one side of her chair" (Tobias Smollett, *Roderick Random*, 1748). Finally, the plural *conveniences* also was one of many nineteenth-century euphemisms for the UNMENTIONABLES that covered the LIMBS of gentlemen. See also TOILET.

conversation. Sexual intercourse. The euphemism goes back a ways, e.g., "The

men hath conuersacyon with the wymen, who that they ben or who they fyrst mete" (*First English Book on America*, ca. 1511). A modern, blander, still-vaguer variant is "socialize," *re* the admission by Sen. Charles Robb (D. Va.) to "socializing under circumstances not appropriate for a married man," which was his way of responding to reports that he had attended some uproarious parties and received a massage in the nude from a former Miss Virginia, (*New York Times*, 5/28/94). See also CRIMINAL CONVERSATION.

convey. To steal. *The Oxford English Dictionary* tracks the euphemism's use from the fifteenth through the nineteenth centuries. For example, from Shakespeare's *The Merry Wives of Windsor* (1597):

> NYM: The good humor is to steal at a
> minute's rest.
> PISTOL: "Convey," the wise it call.
> "Steal!" Foh, a fico [see FIG] for the
> phrase!

From "convey" in this sense it followed naturally that a "conveyer" was a thief, especially an agile one, who carried loot away quickly. The deposed king puns upon both verb and noun in *Richard II* (1594–95) after Bolingbroke (Henry IV) has relieved him of his crown:

> BOLINGBROKE: Go some of you, convey
> him to the Tower.
> KING RICHARD: Oh, good! Convey!
> Conveyors are you all, That rise
> thus nimbly by a true king's fall.

See also APPROPRIATE.

convivial indulgence. Overindulgence with alcohol. "'Convivial indulgence,' admitted an Irish patriot, was the besetting sin of eighteenth-century Ireland" (Elizabeth Longford, *Wellington, The Years of the Sword*, 1969). See also REFRESHMENT.

cony. An aural euphemism for "cunny." See also RABBIT.

coordinator. Assistant coach. Pro football teams nowadays have offensive and defensive *coordinators*, not coaches.

copulate/copulation. Sexual intercourse. "Copulate" and "copulation" originally referred to coupling in a nonsexual way, but by the fifteenth century people were beginning to speak of "carnal copulacyon." In accordance with Gresham's Law, whereby "bad" meanings of words drive out "good" ones, the sexual sense gradually became dominant (as it did with the related COITION), e.g., "The wren goes to 't, and the small gilded fly Does lecher in my sight. Let copulation thrive" (William Shakespeare, *King Lear*, 1605–06).

Sir James Murray, chief editor of *The Oxford English Dictionary*, specified in the relevant section of Volume C (1893) that both verb and noun were "now chiefly a term of Zoology." But this has changed, as evidenced by the goings-on in the swimming pool at Plato's Retreat in New York City: "Two giggling women start to push a third into the water.... It is normal poolside fun, except that everyone is naked and three couples are copulating in the water" (*Time*, 1/16/78). As a result, it is difficult for teachers today to discuss "copulative" verbs without reducing classrooms to snickers. Any teacher who can get through this lesson unscathed may advance to "laylie"; see LIE/LIE WITH. And for more about the varieties of *copulation,* continue with INTERCOURSE.

cordless massager. A term used by those who wish to order a vibrator but are too shy to ask for one by name. The picture accompanying an ad for a *cordless massager* in *House and Garden* (9/77) showed the gadget being used on a foot, but the advertising copy was suggestive of other possibilities: "Battery-operated massager brings satisfying relaxation. Deep gentle penetrating vibrations . . ." This particular brand of *cordless massager* came in four models: 4½ inches long, 7 inches, 10 inches, and 12 inches. See also DILDO, FRIG, and MARITAL AID.

core rearrangement. In the nuclear power biz, the opaque way of describing the explosive destruction of the core of a reactor. "The reaction could be self-propagating, producing a 'core rearrangement'— destruction of the reactor core" (Norman Metzger, *Energy: The Continuing Crisis*, 1977). The people who run the the Nuclear Regulatory Commission also tend to shield their meanings in leaden terms. Other forms of *core rearrangement* used by the NRC include *core disruptive accident, energetic disassemblage* (or *disassembly*), and *rapid disassembly*. A possible scenario would begin with *rapid oxidation* (a fire). This might lead to a *superprompt critical power excursion* (runaway chain reaction in the reactor core), resulting in a *disruptive* or *explosive energy release* (a blast) and a *containment-breaching incident* (in which plutonium "takes up residence," as they say in nuclearese, outside the reactor).

The nuclear-power-plant lingo calls to mind the "unplanned rapid ignition of solid fuel" that was said by Major Michael Griffin to have caused the first stage of a Pershing II missile to ignite, killing three soldiers and injuring sixteen (*Newsweek*, 1/21/85). The United States does not have a patent on this terminology, however. Thus, the official Russian report on the Chernobyl disaster in 1986 described the explosion of the nuclear power plant's core as a "rapid fuel relocation," which was true in the sense that the fuel had relocated itself all over the landscape, forcing the evacuation of 135,000 people from the vicinity. See also ABOVE CRITICAL, ENERGY RELEASE, and MONITORED RETRIEVABLE STORAGE FACILITY.

corporation. A large belly, a big paunch, a.k.a. *bay window*; probably a play on *corpus*, dating from the eighteenth century. "Sirrah! my corporation is made up of good English fat" (Tobias Smollett, *The Adventures of Ferdinand Count Fathom*, 1753). See also PORTLY.

correctional facility. A prison—and the key euphemism in a sweeping change in jailhouse nomenclature to softer, more "professional-sounding" jargon. Thus, New York's famous Sing Sing Prison—established in the 1820s as, of all things, Mount Pleasant—has been known officially since 1970 as a Correctional Facility. (For several years it was called the Ossining Correctional Facility, but "Ossining" was dropped in 1983, at the urgent request of the inhabitants of that Hudson River town, and "Sing Sing" restored.) The Empire State is by no means out in front of the other forty-nine, however. As long ago as 1952, the old National Prison Association, the organization of people whose trade it is to lock other people up, changed its name to the American Correctional Association.

Semantic changes have not affected the underlying reality, of course. As was noted in *Attica, The Official Report of the New York State Special Commission on Attica* (1972):

> Effective July 8, 1970, there were no more prisons; in their places, instead, stood six maximum security "correctional facilities." The prison wardens became "institutional superintendents" . . . and the old-line prison guards awakened that morning to find themselves suddenly "correctional officers." No one's job or essential duties changed, only his title. Certainly the institutions themselves did not change. . . . To a man spending 14 to 16 hours a day in a cell being "rehabilitated," it was scarcely any comfort and no reassurance to learn that he was suddenly "an inmate in a correctional facility" instead of a convict in a prison.

Not all prisons are *correctional facilities* or, more optimistically, *rehabilitative correctional facilities*. (See also FACILITY.) Some are REFORMATORIES, SCHOOLS, and *youth centers*, where guards may be known as *youth leaders*. ("Youth" is not a strict criterion for admittance: After being convicted of rape in 1991, heavyweight boxing champion Mike Tyson, a full-grown man in the eyes of most observers, was sentenced to six years in the Indiana Youth Center.) And there are still some STATE FARMS, as well as such oddities as the California Men's Colony in San Luis Obispo, and Honor Rancho North, a maximum-security prison in Santa Clarita, California. (Military authorities in Uruguay topped this by a considerable margin, however, with their maximum security oxymoron: Penal Libertad, or Liberty Prison.)

As for the INMATES of *correctional facilities,* they are known in correctional newspeak as CLIENTS, RESIDENTS, and even STUDENTS—unless they are political prisoners, in which case they are DETAINEES or INTERNS, and their prisons are CONCENTRATION CAMPS, *detention centers,* and (in the United States during World War II) ASSEMBLY or RELOCATION CENTERS. Particularly bad RESIDENTS usually are housed in the *maximum security dormitories* (cell blocks) of SECURE FACILITIES. When they act up, they may be put into ADJUSTMENT CENTERS (solitary confinement) or SECLUSION (same thing). Sometimes they are tortured; see the *Tucker telephone* in BELL TELEPHONE HOUR as well as the aboveboard AVERSION THERAPY. Those that are scheduled to receive CAPITAL PUNISHMENT may be confined in the *unit for condemned prisoners* (the old "death row").

corrigendum. A mistake to be corrected, especially in print; *corrigenda* in the plural. Thus, from a slip bound into the very front of *An Elizabethan in 1582: The Diary of Richard Madox* (Elizabeth Story Donno, 1976):

> *Corrigendum* to the Half Title
> This volume is not issued for 1976
> but is the second issue for 1974

The Latin (from *corrigere,* to make straight) has the double advantage of allowing the perpetrator (the publisher) to blur the nature of the offense while demonstrating that he is actually a gentleman of immense learning. The psychology is much the same as with ERRATUM.

cosmetician/cosmetologist. Not, as one might be forgiven for assuming, a practitioner of what is known variously as *cosmetic* or *aesthetic* (i.e., plastic) surgery, but a beauty parlor worker who specializes in makeup and skin care. (The even fancier *aesthetician, esthetician,* and *estheticienne* also have been sighted.) The organization in the field is the National Cosmetology Association. (It used to be known as the National Hairdressers and Cosmetologists Association, but "hairdressers" was dropped as the hairdressers themselves metamorphosed into *hairstylists.*) See also BEAUTICIAN.

cosmopolitan. A Jew; a barely encoded code word. "During the last years of Stalin's life a wave of Jews began to be noticeable [in Soviet prison camps]. From 1950 they were hauled in little by little as *cosmopolitans....* It would seem that Stalin intended to arrange a great massacre of the Jews" (Aleksandr I. Solzhenitsyn, *The Gulag Archipelago 1918–1956,* 1974). The usage has survived the breakup of the Soviet Union and the overthrow of Communism in eastern Europe. Thus, quoting Iván T. Berend, a Hungarian economic historian, who also happens to be Jewish: "They [nationalist members of the Democratic Forum] are counting the Jews in leading positions, they are counting the Jews in the mass media, and are saying they are destroying Hungarian culture. They use the word 'cosmopolitan'" (*New Yorker,* 11/20/89). See also HEBREW.

councilor. A lawyer or someone who is trying very hard to enhance the prestige of his or her business, such as a *public relations councilor.* Lawyers like to flatter each other with the fancy form of address, but also find it useful on other occasions: "'Councilor' is the term by which a lawyer addresses a colleague whose name has momentarily escaped him: 'Good morning, councilor,' said Attorney Koskoff, with a slight bow" (David E. Koskoff, personal communication, 12/1/81). See also ATTORNEY, COUNSEL, and PUBLIC RELATIONS.

counsel. A lawyer, or one who yearns for lawyerly status. (PR types have glommed on to this title, along with COUNCILOR.) Among themselves, lawyers go a few steps further, commonly addressing one another as *distinguished counsel* or *learned counsel.* Not even the boldest press agent has yet dared do this. It is a form of grooming behavior—you massage my ego and I'll massage yours—that lawyers have perfected to an unmatched degree.

In the White House, the president's official lawyer is, of course, his *counsel.*

> P—Why don't we just say . . . "He is the White House Counsel and, therefore, his appearance before any judicial group is on a different basis from anybody else . . . with his unique position of being a top member of the President's staff but also the Counsel. There is a lawyer, Counsel—not lawyer, Counsel—but the responsibility of the Counsel for confidentiality." (Richard M. Nixon, 3/27/73, *The White House Transcripts,* 1974)

See also ATTORNEY, ENGINEER, and PUBLIC RELATIONS.

courses of particular interest. Asteroids that travel on *courses of particular interest* are those that cross the orbit of the Earth. They are of "interest" because of accumulating evidence that several massive extinctions of life on this planet may have been caused by asteroid impacts.

courtesan. A medium-priced whore—and a word that has been working its way down the social ladder for the past four or five centuries.

Originally, a *courtesan* was simply "a woman of the court," but the association with high-class prostitution developed early, which says something about life at the top in medieval times. *The Oxford English Dictionary*'s oldest example comes from 1549, and already the reference is to those who "keepe Courtisanes." By the start of the seventeenth century, the following distinction was made: "Your whore is for euery rascall, but your Curtizan is for your Courtier" (Edward Sharpham, *The Fleire,* 1607). As time went on, *courtesans* began taking on commoners, too, though still retaining some traces of their formal social standing. Thus, during the Victorian era, the label was reserved for the most-refined whores of the sort frequently patronized by the anonymous author of *My Secret Life* (ca. 1890), e.g.: "Beyond a voluptuous grace natural to her, she had not at first the facile ways of a French courtesan, they came later on." Today, the term has become further cheapened, so that anyone who doesn't actually walk the streets may class as a *courtesan.* From a report on the world of big-city prostitutes: "They call themselves 'working girls,' or, if they are call girls, 'courtesans'" (*New York Times,* 8/9/71). See also CALL GIRL, WORKING GIRL, and the basic PROSTITUTE.

courtesy chair. A wheelchair. "I heard at Will Rogers Airport in O.K. City, O.K., a *wheelchair* called a *courtesy chair* by American Air Lines employees" (Bernard Arkules, personal communication, 6/16/82). See also DIFFERENTLY ABLED.

cover. A lie, especially in the cloak-and-dagger business; more elaborately, a *cover story.* "The whole question of lying to Congress—you could call it a lie, but for us, that's keeping cover" (David Whipple, ex–CIA agent and head of the Association of Former Intelligence Officers, *Philadelphia Bulletin,* 9/7/91).

The basic "cover" has been employed for several centuries to refer to something that hides, conceals, or disguises, e.g.: "Wicked men have divers covers for their lewdnesse" (Jeremiah Burroughs, *An Exposition of Hosea,* 1643). But "cover story" appears to date only to World War II. Thus, speaking of the Office of Strategic Services, the wartime predecessor of the CIA: "When an agent's training was completed and his mission in Germany or German-occupied territory decided upon, this OSS branch [the authentication bureau] would be given the outline of what was known as an agent's 'cover story.' A cover story is a biography in fiction. It was up to the authentication bureau to make that fiction look like fact" (Stewart Alsop and Thomas Braden, *Sub Rosa—The O.S.S. and American Espionage,* 1946). A biography of this sort, also called a *legend,* often is long and involved, compounded partially out of truths, making the tale easier for the spy to remember and more difficult for the enemy to disprove.

A *cover* or *cover story* may be prepared to conceal an operation as well as a person's identity. For example, after the U-2 piloted by Francis Gary Powers was shot down on May 1, 1960, over Russia (see OVERFLIGHT), the United States announced that one of its weather observation planes was missing—a *cover story* that was shot down, too, when Soviet Premier Nikita Khrushchev announced four days later that the Russians had Powers, "alive and kicking." For many Americans of that innocent era, the blowing of the U-2 *cover story* was the first convincing demonstration that sometimes the Russians told the truth, while their own government lied. See also EMBROIDER THE TRUTH, SCENARIO, STORY, and WHITE LIE.

cover (one's) feet. An ancient and now-obsolete Hebrew euphemism for the relieving of the bowels, e.g.: "And he came to the sheepcotes by the way, where was a cave; and Saul went in to cover his feet" (I Samuel 24:3). See also EASE.

covert action (or operation). A secret, usually illegal governmental action or operation such as—in order of increasing violence—a break-in, burglary, murder, or undercover war. The *action* or *operation,* up to and including the *destabilization* (subversion or overthrow) of a foreign government, whether by political or military means, may be highly publicized, but it is said to be *covert* because of its *deniability*—that is, it cannot be traced back to the responsible party. *Covert action/operation* is one of the leading examples—along with CAPER and, almost inevitably, PLAUSIBLE DENIAL—of how the language and methods of thinking of the intelligence COMMUNITY have contaminated domestic politics.

On the foreign front, referring to the overthrow of Premier Mohammed Mossadegh in Iran: "In 1953 . . . a covert operation so successful that it became widely known all over the world was carried out in Iran" (Ray S. Cline, *Secrets, Spies, and Scholars: Blueprint of the Essential CIA,* 1978). In theory, subversive activities of this sort are supervised by congressional oversight committees. (It seems significant in the context that "oversight" is one of those rare peculiar words that has acquired opposing meanings, referring to the act of supervision as well as the failure to notice what is going on.) In practice, however, presidents have not always chosen to inform Congress of such operations in what the Intelligence Oversight (*sic*) Act of 1980 characterized as "timely" fashion. This has led to some fine distinctions, with participants sometimes preferring for legal reasons to refer to *covert actions* as *secret* (or *special) activities.* Thus, parsing the testimony of Admiral John Poindexter at the Iran-Contra hearings (7/20/87), Sen. William S. Cohen (R., Maine) declared:

> I must tell you that I find it troubling when you say that "I withheld information from Congress but I did not mislead it." Or that the administration's support of the Contras was secret activity but not covert action. [See also WITHHOLD INFORMATION.]

On the home front, meanwhile, a famous *covert operation* was the break-in on September 3–4, 1971, at the office of Dr. Lewis Fielding in Beverly Hills, California. Part of the Watergate scandal, this illegal entry was a key element in the effort to NEUTRALIZE Daniel ("Pentagon Papers") Ellsberg. It was recommended to John D. (DEEP-SIX) Ehrlichman in a memo on August 11, 1971, from Egil "Bud" Krogh, Jr., and David R. Young, cochairmen of the PLUMBERS, who urged that "a covert operation be undertaken to examine all the medical files still held by Ellsberg's psychoanalyst covering the two-year period in which he was undergoing analysis." Ehrlichman approved the memo in virtually the same terms as used in FBI

headquarters for authorizing BLACK BAG JOBS, initialing it and noting, "If done under your assurance that it is not traceable." But it was traced, and Young eventually testified for the prosecution, while Ehrlichman and Krogh were among those who went to jail for their involvement in the break-in. For the conspirators, the choice of words was an important element in their thinking, as implied by Mr. Krogh in his courtroom testimony; see OPERATION.

cover-up. An obstruction of justice or, as a verb, to prevent the detection of a crime; loosely, to conceal a mistake. "The Iran-Contra cover-up, which has continued for more than six years, has now been completed with the pardon of Caspar Weinberger" (Independent Counsel Lawrence E. Walsh, Jr., 12/24/92).

Dated to the 1920s in underworld slang ("'Can he cover up by marrying her?' Archer asked," Raymond Chandler, *The Maltese Falcon,* 1930), the term did not register on the national consciousness until the time of the White House *cover-up* to avoid blame for the 1972 Watergate burglary, or CAPER. As President Richard M. Nixon himself said, in a slip that Freud would have admired:

> That is, because of—because of our—and that is we are attempting, the position is to withhold information and to cover up—this is totally true—you could say this is totally untrue. (3/30/73, *The White House Transcripts,* 1974)

The term acquired so many negative associations on account of the Watergate scandal that participants in subsequent *cover-ups* have tended to shy clear of the expression. Thus, Colonel Oliver North's secretary, Fawn Hall, who smuggled incriminating documents out of the White House as the Iran-Contra scandal was breaking in 1987, told the Select Committee on Secret Military Assistance to Iran and the Nicaraguan Opposition: "I don't use the word 'cover-up'; I would use the word 'protect'" (6/10/87). At another point, asked why she had given the documents to the colonel, after he himself had been discharged from the White House staff, Ms. Hall explained that "I was still very much in my protective mode."

See also CONTAIN and STONEWALL.

cow brute. One of a thundering herd of euphemisms for "bull," a sexually potent word that even earthy farmers and ranchers have tried to avoid over the years, e.g., "I was not fooling with a two-year-old cow brute" (J. M. Hunter, ed., *The Trail Drivers of Texas*, 1920).

It is sometimes thought that *cow brute* and other desexualized synonyms, such as *cow creature, male cow,* and *gentleman cow,* are purely regional curiosities, products of such cultural backwaters as the Ozarks, but this is not so. Thus, Henry Wadsworth Longfellow related in "The Wreck of the Hesperus" (1841) how "the cruel rocks they gored her side, Like the horns of a gentleman cow." A century later, *gentleman cow* was still the most popular of forty-two bullish euphemisms listed in the *Linguistic Atlas of New England* (Hans Kurath, ed., 1939–43). Others, in declining order of popularity, included: *male, toro, sire, animal, gentleman ox, critter* (or *creature*), *gentleman, beast, male animal, male cow, he cow, top cow, roarer, masculine, bison, he animal, seed ox, short horn, he critter, the he, top ox, he ox, male ox, kooter, cow critter, he creature, old man, top steer, gentleman heifer, master, male beast, brute, male critter, man cow, cow man, bullock cow, topper, doctor, bullit, paddy,* and *bungy.*

Nor does this exhaust the possibilities: *big cow, bullette* (a young bull or baby calf), *buttermilk cow, cow's husband, duke, he thing, poppa cow, preacher cow, stock bull, stud,* and *surly* also have been recorded. As long ago and as far away as eighteenth-century England, Capt. Francis Grose explained in his *Classical Dictionary of the Vulgar Tongue* (1796) that a *cow's spouse* was "a bull." The general reluctance to mention the male of the species may also help explain why "cowboy," originally a boy who tended cows (from 1725, *OED*), was applied to the rough and ready fellows in the Old West who were not boys and who did not tend cows.

While the prejudice against "bull" is widespread, it is, admittedly, in the isolated Ozarks that the taboo has been developed into a high art form. Thus, Vance Randolph reported in "Verbal Modesty in the Ozarks":

> It was only a few years ago that two women in Scott county, Arkansas, raised a great clamor for the arrest of a man who had mentioned a *bull-calf* in their presence. Even such words as *bull-frog, bull-fiddle* and *bull-snake* must be used with considerable caution, and a preacher at Pineville, Mo., recently told his flock that Pharaoh's daughter found the infant Moses in the flags: he didn't like to say *bull-rushes.* (*Dialect Notes,* vol. VI, Part 1, 1928)

All this may seem laughable, but before laughing too hard at the quaint ways of the hillfolk, it is well to remember that some very sophisticated people today maintain that "bull" in "bull market" should be avoided because of its sexist connotations. Rather, the politically correct person will speak of a *buy* market or, distancing oneself even further from the underlying B word, an *escalating, improving,* or *rising* market.

The bull is only one of a number of male animals whose name has been euphemized for strictly sexual reasons. See also GENTLE-MAN, HE-BIDDY, ROOSTER, and SIRE, as well as the female SLUT.

cowslip. The common name for the English primrose or marsh marigold has lost its bad odor thanks to the passage of time and popular misapprehension of the term's etymology. Contrary to appearance, it does not derive from "cow's lip," but from the Anglo-Saxon *cu*, cow, plus *slyppe*, slime, which translates as "cow slop" or "cow dung." See also PARSON-IN-THE-PULPIT.

crap. "Crap" is to "shit" as SCREW is to "fuck"—a newer term, considered coarse but not as coarse as its synonym and, so, something of a euphemism for it. Thus, writers could get away with "crap" (as they also could with DRECK and MERDE) back when editors usually were editing out the other one, both in its literal sense, e.g., "There didn't look like there was anything in the park except dog crap," as well as figuratively, e.g., "all that David Copperfield kind of crap" (both from J. D. Salinger, *The Catcher in the Rye*, 1951).

"Crap" is inevitably linked with the name of an English sanitary engineer, Thomas Crapper, who really existed (1837–1910), and who really did make a key contribution to the development of the modern flush toilet. The association is largely fortuitous, however. "Crap" in the

sense of "to defecate" is dated in *The Oxford English Dictionary* to 1874, eight years before Crapper invented his Valveless Water Waste Preventer, which automatically shut off the flow of water to a toilet's holding tank after it was refilled. The *OED* citation, moreover, comes from a slang dictionary, which suggests that the word had been in use for quite some time previously. Buttressing this conclusion is the appearance in 1846, when Thomas Crapper was but a lad of nine, of the adjectival form, e.g., "Which of us had hold of the crappy (shten) end of the stick?" (*Swell's Night Guide*). This same work also mentions a "crapping ken" ("ken" equals "house"), meaning an outdoor PRIVY. (Variations on the theme included *crapping casa, crapping case,* and *crapping castle*.)

"Crapping ken," in turn, is a variant of "cropping ken," used in the same sense as far back as the seventeenth century. The difference in spelling reflects different ways of pronouncing the same word, "crop" representing the southern English pronunciation of "crap," from the Middle English *crap* or *crappe*, chaff, employed since at least the fifteenth century to refer to leftovers, scraps, and residues of other sorts as well as to discarded husks of grain. (In parts of the southeastern United States, "crop" commonly was pronounced "crap" until comparatively recently, and the "a" form is still heard occasionally.) The etymology of the term parallels that for synonymous terms: "turd," from the Indo-European root *der*, to split, hence, that which is separated; "shit," from the Indo-European root *skei-*, to cut, to split; and "excrement," from *ex*, out, plus *cernere*, to separate or to sift.

All this being said, it also seems likely that the appearance of Thomas Crapper's last name on porcelain fixtures helped to popularize the odoriferous sense of the word in the twentieth century, with the result that *crap* itself has come to be euphemized as *frap* and CRUD. In conformance with Gresham's Law of Language, the "bad" meaning of the word also has driven out the original "good" ones. Thus, nobody refers nowadays to the residue formed when rendering fat as "crap" or "crap-cake," or to dregs or settlings at the bottom of a beer barrel as "crap" (except possibly in a metaphoric sense). And not even in the interest of capturing local dialect would Mark Twain today be likely to spell "crop" as "crap," e.g., "'Ole Drake Higgins he's been down to Shelby las' week. Tuck his crap down . . . hit warn't no time to sell, he says, so he fotched it back again'" (with Charles Dudley Warner, *The Gilded Age*, 1873). For similar shifts in meaning of similar words, see DEFECATE/DEFECATION, EXCREMENT, FECES, FERTILIZER, and MANURE.

creative. Inventive, especially in order to deceive or to defraud. "It is part of American tax lore that nearly everybody who claims travel and entertainment expenses . . . resorts to at least some fiction. . . . and many of them perform this creative work the night before the audit" (*Esquire*, 1/73). The term appears in many combinations, including *creative accounting, creative bookkeeping, creative license, creative penmanship,* and *creative amnesia* (also called *convenient memory*). The first of these probably is the most common, e.g., "The kind of figure-juggling that had come to be called 'creative accounting' continued to flourish, and accounting authorities continued to shrug" (*New Yorker*, 8/13/73). See also WHITE LIE.

cremains. Human ashes; an unctuous combination of "cremated" and REMAINS. "In the special language of death, the mortician did not say 'ashes'; he referred to them as 'cremains'" (Lynn Caine, *Widow,* 1974).

Cremains are produced in a *cremation chamber* or *vault* (as opposed to "retort") of a *crematorium* (a late-Victorian word, dating to circa 1880) by means of "calcination— the *kindlier* heat" (Jessica Mitford, *The American Way of Death,* 1963). See also INURNMENT and MORTICIAN.

crepitation. The act of farting; from the Latin *crepitare,* to crackle. "Crepitation contests at staff meetings and unbridled revelry at Las Vegas promotional events did not help matters" (*Publishers Weekly,* 3/22/93, review of Robert J. Burgess, *Silver Bullets: A Soldier's Story of How Coors Bombed in the Beer Wars*). See also BREAK WIND.

crew transfer container. A temporary coffin. NASA used *crew transfer containers* (also known, in the U.S. military, as *aluminum transfer containers*) for the bodies of the seven people killed when the space shuttle *Challenger* blew up in 1985.

The nomenclature is in keeping with the government's tropism toward jawbreaking designations for mundane objects (see ENTRENCHING TOOL), but the denial of death seems to have been the chief motive in this instance for employing the multiword term. Evidence for this comes from NASA's report that "whether or not a cabin rupture occurred prior to water impact has not yet been determined by a superficial examination of the recovered components," where *recovered components* was the agency's way of referring to the contents of the *crew transfer containers* (*Philadelphia Inquirer,* 4/26/86). See also ANOMALY, CASKET, and HUMAN REMAINS POUCH.

criminal conversation. Sex without marriage; adultery, in particular, with the *conversation* being a euphemism for nonspoken INTERCOURSE (see CONVERSATION). The term appears in British common law and in the laws of some states of the United States. It frequently is abbreviated as *C.C.* or *Crim. Con.* in Britain (where the *Con.* may also be construed as standing for "connexion"; see CONNECTION). Thus, the heroine of *Lady Pokingham; or They All Do It,* which appeared in installments in a distinctly underground monthly, *The Pearl,* married a Lord Crim-Con (7/1879–9/1880). In real life in this era, the records (ca. 1860–70) of the Thomas Coram Foundling Hospital in London are replete with such statements by unwed mothers as "He took me by force to his bedroom and gave me Brandy and Water. Crim. Con. was repeated frequently" and "[He] seduced me out of doors and C.C. was repeated in the same way more than once" (from Françoise Barret-Ducrocq, *Love in the Time of Victoria,* 1991).

Private *criminal conversation* may become a public matter when a husband sues another man for having an AFFAIR with his wife. As the anonymous "Member of the Whip Club," who revised Capt. Francis Grose's *A Classical Dictionary of the Vulgar Tongue* and reissued it as the *Lexicon Balatronicum* in 1811, explained:

> CRIM. CON. MONEY. Damages directed by a jury to be paid by a convicted adulterer to the injured husband, for criminal conversation with his wife.

A famous suit for *crim. con.* money involved James Thomas Brudenell, seventh earl of Cardigan, who led the charge of the Light Brigade at Balaclava in 1854. A notorious womanizer, Cardigan was accused in 1843 of adultery with Lady Frances, wife of Lord William Paget, who asserted that he'd been damaged to the tune of £15,000. Paget was supported by the testimony of Frederick Winter, a private detective, who had managed to post himself beneath a sofa in a drawing room adjoining the one in which the *C.C.* allegedly took place. (This forward position was not without peril: At one point the couple perched on the sofa, and Winter was in some danger of being raked by Cardigan's spurs, the latter being attired, still, in full-dress uniform.) Winter told the court that the breathing of the couple subsequently became "hard like persons distressed for breath after running," and that he had no doubt, from what he had heard and seen, that a "criminal connection had taken place between the parties," not once but twice. Despite this evidence, the jury let Cardigan off, apparently because Paget himself was shown to be such a cad that they sympathized with Lady Frances and had no wish to see Lord William enjoy all that *crim. con.* money (from Donald Thomas, *Charge! Hurrah! Hurrah! A Life of Cardigan of Balaclava,* 1974). See also EXTRAMARITAL and SLEEP WITH.

criminal (or illegal) operation. Abortion back when "abortion" couldn't be mentioned in polite society, especially not in FAMILY newspapers, and when the operation was completely against the law. *Criminal operation* seems to have been used mainly in the United States, *illegal operation* in Great Britain. (British newspapers also used to avoid "abortion" with the completely opaque *producing a certain state.*) See also ILLEGAL and MISCARRIAGE.

cripes. Christ; one of many euphemisms for the holy name. Among the others:

cricky, cracky, chrissakes, Christmas, Christopher Columbus, criminey, JIMINY CRICKET, and, most elegantly, *G. Rover Cripes*. Though the reach is rather longer, such quaint expressions as *ever since George Washington* (or *Moses* or *Caesar*) *was a corporal*, meaning "as long as anyone can remember," also look as though they might have begun as roundabouts for "ever since Christ." See also CHRISSAKE; CRYING OUT LOUD, FOR; and GEE.

crispy critter. A person who has been burned to death. Almost certainly adapted from the breakfast cereal of the same name, the term was used during the VIETNAM ERA to describe bodies that had been charred by napalm, a.k.a. SELECTIVE ORDNANCE. (A *Bhuddist barbecue* in this period was a Vietnamese monk who had immolated himself as a protest against the war.) "Crispy critter" has shown considerable staying power, being extended in the 1980s by medical personnel in hospitals to include children with third-degree burns and by smoke jumpers to refer to animals that have been burned to death in forest fires.

croak. To die, to murder. "He croaked a screw at Dannemora [prison]" (Joel Sayre, *American Mercury*, 12/31). The expression has been dated to 1812 (*OED*) and perhaps imitates the gurgling sound of the dying person. Back in the good old days of public hangings, the final speech of a murderer upon the gallows (especially if a confession) was called a *croak*. See also HIT.

cross over. To die; "cross" is synonymous as a euphemism with "pass" (as in PASS AWAY), and it appears in various phrases, all with a deathly meaning, such as *cross over the range, cross over to the other side, cross the bar, cross the border, cross the great divide, cross the river* (or *River Jordan*), *cross the ties* (hobo talk), and *cross the veil*. The best-known literary example is Tennyson's "I hope to see my Pilot face to face/When I have crossed the bar" (*Crossing the Bar*, 1889). More remarkable, for being spontaneous, are the dying words of General Thomas J. ("Stonewall") Jackson, CSA, on May 10, 1863, eight days after having been mistakenly shot by his own troops at the Battle of Chancellorsville: "Let us cross over the river and rest under the shade of the trees." See also FRIENDLY FIRE and REST.

crowd management team. Riot squad. Members of the Metro Toronto Police public-order unit are called the "crowd management team" (Toronto *Globe and Mail*, 5/9/92). When riot squads go into action, they engage in *confrontation management*, which is police-ese for "riot control." See also the *crowd control engineer* in ENGINEER and UNUSUAL OCCURRENCE.

crower. A cock. "I'm going to have the Plymouth Rock crower killed" (Mary E. Freeman, *Six Trees*, 1903). For more about the *crower* and why he got this name, see ROOSTER.

crud. A general term for a number of nasty things (e.g., an intestinal upset accompanied by vomiting and/or diarrhea; dried semen; venereal disease, usually syphilis) that also functions as a euphemism for *crap*, as in "I'll beat the living crud out of you" (*West Side Story*, film, 1961). Science fiction writer Theodore Sturgeon is credited with the observation that "90 percent of everything is crud" (*Playboy*, 2/84). Not surprisingly, given its range of noxious meanings, *crud* itself has been euphemized—as *crut*, e.g., "You miserable little crut" (Ernest Hemingway, *To Have and Have Not*, 1937).

See also CRAP and the *Cairo Crud* in MONTEZUMA'S REVENGE.

crump. To die; hospital-talk, probably from *crumped out*, dead drunk, and the military use of the word to refer to shelling (from WW I and the sound of an explosion). This is one of many current roundabouts employed by doctors and nurses who face death daily but tend to speak about it indirectly, e.g., *flatlined* (as an EKG monitor reading, also called *the Nebraska sign* and, in Europe, *the Holland sign*), *positive O sign* (referring to the open mouth of a corpse or person at death's door), and *positive Q sign* (like the *O sign* but with the tongue sticking out). See also EXPIRE and PASS AWAY.

crying out loud, for. The euphemistic equivalent of "for Christ's sake." This is one of many similar phrases, including *for cat's sake, for cramp's sake, for cripe's sake, for crooning out loud, for crum(p)'s sake, for heaven's sake, for Pete's sake,* and *for pity's sake*. Meanwhile, "for the love of Christ" often comes out as *for the love of Mike* or *for the love of Pete*. See also CHRISSAKE, CRIPES, JIMINY CRICKET, and GEE.

cul-de-sac. Dead end; real estate–ese. The French expression translates literally as "bottom of the bag," the dead end or blind alley being a narrow passageway that is open only at one end, like a sack. In French, *cul* also denotes the human bottom or ANUS, another passageway with only one opening. Shakespeare made various plays on the French word. Thus, in *Love's Labor's Lost* (1588–94), when the affected Armado

describes the "afternoon" as the "posteriors of the day," the schoolmaster, Holofernes, says the phrase is "well culled, chose, sweet and apt." Rather more explicit is Jack Cade's reference to the Dauphin of France in *Henry VI, Part II* (1590–91) as "Monsieur Basimecu" (*baise mon cul*), which translates as Mr. Kiss-my-ass. All of which may be worth remembering next time you spot an ad in the real estate section of the local newspaper for a fancy house on a *cul-de-sac*. See also ENCLAVE and NO OUTLET.

cull. The general term for selecting or picking later acquired the sense of tossing out or removing that which is inferior and, as a noun, "a cull," the rejected object itself. "Cull" is especially favored in agricultural and GAME MANAGEMENT circles to the word it sounds so much like, "kill," as in "The battery boys 'cull' (or liquidate) their hens when they've laid for about a year" (*Listener*, 3/27/69). See also DEPOPULATE, HARVEST, LIQUIDATE, SACRIFICE, SELECT OUT, THIN, and TRIAGE.

culturally deprived. Poor. "What used to be called a 'slum' is now delicately referred to as 'a culturally deprived environment'" (William Safire, *Safire's Political Dictionary*, 1978). See also DISADVANTAGED.

cumshaw. A bribe, a payoff. The English rendering of the Chinese words for "grateful thanks" originally referred to a small gift to a beggar or coolie, but it becomes a euphemism for a bribe when large sums of money are demanded in order to effect a business deal. Dated to 1839 in *The Oxford English Dictionary*, the term is considerably older. Thus, describing an encounter in 1769 near Canton: "The mandarin took up a red morocco case containing combs and a pair of scissors, saying 'Cumshaw.' This I did not understand; but Bob told me the fellow asked for the case as a present" (*The Prodigal Rake, Memoirs of William Hickey*, Peter Quennell, ed., 1962). And in the more expensive sense, a Lockheed Aircraft Corp. employee in Europe reported home, after meeting with the firm's Italian CONSULTANT to discuss selling airplanes in his country, that "Gelac [Lockheed's Georgia company], if it wishes the maximum run for success, must be prepared to go as high as $120,000 *per airplane* for the cumshaw part" (letter, 3/28/69, released 2/4/76 by the Senate Subcommittee on Multinational Corporations). See also BAKSHEESH.

cunnilingus. A relatively new word for an old practice—and one of the greatest examples of the cleansing power of an otherwise dead language, the Latin being printable in many places where the English is not. The Latin, as it happens, is quite straightforward (to Latin-speakers), the term deriving from *lingere*, to lick, and *cunnus,* which means "female pudenda" or, in the vernacular, "cunt." (And that last word is not slang, but legitimate, Standard English; see VAGINA.)

"Cunnilingus" seems to be a late-Victorian invention, with the oldest example in the 1972 supplement to *The Oxford English Dictionary* coming from Havelock Ellis's *Studies in the Psychology of Sex*, of 1897. Ten years earlier, "the obscene act of cunnilinging" was mentioned in J. R. Smither's translation of *Forberg's Manual of Classical Erotology*. During this period, the anonymous author of *My Secret Life* (ca. 1890) also discussed "female cunilingers," but this was exceptional: He was more apt to refer to *gamahuching*. See also BLOW, FELLATIO, MOUTH MUSIC, and SOIXANTE-NEUF.

curiosa. Pornography. The generalized "curiosa," actually meaning "curiosities" or "oddities," is one of the euphemisms used by literate booksellers to describe their dirtier wares. "Curious" also has been used this way. Thus, playing the two off against each other: "She's not . . . the type to pore over literary curiosa unless . . . they were curious in the specialised sense" (Ngaio Marsh, *Final Curtain*, 1947). See also EROTICA.

curiosity delay. A rubbernecking delay (traffic news radio broadcast, 7/23/91).

cushion for flotation. A life preserver on an airplane, also called an *article of comfort*. See also PERSONAL FLOTATION DEVICE and WATER LANDING.

cuspidor. A spittoon; the more ornate word is preferred by those who choose to EXPECTORATE instead of "spit." He whose task it is to empty the contents of the receptacle, and to keep it polished, is, naturally, the *cuspidorian*.

cuss. Damn. "Cuss" is a euphemistic variant of "curse," itself a generalized euphemistic substitute for the more specific "damn." For example: "Not keering a tinker's cuss what meeting house you sleep in Sundays" (C. F. Browne, *Artemus Ward: His Book*, 1862). The present participle is *cussin'*. See also BLESSING, CONTINENTAL, DARN, and SWAN.

custodian. A cleaned-up JANITOR, frequently found in schools; a SUPERINTENDENT. "Custodian" improves upon "janitor," just as JANITOR improves upon "caretaker," "furnace-stoker," and "floor-sweeper." Variations include *custodian-engineer* and, of all things, *engineer-custodian*. The switch to *cus-*

todian has had a ripple effect: "One of the amusing sequels of the shift in terminology from janitor to *custodian* in one American university was that the title of the head of the research library had, in turn, to be changed from *Custodian* to *Director,* since there was some danger of confusing him with the janitor of the place" (Albert H. Marchwardt, *American English,* 1958). The janitorial *custodian* should not be confused with the *custodial officer,* who is really a *correctional officer,* or prison guard. See also CORRECTIONAL FACILITY and ENGINEER.

CYA. Cover (or Covering) Your Ass. Occasionally, for the benefit of those with especially tender sensibilities, the initials are interpreted to mean "Cover Your Aft [end]" and "Cover Your Anatomy." See also ARSE, BEHIND, and DERRIÈRE.

D

d – – –. Damn. The profanity usually was printed in full until the early 1700s, e.g., from 1709, "Call the Chairmen: Damn 'em, I warrant they are at the Ale-house already!" (Sir Richard Steele, *Tatler*, No. 13). In succeeding generations, however, Fielding, Smollett, and other eighteenth-century writers began rendering it as *d – – –, d – – n,* and *d – – – – d* (for the past participle). This resulted in such characteristic pre-Victorian passages as "Lieutenant Minchin . . . roared out in the true style of a British seaman, 'Fire and be d – – – – d'" (Charles William Janson, *The Stranger in America,* 1807). And—more watered-down sailor talk: "'you d – – – – d hay-making son of a sea-cook. Do it again, d – – n your eyes, and I'll cut your liver out'" (Capt. Frederick Marryat, *Peter Simple,* 1834). During this period, too, Henrietta Maria Bowdler converted Lady Macbeth's "Out, damn'd spot!" into "Out, crimson spot!" (*The Family Shakespeare,* 1807).

Censors still delete "damn" from books for children, and TV stations balked initially at running the New York Urban Coalition's "Give money. Give a damn" ad campaign in 1968. For most people, though, the term has lost most of its old power. As a result, it can not only be used freely again but be employed as a euphemism for something even "worse," e.g., from an interview with Ted Williams: "In slightly expurgated form, he answered, 'The reason I became the hitter I was, was due to trial and damn error, trial and damn error, trial and damn error, trial and damn error!'" (Ira Berkow, *New York Times,* 5/1/89). See also A – –, BLANK, DARN, DASH, F – – –, and H – – L.

dad. A euphemistic form of "God," especially useful in forming such mild oaths as *dadblame, dadblast, dadburn, dadfetch, dadgum, dagnab (it), dadrat, dadrot, dadshame, dadsizzle,* and *dadswamp,* where the BLAME, *blast, burn,* etc. all stand for "damn." For example: "'Dad fetch it! This comes of playing hookey and doing everything a feller's told not to do'" (Mark Twain, *The Adventures of Tom Sawyer,* 1876). A common nineteenth-century variant of *dad* was *dod,* which was used in most of the same combinations, e.g., "I'll be dod blamed if I do" (A. B. Longstreet, *Georgia Scenes, Characters, Incidents, etc., in the First Half Century of the Republic,* 1835). See also DOGGONE, EGAD, and GADZOOKS.

daisy-cutter. People-cutter, this being the military term (from WW I) for a fragmentation bomb or shell, designed to explode instantaneously upon hitting the ground or heavy vegetation, thus spraying shrapnel at a low level over a wide area. Technically, a *daisy-cutter* classes as an ANTIPERSONNEL WEAPON. See also PEACEKEEPER.

dang. Damn. "Dang," sometimes euphemized itself as "ding," has a folksy ring, which makes it sound obsolete, but it isn't. "Sure they'll drill holes in wood but the danged things 'walk' all over the place so that you can't put the hole where you want it" (Leichtung ad, *Natural History,* 10/78). Then there was the Connecticut man who objected to his neighbor's homing pigeons: "I'm an animal lover but these pigeons are a dang nuisance" (*Litchfield County,* Conn., *Times,* 3/31/89). See also DARN.

darky (also darkey or dark). A black person, especially a slave. The term dates to the colonial period, with the oldest example in

A Dictionary of American English (Mitford M. Mathews, ed., 1951) coming from a 1775 song that was popular during the American Revolution: "The women ran, the darkeys too; And all the bells, they tolled." This was not just a polite, white euphemism. African-Americans also referred to themselves this way for many years. Thus, "Carry Me Back to Old Virginny," written by a James A. Bland (1854–1911), a black minstrel who also enriched us with "Oh, Dem Golden Slippers" and "In the Evening by the Moonlight," begins:

Carry me back to old Virginny,
That's where the cotton and the corn
   and 'tatoes grow,
That's where the birds warble sweet
   in the springtime,
That's where the old darkey's heart am
   long'd to go.

Bland's use of "darkey" in this song, adopted by Virginia in 1940 as the official state song, parallels that of "coon," another now-derogatory term, whose racial sense was popularized in "All Coons Look Alike to Me," a minstrel song by another African-American, Ernest Hogan. "Darky" remained in widespread use at least through 1915 (e.g., "The Darktown Strutters Ball"), but the euphemism began wearing thin soon thereafter. The *Baltimore Afro-American* launched a crusade in 1936 against "My Old Kentucky Home" because it contains the word. This battle was still simmering a half-century later in Virginia, where L. Douglas Wilder, grandson of a slave, and the state's lieutenant governor (and future governor), made a point of making a grand exit from a public function in 1987 when the state song was sung. (But it is still the official song.)

A very few African-Americans continued to embrace the term into the 1990s when speaking of themselves. "I'm afraid I am a naughty little darkey," said Bessie Delany. "Ha ha! I know it's not fashionable to use some of the words from my heyday, but that's who I am! And who is going to stop me? Nobody, that's who!" But Ms. Delany's "heyday" was a while back. The second black woman to become a dentist in New York State, she was 101 when she said this (Sarah and A. Elizabeth Delany, with Amy Hill Heath, *Having Our Say: The Delany Sisters' First 100 Years* [1993]). See also NEGRO.

darn. Damn. A euphemism of uncertain origin, it appeared first in the 1770s in New England. Some authorities (led by Noah Webster, no less) have maintained that it comes from the Middle English *dern,* secret, while others have argued that it is a corruption of "eternal," as in "eternal damnation," via *tarnal* and *tarnation,* both of which also surfaced as euphemisms for "damn" and "damnation" at about the same time as "darn." Whatever the source, the term's euphemistic nature was immediately recognized, e.g.: "In New England profane swearing (and everything *'similar to the like of that'*) is so far from polite as to be criminal, and many of the lower class of people use, instead of it, what I suppose they deem to be justifiable substitutions such as *darn* it, for d – – n it" (*Pennsylvania Magazine,* 6/20/1781).

While the Puritan blue laws may have helped inspire *darn, tarnal,* and the rest as the preceding example suggests, the sudden appearance of so many euphemisms at about the same time also suggests another cause—in this case, the simultaneous rise of a new middle class and the blossoming of pre-Victorian prudery. Later nineteenth-century developments included *darnation, goldarn, gosh darn,* and such minced combinations as *not by a darned sight,* which, in its turn, was softened to *not by a considerable sight* and *not by a long sight.*

Of course, "darn" is only the most popular of a great many euphemisms for "damn." Among the others, many of which are encountered most often in the past tense: BLAMED, BLAST, *blowed* (as in "I'll be blowed"), *bother* (see BOTHERATION), D., DANG, DASH, *dear* ("Oh dear me!," not to be confused with "Oh, dear!" meaning "Oh, God!"); DEUCE (also a euphemism for Satan); DING; *dog* ("I'll be dogged!" or "Dog my cats!"), *drat, jiggered, switched,* and THUNDER. See also D – – –, DOGGONE, GEE, GOLLY, GOSH, and HECK.

dash. Damn, the Devil, or any other profanity that the speaker, writer, or editor wishes to soft-pedal. Thus, William Dean Howells, editor of *The Atlantic Monthly,* toned down the language in Mark Twain's *Life on the Mississippi,* so what Twain termed the "sublime profanity" of the mate of the *Paul Jones* came out this way: "Don't you hear me? Dash it to dash! . . . Where're you going with that barrel! *For-ard* with it 'fore I make you swallow it, you dash-dash-dash-*dashed* split between a tired mud turtle and a crippled hearse horse!" (*Harper's,* 1/1875). See also BLANK; D – – –; DARN; DEVIL, THE; EXPLETIVE DELETED; and F-WORD.

date. A whore's customer, a.k.a. JOHN or TRICK, or a transaction between them. Quoting a prostitute who had been shown a photograph of a serial killer: "He used to constantly ask me out on dates, but I told him I didn't go out with strangers" (*New*
York Times, 6/30/93). See also WANNA GO OUT?.

daytime drama. A soap opera. See also CONTINUING (or ADULT) DRAMA.

deaccession. To sell or trade, especially when a museum raises funds by selling a work of art—an *accession* when it was acquired. People who think that museums should hold on to what they have object to the word as well as the practice for which it stands: "They call it by the polite name of deaccessioning, but what it amounts to is a legal form of looting. You buy something you cannot afford; you incur expenses you cannot meet; and the inevitable consequence is that you have to liquidate some of your 'assets'" (Hilton Kramer, *New York Observer,* 3/19/90).

"Deaccession" was popularized, so to speak, in the early 1970s, along with "deacquisition," as in "When it was announced seven months ago that Thomas Pearsall Field Hoving's deacquisitions would include Picasso's 'Women in White' and Manet's 'Boy with a Sword,' it aroused the kind of reaction that has made Hoving a controversial figure ever since he was Mayor Lindsay's parks commissioner" (*Newsweek,* 10/16/72).

deballast. To spill oil into the ocean. "Deballast" is what oil tankers are said by oil shippers to do when they get rid of oil at sea, usually while out of sight of land. See also DEEP-OCEAN PLACEMENT and EFFLUENT.

deceased. Dead; the dead person. This is probably the most popular way of not saying "dead." It also is used frequently in lieu of the dead person's name, e.g., "Don't you think the deceased would prefer the mahogany model?" (See DEPARTED for more about the taboo against naming the names of the dead.)

"Deceased" amounts to a verbal flinch — a quick blink of the eye to escape a gruesome sight. It has a FOP Index of 2.25. Even in the original Latin, it is a euphemism, deriving ultimately from *decedere,* which has the bland meaning of "to go away" or "to depart" (*de,* away, plus *cedere,* to go). Strictly speaking, which isn't often done nowadays, "deceased" is a legal term (although not as legal as "decedent") applying only to people. As such, it is the counterpart of DEMISE, which originally related to the transfer of property and property rights. John O'Hara, whose ear for language was notoriously fine, embedded "deceased" perfectly in its proper context at the tragic conclusion of *Appointment in Samarra* (1934): "Fortunately deceased had seen fit to vent his rage and smash the clock in the front part of the car, which readily enabled the deputy coroner to fix the time of death at about eleven p.m."

The *deceased* may also be described politely as the *defunct, the late lamented* (see LATE), the LOVED ONE, and the REMAINS. Slang expressions tend to be more macabre, as well as more picturesque. Among them: *backed* (not used much since the nineteenth century, but of sufficient ingenuity to warrant revival; as explained by Capt. Francis Grose in *A Classical Dictionary of the Vulgar Tongue,* 1796: "He wishes to have the senior, or old square toes, backed: he longs to have his father on six men's shoulders; that is, carrying to the grave"); *cold meat* (in which case the hearse, or PROFESSIONAL CAR, becomes a *cold meat cart* and the CASKET a *cold meat box*); *crowbait; food for worms; morgue-aged property,* and *stiff* (a nineteenth-century Ameri-can clipping of the British *stiff one* or *stiff'un*). For the many ways in which people become *deceased,* without actually "dying," see PASS AWAY.

decent marriage. Dowry required. "Decent marriage" is the code phrase used in India in classified ads for partners in arranged marriages. The code is necessary because such payments are illegal under the Dowry Prohibition Act of 1961.

decision-making. Deciding. The longer term (FOP Index of 2.1) elevates the status of the *decision-maker.* See also OPTION.

deed. A general term for covering up such unseemly specifics as (1) dog shit, and (2) sexual intercourse.

In the the first instance, the term is synonymous with, though marginally blander than, MESS or NUISANCE, e.g., "Tipper did a deed in my bedroom and I found it with my foot" (note from an anguished daughter, 11/4/93). See also DOG DIRT/DO/LITTER/WASTE.

The sexual DEED, meanwhile, forms an exact parallel with ACT. In this case, the operative phrase originally was "with the deed," as in, from a translation from the French, of 1585: "The Adulterer being found with the deed." At about the same time, though, William Shakespeare used the word in the modern way, with Berowne describing Rosaline in *Love's Labor's Lost* (1593?) as "A whitely wanton . . . one that will do the deed/Though Argus were her eunuch and her guard." (See also DO.) Today, in seeking to clarify their use of the euphemism, people sometimes reveal their true feelings about sex, calling it *the dirty deed.* See also COPULATE/COPULATION, INTERCOURSE, and UGLY.

deep-ocean placement. Toxic waste dumping; see also DEBALLAST.

deep-six. To throw overboard, specifically to get rid of evidence—what John W. Dean III, President Nixon's COUNSEL, said he was advised to do by John D. Ehrlichman, the president's chief domestic affairs adviser, with papers found in the office safe of E. Howard Hunt, Jr., the official White House PLUMBER. "I asked him what he meant by 'deep-six.' He leaned back in his chair and said: 'You drive across the [Potomac] river at night, don't you? Well, when you cross over the river on your way home, just toss the briefcase into the river'" (testimony to the Senate Watergate Committee, 6/25/73). Before becoming a euphemism for a criminal act, "deep-six" (for six fathoms' depth, i.e., thirty-six feet) was a relatively innocent naval expression for jettisoning, e.g., "Give that gear the deep six" (Cary Grant, as a submarine captain, *Destination Tokyo*, film, 1941). The expression may have arisen with reference to burial at sea: Vessels that sink, and the sailors that sink with them, also are said *to get* (or *take*) *the deep six*. In this sense, the maritime phrase trades upon the notion of burial on land, "deep six" being another term for a grave, six feet deep. See also SANITIZE and SPACE.

defecate/defecation. The words are long, Latinate, and "printable," but they're not ordinarily used by ordinary people, e.g., "'The only big words I use were taught me in the police academy, Roscoe,' said Baxter. 'Words like hemorrhage and defecation'" (Joseph Wambaugh, *Onionfield*, 1976). Compared to the short word that Baxter would have learned as a boy, i.e., shit, "defecation" has a FOP Index of 3.25.

The prevailing meanings of "defecate"

and "defecation" appear to be products of the nineteenth century. *The Oxford English Dictionary*'s earliest example of "defecation" in the modern sense comes from 1830, seven years before Victoria became queen. (See PASS AWAY, PECULIAR MEMBERS, and ROOSTER for more about the euphemistically important pre-Victorian period.) Originally, "to defecate" was "to purify," both literally, as by removing the sediment (also called the CRAP) from a liquid, or figuratively, as by cleansing the mind or soul of guilt. (EXCREMENT has a similar etymology.) Today, one hardly ever comes across such sentences as "Consider the defecated nature of that pure and divine body" (Thomas Taylor, *Two Orations of the Emperor Julian*, trans. 1793).

Besides the classical Latinate "defecate" and "defecation," there are many other euphemistic expressions for the act and its result, with those for the act often overlapping with the large set of euphemisms for PEE. See, for example: BUSINESS, CALLS (or NEEDS) OF NATURE, CAUGHT (or TAKEN) SHORT, COVER (ONE'S) FEET, DUTY, EASE, ELIMINATE/ELIMINATION, GO, *make* (see MAKE [or PASS] WATER), NUMBER ONE AND/OR TWO, POOP, POWDER MY NOSE, RELIEVE, SIT DOWN, *sit on the* THRONE (see TOILET), and *squat* (see the *diddly-squat* in DIDDLY-POO).

As for the results, the euphemistic synonyms fall roughly into three categories: those relating mainly to people, those relating mainly to animals, and those relating to agriculture. For example:

People: BM, *boom boom* (potty talk), CACA, CRAP, *dead soldier* ("pay a visit to the old soldier's home" is another form of POWDER MY NOSE), DIDDLY-POO (more basic potty talk; see also WEE-WEE), DOO-DOO, DUMP, FECES, *hockey* (especially popular in the southern United States, and also used as a verb and mild expletive, as in "That's a bunch of horse hockey"), NIGHT SOIL, *starch* (as in, "Say that again, and I'll beat the living starch out of you"), STOOL, and *(body) wax*.

Animals: ACCIDENT, BS, BUSHWA, *button* (from a sheep), *chip* (as in *buffalo chip, prairie chip*, etc.), CALLING CARD(S), DOG DIRT/DO/LITTER/WASTE, DROPPING, *heifer dust, horse apple, meadow dressing*, MESS, NUISANCE, POPPYCOCK, *pure* (pure dog-shit in nineteenth-century London, where *pure* was collected for use in tanneries by *pure-finders*), SHY-POKE (the name of a bird), WASTE, and the highly technical WHITE DIELECTRIC MATERIAL.

Agriculture: *brown gold*, FERTILIZER, HONEY, MANURE, MUCK, *(organic) plantfood, poudrette* (a nineteenth-century term for the contents of privies, from the French *poudre*, powder), and the latter's fair-sounding companion, *urette*.

Of course, many of the above, as well as some others, also can be used metaphorically or as euphemistic interjections. See also, for example, BARNYARD EPITHET, BS, BUSHWA, CHICKEN, CRAP, DRECK, HORSEFEATHERS, KHAZERAY, MERDE, NUTS, PISH/PSHAW, S – – –, SHUCKS, SPIT, SUGAR, T – – –, and WHAT.

Defense, Department of. In the beginning —i.e., in 1789, when George Washington was putting together his first cabinet—there was the War Department, later (1798) supplemented by a separate Navy Department. This arrangement lasted until 1947, when the *Department of Defense* was created as the umbrella for the Departments of the Army (erstwhile "War"), Navy, and Air Force. Naturally, the nonaggressive *Defense Department* was formed just as the Cold War was, as the saying goes, heating up—and just as the development of nuclear weapons was giving the ultimate lie to the notion of effective *defense* (see LIMITED WAR

for details). In complete consistency with this new nomenclature, the United States has not fought any "wars" since the *Defense Department* was established—merely the Korean POLICE ACTION and the Vietnam CONFLICT, along with such passing forays into other countries as the "rescue mission" (President Reagan's words, 11/3/83) that toppled a Marxist government in Grenada in 1983, the self-serving "Operation Just Cause" that removed Manuel Noriega as president of Panama in 1989, and the Persian Gulf episode of 1991 (not a war, though it looked like one, Congress merely approving a resolution that authorized "the use of military force"). Language is stretched even further in the case of undercover wars, of course. Thus, the CIA's International Affairs Division engaged in paramilitary operations around the world while the U.S. Department of State's Nicaraguan Humanitarian Assistance Office provided weapons and other military supplies to the Contras seeking to overthrow that nation's government.

The United States has plenty of company when it comes to converting swords into euphemistic plowshares. The military services of Israel, for instance, form the Israeli Defense Forces. When they invaded Lebanon in 1978, Prime Minister Menachem Begin justified the offensive action by declaring that "we should make use of active defenses in order to break the strength of the PLO" (*New York Times*, 3/14/78), and when Israel re-invaded Lebanon in 1982, the attack was known officially as "Operation Peace for Galilee" (and unofficially as "Arik's War," after the nickname of Defense Minister Ariel Sharon). South Africa also has its *Defense Force*, and it, too, has been known to cross borders (e.g., Zimbabwe in 1982). Then there is, or was, the former Soviet

Union, where the Red Army Band was converted into the *Ministry of Defense Band.* For somewhat different reasons (bad memories of World War II), the Japanese Imperial Navy now puts to sea as the *Maritime Self-Defense Force.*

And so it goes. In Grenada in the 1970s, the government kept the opposition in line with its *Volunteers for the Defense of Fundamental Human Liberties* (formerly called the Night Ambush Squad and, before that, the Secret Police); in Uganda, during the reign of Idi Amin (1971–79), the secret police worked undercover as the *State Research Bureau*; in the sultanate of Oman, the secret police are known as the *Research Department*; in Guatemala operations of death squads in the early 1980s were coordinated by an agency known variously as the *Regional Telecommunications Center,* the *Presidential Special Services for Communications,* and, with a modicum of honesty, the *Regional Police*; in Panama, prior to Operation Just Cause, General Noriega's paramilitary squads were known as *Dignity Battalions,* and in Haiti, the military junta that interrupted (1991–94) the presidency of Jean-Bertrand Aristide employed *attachés,* so called because the gunmen were "attached" to the government.

See also COERCIVE DIPLOMACY, ECODEFENSE, FLYING FORTRESS, INTERNATIONAL MARITIME ORGANIZATION, PEACEKEEPER, and PREVENTIVE ACTION/DETENTION/WAR.

defer purchase. Sell! "And then there was Upjohn, the victim of . . . a William D. Witter decision to shift the stock into the 'defer purchase' category, which, in institutionalese, means 'sell quick'" (*Barron's,* 9/16/74). In this particular case, so many people *deferred purchase* that the stock dropped 13⅞ points within a week. See

also GROWTH STOCK, HOLD, NONPERFORMING ASSET, and RANGE FORWARD CONTRACT.

deferred compensation. Alimony. Women who oppose "alimony" because they do not like to think of themselves as living on payments from former husbands have been known to accept *deferred compensation* for their contributions to the home while married.

deficiency. Failure. Thus, a reader reported to the *Quarterly Review of Doublespeak* that her son brought home a note from school announcing that "there will be a modified English course offered for those children who achieve a deficiency in English" (4/86). The "modified" here also is worthy of note. In other words, the oxymoronic *deficient achievers* were to be offered a remedial course. See also DEFICIENT, NEEDS ASSESSMENT, and RETAIN.

deficient. Failing. After Texas enacted a law that prevented students with "F" grades from participating in extracurricular activities, Eddie Joseph, president of the state's High School Coaches Association, attempted an end run around the requirement with the assertion: "They're not failing; they're deficient at grading period" ("MacNeil-Lehrer NewsHour," 10/23/85). Meanwhile, some students may receive low marks because they are *motivationally deficient,* i.e., lazy. See also DEFICIENCY and NONPASSING.

dehire. Fire. "Fire is a rude word but the bouncing of the boss is happening now on such a large scale that Wall Street is mushrooming with firms bearing the weird names of 'Dehiring Consultants, Inc.' and 'Executive Adjustment Advisers.' Their function is to find painless ways of easing company presidents into 'early retirement.' In a depression, the boss is sacked and jumps from a window. In the 'recedence,' he is 'dehired'" (*Manchester Guardian Weekly*, 9/5/70). See also EARLY RETIREMENT, LET GO, and OUTPLACEMENT.

delicate. A dainty reference to a "sensitive" subject: If a woman is in a *delicate* (or *certain* or INTERESTING) *condition* or *state of health,* she is pregnant. "Delicate" flourished in America as a euphemism for pregnancy in the years following the Civil War (a.k.a. LATE UNPLEASANTNESS), according to H. L. Mencken (*The American Language,* 1936). The British also leaned on it: "Mrs. Micawber, being in a delicate state of health, was overcome by it" (Charles Dickens, *David Copperfield,* 1850). See also PREGNANT.

deliver. The proper military term for "drop," when the falling objects come from airplanes. Thus, deciphering the language of U.S. military briefers in Vietnam: "Planes do not drop bombs, they 'deliver ordnance'" (Sydney H. Schanberg, *New York Times Magazine,* 11/12/72). The euphemism operates on two levels, dulling the sense of physical impact of bombs upon people while implying that bombing is an exact business, akin to delivering mail or milk. (Bombers also travel on *milk runs.*) The technique of seeming to hit nothing but military targets is known as PRECISION BOMBING. See also ORDNANCE.

deluxe. A sumptuous euphemism for "first class," especially treasured by manufacturers and hotelkeepers who want to avoid assigning numbers to different models and kinds of accommodations, since this would result in such ignominious, hard-to-market

labels as "second class," "third class," and so on. The Frenchification seems to have been popularized by book publishers, who began offering *éditions de luxe* in the opening decades of the nineteenth century (1819, *OED*). It has been all downhill since. "*Deluxe* . . . means absolutely nothing today. It's like linguistic wallpaper, with one possible exception: 2,000 years hence, grammarians struggling to decipher our long-dead language will find themselves stuck on the meaning of this word. Finally will come a breakthrough. 'I've got it,' one will exult. 'What does it mean?' another will ask. 'With french fries!'" (Bruce Feirstein, *New York Observer,* 4/6/92). See also FIRST CLASS.

demise. Death. The term referred originally (and still does, technically) to the transfer of rights or an estate, usually the sovereignty or property of a monarch, and usually, but not necessarily, by death. Thus, the diarist John Evelyn could note in 1689, "That King James . . . had by demise abdicated himself and wholly vacated his right." The king in this case, James II, of Great Britain and Ireland, was still very much alive and would remain so until 1701. He had, however, fled to France and been replaced on the throne by William and Mary.

Today, "demise" frequently is used when referring to the doings of nonroyals, e.g., "Following the *demise* of her husband, Clara left on a round-the-world trip." While the *demise* may have made the trip possible, the main purpose of the term in such a context is merely to avoid mentioning "death." See also BITE THE DUST, DECEASED, and PASS AWAY.

demi-vierge. The French helps obscure the action, which is hot and heavy, the reference being to a woman whose amorous engagements are such that only on the thinnest of physiological technicalities can she still be called a virgin. (And even this is not complete guarantee against pregnancy; see PENETRATE/PENETRATION.) Once especially common among Roman Catholics, the *demi-vierge* is an endangered species now that most American RC's have parted company with the pope on the question of using artificial means of birth control. The *demi-vierge* should not be confused with the practitioner of *secondary virginity,* which is a woman whose policy is to just say "no," though she has said "yes" at least once in the past. See also DIE and PET.

democracy. Not necessarily democracy; sometimes dictatorship. From an interview over Polish state radio: "In this country for many years words have been deprived of their true meanings. The word 'democracy,' for example, meant the lack of democracy. 'Brotherly help' meant armed intervention. 'Security' was the scariest word I ever heard" (Jacek Kuron, *New Yorker,* 11/13/89). Then there was the mind-bending announcement of João Baptista Figueiredo, following his election as president of Brazil in 1979: "I intend to open this country up to democracy and anyone who is against that I will jail, I will crush." For this, he won a special award for the year's best foreign example of Doublespeak from the Committee on Public Doublespeak of the National Council of Teachers of English. See also PEOPLE'S REPUBLIC.

dentures. False teeth; sometimes further embellished as *artificial dentures* or *alternative dentation.* The Latinate *dentures* presumably makes their owner feel better about having to take them out at night. See also PROSTHESIS.

Nancy Mitford, in her famous essay "The English Aristocracy," in which she introduced the concepts of U (upper-class speech) and non-U to the English-speaking world, held that "*dentures* . . . and *glasses* for *spectacles* amount almost to non-U indicators" (*Noblesse Oblige,* 1956). What happens, according to Ms. Mitford, is that the poor non-U speaker continuously betrays his or her non-U-ness by a fatal tropism toward artificially refined and elegant language. For examples, see HOME, ILL, and SERVIETTE. Americans may take pride in knowing that the essence of Ms. Mitford's discussion of U-ness was anticipated by nearly 120 years by their own James Fenimore Cooper; see SABBATH.

departed. Dead, as in *the departed, the dear departed,* and *the departed one.* "Beth . . . sat making a winding-sheet, while the dear-departed [Pip, a canary] lay in the domino-box" (Louisa May Alcott, *Little Women,* 1871). For more about winding-sheets, continue with SLUMBER ROBE, and for a curious gnarl on the Alcott family tree, see ROOSTER.

"Departed" frequently is used in lieu of the DECEASED person's name, which is tabooed in this as well as other, more exotic cultures. Speaking of the Australian aborigines, for example: "The name of a dead person was not mentioned, for to do so would bring back the spirit which the name represented. . . . After Dawudi, the great artist of Milingimbi, died, I could not mention his name directly to his brother, Djawa, but was obliged to refer to him as '*bunakaka wawa,*' the departed one" (Louis A. Allen, *Time Before Morning,* 1975). A similar aborigine allusion, also mentioned by Allen, is "one gone."

The fear of naming certain names is so widespread as to be almost universal; see ADONAI; DEVIL, THE; and GRANDFATHER.

dependence. Addiction, as to drugs or alcohol. "I entered Long Beach [Naval Hospital's Alcohol and Drug Rehabilitation Service] to rid myself of dependence on drugs" (Betty Ford, *The Times of My Life,* 1978). See also CHEMICAL DEPENDENCY and SOLDIER'S DISEASE.

depopulate. To kill, especially large numbers of animals. After chicken flocks in Pennsylvania were infected with an influenza virus in 1983, the government conducted a *depopulation* program in which more than seven million birds were gassed to death. "We use that terrible word depopulation to avoid saying slaughter," explained David Goodman, a federal information officer (*Time,* 1/9/84). Another word for the mass destruction of chickens is *henicide.* See also CULL and SURPLUS.

derrière. The French, usually feminine, equivalent of the Latin, usually masculine, GLUTEUS MAXIMUS; the ass. "They snuggle close to your waist and hips, and hug your derrière" (ad for Gloria Vanderbilt jeans, WCBS-TV, NYC, 9/6/79). And in a masculine context: "When I quoted Herman J. Mankiewicz's famous line 'Imagine—the whole world wired to Harry Cohn's ass,' he insisted that it be 'Harry Cohn's derrière,'" —the "he" being *New Yorker* editor William Shawn, who eventually backed down in this instance (Pauline Kael, *Pauline Kael for Keeps,* 1994). Then there are SWINGING *derrières,* as in the following classified:

HARTFORD REBELLIOUS LADY WITH VERY SPANKABLE rounded derrière enjoys

reasonable bondage and discipline at the hands of an intell masculine partner. (*Ace,* undated, ca. 1976)

Derrière has been used as a euphemism for the ANGLO-SAXON word since at least the eighteenth century, with the earliest example in *The Oxford English Dictionary*'s 1972 supplement coming from a letter that was written in 1747. Naturally, being British, it also has to do with spanking: *"S'il fait le fier* [If he acts haughtily] . . . I shall give him several spanks upon his derrière." See also ARSE, CYA, and POSTERIORS.

descent with modification. Evolution. Publishers of some science texts have employed "descent with modification" and "diversity" as euphemisms for "evolution" in order to avoid controversies with religious detractors of Darwin (Jerry Resnick, panel, Authors Guild annual meeting, 2/23/83). In the meantime, the oxymoronic "scientific creationists," have come up with "intelligent-design theory," as exemplified in a text, *Of Pandas and People* (1989). The name of the "intelligent agent" who created the "design" is left to the student's imagination (*Wall Street Journal,* 11/14/94). Only time and the courts will tell whether or not this approach satisfies the requirements of a 1987 Supreme Court decision that allows public schools to present alternatives to Darwin's theory but bars them from teaching religious-based creationism.

deselect. To select out, as from a job; to fire. An ex–Peace Corps member reminisces: "I couldn't help recalling my own experience in the Peace Corps in Malawi. Nowhere else can a person be fired by being told he has been 'selected out' or 'deselected'" (*Time,* 10/3/69). The "nowhere else" isn't quite right, however. "Members of [the British] Parliament who fail to get re-elected are 'deselected'" (*Quarterly Review of Doublespeak*, 1/92). See also LET GO.

detain. To imprison. "Queripel's trial [in 1955] lasted only five minutes, and he was sentenced to be 'detained during Her Majesty's pleasure,' a phrase that meant life imprisonment" (Colin Wilson, *Written in Blood*, 1989). See also BOOKED FOR INVESTIGATION and DETAINEE.

detainee. A prisoner; a person in DETENTION. As a rule, *detainees* (sometimes called *restrictees*) are held for political rather than criminal reasons, e.g., from the Republic of South Africa: "Mr. [Steven] Biko was the 45th political detainee to die in the hands of the security police" (*New York Times*, 9/20/77).

The United States also has employed this euphemism. After the invasion of Grenada in 1983, the American military locked up some 1,100 people who had opposed—or were thought to have opposed—the operation. Lacking legal authority for this sweep, the State Department felt compelled to deny that anyone had been arrested. "We are detaining people," said a Department official. "They should be described as detainees" (*Quarterly Review of Doublespeak*, 1/85). See also DETAIN and INTERN.

detention. Arrest and imprisonment without formal charges, often for political reasons. The prison or other enclosure (football stadiums and other buildings occasionally are pressed into service) in which the DETAINEES are confined usually is described as a *detention camp, detention center,* or *detention facility*. The inmates fequently are said to be in *administrative detention*; for example, this was the phrase used by United Nations forces when rounding up Somalis in 1993 and by the Israeli army when arresting militant settlers on the West Bank in 1994. A variant is *custodial detention,* as in, from *New York Post* columnist James A. Wechsler's report on his FBI dossier: "My file reveals that from June 1942 until February 1945, I was on the FBI director's list of Americans targeted for 'custodial detention'" (*New York Post*, 1/4/77). See also CONCENTRATION CAMP, INTERN, PREVENTIVE DETENTION, and PROTECTIVE CUSTODY.

deuce. The Devil, Satan; probably from *deuce,* two, an unlucky throw at dice, perhaps with reinforcement from the Teutonic *duus,* again an unlucky throw at dice and also the Devil. "The deuce we are!" (Owen Johnson, *Stover at Yale,* 1931). And in a variant spelling from *Tom Thumb's Pretty Song Book* (ca. 1744):

> The Wheelbarrow broke
> And give my Wife a fall,
> The duce take
> Wheelbarrow, Wife & all.

"Deuce" doubles as a euphemism for "damn"; see DARN as well as DEVIL, THE.

develop/development. Women and real estate may be said to be *undeveloped, underdeveloped, developing, well-developed,* and *overdeveloped*. In any case, the process is *development*. Great minds are able to reflect upon both topics simultaneously, e.g., "Being Ambassador to India is the nearest thing yet devised to a male chastity belt. But one can still gaze wistfully, leading to the law: 'The more underdeveloped the country, the more overdeveloped the women'" (John Kenneth Galbraith, *Ambassador's Journal,* 1969).

The basic image is by no means new. As Dr. Squills observed of Becky Sharp: "Green eyes, fair skin, pretty figure, famous frontal development" (William Makepeace Thackeray, *Vanity Fair,* 1848). John O'Hara may have had this one in mind when he had a young woman in *Ten North Frederick* (1955) tell a friend, "Oh, she said to me, 'You know you have glorious fronts.'"

In the case of real estate, the positive "develop" helps mask a frequently execrable process, as in "Hogarth's house in Chiswick . . . will probably be purchased by a builder who will do what is called develop the property; we all know pretty well what that means" (London *Times,* 11/6/01). The result of the act of *development* is, inevitably, a *development,* also called a *project,* both terms applying to a variety of structures, including large groupings of ticky-tacky houses as well as neo-Stalinist apartment buildings. See also DEVELOPING, ECODEFENSE, ENCLAVE, GREENLAND, and REALTOR.

developing. Poor, backward, primitive, when applied to countries (as opposed to women, for which see DEVELOP/DEVELOPMENT). In its national, economic sense, "developing" is a third-order euphemism. It replaced UNDERDEVELOPED, which was marginally kinder than "undeveloped," which, in turn, was gentler than the original "poor," "backward," or "primitive." "Developing" also won out over "emerging" and "fledgling" ("fledgling nation" is attributed to Eleanor Roosevelt). In time, as the gloss wears off, developing probably will be replaced by some other, fourth-order euphemism, such as the relatively opaque LDC (Less- or Lesser-Developed Country).

For the domestic equivalent of the international developing, see DISADVANTAGED.

developmentally delayed/disabled/handicapped. Retarded, slow; an optimistic reference to mental development that may occur but—then again—may not. Thus, speaking of changes in nomenclature and practice at the Southbury, Conn., Training School: "The original residents were inappropriately labeled 'idiots' or 'imbeciles.' Clients or residents now are termed developmentally handicapped, and their treatment over the last half century has been more humanized, with emphasis on what can be accomplished by residents, and on integrating a large portion of the population into the community" (Woodbury, Conn., *Voices,* 9/26/90). In other states, such as New York, the Southbury institution would be classed as a *developmental center.* See also EXCEPTIONAL.

device. A bomb. *Devices* come in all sizes. On the lower end of the scale is the 4.5-pound *entry device* that the Philadelphia police dropped on May 13, 1985, on the roof of a house full of anarchists. This started a fire that killed eleven people, devastated two entire blocks, and left some three hundred people homeless. (The plan for evicting the radicals from the house was "perfect, except for the fire," opined Mayor W. Wilson Goode.)

Most *devices* are much larger. For example, James Bond speaking: "He's given you a bomb." Goldfinger: "I prefer to call it an atomic device" (*Goldfinger,* film, 1964). On the upper end of the explosive spectrum, a bomb may be further disguised as a *low-yield thermonuclear device, peaceful nuclear device* (India detonated one of the latter in 1974), or *five-megaton device* (where *megaton* helps muffle "one million tons of TNT"). The explosive core of such a *device* is known to the technicians who assemble (and disassemble) the objects at the Pantex plant near Amarillo, Texas, as the *physics package*. And talking about the way people talk at the headquarters for American bomb-makers in Los Alamos, New Mexico: "An explosion, however large, was a 'shot.' The word 'bomb' was almost never used. A bomb was a 'device' or a 'gadget.' Language could hide what the sky could not. The Los Alamos Scientific Laboratory was 'the Ranch.' Often, it was simply called 'the Hill.' An implosion bomb was made with 'ploot'" (John McPhee, *The Curve of Binding Energy*, 1974).

See also ENHANCED RADIATION WEAPON, GADGET, MININUKE, SPECIAL NUCLEAR MATERIALS, and, for a certifiably mad bomb-maker whose language paralleled that of the certifiably sane ones in Los Alamos, refer to UNIT.

Devil, the. Satan. There are (or are said to be) many devils—Beelzebub, Belial, Mephistopheles, et al.—but the generic term usually is used for Satan, on the theory that it is safer not to mention his real name. As the saying goes: Speak of the *Devil* and he appears.

"He's full of the Old Scratch, but . . . I ain't got the heart to lash him, somehow" (Aunt Polly, in Mark Twain's *The Adventures of Tom Sawyer*, 1876). Of course, "Old Scratch" (from the Old Norse *scratle*, a wizard, goblin, or monster) is only one of many possibilities for the faint of heart. "If you are in Scotland, you call him Clootie or Auld Hornie; in Germany, Meister Peter; in the Shetlands, da black tief; in England, Old Nick; in New England, the Deuce [see DEUCE] or The Old Boy Himself" (Maria

Leach, ed., *Funk & Wagnalls Dictionary of Folklore, Mythology, and Legend*, 1972). Still other alternatives include *The Adversary, The Archfiend* (also *The Fiend* or *Foul Fiend), The Black One, The Dark Stranger, The Evil One, The Good Man, The Great Fellow, The Old Gentleman (in Black), Old Harry, Old Ned, The Old One* (dated to before 1000, as *se ealda*, which means "Old One" in Old English), *Old Red, Old Rip, Old Sam, The Tempter*, and the more prosaic *Bad Guy*, e.g., quoting a resident of New Milford, Conn.: "The problem is there are two kinds of supernatural: the supernatural from God and the supernatural from the Bad Guy" (*Litchfield County*, Conn., *Times*, 12/18/92).

As an interjection, too, "Satan" is euphemized as *the dickens*, e.g., "I cannot tell what the dickens his name is . . ." (William Shakespeare, *The Merry Wives of Windsor*, 1599?). The taboo against naming Satan is carried all the way to its illogical conclusion by the Yezidis, a religious sect of Iran, Armenia, and the Caucasus, who call their devil *Peacock* because that word, in their language, sounds least like his real name. For similar supernatural euphemisms and circumlocutions, see ADONAI; DASH; DEPARTED; GRANDFATHER; and SCOTTISH PLAY, THE.

dick. The penis and, by extension, its use in sex, as in the graffito from the 1970s, "Dick Nixon before he dicks you." The term is dated to 1888 in the *Random House Historical Dictionary of American Slang*, but is certainly much older. For example, consider the plays on the nickname of Martin Van Buren's vice president, Richard M. Johnson, after word got around that he kept a young black slave as his mistress (she succeeded her sister, who had been sold on account of infidelity): "Halstead of New Jersey attacked the administration in 1838 in a speech filled with complicated puns directed at Dickie Johnson, saying meaningfully that 'the Democrats had turned dandies,' and that 'the dandies had a great liking for *dickies*,' and that the '*dickies* had a close affinity to *darkies* or *blackies*'" (Arthur Schlesinger, Jr., *The Age of Jackson*, 1945).

Various etymologies for the sexual "dick" have been suggested, including (1) that it was spawned by the notably well endowed DONKEY, commonly called *donkey dick* in the eighteenth century; (2) that it derives from the name of the large movable boom, a *derrick*, in turn from an older hoisting device, the gallows, also called a *derrick*, after the Derick, or Derrick, who operated the gallows at Tyburn in Elizabeth I's reign; (3) that it is a survival of the Middle English *dighten*, to copulate, where "he dight her" would have been pronounced "he dicked her"; and (4) that it is simply a rhyme on *prick*. Whatever the source, the continuing popularity of the term is in keeping with—and certainly was reinforced by—the tendency to bestow personal names on the PENIS. See also JOHN THOMAS, PETER, and ROGER.

diddle. To accomplish the sex act (see INTERCOURSE); to masturbate, oneself or another, especially a woman ("to digitate sexually and successfully," as Eric Partridge put it in *A Dictionary of Slang and Unconventional English*). In the primary sense, herewith no. 293 in G. Legman's monumental collection (1,700 examples), *The Limerick* (1969):

> There was a young man with a fiddle
> Who asked his girl, "Do you diddle?"
> She replied, "Yes, I do,
> But prefer to with two—
> It's twice as much fun in the middle."

While *diddle* dates to the nineteenth century as schoolboy slang for the PENIS, the sexual senses of the word may actually derive from its aboveground meanings, including "to jerk back and forth," "to waste time," and "to cheat." Certainly, the conjunction in related words of the ideas of sex, sharp motion, wasting time, and cheating is fairly common. See also FIRK, FRIG, MASTURBATION, and SCREW.

diddly-poo. Diddly-shit, the *poo* being an example of children's potty talk carried over into the adult world (see also WEE-WEE). *Diddly-poo* turns up in the oddest places . . . such as the convention of the Associated Press Managing Editors Association, where one hard-bitten newspaper executive opined: "A lot of our guys are small-town editors who don't know diddly-poo about Washington or Watergate" ([MORE], 12/73). Marginally stronger variants include *diddly-squat* and *doodly-* or *doodley-squat*, where the "squat" is at once a positional reference and a phonetic substitute. See also DEFECATE/DEFECATION and POOP.

die. To experience sexual orgasm; a predecessor of the modern COME. "Die" was much favored by poets, who made many plays on it. For example, from the works of John Donne (pre-1631):

> Wee can dye by it, if not
> live by love.
> —"The Canonization"

> Wee dye but once, and who lov'd
> last did die.
> —"The Paradox"

And from Alexander Pope's *The Rape of the Lock* (1712–14):

Nor feared the Chief th'unequal
    fight to try,
Who sought no more than on his
    foe to die.

Then there is the quatrain by Matthew Prior (1664–1721) about a DEMI-VIERGE (giving her the benefit of the doubt), which is still omitted from most collections of early English verse:

No, no; for my Virginity,
    When I lose that, says Rose, I'll die;
Behind the elms, last Night, cry'd Dick,
    Rose, were you not extremely sick?

The metaphor remains current (re the lyric in the pop hit "Annie's Song": "Come, let me love you . . . Let me die in your arms").

"Die" epitomizes the set of associations between sex, death, and violence. See also ACTION, GUN, OFF, and WEAPON, as well as, for nonsexual dying, PASS AWAY.

diet. Die; a nonce use too good not to mention. Complaints about the title of the 1991 film *The Pope Must Die* led the distributor to change it to *The Pope Must Diet.* For more about film titles, see FANNY.

differently (or otherly) abled. Handicapped. "He asserts that . . . if we are ready to call a handicapped person 'differently abled,' then we should be willing to label the dull-witted 'differently smart'" (*New York Times,* review of *In Defense of Elitism* by William A. Henry III, 9/26/94). See also DIFFERING ABILITIES.

differently pleasured. Sadomasochistic, perverse. See also ALTERNATE SEXUAL PREFERENCE.

differently sized. Fat. *People of size,* as they are also called, may be said to be *differently sized.* Discrimination against the *differently sized* is called *sizism.* People who are sensitive to the nuances of such words as "fat" (and "svelte," for that matter) are commendably *nonsizist.* See also KING-SIZE, LARGE, QUEEN-SIZE, and SIZE TEN.

differing abilities. Disabled, handicapped, crippled. "People with differing abilities" was the prizewinning ($50,000!) entry in a 1991 contest sponsored by the National Cristina Foundation to find a positive substitute for "disabled, etc." The winner was B. Freer Freeman, a teacher of SPECIAL education in Virginia.

The DIFFERENTLY ABLED don't much like politically correct euphemisms, however, and they nearly laughed the winning phrase out of court. "Perhaps it was invented by someone with a linguistic disability," said Paul Longmore, a historian and visiting scholar at Stanford University, who had polio as a child (*Philadelphia Inquirer,* 10/19/92). See also DISABILITY, DISABLED, HANDI-CAPABLE, and PHYSICALLY CHALLENGED.

dildo. An imitation erect penis. The term enjoyed something of a vogue as a euphemism several centuries ago, when it was employed commonly in ballads, with more than one meaning in mind, e.g., from William Shakespeare's *The Winter's Tale* (1610–11):

He has the prettiest love songs for maids so without bawdry, which is strange, with such delicate burdens of dildos and fadings, "jump her and thump her."

The origin of "dildo" is obscure. The name of the instrument bears a suspicious resemblance to the name of the dildo bush or tree, an exotic plant that is rather thin and grows straight up, ten or twelve feet high. Likelier possibilities, though, are that the term is either a corruption of "diddle" or of the object's name in Italian, *diletto* (delight). In this connection, it seems significant that the English associated both word and device with Italy from an early date. For example, one of the most charming poems of John Wilmot, second earl of Rochester, tells of the popularity of an Italian gentleman, a certain "Signior Dildo," with the ladies of Charles II's court. Written in December 1673, the poem may have been inspired by the discovery a couple years earlier of a shipment of dildos by customs men, who proceeded to confiscate and burn the nasty foreign items. Nell Gwynne, most famous of the king's mistresses, was among those memorialized:

The countess o' the' Cockpit (Who knows
  not her name?
She's famous in story for a killing
  dame),
When all her old lovers forsake her, I
  trow
She'll then be contented with Signior
  Dildo.

(The Cockpit, a part of Whitehall Palace, included a theater where Ms. Gwynne, who first attracted public attention as an actress, presumably appeared. Rochester intended this poem for the king, but slipped up when delivering it to him; see MEMBER.)

In Italy, the gadget also is called a *passatempo*, or "pass the time," while the French have termed it variously a *godemiché*, from the Latin for "enjoy myself"; a *bientateur*, or "do-gooder," and a *consolateur*,

which should require no explanation. By whatever name, the origins of the instrument are decently lost in the mists of time. From the Bible (Ezekiel 16:17): "Thou has also taken thy fair jewels of my gold and silver, which I had given thee, and madest to thyself images of men, and didst commit whoredom with them."

See also CORDLESS MASSAGE, FRIG, the Shakespearean JUMP, MASTURBATION, and, for more about "whoredom," Noah Webster's handling of that term in PECULIAR MEMBERS.

ding. To kill. "Gibson Hand went to work on surveillance and drew a hot assignment and got to ding some people his first week" (Joseph Wambaugh, *The Glitter Dome*, 1981).

This sense of "ding" seems to have been popularized by the U.S. military in Vietnam, where "ding team" was another name for a "kill team," a.k.a. *Katy* or *KT*, a sniper team composed of two scouts who alternated as spotter and shooter. The deathly sense is in keeping with the word's oldest meanings (pre-1300), involving a heavy blow, a knock, a thump, or a series of such buffets in the phrase "to ding to death." The term has the same euphemistic quality as HIT, which, as it happens, was used in the same way in Vietnam, where *ding teams* also were called *hit teams*.

As a noun, "ding" may also refer to the penis. This sense might stem from any of several factors or some combination of them, i.e., from DING-A-LING below; from the association of *ding* with the penile DONG; or from the old meanings of a heavy blow, etc., since the penis often is portrayed semantically as a WEAPON.

ding-a-ling. The PENIS; adult potty talk. "Lines such as 'I like to play with my ding-a-ling' . . . are intended as deliberate stimulation to self and mutual masturbation" (London *Daily Telegraph,* 11/17/72). *Ding-a-ling* is only the most infantile of a series of related D-words with this same meaning, e.g., DICK, DING, *dingbat, dingdong, dingus, dingwallace,* DONG, *doodad, doodle* (see TIMBERDOODLE), DOOHICKEY, and DOOJIGGER. For more about potty talk, see WEE-WEE.

direct flight. In the airline business, "direct flight" is the indirect way of saying that the airplane you're on will make one or more stops before reaching its final destination. The route will not be the same that a crow would use and passengers may be required to change EQUIPMENT along the way. See also WATER LANDING.

direct mail. Unsolicited mail or, descending one more notch toward reality, junk mail, a.k.a. *bulk mail.* Obviously, "direct mail" has a happier ring to the people in the business, e.g., the members of the Direct Mail-Marketing Association, especially when they are lobbying in Congress for favorable postal rates for junk mail.

directory assistance. The telephone company used to call it "information." See also COIN TELEPHONE ENCLOSURE and SERVICE, NO LONGER IN.

disability. A handicap. The landmark legislation in the field is the Americans With Disabilities Act of 1991. "Disability" has gained favor as many people with impediments have revolted against traditional stereotypes that cast them in meek, passive, dependent roles in society. "I find references to 'the handicapped' offensive. While I have a severe disability, I have never considered myself handicapped" (Deborah Livesey, letter, *New York Times,* 10/10/91).

Some of the more militant persons with *disabilities* are even attempting to reclaim "cripple," on the theory that the blunter word forces society to confront them as individuals. So many changes already have been made in terminology, however—e.g., the Institute for the Crippled and Disabled, now called the Institute for the Chronically Disabled—that it is hard to imagine the linguistic pendulum swinging back in this direction very soon. See also DIFFERING ABILITIES and DISABLED.

disabled. Handicapped, crippled. "The preferred term is 'disabled,' which has replaced 'handicapped' in recent years and is the first such word to emerge by consensus from disabled people themselves. More acceptable still is 'person with a disability' (or 'who is blind,' 'who has mental retardation' and so on) since it emphasizes the individual before the condition" (Joseph P. Shapiro, *Washington Post,* 8/25/91). It follows from this change in nomenclature that the *disabled*—or, softer yet, the *otherly abled*—often refer to those without handicaps as *TABs* (i.e., temporarily able-bodied).

Adoption of "disabled" merely represents a revival of a standard sense of the word. *The Oxford English Dictionary* includes examples of its use in the sense of incapacitation, especially from physical injury, beginning with Wynkyn de Worde's translation of William Caxton's *Vitas Patrum:* "I am all dysabled of my membres" (1491).

See also COURTESY CHAIR, DIFFERING ABILITIES, DISABILITY, INCONVENIENCED, NONDISABLED, and PHYSICALLY CHALLENGED.

disadvantaged. Poor. Sometimes fancied up into *culturally disadvantaged* or *socially disadvantaged,* this is basically the domestic equivalent of the international DEVELOPING. "Poor children have disappeared, if not from the slums, then at least from the language. First, they became 'deprived,' then 'disadvantaged,' and finally 'culturally disadvantaged,' as though they lacked nothing more serious than a free pass to Lincoln Center" (Grace Hechinger, *Wall Street Journal*, 10/27/71). Jules Feiffer broke the progression into even finer gradations in a 1965 cartoon strip in which a *poor* man went from being *needy* to *deprived* to *underprivileged* to *disadvantaged*, winding up broke but with "a GREAT vocabulary" (*New York Post*, 2/17/1965). See also CULTURALLY DEPRIVED, LOW-INCOME, RETENTION, and UNDERPRIVILEGED.

disappear. To kidnap and kill, especially in Central and South America, where, as Joan Didion pointed out in *Salvador* (1983), Spanish-speakers use *disappear* as a transitive verb, as in "The government disappeared the students." Unfortunately, *disappearances* of this sort are not confined to the New World. Speaking of Idi Amin: "I want to confirm here and now that indeed you are personally responsible for the liquidation of all the people who have disappeared in Uganda since you came to power" (Manume Kibedi, former Ugandan minister of foreign affairs, 1974 letter in *New York Times*, 3/4/77). And from the Ivory Coast: "A child reported as having disappeared [on the necrology page of the newspaper] was presumed to have been sacrificed" (V. S. Naipaul, *New Yorker*, 5/14/84). Going back into the 1960s, Charles Dillon (Casey) Stengel also employed the verb transitively, referring to ballplayers who drank too much: "When I had one of these boys I said, 'Well, this man is limited. If he don't want to change, why,

disappear him'" (in Robert Creamer, *Stengel: His Life and Times*, 1984). Casey got rid of unwanted players without killing them, however, and he himself was *disappeared* more than once. See DISCHARGE and RETIRE.

discharge. Cannons are "fired" as well as "discharged"—and so are people. In both cases, the longer, less active word softens the action in much the same way as DELIVER does for "drop." As New York Yankee manager Casey Stengel told the Subcommittee on Antitrust and Monopoly of the Senate Judiciary Committee on July 9, 1958: "I became a major league manager in several cities and was discharged. We call it discharged because there was no question I had to leave." See also DISAPPEAR and RETIRE.

discomfort. Pain. When a dentist asks "Are you experiencing any discomfort?" what he really means is "Am I hurting you?" But the question probably is rhetorical, because your mouth is full of hardware and you can't reply anyway. See also MOTION DISCOMFORT.

disinvestment. Mealymouthed banker's code for the more vivid "redlining," itself financial jargon for the refusal to give mortgages or write insurance policies in city neighborhoods (usually demarcated by zip codes) that have changed, or are in the process of changing, racially and economically (white to nonwhite and middle class to DISADVANTAGED). Reporting on hearings of the Senate Banking Committee: "Both industry and government witnesses steered away from using the term redlining, preferring to talk about 'disinvestment,' an Orwellian term meaning the same thing" (*New Republic*, 6/21/75).

127

dislocate. To fire from a job, especially because the employer is moving to a new location. "Yet there is a work force out there . . . Many of them bought cars, houses and consumer goods, until they found themselves unemployed (or, as today's euphemism has it, 'dislocated')" (Robert Wechsler, letter, *New York Times*, 5/5/83). See also LET GO.

dispatch. To kill. Almost from the time the word came into the English language in the early sixteenth century, it has been used both in the sense of sending someone or something (as a message) off, posthaste, and in the sense of sending someone off, permanently. See also DECEASED, DISPOSE, and HIT.

disperse. To scatter by shooting; a governmental euphemism from the late nineteenth century. "To an observer of languages, it is interesting to note the new signification of the word *disperse*: that when a Black girl is shot down she is said to be *dispersed*" (*The Australian Race,* 1887, in Tom McArthur, ed., *The Oxford Companion to the English Language,* 1992). See also HIT.

dispose. To kill, *get rid of,* or ACCOUNT FOR. *Dispose* is so opaque that its meaning depends largely upon the context in which it is used. And even when the context is known, the term still can be hard to decipher, as pointed out by the CIA inspector general in a 1967 internal report that was cited by the Senate Intelligence Committee in its 1975 report on United States plots to assassinate foreign leaders. Addressing a common feature of euphemisms and doubletalk, the inspector general noted:

The point is that of frequent resort to synecdoche—the mention of a part when the whole is to be understood, or vice versa. Thus, we encounter repeated references to phrases such as "disposing of Castro," which may be read in the narrow, literal sense of assassinating him, when it is intended that it be read in the broader, figural sense of dislodging the Castro regime. Reversing the coin, we find people speaking vaguely of "doing something about Castro" when it is clear that what they have specifically in mind is killing him. In a situation wherein those speaking may not have actually meant what they seemed to say or may not have said what they actually meant, they should not be surprised if their oral shorthand is interpreted differently than it was intended.

In this linguistic morass, high presidential advisers were able to maintain that their bosses never understood from conversations with the CIA that murder was intended, while lower-level CIA officers could assert—as did William Harvey, testifying before the Senate committee in 1975—that they believed their plots had been authorized "at every appropriate level within and beyond the Agency." ("Beyond the Agency" here is a euphemism for "President, the.") See also ASSASSINATION, HIT, TERMINATE/TERMINATION, and, for one of the CIA's cleverer methods of *disposing* of someone, NONDISCERNIBLE MICROBIONOCULATOR.

disturbance. A riot, a.k.a. *disorder.* "The violence—and counterviolence by South African security forces—spread to other black ghettos. By the time the 'disturbances' subsided in December, 618 had died" (*Time*, 6/27/77). "The disturbances which took a toll of 72 lives in the Union of South Africa on March 21 should be viewed in proper perspective" (press release, Information Service of South Africa, 3/28/60). See also ABERRATION.

do. This versatile verb serves as euphemistic shorthand in a variety of constructions, including *do away with, do in*, and *do for*, all meaning "to kill" or "do to death," as well as *do (someone)*, meaning either "to cheat, rob, or beat (someone)" or, in another context, "to do sex (with someone)." This is another of the many terms that combine senses of violence and sex (see ACTION) as well as cheating and sex (see DIDDLE). In street talk, the simple "do" may serve either purpose, e.g., "David kept nagging him, saying, 'This is your chance to do Rev'" (and Rev was later *done* with a .25-caliber pistol, *New York Times*, 5/17/94), and then again, quoting a New York City detective's testimony about a gang rape, "He said that while Steve Ross was on top of her, doing her, he got sick of looking at her face and raised a brick and prepared to smash her face" (*New York Times*, 11/28/90).

The various euphemistic meanings of "do" have been in place for a while. The senses of killing, hoaxing, and cheating have been dated to the seventeenth century and the sexual sense to the sixteenth. The last form of "do" may be shorthand for "do the act of darkness" or "do the deed." (See also ACT, THE and DEED.) Shakespeare knew the word's sexual meanings and employed it in the modern manner in several plays. Thus, in *Titus Andronicus* (1598–94), after Tamora, Queen of the Goths, gives birth to a child by the Moor, Aaron, the queen's sons are properly outraged, leading to the following exchange:

DEMETRIUS: Villain, what hast thou done?
AARON: That which thou canst not undo.
CHIRON: Thou hast undone our mother.
AARON: Villain, I have done thy mother.

doctor. The title comes from the Latin *docere*, to teach, which is something very few *doctors* do. Associated most often with the medical profession, because this is the kind of *doctor* most people see most often, the title becomes ever more euphemistic as it is stretched further to cover ministers and lawyers, as well as chiropractors, naturopaths, and other medical practitioners who may or may not have university degrees.

"There are thousands of protestant ministers whom you'd damn well better address as 'Doctor,' including Billy Graham, Norman Vincent Peale, almost every quack evangelist, and even in some small towns where the Service Board on the church lawn heralds its minister as D.D., Ll. D. . . . The status of that Doctorate to a parish is considerable" (letter, 10/10/91, from Hartzell Spence, son of a Protestant minister, and author of *One Foot in Heaven*, 1940). This is not a new phenomenon: "Why take you no Notice of Sow-gelders and Farriers that take the Title of *Doctor*?" (*New-England Courant*, 12/23–30/1723).

The term also has its euphemistic uses as a verb. Thus, to *doctor* a record is to tamper with it, to falsify it, perhaps in order to SANITIZE it. Then there is the kind of *doctoring* that is sometimes done to male animals even though they are not sick, e.g., "It is necessary . . . to have your male cat doctored when he arrives at the years of discretion" (F. Simpson, *Cats*, 1902). See also ALTER and, for more about the use and abuse of titles, COLONEL, ENGINEER, and HONORABLE.

document. A piece of paper that has been sanctified by a bureaucrat. "When does a sheet of paper metamorphose into a document? . . . Documents are only papers, sometimes classified, or overclassified" (Edwin Newman, *Strictly Speaking*, 1974). In line with this, a *document retention program* is a system for getting rid of old papers and an UNDOCUMENTED WORKER is one without papers. An *energy document* is a monthly utility bill (as from Pacific Gas and Electric Co.). The British have a better word for bureaucratic papers, and the word is *bumf*; see BATHROOM TISSUE.

documentation. Instructions, especially in the computer-program business.

dog dirt/do/litter/waste. By any other name, dog shit smells the same. "The Dog Control Committee of the Carl Schurz Park Association has organized to try to solve the 'dog dirt' problem in their park" (*New York Times*, 2/1/76). This problem also was addressed by Section 1310 of the New York State Public Health Law, which went into effect on August 1, 1978, and required people to clean up after their pets, with the threat of a $100 fine per offense. The statute was variously described, depending on what day you read the *Times*, as the "'canine waste' law" (7/23/78), or the "'Canine Litter Law'" (8/1/78). London has a similar law on the books, with a fine for permitting a dog to "foul the footpaths." See also ACCIDENT, COMFORT STATION, DEED, DROPPINGS, LITTER, MESS, NUISANCE, and WASTE.

doggone. Goddam, itself a euphemistic spelling of the eschatological "God damn." "Doggone" seems to be a genuine mid-nineteenth-century Americanism, but no one is sure of its immediate antecedents. One theory is that it comes from the Scotch *dagone* (gone to the dogs); another is that it is a compression of "dog on it" (similar to the older "pox on it"). Note, too, that "God" spelled backward is "dog." The most likely explanation, however, is that this is just another example of the tropism that English speakers have toward "D" sounds when devising ways to water down their oaths and imprecations, e.g., DAD, DANG, and DARN. See also ADONAI, GEE, GOSH, and HECK.

domestic. A diplomatic condensation of "domestic servant," the "servant" part having become anathema in the early nineteenth century through overuse as a euphemism for "slave." *Domestic* is less common in Britain than the United States, judging from Graham Greene's *The End of the Affair* (film, 1955):

> "We've been able to make contact with the domestic."
> "The what?"
> "The maid, sir."

Note that the verb "domesticate," as commonly applied to plants and animals, carries the same euphemistic connotations as does "domestic" when applied to humans, e.g., "More than nearly any other animal, the raccoon has managed to coexist with man without becoming domesticated, i.e., enslaved" (*Smithsonian*, 8/79). See also HELP, HOUSEKEEPER, MAID, and SERVANT.

donation. A payment, not a true gift. For example, *donations* frequently are requested by organizations and businesses that have legal reasons for not wanting to charge "fees" for the goods or services they provide. Thus, a museum may ask for a *donation* instead of charging for admission, and a bar that is operating as a CLUB may ask for *donations* for drinks. The practice seems to be universal. In India, for example, it is reported that "many prestigious educational institutions in Kerala collect a sum of money as a bribe from every one who seeks admission to them. But a bribe to an institution is called a donation and by calling it that bribing has become a nonobjectionable practice" (George John, "The Land of Euphemism," *Indian Express* [Bombay], 8/3/79). Of course, American colleges and institutions never, never use *donation* in this manner. See also COMMISSION and CONTRIBUTION.

dong. The penis. "I was wholly incapable of keeping my paws off my dong" (Philip Roth, *Portnoy's Complaint,* 1969). Though admissible in publications for adults, the term appeared rarely if ever in newspapers or the electronic media prior to the Senate Judiciary Committee hearings of October 11–13, 1991, when Long Dong Silver, the stage name of a featured actor in pornographic films of the 1970s and early 1980s, figured in the charges of sexual harassment that Ms. Anita Hill brought against Judge Clarence Thomas, then being considered for elevation to the Supreme Court of the United States. Dating from the nineteenth century, "dong" is of mysterious provenance. Perhaps it alludes to the clapper of a bell—the *dong* that goes DING (in the sense of a heavy blow)—or it may simply be another example of the use of D-words for this anatomical organ; see DING-A-LING for others.

donkey. Ass. "C'mon, get your donkey over here" (an example of Clark Gable's "rough talk," according to Yvonne De Carlo, "Gable: The King Remembered," WNET, 11/12/88). Hereby hangs a tale:

The beast's original name (from the Latin *asinus*) was contaminated by the change in the pronunciation of the anatomical "arse," whose "r" was dropped in the sixteenth and seventeenth centuries, so that it sounded the same as the animal's name. (See ARSE for details.) This didn't matter much until about the middle of the eighteenth century, when society started to become more refined. Then people began to shy away from saying the name of the animal because of the bad anatomical thoughts that the word conjured up in their minds. As Capt. Francis Grose explained in *A Classical Dictionary of the Vulgar Tongue* (1785), a "Johnny Bum" was "A he or jack ass, so called by a lady that affected to be extremely polite and would not say jack because it was vulgar, nor ass because it was indecent."

Obviously, a new name was needed for the barnyard animal, which is how "donkey" came onto the linguistic scene. The oldest example of the word in *The Oxford English Dictionary* also comes from Grose, who included an imaginative etymology for the then new word in his 1785 work: "DONKEY, DONKEY DICK. A he, or jack ass: called donkey, perhaps, from the Spanish or don-like gravity of that animal, intitled also the king of Spain's trumpeter." Likelier explanations (all guesses) are that "donkey" comes from "dun," the color, plus "key" (a parallel to "monkey"), or that it represents a familiar form of Duncan (from the Gaelic for "brown head"), one of the personal names (Dicky, Jenny, Neddy were others) commonly bestowed by farmers upon their asses. Whatever the source, by the middle of the nineteenth century, if not before, "donkey" was the word that most nice people used most of the time, except in Ireland, where "ass" was kept, and in Scotland, where the ass was called "cuddie," perhaps from another personal name, Cuthbert. In the case of male donkeys, the "ass" might also be obscured to varying degrees by calling the critter a *jackass, jassack, jack,* or, quaintest of all, *John Donkey,* e.g., "Some one passed the road with a long-eared animal, politely called a John Donkey" (Harden E. Taliaferro, *Fisher's River* [North Carolina] *Scenes and Characters,* 1859).

See also BOTTOM, SMART WEED, and, for the richly euphemistic subject of animal names, begin with ROOSTER.

doodle. (1) A simpleton; (2) a penis, especially a child's; (3) a haystack, especially in midwestern states. The first sense seems to be the oldest (1628, *OED*). The origin of the word is uncertain, but it parallels the Low German *Dudeltopf,* also a simpleton. Use of the same term to denote a penis and a dolt is not unusual. Other words that have acquired both meanings, also from German as it happens (via Yiddish), include "putz" and "schmuck" (see SCHMO).

The penile sense of "doodle" was in place at least by the late eighteenth century. Capt. Francis Grose included "doodle" as a "child's penis"—along with "doodle sack," meaning a bagpipe, but also "the private parts of a woman"—in the 1788 edition of *A Classical Dictionary of the Vulgar Tongue.* The association with a haystack shows up in the same decade in Joseph Atkinson's play *A Match for a Widow,* in which an American character claims that his countrymen are "chaste in their thoughts" and think "a *doodle of hay,* more decent than to call a thing a *cock of hay.*" The *doodle of hay,* also called a *doodle bug* or simply a *doodle,* is another example of the great pre-Victorian

cleanup of the language in general and of the barnyard in particular; see also DONKEY, HAYSTACK, and ROOSTER.

doo-doo. Shit. In the inimitable words of George Bush, when asked by the *Wall Street Journal* in February 1986 what would have happened in the 1970s to any Chinese official who seemed to be too friendly with Americans: "He would have been in deep doo-doo." A variant, also preserved by *WSJ,* is *foo-foo,* as in, quoting John J. Turnbracer, president of Executive Assets, an OUTPLACEMENT firm: "You're in a bigger paradigm, and if you break that, you're in deep foo-foo" (10/18/94). See also APPLESAUCE, BS, DEFECATE/DEFECATION, and WEE-WEE.

draft. A ploy used by insecure authors and artful bureaucrats to obviate criticism, since any comment on a manuscript or report headed "draft" can be deflected with the reply, "That didn't represent my final thought." The intensive form, employed by the most nervous authors and the canniest bureaucrats, is "rough draft." See also NONPAPER.

dreck. Rubbish, filth. Another example of the cleansing power of a foreign language, this is the Yiddish equivalent of the English CRAP and the French MERDE and, like them, it may be used in situations where its literal translation—it comes from the German word for "shit"—would not be allowed. "*Dreck* . . . showed up not long ago in a book review in that great arbiter of English usage in this country, the *New York Times*" (Theodor Rosebury, *Life on Man,* 1969).

droppings. Animal dung, a.k.a. shit. The word for the action, the dropping, stands for that which is dropped, a common euphemistic technique. See also DOG DIRT/DO/LITTER/WASTE, and, for a similar verb turned into a noun, FERTILIZER.

drumstick. The notorious taboo against "leg" was so strong that fowls on the dinner table began sprouting *drumsticks* about the same time the diners became equipped with *limbs*. Like so many of the euphemisms commonly associated with the Victorian era (see ROOSTER, for example), this one actually predates Victoria's ascension in 1837 by several generations. The oldest example in *The Oxford English Dictionary* of a "drumstick" for eating, rather than for banging on a drum, comes from 1764, i.e., "She always helps me herself to the tough drumsticks of turkies" (Samuel Foote, *The Mayor of Garrett*). It was in the United States, however, that the taboo against "leg" reached its grandest proportions. Besides "drumstick," Americans used a variety of other euphemisms for the legs of birds, including *dark meat*, JOINT, and *lower limb.* Still more picturesquely, an excessively polite person at the dinner table might ask for "the trotter of a chicken" (Richard Mead Bache, *Vulgarisms and Other Errors of Speech,* 1869). See also LIMB, PARSON'S- (or POPE'S-) NOSE, WHITE MEAT, and, for meat-eating in general, FILET MIGNON.

duckys. The breasts of a woman. "Wishing my self (specially an Evening) in my Sweethearts Armes whose pritty Duckys I trust shortly to kysse" (Henry VIII to Anne Boleyn, letter, ca. 1533). See also BOSOM.

duff. The ass, as in "Congress needs to get off its duff" (Governor William G. Milliken, R., Mich., WCBS-TV, 11:00 P.M. news, 8/27/78). "Duff" probably is of military origin; a shortening, possibly, of the "duffel bag" on which soldiers sit while waiting for something to happen. (The cloth originally came from Duffel, a town near Antwerp, Belgium.) The anatomical sense within the military might also have been reinforced by "doughboy," since "duff" was a not uncommon pronunciation of "dough" (like "enough" or "rough") in the nineteenth century. See also ARSE.

dump. A defecation; short for "dump a load of a shit." "Every time you take a dump or a leak in a standard john, you flush five gallons of water out with your piddle" (*Last Whole Earth Catalog,* 1972). See also JOHN, LEAK, and PIDDLE, as well as DEFECATE/DEFECATION.

dust. To kill. Thus, former Miami Dolphin star running back Mercury Morris said he had forgiven the informer who caused him to be arrested on a drug charge: "Maybe two years ago I would have wanted the guy dusted, but not now" (*New York Times,* 9/2/82). "Dust" in this sense seems to be a twentieth-century Americanism, perhaps deriving from "dust," meaning "to thrash," as in "So she took and dusted us both with the hickry" (Mark Twain, *Huckleberry Finn,* 1884). The metaphor might well have been reinforced by "dust (someone) off," that is, to cause someone to hit the dust and, by extension, to hit or beat someone. "Dust off" in the sense of "to kill" or "to murder" is dated to 1940 in the *Random House Historical Dictionary of American Slang.* See also BITE THE DUST and HIT.

Dutch treat. Not a treat, since each person is paying his or her own way. "Dutch treat" probably is the most common of the many pejorative uses of "Dutch," many dating to the seventeenth century, when the Dutch contested the English for control of the seas, and the English got back at them by employing "Dutch" to mean "inferior," as in *Dutch bargain* (a one-sided bargain, i.e., no bargain at all), *Dutch courage* (false courage, induced by brandy or other spirits), and *Dutch wife* or *husband* (a bed bolster). Of course, ethnic terms frequently are used in this manner; see also FRENCH.

duty. The act of urinating and/or defecating, often encountered in the phrase "do one's duty," but not only, as one might think, in connection with the doings of children, e.g., "The lamb ran away and stood in the middle of the field doing duties at an adjacent haystack" (A. J. Cronin, *The Stars Look Down*, 1935). See also DEFECATE/DEFECATION and URINATE/URINATION.

E

early retirement. The unexpected loss of a job. Police officers who have been charged with unlawful acts often take *early retirement* in order to keep pensions that would be lost if they were dismissed for cause. In the private sector, too, employees may be required to take *early retirement,* usually because the company is cutting back its work force. See also DEHIRE, LET GO, and RIGHTSIZE.

earth. Hell. "'What *in hell* are you doing?' has its milder version, 'What *on earth* are you doing?'" (*American Speech,* 2/61). See also HECK.

earth closet. A toilet; specifically, a water closet without water—and with various disadvantages, to wit: "The earth-closet, which, because it must of necessity be kept dry, is unsuited to durable comfort for those who experience difficulty in separating their natural functions and therefore [is] a poor place to read" (Reginald Reynolds, *Cleanliness and Godliness,* 1946). See also TOILET and WC.

earthy. Dirty, especially as applied to soiled language. "They [the English] delight in strong earthy expressions . . . coarsely true to the human body" (Ralph Waldo Emerson, *English Traits,* 1856). "One witness noted that Ms. [Bess] Myerson used some earthy language after receiving a subpoena. Afterward, walking out of the courtroom, Ms. Myerson was heard to remark, 'Would a nice Jewish girl from the Bronx use language like that?'" (*New York Times,* 12/11/88). See also ANGLO-SAXON.

ease. A somewhat old-fashioned but not-yet-entirely extinct euphemism for the discharge of excrement. For example, illustrating the customs of the ancient Hebrews (Deuteronomy 23:13):

> And thou shalt have a paddle upon thy weapon: and it shalt be when thou wilt ease thyself abroad, thou shalt dig therewith, and shalt turn back, and cover that which cometh from thee.

From the action, often embellished as *to do one's ease, to ease nature,* and *to ease oneself,* the term was extended to cover the place of performance. Hence: *closet of ease, house of ease,* and *seat of ease.* In the words of that well-known cleric Jonathan Swift ("Strephon and Chloe," 1731):

> Had you but through a cranny spied
> On house of ease your future bride.

Because the English of the Elizabethan period were not as fastidious as the Hebrews of the Bible about where and how they *eased* themselves, a remarkable secondary euphemism, *sir-reverence,* was created. This expression, which translates as "save reverence" or "saving your reverence," meaning "pardon the expression," was used in such contexts as "Watch out—don't step in the sir-reverence," or, an actual example: "Never was a gentle angler so dressed, for his face, his head, and his neck were all besmeared with the soft Sir Reverence, so he stunk worse than a jakes-farmer" (Robert Greene, *The Black Book's Messenger,* 1592). The origin of this euphemism was explained in the following manner by Capt. Francis Grose in *A Classical Dictionary of the Vulgar Tongue* (1796):

REVERENCE. An ancient custom, which obliges any person easing himself near the highway or foot-path, on the word reverence being given him by a passenger, to take off his hat [and hold it] with his teeth, and without moving it from his station to throw it over his head, by which it frequently falls into the excrement: this was considered as a punishment for the breach of delicacy. A person refusing to obey this law, might be pushed backwards.

See also COVER (ONE'S) FEET, DEFECATE/DEFECATION, and TOILET.

eat-in kitchen. Real estate–ese for "no dining room." See also REALTOR.

ecdysiast. A stripteaser—and one of the relatively few euphemisms (INTESTINAL FORTITUDE and REVENUE ENHANCEMENT are others) that can be attributed with confidence to a particular individual. This one was devised in 1940 by H. L. Mencken, at the request of a practitioner of the art, Miss Georgia Sothern, who felt public objections to her profession would vanish if it were given "a new and more palatable" name. Relating stripteasing to "the associated zoölogical phenomenon of molting," Mencken told La Sothern that "the word *moltician* comes to mind, but it must be rejected because of its likeness to *mortician.* A resort to the scientific name for molting, which is *ecdysis,* produces both *ecdysist* and *ecdysiast*" (Mencken, *The American Language, Supplement One,* 1945). The new name quickly caught on, and it continues to be the euphemism of choice, despite various misguided efforts to improve upon it (*ecdysiste*) and to compete with it (*strippeuse* and *stripteuse,* neither of which

should be confused with *scripteuse,* which is, or was, circa 1943, a woman scriptwriter). See also BURLEYCUE and EXOTIC DANCER.

ecodefense. Sabotage against perceived enemies of the environment, a.k.a. *ecotage.* So-called *ecodefenders* employ "defense" in an aggressive sense, giving them an unexpected bond with the brass hats in the Pentagon; see DEFENSE, DEPARTMENT OF. A seminal work in the environmental field is *Ecodefense: A Field Guide to Monkeywrenching* (1987), edited by Dave Foreman and Bill Haywood. "Monkeywrenching" includes such "defensive" measures as slashing tires, disabling machinery, toppling power lines, and interfering with chain-saw cutting by driving six-inch spikes into trees that are scheduled for logging. The term alludes to *The Monkey Wrench Gang* (1975), a novel by Edward Abbey about preservation of the environment by sabotaging those who attempt to DEVELOP it.

ecology. A term that is subject to abuse as businesses and other organizations seek to take advantage of its positive associations. Thus, the Nuclear Engineering Company of Louisville, Kentucky, a firm that disposes of radioactive and chemical wastes, changed its name in 1981 to U.S. Ecology. Then there are the College of Human Ecology (formerly the College of Home Economics) at the University of Minnesota, and the Human Ecology Department (staff clergy) at the Madison (Wisc.) General Hospital. The CIA, meanwhile, used to support research into human behavior modification through an agency conduit known as the Society for the Investigation of Human Ecology. See also ENVIRONMENTAL, *greenwashing* in LAUNDER, and RECYCLER.

economical. Frugal, cheap; see also THRIFTY.

economical with the truth. Not fully truthful, evasive; especially in a legal context. Thus, reporting the testimony of Sir Robert Armstrong, Britain's top-ranking civil servant, in support of his government's attempt to prevent publication in Australia of Peter Wright's *Spycatcher: The Candid Autobiography of a Senior Intelligence Officer*: "Sir Robert had to acknowledge that he had been, as he put it, 'economical with the truth' in earlier testimony in the case. Today, in his fourth day on the stand, Sir Robert was accused of lying by Mr. Wright's lawyer" (*New York Times*, 11/22/86). See also FUNDAMENTAL TRUTH, LESS THAN CANDID, NO RECALL (or MEMORY or RECOLLECTION) OF, TERMINOLOGICAL INEXACTITUDE, and WITHHOLD INFORMATION.

economic experts. A reunion of 800 veterans of the Waffen SS in Bad Harzburg, Germany, in 1984 was billed as "a conference of economic experts" (UPI, 3/5/84). Perhaps they discussed the economics of making soap.

economy class. Second or third class; see TOURIST.

educator. Teacher. "Educator" is to "teacher" as AUTHOR is to "writer." The E-word is preferred by pedagogues because it is of Latin extraction. "Educator" derives from *ēducāre*, to educate, to bring up, while "teacher" has a lowly Anglo-Saxon root, *tǣcan*, to teach, to show. See also ENGINEER.

eff. A euphemistic "fuck," having all the versatility of the word for which it stands. For example: "I have already had several abusive phone calls, telling me to eff off back to effing Russia, you effing, corksacking limey effer. This is because I suggested some time ago . . . that America would be better off for a bit of socialized medicine" (Anthony Burgess, *New York Times Magazine*, 10/29/72). See also F – – –.

effluent. A mellifluent pollutant, typically smoke, sewage, or other outflow of industrial waste; called a "residual effluent" if it remains too long in one place. "Radiation doses from airborne effluents of a coal-fired [power] plant may be greater than those from a nuclear plant" (subhead, *Science*, 12/8/78). See also DEBALLAST, CLEAN HARBOR, DEEP-OCEAN PLACEMENT, and EMERGENCY AND REMEDIAL RESPONSE, OFFICE OF.

egad. A somewhat archaic euphemistic oath that survives in some circles—and on some blocks. From "Sesame Street," for instance: "Egad! It sounds like a job for Sherlock Hemlock, who sees all" (Betty Lou, *Sherlock Hemlock and the Great Twiddlebug Mystery or The Mystery of the Terrible Mess in My Friend's Front Yard*, 1972). The substitution of "Gad" for "God" is common. Near relations to "egad" include BEGAD, *Gadsbodikins, Gads me, Gads my life, Gadsprecious*, and GADZOOKS. See also ADONAI, GOSH, and ODDS BODKINS.

egress. Exit. P. T. Barnum (1810–1891) is said to have made room for new customers in his American Museum by posting a sign, "This way to the egress," thereby keeping the hoi polloi moving along until, suddenly, they found themselves out the back door. In the parlance of the time, they had been "humbugged." The term should never have outlived this usage, but the sign "Not an Accredited Egress" was spotted over a doorway in the Ritz-Carlton Hotel in Boston within living memory (1976). One can't help wondering how many Bostonians have disappeared over the years, searching endlessly for an "Accredited Egress."

eliminate/elimination. The Latinate words are doubly euphemistic, applying to the act of getting rid of waste matter from the body as well as to getting rid of the bodies themselves.

In the first, least objectionable sense, Skylab astronaut Joseph P. Kerwin's self-checklist went like this: "How's my sleeping? Eating? Drinking? Eliminating?" (Henry S. F. Cooper, Jr., *A House in Space*, 1974).

In the second case, people may be *eliminated* from their jobs, or even from life itself, with the two thoughts sometimes reinforcing each other, e.g., "General Electric's chairman, John F. Welch, Jr. . . . earned the nickname Neutron Jack on his reputation for eliminating people while leaving buildings standing." (*New York Times*, 3/4/92). "Neutron Jack" was, in other words, an ENHANCED RADIATION WEAPON.

"Eliminate/elimination" frequently are used synonymously with TERMINATE/TERMINATION as roundabout terms for death by murder. Referring to a suspected double agent in Vietnam, who came to an untimely end (reportedly drugged, shot, and dropped into the sea from a helicopter), a former Green Beret admitted: "He was my agent and it was my responsibility to eliminate him with extreme prejudice" (*New York Times*, 4/4/71). On a more rarefied level, Senate investigators learned that CIA director Allen Dulles signed a memorandum in 1960 advocating that "thorough consideration be given to the elimination of Fidel Castro" (Intelligence Committee report on American plots to kill foreign leaders, 11/77).

Other countries have adopted this same bland terminology. Thus, according to official South African records, the chief of that nation's armed forces met in 1987 with the head of a covert operations unit to discuss the "elimination of specific targets" using "non-standard issue weapons in an unconventional fashion," by which they meant the killing of domestic opponents of apartheid (*New York Times*, 9/2/93). And continuing the parallel (or closing the circle, if you prefer), we have it on the authority of G. Gordon Liddy, the well-known PLUMBER, that in the CIA in the 1970s, a person qualified to undertake an assassination might be described as an expert in "the unorthodox application of chemical or medical knowledge" (1980 interview with Dick Cavett, rerun 9/8/82). See also ASSASSINATION, DEFECATE/DEFECATION, EXECUTIVE ACTION, NONDISCERNIBLE BIONOCULATOR, and WASTE.

embrace. To engage in sexual intercourse. The friendly "embrace" has served for several centuries as a euphemism for hugs that are quite friendly indeed. For example, from Shakespeare's *Much Ado About Nothing* (1598–1600): "I know what you would say: if I have known her, You will say she did embrace me as a husband." (See also KNOW.) And in our own time, from a pamphlet purchased at the castle of William the Conqueror in Normany: "It is in a small rush-strewn cell of the keep that Robert the Magnificent embraced Arlette and made her the mother of William, the founder of an immense empire" (Léonce Macary, *Falaise*, 1958). All of which adds an extra dimension to the song "Embraceable You."

embroider the truth. To lie, ornamentally. The circumlocution acknowledges what every good liar knows: the best lies are composed largely of truths. See also COVER, FUNDAMENTAL TRUTH, STRETCH THE TRUTH, and WHITE LIE.

Emergency and Remedial Response, Office of. The Environmental Protection Agency changed the name of its Office of Hazardous Emergency Response to the *Office of Emergency and Remedial Response* in 1981 as part of an effort to drop "hazard" from its institutional vocabulary. Announcing the name change, John Hernandez, the EPA's second-in-command, said he wanted aides to "talk about 'degree of mitigation of risk' instead of 'degree of hazard'" (*Miami Herald*, 8/30/81). By the mid-1990s, the "remedial" also had gone by the boards, the unit having metamorphosed into the *Office of Solid Waste and Emergency Response*. See also EFFLUENT and LANDFILL.

emergent. Near death. At New York's Bellevue Hospital incoming patients are divided into three categories: emergent, urgent, and routine. *Emergent* patients must be treated right away or they will die. See also TRIAGE.

emerging religion. A cult, especially one whose members withdraw from conventional society and live under the direction of an authoritarian, charismatic leader, à la Jim Jones of Jonestown or David Koresh of the Branch Dravidians. Not only do cultists not like the pejorative "cult" label (and they have been known to sue their critics), but mainstream theologians have difficulty discerning differences between modern cults and the cultlike origins of their own denominations. Accordingly, discussions of "cults" today tend to be cast in terms of *emerging religions* and—other available alternatives—*charismatic groups, dissenting religious groups, exotic religions, minority religions, new religions, new religious movements,* and *unconventional religions.*

emeritus. Retired. "Since [I. I.] Rabi was born on June 29, 1898, his retirement was on June 30, 1967, when he became professor emeritus" (*New Yorker,* 10/25/75). "Emeritus" permits distinguished professors to retain their academic rank after they have ceased teaching. See also HONORABLE and LAUREATE.

emporium. Originally a place, usually a town or city, where merchandise from a wide area was gathered for trade, "emporium" later was applied pompously to stores (e.g., the Food Emporiums that dot New York City) and other business establishments. "The 'weaker' sex will take over once again out at Jimmy Kilshaw's grapple emporium Tuesday night when Nell Stewart, comely Jacksonville, Fla., miss, meets Dottie Dotson, of Houston, Tex., in the weekly main event" (*Baton-Rouge,* La., *State Times,* 2/23/47).

So beloved is the grandiloquent "orium" ending that it has been picked up in other ways, e.g., *corsetorium,* which is where one goes to buy a corset or BODY BRIEFER; *hairitorium,* where one may purchase a HAIRPIECE; *hairporium,* a beauty PARLOR; and, most wonderfully, *ejaculatorium,* which is the room in a sperm bank where a donor goes in order to make a "deposit" (as sperm bankers say). See also LUBRITORIUM and SANITORIUM.

enceinte. This sterling example of the sometimes desperate lunge into another language to avoid a sexually charged term is only of historic interest now that the word "pregnant" can be uttered in polite circles. Sheer force of numbers (i.e., the post–World War II baby boom) cracked the taboo on the P-word, despite the best efforts of arbiters of public morals to enforce it. Thus, TV censors would not permit Lucille Ball, star of the immensely popular "I Love Lucy," to sully the airwaves with "pregnant" in 1952 even though she was visibly so. Hence, the title of the episode in which she officially announced her condition was "Lucy Is Enceinte." (See also FAMILY WAY, IN THE.) And the following year, there was a great uproar when "pregnant" (along with such other highly charged words as "seduce" and "virgin") was included in a film, *The Moon Is Blue*. The administrators of the Motion Picture Production Code refused to give the film an official seal and the Roman Catholic Legion of Decency condemned it, with the almost inevitable result that this otherwise tame little comedy became a box-office smash. Ironically, the word at issue had itself been popularized long before as a euphemism; see PREGNANT.

"Enceinte" comes via the French from Latin, probably from *inciens,* being with young, though some have argued for *in,* not, plus *cinctus,* girdled, i.e., "girdle loosened." The term seems to have been used first in a legal context. The oldest example in *The Oxford English Dictionary* is from 1599 and the last will of one G. Taylard: "Yf my wife be pryvyment insented wt a man-childe." Here, and in other early references, "pryvyment insent" translates as "pregnant but not discernibly so." Today, of course, pregnant persons who are not yet showing may purchase T-shirts that

say it in French. In the words of a 1976 Saks Fifth Avenue ad: " 'Je suis enceinte' announces to the world what I already know about me." A variation is the shirt that says *"le bébe"* up top and has an arrow pointing below. For a parallel Frenchification, see ACCOUCHEMENT.

enclave. A small group of fancy houses; a high-priced project. Speaking of eight houses to be constructed at Wynnewood Estates in Stamford, Connecticut, the broker handling the deal said: "A development, a project, ugh. It sounds so awful. We like to think of this as an enclave. An enclave of great homes that go together" (*New York Times,* 4/1987). See also CUL-DE-SAC, DEVELOP/DEVELOPMENT, ESTATE, GREENLAND, and PLANTATION.

encore. A repeat or rerun, short for "encore presentation"; TV talk. "Now we don't get re-runs in the summer. We get encores. You change the description and suddenly it's not a tired old program but one that's been brought back because the great American public couldn't wait to see it again" (New York *City News,* 9/26/78).

endowed/endowment. The essentially financial terms (from the Latin *dotare,* dowry) become euphemisms for other kinds of riches when used to describe the human body. Usually, the context is feminine and the reference is to large breasts, e.g., in the words of a *Playboy* photography editor, Marilyn Grabowski, "Most men look at a girl's endowments and that suffices" (*New York Times,* 2/26/77). Women may also be "well" or "amply endowed"—as may men, though the meaning then is that they are well HUNG. In the poignant words of a classified from Texas: "HOUSTON VERY PASSIONATE WIDOW wants to meet well-endowed men for dates and fun and games" (*Ace*, undated, ca. 1976). See also BOSOM, FULL-FIGURED, and STATUESQUE.

energy release. Radiation release, as from the explosion of a nuclear reactor. "There was still no realistic estimate as to exactly how many people would be killed, maimed, or come down with leukemia if an 'energy release' hit a populated area" (John G. Fuller, *We Almost Lost Detroit*, 1975). See also ABOVE CRITICAL, CORE REARRANGEMENT, and EVENT.

engineer. A vastly popular title for elevating the status of occupations of all sorts, "engineer" generally should be interpreted as a euphemism for "man" (or PERSON), as in *advertising engineer, cost engineer, patent engineer,* or *sales engineer.* At the behest of real engineers, most states (forty-five at last count) have enacted laws that make it illegal to use the title unless one has been educated and licensed in a recognized engineering discipline, but this is akin to trying to stop the tide. "Engineer" has been sighted in more than 2,000 combinations over the years, among them: *automobile engineer* (a mechanic), *casement window engineer, crowd control engineer* (a four-footed member of the police Canine Corps in Birmingham, Alabama, circa 1963; see also CROWD MANAGEMENT TEAM), *custodian-engineer* (also *engineer-custodian,* see CUSTODIAN), *customer engineer* (a salesperson), *customer service engineer* (a repairer of typewriters), *dansant engineer* (an agent for nightclub dancers and musicians), *dry cleaning engineer, educational engineer* (a school principal), *environmental engineer* (a garbageman),

exterminating engineer (rat and roach killer), *fantasy engineer* (the title adopted by a professional dominatrix, Mistress Jacqueline, author of the seminal *Whips and Kisses*), *footwear maintenance engineer* (a bootblack), *human engineer* (a kind of psychoanalyst, not to be confused with the *Corporate Human Factors Engineering Manager,* who seems to have something to do with personnel), *mattress engineer* (one of many spurious "engineers" recorded by *Engineering News Record,* a trade magazine for real engineers, this one was a bedding manufacturer who later metamorphosed into the even finer *sleep engineer),* *methods engineer* (from the 1957 film *Desk Set*, Tracy: "I'm a methods engineer." Hepburn: "Is that like an efficiency expert?" Tracy: "Well, that term's a little obsolete now."), *petroleum transfer engineer* (a filling station attendant), *publicity engineer* (see PUBLICITOR), *recreation engineer, sanitary engineer* (another garbageman, a.k.a. SANITATION MAN), *software engineer* (computer programmer), *vision engineer* (an optician), *wardrobe engineer* (a person who tells you what clothes to buy, a.k.a. *taste technician),* and *window cleaning engineer.*

Even the engineer who runs a locomotive is something of a euphemism. The dubious nature of the American term was recognized in the nineteenth century by John R. Bartlett, whose *Dictionary of Americanisms* (1860) included this entry: "Engineer, the engine-driver on our railroads is thus magniloquently designated." "Engine-driver" is still the title for this job among the British who, as a seafaring nation, naturally reserve the high-sounding "engineer" for those in charge of marine engines.

For more about the great and continuing effort to upgrade job titles, see, in addition to those entries already cited in passing:

ACCESS CONTROLLER; ADMINISTRATIVE ASSISTANT; AGENT; ASSISTANT TO THE PRESIDENT FOR PUBLIC EVENTS AND INITIATIVES; ASSOCIATE; ATTORNEY; AUTHOR; AUTOMOTIVE INTERNIST; BEAUTICIAN; BEVERAGE HOST; CHAUFFEUR; CLOTHES DOCTOR; CONSULTANT; COSMETICIAN/COSMETOLOGIST; COUNSEL; DOCTOR; EDUCATOR; ECDYSIAST; ENUMERATOR; EXCAVATIONIST; EXECUTIVE; FIRE FIGHTER; FLUEOLOGIST; FOUNTAIN ATTENDANT; FUNERAL DIRECTOR; GARBOLOGIST; HOMEMAKER; HONORABLE, THE; HOUSEHOLD ADMINISTRATOR; INFORMATION SPECIALIST; INVESTIGATOR; LEARNING FACILITATOR; MARKETING; MEDIA SPECIALIST; METEOROLOGIST; MIXOLOGIST; OFFICER; PERCUSSIONIST; PROSTITUTE; PROFESSIONAL PUBLIC MANAGER; REALTOR; REPRESENTATIVE; ROAD CAR INSPECTOR; SECURITY; SERVANT; SHOE REBUILDER; SOFTWARE DOCUMENTATION SPECIALIST; SPECIALIST; TECHNICIAN; TRAFFIC EXPEDITER; TRAIL REPRESENTATIVE; VERTICAL TRANSPORTATION CORPS, and VICE PRESIDENT.

engineering surface facility. A clean name for a tank for storing radioactive wastes from nuclear power plants. Casks of spent fuel may also be stored in a *monitored retrievable storage facility,* which is a fenced-in lot for parking radioactive wastes until someone can figure out what else to do with them. See also ENVIRONMENTAL.

English guidance or **arts** or **culture.** Sadism and/or masochism. "BOW YOUR HEAD! The Mistress is now accepting slaves for English guidance" (personal ad, *Screw,* 8/2/76). According to classified ads on the subject, *English guidance* features (though it is by no means limited to) whips, canes, riding crops, and hairbrushes, which are applied to what the English, in such situations, call the DERRIÈRE or POSTERIORS. See also FRENCH, MISTRESS, and SM.

enhanced (or **enlarged) radiation weapon.** A neutron bomb, a.k.a. *radiation enhancement weapon,* which may be either dropped from a plane or shot from a cannon. (In a miracle of modern engineering, a neutron warhead can be made to fit into an eight-inch artillery shell.) The terminological enhancement won the 1977 Doublespeak Award of the Committee on Public Doublespeak of the National Council of Teachers of English. It was selected, the committee explained, because it concealed so well the true effects of the bomb, i.e.: "The body convulses, limbs shake, the nervous system fails so that all automatic body functions, even breathing, are affected. Death comes within 48 hours." The beauty part is that the *enhanced radiation weapon* produces twice as much lethal radiation as an ordinary nuclear bomb with only a tenth as much explosive power. This means it can kill a great many people while leaving buildings standing. See also CLEAN BOMB, DEVICE, ELIMINATE/ELIMINATION, and TACTICAL NUCLEAR WEAPON.

enob. The penis, from "bone" spelled backward. Similar euphemistic deconstructions include "frab" and "mosob." See also BOSOM, PENIS, and UPCHUCK.

entrenching tool. A small, folding spade in the U.S. Army; also known as a *digging instrument* or *combat emplacement evacuator,* and less formally as an *Army (*or *Irish) banjo.*

The tradition of avoiding the humble "spade" with a fancy phrase is of considerable antiquity. Thus, Roman soldiers did not have spades; rather, Tacitus tells us, they were equipped with "instruments for digging earth and cutting turf" (*Annals* 1:65, ca. 116). Of course, Tacitus was a model of refinement (see also HOUSE) compared to uncouth peoples in the hinterlands of the empire. As noted by Plutarch, writing at about the same time, "the Macedonians are a rude and clownish people that call a spade a spade" (*Apothegms, Philip of Macedon*).

The renaming of ordinary items has since been developed into a high art form by Pentagon procurement officers. Among the choicer military examples:

Electro-optical system. Television.
Emergency exit light. A flashlight.
Frame-supported tension structure (FST). A tent; a key component of the Marine Corps "Expeditionary Soft Shelter System."
Hexaform rotatable surface compression unit. A nut. The Navy was reported in 1986 to have paid $2,043 apiece for steel ones. The official nomenclature has an extremely high FOP Index of 18.7.
Interlocking slide fastener. A zipper.
Manually powered fastener-driving impact device. A hammer.
Multidirectional impact generator. Another hammer; a $450 item in 1985.
Portable handheld communications inscriber. A pen, with a FOP Index of 16.7.
Wood interdental stimulator. A toothpick.

The Pentagon does not enjoy a monopoly on this kind of pseudo-technical talk. For example, astronauts aboard the space shuttles use a "remote manipulator system" (i.e., robot arm) with an "end effector" (clawlike hand). In time, no doubt, the shuttles also will have to be supplied with what government purchasing agents call "rodent elimination devices" (mousetraps). American auto manufacturers equip their cars with "ash receivers," not "ashtrays";

the Gillette company sells a "shaving system," a.k.a. razor, for use in one's "shaving environment," a.k.a. bathroom (National Public Radio, "Marketplace," 11/8/93); and in Canada, government purchasing agents shelled out $123.80 apiece for "user friendly, space effective, flexible, deskside sortation units," which are glorified "wastepaper baskets" (*Toronto Star,* 5/13/92). Meanwhile, the FBI used *combat engineering vehicles* to knock down walls when attacking the compound of the Branch Dravidians in Waco, Texas, in 1993. Observers thought the armored *combat engineering vehicles* looked very much like tanks.

See also ADVANCED LIFE SUPPORT UNIT, AERODYNAMIC PERSONNEL DECELERATOR, COIN TELEPHONE ENCLOSURE, CREW TRANSFER CONTAINER, IDENTIFICATION TAGS, IMPACT ATTENUATION DEVICE, MOTORIZED TRANSPORTATION MODULE, PERSONAL FLOTATION DEVICE, PERSONAL TIME CONTROL CENTER, SINGLE-PURPOSE AGRICULTURAL STRUCTURE, and SPACE TRANSPORTATION SYSTEM.

entry denial fixture. A lock, with FOP Index of 6.5.

enumerator. Counter. The Census Bureau counts people, but the people who knock on doors are, in Census-ese, *enumerators.* See also ENGINEER.

environmental. Like ECOLOGY, the term is a popular one for covering up a variety of messy businesses. For example, speaking of the large operator of large dumps, Waste Management, Inc.: "It carefully sanitizes its image, referring to itself as an 'environmental-service concern,' to garbage dumps as 'sanitary landfills' and to hazardous-waste sites as 'residual management units'" (*Wall*

Steeet Journal, 5/1/91). Another kind of garbage is collected by Environmental Health Research and Testing, an American firm that was hired by Kuwait to clear the desert of mines and explosives left behind after the Gulf War. On a more mundane level, *environmental technicians* (janitors) perform *environmental services* (as they do at the Madison, Wisc., General Hospital). But this is an international phenomenon. Septic tanks in Beijing are pumped out at night by *environmental hygiene workers* (see also NIGHT SOIL), while letters to the London *Times* have noted the transmutations of a janitor into an *environmental hygienist* and of a plumber into an *environmental physicist.* See also CLEAN AIR, ENGINEERING SURFACE FACILITY, JANITOR, RECYCLER, SANITATION MAN, SECONDARY FIBER, and SWIMMING ENVIRONMENT.

episode. A disaster, or the immediate threat of one. For example, in November 1975, Pittsburgh, Pennsylvania, underwent a five-day "air pollution episode," during which the "coefficient of haze" across the Monongahela River from U.S. Steel's Clairton Coke Works reached 7.8, on a scale where 8 indicates "imminent and substantial endangerment" to human health. The Environmental Protection Agency later estimated that the "episode" probably caused fourteen deaths. See also EVENT and INCIDENT.

equestrian center. A stable, e.g., the $1.75-million *equestrian center* at Mount Holyoke College in Massachusetts.

equipment. Airline-ese for "airplane," typically encountered in loudspeaker announcements in the form of "There will be a slight delay in the departure of Flight 707 while we have a change of equipment." The point, of course, is to avoid implying that anything ever goes wrong with an "airplane." Air controllers, meanwhile, relieve stress by saying that they are "pushing pieces of tin," as opposed to guiding planes with people inside them. See also the "late arrival of equipment" in WATER LANDING.

erotica. Pornography (whose root, *porne,* is Greek for "harlot"). Cousins include *esoterica* and *exotica.* When draped in the cloak of science, the term is *erotology* and specialists in the subject are, naturally, *erotologists.* See also ADULT, CURIOSA, FACETIAE, and SEXUALLY EXPLICIT (or ORIENTED).

erratum. Error. No one likes to have to admit publicly to making mistakes, but there are times when this simply has to be done, and in those cases, the confession is easier if cloaked in Latin. Book publishers, for example, do not issue "error slips," but *erratum slips*—or if, horrors, more than one mistake has been made—*errata slips.* See also CORRIGENDUM.

erroneous report. A lie. "The Department of Defense man . . . had no trouble when asked if the Pentagon had lied to the Senate about the bombing of Cambodia. Spokesman Jerry W. Friedheim replied that the Pentagon hadn't lied, it had merely submitted an erroneous report. This is pure Pentagon Doublespeak" (Israel Shenker, "Zieglerrata," *New Republic,* 4/13/74). This particular *erroneous report* omitted any mention of 3,630 B-52 air raids made in 1969–70 over Cambodia, a neutral nation during the VIETNAM ERA. See also MISSTATEMENT, PROTECTIVE REACTION, and WHITE LIE.

escalate. To increase the level of something, especially the violence of a war. The increment of increase is an *escalation, a graduated escalation,* or, sometimes, a *measured response.*

"Escalate" became a vogue word in the VIETNAM ERA, but predates it. For example: "By 1960 . . . the predominant feeling among the critics of massive retaliation was always that limited nuclear war would billow up quickly (in the jargon, 'escalate') into full nuclear war" (Arthur M. Schlesinger, Jr., *A Thousand Days,* 1965). See also LIMITED WAR.

estate. A plot of land, not necessarily very large. Thus, Wynnewood Estates, an ENCLAVE, in Stamford, Conn., consists of eight houses on twenty-six acres, which works out to 3¼ acres per *estate.* Some *estates* have much smaller dimensions, as indicated in the opening of a letter, prepared by the Matthews Memorial Bronze Company (quoted in Jessica Mitford, *The American Way of Death,* 1963):

Dear Friend,

The other day, we and our maintenance crews were out working the section of the cemetery, where your family estate is located. . . . One of the workmen commented that an unmarked grave is a sad thing.

See also CEMETERY and MEMORIAL PARK.

etc. The convenient catchall may take the edge off tabooed terms without totally obscuring them. "'You don't know your etc. from your etc.' A very coarse comparison, such as never before . . . had I used to a woman" (Joyce Cary, *To Be a Pilgrim,* 1942). The construction has been employed in this manner since at least the sixteenth century by Shakespeare, Byron, e.e. cummings, and others. One of the best-known Shakespearean examples may be a misreading, however. The question arises at the opening of the second act of *Romeo and Juliet* when Mercutio exclaims, "O that she were An open *et cetera,* thou a pop'rin pear!" where the shape of the pear made it a metaphor for male genitals. (The name itself came from Poperinhe in Flanders.) This line is from the first quarto (1597), but the text is a rough one, probably based on actors' memories. Modern scholars lean toward another reading, suggested in 1954 by Richard Hosley, who changed "An open *et cetera*" to "An open arse," meaning "sexually loose." The "et cetera" version is the traditional one, however, and, as Philip C. Kolin pointed out in *American Speech* (Spring 1983), this is the example that would have influenced Byron, Carey, cummings, etc.

ethnic. White, but not Wasp; "ethnic" is shorthand for *ethnic group, ethnic minority,* or, plainest, *white ethnic.* "The former 'ethnics', a polite term for Jews, Italians, and other lesser breeds just inside the law" (London *Times Literary Supplement,* 11/17/61). See also MIDDLE CLASS and MINORITY.

ethnic cleansing. The elimination of a particular group by murder or expulsion; specifically, the creation of exclusive Serbian enclaves in large portions of Bosnia and Herzegovina by killing, raping, starving, shelling, and evicting their Muslim and Croat inhabitants. Variants include *cultural cleansing* (practiced in Nepal) and *ideological cleansing* (conducted with less lethal effect in the U.S. Republican party).

"In effect, Mr. Herak's story was the first account given by a perpetrator to outsiders of how the Serbian nationalist forces have carried out 'ethnic cleansing.' ... At Ahatovici, for instance, he said Serbian commanders had described the Serbian operation as 'ciscenje prostora,' or the cleansing of the region, and had told the Serbian fighters to leave nobody alive" (*New York Times*, 11/27/92). The Serbian nationalist leader, Dr. Radovan Karadzic, later denied that many people had been killed. It was not a question of "ethnic cleansing," he told the *New York Times*, but merely of "ethnic shifting" (1/17/93). In the indictment of a Serb concentration-camp commander, Dragan Nikolic, by the Yugoslav War Crimes Tribunal in The Hague in 1994, "ethnic cleansing" was referred to as "illegal deportations." (Mr. Nikolic also was charged with murder, rape, and mutilation of Muslim prisoners.) See also CLEANSE; FINAL SOLUTION, THE; and SPECIAL INVESTIGATION GROUP.

Eumenides or **the Kindly Ones.** The ancient Greek euphemism, popularized by Aeschylus in his play of this name, for the Erinyes or Furies.

euphemism, the. Toilet, the. "Ivan Lendl has gone to the euphemism apparently" (WNBC-TV, 6/9/85, explaining an unexpected break in the French Open tennis final). See also POWDER MY NOSE, I HAVE TO and TOILET.

event. A neutral word that becomes a euphemism when used to soft-pedal "catastrophe," as in *nuclear event* (an accident, up to and including an explosion), *seismic event* (an earthquake), and *vascular event* (a stroke, a.k.a. ACCIDENT). Civil authorities also use the term to downplay riots and other forms of strife, e.g., the 1988 anti-Armenian "February events" in Azerbaijan and "the events of 1956" in Hungary, put down by Soviet tanks.

"Event" is especially beloved in the nuclear power business. Thus, if a truck carrying nuclear wastes runs off the road, this is likely to be passed off as a *transportation event* (kissing kin to the *unscheduled descent* that occurs when a crane accidentally drops fuel rods into a reactor core). And in California, where the Diablo Canyon nuclear plant was built unfortunately close to the San Simeon-Hosgri fault, power company officials resorted to soothing references to "the excitations produced by the larger potential Hosgri event." The tropism of the nuclear-minded toward "event" is typified by the opening sentence of the transcript of one of the hairier meetings of the U.S. Nuclear Regulatory Commission:

As the Three Mile Island situation developed beginning on Wednesday, March 28 [1979], the Commissioners met to discuss the nature of the event.

The commissioners had many things to worry about the *event*-in-progress, including the threats of "rapid oxidation" (fire) and "energetic displacement" of the fuel (an explosion, or BLIP). Neither of these occurred, though plutonium did "take up residence" in the reactor vessel (i.e., contaminate it), leading to permanent closure of the plant. See also ABOVE CRITICAL, ABNORMAL OCCURRENCE, and INCIDENT.

excavationist. An archaeologist with shovel in hand. "This work, too, is temporary and is usually carried out under pressure and against time, typifying the rather harsh conditions under which excavationists work. (The neologism serves to distinguish archaeologists from construction workers and has the positive associations of *conservationist*)" (London *Times,* 10/28/86). See also ENGINEER.

excellent. Not so good. Army officers who receive *excellent* ratings on their efficiency reports had better start shopping around for new careers, as "excellent" probably puts them in the bottom 20 percent of their group. The six army rating categories are: 1. Outstanding; 2. Superior; 3. Excellent; 4. Effective; 5. Marginal; 6. Inadequate. The other services have similarly inflated ranking systems. The navy, for example, has a "top" grade—with four subdivisions—followed by "typically effective," with two subdivisions. In the air force, "meets standard" is the third of six categories, and an officer who gets this rating has, in effect, been given the kiss of death. The marines also have an *excellent* category; it is midway between "above average" and "outstanding," which is the top category. See also FAIR, FINE, and FIRST CLASS.

exceptional. Disturbed, handicapped, retarded, stupid. The term has been applied to extra-bright children, too, presumably to avoid the plainer but elitist "gifted," but usually the reference is to deviations from the norm in the other direction, e.g., "Children who failed to acquire skills expected at their age used to be called 'dull.' Later they were called 'retarded.' Now they are called 'exceptional'" (Anatol Rapoport, *Semantics,* 1975). Then there was the summer camp for boys that advertised itself as having been designed for "individual attention for the minimally exceptional" (*New York Times Magazine,* 2/23/86).

Exceptional children may grow up to become *exceptional* adults. For example: "On the whole, mentally handicapped—or 'exceptional'—workers have an absenteeism rate of one-third or one-fourth that of other workers. This is just one of many reasons for hiring these exceptional workers" (Edwin P. Feldman and George B. Wright, *The Supervisor's Handbook,* 1982). See also CARDINAL, DEVELOPMENTALLY DELAYED/DISABLED/HANDICAPPED, MENTAL, MONOSAVANT, SLOW, and SPECIAL.

excess. To fire someone, not for cause but to cut costs; usually encountered in the past tense, as in "A good friend of mine, a brilliant teacher and first-rate literary critic, was 'excessed' from New York College in early August because he first arrived at the college two years ago, and the rules of seniority must be served" (*New Republic,* 10/2/76). The euphemism appeared first in the public sector in the 1970s but has since been adopted by private enterprise, too. "Excessive" synonyms include *displace* and SURPLUS. See also the British REDUNDANCY and the basic American LET GO.

exchange. War; an amiable term for the nuclear holocaust that would be labeled World War III by any who survived it; in full, an *all-out strategic exchange.* "When that day comes, and there is a massive exchange, then that is the end, because you are talking about . . . 150 million casualties in the first eighteen hours" (John F. Kennedy, quoted by Arthur M. Schlesinger, Jr., *A Thousand Days,* 1965). See also CASUALTY, LIMITED WAR, STRATEGIC, and TACTICAL NUCLEAR WEAPON.

excrement. Shit. "The microfossils look to him like 'little streaks of [excrement]'" (*Sci-*

entific American, 2/91, brackets in the original). Like many words for waste matter from the bowels, this one originally had blander meanings. Deriving from the Latin *ex,* out, plus *cernere,* sift, separate, "excrement" was applied in the sixteenth and seventeenth centuries to dregs, lees, refuse, and other cast-off items, e.g., "Men, beasts and fowles . . . haue outwardly some offensive excrement, as haire or feathers" (Charles Butler, *The Feminine Monarchie; or a Treatise Concerning Bees,* 1609). The modern meaning existed from an early date, however (1533, *OED*), and it thoroughly contaminated the term by the middle of the eighteenth century, if not before. Similar words whose modern meanings evolved in the same way include CRAP, DEFECATE/DEFECATION, and FECES.

excursion. In the nuclear-reactor business, an uncontrolled chain reaction. See ABOVE CRITICAL.

execute. To murder. "Execute" is preferred by terrorists because it lends an aura of legality to their killings. (See also EXPROPRIATION and FREEDOM FIGHTER in this connection.) Such nuances are thought to be especially important when, as is frequently the case, the victim is a helpless captive. For example, "The Irish Republican Army said today . . . police constable William Turbitt, who was kidnapped in a bloody IRA ambush . . . was 'executed' because he was part of the 'British war machine'" (*New York Post,* 6/19/78). See also CAPITAL PUNISHMENT, HIT, and KILL.

execution technician. Executioner. After New Jersey passed a new death-penalty law in 1982, it became necessary to con-

struct a special facility in which state-mandated killings could be carried out "scientifically, with precision" by an "execution technician." See also CAPITAL PUNISHMENT and TECHNICIAN.

executive. Employee. Firms that specialize in *executive counseling* and *executive searches,* for example, are high-toned employment agencies (a.k.a. headhunters) that often fill jobs in middle (and lower) management. Then there are the thundering herds of Wall Street *account executives,* a.k.a. *registered representatives,* who originally were known as "customer's men," and the IBM *client executives,* who are just salespeople. The American College of Healthcare Executives, meanwhile, used to be known as the American College of Hospital Administrators. (Note that the quondam administrators also chose to drop "hospital" from their collegial name; many of them now run *medical centers* instead.) See also ENGINEER, HEALTH, REPRESENTATIVE, and VICE PRESIDENT.

executive action. A CIA euphemism for getting rid of people, especially the leaders of foreign countries, and especially by murder. "Assassination capability (Executive action) . . . the Committee has received evidence that ranking Government officials discussed, and may have authorized, the establishment within the CIA of a generalized assassination capability" (Senate Intelligence Committee report on American assassination plots against foreign leaders, 11/75). David Wise later reported that the agency did form an assassination unit, known in spookspeak as the Health Alteration Committee (*The American Police State: The Government*

Against the People, 1976). Within the COM-MUNITY, a person whose death was arranged so as to appear to be due to natural causes might be said to have *died of the measles.* See also ACTION; ASSASSINATION; CAPABILITY; ELIMINATE/ELIMINATION; HEALTH, REASONS OF; TERMINATE/TERMINATION; WET AFFAIR; and the similarly bland *executive measures* in FINAL SOLUTION, THE.

executive summary. Summary. The "executive" massages the ego of the reader, while producing a FOP Index of 3.0. It also helps executives with short attention spans to justify not reading reports in full. After all, if the summary is for executive, the report itself must be only for corporate underlings.

exfiltration. The opposite of infiltration, i.e., retreat. As defined in the official U.S. *Department of Defense Dictionary of Military and Associated Terms* (1979): "*exfiltration (DOD)*—The removal of personnel or units from areas under enemy control." The relevant verb is "exfiltrate." See also STRATEGIC MOVEMENT TO THE REAR.

ex gratia. The expression translates as "out of kindness" or "as a favor," and it is a convenient dodge for people who are morally obliged to pay damages to others but do not wish to admit legal liability. For example, Chile agreed in 1990 to provide *ex gratia* compensation for surviving relatives of exiled diplomat Orlando Letelier and his aide, Ronni Moffitt, killed in a car-bombing fourteen years earlier. Meanwhile, the United States offered *ex gratia* payments to families of the 290 people killed when an American cruiser shot down an Iranian passenger plane over the Persian Gulf in 1988.

Similar to an *ex gratia payment* is the *condolence award* made during the VIETNAM ERA to the families of South Vietnamese who were killed by American troops by mistake. The standard *condolence award* was $34. More generous was the *missing person gratuity* given to the wife of a Vietnamese who had been working for the Green Berets and was apparently murdered by them (see ELIMINATE/ELIMINATION). The *missing person gratuity* was $6,472. See also BEREAVEMENT FARE, COMFORT WOMAN (for an inscrutable Japanese variant), GESTURE OF GOODWILL, and GRATUITY.

exotic. A stripteaser, a.k.a. *variety dancer,* or that which pertains to the profession of disrobing in public. "'Exotic dancer—' 'A euphemism for stripper'" (R. Hardwick, *The Plotters,* 1965). An *exotic* is one step this side of *exotica,* i.e., EROTICA. See also ECDYSIAST.

expectant. Pregnant, except on a battlefield, where an *expectant* is—also euphemistically—a wounded person who is expected to die. "Expectant" appears to have been applied initially (1861, *OED*) to fathers-to-be in the sense of "having expectations." The first "expectant" woman doesn't crop up in the written record until 1882. Occasionally, the term is still employed in a masculine context, e.g., *Expectant Fathers,* by Sam Bittman and Sue R. Zalk, a book that first saw the light of day in 1978. See also BLESSED EVENT, EXPECTING, and PREGNANT.

expecting. Pregnant, as in a TV ad for Preparation H, "When you're expecting, check with your doctor before using any medicine" (6/22/78). The oldest known example of the basic "expect" in a pregnant sense comes from a letter by Jane Austen: "She *expects* much about this day three weeks, & is generally very exact" (3/23/1817). The emphasis, which is Ms. Austen's, suggests that the euphemistic sense of the word was relatively new at the time. See also EXPECTANT and PREGNANT.

expectorate. To spit. "As Tom wended to school after breakfast, he was the envy of every boy he met because the gap in his upper row of teeth enabled him to expectorate in a new and admirable way" (Mark Twain, *The Adventures of Tom Sawyer,* 1876). Just as boys love to learn to wrap their tongues around the complicated "expectorate" while they are teaching themselves to spit, so, when they are a little older, they are similarly intrigued by OSCULATE. See also CUSPIDOR and SPIT.

expendable. Military-ese for those who are about to die. Before 1900, "expendable" was a fairly rare word, applied more to property and provisions than to men's lives; it took the twentieth century to give it a new meaning. A key work on the subject is W. L. White's *They Were Expendable* (1942). As far back as the eighteenth century, however, the similar "expended" was used by sailors in the sense of "killed." This was an allusion "to the gunner's accounts, wherein the articles consumed are charged under the title of expended" (Capt. Francis Grose, *A Classical Dictionary of the Vulgar Tongue,* 1796). See also BITE THE DUST, CASUALTY, and WASTE.

experience. An opaque word for masking almost anything from private pleasure to public pain. Thus, in what is usually construed as the pleasurable side, "experi-

ence" translates as "sex" when a MASSAGE PARLOR advertises a "$50 Experience" or when a sex therapist talks about the *group experience* or *prostitute experience.* MBAs generally have something else on their minds when they refer to the *career experience,* which is a "job" to someone who has a POSITION. See also CAREER and MORTALITY EXPERIENCE.

experienced. Used, as applied to *experienced tires* or *experienced cars.* When employed in this manner, "experienced" has a FOP Index of 3.5. See also PREVIOUSLY OWNED.

expire. To die; the primary meaning of the longer, softer word, "to breathe out," has been extended to include the unstated thought that this breath is the last one. It should come as no surprise that the euphemistic "expire" is of French-Latin extraction, while the plainer "die" comes from the Middle English *dien,* which corresponds to, and perhaps derives from, the Old Norse *deyja.*

"Expire" is the formal, somewhat technical equivalent of PASS AWAY, and it is preferred by professionals who deal with death at first hand, e.g.: "The word 'death' is seldom heard in hospital wards. Whether from a sense of delicacy or for greater exactness, 'to cease breathing' or 'to expire' are the usual expressions. Upon inquiry, a nurse will say that 'So-and-So did not live' in preference to 'he died'" (*American Speech,* 4/27). Several generations later, hospital personnel—and patients—still talk much the same way: "One of the saddest duties a nurse must perform is *DCing* 'disconnecting' everything . . . after the patient has *expired*" (Frances J. Storlie, R.N., *American Speech,* Spring 1979).

See also CHECK OUT, CODE (OUT), CRUMP,

EXPOSE, GAME, GUARDED, HOSPICE, NO MAY-DAY, MORTALITY EXPERIENCE, *negative patient outcome* in NEGATIVE, NOT DOING WELL, OFF, POST, and TERMINATE/TERMINATION.

expletive deleted. Popularized by its frequent appearance in the transcripts of White House discussions of the Watergate affair, "expletive deleted" has shown considerable staying power as a printable substitute for a wide variety of coarse expressions. Initially assumed to have been designed purely in the interest of preserving public decorum, the phrase actually helped the conspirators maintain the fabric of the COVER-UP, e.g., President Nixon speaking: "(Expletive deleted), get it. In a way that—who is going to talk to him? Colson? He is the one who is supposed to know him?" (meeting with H. R. Haldeman and John W. Dean III, 3/21/73). After members of the House Judiciary Committee got the chance to play the White House tapes, they learned that "(Expletive deleted) get it" in this instance meant "Well, for Christ's sake, get it," the "it" being $120,000 to buy the silence of Watergate burglar E. Howard Hunt, Jr. With the expletive included, Nixon's words sounded like a direct order, not, as his lawyers had argued, a hypothetical discussion. (A similar White House substitution, "characterization omitted," as in "Bobby was a ruthless [characterization omitted]," tape, 2/28/73, does not appear to have withstood the test of time.)

Nowadays, editors commonly use "expletive deleted" in much the same way as the traditional BLANK and DASH. For example, the *Litchfield County,* Conn., *Times* toned down the complaint of a local first selectman this way: "What the hell they got me going for a deposition for? It

pissed the [expletive deleted] out of me, I'll tell you" (10/25/91, transcript of a purported conversation in 1986, given to the newspaper by a rival politician). And note which words the newspaper allowed into print. This is another case (see also A – – and F – – –) in which fine editorial distinctions throw light on contemporary community standards of decency as interpreted by local editors (who, of course, take the heat from their friends and neighbors if they guess wrong).

Either part of "expletive deleted" may be used alone with the same effect as the whole. Thus, the National Transportation Safety Board employs both forms when releasing transcripts of conversations of crew members of airplanes that have been in accidents, e.g., "Unidentified crew member: Oh [expletive]" (Delta Airlines Flight 191, two seconds before crashing, 136 killed, 8/2/85) and "Well, I don't drink, but I'll sure as [deleted] have one" (United Flight 232 crew member, talking about having a beer if the crippled plane landed safely, which it did not—112 of 296 killed, 7/19/89).

As with other evasions of this sort, readers may easily assume the deleted expletive to be worse than it actually was. Thus, in a page-one story on a freedom-of-speech case, the *New York Times* reported that "Miss Dietze, according to court records, called the woman a bitch and her son a dog and threatened to 'beat the [expletive] out of you some day or night in the street'" (12/20/89). Which looks like pretty strong stuff. Readers who plowed through the excerpts from the court decision in the paper's second section, however, discovered that the defendant had merely announced her intention to "beat the crap out of [the complainant] some day or night in the street." It seems the good, gray *Times* just couldn't bear to print "crap" on its first page.

See also ADJECTIVE/ADJECTIVAL, BLEEP, BLIP, F-WORD, and UNPRINTABLE.

expose. To infect in a deadly manner; especially as applied to people who have tested positive for HTLV-III antibodies and are told gently that they have been "exposed" to AIDS, not that the virus has taken up residence in their blood. Randy Shilts nominated this euphemism as "perhaps the most pernicious" addition to AIDSpeak, the "politically facile and psychologically reassuring" new language "forged by public health officials, anxious gay politicians, and the burgeoning ranks of 'AIDS activists'" (*And the Band Played On: Politics, People, and the AIDS Epidemic,* 1987). Shilts quoted Dr. Bruce Voeller, a microbiologist and former executive director of the National Gay Task Force, who parsed the euphemism this way: "When people say 'expose,' I get the feeling that they think the virus floats around the room, like the scent of gardenias, and somehow they get exposed. That's not how it works. If you've got an antibody, that virus has been in your blood. You've been infected." For more hospital talk, see EXPIRE and PEOPLE WITH AIDS.

expropriation. Theft, robbery. Politically motivated people who grab other people's money prefer "expropriation" to "robbery" for the same reason that terrorists prefer EXECUTE to "murder." "In El Salvador, one of the ways they have got funds for the revolution is through bank expropriations" (WPIX-NYC, Independent Network News, 5/25/82). This happens in the United States, too. Thus, a defendant acting as his own lawyer in the trial of three members of

the Black Liberation Army for robbery and murder (two police officers and a guard, killed during an attempted $1.6 million holdup of an armored car), asked a witness: "Are you familiar with the expropriation which occurred in Nyack [N.Y.] on October 20, 1981?" (*New York Times,* 9/13/83). See also APPROPRIATE and FREEDOM FIGHTER.

extended nutritional deprivation. Hunger. "Extended nutritional deprivation," as "hunger" was termed in the report of President Ronald Reagan's Task Force on Food Assistance (1984), has a FOP Index of 6.8.

extramarital. Adulterous, as in *extramarital affairs, extramarital relations,* and *extramarital relationships* (note that all tend to come in the plural). Variants include *comarital sex, extracurricular activity,* and— the technical term when couples take the time to get out of their cars—*extravehicular activity.* In all cases, the Latin takes much of the edge off the violation of the Seventh Commandment. Would you believe: "Thou shalt not commit extramarital affairs"? Deep-thinkers have recognized the euphemistic quality of "extramarital" for at least the last fifty years, e.g.: "We, however, wish to appeal to reason, and we must therefore employ dull neutral phrases, such as 'extra-marital sexual relations'" (Bertrand Russell, *Marriage and Morals,* 1929). See also AFFAIR, CONSENSUAL NONMONOGAMY, FORNICATE/FORNICATION, GROUP SEX, OPEN MARRIAGE, RELATIONSHIP, and SWINGING.

extremity. An arm or a leg, usually the latter, but with a FOP Index of 4.0 in either case. "Even medical students too often in their histories call legs and arms extremities somewhat to the confusion of those who read hospital notes and are compelled to study out which extremities are meant" (Dr. Charles W. Burr, *Annals of Medical History*, IX, 1927). Doctor-talk remains much the same. Thus, when ex-President Nixon suffered from blood clots, one of his physicians characterized the condition as "deep venous thrombosis in the main veins draining Mr. Nixon's left lower extremity" (*New York Times*, 10/29/74). See also LIMB.

F

f – – –; also f – – k, f★★★, – – – –, etc. It hardly takes a genius to figure out that this is the most distinguished of the FOUR-LETTER WORDS—that the meaning is neither "fair" nor "foul," neither "fink" nor "funk," but simply "fuck," a.k.a. INTERCOURSE. Yet the blanks continue to be more printable than the letters for which they stand, e.g., reporting a banquet speech by Roseanne Barr at the annual convention of the American Booksellers Association: "She carefully began reading from the script she was clutching. But within minutes, much to the delight of her almost-dozing audience, she lost her place and shouted, 'F – – – it!' and launched into an ab-libbed 'real story'" (*Publishers Weekly*, 6/30/89).

From the sheer transparency of the dashes, it is obvious that the dasher-outers are more concerned with the imprint of the word upon the page than with the imprint of the thought upon the mind. It is the actual configuration of the letters before the eye that arouses an emotional response, one whose intensity has only recently begun to diminish through familiarity with the sight. As contrasted with ordinary euphemisms, which attempt to improve reality (SANITATION MAN for garbageman, for instance), or even to repress it (SLEEP for death), the dashes for the letters of "fuck" are straight substitutions and, as such, are closer kin to such substitutes for tabooed words as ADONAI, BLANK, DARN, DASH, and DEPARTED. This is true, too, of other dashed euphemisms, such as A – –, c – – t, p – – –, D – – –, G – – D – – – –, and H – – L, as well as aural euphemisms for *f – – –*, such as *firk,*

flog, fork, fratting (see FRATERNIZATION), FREAKING, *frick,* FRIG, FUG, FUNGOO, FUTZ, and PORK.

The origins of "fuck" are not well known on account of the dearth of early examples of the word in print—a reflection, most likely, of the taboo upon it. Folk etymologizers have dreamed up various acronyms to explain the word, e.g., "For Unnatural Carnal Knowledge," "For Unlawful Carnal Knowledge," and "Fornication Under the Consent of the King." These are sometimes said to have been used in medieval rape and sodomy cases, but philologists will be greatly surprised if documentary evidence for any of them is ever found.

The oldest examples of the word in its modern form come from Scottish writings of the early sixteenth century. Sir David Lyndesay employed it thusly in *Ane Satyre of the Thrie Estaits* (1535): "Bischops . . . may fuck thair fill and by vnmaryit." Variants of the period included *fukkit, fucke,* and *ffuck.* The present participle seems to have been *fukkand.* Still earlier, the word appeared in coded form—handled with tongs, in effect —in an anonymous pre-1500 poem satirizing the Carmelite friars of Cambridge, "Flyn, flyys" (from the first line, "Flen, flyys, and freris," i.e., "Fleas, flies, and friars"). The key word here is "gxddbov," where each letter stands for the preceding letter in the alphabet. Taking into account changes in the alphabet and spelling, this is deciphered in *The American Heritage Dictionary of the English Language* (1992) as the fake Latin *fvccant.* The crucial line, *Non sunt in coeli, quia gxddbov xxkxzt pg ifmk,* translates as "They [the friars] are not in heaven because they fuck the wives of Ely [a town nearby]."

The terrible term probably is related to the Middle Dutch *fokken,* to strike, to thrust, to copulate with, and the German *ficken,*

154

with the same meanings. It would be especially satisfying to be able to prove the German connection because *ficken* originally meant "knock," and this would make a neat psychological parallel with the modern KNOCK UP. The Latin *pungere*, to prick, and *pugil*, a boxer, both of which have the root *pug*, to thrust or strike, are presumed to be cognates of "fuck." As Allen Walker Read pointed out, this makes *"pugilist, pugnacious, puncture, appoint*, etc. . . . cousins of our nastiest word"* ("An Obscenity Symbol," *American Speech*, 12/34). The link to "pugilist" et al. also is in keeping with the common conjunction of violent and sexual meanings within the same word; see ACTION, for example.

Whatever its genesis, "fuck" soon became the taboo term, replacing such now-forgotten terms as *jape, sard*, OCCUPY, and *swive*, the last of which was what people did in Chaucer's time ("Thus swyved was this carpenteris wyf," *The Miller's Tale*, ca. 1387–1400) and, even later, as in "The Mock Song" (ca. 1676–77), by John Wilmot, second earl of Rochester:

I swive as well as others do;
I'm young, not yet deform'd
My tender heart, sincere, and true,
Deserves not to be scorned.

By Rochester's time, however, "swive" already was going out of fashion, except as a learned euphemism, while "fuck" was well on its way to becoming the-word-that-couldn't-be-printed. The term does not appear in Shakespeare's plays, for example, though the bard apparently knew it, judging from his use of such F-terms as *firk, foutre*, and *fut*.

The first of these Elizabethan beauties, "firk," had a wide range of meanings, including "to move briskly, to urge oneself forward, to beat." Other playwrights of the period also made sexual plays upon it. *Foutre*, meanwhile, is just archaic French for "fuck." Pistol employs both "firk" and "foutre" in much the same way that "fuck" is used today, e.g., "Master Fer? I'll fer him and firk him" (*Henry V*, 1599), and "A foutre for thine office" (*Henry IV, Part II*, 1596–97). The French term also is the occasion of merriment in *Henry V*, when the French princess, Katharine, learns that the English word for "foot" sounds like the indecent *foutre* in her own language. (She also professes to be shocked by "gown," rendered by her attendant, Alice, as "coun," which sounds like the French *con*; see VAGINA.) "Fut," finally, sometimes is said to be a variant of "foot," in turn a euphemistic clipping of "Christ's foot," an oath that dates at least to Chaucer's time. But it might also be an Anglicization of *foutre*, and the context suggests that Shakespeare had the sexual term in mind when Edmund exclaims in *King Lear* (1605–06): "My nativity was under Ursa Major, so that it follows I am rough and lecherous. Fut! I should have been that [what] I am, had the maidenliest star in the firmament twinkled on my bastardizing." (In some texts, "Fut" here is rendered as "Tut," which hardly seems in keeping with Edmund's anger.) In this connection, see also Shakespeare's use of FIG.

Aside from the bawdy works of Rochester, Robert Burns, and underground productions such as the anonymous *My Secret Life*, "fuck" appears only rarely in writings that have survived from the middle of the seventeenth century to the middle of the twentieth. Nathaniel Bailey and John Ash included it in dictionaries that they published in 1721 and 1775, respectively, but Samuel Johnson, by far the greatest and most influential lexicographer of the age, omitted the word from his *Dictionary of the English Language* (1755). That the good doctor knew the word is apparent, however, from a reminiscence by the actor David Garrick (a student of Johnson's at Litchfield and his longtime friend). "When it was asked what was the greatest pleasure," according to Garrick, "Johnson answered ✳✳✳✳✳✳✳" (from Read, *op. cit.*). Capt. Francis Grose did include the term in his *A Classical Dictionary of the Vulgar Tongue* (1785), but discreetly, in the form of "TO F – – K" and "DUCK F – CK – R. " (The latter was defined as "The man who has care of the poultry on board a ship of war.") When Grose's work was revised by "A Member of the Whip Club" and republished in 1811 as the *Lexicon Balatronicum,* the entry on "TO F – – K" was dropped. And toward the end of the nineteenth century, "fuck" was one of the two most conspicuous omissions (the other was "cunt") from the first edition of the monumental *Oxford English Dictionary* (vol. F being prepared in 1893–97).

The social taboos were reinforced by laws in both Great Britain (the Obscene Publications Act of 1857) and the United States (the Comstock Act of 1873). Offenders ran the risk of prosecution and loss of mailing privileges. For example, a legal investigation was mounted after a prankster embarrassed the London *Times* by putting the word in the attorney-general's mouth, quoting him as having said in Parliament that "he felt inclined for a bit of fucking" (1/23/1882). Despite the best efforts of red-faced management, the perpetrator of this "gross outrage" was never apprehended. The same person, or perhaps a copycat, even had the nerve to strike

again with an ad in the *Times* later that year for a book, "Every-day Life in Our Public Schools," featuring "a Glossary of Some Words used by Henry Irving in his disquisition upon fucking" (6/12/1882).

Not until after World War I, which had a liberating influence generally (see BRASSIERE and PANTIES), did the word begin to reappear in aboveground literature without causing the earth to move. Thus, the editors of *The Oxford English Dictionary,* who had ignored "fuckwind," another name for the kestrel, when putting volume F together in the 1890s, included its alternate, "windfucker," when they came to the Ws in the 1920s. As far as the general reading public is concerned, however, the real breakthrough was made by James Joyce in *Ulysses* (1922) when Private Carr shouted, "I'll wring the neck of any bugger says a word against my fucking king." And almost 200 pages later, Joyce used the word again, this time in the even more shocking literal sense, in Molly Bloom's final soliloquy: "I'll let him know that if that's what he wanted that his wife is fucked yes and damn well fucked yes and damn well fucked up to the neck nearly not by him 5 or 6 times handrunning . . ." Still, it was because of language of this sort that *Ulysses* was banned in the United States until 1933.

The legal precedent established by *Ulysses* was not really confirmed until society had experienced the liberating effects of a second global conflict. (Progress in semantics is sometimes costly in other ways.) In the United States, the great change seems to have occurred about 1950. Where Norman Mailer resorted to FUG in *The Naked and the Dead* (1948), James Jones used "fuck" in *From Here to Eternity* (1951). Which is not to imply that Jones wrote with complete freedom. Speaking of the editing of that book: "In the 859 pages, fuck was reduced from 258 mentions to a mere 50, and *cunt* and *prick* which appeared many times in the original manuscript, were eliminated by the cleansers" (Edward Sagarin, *The Anatomy of Dirty Words,* 1962).

The taboos were tumbling down, however. By 1959 (in the United States) and 1960 (in England), it became legal to publish D. H. Lawrence's *Lady Chatterley's Lover* (1928) as the author originally wrote it. Soon, even dictionary-makers took the blinkers off their eyes. *The Penguin Dictionary* included "fuck" in 1965, *The American Heritage Dictionary* in 1969, and *The Oxford English Dictionary* in its 1972 supplement.

Still, "fuck" retains much of its old power. Though now commonly printed in full in many books, and heard repeatedly in daily life, rap songs, and films (with ratings of PG-13 and above), almost all newspapers and FAMILY-oriented publications continue to dash out the term or euphemize it in other ways. Even the pioneer publisher of *The American Heritage Dictionary,* Houghton Mifflin, has waffled a bit. Thus, *The American Heritage Illustrated Encyclopedic Dictionary,* published in 1987, boasts 180,000 entries, but jumps from "fuchsin," a greenish, synthetic analine dyestuff, to "fucoid," of or belonging to the order of seaweeds known as *Fucales,* with nary a stop in between. FLIP, F-WORD, the abbreviated MOTHER, and the acronymic SNAFU also are acceptable in many situations where the terms for which they stand are not. Meanwhile, otherwise bold denizens of singles bars have been heard to say "FM?" when they mean "Fuck me?"; kids still write "FTL" on walls instead of "Fuck The Law"; and soldiers commonly speak in barely encoded terms, e.g., FNG, FOXTROT YANKEE, and FTA. Then there was the little old lady

in the West Country of England, a widow in her seventies, who had been taken to the cleaners as an investor in Lloyd's of London. She let the world know what she thought about the insurance syndicate by posting a new nameplate on her house: "This dwelling, [the sign] tells you, is called SDYOLLKCUF, which has a Celtic, perhaps Cornish, feel to it, though if you read it backward you find it altogether more Anglo-Saxon" (*New Yorker,* 9/20/93).

See also A – – and EXPLETIVE DELETED.

fabrication. A long-winded, Latinized lie. "In the strongest word I can use politely on the telephone, I want to say that is untrue, a fabrication, poppycock" (Dr. William Roper, head of the Centers for Disease Control, responding to charges by AIDS groups that for political reasons he had killed government ads urging use of condoms, *New York Times,* 7/1/92). "Fabrication" originally referred to the process of making something, but the word has been somewhat tarnished by the later sense of making up something. It has a FOP Index of 4.7. See also POPPYCOCK and WHITE LIE.

facetiae. A euphemism among learned bookmen for pornography. "Facetiae" once were just witty, refined, or facetious sayings, considered collectively. Thus, from a 1657 book on rhetoric: "The merry and pleasant sayings incident hereunto are called Facetiae." The word seems to have taken its turn for the worse during the nineteenth century. "He puts to the end of his catalogue . . . two pages that he calls 'Facetiae' . . . indecent books, indeed" (Henry Mayhew, *London Labour and the London Poor,* 1851). See also EROTICA.

facility. (1) A toilet; (2) a building.

The generalized "facility" has several advantages. In the case of "toilet," it simply blots out the embarrassment. Meanwhile, in the larger, structural sense, the Latinate term also is preferred by those who believe that they will seem to be more profound if fewer people understand what they say. Thus, "sports facility" is preferred to "sports arena" or "stadium," either of which presents a much clearer picture of what is meant, while "ancillary facility," which is how a soldier might describe a "bomb shelter," is hard to beat. Another, subtler advantage of "facility" is that it also means "ease of performance," "ability," and "dexterity," thus suggesting subliminally that someone may actually be accomplishing something in the building concerned. See also TOILET, and the specialized CORRECTIONAL FACILITY.

fact-finding trip. Junket. "Meantime, with five other senators [Harry S Truman] flew off to Mexico and Central America on a so-called 'fact-finding' trip—'a pleasure trip,' he was frank to admit" (David McCullough, *Truman*, 1992). In Great Britain, government officials refer to such excursions as "facility trips" (Jonathon Green, letter, 6/23/83).

fair. The dictionary definition of "moderately satisfactory or acceptable; passably good," is belied by the word's actual meaning in ratings of various kinds, where "fair" generally is a failing grade. An especially flagrant "fair" got A. J. Spano, a Colorado state representative, an honorable mention when the Committee on Public Doublespeak of the National Council of Teachers of English handed out its awards in 1979. Mr. Spano had proposed that air quality in Denver be improved by changing federal pollution standards so that hazardous would be redefined as "poor," dangerous as "acceptable," very unhealthy as "fair," unhealthy as "good," and "moderate" as very good. See also EXCELLENT, FINE, and FIRST CLASS.

fair trade. Restraint of trade; fixed price; unfair trade. "The Corning Glass Works announced today that it was discontinuing so-called 'fair trade' price fixing arrangements that have come under attack by consumer advocates" (AP, 4/7/75). "Fair trade," with its overtones of "free trade," is a good example of Reverse English, or the power of the euphemism to imply exactly the opposite of its actual meaning. "Fair trade" fits hand-in-glove with FREE ENTERPRISE.

faith. An archaic interjection, once used essentially as a euphemism for "God" in such phrases as "By my faith" and "On my faith." "Weapons outflourished in the wind, my faith!" (Robert Browning, *Prince Hohenstiel-Schwangau*, 1871). See also GOSH.

fall/fallen. To die, especially in combat; to be dead. When applied to soldiers who "drop down" on the battlefield, "fall" actually is a euphemistic shortening of "fall dead." The expression probably originated soon after the first soldier fell. As Aias said after Patroklos was killed: "I think he [Achilles] has not yet heard the ghastly news, how his beloved companion has fallen" (*The Iliad of Homer*, ca. 750 B.C., trans. Richmond Lattimore, 1951). See also BITE THE DUST.

fallen woman. An archaic euphemism for a woman who is not married and who is not a virgin. In the nineteenth century, this was one of the polite terms for a whore, or PROS-TITUTE. "The once fall'n woman must for ever fall" (George Gordon, Lord Byron, *Marino Faliero, Doge of Venice,* 1820). Rarely heard in the United States nowadays, the expression lingers on as a colloquialism for becoming pregnant in Britain, where a woman might say, "We were married nearly a year before I fell." For a similar *fall,* see ANKLE, SPRAIN AN.

family. No sex, as distinguished from ADULT. "Most newspapers still use the cliché 'a family newspaper' to describe them-selves, although the kind of family to which they are presumably dedicated disappeared during the sixties, except at certain levels. Broadcasting shares this dedication. . . . In both media, 'family' applied to 'newspaper' or 'entertainment' means 'no sex'" (John Tebbel, *The Media in America,* 1974).

Of course, the publishers of *family* news-papers, the TV broadcasters of "Family Hour" shows, and Dr. Donald E. Wild-mon's American Family Association (which campaigns against profanity and violence as well as sex) are just tippytoeing along in the giant footsteps of Henrietta Maria Bowdler and her brother Thomas, whose expurgated edition of Shakespeare, called *The Family Shakespeare* (naturally), quickly made their own family name synonymous (by 1836, *OED*) with prudish censorship. As Thomas explained in the preface to the enlarged, second edition of their work, published in 1818:

"Nothing is added to the original text; but those words and expressions are omitted which cannot with propriety be read aloud in a family." Because his name appeared as editor of the 1818 edition, Thomas usually has been given all the credit for the squea-mishness that made bowdlerism a house-

hold word. Modern scholarship has revealed, however, that the true culprit was Henrietta Maria ("Harriet" to her family), who produced the first edition of *The Family Shakespeare* in 1807 but didn't sign it. Proba-bly, as a maiden lady, she didn't want to admit publicly to knowing the meanings of all the words she had excised.

See also FAMILY VALUES and, for more about taking the bite out of the Bard, LIE/LIE WITH. For the comparable job that Noah Webster did on the Bible, continue with PECULIAR MEMBERS.

family jewels. The balls or TESTICLES, which are precious and must be protected, not only because of the progeny that descends from them but because of the pain that occurs when they are injured. The phrase is of uncertain antiquity; "jewels" alone has been used in the testicular sense since before 1500. In the CIA, the expression gained another euphemistic meaning when employed in 1973 by "a wag" (ex-director William Colby's characterization) to de-scribe the agency's most sensitive (i.e., ille-gal) secrets, such as its domestic MAIL COVER and SURVEILLANCE programs. Colby main-tained that he himself referred to the *family jewels* as "our skeletons in the closet" (*Honorable Men,* 1978). See also PRIDES, ROCKS, and SCHMO.

family lawyer. Divorce lawyer; a practi-tioner of *family law.* "Q. Before you were a judge, you had a very lucrative practice as a divorce lawyer. *A.* We call it family law" (interview with California Superior-Court Judge Howard Broadman, *Time,* 3/9/92). See also MATRIMONIAL LAWYER.

family planning. Birth control in positive guise. "Family planning" is to "birth control" as PRO-CHOICE is to "abortion." "It was members of this committee [the Birth Control Investigation Committee] who persuaded Lady Denman to form what is now called the Family Planning Association to coordinate the work" (London *Times*, 4/30/70). See also PLANNED PARENTHOOD.

family values. Conventional heterosexual sex within the bonds of matrimony; frequently combined with opposition to sex education, abortion rights, and gay rights, e.g., Colorado for Family Values, which campaigned successfully in 1992 for the repeal of local ordinances barring discrimination against homosexuals. "There are some who feel that the phrase 'family values' is a kind of code and an indirect condemnation of people who choose different lifestyles, like homosexuals" (Stone Phillips, NBC-TV News, interview with President George Bush, 8/11/92). See also FAMILY.

family way, in the. Pregnant. "The Countess was again in the family way" (Mrs. Eliza Parsons, *The Mysterious Warning*, 1796). This relic of the period of pre-Victorian prudery was still being employed regularly in the 1960s, according to Johnny Carson, who cited it and WITH CHILD as euphemisms for "pregnant," a word that "couldn't be used on TV ten years ago" ("The Tonight Show," WNBC-TV, 11/19/74). See also ENCEINTE and PREGNANT.

family with service needs. Family that abuses its children; a tactful legalism in Connecticut.

fancy. A precious euphemistic building block. Thus, over the years, *fancy house* has meant whorehouse, while *fancy woman* and *fancy girl* have stood at different times for sweetheart, mistress, and whore (or PROSTITUTE). The history of *fancy man* is even more tangled, having been applied to gigolos, to sweethearts generally, to pimps, and to homosexuals. Speaking of the last: "The 'fancy men' are homosexuals, usually passive, of whom there are always several on any windjammer even in these days and who cater to the desires of the officers (and often the men) in return for money, special privileges, etc." (David W. Maurer, *American Speech*, 10/42). In rhyming slang, a *fancy man* might also be known as a *nancy*. See also GAY.

fanny. The buttocks or ass. "If a senator is putting his hand on my fanny and telling me how he's going to vote on impeaching President Nixon, I'm not so sure I'm going to remove his hand no matter how demeaning it is" (Sally Quinn, in *Media People*, magazine, mailing, rec'd 11/29/79).

The blossoming of "fanny" in the public prints is a comparatively new phenomenon. This sense of the word is dated to 1919 in the *Random House Historical Dictionary of American Slang* (J. E. Lighter, 1994). It must be a good bit older, however, since it was understood widely enough in the 1920s to be worked into vaudeville routines—and then to be banned from the Keith circuit in 1929. Other words and expressions on the Keith Index included: ARAB, *belly* (see ABDOMEN), *cockeyed, dammit, to hell with, lousy, pushover,* and *wop* (H. L. Mencken, *The American Language, Supplement One*, 1945).

The origin of "fanny" is a minor lexicographical mystery. One school of thought holds that the term is an eponym, commemorating a particular Fanny with a very large one. In this connection, note that the personal name now is usually avoided. Thus, Fanny Rose Shore metamorphosed into Dinah Shore, while the diminutive of Frances today commonly is Fran or Franny. The general shift away from "Fanny" almost certainly reflects the increasing taint of the anatomical connotation. Although the government has refrained from articulating the reason, this also appears to be why the Federal National Mortgage Association is known in short as *Fannie* Mae, not *Fanny* Mae.

Several other etymologies have been proposed. One possibility is that the anatomical "fanny" derives from the punishment sometimes administered to it, i.e., "to fan," in the sense of "to spank." More likely, though equally unproved, is that the human "fanny" comes from the nautical "fantail," the overhanging stern of some ships. (There is a strong convergence here, since people also have TAILS, while both ships and people are said to have *poops* and *sterns*.) Finally, this may be simply a case of displaced meaning, since "fanny" was employed in British slang from the first half of the nineteenth century to refer to the vulva (or VAGINA). Here, too, the word might be an eponym, deriving in this case from Fanny Hill, heroine of John Cleland's *Memoirs of a Woman of Pleasure* (1749). "Fanny" in the vulvar sense—still current in British English—may sound odd to American ears, but it is by no means the only word to have managed to carry both meanings; see KEISTER and TAIL. The curious thing here is that the diminutive "Fanny" appears to be less objectionable in Great Britain than the United States. Thus, the British film *Fanny by Gaslight* was retitled for display on American theater marquees as *Man of Evil* (1944).

See also ARSE, BOO-BOO (for another con-troversial "fanny"), and TRAMP (for a similar film retitling).

fatigue. "Battle fatigue" is World War II's enervated version of World War I's "shell shock," while "mental fatigue" closely resembles "mental depression," as in: "Six days earlier, Eagleton [Sen. Thomas E. Eagleton, D., Mo.] had revealed that he had undergone electric shock treatment for mental fatigue in the 1960's" (Bob Woodward and Carl Bernstein, *All the President's Men,* 1974). Then there is the original French *fatigué,* which is not only acceptable but "smart" in places where plain English would never do, e.g., from an ad for a woman's T-shirt with *"Je suis fatigué"* emblazoned across the chest: "'I'm tired!' says the tee—so much more expressive in French, isn't it?" (Lillian Vernon catalog). See also MENTAL, NERVOUS EXHAUSTION, and POSTTRAUMATIC NEUROSIS.

faux. False, fake, counterfeit, bogus. French is always finer, as in "Princess Diana wears Mr. Lane's 'Princess Necklace' of faux pearls, diamonds, and blue sapphire. Now you can wear it, too" (for $95, ad, *New Yorker,* 10/21/91).

favors. To enjoy the favor of a woman's company is one thing, but to enjoy her *favors* is quite another, since the word that in the singular may refer to a "little gift or remembrance given as a token of esteem, affection, or hospitality," becomes in the plural a euphemism for some form of sexual INTERCOURSE or SERVICE. For example, speaking of a once-powerful congressman from Ohio: "Mr. [Wayne L.] Hays today admitted having a relationship with the woman, but denied that she had been hired for her sexual favors" (*New York*

Times, 5/26/76). His denial was undercut somewhat by the admission to reporters of the woman in question, Ms. Elizabeth Ray, that "I can't type. I can't file. I can't even answer the phone." For this she was paid $14,000 a year (which obviously bought more in 1976 than it does today).

Careful writers have been making use of "favors" for many years. Thus, speaking of the Flathead Indians: "Chastity is particularly esteemed, and no woman will barter her favors, even with the whites, upon any mercenary consideration" (*Alexander Henry's Journal,* 1811). The euphemism dates at least to the sixteenth century, when the term was used more or less synonymously with CHARMS, e.g., the bawdy exchange between Hamlet and the courtiers, Rosencrantz amd Guildenstern:

> GUILDENSTERN: On Fortune's cap we are not the very button.
> HAMLET: Nor the soles of her shoe?
> ROSENCRANTZ: Neither, my Lord.
> HAMLET: Then you live about her waist, or in the middle of her favors?
> GUILDENSTERN: Faith, her privates we.
> HAMLET: In the secret parts of Fortune?
> Oh, most true, she is a strumpet.

On this topic, the last word, so to speak, is what our ancestors called "the last favor." As Moll Flanders reports: "However, though he took these freedoms with me, it did not go to that which they call the last favour." (Daniel Defoe, *Moll Flanders,* 1722). See also PRIVATE PARTS, PUT OUT, and RELATIONSHIP.

feature. A bug in a computer program, as in "This new program has several interesting features" (Stephen Manes, personal communication, 5/11/94).

feces. Normal people do not normally use this word or its variant, "faeces" (the chiefly British spelling), but when they do, it is as a euphemism for "shit." "Next to the word 'damn,' the most common expletive in the English language is the four-letter word for feces" (Leonard Feinberg, "The Secret of Humor," *Maledicta,* 1978). "Feces" originally meant "dregs" (or CRAP) and the earliest examples of the word's use in English (ca. 1465) deal with the "feces" of wine, salad oil, etc. The term began to be used for excrement in the seventeenth century and now, of course, the "bad" meaning has driven out the "good" one, so this is its only meaning. See also DEFECATE/DEFECATION.

fellatio. A relatively new and printable term for an old and unprintable act, the sucking or licking of the PENIS—"penilingus," to lapse into another Latinate term, or "corksacking," as Anthony Burgess euphemized it in EFF. "Fellatio," deriving from the Latin *fellare,* to suck, and so, through the root, *fe,* to suckle, is related to such relatively innocuous words as "fecund," "fetus," "filial," and FEMALE. (The etymology parallels that of the synonymous but more esoteric "irrumation," from the Latin *irrumo,* to give suck.) The oldest example of "fellatio" in *The Oxford English Dictionary* comes from H. Havelock Ellis's *Studies in the Psychology of Sex* (1897), a work that also supplies—by a not-so-remarkable coincidence—the oldest CUNNILINGUS. During the preceding decade, dating back to 1887, other writers had used "fellation" for the act, and "fellator" and "fellatrix" for those who perform it, male and female, respectively. The proper adjective is "fellatory" and the verb is "fellate," as in "Lazily she fellated him while he combed her lovely hair" (John Updike, *Couples,*

1969). See also BLOW, MOUTH MUSIC, and SOIXANTE-NEUF.

felo de se. A suicide or the act of committing suicide; a legalism (from the Anglo-Latin *felo,* felon, plus *de,* of, plus *se,* self). Herewith, a taste of the humor that apparently reduced our ancestors to helpless laughter, from the original *Joe Miller's Jests* (1739):

> An under Officer of the Customs at the Port of Liverpool, running heedlessly along a Ship's Gunnel, happened to tip overboard and was drown'd; being soon after taken up, the Coroner's Jury was summoned to sit upon the Body. One of the Jury-Men returning home, was call'd to by an Alderman of the Town, and ask'd what Verdict they brought in, and whether they found it *Felo de se: Ay, ay* says the Jury-Man shaking his Noddle, he fell into the Sea, sure enough.

See also BRIEF ILLNESS and SELF-DELIVERANCE.

female. One of two (with LADY) main euphemisms in nineteenth-century America for WOMAN. Thus, when Emma Willard, pioneer of education for women, began founding schools, the operative word was always "female," as in the Middlebury (Vermont) Female Seminary (1814) and the Waterford (New York) Female Academy (1819). But gradually, of course, "female" began to acquire some of the base sexual associations of the word it had replaced. By 1861, the pendulum had swung so far that when Vassar Female College was established, the editor of *Godey's Lady's Book,* Mrs. Sarah Josepha Hale, protested loudly.

She argued that "female" was not in good taste because "many writers employ the word as a noun, which, when applied to women, is improper and sounds unpleasantly, as referring to an animal. To illustrate: almost every newspaper we open, or book we read, will have sentences like these: 'A man and two *females* were seen,' etc. . . . 'The *females* were much alarmed.' . . . It is inelegant as well as absurd." Mrs. Hale won the day; the offending "female" was expunged from Vassar College (just as well, now that males are admitted) and her argument was generally accepted. At the end of the century, *The Oxford English Dictionary* noted that "female" as a synonym for "woman" was "now commonly avoided by good writers, except with contemptuous implication."

Today, "female" still seems irredeemably biological (N.B.: *female complaint,* not "women's complaint"), and so is still avoided except when constructing classified ads, e.g.: "Female, 32, attractive, sensitive, warm, alive, seeks intelligent, sincere, stable mate." Even in this context, however, "female" appears less often than "woman." For example, in a randomly selected issue of *The New York Review of Books* (2/3/77), references to feminine gender in the personal ads broke down this way: woman, 22; female, 9; lady, 4; blonde, 1; femme, 1; girl, 1; person, 1; one, 1. In the 1990s, "woman" was still the preferred term. Thus, from the same department in the same publication (10/7/93): woman, 16; female, 6; lady, 3; widow, 2; writer, 2 (one of them a "redhead writer"), and—a mixed bag, indeed—an academic, damsel, dominatrix, feminine package, grande dame, Southern belle, and surfer (1 each).

Aside from its essential sexual aspect, another strike against "female" in the minds of some liberated PERSONS is that the word implies by its formation that "females" are in some way derived from, or subordinate to, "males." But this is a mistake. "Female" does not come from its "obvious" root any more than "woman" comes from its apparent source. Rather, "female" derives from the French *femelle,* which, in turn, comes from the Latin *femella,* the diminutive of *femina,* meaning "woman" (literally, "one who suckles"), from *fe,* to suckle. The present spelling of "female" is the result of a fourteenth-century confusion with the sound-alike "male," which actually has an entirely different Latin ancestor, *masculus.* See also HERSTORY and MALE.

fertilizer. MANURE; a second-order euphemism, *manure* itself standing for something worse. "The fertilizer really hit the fan" (CNN weather report, 3/26/85).

There is a famous story about Harry S Truman, which may be apocryphal but has the ring of truth:

> "I grew up on a farm," the president is said to have said, "and I know that farming means manure, manure, and more manure." At which a friend of the president's wife leaned over, saying, "Really, Bess, you should teach Harry to say 'fertilizer,' not 'manure.'" "Mrs. Truman shook her head sadly. "Good Lord," she replied, "do you know that it has taken me thirty years to get him to say 'manure'?"

"Fertilizer," which is sometimes further disguised as BIOSOLIDS, NIGHT SOIL, and *plantfood* (or even *organic plantfood*), did not come into its present meaning until the nineteenth century. Originally, the word

applied only to the person or other agency that enriched the soil, perhaps even, in a sentence that was composed as late as 1872 but which only an irreverent writer would produce today, the Lord himself: "The march of Jehovah, the Fertiliser, may be traced by the abundance which he creates" (Charles Haddon Spurgeon, *The Treasury of David*). The extension of the word's meaning, from the action of fertilizing to include the material, is standard euphemistic operating technique; see DROPPINGS.

festival seating. General admission, unreserved seating. Popularized by promoters of rock concerts in the 1970s, the term and the practice have led to periodic tragedies when holders of *festival seating* tickets have stampeded, e.g., in Cincinnati, Ohio, where eleven people were trampled to death on December 12, 1979, while trying to get into a concert by The Who in Riverfront Coliseum. See also REAR MEZZANINE.

fib. A lie or to lie. Deriving perhaps from "fibble-fable," itself a reduplication of "fable," the "fib" implies that the lie is trivial or childish, except, of course, when the word is being used euphemistically, e.g., "I do not say he lyes neither: no, I am too well bred for that: but his Lordship fibbs most abominably" (John Dryden, *Amphitryon, or The Two Sosias,* 1690). Keeping company with John Dryden is William Safire, who reports: "Newspapers, magazines, and broadcasters harped on news management as soon as the worst of the [1962 Cuban] missile crisis was over, with much justification. There had been some fibbing in high places. Assistant Defense Secretary Arthur Sylvester later talked about the 'government's right, if necessary, to lie'" (*Safire's Political Dictionary,* 1978). See also WHITE LIE.

field interview. Field interrogation; questioning by police on the prowl of people who look suspicious for one reason or another. "Police Maj. Colin McCormack said such stops are called 'field interviews,' and in the past two years police have done 3,500" (*Litchfield County*, Conn., *Times*, 5/13/94). This was in New Milford, Connecticut, which must be teeming with suspicious people, considering that the constabulary had found reasons for conducting *field interviews* with what amounts to about 15 percent of the town's 1990 population of 23,629. Some individuals had been stopped more than once, of course, and they tended to regard the *field interviews* as harassment. See also BOOKED FOR INVESTIGATION and POLYGRAPH INTERVIEW.

fig. A multipurpose imprecation, much favored by Shakespeare and other Elizabethans, e.g., "When Pistol lies, do this, and fig me like The bragging Spaniard" (*Henry IV, Part II*, 1596–97). Sometimes rendered as "fico" and "figo," the term is short for "fig of Spain." The reference is to a standard gesture of contempt in Mediterranean lands, wherein the thumb is inserted between two fingers. It is a visual pun. The words for "fig" and "vulva" (see VAGINA) are the same in Italy and other fig-growing countries, and the fruit has long been freighted with sexual associations. From Aristophanes' *The Peace* (422 B.C.): "Now live splendidly together,/Free from adversity./Pick your figs./May his be large and hard./May hers be sweet." Judging from the contexts in which the Elizabethans used the term (see also CONVEY), it seems likely that they latched on to the foreign word as a substitute for their own, already unprintable F-WORD. In turn, this may have helped popularize "not give (or care) a fig," which,

on the face of it, makes more sense as a expression of unconcern in lands where figs grow profusely, and have relatively little value, than in England, where they are imported delicacies.

figure. Breasts. "A modiste will insist on a brassière to support the figure and give it the proper up-to-date shape" (*Queen* magazine, from 1916, in C. Willett and Phillis Cunnington, *The History of Underclothes*, 1992). See also BOSOM, BRASSIERE, and FULL-FIGURED.

filch. Steal. The connotations of "filch" suggest petty thievery—the *filching* of towels from fancy hotels, say—and so make the term useful for downplaying more serious crimes. "Apparently a Reagan mole in the Carter camp had filched papers" (Laurence Barrett, *Gambling With History*, 1988). The "filch" works because the papers themselves had little intrinsic value; it was because of what was on them—briefings for the president—that the FBI investigated the crime. Shakespeare exploited the same dynamics of "filch," applying it to something of little apparent value which, in fact, is most precious. Thus, Iago—that soul of virtue—protests in *Othello* (1604):

> Who steals my purse steals trash; 'tis
>   something, nothing;
> 'Twas mine, 'tis his, and has been slave to
>   thousands;
> But he that filches from me my good name
> Robs me of that which not enriches him
> And makes me poor indeed.

See also APPROPRIATE.

file. Forget. "Let's put that in the circular file" (i.e., wastebasket) translates as "Let's forget it." Naturally, since "file" means "forget," it follows that "do not file" must mean "remember." Thus, J. Edgar Hoover's FBI filed some 10,000 pages of material on the American Civil Liberties Union in what it called "do not file files."

filet mignon. The foods we eat almost always seem tastier when served with French names. In part, this is due to the general euphemistic rule that "French is always finer." Frenchification has the additional advantage in the case of meat dishes of blurring the diner's mental image of the creature being consumed. A relatively new entrant into English (1906), "filet mignon" translates literally as "delicate" or "dainty slice," but actually, as semanticist-turned-senator S. (for "Sam") I. Hayakawa pointed out: "finest-quality filet mignon" really is just another way of saying "first-class piece of dead cow."

The use of French terms for cooked animals stems from the Norman conquest of England. As noted by Wamba, the not-so-foolish jester in Sir Walter Scott's *Ivanhoe* (1819), Saxon serfs herded Saxon animals, whose names were translated for the delectation of French-speaking lords:

Pork, I think, is good Norman-French; and so when the brute lives, and is in charge of a Saxon slave, she goes by her Saxon name [swine]; but becomes a Norman and is called pork [*porc*], when she is carried to the castle hall to feast among the nobles. . . . I can tell you more . . . there is old Alderman Ox continues to hold his Saxon epithet while he is under charge of serfs and bondsmen . . . but becomes Beef [*boeuf*], a fiery French

gallant, when he arrives before the worshipful jaws that are destined to consume him. Mynherr Calf, too, becomes Monsieur de Veau [veal] in the like manner: he is Saxon when he requires tendance, and, takes a Norman name when he becomes a matter of enjoyment.

Other animals whose names are converted from English, when they are on the hoof, to French, when they appear on the plate, include deer, which becomes VENISON (*venaison*), goat, which becomes CHEVON, and sheep, which becomes mutton (*mouton*). Then there is fat liver paste, which is much more appetizing when presented as *pâté de fois gras*.

For more about eating meat, see CHEVALENE, DRUMSTICK, FRAGRANT MEAT, FRY, HOOVER HOG, JOINT, PARSON'S-NOSE, PENGUIN, PRAIRIE OYSTERS, RABBIT, SALISBURY STEAK, SWEETBREAD, TUBE STEAK, VARIETY MEATS, and WHITE MEAT. Fish-eaters should consult CAPE COD TURKEY.

fille de joie. A whore. "Bill Novak and Norman MacArthur . . . bought their 1881 Neo-Grec style house seven years ago when it was a rooming house with two *filles de joie*" (*Park Slope*, Brooklyn, *Civic News*, 4/77). *Filles de joie* may also be said to live and work in a *maison, maison de joie*, or *maison close* (closed house). See also HOUSE and PROSTITUTE.

Final Solution, the. The best known of the opaque Nazi allusions to the program for exterminating Europe's Jews during World War II. Besides "Final Solution" (*Endlösung*), the Nazis also used "evacuation" (*Aussiedlung*), "special treatment" (*Sonder-*

behandlung), and "resettlement" (*Umsiedlung*) in the same way.

Just when "Final Solution" became a euphemism for mass murder is not known. The term was used as early as September 1938 by Franz Stuckart, who had drafted the Nuremberg Laws of 1935. He wrote that the decisions embodied in these laws, which stripped German Jews of their citizenship and placed many restrictions upon them, would "lose their importance as the 'Final Solution' of the Jewish problem is approached." At this date, Stuckart probably was referring to the purging of the Reich of Jews by deportation rather than by killing. After the war began, however, the genocidal meaning was attached to the phrase. The original version of what became known as the "Führer Order on the Final Solution" probably was issued verbally by Hitler to Hermann Göring, Reinhard Heydrich, and Heinrich Himmler, who passed it down the line. This apparently occurred as plans were being made to attack Russia on June 22, 1941. During May, the army and the SS reached an agreement allowing the invading forces to be accompanied by the *Einsatzgruppen,* roving units charged with taking "executive measures affecting the civilian population." The "executive measures" (see also EXECUTIVE ACTION) involved the summary execution of eleven categories of people: Russian officials, "fanatical" Communists, etc., with "Category Number 10" including "All Jews." Adolf Eichmann seems to have understood the euphemism as early as May 20, 1941, when a memo from his office advised German consulates that Jewish emigration from Belgium and France was banned because "the final solution of the Jewish question" was in sight. And by July 31, 1941, when Göring wrote Heydrich, who was in charge of the *Einsatzgruppen,* saying, "I request, furthermore, that you send me an overall plan . . . for the implementation of the desired final solution of the Jewish question," Heydrich almost certainly knew just what Goring had in mind (quotes from Nora Levin, *The Holocaust,* 1968).

See also ETHNIC CLEANSING, LIQUIDATE/ LIQUIDATION, PROCESS, PROTECTIVE CUSTODY, and SPECIAL TREATMENT.

fine. Not so fine. Everything is relative when it comes to grading the condition of coins, books, and other items. A "fine" coin, for example, may have been knocked around quite a bit. "*Fine:* The wear is considerable although the entire design is still strong and visible" (*Coin World Guide to U.S. Coins, Prices & Value Trends,* 1993). On a scale where mint state equals sixty, a *fine* coin would have a numerical ranking of twelve. See also EXCELLENT, FAIR, and FIRST CLASS.

finger wave. A rectal exam, as for drugs. "Apparently annoyed at discovering nothing illegal, they decided to give him a 'finger wave.' One customs man approached Lenny—pulling on a rubber glove and carrying a tube of K-Y jelly" (Albert Goldman, from the journalism of Lawrence Schiller, *Ladies and Gentleman, Lenny Bruce!!,* 1974).

fire fighter. A fireman—and a rarity among genderless job designations for appealing to men as well as to women. The women like it because it desexualizes the occupation, e.g.: "Terms incorporating gender reference should be avoided. Use fire fighter instead of fireman, business executive instead of businessman, letter carrier instead of mailman" (*The Bulletin,* American Society of Newspaper Editors, 9/76). Meanwhile, the firemen, who are among the staunchest resisters to admitting women into their occupation, also prefer "fire fighter," which emphasizes the dangers of their work (helpful when it comes to negotiating new contracts). Hence, most of the "firemen" in the United States and Canada belong to the International Association of Fire Fighters. See also ENGINEER and PERSON.

first class. A euphemism in the travel business for second class.

"First class" became second class in fact, though not in name, following the creation of DELUXE. Thus, a *first-class* hotel charges less than a *deluxe* one. Such a displacement has ripple effects throughout the classification systems, with *second class* in name becoming third class in fact, and so forth.

See also COACH, FAIR, LARGE, TOURIST, and WORLD-CLASS.

first-year student. A freshman on politically correct campuses where the generic "man" is to be avoided at all costs. See also FRESHPERSON.

five-finger discount. Shoplifting. A correspondent who prefers to remain anonymous tells how she first heard this term in the early 1960s after a mall opened in Richmond, Virginia: "It was *the* place to go— including kids. To my horror my children told me that some of their acquaintances thought it was a lark to obtain merchandise by the method of five-finger discount. . . . I just had to insist that shoplifting is stealing no matter what fanciful name was given to it" (letter, 3/31/82). See also APPROPRIATE, HOOK, and SWIPE.

fix. A neutral word for concealing various unmentionable operations, such as neutering ("Has kitty been fixed?"), bribery ("The legislature's been fixed again."), tampering of various kinds (*fixing* a race, say, by *fixing* a horse), and even killing, e.g., "McDonald got up and said, 'I'll fix you, Fiddler Neary.' He drew a weapon" (*Chicago Tribune,* 9/25/1875). See also ALTER and HIT.

flatulence. Deriving from the Latin *flatus,* a blowing, "flatulence" is another gold-plated term, comparable to CREPITATION, for the body's interior turbulence. See also BREAK WIND.

flight attendant. While airlines also employ stewards, most *flight attendants* are women, and they are what used to be known as "stewardesses." The union in the field is the Association of Flight Attendants. The adoption of the neuter "flight attendant" is part of the current, sweeping desexualization of job titles (see PERSON), but the stewardesses had another, specific gripe, this title often being shortened to "stew," an old word for "brothel" as well as for the woman who worked in one. See also ENGINEER, FOUNTAIN ATTENDANT, and STEW.

flip. "Flip" is an acceptable swear word (along with "pick" and "scrud") among Mormon missionaries around the world (Kary D. Smout, *American Speech,* Summer 1988). As adverb and participle, "flipping" also makes a mild substitute for a stronger term, presumably also beginning with "F." Thus, from an interview with an Englishman who raised maggots as bait for fishermen: "'I wish fishing were as popular as flipping darts,' he says. 'I'd be a flipping big star. I'd be riding around in a flipping limousine'" (*Wall Street Journal*, 9/13/83). See also F – – –.

FLK. Funny Looking Kid. The abbreviation is used in pediatric wards to refer to babies whose appearance suggests the existence of a genetic defect.

flueologist. A British chimney sweep, noted by John Moore in *You English Words* (1961). See also ENGINEER and GARBOLOGIST.

Flying Fortress. The B-17 long-range bomber, of World War II fame. Its name to the contrary, the plane was designed strictly as an offensive weapon for striking the enemy behind his lines. "In 1936 the Army agreed to buy thirteen such planes, which it designated the B-17 and called the Flying Fortress, in politically expedient but ironic suggestion that the purpose was thoroughly defensive" (Russell F. Weigley, *The American Way of War*, 1973). See also DE-FENSE, DEPARTMENT OF; PEACEKEEPER; and PRECISION BOMBING.

FNG. Fucking New Guy; a military term in Vietnam and later for a replacement, a new man in an outfit; pronounced "fenugie," a.k.a., among other things, a *newbie* (from "new baby"), *newfer,* and *new meat.* See also F – – –, FTA, and SNAFU.

folk art. Primitive art. "It is perhaps understandable that Klaus Perls justifies his lifelong pursuit of only the art of Benin by labeling the rest of the art of Africa 'folk art.' Thankfully, the often used slanderous and possibly racist term 'primitive' was not used, but admirers of the greatness of African tribal life and art catch his

drift" (George Lois, letter, *New York Times*, 2/9/92).

It has been quite some time—from the 1960s, at least—since art collectors, anthropologists, or anyone else, for that matter, could get away with such a sentence as "The three primitive peoples described in this volume . . . ," which is how Ruth Benedict began her acknowledgments in *Patterns of Culture* (1934). See also PRELITERATE.

foreigner. Italian. "Don't use 'Italian' in crime stories; say foreigner" (from the "Don't List" of the *New York Herald*, during the long editorial reign—1867–1918—of James Gordon Bennett, Jr.). See also ORGANIZED CRIME.

fornicate/fornication. Whether as a verb or a noun, the technical, Latinate terms for voluntary sexual intercourse between people who are not married to each other serve also as euphemisms for the prototypical FOUR-LETTER WORD. Thus, the anonymous author of *My Secret Life* (ca. 1890) describes the pictures owned by a London whore (or GAY woman) back in the days when the world had not yet been blessed with color photography: "She had . . . a selection of thoroughly good, coloured, cock rousing lithographs of fornication." In our own time, the greater acceptability of the Latin was well illustrated by public reaction to Jimmy Carter's indiscreet interview in *Playboy* (11/76). While many bluenoses wrinkled theirs at Carter's use of SCREW and SHACK UP, hardly anyone objected to the future president's remark that, as governor of Georgia, "I didn't run around breaking down people's doors to see if they were fornicating."

"Fornication" is distinguished for having an unusually piquant etymology: It comes from *fornix*, the Latin word for "arch" or "vault." Roman brothels, it seems, often were located in basements with arched ceilings. Because of this, *fornix* acquired the additional meaning of "brothel"; "to frequent brothels" became *fornicari*, and the noun, for the act, followed naturally. See also EXTRAMARITAL, F – – –, INTERCOURSE, and, for Noah Webster's euphemism for "fornication," PECULIAR MEMBERS.

forward observer. A sniper. Prosecutors at the Texas trial of the Branch Dravidians in 1994 called FBI man Mike Toulouse a "forward observer," apparently in an effort to minimize the government's responsibility for the deaths that occurred when federal agents assaulted the sect's compound in Waco. When called to the stand, however, Mr. Toulouse described himself as a "sniper."

fouled up. Fucked up. See also SNAFU.

foundation garment. A corset, corselet, or girdle, sometimes abbreviated to "foundation," as in "Abraham and Straus Semi-annual Foundations Sale, June 4 to July 4" (flyer, 1978). See also BODY BRIEFER.

fountain attendant. A soda jerk. The longer title enables the functionary to escape the associations of "jerk" with "fool," "dummy," and, even worse, the "jerkoff," who is a masturbator as well as a stupid person. See also FLIGHT ATTENDANT.

four-letter word. A "dirty" word, usually an ANGLO-SAXON one; a MONOSYLLABLE. "The obscene 'four-letter words' of the English language are not cant or slang or dialect, but belong to the oldest and best-established element in the English vocabulary. They are not even substandard, for they form part of the linguistic equipment of speakers of standard English" (Allen Walker Read, "An Obscenity Symbol," *American Speech*, 12/34). "'Four-letter words' (itself a euphemistic expression to skirt having to use other words) are more strictly taboo than any others in the English language" (Peter Farb, *Word Play: What Happens When People Talk*, 1974). "Slang has an aggressive, macho quality. In Ireland, it is largely confined to the use of one multi-purpose four letter verb and the noun and adjective derived from it—often all three occur in a single sentence" (Eileen Battersby, *Irish Times Weekend*, 9/29/90).

The phrase "four-letter word" was dated to 1929 by Eric Partridge, who linked it to the furor over the appearance the previous year of *Lady Chatterley's Lover* by D. H. Lawrence. It was preceded, and perhaps inspired, by *four-letter man*, which was a euphemism of World War I for a very objectionable or obnoxious person (i.e., a "shit"). Later, around 1930, "four-letter man" also came to mean "homosexual" (from "homo"). See also THREE-LETTER MAN.

Authorities are divided as to the exact number of four-letter words, with different lists varying according to the fastidiousness of the list-maker. For example, "guts" has four letters, and some have believed it revolting enough to deserve euphemizing (see INTESTINAL FORTITUDE and PLUCK). The term also may be extended in such phrases as "Work is a four-letter word." Still, "guts" and "work" seem lily-livered in comparison to some of the other *four-letter words* that may possibly come to the reader's mind. In fact, all the true *four-letter words* deal with the most intimate parts of the human body, and the excretory and sexual functions thereof. Partridge gave the following list in his *Dictionary of Slang and Unconventional English* (1970): arse, ball(s), cock, cunt, fart, fuck, piss, quim, shit, and twat. To this, some would add "turd" (see T – – –). The most powerful, most versatile of the group generally is conceded to be "fuck"; it was, in fact, the subject of Allan Walker Read's "The Obscenity Symbol," although not once in the course of that entertaining, erudite, fifteen-page article did he actually use the F-WORD, as it is often called. (This was 1934, remember.)

The determination of just which words constitute the group of *four-letter words* was complicated immensely by the Supreme Court's "seven dirty words" ruling in the WBAI–George Carlin case in 1978. Writing for the majority in the 5–4 decision upholding the Federal Communication Commission's authority to ban the terms from the airwaves, Justice John Paul Stevens referred to "contemporary attitudes about four-letter words," even though three of the words at issue were either longer or shorter. The sinful seven (not well publicized at the time, since newspapers throughout the land reported the landmark decision without naming them) were "cunt," "fuck," "piss," "shit," and the non–four-letter words, "cocksucker" (see FELLATIO), "motherfucker" (see MOTHER), and "tit" (see TITTIE).

On a more profound level, the ultimate obscenity is none of the above *three-to-twelve-letter words,* but the banning of the very phrase "four-letter words." Thus, Cole Porter wrote in "Anything Goes" (1934) that "Good authors too/Who once used better words/Now only use four-letter words." When this song was featured in a duet medley by Mary Martin and Noel

Coward, on a CBS telecast on October 22, 1955, however, the operative line was changed to "Now only use three-letter words." And just what the audience was supposed to make of this—one of the stranger euphemisms of our time—only the CBS censor knew.

For more about the nature of taboos surrounding the *four-letter words,* see the short history of F – – –.

foxtrot yankee. Fuck you; from the phonetic alphabet used in the military; also rendered as *FU,* where the "U" stands for "You" or, in other contexts, "Up." (The British equivalent is *F.U.J.,* Fuck You Jack.) "Foxtrot" alone also has multiple meanings: fuck, fucker, fucking—depending upon context. Meanwhile, "foxtrot bravo" denotes a woman, where "bravo" stands for the second letter of the alphabet, probably, in this instance, the "B" of "bitch." See also F – – –, FTA, and SNAFU.

foxy. Sexy, as in "I have a date with a foxy lady tonight" or, a film title from 1956, *The Foxiest Girl in Paris.* The basic "fox," meaning an attractive, desirable woman, was popularized during 1963 by the boxer Muhammad Ali, then known as Cassius Clay (Harold Wentworth and Stuart Berg Flexner, *Dictionary of American Slang,* 1975). "Fox" appears to be a back-formation, a clipping of "foxy," whose oldest known examples in the sexually desirable sense (1895) predate the "fox" that is a woman (1961) by several generations (J. E. Lighter, *Random House Historical Dictionary of American Slang,* 1994).

"Foxy" was certified officially as a euphemism by the Advertising Acceptability Department of the *New York Times* when presented with an ad for the Labor of Love

Company's "exclusive New York Times Crossword Puzzle T-shirt." The proposed ad showed a young man, looking for an eleven-letter word as he filled out a puzzle on the well-filled-out T-shirt of a woman. The caption read "What's another word for sexy?" The *Times* balked at this, however, and changed the line to "What's another word for foxy?" (*MORE*, 10/76). The answer, by the way, is "stimulating."

See also SEX.

fragrance. Once upon a rather long time ago (ca. A.D. 700–1200), people did not always wrinkle their noses at "stink." Originally, that word was used to characterize sweet smells as well as foul ones. Thus, a rose might be said to have "a good stink." However, as usually happens when words bear both "good" and "bad" meanings, the bad ones took over, with the result that "stink" became practically unmentionable. (Noah Webster omitted every "stink" in the Bible when he rewrote it in 1833; see PECULIAR MEMBERS for details.) To replace "stink" in the original, neutral sense, people first used "smell," but this, too, became contaminated, and so they turned to "odor," which, in its turn, acquired noxious connotations; see BO. Almost certainly, the same thing eventually will happen to "fragrance," despite its present entrenchment as a byword for ye olde "good stink." See also MATRON and SCENT.

fragrant. More-or-less rhyming slang for those who are too embarrassed to say "pregnant." See also PREGNANT.

fragrant meat. A Chinese hot dog (the kind that is man's best friend). "Last November . . . Taiwan's first full-size restaurant offering 'fragrant meat,' the standard euphemism, opened on a major thoroughfare" (*New York Times*, 4/22/73).

Eating dog is an ancient Chinese custom. Recipes for dog flank and liver were found in the tomb of the honorable lady of Marquis of Tai, who died circa 160 B.C. The meat is thought to act as a general constitutional pick-up, relieve stomach trouble and rheumatism, and increase sexual potency. Older men, in particular, favor this culinary delight. The family of General Charles George "Chinese" Gordon did not know all this when they presented a prize pedigree dog to the visiting statesman Li Hung-Chang in 1896, and so were startled by his thank-you note: "As I am advanced in age, I usually take little food. Therefore, I have been able to take a very small portion of your delicious meat which, indeed, has given me great gratification." See also FILET MIGNON.

frank. A euphemism among swingers and a circumlocution among diplomats. Among the former, it stands for openness in sexual talk, e.g.: "The booze had had its effect and we became franker and franker. We admitted our fantasy about making it together with [another couple]. Martha and Sal admitted that they had been in that scene already" (*Forum*, 12/76). In a sexual context, "frank" once applied to actions that spoke even louder than words, as in Alexander Pope's *Epistle to a Lady* (1735):

> See Sin in State, majestically drunk;
> Proud as a Peeress, prouder as a Punk;
> Chaste to her Husband, frank to all
>   beside,
> A teeming Mistress, but a barren Bride.

"Punk," by the way, meant PROSTITUTE in Pope's time. Fortunately for him, and for literature, he did not have to reckon with modern libel laws, since he probably had a real person in mind when he tossed off these lines: Lady Godolphin, daughter of the duke of Marlborough.

Meanwhile, statesmen (on official business, at any rate) use "frank" and, for emphasis, "full and frank," to paper over their differences, e.g., "The White House spokesman, John W. Hushen, told newsmen afterward that the meeting included a 'full and frank' discussion of the full range of CIA activities" (*New York Times*, 9/21/74). As later revealed, however, the meeting between Secretary of State Henry Kissinger and congressional leaders was neither full nor frank, the secretary neglecting to mention the CIA's subsidization of strikers in Chile as part of its program to overthrow ("destabilize") that nation's elected government.

Diplomats at "full and frank" meetings do not usually come to blows, but the essentially antagonistic implications of the phrase were revealed clearly when, prior to a professional football play-off game between the Washington Redskins and the Dallas Cowboys in January 1983, banners appeared on the walls of the State Department headquarters in Washington, D.C., with the hometown boast, "We'll have a full and frank discussion on the field."

See also SERIOUS AND CANDID, SWINGING, and UNACCEPTABLE ACTIVITIES.

fraternization. Originally an all-male word for a close, brotherly association (from the Latin *frater,* brother), the term has become a euphemism for nonbrotherly RELATION-SHIPS. Popularized in the latter sense in the military (General Dwight D. Eisenhower's Proclamation No. 1, issued in 1944, forbade "fraternization" with German civilians), the term has crept into civilian life. For example, Wal-Mart's company handbook, issued in 1989, contains a section on "fraternization," which prohibits a married ASSOCIATE from entering into a "dating relationship" with "another associate other than his or her own spouse."

In its original military setting, "fraternization" was abbreviated in various ways, e.g., *fratting* for dating the former enemy, *frat* and *piece of frat* for the former enemy herself, and *fratter* for the soldier doing the *fratting.* The sexual implications remained strong in the short forms, making "fratting" essentially a euphemism for another participle with a strong "f" sound; see F – – –.

freaking. A euphemistic intensifier, standing for "damn" or, more often, "fucking," as in "Am I out of my freaking mind?" ("Jack's Place," WABC-TV, 8/3/93). See also F – – –.

freedom fighter. Terrorist, revolutionary; one who uses force in an effort to overthrow an established government. Thus, Lt. Col. Oliver L. North continually referred to the rightist Nicaraguan Contras as "freedom fighters" in his testimony to Congress in 1987. Meanwhile, the leftist members of the Black Liberation Army who killed three people in 1981 while attempting a $1.6 million EXPROPRIATION in Nyack, New York, also referred to themselves as "freedom fighters."

It is easier to get away with the "freedom fighter" label, of course, if one winds up on the winning side. For example, members of the Jewish underground military organization, Irgun Zvai Leumi, commanded by Menachem Begin (1943–48), generally were described as "terrorists" when they attacked the British in Palestine, but Mr. Begin objected vehemently when reporters used that word after he became Prime Minister of Israel in 1977. "'Freedom fighter' is the correct description, he insisted" (*New York Times*, 5/22/77).

free enterprise. Private enterprise. While the "free" has an open, competitive, equitable sound to it, cynics maintain that "free enterprise" amounts to "freedom to cheat." It would be easier to dismiss them as socialistic spoilsports if it were not for the advice of Adam Smith: "People of the same trade seldom meet together, even for merriment and diversion but the conversation ends in a conspiracy against the public, or in some contrivance to raise prices" (*The Wealth of Nations*, 1776). See also FAIR TRADE, FREE GIFT, and SPECULATE.

free gift. Since a true "gift" does not require any elaboration about its being "free," the redundancy should set antennae quivering. A bank that offers a *free gift* for making a deposit will manage to get back its value—or more—by reducing interest on the account if the recipient withdraws the money before a certain amount of time has passed. In truth, the *free gift* is a conditional gift. As with FREE ENTERPRISE, it would be easier to laugh this construction out of court if it were not for a distinguished, somewhat worrisome precedent. Thus, St. Paul speaks of the grace of God abounding: "Therefore as by the offence of one [Adam] *judgment came* upon all men to condemnation; even so by the righteousness of one [Jesus] *the free gift came* upon all men to the justification of life" (Romans 5:18).

Free World. Any anti-Communist country, no matter how repressive the regime, back in the 1950s when the United States was not too particular about its allies, e.g., Spain under Franco, Taiwan under Chiang, and Greece under various colonels. "There was often not much that was 'free' about many of the states that made up what we used to call the Free World" (Arthur M. Schlesinger, Jr., *Today's Education*, 9/10/74). The expression enjoyed a minirevival during President Ronald Reagan's first term, when neoconservatives formed the Committee for the Free World (founded 1981). Brutalitarian allies of the United States in this period became "authoritarian governments," as Jeanne T. Kirkpatrick gently characterized them when defending this country's choices of its friends (*Commentary*, 11/79). Of purely historical interest, now that Communism has crumbled practically everywhere, the "Free World" rallying cry is included here just as an example of the kind of oversimplified thinking above which we have, of course, completely risen.

French—culture, disease, kiss, leave, letter, pill, postcard, pox, prints, vice, way, etc. Over the years, English speakers have attached many meanings to "French," almost all of which reduce ultimately to some form of "wrong," or "sexy," or—most often—some evil combination of the two. For example:

"French" is a euphemism for "profanity" when someone says "Pardon my *French*," or "Excuse my *French*." And since at least the eighteenth century, *French novels*, *French prints*, and, of course, *French postcards* have had a reputation for raciness if not downright dirtiness. (The French have been known to purchase what they call *American* postcards, but that is another matter.) Then there is *French leave*, which is what people take when they duck out of a party without saying goodbye to the hostess—or go AWOL from the military. (Strangely, the French expression for "to slip away" is *filer a l'anglaise*.) To do one's visitors *the French courtesy* is (or was—the custom is believed to be obsolete) to show special favor to one's guests by receiving them while sitting upon one's close STOOL.

Today, "French" commonly connotes "perversion" in the sense of oral-genital sex. (See SOIXANTE-NEUF.) As a euphemism for sexual practices that could not be named, "French vice" first appeared in the British press in 1885 in accounts of the celebrated divorce case in which Sir Charles Dilke was named as corespondent, thus putting a permanent crimp in what had been a very promising political career. In the United States, this kind of "French" apparently dates to about the time of World War I. Popularity of the expression may be due in part to the experiences in France of the boys in the AEF. As early as 1918, the term was being used in Chicago. Thus, recalling life at the Roamer Inn, a famous whorehouse owned by Al Capone's SYNDICATE:

> Those girls were always competing with each other; one would come up to you, switching her hips like a young duck, and whisper in your ear, "Want to go to bed, dear, I'll show you a good time, honey, I'm French," and a minute later another one would ease along and say coyly, "Baby, don't you want a straight girl for a change?" (Milton "Mezz" Mezzrow and Bernard Wolfe, *Really the Blues,* 1946)

The oral-genital "French" appears in many forms, including *to French* (someone), *French jobs, French kiss* (also used, confusingly, for an open-mouthed kiss in which the tongue or tongues come into play), and *French way*. In the more-or-less underground classifieds, *French culture* is distinguished from ENGLISH CULTURE (the subdivision of SM that relies upon the cane or riding crop), GREEK CULTURE (anal INTERCOURSE), and ROMAN CULTURE (group sex, an orgy). The various terms often are abbreviated to *French* (or *fr.*), *English, Greek* (*gr.*), and *Roman*. Not infrequently, national and cultural differences dissolve within a single, very hot, melting pot:

> HORNY BLUE-EYED DIVORCEE, 24, seeks bi gals, married or sgl select males or cpls. Clean discreet and can travel. Love fr gr roman mild bd [bondage and discipline] or sm in fact love it all. (*Ace,* undated, ca. 1976)

Then there is syphilis, which was known for many years as the *French crown, French disease, French gout, French malady,* or *French pox,* with *French pox* being recorded as early as 1503, while the modern name comes from a literary production of 1530, entitled *Syphilis: Or, a Poetical History of the French Disease.* Not translated into English until 1686, the poetical history is about an unfortunate shepherd named Syphilis, who suffered from this SOCIAL DISEASE. The origin of the disease itself is not well understood (it may have been brought back from the New World to the Old by Columbus's crews), and this uncertainty is reflected in the terminology: The complaint also has been called the *Italian disease,* the *Neapolitan disease,* the *Polish disease,* the *Spanish disease,* the *Canton disease* (in China), the *Chinese disease* (in Japan), and even (in France) the *English disease.*

For those who want to be sure of avoiding the *French disease* (as well as pregnancy), there is always the *French letter,* or condom. Again, the French return the favor, calling the same article *une capote anglaise,* a *capote* being a hooded cloak. Casanova, an enlightened lover (he was one of the first to use condoms to protect his partners "from anxiety" as well as himself from disease) called them *redingotes d'Angleterre* (English overcoats). At other times and places, they have been called *Spanish, Italian,* and even *American letters.*

Once more, the origin of the basic item, the condom, is something of a mystery. The oldest known example of the word in print comes from 1706. Since it reeked of sex, however, the term often was blanked out in the early eighteenth century as C – – – – – or, in the interest of great clarity, C – – – –m. As explained at an early date in the The *Tatler*: "A Gentleman of this House [Wills Coffee-House] . . . observ'd by the Surgeons with much Envy; for he has invented an Engine for the Prevention of Harms by Love-Adventures, and has . . . by giving his Engine his own Name, made it obscene to speak of him more" (No. 15, 5/14/1709). Later research has turned up no independent evidence that Condom, rumored to be either a doctor or a colonel, ever existed, so perhaps Condom, the man, never was. Whatever the truth of this matter, the name certainly did become too "obscene to speak," and the editors of *The Oxford English Dictionary* could not even bring themselves to write it until 1972, when "condom" belatedly appeared in that year's revised supplement. In the intervening centuries, not having a proper word available, gentlemen who used such things had to speak of *French letters,* or of *purses* that were carried in a *bishop* (an extra-large condom), or of donning their *armour.* As noted in an old limerick:

There was a young man of Cape Horn,
Who wished he had never been born.
And he wouldn't have been
If his father had seen
That the bloody French letter was torn.

Finally, in the event of a tear in the *French letter,* a woman might wish to induce an abortion by means of *French Lunar Pills, French Renovating Pills,* or even *Portuguese Female Pills.* Thus, a January 1845 ad in the *Boston Daily Times* carefully explained that "Dr. Peter's French Renovating Pills" were "a blessing to mothers . . . and although very mild and prompt in their operations, pregnant females should not use them, as they inevitably produce a miscarriage" (from James C. Mohr, *Abortion in America: The Origins and Evolution of National Policy, 1800–1900*). See also MISCARRIAGE.

freshperson. A freshman; a.k.a. FIRST-YEAR STUDENT. In the plural, both *freshpersons* and *freshpeople* are (politically) correct, as in "Merit Grants Lure Freshpeople Away" (headline, *Yale Daily News,* 11/4/93). See also PERSON.

friend. A lover; a COMPANION of either sex; frequently a PARTNER or PARAMOUR. "He hath got his friend with child" (William Shakespeare, *Measure for Measure,* 1604). "Friend is a word of somewhat doubtful connotations where a lady and gentleman are concerned" ("Sergeant Cribb: Murder Old Boy," WNET-TV, 2/3/83). Of course, some friendly persons have more than one *friend.* "Helen Gurley Brown suggests that a woman who sleeps with two or more men in one week can simply be called 'multifriended'" (*Time*, 12/27/82). In Ms. Brown's lexicon, the *multifriended* woman's encounters class as *one-night friendships*. See also BOYFRIEND, GIRLFRIEND, LIAISON, and SLEEP WITH.

friendly fire. A contradiction in terms: No matter what the military says, the "fire" is not "friendly" when it hits you. "In its accounting this week of American casualties [in the Gulf war], the Pentagon said 27 of the 35 tanks and armored vehicles damaged or destroyed were the victims of American fire—so-called 'friendly fire'" (*New York Times*, 8/15/91).

The expression was epitomized in C. B. D. Bryan's *Friendly Fire* (1976), about the circumstances surrounding the death of Michael Mullen, an American soldier in Vietnam in 1970. He was killed by a so-called "defensive round" from an artillery battery commanded by Col. H. Norman Schwartzkopf, future generalissimo of the Gulf war. Investigation revealed that the cannon had been aimed too low because an officer, working from elevations on a map, forgot to take into account the additional height of foliage when computing the shell's desired trajectory. The round hit a tree above the American position and a piece of shrapnel killed Mullen while he slept in a foxhole. For this he received a Bronze Star, posthumously.

Soldiers as well as civilians in Vietnam also became *friendly* (or *nonhostile*) *casualties*, sometimes escaping with nonlethal *friendly wounds*. The errant bombs and shells that did this harm were categorized as *incontinent ordnance* and *short rounds*. Such accidents, or MISADVENTURES ("fate" was Col. Schwartzkopf's explanation for Mullen's death), occurred so often that the line "Fuck 'em if they can't take a joke"

became a catchphrase for dismissing almost any tragedy.

The phenomenon of death by *friendly fire* is by no means new. John Keegan noted in *The Face of Battle* (1976) that "there are numerous authentic accounts of losses by 'friendly' fire—or even 'friendly' sword-cuts—at Waterloo." Ever since men with weapons have been bunched together in armies, in fact, soldiers have run the risk of being killed or wounded by their companions. Thus, from Book 18 of *The Iliad* of Homer (ca. 8th century B.C., as translated by Richmond Lattimore, 1951):

> Three times across the ditch brilliant
>   Achilles gave his great cry,
> and three times the Trojans and their
>   renowned companions were routed.
> There at that time twelve of the best
>   men among them perished
> upon their own chariots and spears.

See also CASUALTY, ORDNANCE, and, for a famous death by *friendly fire,* CROSS OVER.

frig. An old euphemism for "masturbate" that evolved into a euphemism for "fuck." Probably deriving from the Middle English *friggen,* to quiver (the Latin *fricare,* to rub, is another possibility), the original, above-ground meaning of "frig" was "to move about restlessly," "to rub," or "to chafe." By the end of the sixteenth century, the general term for rubbing was being used for the particular action. Thus, in an age that was even more liberated than our own, John Wilmot, the bawdy second earl of Rochester, who lived a merry life but a short one (1647–1680), could write the following verse (ca. 1677) about a famous beauty, Cary Frazier, daughter of King Charles II's principal physician:

Her father gave her dildoes six;
   Her mother made 'em up a score
But she loves not but living pricks,
   And swears by God she'll frig no more.

The change in the euphemism's meaning apparently occurred around the turn of the twentieth century. For example, Frank Harris, recalling his youthful struggles to improve his athletic prowess, circa 1868, used the term in the older sense, e.g.: "I soon noticed that if I frigged myself the night before, I could not [high] jump so well, the consequence being that I restrained myself, and never frigged save on Sunday, and soon managed to omit the practice three Sundays out of four" (*My Life and Loves*, 1925). The anonymous but immensely authoritative author of *My Secret Life* (ca. 1890) also used "frig" in its masturbatory sense. Meanwhile, the earliest example of the modern meaning in *The Oxford English Dictionary* comes from a letter that James Joyce wrote in 1905: "Cosgrave says it's unfair for you to frig the one idea about love, which he had before he met you." Even after laws were relaxed to permit "fuck" to be printed, the euphemistic "frig" continued to see service. Thus, *The American Thesaurus of Slang* (Lester V. Berry and Melvin Van Den Bark, 1953), which does include "fuck," also defines "the four F's" as "find 'em, fool 'em, frig 'em, and forget 'em." See also DILDO, EFF, F – – – , and MASTURBATION.

fry. A testicle or other internal part of an animal (such as the PLUCK) that is about to be fried and eaten. Because people usually eat more than one at a sitting, the term usually is encountered in the plural, e.g., "The products of lambs' castration are called lamb's fries" (Frederick T. Elworthy, *The West Somerset Word Book*, 1886). See also FILET MIGNON, PRAIRIE OYSTERS, and TESTICLES.

FTA. Fuck The Army; a ubiquitous abbreviation in and around military installations, from the 1960s, memorialized in a film, *F.T.A.*, a 1972 documentary of an antiwar review, *Free (or F – – –) the Army*, presented by Jane Fonda and Donald Sutherland near Army bases during the VIETNAM ERA. When challenged by a superior for having emblazoned "FTA" on a piece of equipment or clothing, a soldier might hope to defend himself by claiming that the initials stood for "Fun, Travel, Adventure," used in army promotional material. A spin-off for the truly disenchanted is *FTW*, Fuck The World.

See also F – – – , FNG, FOXTROT YANKEE, and SNAFU.

fudge. An interjection for "stuff and nonsense" that sometimes serves as a euphemism for stronger stuff, usually but not always another F-WORD. Speaking of the Battle of Trenton in the American Revolution: "The Hessians had been caught completely by surprise. When he had been urged several days before to take precautions, the commanding officer, Colonel Johann Gottlieb Rall, had (according to a Victorian translation of the official Hessian investigation) stated 'Fudge! These country clowns cannot whip us'" (James Thomas Flexner, *George Washington in the American Revolution, 1775–1783*, 1968).

"Fudge" is of unknown origin. The sense of "nonsense" may derive from the verb, "to fudge"—that is, to put together in a clumsy, makeshift way, or to shade the truth. Connection with a seventeenth-century seaman, Captain Fudge, also known (in a letter of 1664) as "Lying Fudge," has not been proven. Because it also is the name of a candy (from 1896), "fudge" makes a fit euphemistic companion for SUGAR.

fug. Fuck; a historical curiosity, popularized by Norman Mailer before it was safe legally to print the real word in full. "'Go fug yourself,' Gallagher yelled" (Mailer, *The Naked and the Dead,* 1948). "Fug" continued in service for some years after the ban on "fuck" began to be relaxed. Thus, describing the memorial service for Lenny Bruce (1927–66): "The Fugs came on. They are a rock 'n' roll group, named after Norman Mailer's most famous typographical euphemism" (Dick Schaap, in the afterward to Lenny Bruce's *How to Talk Dirty and Influence People,* 1972). Joseph Heller's "furgle" never had a good chance to catch on because *Catch-22* appeared in 1961, just as "fuck" was starting to become generally printable. See also F – – –.

full-figured. Fat, especially with large breasts. "'Full-figured,' which seems to have been invented by makers of bras to flatter a certain, uh, fodgel [fat] clientele, is also out, and good riddance" (Walter Goodman, *New York Times Book Review,* 1/27/91).

Well, maybe down, but not entirely "out," e.g., the self-descriptions in personal ads: "DWF, 46, 5'1", full-figured" and "5'2", full-figured" (Waterbury, Conn., *Sunday Republican,* 10/28/93). See also BOSOM, FIGURE, and STATUESQUE.

full of applesauce, etc. Nonsense, bullshit. Synonymous phrases include *full of baloney, -beans, -crap, -horsehoe nails, -hot air,* and *-prunes.* The essentially excremental nature of the "full of" construction is apparent from New York governor Mario Cuomo's preconvention declaration in 1988 that anyone who said he had pledged his support for Massachusetts governor Michael S. Dukakis was "full of what makes the grass green" (*New York Times,* 7/15/88). A variant is Jean Harlow's "Ain't that a load of clams?" (*Bombshell,* 1933). See also APPLESAUCE, BALONEY, BS, and CRAP.

fully dressed. Armed. A *fully dressed* person may wear a SIZE-38 DRESS.

fun. A general-purpose substitute for something naughty—sex, for instance. "Miss Hamblin said that she asked Representative Howe what he was doing and he told her, 'Looking for a little fun'" (UPI, 7/7/76). In this case, Mr. Allan Howe, Democrat of Utah, did not have any *fun,* since Ms. Margaret Hamblin turned out to be a police decoy posing as a PROSTITUTE. Here, the prospective customer's search for *fun* is the counterpart to the prostitute's opening line: "WANNA GO OUT?"

funch. Sex during the lunch hour, also called a *nooner.* A portmanteau word, "funch" was popularized at the edges of cities, where offices and motels are close together. It can be employed both as noun ("It was a fun funch") or verb ("Miss Otis regrets that she is unable to funch today"). See also MATINEE and MOTEL.

fundament. The ass or ANUS. "Fundament" has been used to refer to the bottom, foundation, or seat of the body, since medieval times, e.g.: "He . . . with a spere smote the noble knyght in to the foundament soo that his bowels comen oute there" (William

Caxton, *The Chronicles of England,* 1480). See also ARSE, BOTTOM, and SEAT.

fundamental truth. Not the full truth; untruth. "Now under all these circumstances, my reactions in some of these statements and press conferences and so forth after that, I want to say right here and now that some of them were not true. Most of them were fundamentally true on the big issues but without going as far as I should have gone" (Richard M. Nixon, interview with David Frost in *I Gave Them a Sword,* 1978). The point, of course, is that "truth" should never have to be qualified; when it is, the buyer should beware. Variants include *essential truth* and *symbolic truth.* See also ECONOMICAL WITH THE TRUTH.

funeral director. An undertaker; the person who operates a FUNERAL HOME or memorial CHAPEL.

Undertakers have come a long way. In England, in the eighteenth and early nineteenth centuries, they were known commonly as *carrion hunters, death hunters,* and *cold cooks.* (The *funeral home* then was a *cold cookshop.*) Even "undertaker" is something of a euphemism; "taker-under" would be more precise. As a general term for someone who takes on some job, challenge, or enterprise, "undertaker" has been applied in a wide variety of fields; book publishers, for instance, were once known as "undertakers." The first funeral "undertaker" to be recorded in *The Oxford English Dictionary* comes from 1698. Previously, funerals usually were stage-managed by the family rather than by outside professionals. The new calling was not especially dignified, as indicated by the following couplet from Edward Young's *Love of Fame* (1728):

While rival undertakers hover round,
And with his spade the sexton marks
the ground.

In the United States, meanwhile, development of the undertaking trade lagged behind that of England. (The Americans have since made up for lost time.) At the start of the nineteenth century, even in such a citadel of culture as Charleston, South Carolina, hardly anyone knew what an undertaker was. As a tourist of the period reported: "A few months before the yellow fever raged in that city, in 1807, an undertaker made his appearance, which was so great a novelty to the inhabitants that he was obliged to explain what was meant by the term undertaker in an advertisement" (John Lambert, *Travels Through Lower Canada and the United States of North America,* 1810).

Toward the end of the nineteenth century, American undertakers began to get their act together. (The Civil War had given business a big boost, with CASKET, a somewhat earlier invention, catching on, circa 1863.) By the 1880s, some of the more forward-looking undertakers were calling themselves "funeral directors." Thus, from a trade publication, *Sunnyside* (now *Casket and Sunnyside*), of 1885: "Funeral directors are members of an exalted, almost sacred calling . . . the Executive Council believed that a cut in prices would be suicidal, and notified the manufacturers that better goods, rather than lower prices, were needed."

Starting about 1925, undertakers began campaigning to have Rotary and the Yellow Pages list them as "funeral directors." In this, they have been successful, as a glance at any current telephone classified section will show. Entries for "undertakers" and "morticians" are just cross-references to the main listings at "Funeral Directors."

Other terms for "undertaker" have been used at different times with varying degrees of success, including *counselor* and *funeral counselor; mortuary consultant* (see MORTUARY and CONSULTANT), and *sanitarian.* If "funeral director" is ever replaced—and, given the continual flux in titles of this sort, chances are it will be—the most probable successor is *funeral service practitioner,* which was proposed in 1959 by the Commission on Mortuary Education as a replacement for "embalmer" and "funeral director." The beauty part of *f.s.p.* is the "practitioner," which appeals to the long-standing, deep-felt wish of undertakers to have their trade regarded as a profession akin to, if not on a par with, medicine. This desire has been articulated in many ways over the years. Undertakers have referred to themselves as *Dr. So-and-So,* and as *embalming surgeons;* they have embalmed *cases* and *patients,* rather than cadavers or corpses, and they have done their work in *operating rooms* and *parlors.* Some are even reported to have transported dead bodies in *ambulances* and *invalid coaches* instead of hearses (see PROFESSIONAL CAR). And, of course, it was the desire to emulate physicians that spawned MORTICIAN, a famous euphemism that seems to have failed, partly because it was cheapened by success. Meanwhile, waiting in the wings, on the chance that "funeral service practitioner" will not catch on, are *grief therapist* and *thanatologist* (see THANATOLOGY).

funeral home/parlor. An undertaker's place of business, especially when under the same roof as his residence; a MORTUARY; a deadhouse.

The oldest "funeral parlor" in *The Oxford English Dictionary* comes only from 1927. In the case of "funeral home," we have it on the authority of the *Tishomingo,* Okla., *Capital-Democrat* (6/10/48) that "the Chapman Funeral Home, established by Russell's father, has been operating under the same name for 50 years." Both terms probably go back at least to the closing decades of the nineteenth century, which seems to have been a period of great ferment in this particular field, with FUNERAL DIRECTOR and MORTICIAN also surfacing then.

Today, the operation of deadhouses is no longer a cottage industry but big business, with many of the old-line *funeral homes* and *funeral parlors* having been replaced by *funeral directors* and chains of funeral and mortuary CHAPELS. Still, *funeral homes* are not only surviving, thank you, but actually breaking new ground (if you'll pardon the expression). Some have gone so far as to offer discounted, no-frills funerals; they are known in the trade as *Wal-morts.* Others provide drive-through facilities. As far back as 1976, the Pointe Coupee Funeral Home, of New Roads, La., opened such an establishment. It featured a window, seven feet by five feet, through which grief-stricken motorists could view the DECEASED in an open coffin, bathed in the light of a small blue neon cross. Drivers could even sign the mourners register without getting out of their cars. Another drive-through in Kentucky has provided tanks of tropical fish, which are soothing as well as educational; local schoolchildren began stopping by between funerals to learn about marine life.

The funeral business is based upon death, but that is the last word that anyone in the trade wants to mention. As a result, the well-spoken undertaker will say:

Baby or *infant*, not stillborn
Case, patient, or Mr. Smith—anything but corpse or dead person
CASKET, not coffin (displayed in a *selection room,* not showroom)
CEMETERY or MEMORIAL PARK, not grave-yard
CREMAINS, not ashes
Cryobiological preservation, not freezing dead bodies
DECEASED or DEPARTED, not dead or dead person
ESTATE, not grave plot
floral tribute, not flowers for the dead (carried in a *flower car,* not a flower truck)
FUNERAL OBSEQUIES, not funeral
INTERMENT, not burial
INURNMENT, not potting
LOVED ONE, not corpse
Memorial or *monument,* not gravestone or tombstone
Memory picture, not last look
Mortuary couch or *preparation couch,* not embalming table
NEGLIGÉE or SLUMBER ROBE, not shroud
OBITUARY, not death notice
Operating or *preparation room,* not embalming room or cellar
PASS AWAY, not die
PROFESSIONAL CAR or *coach,* not hearse (in which case, the occupant is a *passenger* or *silent passenger*)
Reposing room or *slumber room,* not laying-out room (see REPOSE)
Service, not funeral (in which instance, the undertaker may be called a *Doctor of Services*)
SPACE, not grave
Vital statistics form, not death certificate

Of course, the operators of *funeral homes* and *parlors* are by no means the only busi-nesspeople to have traded on the positive connotations of those terms; see HOME and PARLOR.

funeral obsequies. "Obsequies" (the singular "obsequy" is rarely used) comes from the Latin *obsequiae,* funeral rites, so "funeral obsequies" is a pretentious redundancy. (Related terms include "obsequious," from the Latin *obsequium,* compliance, dutiful service, and "sequel," from the Latin *sequi,* to follow.) "Funeral obsequies" somehow survived Mark Twain's ridicule. As the king explained in *Huckleberry Finn* (1884), when challenged by the duke on his use of "orgies" in place of "obsequies":

I say orgies, not because it's the common term, because it ain't—obsequies bein' the common term—but because orgies is the right term. Obsequies ain't used in England no more now—it's gone out. We say orgies now in England. Orgies is better, because it means the thing you're after, more exact. It's a word that's made up out'n the Greek *orgo,* outside, open, abroad; and the Hebrew *jeesum,* to plant, cover up; hence *inter.* So, you see, funeral orgies is an open er public funeral.

See also FUNERAL HOME/PARLOR.

fungoo. Frequently employed by schoolchildren as an aural euphemism for "fuck you" ("Ah fungoo to you, too"), the term actually has a more vulgar meaning—of which its users are generally unaware. It derives from the dialectical Italian *fa'n'gul,* in turn from *affanculo,* "I fuck (you) in the ass." See also F – – –.

furlough. In civilian life, a layoff from work. The civilian usage trades on the happy associations of the word in its military sense, where it means a leave of absence—in effect, a holiday from work. "Many of the pilots now being laid off . . . are experiencing their second 'furlough,' the airline euphemism for layoffs, in two years" (*New York Times*, 12/24/73). See also AT LIBERTY, BETWEEN ASSIGNMENTS, and LEAVE.

futz. Thanks to its sound and initial "f" the Yiddish *futz,* to loaf, waste time, or goof off, may be employed as a euphemism for "fuck," especially in such phrases as "to futz around" or "to futz up." "I've got her all futzed up. She does everything I tell her" (Calder Willingham, *End as a Man,* 1947). In the Yiddish, the term also has a low, though noncopulative, meaning. It is a clipping of *arumfartzen,* to fart around. See also F – – –.

F-word. Many words begin with "F," but there is only one "F-word." The word is "fuck," and it is used all the time, though still not printed in many publications. Thus, from the Sheriff's Log of the *Brown County,* Ind., *Democrat* for August 14, 1993:

> 8:31 P.M. Mount Liberty woman wants officer to do something about neighbors that have been going at each other for about the last two hours. A male and female using F-word.

The most surprising thing about this euphemism is how recently it surfaced in print. The earliest example of the term that John Algeo and Adele Algeo included in their "Among New Words" column in *American Speech* (Winter 1988) came from *Time* magazine of December 7, 1987—and *Time* has a history of creating and popularizing new expressions. This particular one sounds as though it might have been devised by kids who sensed that it would be wrong to use the actual word in front of their elders, as in "Her first grader once asked her 'what the "F" word means,' she recalled" (Bill Duryea, *New Milford,* Conn., *Times,* 4/6/89).

Whatever its source, "F-word" began to be employed widely in the late 1980s and early 1990s. It seems likely to have a relatively long life because it improves upon similar euphemisms in important ways: It can be articulated where F – – –, "****," "*&$%#!," and other dingbats are restricted to print; it is more down-to-earth (less literary) than ADJECTIVE/ADJECTIVAL, and it is more pointed than BLANK, BLEEP, DASH, and EXPLETIVE DELETED (as well as, in the case of the last, a lot easier to say and to write).

The staying power of "F-word" also is suggested by its remarkable fecundity. Within a few years of its appearance, it spawned a veritable alphabet of other "-words." Some were introduced with tongue in cheek and many had more than one meaning, but all traded on the power of the tabooed *F-word.* Among them: *A-word,* "A" was for "adultery" back in Hester Prynne's time, but now it usually stands for "abortion" or "ass"; *C-word,* cancer (see also C, THE BIG), capitalism, conservative, crap, cunt; *D-word,* death, debt or deficit (meaning the federal government's), depression (economic), detente; *F-word,* fraud as well as fuck; *H-word,* Harvard; *I-word,* impeachment (as of a president); *J-word,* junk; L-WORD, liberal (whose earliest written examples actually predate those of the *F-word*); *M-word,* meltdown; *N-word,* nigger, nuclear; *P-word,* penis, plagiarism, please; *Q-word,* quagmire, quota; *R-word,* recession (economic); *S-word,* selfish, sex, sharing, shit, socialism, suicide; T-WORD, tax; *V-word,* values, veto (as by a presi-dent); and *W-word,* wife, as in "1989 April 14 female age ca 30 conversation San Francisco [upon being introduced as so-and-so's wife] 'Ah, the W-word'" (Martha Cornog and Timothy Perper, *American Speech,* Fall 1991).

G

gadget. An atomic bomb, in the patois of Los Alamos, New Mexico, where they were made. For instance, *Gadget* was the title of a 1977 suspense novel by Nicholas Freeling involving such a weapon. In other contexts, the versatile "gadget" has also been made to stand for "girl" and for "penis," and it is of additional interest for being a relatively new word. The earliest citation for "gadget" in *The Oxford English Dictionary* comes from as recently as 1886. The term seems to have originated among seamen, who applied it to any small contrivance, fitting, or mechanism whose real name they did not know or had momentarily forgotten. It may come from the French *gâchette,* also applied to various mechanical items. See also DEVICE, DING-A-LING, and THING.

gadzooks. The "gad" is a euphemistic pronunciation of "god"; the "zooks" probably derives from the "hooks," or nails, used in the crucifixion of Christ. See also DAD, EGAD, ODDS BODKINS, and ZOUNDS.

gal/guy Friday. Secretary-servant, general factotum, gofer; an ADMINISTRATIVE ASSISTANT. "Gal/Guy Fri—To 2 Executives. Exp. motivated . . . Heavy clerical, excel w/figures, A/R, inventory, typing" (*New York Times,* 10/17/93).

The "Friday" part of the "gal/guy Fri" construction comes from Robinson Crusoe's Man Friday. The "guy" is much newer; the usual request was just for a *gal Fri* before equal opportunity laws forced advertisers and employers to at least pretend to open all jobs to all persons. "Guy" itself, as a general term for "man" or "fellow," seems to be a nineteenth-century Americanism. It may have developed from the older English "guy," meaning someone of grotesque appearance, and possibly was influenced by the Yiddish *goy,* Gentile. The grotesque "guy," in turn, derived from the effigies of Guy Fawkes, burned annually on November 5 to commemorate the foiling in 1605 of his Gunpowder Plot to blow up the Houses of Parliament. As for the "gal" of "gal/guy Fri," this slangy mispronunciation of "girl" dates from the late eighteenth century. Once a common term of affection for a young or pleasant woman, a sweetheart, it must be employed cautiously outside help-wanted ads because of the free-and-easy connations it has acquired, e.g., "Sal, of 'My Gal, Sal' was the madam of a sporting house in Evansville, Indiana" (Bergen Evans and Cornelia Evans, *A Dictionary of Contemporary American Usage,* 1957). And as Tom Sawyer quickly replied, when Huck Finn asked him the name of the "gal" he intended to marry: "'It ain't a gal at all—it's a girl'" (Mark Twain, *The Adventures of Tom Sawyer,* 1876). See also SERVANT.

gallantry. "Gallantry" is out of fashion now, except among soldiers who occasionally display it under fire, but at one time the chivalrous word was a byword for sexual intrigue. It derives from "gallant," originally meaning a fine-looking man, woman, or ship that came to include those gentlemen who spent excessive amounts of time chasing ladies. Thus, succinctly explaining the conditions surrounding the initial conquest of the protagonist of *Don Juan* (1819–24), George Gordon, Lord Byron explained:

> What men call gallantry, and gods adultry,

Is much more common where the climate's sultry.

Byron was referring to Spain, of course, but *gallantry* knew no national boundaries. Lady Mary Wortley Montagu had much the same opinion as Byron, though referring to the rather less sultry climate of Austria: "Thus, you see, my dear, gallantry and good breeding are as different in different climates as morality and religion" (letter to Lady Rich, 9/20/1776). Meanwhile, Capt. Francis Grose defined the word "pray" in this manner: "She prays with her knees upwards; said of a woman much given to gallantry and intrigue" (*A Classical Dictionary of the Vulgar Tongue*, 1796).

gallery. A store or shop, such as Meghan's Hair Gallery (Danbury, Conn., Yellow Pages, 1994–95). See also CLINIC and SALON.

game. Whether games imitate life or life imitates games is a matter of debate, but the overlap is indisputably great as evidence by use of "game," "game plan," and a host of other game-playing metaphors as euphemisms and circumlocutions in politics, war, business, and other nonsporting activities. Take politics, for example:

On the assumption that the proposed undertaking by Hunt and Liddy would be carried out and would be successful, I would appreciate receiving from you by about Wednesday a game plan as to how and when you believe the materials should be used. (Memo from John D. Ehrlichman to Charles W. Colson, 8/27/71)

"Game plan," a legitimate expression for a football coach, is pseudo-macho doubletalk for "plan" in board rooms and other nonathletic contexts. (The *game plan* in the above instance was the White House plot to smear Daniel Ellsberg; see COVERT OPERATION.) Of course, the chief gamester in this, the Nixon administration, was the president himself. He used "game plan" frequently in private conversation, usually as a verb, e.g., "We have to game-plan this" (William Safire, *Safire's Political Dictionary*, 1978). The president also was a great advocate of *hardball* tactics, which is playing the *game* of politics with few if any holds barred, and he switched easily into other sports, preparing for an aggressive defense of the White House role in the Watergate CAPER with the remark that "this is a full court press, isn't it?" (Appendix 35, *The White House Transcripts*, 1974).

In the main, American politicians seem to have been a relatively sedentary breed, drawing their game-playing metaphors from the card table, e.g., Harry Truman's *Fair Deal*, FDR's *New Deal*, and Teddy Roosevelt's *Square Deal*. In the nineteenth century, a great American original, Col. David (Davy) Crockett said in his *Life of Martin Van Buren* (1835): "Statesmen are gamesters, and the people are the cards they play with . . . the way they cut and shuffle is a surprise to all beginners." And so it goes, back into the mists of time. The oldest citation in *The Oxford English Dictionary* for "game" in the sense of "a proceeding, scheme, intrigue, undertaking," is from a song, "The Story of Genesis and Exodus," dating to about 1250: "Ysmael pleide hard gamen." And one can't help but suspect that the gamen Ysmael pleide was *hardball*.

War, like politics, has been long thought of as a game: "War's a game which were their subjects wise/Kings would not play at" (William Cowper, "The Winter Morning

Walk," *The Task*, 1785). However, it remained for the Prussians (who else?) to formalize the war-game equation with the invention (ca. 1824) of *kriegspiel,* a war game for training people to fight real ones. Later in the nineteenth century, the contest for power in Asia between Great Britain and Russia was known as "the Great Game," as memorialized by Rudyard Kipling in *Kim* (1901): "Now I shall go far and far into the North, playing the Great Game."

Practice at *games* of this sort has encouraged global politicians to regard nations as inanimate objects (e.g., the *domino theory* that all of Southeast Asia automatically would become Communist following South Vietnam's fall); to justify air raids, as in "The bombing campaign is one of the two trump cards in the hands of the president" (memo from the chairman of the Joint Chiefs of Staff to the secretary of defense, 10/14/66, *The Pentagon Papers*, 1971); to think of weapons systems as bargaining *chips* in arms limitation treaties, and to play off one country against another, e.g., the China *card,* where closer ties with China (in turn the product of *ping-pong diplomacy*) were viewed as a means of putting more pressure on the USSR. This cast of mind seems to be well-nigh universal. Thus, quoting "a senior Iranian official" on the subject of his nation's rapprochement with its bitter enemy, Iraq: "As long as we do not get from the West the sort of normalization and concessions we have been asking for and which we are entitled to, we will use other cards to exact them" (*New York Times,* 1/9/91).

If the *game*-playing indoctrination is good enough, even the soldiers in the field may come to think of what they're doing as an athletic contest. For example, pro football coach Mike Holovak recalled his World War II service this way: "He refers to those years as the time he was on 'the first team' in the 'South Pacific playground' where tracers arced out 'like a touchdown pass' and the artillery fired 'orange blobs—just like a football'" (*Natural History,* 10/75). This is the same Mike Holovak, by the way, who, as general manager of the Houston Oilers, docked tackle David Williams $111,111 (his weekly pay) in 1993 for missing a game in order to be with his wife while she gave birth. And closing the circle: Bob Young, the Oilers' offensive (read that however you choose) line coach, compared Williams's action to a soldier missing a combat mission.

Businessmen, too, like to think of themselves as *players* or even *major players*, especially when they put down *chips* or *markers* in *high-stakes* contests to gain control of other companies. The target company in such a case is said to be *in play.* An unwilling victim may strike back by purchasing stock of the would-be acquisitor. This became known as the *Pac-Man defense,* after the video game in which an attacker must gobble up opponents or itself be consumed.

The "game" metaphor also helps gloss over thoughts of death. This adds to its attraction for soldiers, who rarely discuss death directly (see CASUALTY) as well as for hospital workers (see EXPIRE). For example, here are some snippets from conversations between doctors and patients with fatal illnesses, as recorded by Andrew H. Malcolm in the *New York Times* (2/14/86):

"We'll be very honest with you about the outlook. But I won't have all the information for a day or so . . ."
"Yup. Keep right on it, Doc."
"I will but—are you a football fan?—well it's fourth down, Mr. Anderson."

And the next day:

"I'm afraid things are not going to improve. The outlook is, uh, well, the two-minute warning is in."
"I understand."

Then there is the *game* of love, or sex, also known as *The Mating Game* (film, 1959). The euphemism does not always guarantee protection for the user; however, Earl L. Butz, agriculture secretary, jumped headfirst into boiling water in 1974, with a joke that quoted an Italian woman as justifying her dissent from the pope's ban on artificial means of birth control by saying, "He no playa da game, he no make-a da rules." (For the last words on Butz, who seems to have had a political death wish, see OBSCENE, DEROGATORY, AND SCATOLOGICAL.)

Linking sex to game playing is by no means new. For example, the virile James Boswell confided to his journal for January 12, 1763, the details of his first night with Louisa, a young actress: "Proud of my godlike vigour, I soon resumed the noble game. . . . Five times was I fairly lost in supreme rapture. Louisa . . . declared I was a prodigy, and asked me if this was not extraordinary for human nature. I said twice as much might be, but this was not, although in my own mind I was somewhat proud of my performance" (Frederick A. Pottle, ed., *Boswell's London Journal, 1762–63*, 1950).

P.S. Boswell was twenty-two. If he were living today, he might have said he had SCORED or *hit a home run*. (He certainly got way beyond *first base*, which is just hugging and kissing.) As it was, he later had cause to rue the CONNECTION.

Finally, there is the ultimate game, which is life itself (with all due respect to Stephen Potter, who defined "lifesmanship" as the application of the principles of gamesmanship to the smaller world of life). In the words of Ralph Waldo Emerson: "Play out the game, act well your part, and if the gods have blundered, we will not" (*Journals*, 1856). Of course, this is pretty much a restatement of Saint Paul's advice: "Know ye not, that they which run in a race, run all, but one receiveth the prize? So run, that ye may obtain" (I Corinthians 9:24). Still another, more informal version is set forth in a song that was played frequently by radio stations in the Bible Belt in the mid-1970s, but which must be considerably older, judging from the reference to a football tactic that went out of fashion in the 1930s:

I've got the will Lord, if you've got the toe.
Drop-kick me, Jesus, through the goalposts of life,
End over end, neither left nor to the right,
Straight through the heart of them righteous uprights;
Drop-kick me, Jesus, through the goalposts of life.

A few dyspeptic souls refuse to go along with the life-as-a-game analogy. For example, consider Holden Caulfield's meditation on the subject of life as a *game*:

Game, my ass. Some game. If you get on the side where all the hot-shots are, then it's a game all right—I'll admit that. But if you get on the other side, where there aren't any hot-shots, then what's the game about it? Nothing. No game. (J. D. Salinger, *The Catcher in the Rye*, 1951)

game management. Killing animals; hunting. Modern *game managment* is a highly rationalized business, with an appropriate storehouse of bloodless words. "Instead of shooting bears the [Pennsylvania Game] commission spoke of harvesting bears, which it called a wildlife resource. And the process of putting a bullet in the head of a bear cub was called 'bear management'" (William Ecenbarger, *Philadelphia Inquirer,* 5/12/80). See also CULL and HARVEST.

gaming industry. Gambling industry. Principal industries of Nevada include "gaming, tourism, [and] mining" (*The World Almanac and Book of Facts,* 1993). See also INVEST.

garbage. Shit. When Mark Harris's novel, *Bang the Drum Slowly,* was presented as a television drama (starring Paul Newman) on September 26, 1956, locker-room repartee came out this way:

"How tall are you?"
"Six two and a quarter."
"I didn't know they piled garbage that
    high."

garbologist. A garbageman. "Sanitation worker, Ronald Whatley, has suggested a new title for workers in his profession— 'Garbologists'" (*New York Times,* 9/16/68). Earliest sighting of this term comes from New Zealand in 1965 in the form of "garbiologist" (*OED*). The similar "garbician," noted in *American Speech* (12/56), seems to have died a stillbirth. See also ENGINEER, FLUEOLOGIST, and SANITATION MAN.

garçon. A man; specifically, a waiter in an expensive French restaurant. "Garçon," meaning "boy," is a conspicuous exception to the rule against using that word anymore. The fact that it's in French makes it okay. See also BOY and MAN.

gay. Homosexual; once a code word, used primarily among *gays,* the term has not only come out of the closet but managed to preempt the word's older meanings. Thus, so-called straight people hardly ever dare talk anymore about having "a gay old time" at "gay parties." Nor would Mark Twain, if he were alive today, say of himself, as he did in the *Virginia City,* Nev., *Territorial Enterprise,* "I must have led a gay life at Lake Bigler, for it seems a month since I flew up there on the Pioneer coach, alongside of Hank Monk, the king of stage drivers" (8/19/1863). The word's now dominantly homosexual associations also have inspired various name changes, such as *Garden Bouquet Beauty Soap,* formerly called Gay Bouquet soap, and *Fawn Trail* in West Seneca, N.Y., formerly called Gay Street.

The rise of "gay," supplanting such terms as *faggot, fairy, fancy man* (see FANCY), *homo, queer,* and THREE-LETTER MAN, is a fairly recent phenomenon. In 1961, for example, the term was still being employed in its older senses, without anyone—non-gays, at least—giving the word a second thought. That year saw the opening on Broadway of a musical, *The Gay Life,* by Michael and Fay Mitchell Kanin, and publication of *The Gay Place,* a novel about Texas politics by Billy Lee Bramer. When the novel was reissued in 1978, however, the "gay" in the title caused one to blink— showing how much the word's meaning had changed, and in how short a time.

The loss of "gay's" older senses occasioned much hand-wringing among language purists and other conservatives in the late 1970s and early 1980s. Their distress was aggravated by such jarring head-lines as "'Post' Won't Say Who Died in D.C. Gay Fire," referring to a conflagration in a theater catering to *gays* that claimed nine lives (*MORE,* 12/77). Many homosexuals themselves had doubts about the appropri-ateness of the term. Christopher Isherwood said in a televised interview with Dick Cavett that he didn't mind being called "queer or fag or anything but gay," while Truman Capote told *Newsweek* that "I do hate the word *gay.* It's so inept and inaccu-rate" (Leonard R. N. Ashley, *Maledicta,* Win-ter 1979). At this point, Mr. Ashley could still pose the queston, "Will *gay* triumph as a word?"

Typical of the outraged "straight" pro-tests of the period was a "Dear Abby" let-ter: "I am an Illinois state senator . . . it galls me that sexual deviates are called 'gays.' The word 'gay' means joyous, merry, happy and cheerful . . . to describe homo-sexuality as 'gay' is a perversion in itself, and I respectfully request that you discon-tinue the use of the word in that context. Instead of 'gay', the word 'queer' would be more appropriate . . . NAME WITHHELD ON REQUEST" (8/9/82). Ms. Abigail Van Buren gave short shrift to NAME WITHHELD, how-ever, totally rejecting "queer" and implying that "gay" should be used if that was the label homosexuals themselves preferred.

By the end of the decade of the 1980s, the linguistic battle was over, as indicated by the capitulation in 1989 of Nynex, a pillar of middle-class morality, to pressure from the Gay and Lesbian Alliance Against Defama-tion to admit homosexual groups and ser-vices into the Yellow Pages under "G" and "L" (for "Gay" and "Lesbian," respec-tively). The assistant director of the alliance, Karin Schwartz, explained that "H" for "Homosexual" was rejected because "it seems to relegate the fact you are gay to sex. Gay is our word of choice" (*New York Times,* 1/18/89).

"Gay" had come a long way. Ironically, the word does not have the happiest of his-tories. The French *gai* sometimes is cited as the source of the word's homosexual sense, which is in keeping with general sexual stereotypes about the FRENCH, but the term's history in English provides suffi-cient explanation for the modern meaning.

"Gay," in the sense of "addicted to social pleasures," was used from the seventeenth century as a euphemism for a "loose or immoral life" (*OED*). Thus, when a "lady" remarked in *Lady of Pleasure* (1637) that "gay men have a privilege," it seems that only heterosexual privileges and pleasures were contemplated.

Proceeding from euphemism to slang, "gay" came to imply "whore." For exam-ple, the anonymous author of *My Secret Life* (ca. 1890) recalled an encounter of per-haps forty years before in this manner: "I saw a woman walking along Pall-Mall dressed in the nicest and neatest way. I could scarcely make up my mind whether she was gay or not, but at length saw the quiet invitation in her eye, and slightly nodding in reply, followed her to a house in B**y Street, St. James."

Gay women of this era also were said to lead the *gay life,* to work in *gay houses,* to be *gay in the arse* (another way of saying a woman was "loose"), and to *gay it* (either sex might *gay it,* this simply meaning "to copulate"). The application of "gay" to prostitutes and their way of life was not restricted to the British Isles. Thus, "Gay Girls' Actions" was the first subhead in the "Scarlet World" column of the New Orleans *Sunday Sun* (1/31/1904), a New Orleans scandal sheet that reported "Interesting Items About the Every-Day Life of Women of Crimson Circles."

The frequent assumption is that the simple "gay" in the modern manner dates just to the 1950s, as in "Where the gay set met for dinner," a 1951 ad for the Cyrano Restaurant in New York's Greenwich Village (Cherry Grove Arts Council Theater program, in George Chauncey, *Gay New York,* 1994). The assumption is wrong, however. For example, in *Bringing Up Baby* (1938), when Cary Grant (a euphemism for Archibald Alexander Leach) is asked what he is doing wearing Katharine Hepburn's peignoir, he jumps up and down and shouts: "Because I just went gay all of a sudden." The term also made early appearances in the lyrics of Noel Coward and Cole Porter, both of whom were *gay.* For example, in Coward's "Mad About the Boy" (1932) the word appears in what can only be described as suspicious circumstances even though the lyric in the original revue was sung by a streetwalker:

It's pretty funny, but I'm mad about
   the boy,
He has a gay appeal
That makes me feel
There's maybe something sad about
   the boy.

Porter was more explicit in "Farming," from *Let's Face It* (1941), but it is likely that only *gays* got the full import of the lyric:

Don't inquire of Georgie Raft
Why his cow has never calfed.
Georgie's bull is beautiful, but he's gay!

Eric Partridge listed "gay boy" as Australian slang for "homosexual" since about 1925 and suggested that "gay" might have been used a long time before this within the homosexual community (*A Dictionary of Slang and Unconventional English,* 1970). Indeed, it seems likely that the word was adopted by the males who inhabited the homosexual underworld that flourished—complete with houses of male prostitution, drag balls, etc.—alongside the heterosexual *gay* underworld in most major cities on both sides of the Atlantic, from the mid-nineteenth century if not before. Thus, John Saul, a male PROSTITUTE who played a leading role in the Cleveland Street Scandal of 1889 (it involved post office boys in a male brothel in London's West End), apparently used the word both ways. On the witness stand, Saul testified that he once earned part of his living by "cleaning out the houses of the gay people," by which he seems to have meant "the gay ladies on the beat," not homosexuals (H. Montgomery Hyde, *The Cleveland Street Scandal,* 1976). In a deposition to the police, however, Saul also referred to his male friends as "gay," and he is credited with the earliest known use of the word in its currently dominant sense by Philip Howard, in *New Words for Old: A Survey of Misused, Vogue & Cliche Words* (1977).

Though the present meaning of "gay" now seems firmly entrenched, one can never tell what the future holds. *Gays* have begun to reclaim the older terms as part of the process of coming to grips with their own identities. For example, Larry Kramer entitled his semiautobiographical novel *Faggots.* Published in 1978, its opening line is "There are 2,556,596 faggots in the New York City area." Other straws in the wind, noted by Mr. Ashley in *Maledicta* (op. cit.), include the formation of such groups as Dykes Opposed to Nuclear Technology and, an organization of lesbians with children, Dykes and Tykes, along with the founding of the New York City newspaper *Big Apple Dyke News*. Even "queer," long regarded as highly pejorative, seems to be making a comeback, as evidenced by the chant of gay rights marchers in New York City, "We're here. We're queer. Get used to us!" (in Ms. Madonna's *Truth or Dare*, 1991).

If "gay" were to be replaced by one of the older words, it would not be the first time that this kind of linguistic change has taken place. See also NEGRO and, for other "gay" terms, BISEXUAL; CONFIRMED BACHELOR; GREEK ARTS; LOVE THAT DARE NOT SPEAK ITS NAME, THE; MALE; QUEEN; SEXUAL ORIENTATION DISTURBANCE; and STERILE.

gay deceivers. Not a couple of police officers trying to entrap gays but a padded brassiere for entrapping guys; a PALPITATOR. See also BRASSIERE.

Adoption by women in the 1940s and 1950s of *gay deceivers*, a.k.a., *cheaters* and *falsies*, was only fair play; traditionally, a *gay deceiver* was the somewhat euphemistic description for a deceitful rake. "Says he, 'I'm a handsome man, but I'm a gay deceiver'" (George Colman, the Younger, *Love Laughs at Locksmiths*, 1808). See the earlier meanings of GAY.

GD. God damn. The abbreviation mitigates the oath, supposedly. "That's what George is. A bog. . . . A fen. . . . A GD swamp. Ha, ha, ha, HA!" (Edward Albee, *Who's Afraid of Virginia Woolf*, 1962). See also ADONAI, GODDAM, and GOSH.

gee (or geez). Jesus. "It's the most exciting thing that's happened in—geez—maybe ever, in mathematics" (Dr. Leonard Adelman's reaction to the news of the apparent solution by Dr. Andrew Wiles of the 350-year-old problem of Fermat's last theorum, *New York Times*, 6/24/93).

The oldest citation for "gee" in *The Oxford English Dictionary* comes from as recently as 1895: "Gee rod! how we will thump'em!" (Stephen Crane, *The Red Badge of Courage*). Other "gee" substitutes for "Jesus" include *gee-hollikins, gee-my-knee, geewhilliker(s), geewhillikins* (possibly the progenitor of "gee"), *geewhittaker(s), gee whiz* (perhaps from "gee ziz"), and *geewizard*, as well as such sound-alikes as *Jee, Jeez, jeepers (-creepers), jeezy peezy,* JIMINY CRICKET, and JINGO. For purposes of profanity, the holy name also has been extended in many ways, e.g., *holy jumping Jesus, holy jumping mother of Jesus, Jesus Christ and his brother Harry, Jesus H. Christ, Jesus H. Particular Christ,* and *Jesus Christ on a Bicycle.* It is likely that these oaths have been employed for some years. About 1848, one of Mark Twain's fellow apprentices at the *Missouri Courier* in Hannibal—Wales McCormick by name, a "reckless, hilarious, admirable creature"—caused an uproar by inserting an "H." into the Savior's name when setting into type a sermon by a well-known preacher of the time (*Mark Twain's Autobiography*, 1924).

See also CHRISSAKE; CRYING OUT LOUD, FOR; CRIPES; GOSH; MARRY, and, for background on avoiding the name of God, ADONAI.

generation. Sex; especially in such phrases as *act of generation, members of generation,* and *organs of generation.* "Masochism appears when the afflicted person allows himself to be ill-treated by his partner, in order to be sexually excited or to attain the full enjoyment of the act of generation" (Hans Gross, *Criminal Investigation*, Norman Kendal, ed., 1934).

Our Victorian ancestors leaned on this one even in underground novels when "generation" in the true sense of "generating" another generation was most definitely not the purpose of the exercise. For example, from the anonymous *A Man with a Maid*: "For certainly half a minute, Alice intently inspected my organs of generation . . . I wondered what thoughts passed through her mind as she gazed curiously on what very soon would be the instruments of her violation and the conquerors of her virginity!"

The basic expression was already old in Victoria's time, however. Geoffrey Chaucer referred to the "werk of generacion" in his translation of Boethius's *The Consolation of Philosophy* (ca. 1374). See also ACT, F – – –, MEMBER, and ORGAN.

genitals. The external sexual organs, a.k.a. PRIVATE PARTS. For those who prefer to retreat further into fake Latin, the word becomes "genitalia." The real Latin *genitālis* (of generation) comes from the past participle of *gignere* (to beget), which makes "genitals" a misnomer when precautions are taken to avoid procreation. See also GROIN, NATURAL, PENIS, POSSIBLE, PUDENDUM, TESTICLES, and VAGINA.

gentleman. Man; male. Though its career is not as checkered as that of LADY, the "gentle" term has been used to paper over a wide variety of low, impolite, indecent, rascally, and altogether ungentlemanly conditions, creatures, and occupations. Following is a selection of these usages, most of them now obsolete due to the egalitarian, nongentlemanly spirit of our own age.

First, and perhaps least euphemistic, is the "gentleman" that is routinely extended to practically anything that is male and walks on two legs. In this category are the *gentleman-caller, gentleman-lodger, gentleman-tailor, gentleman-volunteer,* and *gentleman-waiter* — among many others. Other, more picturesque "gentlemen" have included the policeman, who was known as the *gentleman in blue* (or *of the short staff*); the soldier, who was the *gentleman in red* (before the British realized what good targets redcoats made and changed their uniforms); the *gentleman of fortune,* who was a pirate; the *gentleman of the road,* who was either a highwayman, gypsy, or traveling salesman; and the *gentleman's master,* who was definitely a highwayman because he made real gentlemen obey his command to "Stand and Deliver." Then there is the *gentleman at large,* originally a court attendant with no specific duties, but later a person out of work (i.e., AT LIBERTY); the *gentleman's gentleman,* who was a valet (the French *valet,* in turn, being a nicefied way of saying "servant"); the *gentleman of the back (door),* a sodomist, and the simple *gentleman,* who was a smuggler, as in "Watch the wall, my darling, while the Gentlemen go by!" (Rudyard Kipling, *Puck of Pook's Hill,* 1906).

The old gentleman or *the (old) gentleman in black* is Satan, who is not usually called by his real name for fear that he will hear it and come (see DEVIL, THE). A *gentleman of the three ins* was a person who was "In debt, in gaol, and in danger of remaining there for life; or, in gaol, indicted, and in danger of being hanged in chains" (Capt. Francis Grose, *A Classical Dictionary of the Vulgar Tongue,* 1796). This contrasted with a *gentleman of the three outs,* who was "without money, without wit, and without manners" (Grose, op. cit.), or "out of pocket, out of elbows, and out of credit" (Edward G. E. L. Bulwer-Lytton, *Paul Clifford,* 1830).

Finally, "gentleman" also has been awarded to various creatures that aren't necessarily male and that sometimes have four—or more—legs. The *gentleman that (or who) pays the rent* was a pig, in England, where a *gentleman's companion* was a body louse, and a *gentleman in brown,* a bedbug. In the United States, the turkey cock has been called a *gentleman turkey* and the bull has been dignified as a *gentleman cow.* Sharp-eyed lexicographers also have spotted *gentleman hounds* and *gentlemen sheep.* This same fastidiousness was responsible for turning the ancient "ass" into the familiar DONKEY and the original "cock" into the contemporary ROOSTER.

See also COW BRUTE, LADIES/GENTLEMEN, and MAN.

George/Godfrey. Two given names for "God." Dating from the sixteenth century, "George" may actually derive from Saint George, but it usually is used in contexts where a true oathsayer would say "God," e.g., "'By George, he *has* got something to tell'" (Mark Twain, *The Adventures of Tom Sawyer,* 1876). "Godfrey," meanwhile, is a simple, euphemistic extension of "God," dating to around the turn of this century, and probably used most frequently by sailors who say they are steering "by guess and by Godfrey" when they are proceeding without a set course or the aid of landmarks. See also GOSH.

gesture of goodwill. A payment that one is required to make. Thus, I. G. Farben, the German combine, having already lost a suit to one of the people who had been a slave laborer for the company during World War II, tried to evade its responsibility by insisting that reparations to survivors be considered a "gesture of goodwill," not the "discharge of an obligation" (*New York Times Book Review,* 12/9/79). A *gesture of goodwill* is essentially the same as an EX GRATIA payment.

girlfriend. Lover, mistress. "Those indicted were James McElroy, 36 years old, a gang leader who has been jailed on a separate murder charge; his girlfriend, Francine Mostyn, 40" (*New York Times,* 3/21/87). How old, one wonders, does one have to be to become a "woman friend"? See also BOYFRIEND and FRIEND.

glands. The testicles; also called *sex glands* or *interstitial glands.* "Glands," from the Latin *glans,* acorn, was favored in the 1920s and 1930s by newspapers that didn't dare print "testicles." Women have glands, too —MAMMARY GLANDS. See also TESTICLES.

glow. Sweat. "Horses sweat, men perspire, women glow" (old saying, ca. Queen Victoria). See also PERSPIRE.

gluteus maximus. The ass; technically only the largest of the three muscles (*g. medius* and *minimus* are the others) that form the buttock of a person, but often used as a fancy euphemism for the entire affair. Generally, the Latin "gluteus maximus" is reserved for men, while women are awarded the French DERRIÈRE.

go. One of the most versatile words in the English language, "go" naturally has many euphemistic applications. For example, "to go" may be shorthand for "go to the bathroom" (see also BATHROOM), as in, discussing the need for portable toilets following hurricane Andrew in Florida: "We're talking about fifty thousand people and they have no place to go" (WABC-TV, "Eyewitness News," 8/30/92).

In quite another context, "to go" may

mean "to die," as in "I'm afraid he's about to go." In the latter case, it is also possible to *go* with flourishes, such as *go down hill with no brakes, go home, go off, go out, go the way of all the earth,* and *go the way of all flesh.* (The latter two are biblical, the "earth" form appearing in the King James Bible of 1611, e.g., Joshua 23:14, and the other in the Douay Version of 1609, III Kings 2:3.) After *going* in this way, one may be said to have *gone,* as in the exchange from Shakespeare's *The Winter's Tale,* (1611):

> SERVANT: The Prince, your son . . . is gone.
> LEONTES: How? Gone?
> SERVANT: Is dead.

Or as Stalin told Truman at Potsdam in 1945, when Truman asked what had happened to the Polish officers who were massacred in Katyn Forest in 1940: "They went away" (David McCullough, *Truman,* 1992). See also GO WEST; HAPPY HUNTING GROUNDS, GONE TO THE; and PASS AWAY.

Other kinds of euphemistic "go's" include:

go all the way (or *the limit* or *the whole route*), for sexual INTERCOURSE; see ALL THE WAY.

go down (on), for oral-genital sex (CUNNILINGUS or FELLATIO), but also, as "go down," without the "on," a euphemism in some parts of the country for conventional COPULATION.

go down like a submarine, for someone who submerges sexually with especial speed and enthusiasm.

go out, for an engagement with a whore; see WANNA GO OUT?

Finally, there is the very basic "go on,"

elegantly illustrated by George Gordon, Lord Byron in *Don Juan* (1819–24), when the beauteous Julia berates her suspicious husband:

> Ungrateful, perjured, barbarous Don Alfonso,
> How dare you think your lady would go on so?

Strong words but—alas—even as Julia speaks, sixteen-year-old Juan is hiding in her bed, and as the reader knows from a previous verse, the lady is not as innocent as she pretends:

> A little she strove, and much repented
> And whispering, "I will ne'er consent"— consented.

goddam (or **goddem).** A euphemistic "God damn"; also, from the fifteenth century, an Englishman (to a Frenchman). Or to a Frenchwoman—Joan of Arc, say, who commonly referred to the English as the "Goddems." English soldiers of the period gained the sobriquet by their frequent use of the expression. See also DOGGONE, GD, GOSH, and SOB.

golden age/years. Old age; the "golden years" variant probably is a half-breed ("hybrid," if you prefer), compounded of "golden age" and SUNSET YEARS.

The myth that the golden years are the best years is rooted in the concept of the Golden Age as the first and best of the ages of the world. The Golden Age was supposed to be a time of innocence and happiness, when truth and justice prevailed. Spears and swords had not yet been invented, perpetual spring reigned, and the rivers flowed with milk and wine. Thus, the euphemism completes a metaphorical circle, returning the oldster to the infancy of the species—another example of ontogeny recapitulating phylogeny.

"Golden age" appears to have been a product of the golden 1950s. The first example in the 1972 supplement to *The Oxford English Dictionary* is from 1961. Of course, the base metal beneath the gilding was recognized by some people from the start: "The brochure writers and the publicists talk of the 'golden years' and of 'senior citizens.' But these are euphemisms to ease the conscience of the callous. America tends to make people miserable when they are old and there are not enough phrases in the dictionary to gloss over the ugly reality" (Michael Harrington, *The Other America*, 1962). See also KEEN AGE, MASTER, MATRON, MATURE, and SENIOR CITIZEN.

golly. A euphemistic deformation of "God," often encountered in the form of "By Golly!"

People have been exclaiming "Golly" since at least the eighteenth century; an early variant was "goles," e.g., "Why then, by goles, I will tell you—I hate you" (Henry Fielding, *Virgin Unmasked*, 1734). The "golly," in turn, has helped produce a raft of other euphemistic expletives, such as *goldamn, goldang, goldarn, gollydingwhiz, golly gee,* and *golly Moses.* See also DARN, GD, GEE, and GOSH.

good fellow. A criminal; specifically, a member of *organized crime,* as the Mafia is often termed in deference to Italian-Americans who object to being associated with gangsterism. "Mr. McDonald said, however, that Mr. Bolino had referred to himself as 'a good fellow,' and in the lexicon of law enforcement, this meant being a member of organized crime" (*New York Times,* 6/24/80). The classic treatment of the subject is Martin Scorsese's film *GoodFellas* (1990), based on Nicholas Pileggi's book *Wiseguy* (1987). "Good fellow" also is a nineteenth-century euphemism for a soft-brained person, a dummy, but it probably is not advisable to use the term in this sense when speaking to a member of the mob. See also SYNDICATE.

good grief. Good God—as in the famous line in Charles Schulz's "Peanuts" comic strip, "Good grief, Charlie Brown." Functional equivalents include *good gosh, good gracious, good gracious to Betsy, good gravy,* and *goodness sakes alive.* See also GOSH, GREAT SCOTT, and GRIEF.

good people, the. Fairies, gnomes, leprechauns, goblins, and other little people. These are not especially malevolent spirits. They often help mortals accomplish their tasks, give them valuable presents, and warn them of danger. Still, they love to play tricks on people, and they have a disturbing fondness for human babies—sometimes stealing them and leaving fairy babies in their places. Because they are what they are, people have felt it wise to propitiate them with gifts and, of course, never to say anything bad about them.

In medieval Europe, the common folk believed themselves constantly beset by supernatural pests, but took care never to risk offending them with a bad name. In Scotland, for instance, they were always *daoine sithe,* "the little men of peace," and in Spain *las estantiguas,* "the venerable ones." In

India to this day the native fiends and imps are called *punyajanas,* "the good people." (Gary Jennings, *Personalities of Language,* 1965)

Some animals, too, are commonly approached indirectly and euphemistically; see GRANDFATHER. Of course, the short, *good people* should not be confused with LITTLE PEOPLE.

gosh. Along with GOLLY, probably the most common of the many euphemisms still used for "God," e.g., " 'Oh gosh,' murmured the darling close-eyed girl, biting her lip as . . ." (Maxwell Kenton, a.k.a. Terry Southern, *Candy,* 1965).

"Gosh" seems to be a product of the eighteenth century, with the oldest example in *The Oxford English Dictionary* coming from 1757. However, it was preceded by the similar *gosse,* recorded as "by gosse," circa 1553. Like DARN, GEE, and GOLLY, "gosh" has been developed into many picturesque combinations, such as *gosh-almighty, gosh-all-fishhooks, gosh-all-hemlock, gosh-all-Potomac, gosh-awful, gosh-dang, gosh-durn, goshwalader, by-guess-and-by-gosh, holy gosh,* and *ohmigosh.*

For the root reason for avoiding "God," see ADONAI, and for other ways of swearing without actually taking the sacred name in vain, continue with BEGORRA(H), CAIN, DAD, DOGGONE, EGAD, FAITH, GADZOOKS, GD, GEORGE/GODFREY, GODDAM, GOOD GRIEF, GRABS, GREAT SCOTT, HEAVENS, JOVE, LAW, MAN, ODDS BODKINS, and ZOUNDS.

go west. To die, or PASS AWAY. Usually encountered in the past tense, after a person has DEPARTED, "gone west" was popularized, so to speak, in World War I. It may have originated in the American West,

though it also has been reported to have been used in the Boer War. A variant was "send west," as in "the Huns came pretty near sending me 'west'" (*Literary Digest,* 8/17/18). Whatever the source of the precise expression, the association between the West, where the sun sets, and death is extremely ancient. The Celtic Otherworld was in the West, and "occident," the word we have inherited from the Romans for "the West" (as opposed to "the Orient") comes from *occidere,* to fall down—or to die. J. R. R. Tolkien drew on this association when he concluded the trilogy of *The Lord of the Rings* (1956) with Bilbo and Frodo going to the Grey Havens, where they boarded a white ship, and "went out into the High Sea and passed on into the West." The same idea is echoed banally in the euphemism of old age as the SUNSET YEARS. See also BITE THE DUST; GO; and HAPPY HUNTING GROUNDS, GONE TO THE.

grabs. God, usually in the form of "by grabs" or "good grabs." "We ain't dead, by grabs, and nowheres nigh it" (Joel Chandler Harris, *Tales of the Home Folks,* 1898). See also GOSH.

grandfather. A common euphemism among many peoples (and not only PRELITERATE ones) for any of a number of animals. "Depending on where you live, the euphemism grandfather may mean the bear, the tiger, the elephant, or the alligator" (Maria Leach, ed., *Funk & Wagnalls Standard Dictionary of Folklore, Mythology and Legend,* 1972). The bear, for example, is *grandfather* to the Ural-Altaic peoples of Siberia, to those who live near the Baltic Sea, and to the Tête de Boule Indians in Quebec. And this is only one of many euphemisms for the bear. "The Russian linguist A. A. Reformatsky notes the variety of euphemisms for 'bear' among Russian commercial hunters. Actually even the common word *miedvied* is an old euphemism; its literal meaning is 'honey eater.' Eventually secondary euphemisms developed: *khoziain* (landlord or boss), *lomaka* (he who breaks things, like bones maybe), *mokhnach* (the shaggy one), *liesnik* (the forest dweller) or simply *on* (he)" (Anatol Rapoport, *Semantics*, 1970). Other euphemisms for "bear" include *Little Old Man, Dear Uncle, Wise One, Beautiful Honey-Paw,* and *Broad Foot.* In Lappland, the bear is often referred to as *the old man in the fur coat.*

The set of euphemisms is ancient as well as widespread; speakers of Indo-European languages have almost always used them. "The name of the bear was likewise subject to a hunter's taboo; the animal could not be mentioned by his real name on the hunt. . . . All the northern [Indo-European] languages have a substitute term: in Slavic he is the 'honey-eater,' in Germanic the 'brown one'" (*The American Heritage Dictionary of the English Language,* 1969).

Several intertwined and to some extent competing reasons exist for using euphemisms in place of the true names of animals that are feared, revered, or desired. The euphemistic or metaphoric name may be intended to flatter or propitiate the animal or, conversely, and not so flatteringly, it may be intended to deceive, the idea being that the animal won't realize hunters are talking about it if its true name is not mentioned. On another level, there is the deep-seated human belief that words are extensions of the objects for which they stand, and hence, that to name an object is to establish contact with the object named. (This principle applies to beings and things of all kinds, not just to animals; see ADONAI; DEVIL, THE; and GOOD PEOPLE, THE.) Because words are thought to have this quality, people in many cultures will not speak the real name of another person, especially not a king or a dead person (see DEPARTED). To speak the name of a dead person may raise a ghost; to say the true name of the bear may make him appear when he is not wanted. This belief in the magical power of words to affect the course of events helps explain the universal use of curses and blessings, of spells and of prayers. For other euphemisms for other animals, see STRIPED ONE.

grand master. An athlete beyond his or her prime. "Founded by Al Bunis, the Grand Masters is a world tour of men tennis stars over 45" (*Hall of Fame News,* Fall 1981). See also MASTER.

grand prize. Second prize at the Cannes Film Festival, where the first prize is the Palme d'Or.

gratuity. A relatively innocuous grandiloquency, parallel to HONORARIUM, when the amount is added to another bill, as in "taxes and gratuities extra," but a byword for "bribe" when a larger gift is made to a person in a public post, as in "A Federal jury today found a top aide to former Housing Secretary Samuel R. Pierce Jr. and two other men guilty of offering gratuities to Federal housing officials" (AP, 1/5/93). See also EX GRATIA.

Great Scott. Good God. Dated to 1885 (*OED*), "Great Scott" may have been inspired partly by General Winfield Scott, whose achievements kept him in the public eye from 1812, when he was a hero in the war with Great Britain, to 1865, when he commanded the Union army at the start of the Civil War. "Scott" is only one of many variants, however. Other "Great"s all with the same euphemistic meaning and all dating from the ultrapolite nineteenth century, include *Great Caesar, Great Caesar's Ghost, Great Grief, Great Guns, Great Horn Spoon, Great Shakes,* and *Great Sun.* Like CRIPES, JOVE, and other "oaths" of this ilk, "Great Scott" survives mainly in the comics, e.g., "Great Scott! Ya mean this is the year 2430?" (Robert C. Dille, *The World of Buck Rogers,* 1978). See also GOSH.

Greek arts/culture/way. The code in personal ads for anal intercourse, heterosexual as well as homosexual; frequently abbreviated to a space-saving *Greek* or *gr.* The association of the Greeks with homosexuality—pederasty in particular—goes back to classical times. Thus, Herodotus (ca. 480–425 B.C.) reflected on the cultural adaptations of the Persians: "They have taken the dress of the Medes, considering it superior to their own; and in war they wear the Egyptian breastplate. As soon as they hear of any luxury, they instantly make it their own, and hence, among other novelties, from the Greeks, they learnt to go to bed with boys" (*The Histories*). See also BISEXUAL, the "horny blue eyed divorcee" in FRENCH, and Oscar Wilde's citation of Plato in LOVE THAT DARE NOT SPEAK ITS NAME, THE.

Greenland. This has to be the world's most deceptive name for a piece of real estate. Though frequently colored green on maps, *Greenland* is anything but. Some 60 percent of the island is covered by glaciers; the rest alternates between barren rock and arctic prairie. True, when Eric the Red explored the island in 981–84, the climate was somewhat warmer than now, and the land pre-

sumably somewhat greener. Still, the Norsemen who followed him took one look and concluded that a shrewd promoter had picked this name. As Ari Thorgilsson put it in the *Islendingabok,* a history compiled in the early twelfth century:

The country which was called Gronland was discovered and settled from Iceland. Erik the Red was the name of the man from Breidafiord who went there and took possession of the land at the place since called Eriksfiord. He called the country Gronland, saying people would desire to go there if the country had a good name.

Vínland hit góda, or Wineland the good, the name of the Norse settlement in Newfoundland, probably was selected by Eric's son, Leif the Lucky, with the same thought in mind. Grapes did not grow so far north, though a very thirsty Viking might have made something drinkable from wild red currants, gooseberries, or mountain cranberries in the area.

While motives vary from case to case—greed, pride, prudishness, and superstition are common ones—the drive to dress up one's surroundings with fair-sounding names is a basic human trait. And this is ignoring such politically motivated names as *Arabian Gulf* for Persian Gulf; *Samaria* and *Judea* for the West Bank; *Kitchner,* Ontario, for Bismarck; *General Pershing Street* in New Orleans for Berlin Street (see also LIBERTY CABBAGE); and the serene *Place de la Concorde* in Paris for *Place de la Révolution,* as it was called when MADAME, the guillotine, operated there (in prerevolutionary days it was *Place Louis XV*).

Frequently, as in the case of Eric and Leif, it is a question of real estate operators at work. This is why—in New York City, for example—Hell's Kitchen was renamed the *Clinton* district; why Welfare Island (formerly Blackwell's Island) became *Roosevelt Island;* why the Lower East Side was reincarnated as the *East Village;* why Punkiesberg, the solid Dutch name of a Brooklyn neighborhood, was discarded in favor of *Cobble Hill;* why the adjacent neighborhood, North Gowanus, became *Boerum Hill,* and why, across the Hudson in New Jersey, East Paterson became *Elmwood Park* and bucolic Passaic Township metamorphosed into *Long Hill Township* (no more confusion with the urban decay of the city of Passaic, some twenty miles away). This is also why proper Bostonians tried to convert their city's ADULT entertainment (or "combat") zone into the *Liberty Tree Neighborhood;* why Hog Island in the Bahamas was renamed *Paradise Island;* why Billygoat Hill, in Nashville, Tennessee, was developed into *Angora Heights;* and why, in a more general sense, apartment houses are blessed with names like Castle *Arms* and Haddon *Hall,* why auto camps are MOTELS, why hotels are called *houses* (as in Parker House, Palmer House, or the generic *guest house*), why houses are called HOMES, why a group of high-priced ones is called an ENCLAVE or PLANTATION, and why a swamp may be developed as a MEADOWLANDS.

The desire to escape rude and humble origins often seems to be as important a motive as boosting property values when it comes to selecting new place names. Thus, the good citizens of Vanderheyden's Ferry, New York, inaugurated the age of classical place-naming in the United States when they gathered together on January 5, 1789, and voted to change the name of their burg to *Troy.* Other examples of the grasping for

grandeur include the conversions of Mole Hill, West Virginia, into *Mountain;* Mud Creek, Nova Scotia, into *Wolfville;* France's lower Loire, the *Loire Inférieure,* into *Loire Atlantique,* and the Central African Republic (during the reign of the self-styled Emperor Jean-Bedel Bokassa) into the *Central African Empire.* In a general way, too, this is why normal schools become *colleges;* why colleges promote themselves into UNIVERSITIES; why small towns pretend to be CITIES, and why, finally, stores and shops advertise themselves as EMPORIUMS, PARLORS, SALONS, and SHOPPES.

Names often are changed simply for reasons of refinement, e.g., *Scranton,* Pennsylvania, née Skunk's Misery; *New Hope,* Mississippi, formerly Dirty Corners; *Cabot Island,* off Newfoundland, first known as Stinkard Island; *Contentment Island,* off Darien, Connecticut, once Contention Island; *Placerville,* California, originally known as Hangtown; *Tuckahoe Creek,* New York, the erstwhile Turkey Hole Rivulet, and *Sob Rapids,* Utah, cleverly devised after the U.S. Board on Geographical Names disallowed SOB Rapids. (The board is not inflexible, however. It has permitted Cat House Creek, Montana; Pleasure House Creek, Virginia; and it reversed itself in the case of *Naughty Girl Meadow,* Oregon, allowing mapmakers to restore the original Whorehouse Meadow.) In its single most sweeping move, the board ruled in 1963 that "Nigger" should be replaced by "Negro" on all state maps. This merely ratified a national trend, "Nigger" already having been dropped in many cases, e.g., *Negro Mountain,* Maryland (once Nigger Mountain, after the death there of a giant black man in the French and Indian War), or completely blotted out, as in *Borrego Springs,*

California, originally Nigger Springs (after Jim Green, an early settler).

Superstition also plays a role in the naming, or renaming, of places, just as it does in the formation of euphemisms for death, the dead, dreaded illnesses, and so on. Thus, the Romans changed the name of a Greek colony in Italy from Malowenta (which meant "rich in sheep," but which they misinterpreted in Latin as Maleuentum, or "ill-come") to the more auspicious *Beneuentum* ("welcome"). The ancient Greeks, meanwhile, referred to the cold and treacherous Black Sea as the Euxine, or HOSPITABLE SEA.

In modern times, too, people avoid words with unlucky associations. In the aforementioned Brooklyn, for example, a yellow fever epidemic in 1848 put Yellow Hook in such bad repute that its name was changed to *Bay Ridge,* while a terrible subway accident at Malbone Street in 1918, the worst in the city's history (97 killed, some 250 injured) resulted in that thoroughfare being renamed *Empire Boulevard.*

And so it goes. In June of 1974, when President Richard M. Nixon met with Soviet Secretary-General Leonid I. Brezhnev at Yalta, the Americans insisted that the site of the meeting be referred to as *Orleans,* the district of the city in which Mr. Brezhnev's dacha was located. This avoided any unfortunate associations with the Big-Three Yalta conference in 1945 at which the allies allegedly "sold out" eastern Europe to the Russians. (Nevertheless, the exercise in summitry did not save Nixon from having to resign two months later.) Then there was the oil tanker *Exxon Valdez,* all 987 feet of her and therefore large enough to qualify for treatment as a place name, which caused the nation's largest oil spill when it ran aground in Alaska in 1989. It began plying the seas again in 1990 after being repaired—and whitewashed with a new name, the *Exxon Mediterranean.*

grief. Disaster, especially pregnancy; what unmarried women used to come to. "Have you ever heard of a typewriter girl who has come to grief, and who wasn't beautiful?" (A. Dale, *Wanted, A Cook,* 1904). See also GOOD GRIEF and PREGNANT.

groin. A slight anatomical displacement, the term for the depression where the thigh joins the abdomen serving as a euphemism for the adjacent GENITALS. "The man returned the compliment by kicking him in the groin" (Charles Dickens, letter, 11/13/1865). More recently, from an interview with the fourteenth Dalai Lama: "Then, of course, sometimes beautiful women.... But then, many monks have the same experience. Some of it is curiosity: If you use this, what is the feeling? [Points to his groin.]" (*New York Times Magazine,* 11/28/93). Women have *groins,* too. In medical schools and hospitals, another term for "gynecology" is *groinecology.*

growth stock. When the market is going down, a *growth stock* "is a stock the bank trust departments hold too much of" (*Barron's,* 2/12/73). See also DEFER PURCHASE, NONPERFORMING ASSET, and RECESSION.

guarded. Hopeless; medical talk. "It is usual for a physician confronted by a hopeless or near-hopeless case to note on the patient's chart some easy euphemism like 'The prognosis is guarded'" (*New Yorker,* 1/25/82). See also NOT DOING WELL.

guest. Customer, especially in the hotel business, where smaller establishments frequently are known as *guest houses*. A departing *guest* at the Plaza Hotel in New York City may awake to find that a *guest folio* has been slid beneath the door of his or her room. The *guest folio* lists all charges as of daybreak, and it can be quite an eye-opener, with the cost of a suite facing Central Park running to $1,100 a night (1992), plus a 19.25 percent hotel and sales tax.

"Guest" also is employed in other commercial operations involving shorter stays, e.g., "We welcome only guests using condoms" (sign in brothel window in Chiang Mai, Thailand, 1991).

guidance counselor. A redundancy. What does a "counselor" do but offer "guidance"? The addition of "guidance" gives the title a FOP Index of 2.2. See also ENGINEER.

gun. The penis. A traditional punishment in the U.S. Marine Corps for a recruit who makes the grievous mistake of referring to his "rifle" as a "gun" is to require him to walk the area, holding his rifle in one hand and his penis in the other, while reciting the quaint quatrain:

> This is my rifle,
> This is my gun.
> This is for shooting,
> This is for fun.

The penis-as-gun is a classic example of the close connection that exists between sex and violence (see ACTION). John Lennon's song, "Happiness Is a Warm Gun," also trades on this association. The metaphor often is extended. "Guns" of both types go BANG and both may cause someone to DIE.

The modern "gun" seems to have taken over the historic role of "pistol," which stood for "penis" as far back as the sixteenth century. For example, Shakespeare's *Henry IV, Part 2* (1598) is loaded with puns on the name of Pistol, as in, Falstaff speaking: "Here, Pistol, I charge you with a cup of sack. Do you discharge upon mine hostess." See also PENIS and TOOL.

H

Hades. Hell. "We prefer our coffee as strong as love, as black as sin, and as hot as Hades" (Rep. T. Hale Boggs, D., La., tariff bill debate, 1960). Mr. Boggs resorted to "Hades," the ancient Greek name of the underworld and its god, because House rules forbade mention of "Hell." His point was that chicory, a key ingredient of coffee in New Orleans, should be included on the duty-free list. See also HALIFAX, HECK, and H – – L.

hail Columbia. Hell, often in the phrases *to catch* or *give (someone) hail Columbia*; from the title of the song (1798) by Joseph Hopkinson, with the "h" sometimes capitalized as a result, e.g., "I got Hail Columbia from Father for that escapade" (*New Yorker*, 5/25/46). Variants include *hail Columbus* and *hale Columby*. See also HECK.

hairpiece. A wig; also called a TOUPEE or *rug*. "A hairpiece by any other name is still a cover-up" (ad for Thomas hair transplants, New York *Village Voice*, 8/21/78). A store that specializes in hairpieces is known, at its fanciest, as a *hairitorium*. See also EMPORIUM.

hair rinse. Hair dye. See also BEAUTICIAN and COLOR.

Halifax. Hell. "I'd see you in Halifax, now, before I'd do it" (Mark Twain, *Old Times on the Mississippi*, 1875). The expression dates to the seventeenth century and probably refers to Halifax, England, where judges practiced what was known as "Halifax Law," the guiding principle of which was purported to be "Hang first, try afterward." Other euphemistic but hellish locations to "go to" include *Guinea, Jericho,* and *Putney.* A variant is "Havana," as in "She can wait until Havana freezes over" (Henry Fonda, referring to Barbara Stanwyck, *The Lady Eve*, 1941). See also HADES, HECK, and H – – L.

halitosis. Scientific bad breath. "What else can ruin romance so quickly as halitosis (bad breath)? And the worst of it is that if you yourself have this insidious condition you may not even know it . . . or even realize that you are offending" (Listerine ad, *Red Star Mystery*, 10/40). "Halitosis" was popularized in the 1920s by advertising copywriters, who plucked it from medical literature, where it had been used since at least the 1870s. In Britain, the functional equivalent of "halitosis" is *oral offense.* See also BO.

ham every Saturday. A code phrase used prior to World War II in ads for resort hotels to indicate that Jews were barred. A synonymous phrase, with the same restrictive meaning, was "near church."

handi-capable. A second-order euphemism, putting the most positive spin possible on "handicapped," itself a soft-pedaling of "crippled." Recalling his introduction as "handi-capable" on a TV show, John Callahan, a cartoonist, author, and also a quadriplegic, said, "I couldn't help but laugh. 'Handi-capable' sounds like I should be dressed up in a clown suit. I rebel against any politically correct terms. I'm paralyzed. Why mince words?" (*Philadelphia Inquirer*, 10/19/92). See also DIFFERING ABILITIES.

handkerchief. A wipe—for the nose, eyes, face, or, as implied by the name, the hand; a "pocket handkerchief" in full. The term is a comparatively new one (from 1530, *OED*), composed of "hand" plus "kerchief," which comes, in turn, from the Old French *cuevrechef,* (it) covers (the) head. Thus, "pocket handkerchief" translates as "pocket hand covers head," which is not terribly explicit. In the past, even "handkerchief" has been regarded by some as too gross for words. Mary Evelyn, daughter of the diarist John, opted for *mouchoir,* the French term for the wipe, contending that "It were Rude, Vulgar, and Uncourtly, to call it a handkerchief" (*The Fop's Dictionary,* 1690). Nor was this just a passing whim. A century and a half later, Thackeray referred to "mouchoirs, aprons, scarfs . . . and other female gimcracks" (*Vanity Fair,* 1848). Meanwhile, the French also were put off by their own word, with utterance of *mouchoir* in an adaptation of *Othello* precipitating a riot at the Comédie Française in 1829. See also CHEMISE.

handyman's special. In the real estate business, a building that may have four walls but not much else, a.k.a., a *fixer-upper.* "'handyman's special' may walk you into, the shell of a house, 'al afresco,' roofless" (Brooklyn, N.Y., *Phoenix,* 7/26/79). See also NEEDS SOME WORK and REALTOR.

hanky-panky. The general allusion to trickery may help cover up more serious matters. For example, speaking of plans for a break-in, a.k.a. SURREPTITIOUS ENTRY:

> "There's no hanky-panky about this, is there?"
> "Neither hanky nor panky. Nothing is to be abstracted from the house and nothing upset."
> (Josephine Tey, *The Singing Sands,* 1953)

Or, as President Richard M. Nixon said, when sorting out the reasons for getting the CIA to tell the FBI to call off its investigation of the Watergate CAPER:

> It would be very detrimental to have this thing go any further. This involves these Cubans, Hunt and a lot of hanky-panky that we have nothing to do with ourselves. (Tape of June 23, 1972, six days after the break-in)

"Hanky-panky" also is useful for downplaying sexual high jinks, as in the following light verse by Balzac Schwenk about a great Transcendentalist:

> Thoreau, the misogynist Yankee
> Claimed that women and girls made
>   him cranky;
>   So both brunette and blonde
>   He barred from his pond
> To make sure there was no hanky-panky.

The origin of "hanky-panky" is obscure. The "hanky" may come from the magician's handkerchief, with the "panky" being a repetition (or reduplication, as linguists say) of the first word's sounds. The term may also have been influenced by "hocus-pocus," a repetitious, pseudo-Latin incantation, popularized by magicians, and perhaps based on the "poke," or bag, into which objects are placed and from which— lo and behold!—they vanish. See also JINGO and MONKEY-BUSINESS.

Hannukah bush. A Jewish Christmas tree. "Hannukah bush" is essentially facetious and some Jews eschew the linguistic dodge and just say it like it is. By whichever name, the object itself is devoid of Christian religious symbols. See also HEBREW.

happy hour. A period of time, not necessarily limited to sixty minutes, that is set aside for consuming alcohol—often in large quantities and at cut rates in military service clubs, bars, and similar WATERING HOLES; also called an *attitude adjustment hour.* "The October Commander's call will be held at 1530, 20 October 1976. . . . The guest speaker will be Mr. Daniel J. Crowe, Indiana State Division of Addiction Service, who will discuss Industrial Alcoholism. . . . At the conclusion of the question and answer session, there will be a 'Happy Hour' in the Ballroom to afford everyone an opportunity to meet Mr. Crowe" (memo from the assistant chief of staff, Fort Benjamin Harrison, Indiana, in *Washington Monthly,* 12/76). See also HIGH.

Happy Hunting Grounds, gone to the. Dead. The pleasant circumlocution commonly is credited to the American Indians, but one wonders if the idea wasn't foisted off on them, considering that the earliest examples of the phrase's use in *A Dictionary of Americanisms* come from such native American non-Indians as Washington Irving, who worked it into the *Adventures of Captain Bonneville* (1837), and James Fenimore Cooper (*The Pathfinder,* 1840). Meanwhile, during this same period, whites were referring to their heaven as "a happy land."

The *Happy Hunting Grounds* are only one of many possible places to which the DECEASED may be said to have traveled, depending on the persuasions of those left behind. These figures of speech were especially popular during the nineteenth century, when people stopped talking plainly about death. Among the others:

Abraham's bosom, as in Luke 16:22: "The beggar died, and was carried by the angels into Abraham's bosom."

Note that this seventeenth-century "bosom" is masculine; see also BOSOM and *Arthur's bosom* below.

angels, joined the or *with the.*

another place. "The time has come to meet in another place" (tape recording, the Rev. Jim Jones, prior to the mass suicide of 913 members of his flock at Jonestown, Guyana, 11/17/78). An exception: When members of the British House of Commons refer to "another place," they usually mean the House of Lords.

Arms of God, asleep in the. Variants include *with God, asleep in Jesus,* and *safe in the arms of Jesus.*

Arthur's bosom. "He's in Arthur's bosom, if ever a man went to Arthur's bosom" (Hostess Quickly on the death of Falstaff, *Henry V,* 1599).

better land/life/place/world, usually in the form of "He has gone to a better . . ."

beyond or *Great Beyond,* as in "He has been called to the beyond."

big PX in the sky, as in "He has gone to the big PX in the sky," a post exchange for dead soldiers.

Chicago. "FISHMAN—Anna. 'Went to Chicago' Saturday, February 27" (death notice, *New York Times,* 2/28/82).

Confucius, seeing. An old Chinese saying, reportedly updated by Prime Minister Zhou Enlai, who told visitors, shortly before his death (1/8/76): "I shall soon be seeing Marx."

country up there. From "A Cowboy's Prayer," included in the program for the funeral of Commerce Secretary Malcolm Baldridge (7/29/87): "Help us, Lord, to live our lives in such a manner that when we make that last inevitable ride to the country up there, where the grass grows lush, green, and stirrup high and the water runs cool, clear and deep, that You, as our last judge, will tell us that our entry fees are paid."

Davy Jones's locker. A sailor's grave. "Davy Jones," as the Devil or evil spirit of the sea, has been dated to 1726. The "Davy" may come from the West Indian *duppy* (devil) and "Jones" from "Jonah," the idea being that the *duppy Jonah* was a devil that brought bad luck.

Eternal rest, heavenly rest, well-earned rest— all places, or states, to which one may be "called" or said "to have gone to."

Eternity, launched into. A nautical, not astronautical, expression.

Fathers, gathered to one's. Or simply "gathered," as in "I used to stay with my mother until she was gathered" ("Rumpole's Return," WNET-TV, 8/29/85).

glory, gone to.

Great majority, joined the. The phrase has been around for a while. Petronius (ca. 26–66) used it (*Abiit ad plures*) in the *Satyricon* and there is no reason to think he coined it. A more elaborate, more political variation is *slipped into the great democracy of the dead.*

Great Adventure, gone to the. Not an amusement park.

Green River, up. Among mountain men in the West in the nineteenth century, to send a man "up Green River" was to kill him. The phrase probably referred not so much to the Green River in Wyoming as to "Green River" knives, so stamped because they were made at the Green River works.

heaven. The place in the sky for good people, as opposed to hell, beneath the surface of the earth, where bad ones go.

hereafter, gone to the.

higher sphere (or *another world*), *translated into.* Note the elliptical verbs that are being used: *called, gone, joined, launched, slipped,* and now, *translated* (originally a removal into heaven without dying, as indicated in PASS AWAY).

home or *last home.* Informally: *go home feet first* or *go home in a box.* "'Be I going doctor?' he asked. 'Tom, my man,' said I, 'you're going home'" (Redruth's death, in Robert Louis Stevenson, *Treasure Island,* 1883). See also GO.

immortals, join the.

infinite varieties, as in the poetic "He has passed from earth's uncertainties into the infinite varieties."

invisible choir, joined the.

Jordan's banks, gone to. Or *to cross* (or *pass over*) *the River Jordan.*

kingdom come, gone to.

land of the heart's desire, gone to the.

mansions of rest, gone to the. "I shall also carry with me the hope that . . . the faults of [my] incompetent abilities will be consigned to oblivion, as myself must soon be to the mansions of rest" (George Washington, Farewell Address, published 9/19/1776). The expression comes from John 14:2: "In my Father's house are many mansions: if *it were* not *so,* I would have told you. I go to prepare a place for you."

outer darkness. As a rule, bad people are said to be "cast into outer darkness," while good ones "slip into" it.

paradise, taken to.

reward, often embellished as *final reward* or *great reward.* "Unfortunately the great leader who had taken the nation through the peacetime and wartime emergencies passed to his great reward just one month before the German surrender" (President Harry S Truman, diary note, 10/26/46, in David McCullough, *Truman*, 1992).

safe anchorage at last. A common epitaph for sailors.

Tap City. The place where high-rolling gamblers go; for a gambler, to be "tapped out" is to be broke.

undiscovered country, the. From a famous image in Shakespeare: "Death, The undiscovered country from whose bourn [border] No traveler returns." (*Hamlet*, 1602).

valley, as in "He is asleep in the valley"; probably a discreet condensation of the Twenty-third Psalm, "Yea, though I walk through the valley of the shadow of death."

wayside, fallen by the. While the rest of us go marching on?

west. The association between death and the West is old; see GO WEST.

And see also EXPIRE, PASS AWAY, REST, and SLEEP.

hard landing. Crash. When a helicopter slammed to the ground during a training exercise at Camp Lejeune, North Carolina, officials described the event as a "hard landing" rather than a "crash" (*Seattle Press-Inquirer*, 11/21/84). Six people were killed and eleven injured in the *hard landing*. A still-longer roundabout was noted in the Dublin *Irish Times*: "Ponder 'uncontrolled contact with the ground' as a way of announcing that a plane has crashed" (9/29/90). See also WATER LANDING.

hard of hearing. Deafened, sometimes totally. "In 1970, I contracted meningitis, which left me completely deaf. . . . Some folks call it very hard of hearing, or very hearing impaired or, perhaps more accurately, deaf as a brick" (Thomas Mitchell, *New York Times*, 7/12/89). See also HEARING IMPAIRED.

harlot. A late bloomer, comparable to PROSTITUTE for avoiding the older, harsher "whore." For example, where the first English translations of the Bible, the Wyclif versions of the fourteenth century, bluntly used "hoore," translations of the sixteenth century frequently had "harlot," and when Noah Webster rewrote the Bible in 1833 (see PECULIAR MEMBERS for details), he cut out every single "whore," using "harlot" and other, still-blander expressions instead (e.g., *lewd woman*).

A "harlot" (from the Old French *(h)arlot, herlot,* i.e., vagabond) was originally a male, not a female—usually a boy or servant, in the sense of a buffoon, rascal, or fornicator, but also sometimes a regular fellow, a good guy. Geoffrey Chaucer employed it in the last sense when he wrote of the Somnour in the *Prologue* to *The Canterbury Tales* (1387–1400):

He was a gentil harlot and a kynde,
A bettre felawe sholde men noght fynde.

"Harlot" was not applied to women until the fifteenth century, and then it encompassed such examples of feminine low life as jugglers, dancers, strumpets, and whores. As usually happens, the "worse" meanings became dominant: The term gradually was limited to women only, and to the worst kind of women at that.

"Harlot" also is distinguished for having one of the quaintest of all spurious etymologies, i.e., the supposition that it derived from the name of Arlette, or Herleve, daughter of Fulbert, a tanner of

Falaise, and mother of William the Bastard, who became William the Conqueror. This etymology, favored for a long time by many students of language, was first proposed toward the end of the sixteenth century, which just goes to show that the whorish meaning of *harlot* had become dominant by that time.

harmonious. As applied to neighborhoods, "segregated." From a 1971 ruling in which a federal judge blamed segregation in Detroit schools on other institutions besides the school board: "For many years, Federal housing administrators and the Veterans Administration openly advised and advocated maintenance of 'harmonious' neighborhoods, i.e., racially and economically harmonious." *Harmonious* neighborhoods have NEIGHBORHOOD SCHOOLS. See also MIDDLE CLASS, SEPARATE BUT EQUAL, and TURN.

harvest. Kill. The agricultural term becomes a euphemism when applied to animals instead of vegetables. Deer hunters have been especially adept at developing nonlethal lingo. For example, an article on "Managing White-tailed Deer," in a New York State publication, *The Conservationist* (9–10/79), referred to the "harvesting of adult does," the "exploitation of the deer," the "annual buck take," and the issuance of "deer management permits," but not once to the "killing" of these animals. Hunters of other animals use similar terminology. Thus, seals and gray whales are *harvested*, and if too many whales, say, are slaughtered in any one year, the species is said to have been *overcropped*. It is okay, of course, to "kill" animals that are of no value, as noted by an assistant secretary of the Interior Department, G. Ray Arnett: "You kill rats, but you harvest game" (*Philadelphia*

Inquirer, 6/21/81). The same thought was expressed in a somewhat different way by President George Bush, who said, when confronted by animal rights advocates while on a quail hunt in Beesville, Texas, on December 28, 1991: "These aren't animals. These are wild quail." See also CULL, GAME MANAGEMENT, RESEARCH, and SLUICE.

haystack (or hayrick). A haycock—and one of the many different kinds of "cocks" that Americans expunged from their language, starting in the second half of the eighteenth century. See also DOODLE and ROOSTER.

head. A toilet; a nautical term now used on land as well as on sea, e.g., "'The head,' by which she meant the toilet, 'is just over there,' and she pointed to a little bucket behind a screen in the corner" (Maxwell Kenton, a.k.a. Terry Southern, *Candy*, 1965). In its original seagoing form (from 1748, *OED*), "head" was a topographical euphemism, alluding to the positioning of toilets on a sailing ship at the head of the vessel, usually on either side of the bowsprit, with the sea in front and the wind behind. The direction of the wind is critical, as anyone who has ever tried to PEE into it can testify. See also TOILET.

head of school. Headmaster, or "head," for short, eliminating the noxious "master" and avoiding the bad thoughts that may arise from "headmistress." For example, trustees of Philips Academy in Andover, Mass., voted to change the title of the office from "headmaster" to "head of school"—four months before appointing the first woman to fill it. See also PERSON.

health. Absence of health, especially in the case of the *health* or *healthcare industry,* which is how *providers of healthcare,* including some MDs, refer to the practice of medicine. Those who think of themselves as *providers* tend to regard their patients as *consumers of healthcare.* Meanwhile, the people who run hospitals have become *healthcare executives*; see EXECUTIVE. Lewis Thomas blew the whistle on "health" in *The Lives of a Cell* (1974), but the medical establishment wasn't listening. Said Dr. Thomas:

> Sooner or later, we are bound to get into trouble with this word. It is too solid and unequivocal a term to be used as a euphemism and this seems to be what we are attempting. I am worried that we may be overdoing it, taxing its meaning, to conceal an unmentionable reality that we've somehow agreed not to talk about in public. It won't work. Illness and death still exist and cannot be hidden.

See also CAREGIVER, IATROGENIC, MEDICAL CENTER, and MENTAL HEALTH CONSUMER.

health, reasons of. While people sometimes do have to leave jobs for *reasons of health,* this is a standard face-saving excuse for those who hadn't feared for their health until they were LET GO. In the words of George Cassidy, telling why he was no longer race starter at Hialeah Park, then operated by Gene Mori: "I left for reasons of health. Mori got sick of me" (Red Smith, *New York Times,* 8/5/77). A marginally plainer variant is "poor health," cited in 1992 as the reason for the departure of seven members from Saudi Arabia's Supreme Authority of Senior Scholars. King Fahd replaced them without explaining the exact nature of the malady that

mysteriously struck down only the older, more conservative members of the nation's highest religious body.

See the CIA's use of "health" in EXECUTIVE ACTION as well as ILL/ILLNESS.

healthy girl. A woman with large breasts; see also STATUESQUE.

hearing impaired. Deafened, a.k.a. *auditory impaired.* From an interview by New York Knicks announcer Cal Ramsey with player Mike Glenn about running a basketball camp for the deaf:

> Q: Does it take special skills to teach the deaf?
> A: I don't think it takes special skills to teach the hearing impaired.

See also HARD OF HEARING and ORTHOGRAPHICALLY IMPAIRED.

hearts. Sons. Proving that the United States does not have a monopoly on political correctness, John Nunziata, a Liberal member of the Canadian Parliament, introduced a bill in 1993 to change "O Canada," the nation's national anthem, so that the phrase "true patriot love in all thy sons command" would be changed to "in all our hearts command." See also PERSON.

heavenly deception. A lie, as told by a member of the Unification Church (a.k.a. a Moonie) to a nonmember. "He learned more about 'heavenly deception'—the Moonie euphemism for lying, for doing whatever is necessary to further the goals of the church" (review of Christopher Edwards's *Crazy for God,* in *The Sunday Record,* Bergen/Passaic/Hudson Counties, N.J., 4/1/79). The *heavenly deception* is permissible because nonmembers of the church are, by definition, members of the world of Satan. "Heavenly deception" has a FOP Index of 7.7. See also WHITE LIE.

heavens. God, as in *good heavens!* or *for heaven's sake.* Thus, Desdemona exclaims in the first folio edition of *Othello* (1623), "Then would to heaven that I had never seen't," where the reading in the first quarto (1622) is "Then would to God that I had never seen't." This is one of a number of differences between the two editions, with the quarto generally preserving oaths from Shakespeare's original draft (1604) that were watered down in accordance with an act of Parliament in 1606 prohibiting swearing on stage (though not in books). Other changes of this sort included "By'r Lady" to "Trust me," "God bless" to "bless," "God save" to "save," "'Sblood but" to "but," and "Zounds" to "come." "Heaven" itself was dropped when used as an exclamation, so that Desdemona's "Heaven bless us!" in the quarto became "Bless us" in the folio. Oaths also were removed in the folio texts of Shakespeare's other plays. For example, in the case of *Henry IV, Part II,* the folio text of 1623 employs "Heaven" and "in good earnest," where the quarto edition of 1600 uses "God" and "God save me." See also GOSH and ZOUNDS.

he-biddy. A nineteenth-century rooster or, more to the point, a cock, a.k.a. *he-chicken.* The euphemism was formed on the same principle as *he-cow* (bull), *he-hog* (boar), and *he-sheep* (ram). See also COW BRUTE and ROOSTER.

Hebrew. Jew; once the standard euphemism, but verging on obsolescence. "Well, I explained to him that I dident hardly expect Trotzky to make any faces for me or to turn a few somersaults or tell the one about two Hebrews named Abe and Moe" (Will Rogers, *There's Not a Bathing Suit in Russia & Other Bare Facts,* 1927). Only rarely is "Hebrew" now encountered in its euphemistic sense. A comparatively recent example is the statement by the Panamanian consul general in New York: "The Government of the Republic of Panama echoes the preoccupation of important sectors of the Hebrew community and the rest of the world that, as well as our country and our Government, reject and condemn the crimes committed by the fascism" (*New York Times,* 4/16/82).

Theoretically, "Hebrew" should be reserved for discussions of the Jewish people of the distant past (i.e., the Hebrews of the Bible) or their language (Hebrew is the official language of the State of Israel). Its use as a euphemism for "Jew" probably was a function of Gresham's Law, as it applies to language (i.e., "bad" meanings drive out "good" ones), "Jew" having acquired many offensive associations through its misuse as a verb and adjective ("to jew down," "Jew boy," etc., ad nauseam). The result was that fastidious people, and nervous ones, began avoiding "Jew" even in proper contexts. Thus, as H. L. Mencken noted, "one often encounters" in newspapers "such forms as *Hebrew comedian, Hebrew holidays,* and even *Hebrew rabbi*" (*The American Language,* 1936).

Use of the euphemism was by no means limited to non-Jews. A study of Jewish applicants to Yale in 1927 showed that fourteen out of ninety-one (15 percent) answered "Hebrew" to the question "Church [sic] affiliation?" (Mencken, *The American Language, Supplement I,* 1945). This indecisiveness is perpetuated in institutional names, e.g., Hebrew Union College (founded 1875) and Jewish Theological Seminary of America

(1876), and in the contrast between the many Young Men's (and Women's) Hebrew Associations and the various Jewish Councils and Jewish Community Centers. Increasing pride in Jewishness has virtually overcome the word's older, negative associations, but the unusual amount of anxiety caused by "Jew" is suggested by the tendency, even today, for sensitive speakers to use "Jewish person" instead of the simple noun. See also ANTI-SEMITIC, ARAB, COSMOPOLITAN, ISRAELITE, JUICE HARP, and ZIONIST.

heck. Hell—as in "What the *heck*," "We had a *heck* of a time," "Just for the *heck* of it," "By *heck*," etc. "Merlini, a magician, gets in a heck of a lot of trouble as he tries to solve a circus murder" (*Columbus*, Ohio, *Citizen*, 9/22/40).

First recorded in the middle of the nineteenth century, the term may derive from the dialectical *ecky* or *hecky*, or—another suggestion—from *By Hector*, referring to the blustering Trojan hero. Whatever the immediate source, it is essentially an alteration of "hell," and probably the most common euphemism today for the infernal regions, e.g., "Cuomo to 'Fight Like Heck' to Revive Drinking-Age Bill" (headline, *New York Times*, 5/31/84) and "Is Our Language Going to Heck?" (headline, Danbury, Conn., *Express Line*, 11/21/92). Then there was the editorial about Abbie Hoffman in the Newark, N.J., *Star-Ledger*, following the radical activist's death, which mentioned that he had written a book entitled *Revolution for the Heck of It* (*Columbia Journalism Review*, 7–8/89). Was it General Sherman who said "War is heck"?

See also BLAZES, CAIN, EARTH, HAIL COLUMBIA, HALIFAX, HEY, H––L, HOT PLACE, JESSE, PISH/PSHAW, SAM HILL, and THUNDER.

help. A euphemism both as a verb and a noun. As a reflexive verb, it means "to steal," in much the same sense as LIBERATE. "They helped themselves freely to the furniture of an uninhabited house" (E. Blackwell, *Booth*, 1883). As a noun, "help" quickly came to stand for "servant" in America because "servant" stood for "slave." This was made clear by a female *help* to Charles W. Janson, an early English visitor to the United States, who included her comments in the following passage from *The Stranger in America* (1807):

> The arrogance of domestics in this land of republican liberty and equality, is particularly calculated to excite the astonishment of strangers. To call persons of this description *servants* or to speak of the *master* or *mistress* is a greivous affront. Having called one day at the house of a gentleman of my acquaintance, on knocking at the door, it was opened by a servant-maid, whom I had never before seen, as she had not been long in his family. The following is the dialogue, word for word, which took place on this occasion:—"Is your master at home?"—"I have no master." "Don't you live here?"—"I stay here."—"And who are you then?" —"Why, I am Mr. – – – – –'s *help* I'd have you know, *man*, that I am no *sarvent*; none but *negers* are *sarvants*."

"Help" of this sort naturally led to *Help Wanted Ads*, frequently for such specialized positions as *Lady Help*, meaning a servant who assisted the lady of the house, or *Mother's Help*—nowadays a *helper*, or, straying further from the utilitarian term (and into the safety of a foreign language) an *au pair*. Even *hired help* (or, more specifically, hired man or hired girl) was accepted by the help or helps themselves, where a mumbled servant would have caused them to walk off the job. See also BOSS, DOMESTIC, HOUSEHOLD ADMINISTRATOR, MAID, and SERVANT.

hemp. Marijuana, to those who favor its legalization. "They say hemp, the less politically charged word they prefer to 'marijuana,' could be used in textiles, as pulp for building materials and paper, for cooking oil and birdseed, and even as a fuel" (New York Times, 4/10/91).

henfire. Hellfire. This was one of the more picturesque of the weakened substitutes for "hell" that were collected by interviewers for the Dictionary of American Regional English. A synonym, but more disguised, is "hoe handle," as in "What the hoe handle!" The latter expression, however, must be used with care in the Ozarks, since a "hoe handle" is also a "long tool," and "tool" is another word for PENIS. See also HECK and TOOL.

herstory. History, as told by women. "I have tried to write a herstory of the inner psychic meaning of the ancient religion" (Peace News, 10/2/81). Specialists in herstory are known, naturally, as herstorians. The etymologically unsound effort to take the "his" out of "history" (which has nothing to do with the male pronoun but comes from the Latin and Greek historia, narrative) is in keeping with the equally misplaced concerns over the superficially masculine elements in FEMALE and WOMAN.

hey. Hell. "Oh, what the hey" (radio ad for Michelob Lite beer, 7/27/91). See also HECK.

hiatus. Canceled. "CBS insists that 'Brooklyn Bridge' is only 'on hiatus,' a term that has evolved into a euphemism for canceled" (New York Times, 12/13/92).

hieronymous. A quaint euphemism for the buttocks or nearby unmentionable parts, as in "Her dress was so short you could pret' near see her hieronymous" (Sarah Lawson, recalling her Indiana grandmother's use of the term, American Speech, Fall, 1969). The Dictionary of American Regional English suggests that the word may derive from the Greek hierón ostéon, sacrum (i.e., the fused vertebrae at the base of the spine). Considering the nature of euphemisms, however, the term appears more likely to be an eponym, from Hieronymous, the Latin form of the personal name Jerome, in turn from the Greek Ieronumus, i.e., "sacred name," the point being that a sacred name also is an unmentionable one. See also ADONAI and ARSE.

high. One of the older of the truly immense number of terms for describing a person who is feeling the effects of alcohol or another drug. The oldest citation for "high" in the drunken sense in The Oxford English Dictionary is from 1627: "He's high with wine" (Thomas May, Lucan's Pharsalia). Other kinds of "high" in the seventeenth and eighteenth centuries included altitudes and elevated, as in "The man is in his altitudes, i.e., he is drunk!" (Capt. Francis Grose, A Classical Dictionary of the Vulgar Tongue, 1796). Today, the altitudinal metaphor may be reinforced by elaborating "high" into such phrases as high as a kite and high spirits, e.g.: "Once [in] a while a reporter writes that a Senator appeared in the Senate in 'high spirits.' Those on the in know the reporter means the Senator was drunk. The reader doesn't" (New York Times, 9/8/74).

Use of "high" to refer to the euphoria produced by narcotics and other drugs seems to be a twentieth-century innovation. The narcotic sense may have been influenced by the "high gear" of a motor vehicle. Thus, David W. Maurer's list in *American Speech* (4/36) of synonyms used by dope addicts for "all lit up" included *"coasting, floating, hitting the gow, in high, on the gow, on the stuff,* [and] *picked up."* (It was said of Maurer, a pioneer student of the specialized vocabularies of drug users, prostitutes, pickpockets, and other subcultures, that "if Dave wasn't the actual father of American sociolinguistics, he was on hand the night when linguistics got knocked up.") *The Oxford English Dictionary*'s earliest example of the word in its narcotic sense, from 1932, is for the unadorned "high," however, and it is clear from other sources that drug users in this period employed the word in the same way as did those who got *high* on alcohol, e.g., the lyrics for "Reefer Man," as sung by Cab Calloway in *International House* (1933): "Have you met that funny, funny reefer man? . . . smokes a reefer and gets high as the sky." Other alcoholic terms that were adopted by users of marijuana and other narcotics at about the same time include *buzzed, gassed, loaded, stoned,* and *zonked.*

Demonstrating our culture's traditional dependence upon alcohol, more synonyms are listed for "drunk" than for any other word in the *Dictionary of American Slang* (Harold Wentworth and Stuart Berg Flexner, 1975). The appendixes to this work include 356 terms for "drunk," and this listing is necessarily incomplete, since the set of drunken synonyms is continually changing, with old terms fading from use and new ones being created. Still, the Wentworth-Flexner listing suggests a considerable expansion in the drinker's working

vocabulary from 1737, when Benjamin Franklin published a similar list of 228 terms. Franklin's listing, a continuation of a project that he had begun in 1722, at the tender age of sixteen, when he could find but nineteen synonyms, included many words and phrases that are rarely, if ever, heard nowadays, e.g., *afflicted, been to Barbados* (where the rum came from), *cherry-merry, cherubimical, disguised, has his flag out, gold-headed, lordly, nimptopsical,* and *pigeon-eyed.* Other terms on his list are hardy perennials. Among them: *boozy, cockeyed, mellow, muddled, oiled, soaked, stewed, stiff, has a skin full,* and *half seas over (American Speech,* 2/40).

For other facets of what social scientists call "the drinking custom," see BEVERAGE HOST, INEBRIATED, LIBATION, SALOON, TEMPERANCE, and WOOD UP.

highly confidential (or **sensitive) source.** A hidden microphone or wiretap, a bug; FBI-ese, from the long (1924–72) reign of J. Edgar Hoover as director of the Bureau. Such bugs often were emplaced during illegal BLACK BAG JOBS, with the result that information from them had to be reported discreetly. For example, an agent might say that "a highly placed sensitive source of known reliability was contacted and furnished items of personality" (*New York Times,* 9/23/80). Inanimate *highly confidential sources,* used in TECHNICAL SURVEILLANCE, should not be confused with the animate though usually cold-blooded CONFIDENTIAL INFORMANT or SOURCE and SOURCE OF INFORMATION, i.e., an informer, a.k.a. INFORMANT. See also SENSITIVE.

highly (or **usually) reliable source.** Journalese, in which "reliable" translates as "this source has supplied information before," while the qualifiers, "highly" and "usually," imply that "the information has not always been correct." Variations on the "source" theme include *highly-placed source, well-placed source,* and *responsible* or *well-informed source* (as opposed to "irresponsible or uninformed sources"?) See also CONFIDENTIAL INFORMER or SOURCE, HIGHLY CONFIDENTIAL SOURCE, and SOURCE OF INFORMATION.

high-risk group. Those infected with AIDS, a.k.a. PEOPLE WITH AIDS. As Charlton Heston said, following the death from AIDS of Rock Hudson, who had played love scenes on the TV show "Dynasty" though almost certainly aware of his illness: "I think a member of that lovely euphemism—'a high-risk group' —has an obligation to refuse to do kissing scenes" (*New York Times,* 11/7/85). Avoidance of the terrifying "AIDS" extends to the Agency for International Development, which prefers to be known by its full name nowadays rather than its once-standard acronym, AID. And plummeting sales of the diet candy Ayds caused the manufacturer to change the name of the product to Aydslim. See also C, THE BIG, and TB.

high-yield securities. Junk bonds.

hiney (also heinie, hinie). The buttocks. "The whole point about being the gender in power is that you don't have to be shapely to be attractive. Power that worries about whether its hiney is beautiful is not power" (Roy Blount, Jr., *What Men Don't Tell Women,* 1984). See also ARSE.

hit. Murder, or the person who is murdered. The understated "hit" is a rare example of an evasion that is shorter than the word for which it stands. It has a negative FOP Index of −2.3. Of course, it comes from the underworld where, by definition, normal rules do not apply. "A murder is a contract. A hit is the sucker that gets killed. Remember those words, and use them. Then, even if the cops tap a phone, they won't know what you're talking about" (*The Enforcer,* film, 1950).

Even in its principal sense of a blow, a stroke, a knock, "hit" qualifies as a euphemism in that it started out as a soft substitute for a stronger word. It developed from a Scandinavian term, comparable to the Old Icelandic *hitta,* to light upon, to meet, via the Anglo-Saxon *hyttan,* to get at, to reach, or not to miss (as an arrow). Subsequently, "hit" also acquired a sexual component, as commonly happens with words that denote aggressive ACTION. From *Love's Labor's Lost* (1588–94):

MARIA: You still wrangle with her, Boyet, and she strikes at the brow [where the cuckold wears his horns].
BOYET: But she herself is hit lower. Have I hit her now?

An underworld *hit* (usually performed by a *hit man* or *hit team,* perhaps working from a *hit list*) is the linguistic and functional equivalent of a governmental EXECUTIVE ACTION. As noted in one of the classic works of criminology:

Persons with an extensive acquaintance with men of the lowest character know only too well what repugnance they feel in employing the correct expression. . . . Persons of a somewhat higher moral grade often shrink from using the word "steal," while the number of periphrastic expressions employed to avoid uttering the simple word "kill" is extraordinary. (Hans Gross, *Criminal Investigation,* Norman Kendal, ed., 1934)

Of course, avoiding the simple, correct words can lead to confusion, as in the following exchange among some of President Nixon's men—Jeb Stuart Magruder, deputy director of the Committee to Re-Elect the President; G. Gordon Liddy, the CREP COUNSEL; and Robert Reisner, Magruder's assistant—in the televised *Watergate* series (Discovery Channel, 1994):

MAGRUDER: Liddy was in my office. I said something as an aside, "Wouldn't it be good if we could get rid of [newspaper columnist] Jack Anderson?"

REISNER: Gordon Liddy emerged from the office. He brushed by me and he said, "Jeb just told me to take care of Jack Anderson."

LIDDY: I said I am to kill Jack Anderson. I am on way to kill Jack Anderson. . . .

REISNER: I then went into Magruder's office and I said, "Jeb, did you just tell him to rub out Jack Anderson?"

MAGRUDER: [Liddy] came back into the office and I said to Gordon, "I was just talking off the cuff. I wasn't serious." Liddy looked at me with that stern, macho look, and said, "Never give me an order for a hit job that you don't mean, because I'll do it."

For more about the circumlocutions of the Watergaters, as well as other periphrastic expressions, consider BLOW AWAY; BUCK; *bump off*; BURN; *cancel one's ticket (permanently)*; CARE OF, TAKE; CONTACT; CONTRACT; CROAK; DING; DISPATCH; DUST; DISPOSE; *erase*; EXECUTE; FIX; *frag; give the business/heat/rap*; HOSE (DOWN); ICE; JUMP; KILL (in very special circumstances); *light up*; LIQUIDATE; MASSAGE; OFF; POP; PUT OUT; REMOVE; RUB OUT; SCORE; *silence*; SMOKE; SNUFF; SPANK; *take for a ride*; TOUCH (OFF); USE UP; WASH AWAY; WASTE; WHACK; *wipe out,* and ZAP. For avoiding death generally, see PASS AWAY.

h – – l. Hell. Though the name of Satan's domicile usually is printed in full nowadays, the dash survives in some sanctimonious circles. Thus, Ronald Reagan quoted one of his own diary entries in his memoir, *An American Life* (1990): "I firmly said to h – – l with it." (An easier thing to say firmly would have been "G.T.H.," meaning "Go To Hell," or "H. E. double toothpicks," another quaint allusion to the HOT PLACE.)

Footnote to American literary history: *Huckleberry Finn* was banned in 1885, the year after its publication, by the public library in Concord, Mass., home of Thoreau and Emerson, partly because Huck was a liar and partly because Mark Twain declined to use dashes, allowing Huck to decide he'd rather "go to hell" than betray Jim. Such profanity, according to the library, rendered the book "trash and suitable only for the slums." To Concord's credit, the town's Free Trade Club quickly elected Twain to honorary membership.

See also A – –, BLANK, DASH, D – – – D, HADES, HECK, and, for another word that got Huck in trouble, PERSPIRATION.

hold. Don't hold; get rid of. "And the analysts' opinions on Dell tracked by Zacks Investment Research Inc. are mainly 'hold', which in Wall Street euphemism typically means sell" (*New York Times*, 11/29/93). See also DEFER PURCHASE.

holy cow. New York Yankee announcer Phil Rizzuto's favorite oath (on the air, at least) and one of the most common of the many "holy" constructions available to those who wish to register shock, amazement, or whatever, without actually being profane. Others include *holy bilge water, holy cats, holy cripes, holy Egypt, holy gee, holy gosh, holy gumdrops, holy heck, holy hoptoads, holy moly, holy Moses, holy smoke, Holy H. Smoke,* and *holy snakes.* Many of the combinatorial terms are euphemisms in their own right: see CRIPES, GEE, GOSH, and HECK.

homage, to pay. Plagiarize. "Biden aides say that borrowing thoughts and phrases is a common speechmaking convention and is a way of paying homage to leaders of the past" (*New York Times,* 9/6/87). In this case, the "homage" amounted to wholesale appropriation by Sen. Joseph R. Biden, Jr. (D., Md.), of a speech by British Labor leader Neil Kinnock. Public revelation of the private *homage* fatally damaged Mr. Biden's campaign for the 1988 Democratic presidential nomination. See also SAMPLING.

home. When used to describe a private, detached dwelling, a genteelism for "house"; in all other instances, an out-and-out euphemism.

In the genteel sense, "home" was among the key words cited by Nancy Mitford as examples of the elegant and euphemistic speech by which non-Upperclass people betray their non-U-ness. Where non-U's say "they have a lovely home," the U person has "a very nice *house*" (*Noblesse Oblige,* 1956). For more about U-ness and non, see DENTURES.

The tendency to drop the plainer "house" in favor of the more luxurious "home" shows up in many other ways. Contractors build *homes,* not *houses;* the people who buy the houses call themselves *homeowners,* not householders; the owners obtain the funds to enlarge their quarters with *home* (not house) *improvement loans;* they take out *homeowner's* (not house-

owner's) *insurance policies,* and they fill their houses with *home furnishings* and *home appliances.* Still more euphemistically, "home" never really means "home" when used to describe quarters for unrelated people in an INSTITUTION. Thus, a *boys' home* or *girls' home* is a kind of jail; a *home for infants* or *children* is an orphanage; a *mental home* (see MENTAL) is a madhouse; a NURSING HOME or *rest home* is a combination hospital-dormitory-warehouse for old people (see CONVALESCENT HOSPITAL), and a *memorial* or FUNERAL HOME is the living end.

See also HOMELESS, HOMEMADE, HOME-MAKER, and, for a notorious exception to the rule that the fancier houses are always homes, refer to HOUSE.

homeless. Houseless; derelict. The social problem, as noted by George Carlin, is "not homelessness" but "houselessness" ("Live at the Paramount," HBO, 5/3/92). See also HOME.

homely. Ugly. "*Ugly* is replaced in English by *plain* and in American by *homely*" (Ernest Weekley, *The Romance of Words,* 1912). The American English here preserves a sense that was once more common in British English. As John Milton proclaimed in *Il Penseroso* (1632):

Beauty is Nature's brag and must be
  shown . . .
It is for homely features to keep home—

homemade. When pie—or anything else, for that matter—is described on a restaurant menu as "homemade," about the best the diner can hope for is that it was made by human hands in the restaurant's own kitchen rather than by machines in a factory. The same principle applies in other fields. For example, the "homemade" signs displayed at political rallies usually are produced on an assembly-line basis. And the "homemade mines" (President Ronald Reagan's words) that were deployed in Nicaraguan harbors in 1984 actually were company-made (by the CIA). See also COMPANY and HOME.

homemaker. Housewife; the relevant committee of the National Organization for Women (NOW) is the National Homemakers Committee. (A housewife who has lost her means of support because of divorce, separation, or the disability or death of her spouse is known technically as a *displaced homemaker.*) In avoiding "housewife," NOW is just following the example of other organizations. As early as 1939, the Long Island Federation of Women's Clubs "decreed that housewives should cease to be *housewives* and become *homemakers*" (H. L. Mencken, *The American Language, Supplement I,* 1945).

The shift to "homemaker" seems almost ordained, given the term's many advantages. Not only is it in keeping with the general preference for HOME instead of "house," but the "maker" puts the emphasis on the job while converting the role into a gender-neutral one. Finally, almost subconsciously, "housewife" may be avoided because it comes from the Old English *huswif,* which also has given us the modern "hussy." See also ENGINEER and PERSON.

honey. Excrement that is to be used as fertilizer. The term appears in many combinations, referring to its collection and transportation, e.g., *honey barge, honey bucket, honey cart, honey dip, honey house, honey pot,* and *honey wagon.* "The honey barges moved by and the air was clean

once more" (Richard McKenna, *The Sand Pebbles,* 1962). Some of the terms are freighted with more than one meaning. Thus, a *honey wagon* may be a portable toilet, a vehicle for transporting or spreading manure, or, by extension, a truck for hauling ordinary garbage. A *honey-dip* may be a toilet, outdoor privy, or, as a verb, the act of cleaning out the latter—whence the occupational designation *honey-dipper* (also *honey-digger*). See also EXCREMENT, MANURE, NIGHT SOIL, and TOILET.

honorable, the. Mister or, with increasing frequency, Mrs. or Ms. (e.g., *The Honorable* Nancy Landon Kassebaum, Senator from Kansas).

"Honorable" is the standard honorific in a democratic society that abjures titles in theory, but not in practice. It is awarded routinely to public servants from ratcatcher on up and, once given, is never given up. As Elizabeth L. Post has noted, "'The Honorable' is an expression that causes considerable confusion" (*The New Emily Post's Etiquette,* 1975). See also COLONEL, EMERITUS, GENTLEMAN, and MADAM.

honorarium. A payment. The Latin conceals with "honor" the grubby monetary transaction. The term was popularized in the eighteenth and nineteenth centuries when doctors, lawyers, architects, and other professionals accepted *honoraria* instead of fees because they thought of themselves as gentlemen, and gentlemen, of course, did not discuss the value of their services. See also EX GRATIA, GRATUITY, PRO BONO, and REMUNERATION.

hooey. Nonsense, but often used as a substitute for horseshit, as in "The tobacco barons' 'scientific' claims about the lack of evidence regarding the lethal effect of smoking are self-serving hooey" (*Wall Street Journal*, 6/7/94). Perhaps a spin-off from the exclamation "phooey" (itself from the German *pfui*), "hooey" has been used widely since the 1920s. Its range of meanings, from nonsense to the stronger stuff, makes it essentially synonymous with BALONEY. See also BS.

hook. To steal. An old English slang term (it goes back at least to the seventeenth century, when HOOKERS, or *anglers*, used hooks to steal merchandise out of shop windows), the expression survives among modern youth, who dare one another to *hook* small items from retail stores. The euphemistic value of "hook" ("stealing" is bad, but *hooking* is okay) has been appreciated by the younger set for at least a century. Consider those conscience-stricken pirates, Joe Harper and Tom Sawyer: "It seemed to them, in the end, that there was no getting around the stubborn fact that taking sweetmeats was only 'hooking,' while taking bacon and ham was plain simple *stealing*— and there was a command against that in the Bible" (Mark Twain, *The Adventures of Tom Sawyer*, 1876). See also APPROPRIATE, FIVE-FINGER DISCOUNT, LIGHT-FINGERED GENTRY, and SWIPE.

hooker. A whore; the slang term is more acceptable in print and conversation than the honest Old English monosyllable, and so stands as a euphemism for it. "A doctor is dead—and a hooker is charged with murder! Jim Rockford is back" (NBC ad, *New York Daily Metro*, 9/29/78). Even the whores themselves seem to prefer it, e.g., " 'Well, I'm not a cocktail waitress, I'm a hooker, but I guess you sort of knew that' " (New York *Village Voice*, 1/2/78).

A rare, direct comparison of "hooker" and "whore," illustrating the greater acceptability of the former, comes from an article in [*MORE*] (5/77) about celebrities who hawk consumer products. There, the word "hooker" was always presented to readers without editorial qualification, i.e., "Nine years ago, says Jane Trahey . . . 'Nobody but hookers and Hadassah ladies wore dark fur' " or, again, referring to the many commercials for many different products by Joe Namath and Bill Cosby, "Too many hooks [meaning logical connections between celebrity and product] and one begins to smell a hooker." Whenever "whore" was used, however, the magazine carefully enclosed the stronger term in quote marks, i.e., "He [meaning Cosby] threatens to replace Arthur Godfrey as the 'whore' of endorsers."

The origin of "hooker" is shrouded in mystery. Credit often is given to Gen. Joseph ("Fighting Joe") Hooker, who commanded the Union armies for a short time during the Civil War, and it is true that he may have helped popularize the whorish sense. His headquarters was described by Charles Francis Adams, Jr., as a combination "barroom and brothel," and Washington's prostitutes in this era were known as "Hooker's Division" or "Brigade." However, the earliest use of the word in this sense predates the Civil War by fifteen years (1845, *OED*). Other suggestions are that "hooker" comes from Corlear's Hook, a notorious section of New York City in the nineteenth century; or from the British use of "hooker" to mean a thief (see HOOK); or from "hooker" referring to a fishing boat (the parallel here would be to the "tramp" that is a vessel as well as a woman); and finally—and most likely—that the noun stems from the way in which working women troll for customers. Thus, quoting an English prostitute of the pre–General Hooker period: "I've hooked many a man by showing him an ankle on a wet day" (Henry Mayhew, *London Labour and the London Poor,* 1857). It may be purely a coincidence—an example of evolutionary convergence—but in Paris, the man who tries to steer pedestrians to the whorehouse for which he works is called an *accrocheur,* literally "hooker," from the verb *accrocher,* to hook. See also PROSTITUTE.

hoor (also **hooer** or **ho).** Whore; the various mispronunciations class as aural euphemisms. See also BURLEYCUE and PROSTITUTE.

hooter. The penis. Thus, a transvestite dancer explained that he got a private laugh out of fooling other men when "I have a hooter that's probably bigger than theirs" ("Real Sex," HBO, 2/21/93). In the plural, *hooters,* the term may also refer to female breasts, proving once again that context is everything. See also BOSOM and PENIS.

Hoover hog. Depression-era rabbit, except in the Southwest, where the term was more likely to refer to an armadillo. "In spite of both the belief that armadillos feed on corpses and the animal's susceptibility to leprosy, poor whites ate them with greens and cornbread during the Depression and called them 'Hoover hogs' or 'Texas turkeys' (on the Christmas table)" (William Least Heat Moon, *Blue Highways,* 1982).

"Hoover hog" was only one of a number of ways in which the name of the thirty-first president was used to dress up foods following the crash of '29. Among the others: *Hoover gravy,* made with fat, flour, and milk, and served as a main course; *Hoover ham,* salt pork; *Hoover pork,* rabbit, and

Hoover steak, land turtle. See also CAPE COD TURKEY.

horse. To play around in general, and to be frisky sexually, up to and including romps in bed, especially when the participants are not married (to each other, at least). "The leader called up all the men and girl singers and piano players together. 'This is a respectable band,' he said, 'and there ain't goin' to be any immoral horsin' goin' on. Whoever you start sleepin' with this trip, that's how you end the tour!'" (Stephen Longstreet, *The Real Jazz Old and New,* 1956). The expression dates at least to Elizabethan times. Shakespeare used this and other equine terms in a sexual sense, e.g., "to colt" and "to mount." Falstaff speaks: "An I could get me a wife in the stews, I were mann'd, horsed, and wived" (*Henry IV, Part 2,* 1596–97). See also INTERCOURSE and STEW.

horsefeathers. Horse shit, a.k.a. *horse chestnuts, horse manure* (see also MANURE), *horse puppy,* and *horseradish.* The term's origin is uncertain. Charles Earle Funk reported in *Horsefeathers & Other Curious Words* (1958) that old-time builders in New England and New York used "horsefeathers" to mean the tapered boards that were laid over rows of shingles or clapboards to provide a flat surface for the attachment of new roofs or siding. Possibly, the feathering strips, as they also were called, started off as a joke for "house feathers." The presumed ancestral term has yet to be found in writing, however. The sense of "nonsense" or "hogwash" was popularized in the 1920s, with credit for this generally given to William De Beck (d. 1942), a comic-strip artist, who also coined or popularized *heebie-jeebies, hot mama,* and *hotsy-totsy.* The euphemistic flavor of the expression is best conveyed by setting it in context. From John O'Hara's *Appointment in Samarra* (1934):

> "And my orders is to see that you keep your knees together, baby."
> "Horse feathers," she said.

hose. Describing "hose" as a "western" term in his *Dictionary of Americanisms* (1859), John Russell Bartlett explained: "Stockings is considered extremely indelicate, although long socks is pardonable." Even today, the entry for "Stockings-Women's" in the Manhattan, New York, Yellow Pages redirects one's fingers to the more genteel "Hosiery-Retail." See also LIMB and LINGERIE.

hose (down). To kill, especially by spraying an area with bullets from an automatic weapon. The expression was popularized during the VIETNAM ERA. "A lot of them are going to killed, hosed down, no questions asked" (Josiah Bunting, *The Lionheads,* 1972). See also HIT, WASH AWAY, and WET AFFAIR.

hospice. A hospitable place to die. Originally a place of rest and entertainment for pilgrims or other travelers, and later a refuge for the poor or the sick, "hospice" was given its latest twist in Great Britain in the 1970s. A hospice within a hospital is, technically and euphemistically, a *palliative care unit.* See also EXPIRE.

Hospitable Sea. The *Euxine*—the ancient Greek name for the Black Sea, originally (and far more accurately) known as the *Axeinos* (inhospitable) sea. "Greeks were fond of describing the strange customs of the peoples of the Euxine, or 'Hospitable Sea', as they euphemistically called it" (A. R. Burn, *A Traveler's History of Greece,* 1965).

And what was life like in that part of the world? Burn continues: "The climate was described as 'four months cold and eight months winter', when (though really it was only true of some winters) the very sea froze, and metal wine amphoras had been known to crack, leaving the contents standing up.' If you pour water on the ground, you will not make mud', says Herodotus, 'but if you light a fire, you will.'" Well over 2,000 years later, the Black Sea still retained its inhospitable reputation. As George Gordon, Lord Byron noted in *Don Juan*:

> There's not a sea the passenger
> e'er pukes in,
> Turns up more dangerous breakers
> than the Euxine.

For more about geographical euphemisms, see also GREENLAND.

hot place. Hell. "We don't give two hoots in a hot place what you do now" (*Ann Vickers,* film, 1933). See also HECK.

hot seat. The electric chair; perhaps the most common of the many oblique references to this article of furniture. More picturesque is the rhyming variant "hot squat," as in "You couldn't ever rise from the hot squat" (A. Hynd, *Public Enemies,* 1949). In "American Euphemisms for Dying, Death, and Burial" (*American Speech,* 10/36), Louise Pound noted that the euphemisms for electrocution "are more terse and forbidding than the word itself, yet somehow suggestive of nonchalance in the face of punishment." In addition to the basic *burn, cook, fry, roast, sizzle,* and *toast,* metaphors for the electric chair and the act of electrocution include *the chair, (take the) electric cure, electric stool, flame chair, (get a)* *permanent wave, hot plate, juice chair, (ride) Old Smoky,* and *(have an appointment with) Ol' Sparky.* See also CAPITAL PUNISHMENT.

house. A brothel or whorehouse, with many variants over the years. Among them: *accommodation house, assignation house* (see ASSIGNATION), *barrelhouse* (originally just a drinking place), *bed house, boarding-house, call house,* (see CALL GIRL), *can house, case house,* CAT HOUSE, *crib house, disorderly house, disreputable house, doss house, fancy house* (see FANCY), *flophouse, funhouse, house of ill fame, house of ill repute, joy house, juke house* (see SWINGING), *naughty house* (see UGLY), *occupying house* (see OCCUPY), *parlor house* (see PARLOR), *quean house* (see QUEEN), *sporting house* (domicile of SPORTING GALS in the *sporting district* of town), and *vaulting house* (another Elizabethan term). Then there are the French *maison close* (closed house, occupied by FILLES DE JOIE), the "little house" or BORDELLO, the architecturally related *romansion* (see ROMANCE), and the less formal LOVE NEST.

Many of the *houses,* e.g., *disorderly house, house of ill fame, house of ill repute,* and *sporting house,* came into vogue as printable euphemisms in American newspapers following the Civil War. Not everyone agreed on which euphemism to use when, however. Thus, one of the admonitions in the "Don't List" of James Gordon Bennett, Jr., proprietor of *The New York Herald* from 1867 to 1918, was "Don't say 'disorderly house' when you mean 'disreputable house.' A house cannot be disorderly. Do not print the numbers of such houses." Some of these terms are still current. For instance, quoting the town historian of Roxbury, Conn., Elmer Worthington: "At Roxbury Station around 1800, there was one drug store, a house of ill fame—one of the biggest in the area—

hotels. . . . It was a very busy place" (*Litchfield County,* Conn., *Times,* 11/18/88).

All the English *houses* probably derive from the STEW, or "hothouse," originally a public bathhouse. In William Shakespeare's *Measure for Measure* (ca. 1604), Mistress Overdone "professes a hothouse, which I think is a very ill house, too." The Elizabethans were not the first to blink at "brothel," however. Tacitus evaded it in his *Histories* (ca. 116) with *inhonesta dictu,* which translates as "places unseemly to mention." But Tacitus was not the type to call a spade a spade; see ENTRENCHING TOOL.

household administrator. A butler. "Who were they? Household administrators. The term 'butler' is archaic and demeaning" (*Matlock,* WNBC-TV, 9/22/87). See also ENGINEER and HELP.

housekeeper. Maid. "If you want maid service at a hotel, you punch 'housekeeper'" (William Safire, *New York Times Magazine,* 9/4/94). This is a revival of sorts. *Housekeepers* have long performed DOMESTIC chores, as evidenced by a reference in James Fordyce's *Sermons to Young Women* (1766) to "Mistresses that leave all to housekeepers and other servants." Shakespeare also had a glimmer of what housekeeping was all about: "I may call him my master, look you, for I keep his house; and I wash, wring, brew, bake, scour, dress meat and drink, make the beds, and do all myself" (Mistress Quickly, servant to Doctor Caius, *The Merry Wives of Windsor,* 1597). See also SERVANT.

housemate. A live-in lover, lacking a marriage license. "After talking with my manfriend and housemate of six months about my doing most of the housework, I finally presented him with a bill today for 'Domestic Services': approximately four hours a week at $3.50 an hour. This so-called liberated male . . . thought about this for two minutes, then drew up his own bill. 'Sexual Services': approximately four hours a week at $5 an hour" (*Ms.,* 7/77). See also ROOM-MATE and SERVICES.

human/humankind. Man/mankind.

The *Random House Webster's College Dictionary* (1991) recommends that writers and speakers consider using "humankind, humanity, people, human race, human species, society, [and] men and women" instead of the collective "man" or "mankind." This recommendation is in keeping with the effort to desexualize the language, which has been gathering momentum since ca. 1970. It has had many reverberations. Thus, Paul Grossman, a lawyer in the Education Department's Office of Civil Rights, complained about the use of "fossil man," "mankind," and "manpower" in various courses offered by the University of California at Berkeley. He urged that the odious terms be replaced by such phrases as "human fossils," "humankind," and "human resource development" (*New York Times,* 5/10/85).

The popularity of "human" also is evidenced by such changes as "Unemployment Office" to "Human Resources Development" (in California), "Welfare" to "Human Services" (Bradley County, Tenn.), and "Department of Home Economics" to "School of Human Resources and Family Studies (University of Illinois). Meanwhile, a juror at a New York City trial "insisted he was not a 'social worker,' as stated on his card, but a 'supervising human resources specialist'" (Paul Hoffman, *What the Hell is Justice,* 1974). For other "human" examples, see KINETICS and WELFARE.

The more ardent linguistic police people would go a step further and avoid "human," too, because of its noxious second syllable. They are misguided, however. There really isn't any "man" here. "Human" comes from the Latin *humanus,* in turn from *humus,* earth, soil. Thus, "human" translates as "earthling," and "human being" qualifies as a redundancy. As noted by an Australian correspondent: "You never hear people say 'dog being', 'cat being' etc." (A. A. Stone, letter, 5/25/83). See also HUMAN RESOURCES, PERSON, and, for more on the checkered history of "man," the antithetical WOMAN.

human remains pouch. Body bag, a.k.a. *glad bag* or *mummy sack*; a plastic or rubber bag for transporting a corpse. "Lite Industries has a rush order for 4,000 body bags, part of a contract for 16,099. . . . The Pentagon, which now prefers to call the product 'human remains pouches,' would like to say as little about this aspect of the gulf deployment as possible" (*New York Times,* 1/16/91). See also CREW TRANSFER CONTAINER.

human resources. A second-order euphemism, replacing PERSONNEL, itself popularized by the military-industrial complex as a substitute for "people." The new term has measurable attractions: "What's in a name? At least 30 percent higher pay and more prestige for personnel workers if a company used the trendy 'human resources' label instead of the usual personnel department designation. A survey of 300 major companies by Goodrich & Sherwood, New York consultants, also finds more VPs heading human resources" (*Wall Street Journal,* 4/26/83). See also HUMAN/HUMANKIND and RESOURCE.

hung. The generalization qualifies as a euphemism though it might also be described as a dangling past participle. Usually referring to male sexual equipment, the term appears in such combinations as *hung like a bull, hung like a chicken, hung like a horse,* and *hung like a rabbit* (the last refers not to size but to being continuously on the make). The basic expression is at least a couple hundred years old. The *Lexicon Balatronicum* (Anon., "A Member of the Whip Club," 1811) translates the following sentence, "The blowen was nutts upon the kiddey because he is well-hung," as "The girl is pleased with the youth because his genitals are large." See also GENITALS.

I

iatrogenic. A fancy medical obfuscation that hides a doctor's responsibility for a patient's complaint. "Difficulties arising from medical clumsiness in the handling of patients are common enough to have originated the diagnosis of iatrogenic, or physician-determined, conditions of health" (L. Kanner, *Child Psychiatry,* 1948). The phenomenon is as old as the practice of medicine but the term is relatively new (1924, *OED*). Its root is the Greek *iātrós,* healer, physician. See also HEALTH and MISADVENTURE.

ice. To kill. "A friend of his had come to his apartment . . . in clothes that were splattered with blood, and announced, 'I just iced two girls'" (*New Yorker,* 2/15/69). See also HIT.

identification tags. Dog tags. The official nomenclature has a FOP Index of 3.3. See also ENTRENCHING TOOL.

ill/illness. Sick—or worse, even unto death. For example, there was the announcement on October 9, 1979, on Radio Kabul, Afghanistan, that former President Noor Mohammad Taraki had died "of a serious illness he had been suffering for some time." Later, it developed that Mr. Taraki had been either shot, or strangled, or perhaps, both.

"Ill" also is one of the key indicators, or class markers, that Nancy Mitford cited as distinguishing non-Upperclass people from those Upperclass types who are "sick," have "false teeth," not DENTURES, and who live in "houses," rather than HOMES (*Noblesse Oblige,* 1956). The example Ms. Mitford gave in this instance, "I was *ill* on the boat," actually referred to a form of MOTION DISCOMFORT. As elucidated by Madame Christian Gaignault, of Princeton, N.J.: "The non-U British speaker wishes to spare his listener the mental picture of the speaker's being *seasick* on the boat, id est puking his guts out over the leeward rails, and so substitutes the word 'ill' in hope of conjuring a less vivid image" (letter, 5/22/86).

See also BRIEF (or SHORT) ILLNESS; HEALTH, REASONS OF; and LONG ILLNESS.

illegal. Criminal. Thus, Ronald Reagan, when governor of California, asserted that "criminal" was too harsh a word to apply to the burglars who pulled off the Watergate CAPER. "Illegal is a better word than 'criminal' because I think criminal has a different connotation," said Reagan, adding that it had been "sort of ignored" that those arrested were "well-meaning individuals" (UPI, 5/2/73). Later, Richard M. Nixon used the same term when defending his actions. Asked by David Frost about his approval of the Huston plan, entailing such criminal activities as burglary (SURREPTITIOUS ENTRY) and mail opening (MAIL COVER), Nixon replied: "Well, when the President does it, that means that it is not illegal" (Frost, *I Gave Them a Sword,* 1978). See also CRIMINAL (or ILLEGAL) OPERATION and IMPROPER.

imbibe. To drink alcohol, elegantly. "Imbibe" was once a general term for absorbing other things besides liquid—air, tobacco smoke, and knowledge among them. For example: "Young women are apt to imbibe another bad habit, namely the use of slang" (Josiah

G. Holland, *Timothy Titcomb's Letters to the Young*, 1858). Today, however, the other meanings have been routed by the overuse of the affected "imbibe" for the act of consuming liquor, as in "What's wrong? Did you imbibe too much last night?" As a rule, those people who imbibe instead of "drink" become INEBRIATED instead of "drunk." One hopes their heads hurt just as much. See also HIGH and LIBATION.

impact attenuation device. A crash cushion, a.k.a. *impact attenuator*; often just a plastic barrel filled with sand or an old oil drum, placed between some unyielding highway obstruction and oncoming traffic. "Impact attenuation device" cushions "crash cushion" with a FOP Index of 2.5. See also ENTRENCHING TOOL, MEDIAN DIVIDER, and PERSONAL FLOTATION DEVICE.

improper. Wrong; not right. The prefix "im" comes from the Latin *in,* not, but "im" doesn't sound nearly as bad as "not" in English. So, for those who wish to obscure a misdeed, the first step is to call it "improper." The psychology is the same as when ILLEGAL is substituted for "criminal."

Extremely artful use of "improper" was made by Patrick J. Buchanan, then a speechwriter for President Nixon, in testimony to the Senate Watergate Committee in 1973 about the strategy he had advocated of interfering in the internal affairs of the Democratic party. The questioning went like this:

SEN. DANIEL K. INNOUYE (D., Hawaii): Do you think it's ethical?
BUCHANAN: I don't think it's unethical.
SEN. JOSEPH M. MONTOYA (D., New Mexico): Do you think it's proper?
BUCHANAN: I don't think it's improper.

Similarly, during the 1987 Iran-Contra congressional hearings, Lt. Col. Oliver North had second thoughts about describing a million-dollar bribe offer as "expected" (see BAKSHEESH). He backpedaled this way: "Actually, it wasn't expected; it was un—it was not unexpected."

As Hugh Rank pointed out in *Language and Public Policy* (1974), a landmark publication of the Committee on Public Doublespeak of the National Council of Teachers of English, this testimonial technique is based on what George Orwell called the "not un-" formation. In Orwell's words: "It is easier—even quicker, once you have the habit—to say *In my opinion it is not an unjustifiable assumption that* than to say *I think*" ("Politics and the English Language," 1946). Orwell suggested, in a rare moment of naiveté, that it should be possible to laugh the *not un-* formation out of existence. He believed people might cure themselves of the habit by memorizing the sentence: "A not unblack dog was chasing a not unsmall rabbit across a not ungreen field." Unfortunately, this formula works only for those who actually want to kick the *not un-* habit—and not everyone does.

For example, when Herman Kahn, of the Hudson Institute, asserted on "Nightline" (WABC-TV, 4/22/82) that the United States should achieve a "not incredible" first-strike capability (i.e., the ability to demolish the Soviet Union with a sneak attack), the show's interlocutor, Ted Koppel, asked if it was possible to avoid the double negatives and "put that into a straightforward sentence." Replied Professor Kahn:

Absolutely not. . . . The attempt to put these in straightforward sentences simply confuses. Take the concept of "not probable." Not probable is, say, less than .5; improbable is less than .1. Therefore, not improbable is quite different from probable.

Of course, this is the same Professor Kahn who specialized in thinking the oxymoronic unthinkable (*On Thermonuclear War*, 1959; *Thinking About the Unthinkable*, 1962), and who decided, after thinking about it in mind-bending detail, that nuclear war was tolerable ("people can and do rise to the occasion"). This conclusion would not have seemed incredible to Orwell, given the professor's approach. He probably would not have expected much better of Mr. Buchanan, either.

improperly dependent. Copied, plagiarized. "*The New York Times* in a page 3 editor's note on July 11 . . . confessed that its July 3 article had contained 'a passage of five paragraphs that closely resembled five paragraphs in the [*Boston*] *Globe* article' involving comparison 'of the same sets of quotations from the disputed texts' and was therefore 'improperly dependent on the *Globe*'s account'" (*Columbia Journalism Review*, 9–10/91). Ironically, the plagiarized story was about a case of plagiarization, the *Globe* having been the first to blow the whistle on the dean of communications at Boston University, whose commencement address had repeated portions of an article by a film critic, nearly word for word and without acknowledgment. The dean's audience consisted, of course, largely of future journalists. See also SAMPLING.

incapacitation. Death. Soldiers who are radiated by nuclear weapons need not worry about dying slow and painful deaths; rather, according to a U.S. Army field manual, they will sustain "immediate permanent incapacitation" (*Detroit News*, 11/23/91). See also BUY THE FARM.

incident. A generalized term, whose value for covering up crisis, catastrophe, disaster, etc., has received worldwide recognition. For example, the Japanese referred to the war that they started with China on July 7, 1937, as "the China incident," and to the massacre and rape of tens of thousands of civilians in Nanjing that year as "the so-called Nanjing incident." (See also ADVANCE.) And some forty years later, when Japanese politicians were caught with wads of American money in their pockets, the scandal was called the *Rokkiedo Jiken*, or Lockheed incident. (See CONSULTANT.) On a more elementary level, an *incident* might be a fight, an automobile accident, or even a single death. Thus, a psychiatrist, Dr. Milton C. Holar, told a Brooklyn, New York, court that some modest conditions might be attached to the release of a former New York City police officer from a mental institution (see MENTAL) because there had been an "incident"—meaning in this case the unprovoked killing of a youth by the officer (*New York Times*, 12/2/78).

The potential of "incident" seems to have been realized most fully in the nuclear power business, however. The Nuclear Regulatory Commission treats *incidents* as *unusual occurrences*, although they are not all that unusual, e.g., the headline "Atomic Plants had 2,835 Incidents in '78" (*New York Times*, 4/15/79). Nor are they merely "incidental." Thus, practically everybody and his brother, from President Jimmy Carter on down, managed to refer to the 1979 crisis at the Three Mile Island nuclear plant in Pennsylvania as an *incident*. (Carter did so on April 1.) The initial Russian reaction to the meltdown at Chernobyl was much the same. As the Russian ambassador to Libya said, "There is bound to be a technical incident" in a nuclear power station on occasion, just as in any factory or plant. "We can say," he continued, "that this is a normal incident, and there is nothing abnormal" (*The Ottawa Citizen*, Canada, 5/12/86).

See also ABERRATION, ABNORMAL OCCURRENCE, ACCIDENT, BROKEN ARROW, EPISODE, EVENT, INVOLVEMENT, IRREGULARITY, PROBLEM, SITUATION, and THING.

inconvenienced. Crippled. The National Inconvenienced Sportsmen's League sponsors athletic competitions for people (women, too, despite the association name) who have lost—or lost the use of—their legs, arms, or eyes. See also DISABLED, HARD OF HEARING, and SIGHT-DEPRIVED.

incursion. Invasion. The invasion that made the euphemism famous occurred in February 1971, when 16,000 South Vietnamese soldiers, supported by American artillery and airplanes, invaded Laos. The operation was called an *incursion*, apparently in an effort to avoid the demonstrations (four students killed at Kent State University) that had been provoked by a similar invasion the previous year of Cambodia. As Edwin Newman reports: "Rarely had the importance the government attached to language been made so clear. An incursion, Washington called it, and there were official objections to our calling it an invasion, evidently in the belief that incursion implied something softer than invasion did, and that an incursion was permissible where perhaps an invasion was not" (*Strictly Speaking*, 1974). In point of fact, the terms always have been considered to be essentially synonymous. For

example, *Funk & Wagnalls Standard College Dictionary* (1974) defines "incursion" as "A hostile, often sudden entrance into a territory; an invasion." For other forms of *incursion*, see ADVANCE; DEFENSE, DEPARTMENT OF; OVERFLIGHT; and PROTECTIVE REACTION.

independent school. Private school. The exclusive connotations of "private school" do not sit well with liberal parents, many of whom attended public school themselves, so they prefer to bundle their kids off to *independent schools*, so named because they are "independent" of the public system. The private schools have even organized themselves into the National Association of Independent Schools.

in-depth treatment. An additional thirty seconds on a TV network news show, where ordinary stories are covered in one minute, fifteen seconds, and more complicated, more important subjects, such as the state of the nation's economy, may get the *in-depth treatment* of one minute, forty-five seconds. For more TV talk, see ACTION and PROTECTIVE COVERAGE.

Indian. Nigger, as in the old counting rhyme, "Eenie, meenie, meinie, mo/Catch an Indian by the toe." It is significant, too, that the title of Agatha Christie's *Ten Little Niggers* (1939) was changed for American consumption to *Ten Little Indians* before the book's publishers settled on the still more innocuous *And Then There Were None*. See also TIGER and TRAMP.

Indian goods. Bad goods. "Indian diamantairs . . . are sensitive to references to 'Indian goods,' which they know to be a euphemism for 'worst quality'" (David E. Koskoff, *The Diamond World*, 1979).

indicate. To say. The vague "indicate" (FOP Index of 3.3) makes a useful protective hedge for those who are speaking under oath. By testifying to what other people *indicated,* as opposed to what they actually "said," the witness gains a great deal of freedom in reconstructing events, while minimizing the possibility of a perjury charge. So useful is the device that it tends to trip off the tongue even when there is no real need for it. Thus, during the Senate Watergate hearings in 1973, Jeb Stuart Magruder, deputy director of the Committee to Re-elect the President, recalled an exchange with G. Gordon Liddy, CREP (pronounced "creep") counsel and its chief resident burglar: "Well, I simply put my hand on Mr. Liddy's shoulder, and he asked me to remove it, and indicated that if I did not, serious consequences would occur." Here, the "consequences" also were something of a euphemism. What Mr. Liddy *indicated* was that if the offending hand was not removed, he would kill Mr. Magruder.

See also AT THIS/THAT POINT IN TIME and NO RECALL (or MEMORY or RECOLLECTION) OF.

indigent. Poor. "'Indigent circumstances'! sneered the other. 'Fine fancy words for saying he was hard up'" (John Dickson Carr, *The Bride of Newgate,* 1950). See also LOW-INCOME.

indiscretion. Admission of lack of discretion may cover a more serious transgression, especially of a sexual nature. "When and where the first act of indiscretion (this is the holiday term for vice) occurred, we know not" (W. Oxberry, *Dramatic Biographies,* 1825). Or as the anonymous author of *My Secret Life* (ca. 1890) put it in his typically uninhibited way: "When I recom-menced indiscretions (to use the accepted and modest term for going on the loose and fucking others than the legitimate one), I sought Camille." See also LIAISON.

indisposed/indisposition. People who are *indisposed* are usually slightly or just euphemistically sick. For example, when a woman is said to be *indisposed,* chances are she is suffering from an unmentionable *female complaint* (see MENSTRUATION), from an unspeakable diarrheal infection (see MONTEZUMA'S REVENGE), or from a fictitious illness that serves as an excuse for putting off unwelcome visitors of various sorts. The last was the case with Fanny Hill when Mr. H., her keeper of the moment, suddenly appeared and began making advances over terrain that a lusty servant boy had occupied but a few minutes before. In Miss Hill's words: "I pretended a violent disorder of my head, and a feverish heat, that indispos'd me too much to receive his embraces. He gave in to this, and good-naturedly desisted" (John Cleland, *Memoirs of a Woman of Pleasure,* 1749). Of course, men also may become *indisposed* or suffer *indisposition.* Male *indisposition* often comes out of a bottle, e.g., "There had been an officer 'staggering on parade' through 'indisposition'" (Elizabeth Longford, *Wellington, The Years of the Sword,* 1969). See also NOT AT HOME.

industrial relations. Labor relations. Some magnates are reluctant to pronounce the word "labor." The "industrial" avoids recognizing the existence of "the opposition" even while dealing with it. "Elizabeth Stanton Haight . . . was married yesterday afternoon to Matthew McGowan O'Connell . . . his father is vice president in charge of industrial relations for the Bethlehem Steel

Corporation" *(New York Times,* 6/11/78). See also TECHNICIAN.

inebriated. Drunk; INTOXICATED. The long-winded "inebriated," with a FOP Index of 2.8, is something of a caste mark: As a rule, gentlemen are said to be *inebriated* (or *in their cups* or *under the weather* or *feeling no pain,* etc.), while the lower classes are "blotto," "stinko," "stewed," or "falling-down drunk." The basic principle was expressed as early as 1839 in an essay by Henry Rogers: "To be 'drunk' is vulgar; but if a man be simply 'intoxicated' or 'inebriated', it is comparatively venial." See also HIGH and IMBIBE.

inexpressibles. Trousers, breeches; in extended usage, any form of underwear. "Inexpressibles" seems to be the oldest of a series of breathless euphemisms for the garments that cover—dare one say it?—the LIMBS. The series includes *indescribables, indispensables, ineffables, . . . unwhisperables.* For the full listing, see the reigning champ: UNMENTIONABLES.

"Inexpressibles" comes out of the remarkable period of prudery that preceded Queen Victoria's long reign (from 1837). The oldest example of the euphemism in *The Oxford English Dictionary* is from *Rowland for Oliver* (1790), by Peter Pindar (John Wolcott):

I've heard that breeches, petticoats, and
   smock
Give to the modest mind a grievous
   shock,
And that the brain (so lucky its device)
Christ'neth them inexpressibles, so nice.

informant. One who provides information; an informer, snitch, stoolie, or rat.

Anthropologists routinely speak of their *informants* and so do the police. The more professional-sounding term, with its soft, French *-ant* ending, has been popular in legal circles since at least the eighteenth century, e.g., "It was the last evidence of the kind. The informant was hanged" (Edmund Burke, *Report on the Affairs of India,* 1783). No one likes a rat, however, not even the police who depend upon them, and "informant" has begun to pick up pejorative connotations as a result. "Most law enforcement officers recognized only one category of informant: the no good one in search of a reward—if not money, then leniency. [David] Durk didn't like the term 'informant'—he preferred the more respectful 'source'" *(New Yorker,* 7/12/93). Other replacement terms that have been bruited about include *intelligence operative,* INVESTIGATOR, and *undercover operator.* See also the *field associate* in ASSOCIATE, CONFIDENTIAL INFORMANT or SOURCE, MONITOR, OPERATIVE/OPERATOR, and SOURCE OF INFORMATION.

information specialist. A librarian. *Information specialists,* also called *information retrieval specialists,* work in *information* (and *resource) centers,* not libraries. See also LEARNING FACILITATOR, MEDIA SPECIALIST, and SPECIALIST.

inhabitance. Haunting, as by a ghost or, in modern paranormal jargon, a SPIRIT.

inheritance tax. This puts the most beneficial construction on what is, in truth, a death duty. See also LIFE INSURANCE.

inmate. A convict in correctional newspeak. "'How does your institution function in regard to prisoners?' 'We call them inmates'" (*The Jericho Mile*, WABC-TV, 3/18/79). See also CORRECTIONAL FACILITY.

inoperative. False; a famous Watergate word that resurfaced, most improbably, in the 1990s amid the ripples of Whitewatergate: When records were found of Hillary Rodham Clinton's commodities trades, showing that she had stayed in the market for longer than previously stated, a so-called "senior official," presumably a young one, with no memory of the word's horrible history, characterized the earlier White House account as "inoperative" (*New York Times*, 4/12/94).

The original, probably immortal "inoperative" was uttered by Ronald L. Ziegler, press secretary to President Richard M. Nixon, on the afternoon of April 17, 1973: "This is the operative statement. The others are inoperative." Those "others" were all the denials the White House had been making for months of any involvement in the Watergate COVER-UP. The occasion of Ziegler's great *mot* was a press conference, following an announcement by the president that there had been "major developments" and "real progress . . . in finding the truth" about Watergate. Prior to the announcement, Ziegler had consulted with the president about how to handle the questions he was bound to be asked. In particular, Ziegler was concerned about reconciling the new announcement with one by the president on August 29, 1972, in which he had said—citing a nonexistent report by John W. Dean III—"I can state categorically that his investigation indicates that no one in the White House staff, no one in this Administration, presently employed, was involved in this very bizarre incident." Their conversation foreshadowed the famous reply:

NIXON: You could say that the August 29 statement—that . . . the facts will determine whether that statement is correct.

ZIEGLER: I will just say that this is the operative statement. (*The White House Transcripts*, 1974)

Which is what Ziegler tried to do at the press conference. A half-dozen times, he repeated, "This is the operative statement," until R. W. Apple, of the *New York Times*, asked if it would be fair to infer from this that the other statement "is now inoperative." Ziegler agreed and thus, in one glorious gulp, ate practically every word he'd said about Watergate for the previous ten months. The overwhelming reaction of the press corps was summed up at a briefing the next day by Clark Mollenhoff, of the *Des Moines Register*, who shouted at Ziegler: "Do you feel free to stand up there and lie and put out misinformation and then come around later and say it's all 'inoperative'? That's what you're doing. You're not entitled to any credibility at all" (*New York Times*, 4/19/73).

"Inoperative" had been used prior to Watergate, but mainly by lawyers when referring to clauses in contracts and other documents that were invalid or without practical effect. For example, various amendments to the U.S. Constitution specify that the pertinent articles "shall be inoperative" unless ratified by the requisite number of state conventions within the Constitutionally prescribed seven-year period. Abraham Lincoln also leaned on "inoperative" when telling a group of clergymen on September 13, 1862, why he was not ready to free the slaves: "When I cannot even enforce the Constitution in the rebel states . . . what good would a proclamation of emancipation from me do? . . . I do not want to issue a document that the whole world will see must necessarily be inoperative." Four days later, Lee's invasion of the North was halted at Antietam, in the Civil War's bloodiest single day of battle. A standoff on the field, but a strategic victory for the North, it provided Lincoln the occasion for which he had been waiting to issue an operative Emancipation Proclamation.

See also CLARIFY, MISSPEAK, PLAUSIBLE DENIAL, and WHITE LIE.

insane. Crazy; a euphemistic stopover on the road from "mad" to *mentally ill*. See also MENTAL.

institute/institution. High-class names for such more-or-less grubby entities as industrial lobbies (the Manufactured Housing Institute represents the companies that make MOBILE HOMES); for schools of various sorts (from New York's Stenotype Institute and Speedwriting Institute to Princeton's Institute for Advanced Study); for jails, or penal *institutions,* for adults as well as for young people (Root-ee toot-toot/Root-ee toot-toot/We're the girls from the Institute); for madhouses (mental *institutions),* and for other places, a.k.a. HOMES, in which the crippled, the deaf, the blind, the retarded, the old, and the orphaned may be confined or, as they say, *institutionalized* (e.g., Elwyn Institute, formerly known as the Pennsylvania Training School for Idiotic and Feeble-Minded Children).

Special cases are the Institute for Religious Works, which is the official title of the Vatican Bank, and "the peculiar institution," which is how nineteenth-century Americans, mainly Southerners, referred to the local custom of keeping slaves. See also SERVANT.

instrument. (1) A test or questionnaire; (2) an old-fashioned penis or vagina.

(1) When applied to a set of questions, the chrome-plated "instrument" reflects the user's desire to appear to be working with scientific precision. "Central to the study was what social scientists call an 'instrument,' this one containing 229 questions with 300 subitems" (*New York Review of Books*, 2/3/77). See also NEEDS ASSESSMENT.

(2) *Instruments* of the anatomical sort have been employed at least since the time of Geoffrey Chaucer. For example, from *The Wife of Bath's Prologue* (ca. 1387–1400):

> In wyfhode wol I use myn instrument
> As frely as my Makere hath it sent.
> If I be daungerous [stingy], God yeve
>   me sorwe!
> Myn housbonde shal it have bothe
>   eve and morwe.

As for masculine instruments, we have it on the authority of Ms. Fanny Hill that bigger is not necessarily best: "Then I saw plainly what I had to trust to: it was one of those just true-siz'd instruments, of which the masters have a better command than the more unwieldy, inordinate siz'd ones are generally under" (John Cleland, *Memoirs of a Woman of Pleasure*, 1749). See also PENIS, VAGINA, and WEAPON.

intercourse. Short for "sexual intercourse," as in "One fifth of our eight million 13 and 14 year olds are believed to have had intercourse" (Planned Parenthood-World Population, fund-raising leaflet, rec'd 11/78). N.B.: The term may also apply to BISEXUAL doings, e.g., "Incredible as it may sound now, I still didn't accept that intercourse was possible between two men" (David Kopay and Perry Deane Young, *The David Kopay Story*, 1977). "Intercourse" probably is the most common evasion today for what usually is known technically as COITION or COPULATION (as opposed to OUTERCOURSE) and informally as f – – – or making love (see F – – – and MAKE LOVE). The sexual connotations of "intercourse" are dominant today, but it was not always thus. The word's original meanings revolved around communication, as between countries or the inhabitants of different localities, especially with regard to commercial traffic. (See also COMMERCE.) The oldest sexual "intercourse" in *The Oxford English Dictionary* comes from 1798, when the granddaddy of all population planners had occasion to refer to "an illicit intercourse between the sexes" (Thomas R. Malthus, *An Essay on the Principle of Population as It Affects the Future Improvment of Society, etc.*). Once the sexual meaning of "intercourse" was established, other meanings began to fall by the wayside. Exceptions to the trend include Intercourse, Pennsylvania, founded in 1813 (the original settlers are credited with having "commerce" or "trade" in mind) and the various nineteenth-century "intercourse laws," regulating trade between whites and Indians. Today, the sexual meaning is so dominant that it is asking for trouble to use the word in any other context—as evidenced by the brouhaha that was raised when the Swarthmore College catalog carried the announcement (ca. 1950) that "intercourse between male and female students will be under the direct supervision of the Dean of Women" (Mick Hill, MD, personal communication, 1977).

As with other basic bodily functions, a great many euphemistic synonyms for "intercourse" exist. They can be divided into three somewhat overlapping categories: the Latinate, the bland metaphoric, and the slangy. Besides those already mentioned, they include:

The Latinate: CARNAL KNOWLEDGE, *conjugal rights* (see CONJUGAL), CUNNILINGUS, FELLATIO, and FORNICATION.

The bland metaphoric: ACT, ACTION (one of many terms that embrace violence as well as sex; see the entry for details), BUSINESS, CONCOURSE, CONGRESS, CONNECTION, CONVERSATION, DEED, EMBRACE, FAVORS, FRATERNIZATION, GENERATION, INTIMACY, KNOW, LIE WITH, OCCUPY, RELATIONS, SERVICE, SLEEP WITH, and TOUCH.

The slangy (more commonly encountered in active form, as verbs): BALL, BANG, BOINK, BOUNCE, *cop some Os* (see O), DIDDLE, *dip* (or *wet*) *one's wick* (and one of many similar phrases that allude to the PENIS, e.g., *bury the weenie, dip in the honey pot, get one's oil checked, play hide the salami*), DO, FRENCH, FRIG, *get into, get physical,* GO (as in *go all the way, go the limit,* and *go on*), HIT, HORSE, IT, *jazz* (music and sex also go together; see SWINGING), JUMP, LAY, MAKE, MAKE OUT, *make whoopee, mess with, nooky* (see VAGINA), *play bouncy-bouncy, play house, play the organ* (see ORGAN), *play the virginals* (a musical image from the Elizabethan era, employed by William Shakespeare and John Fletcher in *The Two Noble Kinsmen*, 1613), *plow* (an agricultural image, used by Shakespeare in *Antony and Cleopatra*, 1606–07, but dating at least to Roman times and still current; the similar *mow* appears to be obsolete), POP, PORK, ROGER, ROLL (or ROMP) IN THE HAY, SCORE, SCREW, SHACK UP (WITH), SPARK, TRICK, UGLY, WILD THING, and YENTZ.

interesting. Uninteresting, boring, dull. "You can always tell when you're not hitting down the center of the fairway by the coded responses of those who speak to you afterwards: 'Congratulations on your play.' 'I had an interesting time'" (A. R. Gurney, *New York Times*, 10/27/91). Still less *interesting* is an "interesting fact," which actually means "drivel" (Henry A. Barnes, "The Language of Bureaucracy," in Neil Postman et al., eds., *Language in America*, 1969).

interesting condition (or **situation** or **state).** Pregnant. Dating to the mid eighteenth century, the euphemism was particularly popular in the nineteenth. "'Mrs. Bunny's in an interesting situation—faith, and she always is, then—and has given the Lieutenant seven already'" (William Makepeace Thackeray, *Vanity Fair*, 1848). See also EXPECTANT and PREGNANT.

interfere with. The British equivalent of the American MOLEST and, like it, both a euphemism for rape and a generalization for sexual assaults other than rape. The noun is "interference," as in "Before the War . . . the rape would have been mentioned delicately. 'Any sign of—interference?'" (Julian Symons, *Bloody Murder*, 1972). See also ASSAULT.

interment. A fancy burial, much favored by undertakers (FUNERAL DIRECTORS) and others in related businesses. A New Jersey grave digger specializes in "Interment Excavation," according to the sign on the side of his truck (Burlington, N.J., *County Times*, 1/16/83). In general, *interment* involves the disposition of a CASKET in a CEMETERY or MEMORIAL PARK, while "burial" is of a "coffin" in a "graveyard." Techni-

cally, too, in *interment*, the grave, or SPACE, is neither "dug" nor "filled," but *opened* and *closed*. Variations on the "interment" theme include *entombment, inhumation*, INURNMENT, and, most beautifully, *sepulture*. "Interment" may be on the way out, however, judging from the example of the Interment Association of America, which dropped that word in 1987, following its merger with another association, becoming the Pre-Arrangement Association of America. The Pre-Arrangement people can be reached, by the way, at 6321 Bury (*sic*) Drive, Eden Prairie, Minn. See also PASS AWAY, PLANT, and PRENEED.

intermission. Another term for yet another commercial break; usually qualified as a "brief intermission." See also MESSAGE.

intern. A prisoner or, as a verb, to hold prisoner, during time of war. Sometimes fancied up into "internee" (analogous to DETAINEE), the term is usually but not necessarily restricted to enemy nationals. Among the exceptions were Japanese-Americans in World War II, e.g., "Mr. [Frank] Tomori was interned at a Twin Falls, Idaho, detention camp because he was Japanese" (UPI, 4/29/76). See also DETENTION.

Internal Revenue Service. See SERVICE, INTERNAL REVENUE.

international. Foreign. R. E. "Ted" Turner issued an edict in 1990 that "international" be used instead of "foreign" on his CNN. He explained in a memo to employees that "The word 'foreign' implies something unfamiliar and creates the perception of misunderstanding. In contrast, 'international' means 'among nations' and promotes a sense of unity" (*New York Times*, 3/18/1990). Mr. Turner's ban extended to conversations on company time as well as to CNN broadcasts. The memo specified that offenders would receive warnings the first time they used the F-WORD, but risk fines of up to $100 for subsequent infractions.

international dining. Nonkosher. As part of an effort to attract more non-Jewish students, Brandeis University broadened its dining hall menus in 1987 to include *international dining,* featuring shellfish, pork, and other nonkosher foods. See also PENGUIN.

international maritime organization. From a help-wanted ad that ran in many newspapers in 1986: "Deck Hands. Immediate opening with international maritime organization seeking to man rapidly expanding fleet. Relocation necessary at our expense. On the job training, good salary, excellent benefits, world travel." The prospective employer was the U.S. Navy.

One hopes the *international maritime organization* will never again come into conflict with the *maritime self-defense force,* which is the post–World War II equivalent of the Japanese Navy. See also DEFENSE, DEPARTMENT OF.

international wildlife conservation park. A zoo, with a FOP Index of 17.0.

The New York Zoological Society decided in 1993 that "zoo" had become a bad word on account of its secondary connotations of confusion and disorder. The criticisms of animal liberationists may also have contributed to the negative image of the Z-word, but the Society did not address this question when announcing that it was changing its smaller "zoos" into "wildlife

conservation centers." The Central Park Zoo, for example, became the Central Park Wildlife Conservation Center. Meanwhile, the famed Bronx Zoo metamorphosed into the International Wildlife Conservation Park. The organization even changed its own name to NYZS/The Wildlife Conservation Society. No more "Zoological." No more "zoo." And no more "Bronx" either.

See also ANIMAL COMPANION.

interpret. Stylish plagiarism in the fashion business, i.e., to knock off, to copy, or—if one is being exceedingly honorable—merely to adapt, as in, "Let's interpret the mood of Laurent's latest." As more than one buyer has noted: It is hard to find an original design in apparel, and only the most outlandish design is theoretically copyrightable. See also APPROPRIATE; HOMAGE, TO PAY; REVERSE ENGINEERING; and SAMPLING.

interrogation. The general term for questioning often conceals the means by which the answers are elicited, e.g., "Trained Brazilian torturers traveled to military academies in neighboring countries to conduct courses in what is euphemistically known as 'interrogation'" (Jean-Pierre Clavel, *New York Times*, 8/4/74).

Traditional forms of *interrogation* include beatings (a.k.a. the *third degree),* the application of electrical shocks (BELL TELEPHONE HOUR), and various forms of water torture (or WATER CURE). Beatings also may be glossed over as *energetic interrogation, physical contact during interrogation, reinforced interrogation,* and (a 1987 recommendation of an Israeli governmental commission that was adopted as offical state policy) a *moderate degree of physical pressure.* More subtle is *deep* or *special inter-*

rogation, which borrows some of the techniques of brainwashing (e.g., sensory- and sleep-deprivation, starvation, and fatigue) to break victims psychologically. See also AVERSION THERAPY, BRAINWASH, and *the question* in AUTO-DA-FÉ.

intestinal fortitude. An elegant substitute for "guts," itself the mildest of the FOUR-LETTER WORDS. "Intestinal fortitude" is a rarity—a common euphemism whose invention can be attributed with some confidence to a particular person, in this case to Dr. John W. Wilce, who doubled as football coach and professor of clinical and preventive medicine at Ohio State University. Two or three years after joining the faculty in 1913, the phrase popped into Dr. Wilce's head while traveling by streetcar between his football office and a class at the Medical College. No doubt the streetcar was near the midpoint of its journey and his mind was half on football and half on medicine. The invention was spurred by Dr. Wilce's dislike of swearing by athletes. He used the phrase initially in a lecture to the football squad and the expression proved striking enough to be remembered and reused (Tom Burns Haber, *American Speech,* 10/55). For those who lack the *intestinal fortitude* to say "guts," other possibilities include PLUCK and the rather riskier COJONES. See also ABDOMEN.

intimacy/intimate. Euphemisms, as noun and adjective respectively, for sexual relations, usually illicit and usually heterosexual. In divorce proceedings, *intimate relations* amount to CRIMINAL CONVERSATION. People who enjoy *intimate relations* frequently are said to be *intimately acquainted.* Naturally, they get to know each other at *intimate meetings* (trysts). A very partial exception to the strictly sexual meaning of "intimate" occurs in the case of *intimate apparel,* a.k.a. *intimacies* or *intimates,* denoting the last feminine barriers to *intimacy.* See also INTERCOURSE and, for more about the euphemisms women wear next to their skin, continue with LINGERIE.

intoxicated. Drunk; typically encountered in police reports in the form of DWI, the abbreviation for Driving While Intoxicated (cousin to the equally vague DUI, which stands for Driving Under the Influence). "Intoxicated" derives from the Latin *toxicum,* poison, in turn from the Greek *toxikon,* for-the-bow-and-arrow, referring to the poison that Homer's heroes put on arrowheads. (*Toxón* is Greek for "bow.") In the original sense, then, arrowheads were intoxicated, not people, and the word implied that the poison was smeared on, not IMBIBED. See also HIGH.

inurnment. The process of placing the ashes of a burnt body (the CREMAINS) into an urn and depositing it in a *cinerarium* or *columbarium* (CEMETERIES for pots); the act of *inurning,* or potting. "Inurnment" has flourished at least since the 1930s, especially in the hothouse atmosphere of Southern California, and not even Evelyn Waugh was able to kill it, though he gave it a good shot in *The Loved One* (1948): "Normal disposal is by inhumement, entombment, inurnment or immurement, but many people prefer insarcophagusment." See also INTERMENT and LOVED ONE, THE.

inventory leakage (or shrinkage). Theft, as from a department store or other business. See also APPROPRIATE and MONITOR.

invest. To bet. "In bookie parlance, one does not bet on a horse; one invests" (London *Times*, 4/21/73). There is, of course, absolutely no relationship between *investing* at the track and *investing* on Wall Street . . . as any good broker will tell you. See also GAMING INDUSTRY.

investigative phase. Experimental. Asked how he got patients to agree to experimental operations, Dr. Denton Cooley, famed for his daring PROCEDURES, replied: "You don't tell patients it's experimental; you say it's in the investigative phase" ("Nova," WNET-TV, 2/23/78).

investigator. A detective. Sherlock Holmes, the greatest detective ever, was a private detective ("unofficial consulting detective," in his own words), but if he were detecting today, he would be listed in the Yellow Pages under "Investigators, Private." Even the police, who are public detectives, seem to be catching the disease, e.g.: "The detectives (now called 'investigators') resented the encroachment of younger patrol officers in the investigative work" (Joseph Wambaugh, *The Choirboys*, 1975). Scientists also like to dress up as "investigators," but the scientific "PI" stands for "Principal Investigator," not "Private Investigator." See also AGENT, CONSULTANT, and OPERATIVE/OPERATOR.

invigorating. Cold. "Come on in; the water's invigorating" is the standard cry of shivering swimmers to warmer, smarter friends on the shore.

Invincible Armada, the. A gloriously exaggerated name for a most ingloriously fated fleet.

In Lisbon, in 1588, the Spanish collected a fleet of 130 ships for the invasion of England. Before sailing, the captain general of the armada, the duke of Medina Sidonia, issued a report on the strength of his forces. It was a detailed report, the kind that would be stamped "top secret" today, but which the Spanish pridefully published, so that the whole of Europe, including the English if they cared to read it, would tremble at the armada's strength. Garrett Mattingly continues: "In the official publication . . . the fleet is called 'La felicissima armada'—the most fortunate fleet—but popular parlance at once substituted 'invincible' in tribute to its awesome strength. Thanks to the Spanish taste for irony, this armada has been known as 'La Invincible' ever since" (*The Armada*, 1959).

Of the 130 ships that left for England, barely half got back to Spain. Of course, the Spanish sense of irony is almost as exquisite as their tortures; see AUTO-DA-FÉ.

involved with/involvement. Whatever the context, the studiedly neutral "involved" ordinarily conceals more exciting action. Typically, the reference is to an AFFAIR. As Emily Post puts it: "A sensible executive who wishes to go far in his company does not become 'involved' with a woman in his office unless they are both free to do as they please" (Elizabeth L. Post, *The New Emily Post's Etiquette*, 1975). The meaning of "involvement" varies somewhat. A person who is *involved with* another person may be said to have an *involvement*, but when a nation has an *involvement*, it usually is fighting a war, such as the long American *involvement* in Southeast Asia. (See also VIETNAM ERA.) Then there is the nondescriptive "involvement," which can easily be a crime. For example: "Haldeman said that what he considered to be the real problem for the White House had nothing to do with the Watergate break-in itself, but concerned what he called 'other involvements'—things that an investigative fishing expedition into the break-in could uncover and exploit politically" (Richard M. Nixon, *RN: The Memoirs of Richard Nixon*, 1978). See also PROBLEM and THING.

irregularity. An omnibus term, useful for glossing over a wide range of unspeakable conditions or actions. For example:

1. Constipation, as in the adman's discreet query, first posed in the 1930s, "Are you suffering from irregularity?"
2. Dishonesty, as when a spokesman for Canadian Prime Minister Pierre Elliott Trudeau's office said the PM would reimburse Air Canada for his wife, Margaret's, travel expenses if there were any "irregularities" in her use of her free pass for nonofficial trips (UPI, 4/2/77).
3. Pregnancy, as in the following advertisement by a nineteenth-century abortionist: "Madame Restell's experience and knowledge in the treatment of cases of female irregularity is such as to require but a few days to effect a perfect cure. Ladies desiring proper medical attendance will be accommodated during such time with private and respectable board" (*Boston Daily Times*, 1/2/1845).

See also ACCIDENT, INCIDENT, and REGULAR.

Israelite. A Jew. "'The only Israelite theater director . . .' 'You may say Jewish'" (*The Last Metro*, film, 1980). See also HEBREW.

it. The neuter pronoun obviously can be made to stand for almost anything one prefers not to discuss in colorful detail and, over the years, "it" has. A century or so ago, when chamber pots were more common than they are today, "Fetch it," could mean "Get the CHAMBER." "It" also has served as a euphemism for the sexual organs, male and female, and for their mutual operation, e.g.: "The thing is, most of the time when you're coming pretty close to doing it with a girl— a girl that isn't a prostitute or anything, I mean—she keeps telling you to stop. The trouble with me is, I stop" (Holden Caulfield in J. D. Salinger's *The Catcher in the Rye*, 1951). Here, Holden is using "it" in precisely the same sense as Randle Cotgrave did more than 300 years previously, when defining *frétiller* as "to . . . lust to be at it," in his French-English dictionary of 1611. (This is the earliest "it" of this sort in *The Oxford English Dictionary*, but see ROOSTER for Shakespeare's prior use of the term in *Hamlet*.) Today, the euphemistic "it" appears frequently in public, e.g., bumper stickers such as "Secretaries do it 8–5" and "Lawyers do it in their briefs," and the ads for the 1982 film *Some Kind of Hero*: "The Army is doing it to him in the daytime. His wife isn't doing it to him at night. And his girlfriend charges him by the hour." Of course, much remains in the mind of the beholder, and self-appointed censors have attacked *Make It With Mademoiselle* (1977), which is not a hot French romance but a sewing guide from *Mademoiselle* magazine. See also MAKE.

As a personal sobriquet, "it" is most closely associated with Clara Bow, who became the "It Girl" by starring in the movie *It*, based on Elinor M. Glyn's best-selling novel, *It*, of 1927. Clara's "It" was "sex appeal," sometimes coyly abbreviated to

S.A. So strong is the association with La Bow that it often is forgotten that Madame Glyn did not limit her definition of "it" in *It* to women, e.g., "He had that nameless charm, with a strong magnetism which can only be called 'it.'" It seems possible, too, that Glyn lifted "it" from Rudyard Kipling's *Traffics & Discoveries* (1904): "'Tisn't beauty, so to speak, nor good talk necessarily. It's just It. Some women'll stay in a man's memory if they once walk down a street."

See also AFFAIR, BUSINESS, OOMPH, SA, and THING.

J

janitor. A caretaker; the person charged with cleaning and heating a building. Deriving from the Latin *janua,* door, which also gives us the god Janus and the month January, "janitor" originally meant a porter or doorkeeper, as in "The Keys for St. Peter, reputed the Janitor of heaven" (Robert Plot, *The Natural History of Staffordshire,* 1686). Caretakers began to assume the janitorial title about the beginning of the eighteenth century. The trend was especially noticeable in egalitarian America; the class-conscious English, by contrast, tended to retain "caretaker" and "porter," thus helping to keep those functionaries in their places. Of course, the upgraded *janitors* looked down upon those they had left behind, including feminine members of their—er—profession, e.g.: "The janitors object to allowing the janitresses to be so styled. 'Scrubwoman' is the term they insist on applying to their female rivals" (*New York Sun,* 11/29/03). In time, the grimy connotations of the job wore off on "janitor," too. See also CUSTODIAN and ENVIRONMENTAL.

jeopardy. Violence on the tube. "'St. Elsewhere' lacks 'jeopardy,' the network euphemism for action and violence that comes naturally to a police show" (*New York Times,* 12/29/82). See also ACTION.

Jesse. Hell; a popular nineteenth-century euphemism, frequently used as a threat when about to scold or thrash a person, in such phrases as "If you don't watch out, you are going to catch Jesse," or "I'm going to give you most particular Jesse." The origin of the term is obscure. Since earlier examples exist, it definitely does not come, as some have thought, from the name of the wife of Gen. John C. Frémont, whose campaign for president in 1856 featured the slogan "Give them Jessie!" The allusion may be to the biblical "rod out of the stem of Jesse" (Isaiah 11:1). "Give him Jesse" may or may not be entirely extinct; it has been a few years since it was last reported officially: "In February, 1946, I heard the expression used in a game of bridge by a player from Sidney, Nebraska, when her partner was ruffing an opponent's suit" (*American Speech,* 4/46). See also HECK.

Jiminy Cricket. The cute Walt Disney character notwithstanding, this is a euphemism for "Jesus Christ," on a par with CRIPES, JINGO, and JUDAS PRIEST. The "Jiminy" comes from "Gemini," which goes back to at least 1664, and which may derive from the Latin *Jesu domine.* "Jiminy" sometimes is used alone, as in "By Jiminy" or—perhaps a transitional form—"'Oh, geeminy, it's *him,*' exclaimed both boys in a breath" (Mark Twain, *The Adventures of Tom Sawyer,* 1876). "Cricket" is only one of a number of possible finishers for "Jiminy," e.g., *Jiminy Christmas, Jiminy crackers, Jiminy criminy, Jiminy cripes,* and *Jiminy whiz.* Yet another way to euphemize the holy name is to reduce it to initials as in, quoting a World War I drill instructor: "'May the Lord Jaycee take you into his merciful and perpetual keeping'; for I have done with you. Class, dismiss!" (Robert Graves, *The Future of Swearing and Improper Language,* 1936). See also the basic GEE.

jingo, by. A euphemism for "By Jesus," the nonsense word having been substituted for the sacred name. ("Jingo" also has been used by conjurers for some hundreds of years; "hey jingo," for making objects suddenly appear, is the opposite of "hey presto," for making them vanish.) The euphemistic meaning is demonstrated clearly in the oldest of the citations for the word in *The Oxford English Dictionary:* Translating *Rabelais* in 1694, Peter Motteux began a sentence "By jingo quoth Panurge," where the French original started *"Par Dieu."* Today, "jingo" more often refers to a bellicose patriot or warmonger. The modern meaning derives from the euphemism, as it was used in a British music hall ditty of 1878, written by G. W. Hunt, and popularized by "The Great MacDermott." The song was seized upon by home-front warriors who wanted England to fight Russia, then making one of her recurring expressions of interest in Turkey and the warm-water port of Constantinople. The chorus went:

> We don't want to fight yet by Jingo!
>   if we do
> We've got the ships, we've got the
>   men, and got the money too.
> We've fought the Bear before, and
>   while we're Britons true,
> The Russians shall not have Constan-
>   tinople.

To their great disappointment, no doubt, the original *jingoes* never got to fight. Great Britain sent its Mediterranean fleet into Turkish waters and Russia backed down. The euphemistic sense, however, is by no means obsolete. When Gen. Mohammad Zia ul-Haq, leader of the military government of Pakistan, was asked if he intended to yield power to civilians by holding elections, he replied: "By jingo, yes, unless the heavens fall, unless a new situation emerges that I have not foreseen and which I do not

anticipate" (*New York Times,* 9/7/77). See also GEE and HANKY-PANKY.

job action. A strike or slowdown by public employees. Apparently created in response to laws forbidding public employees from going on strike, "job action" is a deliciously perverse phrase, a truly fine example of Reverse English, with its apparent, literal meaning being precisely the opposite of the actual meaning, i.e., job *in*action. A similar roundabout for "strike" in Britain is "industrial action." A wildcat strike in the United Kingdom is, by this token, an "unofficial industrial action." See also ACTION, SICK OUT, and WORKING TO RULE.

john. The most common American euphemism for (1) the toilet, and (2) a whore's customer or TRICK.

The first kind of "john" is much the older. A Harvard College regulation of 1735 put it this way: "No freshman shall mingo against the College wall or go into the fellows' cuzjohn." ("Mingo" is Latin, the first-person singular of *mingere,* to piss.) This colonial "cousin john," to give it its full title, is a close relative of *jakes, jacques, jaques,* and *jack's house* (or *place),* all deriving from the masculine "John" and all venerable nicknames for a PRIVY, e.g., "I will tread this unbolted villain into mortar, and daub the wall of a jakes with him" (William Shakespeare, *King Lear,* 1605–06). Use of "john" in this sense led to similar proper-name euphemisms. Thus, nineteenth-century Americans sometimes spoke of going to the *Joe* and even today a woman's toilet may be referred to as a *jane.* Other proper names for the improper place include *Ruth,* MISS WHITE, and *Jones,* as in *Jones's place, Mrs. Jones,* and *Widow Jones.* See also AMENITIES and TOILET.

The "john" who patronizes a whore is a faceless person, in the sense of "John Doe," the fictional anyman and everyman created some centuries ago for use in court proceedings. Here "John" merely denotes "male," just as it does in such other expressions as *John Lack-Latin, John-of-all-trades, John China-man, Johnny-come-lately,* and JOHN THOMAS.

As a purchaser of sexual FAVORS, "John" once implied a steady, fairly durable RELATIONSHIP, in which the man paid for the woman's upkeep. (In this sense, "John" paralleled "Sugar Daddy" and the abbreviated "Daddy," as in Cole Porter's "My Heart Belongs to Daddy," 1938.) As time wore on, and the pace of modern life quickened, the term began to be applied to the male participants in relationships of only a few minutes' duration, e.g., "One night she brought in $1,000. Conventioneers make generous johns" (New York *Village Voice,* 1/2/78). See also SEX WORKER.

John Thomas. The penis—and the most elegant of the various Christian names (e.g., DICK, PETER, and ROGER) commonly bestowed upon it; perhaps from *John Thomson's man,* a Scottish expression, dating to the sixteenth century, for a man who was so devoted to (or browbeaten by) his wife as always to be guided by her. The penile sense was popularized by D. H. Lawrence: "'John Thomas! John Thomas!' and she quickly kissed the soft penis" (*Lady Chatterley's Lover,* 1928). Variations on the "John Thomas" theme, all with the same meaning, include *Jack, John, Johnnie, Johnson,* and *Dr. Johnson.* See also ATHLETIC SUPPORTER, JOHN, and PENIS.

joint. The leg of a fowl in nineteenth-century America; one of many bywords for the human PENIS in the twentieth. The earlier version of the euphemism amused and confused British travelers, who thought of a "joint" in terms of beef or VENISON. Thus, W. F. Goodmane wasn't sure what to do when asked "by a lady, at a public dinnertable, to furnish her with the first and second joint" (*Seven Years in America,* 1845). See also DRUMSTICK and WHITE MEAT.

journalist. Newspaper and magazine reporters can be forgiven for elevating themselves into "journalists," but there is no excuse for that oft-encountered contradiction in terms, the journal-less "TV journalist." See also ENGINEER.

Jove. The name of the supreme Roman deity serves as a euphemism for "God" in such exclamations as "By Jove! here comes the Coroner" (Mary E. Braddon, *Wyllard's Weird,* 1885). "Jupiter," which means "father of the Gods" (from *Jovis* plus *pater*), has been used in the same euphemistic way: "By Jupiter, I had it from her Arme" (William Shakespeare, *Cymbeline,* ca. 1610). Both forms remain current, at least in the comics. For example: "Jumpin' jupiter, Buck. Barney and I need your help if we're gonna' claim all this uranium for earth before other planets find it. . . . [and later] By Jove, that will be the end of the evil Pounce!" (Robert C. Dille, *The World of Buck Rogers,* 1978). See also GOSH and GREAT SCOTT.

Judas Priest. A roundabout for "Jesus Christ." Thus, remembering baseball executive Branch Rickey (1881–1965): "His strongest expression was 'Judas Priest'" (Red Barber, "Baseball," WNET-TV, 9/26/94). Variants include *by Judas* and *Judas Christopher.* See also JIMINY CRICKET.

juice harp. Jew's harp. The name of the instrument has been associated with the Jews for some 400 years. It also used to be called a *Jew's trump* (or *trounk*). Whether or not the name was intended originally to be derogatory is not known, but it almost certainly was uneasiness over saying "Jew" that inspired the much later development of "Juice harp," which was the standard euphemism in the 1940s and 1950s on radio and TV broadcasts. Other alternatives include *jaw harp* and, more discreetly and perhaps not even euphemistically (ignorance of the instrument's true name may be the cause), *mouth harp.* For background on avoiding "Jew," see HEBREW.

jumbo. Popularized by the mammoth—so to speak—elephant exhibited by P. T. Barnum from 1882 until its death in 1885 (hit by a railroad engine), this is an honest enough adjective when applied to truly large items, *jumbo* jets, for example, but one-half of a contradiction in terms—an oxymoron—when used to market *jumbo* shrimp, olives, and other items of considerably less than elephantine proportions. See also LARGE.

jump. To have sexual intercourse or the act thereof; another of the many expressions that combine sex and aggression, "to jump" someone also being to assault someone. "Then you get cockeyed and take her out for a quick jump and ruin the whole works" (John O'Hara, *Appointment in Samarra,* 1935). The metaphor is old. Shakespeare used it; see CORDLESS MASSAGER for an example from *A Winter's Tale.* He also employed "leap" and "vault" as synonyms for the sexual "jump." Today, the term frequently appears in the phrases *jump* (or *jump on*) *someone's bones,* e.g., "Have I tried to . . . jump your bones" (*The Gauntlet,* film, 1977). A variant is *crush someone's bones,* as in "Now, from Lemberg's point of view it's all very clear—he wants to crush her bones" (*New Yorker,* 1/11/93). See also ACTION, BONE, HIT, and INTERCOURSE.

K

Kamikaze. The Japanese word translates as *divine wind,* or *wind of the gods,* hardly suggesting to the uninitiated the terrible, suicidal airplane attacks to which it was applied. The Kamikaze Corps was organized in 1944. It was the Japanese response to the increasing skill of American pilots and the development of the proximity fuse, which caused antiaircraft shells to explode whenever they passed near their targets. The two factors had combined to make it virtually impossible for Japanese planes to get close enough to U.S. ships to damage them by conventional means. The World War II *Kamikaze* took the name from the *Kamikaze* of 1281, a real divine wind—a typhoon that wrecked an invading Mongol fleet. The explosive-laden Kamikaze planes often attacked in mass formation, inscrutably called *Kikusui,* or *floating chrysanthemum.* They exacted a fearful toll: In the Okinawa campaign alone, they sank twenty-one ships outright, damaged forty-three others so badly they had to be scrapped, and put another twenty-three out of action for thirty days or more.

keen age. Old age. "The Ms. Keen-Age America-Senior USA Pageant program is dedicated in [*sic*] prolonging the vigor, vitality, and promise of older adults and in joyously honoring the contributions that have been made by all our senior citizens" (Danbury, Conn., *Advertiser,* 6/20/87). See also GOLDEN AGE/YEARS and SENIOR CITIZEN.

keister (also **kiester, keyster, keester, kister).** An acceptable substitute for "ass," where the three-letter word might still be frowned upon. "A swift kick in the keester" (Garson Kanin, *Born Yesterday,* film, 1951). "If he moves his keister . . ." ("Kojak," CBS-TV, 9/2/77). "I've had it up to my keister with these leaks" (President Ronald Reagan, *New York Times,* 1/14/83).

Of Yiddish extraction, "keister" is a low slang term that has been generalized considerably. The original anatomical reference was to the ANUS or VAGINA. This is because a "keister" (probably from the German *Kiste,* chest or box) also was a suitcase, satchel, trunk, or similar container—and people have often used their lower orifices as hiding places for jewels, heroin, skeleton keys, and what-have-you. The older senses of the word are retained in such underworld expressions as *keister buster* (a safecracker), *keister mark* (the victim of a luggage thief), and *keister plant* (narcotics concealed in the rectum). See also ARSE.

kept. Maintained or supported for sexual reasons or SERVICES. Traditionally, it was women, misses, mistresses, HARLOTS, and others of the feminine persuasion who were *kept,* as in "A kept mistress too! my bowels yearn to her already" (John Dryden, *The Kind Keeper; or Mr. Limberham, A Comedy,* 1678). Men, too, may be *kept* (see SERVICE for a late-eighteenth-century example), but today thay are usually called *gigolos,* which is the masculine counterpart of *gigole,* French for a tall, thin woman; a STREETWALKER, or dance-hall girl. See also MISTRESS and PROSTITUTE.

khazeray (or **khazerei).** Shit; Yiddish, from the Hebrew *khazer,* pig.

Gen. William Westmoreland's lawyer, Dan Burt, didn't think much of CBS's offer of free broadcast time as part of a proposed settlement of his client's libel suit against the network: "All that air time talk—all that khazeray—wasn't worth doing" (*New York Times*, 2/24/85). The case went to trial, but was settled out of court. The settlement did not provide for any *khazeray*. See also DEFECATE/DEFECATION.

kickback. A bribe. The distinction is fine, akin to that between ILLEGAL and "criminal," but nevertheless important to those in the business of disbursing them, since "kickback" puts the blame on the recipient, while "bribe" places the onus on the giver. For example, take Lockheed Aircraft Corp. and the $22 million in grease that it applied to palms abroad: "Daniel J. Houghton, Lockheed's chairman, in his testimony before the [Emergency Loan Guarantee] board refused to characterize the payments as bribes, explaining that one of his lawyers . . . preferred to call them 'kickbacks.'" In this instance, the translation was supplied immediately by Secretary of the Treasury William E. Simon, who, doubling as chairman of the loan guarantee board, took exception to Houghton's remarks and criticized Lockheed's "apparent long-standing practice of resorting to bribery to sell its products in foreign markets" (*New York Times*, 8/26/75). See also COMMISSION.

kill. Murder. As grim as it is, "kill," meaning "to deprive of life" (and in its very oldest recorded sense merely "to strike" or "to hit"), is a blander, less personal word than "murder," a legal term for an "unlawful, malicious, and intentional killing." Hence, in certain very special situations, "kill" can be used as a euphemism for taking the edge off "murder." Thus, commenting on the bombing that caused the death of Earl Mountbatten of Burma, a seventy-nine-

year-old off on a family yachting outing, Tom Duffy, a spokesman for the Irish Republican Army in the United States, opined: "I think the killing—not the murder —was just part of the war that is going on" (*New York Times*, 8/29/79). See also EXECUTE, FREEDOM FIGHTER, HIT, SHOT, and YAH! YAH!

kinetics. A branch of mechanics whose name has been purloined by gym teachers. As far back as 1982, the phys. ed. department at Rutgers College had metamorphosed into the *Department of Human Kinetics*. (Its offerings included "Scuba Diving" and "A Crash Course in Social and Disco Dancing.") The University of Minnesota topped this in 1990 when it converted its School of Physical Education and Recreation into the *School of Kinesiology and Leisure Studies*. Other glorified synonyms for "physical education" include *Applied Life Studies* (University of Illinois, where Home Economics is called *Human Resources and Family Studies*), *Exercise and Sports Science* (Colorado State University), *Human Performance* (Foothill College in California), and *Movement Science* (William Paterson College in New Jersey). High school gym teachers were slow to catch on, but the 1994 decision at New Trier High School in Winnetka, Ill., to convert its phys. ed. staff into a *Department of Kinetic Wellness* suggests the shape of the future. See also HUMAN.

king-size. Doubletalk for longest, largest, biggest, in the case of products; a euphemism for fat, in the case of persons.

Bedding manufacturers turn out *king-size*, *queen-size*, and *regular* beds, with the royal nomenclature eliminating the necessity of ever having to refer to one of their items as "medium" or, worse yet, "small." *King-size* cigarettes work on the same principle. With people, though, the motive is different. In the words of Bernard Levy, a clothier whose stores cater to "men of royal proportions" (sizes 44 to 60 regular): "Fat is one word we'd never, never dream of using. Nor are we fond of portly, oversized or heavyset. When referring to our customers, we much prefer to say king-sized" (*New York Times,* 5/5/78). See also DIFFERENTLY SIZED, LARGE, PORTLY, QUEEN-SIZE, and REGULAR.

knight of the road. A bum. See also TRAMP.

knock up. To render pregnant—the most common informal description of the DELICATE condition; usually encountered in the past tense. "Nicky is 14. She is one of Jolly Jim's main girls. She earns him $300 a night. And she's managed to get herself knocked up" (New York *Village Voice,* 1/2/78).

The sexual "knock," minus the dangling preposition, is dated to 1560 in *Slang and Its Analogues* (J. S. Farmer and W. E. Henley, 1896). Meanwhile, the oldest example of this meaning of the word in *The Oxford English Dictionary* comes from John Florio's Italian-to-English dictionary of 1598, which translated the suspicious-looking *cunnuta* as "a woman nocked." (This is from an *OED* 1976 supplement; Dr. James A. H. Murray omitted the word's sexual senses when he prepared the entries for the letter K at the turn of the century.) It is tempting to think that the sexual "knock" stems from "knock" in the sense of a sharp blow or rap, since this would tie in with the etymology of F – – –, but it is also possible—as suggested by Florio's example—that it comes from "nock," in turn, most likely, from "nock" in the sense of "notch" (e.g., the nock in the butt end of an arrow). The nock-that-is-a-notch is an old slang term

both for the VAGINA and for the POSTERIORS, especially the cleft between them, as in "Yf hys tale be not lyckly Ye shall lycke my tayle in the nocke" (John Heywood, *The Play of the Wether,* 1533). The etymological line is muddied by the fact that "nock" and "knock" were used interchangeably for many years. Thus, John Ash spelled it "nock" when defining the term ("To perform the act of generation on a female") in his *New and Complete Dictionary of English* (1775), while Capt. Francis Grose used the "k" spelling ("To knock a woman; to have carnal knowledge of her") in his *Classical Dictionary of the Vulgar Tongue* (1796). See also CARNAL KNOWLEDGE and GENERATION.

Derivatives of the sexual "knock" in British English have included *knocking-shop* (or *-house* or *-joint*) for brothel; *knocking jacket* for nightgown; and *knocker* for the male thing that does the *knocking.* This contrasts with American usage, where *knockers* are breasts or, in the Ozarks, testicles, as in "Some people think pig's knockers are a powerful aphrodisiac." (See also BOSOM and TESTICLE.)

Conspicuously absent from British English is "knocked up" in the sense of pregnant. To the British, this phrase has entirely different meanings. For example, when Madame D'Arblay (Frances Burney) indited in her diary on February 7, 1770, "Here is a lady who is not at all tired . . . and here am I knocked up," she meant only that she herself was tired. For a time, this usage coexisted with the other in America. Thus, in 1864, Mary A. Dodge could mourn the language to which she, as a woman, was restricted by convention, complaining: "Men can talk slang. . . . But between women and these minor [slang] immoralities stands an invisible barrier of propriety —waves an abstract flaming sword in the hand of Mrs. Grundy. . . . I should like to call my luggage *traps*, and my curiosities *truck* and *dicker*, and my weariness being *knocked up*" (*Country Living and Country Things*). Obviously, Ms. Dodge hadn't read *The Life of Col. David Crockett, Written by Himself*, (1836). In it, Colonel Davy noted: "Nigger women are knocked down by the auctioneer and up by the purchaser." (For a scholarly rewrite of Crockett's words, see NEGRO.) Within twenty years, however, the "bad" meaning of "knocked up" was well enough known that polite Americans were avoiding the phrase altogether. As Mark Twain explained to an Englishman: "When you are exhausted, you say you are 'knocked up.' We don't" ("Concerning the American Language," *The Stolen White Elephant*, 1882). Nor would an American host today ever say to a woman guest, as an Englishman might, "I'll knock you up at eight o'clock tomorrow," meaning only that he'll awaken her by knocking on her door at that hour. Numerous are the shoals of slang between England and the United States; for two of the most treacherous, see PECKER and SCREW.

know. The biblical verb for sexual INTERCOURSE, the reference being to knowledge in its fullest carnal sense. "And Adam knew Eve his wife; and she conceived, and bore Cain, and said, I have gotten a man from the Lord!" (Genesis 4:1). Though Eve assigned less than full responsibility to Adam, it is clear that from Adam's point of view, to know Eve was to love her. See also CARNAL KNOWLEDGE.

L

labor organizer. "This is the age of public relations. [He] is not a goon; he's a labor organizer" ("Rockford Files," WPIX-TV, N.Y., 1/3/80). See also REPLACEMENT WORKER.

ladies/gentlemen. The politest of the various sex-related designations for public toilets; others include *ladies/gents; women/men; hers/his; (little) girls'/boys' room*, as well as such cutesy, fortunately rarer variants as *does/bucks, gulls/buoys, fillies/colts, gals/guys, lassies/lads, mermaids/mermen, princesses/princes*, and *Juliets/Romeos*. Restaurants also often turn to foreign languages on toilet doors even when their menus are in English, e.g., *damen/herren; femmes/hommes; señoritas/señores*.

For sheer subtlety, however, the United States is unable to hold a candle to the British (see RETIRING ROOM and YERTIZ), let alone the South Africans during the heyday of apartheid (also known officially as *separate development, separate freedoms*, and *plural democracy*). Consider the fine gradations on a row of twelve(!) WCs at a railroad station outside Capetown (from *American Speech*, 10/49): First-Class European Ladies; First-Class European Gents; First-Class non-European Ladies; First-Class non-European Gents; Second-Class European Ladies; Second-Class European Gents; Second-Class non-European Ladies; Second-Class non-European Gents; Third-Class European Ladies; Third-Class European Gents; Third-Class non-European Ladies, and, finally, Third-Class non-European Gents. A visiting American would, of course, have been classified as "European" under this system (provided he or she were white). See also LATRINE, REST ROOM, and TOILET.

lady. Once a popular euphemism for WOMAN in the United States and Great Britain, "lady" is not much used in ordinary discourse nowadays and, when it is, the term may give more information about the social class and mind-set of the speaker than of the referant. As Eric Partridge has pointed out: "Only those men who are not gentlemen speak of their women friends as *lady friends*, and only those ladies who are not ladies speak of themselves as *charladies* and their men friends as *gentlemen friends*" (*Usage and Abusage*, 1973).

"Lady"—from the Old English word *hlāefdīge*, loaf-kneader—originally denoted the wife of a lord or another woman of comparatively elevated rank in life. The term has been applied loosely for quite some time, however, its social descent paralleling that of MADAM. Thus, the euphemistic *lady of the night, lady of pleasure*, and *lady of easy virtue* all go back several centuries in the sense of PROSTITUTE. Samuel Pepys had the broader meaning in mind when he confided ruefully to his diary on May 30, 1668, that it "did make my heart ake" to hear the bawdy details of a friend's visit to "my Lady Bennet and her ladies; and there their dancing naked, and all the roguish things in the world" (*The Diary of Samuel Pepys*, Henry B. Wheatley, ed., 1893–99). See also LANDLADY.

In the United States, the widespread use of "lady" for women who were, strictly speaking, not ladies, coincided with the Golden Age of euphemism—circa 1820–80, by H. L. Mencken's reckoning. A number of foreign visitors remarked on this usage.

247

Mrs. Frances Trollope, mother of novelist Anthony, recalled with considerable irritation in *Domestic Manners of the Americans* (1832) that the residents of Cincinnati, Ohio, referred to every female in sight as a "lady," with the notable exception of herself. Speaking of themselves, the townfolk might say "the lady over that way takes in washing" or "that there lady, out on the Gulley, what is making dip-candles," but she herself was just "the English old woman." Several years later, Miss Harriet Martineau, another British tourist, was startled when a jailer in Nashville, Tennessee, replied to her request to see the "women's" cells by saying: "We have no ladies here at present, madam. We have never had but two ladies, who were convicted for stealing a steak." And so it went. In 1838, James Fenimore Cooper inveighed against "lady" in *The American Democrat* (see SABBATH for details), but even he was unable to stem the tide. By 1845, New York City boasted such establishments as a Ladies Oyster Shop, a Ladies Reading Room, and a Ladies Bowling Alley.

Another development of this period was the rise of magazines for "ladies." *Ladies Magazine*, founded in 1828, merged nine years later with its leading rival, *Godey's Lady's Book*, whose publisher, Louis A. Godey, always spoke of his audience as "fair Ladies" or "fair readers." Declared Mr. Godey: "Nothing having the slightest appearance of indelicacy, shall ever be admitted to the *Lady's Book*" (John Tebbel, *Media in America*, 1974). *Ladies' Home Journal* came at the end of the Golden Age, growing out of a newspaper supplement started in 1879, but "woman" already was being pushed to the fore by suffragists (not "suffragettes"; they were English). "Sales ladies" were being replaced by "sales-women," and in 1897, when *Home* magazine took a new name, it became *Woman's Home Companion*. The English, by this time, had caught the "lady" disease themselves, but where the English used, and overused, *charlady, lady-doctor, lady-dog, lady-golfer, lady in distress* (unwed but pregnant), and *lady dog*, Americans tended in the twentieth century toward woman doctor, woman golfer, women's wear, and so on.

"Lady" still appears in special situations, all of them more or less euphemistic. Among them: formal addresses ("Good evening, ladies and gentlemen," giving everyone in the crowd the benefit of the doubt); public signs (see LADIES/GENTLEMEN); in sports (the Ladies Professional Golf Association and such teams as the Lady Dogs and Lady Longhorns, who play basketball, elbows and all, for the Universities of Georgia and Texas, respectively); in the names of the many Ladies Centers and Ladies Clinics to which women repair for abortions; in tabloid headlines, where short words are needed, as in "Lady Cop Shot in Ambush" (*New York Post*, 2/26/82); in canine contexts, e.g., speaking of a border collie in a genetic study, "Mendel's first lady is likely to be a Newfoundland" (*New York Times*, 12/3/91); and in personal ads of different kinds, such as "Lady blacksmith wants to rent small house or apartment" (*Brown County*, Ind., *Democrat*, 10/1/86), "Live talk with hot ladies!" (flyer for a "900" telephone number, rec'd 6/91), and "Boston, lovely WASP lady, 52, fine mood, good body . . . seeks loving man" (*New York Review of Books*, 10/7/93). Then there is the "First Lady" who lives in the White House, but some of the more ardent feminists would replace this epithet with "First Woman" (confusing her with Eve, mother of us all).

For more about the ups and downs of our words for human beings of feminine gender, see FEMALE, WOMAN, and, for comparison's sake, consult GENTLEMAN.

ladybird. An English or somewhat affected American ladybug. The English aversion to "bug" probably stems from the desire to avoid saying even one syllable of the dread word "buggery." Thus, the title of Edgar Allan Poe's *The Gold Bug* was once changed for publication in the United Kingdom to *The Golden Beetle* (Falk Johnson, *The American Mercury*, 11/50). The English also have euphemized the common bedbug as a *B, B flat, gentleman in brown,* and, most grandly, as a *Norfolk Howard.* (The last one stems from a Joshua Bug, landlord of the Swan Tavern in Wakefield, who took an ad in the London *Times* of June 26, 1862, to announce that he had changed his name to Norfolk Howard.) "Bug" itself has a curious origin: It stems from, or was heavily influenced by, the Middle English *bugge,* meaning an object of terror, such as a hobgoblin or scarecrow. This sense of the word survives in "bogey," "bogeyman," "bugaboo," and "bugbear." The "bugger" of buggery, meanwhile, comes from *Bulgarus* (Bulgarian), a term applied to a number of heretical sects, particularly the Albigensians of the twelfth and thirteenth centuries, who were accused of practicing this particular method of birth control. See also BEGGAR.

As for "ladybird," it is an old possessive form, equivalent to Our Lady's Bird (or Bug). As a term of endearment (e.g., Claudia Taylor "Ladybird" Johnson), it has been around for a while: "What, lamb! What, ladybird! God forbid!—Where's this girl?" (Shakespeare, *Romeo and Juliet,* ca. 1594). But here the Bard was, as so often, playing with words: "Ladybird" in his time could mean a tart or lewd woman as well as a pretty little thing. Which is why the Nurse, suddenly aware of the double meaning, follows the endearment with "God forbid!"

land. Lord; often in such minced oaths as *Land alive!* and, for emphasis, *Land's sake alive!* "When I told her how I'd come to see Miss May Pennock, she says, 'Good land a mercy, she' been gone to New York these three months!'" (Patience Stapleton, *The Major's Christmas, and Other Stories,* 1886). See also LAW.

landfill. Garbage, or the place where it is put, i.e., a dump, often cleaned up even further as a *sanitary landfill.* The basic "landfill" is verging on obsolescence now that many communities are running out of space for dumps and have been required by law to convert them into *recycling centers* and *transfer stations.* Garbage that can't be recycled may be sent to a regional *landfill,* a *solid waste* (N.B.: not "garbage") *treatment facility* or a *resource recovery facility* (incinerator). See also EFFLUENT, RECYCLER, SANITATION MAN, and WASTE.

landlady. The mistress of a rooming house —specifically, a whorehouse. "MISS WHITE is one of the finest landladies in the District, known to one and all as a prince of good fellows" (advertisement, New Orleans *Blue Book,* ca. 1905). For the benefit of those who may have doubt about Miss White's true profession, the ad continues: "She has surrounded herself with a bevy of charming girls, each one a star, who are always willing to meet you half way and make you feel that you are welcome." See also LADY and MADAM.

landscape architect. What the artful "gardener" blossoms into. The *landscape architect* plans gardens; those who tend them also have titles: "A reader reports that . . . his son had held a summer job mowing grass and weeding flower beds at a local factory as an 'Industrial Landscape Manager'" (*Quarterly Review of Doublespeak,* 4/84). See also ENGINEER.

lane. Alley. From the fourteenth through the mid-twentieth centuries, people bowled in "alleys," e.g., "An hundredth knightes, truly tolde/Shall playe with bowles in alayes colde" (*The Squyr of Lowe Degre,* pre-1400). Today, however, most "alleys" are called "lanes," thus dispensing with the grimy, back-alley connotations of the original term. At the same time, the "gutters" of the alleys have been converted to *channels.* It is probably no coincidence that these changes occurred as bowling was becoming a FAMILY recreation. See also LONG JUMP.

language arts. Educationese for what used to appear on report cards as "English"; variants include *language skills* and *communications arts.* "'Language Arts Dept.' is the English office" (Bel Kaufman, *Up the Down Staircase,* 1964).

large. All things are relative, but "large" is more relative than most, especially in stores and supermarkets. Olives, for example, are marketed in a host of exotic sizes, such as *behemoth, giant, mammoth,* and *supercolossal,* all of which make *large* olives look pretty small. In another context, when gauging the sizes of women, the *large* or *larger* woman is heavyset, to say the least: "Woman photographer needs models size 16 plus—all ages, for photographs presenting a positive image of large women in everyday settings"

(ad, Brooklyn, N.Y., *Phoenix,* 11/30/78). An organization has been formed to fight discrimination against *large* people; its name is Largesse. As with DELUXE and FIRST CLASS, the relativistic "large" causes displacements all along the scale. See also JUMBO, KING-SIZE, MEDIUM, PERSONAL, POUND, QUEEN-SIZE, REGULAR, and SIZE TEN.

late. Dead—as in "the late lamented" or in the title of John P. Marquand's Pulitzer Prize–winning novel, *The Late George Apley* (1937).

The main difficulty with "late" is knowing when to stop using it. It seems ridiculous to refer to "the late Mr. Jones," when Mr. Jones has not been on the premises for twenty years or more. Yet this is done regularly. Consider the following invitation:

You are cordially invited to attend
the second
"COLONEL CHARLES LEWIS DAY"
in
Bath County, Virginia
honoring the 242nd Anniversary of
the birth of
COLONEL CHARLES LEWIS
late Commander of the Augusta County Regiment
who fell at
The Battle of Point Pleasant
October 10, 1774
opening engagement of the American Revolution

About the best to be said for "late" is that it is by no means a late invention, e.g., from William Caxton's *The Book yf Eneydos* (1400): "Her swete and late amyable hosbonde." See also DECEASED.

latency period. This is how psychoanalysts manage to drain the magic out of "youth." See also YOUNG.

latent humeral epicondylitis. Tennis elbow; doctor-talk, with a FOP Index of 3.1.

late unpleasantness. A war, specifically the American Civil War, a.k.a. THE WAR BETWEEN THE STATES. Popularized by Petroleum Vesuvius Nasby (David Ross Locke, 1833–88), who meant it satirically, the phrase was taken seriously by Southerners who preferred not to discuss the lost war by name. Reports of the euphemism's death are probably premature. Thus, quoting Senator Wyche Fowler, Jr. (D., Ga.): "Because of our long history of suffering, dating back to the late unpleasantness some refer to as the Civil War, I do have a nose for Yankee traps" (*New York Times*, 6/29/90).

The Civil War has also been called by many other names, depending on the sympathies of the caller. Among the labels compiled by George Johnson, of Wausau, Wisconsin: *War to Free the Slaves, War to Preserve the Union, War of Emancipation, Second American Revolution, War Between the Lords of the Loom and the Lords of the Lash, Mr. Lincoln's War, Jeff Davis's War, War for Southern Independence*, and *War of the Rebellion* (letter, 3/15/82). The phenomenon is not unique to this conflict, however. Thus, some Anglophiles refer to the American Revolution as "the dissension of 1776."

See also TROUBLE and UNFORTUNATE INTERRUPTION/PERIOD.

latrine. A military toilet. The term comes immediately from the French, whose army has had more influence linguistically than militarily in history's long run (see PERSONNEL, SORTIE, and TRIAGE), but it is rooted ultimately in the Latin *latrina*, a contraction of *lavātrina*, which, in turn, comes from *lavāre*, to wash. See also LAVATORY and TOILET.

launder. A clean word for dirty business: For example, when dealers in used (or PREVIOUSLY OWNED) cars turn back odometers as, rumor has it, they do from time to time, it is correct to say that the mileage on the vehicles has been *laundered*. In politics, business, and criminal activities, it is cash that is *laundered* so as to conceal its illegitimate origin. Thus, speaking of the funds used to finance the burglars who (almost) pulled off the Watergate CAPER: "They traced one check to a contributor named Ken Dahlberg. And apparently the money was laundered out of a Mexican bank and the FBI has found the bank" (H. R. "Bob" Haldeman, quoting John W. Dean III in *The Ends of Power*, Haldeman with Joseph DiMona, 1978). The term was used by conventional criminals for some years before being popularized by Watergaters, e.g., "It was [Meyer] Lanksy who developed the worldwide network of couriers, middlemen, bankers, and frontmen that allows the underworld to take the profits from illegal enterprises, to send them halfway around the world and then have the money come back laundered clean to be invested in legitimate businesses" (*Atlantic*, 7/70). Another, more specific name for the same operation is "moneywashing," which is not to be confused with "greenwashing," i.e., spurious claims by manufacturers that their products are good for the environment. See also CONTRIBUTION, ECOLOGY, PREOWNED, and SANITIZE.

laureate. Former, retired. "Laureate," from the Latin *laureātus,* crowned with laurel, is an entirely appropriate label for those who have received great honors as, say, poet laureates or Nobel laureates. It is stretching things, however, to apply the term to people who have simply served, with however much distinction, in a particular post—as in "Lukas Foss is conductor laureate of the Brooklyn Philharmonic" (WSHU radio, Fairfield, Conn., 6/14/93). See also EMERITUS.

lavatory. A Latinate WASHROOM, occasionally used for the principal fixture as well as for the place, e.g., "Albert closed the door and sat down on the lavatory" (J. T. Story, *Something for Nothing,* 1963). "Lavatory," sometimes abbreviated in Britain to "lav," comes from the Latin *lavāre,* to wash, as does LATRINE. Prior to the mid-nineteenth century, a *lavatory* or *lavatorium* really was a place for cleaning up. Thus, the typical medieval monastery or convent had a *lavatorium,* which was for washing, and a *reredorter* (behind the dormitory) or *necessarium,* which was not for washing. See also NECESSARY, REST ROOM, and TOILET.

law. The Lord, or *Lawd;* popular variations in the nineteenth century included *laws, lawsy, lawdy,* and *law sakes alive.* "But laws-a-me! he's my own dead sister's boy" (Aunt Polly, speaking of the hero of Mark Twain's *The Adventures of Tom Sawyer,* 1876). In modern secular circles, "Lord" itself has been drawn into service as a euphemism. Thus, in the comic book version of *Indiana Jones and the Temple of Doom,* the hero exclaims, "Oh . . . My . . . Lord" at the point where the film (1984) has "Oh shit!" See also ADONAI, GOSH, and LAND.

law and order. Use of the apparatus of the state to resist political, social, and economic change; doubletalk frequently employed by conservatives who want to keep the lower classes in their place. An old phrase, dating to at least the sixteenth century, its true meaning generally is revealed by the context in which it appears. For example, in 1842, when Rhode Island presented the curious spectacle of having two sets of elected officials at the same time, one group having been elected "illegally" under a new constitution that gave the vote to all adult males, and the other having been elected "legally" under the state's seventeenth-century constitution, which restricted suffrage to property-owners (and which virtually disenfranchised Providence and other cities in the bargain), the party that opposed the more democratic system was "The Law and Order Party." In the next decade, another such party surfaced, this time in poor, bleeding Kansas. It, too, was highly antidemocratic: "The pro-slavery party agreed . . . to change the name of the party from pro-slavery to the law and order party" (*Lawrence,* Kans., *Republican,* 8/6/1857).

In our own century, *law-and-order* signs sprouted on the floor of the 1920 Republican National Convention during a demonstration for Calvin Coolidge, whose main claim to fame was his declaration during the Boston police strike in 1919: "There is no right to strike against the public safety by anybody, anywhere, anytime." More recently, in the tumultuous 1960s, "law and order" was repopularized by rightists, usually when attacking civil rights and antiwar demonstrators, Chief Justice Earl Warren and the Supreme Court, and "crime in the streets." Those on the receiving end of "law and order," 1960s-style, saw things differently: "As black activist Floyd McKissick has remarked, 'Law and order really means "Let's keep the nigger in his place"'" (*New York Times Encyclopedic Almanac,* 1970). This particular code phrase has been adopted internationally. Thus, apartheid in South Africa was enforced by the Ministry of Law and Order, while the military clique that took over Myanmar (former Burma) in 1988 exercised power through the State Law and Order Restoration Council.

See also SAFETY IN THE STREETS.

lay. An informal but printable three-letter euphemism for the greatest of the FOUR-LETTER WORDS, as a verb and as a noun. Thus, *New York* magazine, while dashing out F – – – into the 1990s, never blinked at "lay," e.g., quoting TV producer Liz Bolen: "I want to show ballsy women who get laid—or who can say 'No I don't want to'" (5/29/78).

The most interesting thing, etymologically, about the sexual "lay" is its apparent newness, with the oldest example in the *Dictionary of American Slang* (1975) coming from as recently as 1930. The term probably was bandied about for many years previously, as the related LIE WITH is of considerable antiquity. The King James Version of the Bible (1611) uses both in the same passage, quoting one of Lot's daughters as saying to the other: "Come, let us make our father drunk with wine, and we will lie with him, that we may preserve the seed of our father . . . and the first-born went in and lay with her father" (Genesis 19:32–33). Similar constructions are "lay down," with reference to getting a woman off her feet, and "lay it," where "it" refers to an erect penis that is laid low by a woman. Shakespeare used both, e.g., "The sly whoresons have got a trick to lay down ladies" (*Henry VIII*, 1613), and, in a panoply of bawdy puns, "'Twould anger him/To raise a spirit in his mistress' circle/Of some strange nature, letting it there stand/Till she had

laid it and conjured it down" (*Romeo and Juliet*, ca. 1595).

The second most interesting thing, etymologically, about "lay" is that, in keeping with our increasingly liberated age, the term is no longer restricted to feminine objects. As one of the heroines of the British TV series, "Rock Follies" (aired in the United States on WNET-TV in 1977), said to a once and future (male) bedmate: "As a human being you're a disaster area, but as a bundle of sexual energy, you're a great lay." See also INTERCOURSE and MAKE.

leak. Crude perhaps, but less so than "piss," and so marginally more acceptable. "Leak" has graced the writings of some of the greatest writers of all time, William Shakespeare among them: "Why, they will allow us ne'er a jordan [a chamber pot, or CHAMBER], and then we leek in your chimney" (*Henry IV, Part I,* 1597). Then there is Jonathan Swift on the perils of consuming too much liquid on one's wedding night: "Twelve cups of tea (with grief I speak)/Had now constrain'd the nymph to leak" (*Strephon and Chloe,* 1731). Shakespeare also provided an elegant euphemism for the euphemism in *The Winter's Tale* (1610–11) when the rogue Autolycus, putting on the manner of a courtier, instructs Old Shepherd and his son: "Go. I will but look upon the hedge and follow you." See also PEE.

learning facilitator. A teacher. The *learning facilitator* manages the *learning process,* formerly called "teaching," in a *learning situation,* or classroom, with occasional excursions to the *learning resource center,* or library. See also ENGINEER and INFORMATION SPECIALIST.

leave. Rank hath many strange and wonderful privileges: "An enlisted man goes on furlough; an officer goes on a leave" (Anatol Rapoport, *Semantics*, 1975). See also FURLOUGH and OTHER THAN HONORABLE DISCHARGE.

lechery. Rape, Italian-style. "There are no reliable statistics on the number of rapes in Italy because most do not get reported. When they are, they are often listed as lechery" (*New York Times*, 12/5/76). See also MOLEST.

legislative advocacy leadership. Lobbying. "Learning the nuts and bolts of lobbying, students . . . attend classes in legislative advocacy leadership at Georgetown University" (picture caption, *Front Line*, 1/2/78). It follows from this that the person who engages in *legislative advocacy leadership* is not a lobbyest but an *advocate*.

le mot Cambronne. *Merde*; see SHORT FRENCH EXPLETIVE, A.

less than candid. Misleading, up to and including the telling of lies. "I was less than candid because I viewed the President's order as ill-conceived, quickly retracted, and in my opinion privileged" (former attorney general Richard Kleindienst, pleading guilty to contempt of Congress, 5/16/74). In this instance, Mr. Kliendienst had been *less than candid* with the Senate Judiciary Committee by concealing President Nixon's effort to influence the Justice Department's handling of antitrust cases against International Telephone and Telegraph Corp. See also ECONOMICAL WITH THE TRUTH, TERMINOLOGICAL INEXACTITUDE, WHITE LIE, and WITHHOLD INFORMATION.

let go. To fire. "The agency said Bruce Murray of Newport, R.I., had been let go because it was the policy of the Peace Corps not to involve itself in politics" (AP, 6/29/67). "Dean Witter let the couple go after it learned that Ms. Thomas and her husband . . . were negotiating a deal to move to Merrill Lynch" (*Wall Street Journal*, 9/28/94).

"Let go" probably is the most common of the many euphemisms for dismissal from a job. Their number says much about the increasing frequency with which people are fired as companies merge, move, and RIGHT-SIZE themselves. This set of euphemisms rivals, and overlaps to some extent, those for death itself (see PASS AWAY), which says much about the importance of work in our society. Euphemisms for firing people include:

BLOW AWAY

candidacy not granted (in academia, the pleasant way of saying that someone has been denied tenure and must look for a new post); COLD, HAVE A; *contract not renewed*

DEHIRE; DESELECT; DISCHARGE; *disemploy; displace*

EARLY RETIREMENT; ELIMINATE; EXCESS FURLOUGH;

indefinite idling (the motive behind this one, used by LTV Corp. in 1985, was to avoid paying pension and other benefits to workers, as required by contracts if they were permanently fired); *involuntarily sever* (in which case the dismissed workers are said to be *involuntarily leisured*)

LOSE (as though the job were absentmindedly misplaced)

manage down (as a Sun Oil spokesperson told the *Philadelphia Inquirer*, 12/19/85:

"We don't characterize it as a layoff. We're managing our resources. Sometimes you manage them up, and sometimes you manage them down")

nonretain; nonrenew (as in "Cleveland Nonrenews 141 Administrators," *Firing Line,* 4/82)

reduce duplication; RELEASE; RELIEVE; *request departure; resign involuntarily; resign voluntarily* (see VOLUNTARY); RETIRE; RIF

SELECT OUT, SEPARATE; SHED; *superannuate* ("15 employees superannuated by the newly installed on-line data processing," *Publishers Weekly,* 2/8/80); SURPLUS

TERMINATE.

See also AT LIBERTY, BETWEEN ASSIGNMENTS, LOSE, OUTPLACEMENT, REDUNDANCY, RESTRUCTURE, and TRANSITION

liaison. Illicit sexual relations; lovemaking without marriage and, sometimes, without love, e.g.: "Of course it is manifest that my liaison with Mrs. Mayhew had little or nothing to do with love. It was demoniac youthful sex-urge in me and much the same hunger in her" (Frank Harris, *My Life and Loves,* 1925). Some *liaisons* are passing encounters, in which case they may be described as *instant liaisons* (a.k.a. *one-night friendships*). See also AFFAIR, FRIEND, and INDISCRETION.

libation. An overly fancy drink, almost always alcoholic; a verbal pink lady for those who can't take their language straight. "Have you time for a brief libation, Martin? says Ned" (James Joyce, *Ulysses,* 1922).

In ancient times, a "libation" was the wine or other drink poured out for the gods, but mere mortals have been taking sips for themselves for some centuries:

"Libations to his health, or, in plain english, bumpers were poured forth to the Drapier" (John Boyle, fifth earl of Orrery and Cork, *Remarks on the Life and Writings of Dr. Jonathan Swift,* 1751). See also HIGH, IMBIBE, REFRESHMENT, SMILE, and WOOD UP.

liberate/liberation. To take what isn't yours—and the act thereof; ironically, to destroy, especially a town.

The euphemistic noun seems to have come first, during World War II, when a patriotic editor of the *Richmond News-Leader* suggested that the Allies substitute "liberation" for "invasion." The idea was picked up by FDR. "At a press conference in May 1944, a month before D-day, President Roosevelt said that when our expected invasion of Europe began we would be using the word 'liberation—not invasion'" (Stuart Berg Flexner, *I Hear America Talking,* 1976). Thus, with the best of intentions, the word was *liberated* from its traditional moorings. Soon, soldiers in the armies of *liberation* began to speak of *liberating* chickens, bottles of wine, watches, and practically everything else that wasn't nailed in place. In this way, "liberate" became World War II's counterpart of World War I's SALVAGE and the Civil War's APPROPRIATE. In the ironic sense, cities sometimes were *liberated* so thoroughly as to be hardly recognizable, e.g., "'This place sure has been liberated,' said an American MP . . . when eventually they reached the waste of brick and stone which had been Vire" (A. McKee, *Caen,* 1964).

The euphemism has withstood the test of time. Thus, in Israel, the territories that were taken from the Arabs during the Six-Day War of 1967 were never described by expansionists as "annexed," "occupied," or "administered," but as *liberated,* while in Cambodia, amid the confusion that attended the fall of Phnom Penh to Communist forces, Sydney H. Schanberg noted that "I even had time to 'liberate' a typewriter someone had abandoned, since the troops had 'liberated' mine earlier" (*New York Times,* 5/9/75). Mr. Schanberg also noted that the Communist troops called their military units "rumdos," which translates as "liberation forces." (When the Vietnamese invaded Cambodia in 1979, they also styled themselves as *liberation* forces.) In the United States, meanwhile, adoption of the term helped the Black Liberation Army (see EXPROPRIATION) and the Symbionese Liberation Army, who murdered a school superintendent and kidnapped Patty Hearst, to justify violent actions—in their own minds at least.

For more about invasions, see INCURSION.

liberty cabbage. Sauerkraut—the best known of the super-patriotic attempts during World War I to prevent the American tongue from being sullied by Germanic words. Similar euphemisms included *liberty sandwich* for hamburger sandwich and *liberty measles* for that other kind of measles. During this period, too, German shepherd dogs were transmuted into *Alsatians*; frankfurters were sold more often as *hot dogs*; German toast was dropped as an alternate name for *French toast*; and Berlin, Ontario, was renamed *Kitchener*. People even went and changed their family names, most notably in Great Britain, where the Battenbergs became the *Mountbattens* and the English division of the Saxe-Coburg-Gotha branch of the Wettin family metamorphosed into the House of *Windsor*.

There seems to have been less of this

semantic tomfoolery in World War II. True, the Mikado pencil became the *Mirado,* the collaborationist Vichy government in France gave VICHYSSOISE a bad name for a while, and some people had doubts about sending their children off to "kindergarten." Swastika, Ontario, held on to its name, however; the proposal to change hamburger into *defense steak* was not approved by the National Association of Meat Merchants, and no one seems to have taken seriously the suggestion that Bismarck herring be relabeled *Eisenhower herring* (which would have been a dubious victory at best, one German name being substituted for another). See also SALISBURY STEAK.

lie with. Because of the sexual connotations of LAY, squeamish souls tend to avoid "lie" in any context, which results in such grammatical errors as "He has lain the newspaper down," where "laid down" is correct. The future, however, almost certainly belongs to the squeamish: "Lie" will become Standard English because the rules for using the ordinary, nonsexual "lay" are hardly ever taught anymore. As Sylvia Barrett was advised at the outset of her teaching career at Calvin Coolidge High: "Never turn your back to the class when writing on the board. . . . Never give a lesson on 'lie and lay'" (Bel Kaufman, *Up the Down Staircase,* 1964).

As for "lie with," there should be no confusion, since it has stood for sexual INTERCOURSE since at least the twelfth century. (Time-honored variants include *lie by, lie long,* and the less opaque *lie on.*) The basic construction appears in many of Western culture's basic texts, including the Bible (see LAY for an instance) and Shakespeare's plays and sonnets, e.g., in *Henry VI, Part III*

(1590–92), wherein King Edward IV says to Lady Elizabeth Grey: "To tell thee plain, I aim to lie with thee." (He did marry the lady.)

Inevitably, "lie with" itself was further euphemized. Thus, Romeo's "Well, Juliet, I will lie with thee tonight" has been rewritten for high school students as "Well, Juliet, I will be with thee tonight." Then there was the Reverend James Plumptre, a colleague of the Bowdlers, who did for Shakespeare's songs what Dr. B. and his sister did for the plays. For example, act II, scene 2 of *As You Like It* begins with Amiens entering singing:

> Under the greenwood tree
> Who loves to lie with me

But Plumptre, thinking this too suggestive for FAMILY consumption, improved the verse thusly:

> Under the greenwood tree
> Who loves to work with me

life insurance. Death insurance; the policies are a provision against death, not continuing life. See also INHERITANCE TAX, LIVING WILL, MORTALITY RATE, and SUDDEN VICTORY.

light-fingered gentry. Pickpockets. "Light-fingered" is an old epithet for pilferers (1547, *OED*); the "gentry" part is a nineteenth-century addition. Speaking of London: "Many light-fingered gentry [are] about. The quantity of vatches and harticles of value vich were lost ven I walked in Bond Street in former times is incredible" (Capt. Frederick Marryat, *Mr. Midshipman Easy,* 1836). In New York City, meanwhile, the NYPD Pickpocket and

Confidence Squad was established in 1867 as the Light-Fingered Gentry Squad. See also HOOK.

limb. Leg. Considered more discreet for being more general, "limb" is widely acclaimed as one of the greatest euphemisms of the nineteenth century. Less often recognized is that it has persisted well into the twentieth; thus, describing Josephine Baker's memorable debut in *La Danse de Sauvage* at the Théâtre des Champs Élysées on October 2, 1925: "She made her entry entirely nude except for a pink flamingo feather between her limbs; she was being carried upside down and doing the split on the shoulder of a black giant" (Janet Flanner, *Paris Is Yesterday,* 1972).

Though associated mainly with the Victorian era, "limb" had a previous euphemistic incarnation: Men once had *privy limbs,* where the "privy" equaled the "private" in PRIVATE PARTS. Even in the leggy sense, "limb," like the related DRUMSTICK, came into fashion before Victoria became queen in 1837. It seems, too, that credit for popularizing "limb" must go to Her Majesty's former subjects, the Americans. This is evident from the confusion of such British visitors as Capt. Frederick Marryat, who reported in *A Diary in America* (1839) on the following incident at Niagara Falls:

> I was escorting a young lady with whom I was on friendly terms. She had been standing on a piece of rock, the better to view the scene, when she slipped down, and was evidently hurt by the fall. . . . As she limped a little in walking home, I said, "Did you hurt your leg much?" She turned from me, evidently much shocked, or much

offended . . . I begged to know what was the reason of her displeasure. After some hesitation, she said that as she knew me well, she would tell me that the word *leg* was never mentioned before ladies.

The captain apologized, attributing his "want of refinement" to his "having been accustomed only to English society" and asked how, if the occasion ever arose when he simply had to mention "such articles," he could do so without "shocking the company."

> Her reply was, that the word *limb* was used; "nay," continued she, "I am not so particular as some people are, for I know those who always say limb of a table, or limb of a piano-forte."

Some of Marryat's English readers probably thought he was pulling their—er—*limbs*, which he might have been, but only slightly, since this was also the age of the BENDER, the BOSOM, the JOINT, and such other quaint roundabouts as: "A bit of the wing, Roxy, or the—under limb?" (Oliver Wendell Holmes, *Elsie Venner: A Romance of Destiny*, 1860). See also EXTREMITY, HOSE, UNDERPINNING, and UNMENTIONABLES.

limit, the. Sexual intercourse, the "limit" being the boundary that formerly (in stricter times than today) separated "nice" girls from those who weren't. "On the one hand, the all-American girl must not, as the poetry of our love-lore has it, 'go the limit.' On the other hand, she can't be prissy. She ends up a kind of perfumed puritan" (*Holiday*, 3/57). See also ALL THE WAY and, for the last stop before reaching the *limit*, DEMI-VIERGE.

limited war. Anything short of thermonuclear world holocaust, a.k.a. *obliterative conflict*. The comforting "limited" made the idea easier to live with in the Cold War era, but the details were never very pretty to look at: "A new Congressional study . . . says that even in a limited conflict as many as 20 million people would be killed in both the United States and the Soviet Union" (*New York Times*, 5/23/79). On a smaller scale, the Vietnam CONFLICT also was billed as a *limited war*, with the result that the very word has left a very bad taste in the mouths of some professional soldiers. Thus, Gen. Colin L. Powell, Chairman of the Joint Chiefs of Staff, angrily rejected suggestions that *limited* air strikes be used to deter Serb attacks on Sarajevo: "As soon as they tell me it is limited, it means they do not care whether you achieve a result or not. As soon as they tell me 'surgical,' I head for the bunker" (*New York Times*, 9/28/92). See also CLEAN BOMB, ESCALATION, MININUKE, SELECTIVE STRIKE, and SURGICAL STRIKE.

lingerie. Women's underwear, French-style. In the original French, the primary meanings of "lingerie" have less to do with underclothing than with linen as a material, the true French equivalent of the English "linen" being *linge*. Our own "linen," of course, also is a euphemism for various items worn next to the skin:

> MISS PRUE: I'm resolv'd I won't let Nurse put any more Lavender among my Smocks . . .
> FRAIL: Fie, Miss; amongst your Linnen you must say—You must never say Smock. (William Congreve, *Love for Love*, 1695)

The fancier "lingerie" is traced to 1835 in *The Oxford English Dictionary* as a collective term for all the linen items in a woman's wardrobe or trousseau. It took less than twenty years for the term to acquire its euphemistic meaning, circa 1852. Credit for popularizing "lingerie" in the modern sense is given to Sara Josepha Hale, longtime editor (1837–77) of *Godey's Lady's Book,* by Mary Brooks Picken, in *The Fashion Dictionary* (1973). Today, "lingerie" often classes as doubletalk as well as a euphemism, since the particular item in question may well be made of silk, nylon, rayon, or some other nonlinen material.

For another example of the influence of Mrs. Hale upon American English, see FE-MALE, and for more about women's wear, continue with BODY BRIEFER, BRASSIERE, CHE-MISE, HOSE, INTIMACY/INTIMATE, NIGHT APPAREL, PANTIES, SLIP, UNDIES, and UNMEN-TIONABLES.

liquidate/liquidation. To kill or the act of killing, frequently on a mass basis. "In Russia, after the revolution, massive killings of people accused of obstructing the regime were called 'liquidations,' a word previously meaning the disbanding of business enterprise" (Anatol Rapoport, *Semantics,* 1975). The original Russian word was *likvidirovat* (to wind up). The euphemism was converted into English at least by 1924, e.g., "In this way the 'Labor Opposition,' the 'Workers *Pravda,*' and a few other recalcitrant groups were all 'liquidated'" (*Yale Review,* XIII/24). Soon thereafter it was adopted in nonpolitical contexts. As the wonderful wizard said to Dorothy, upon being told how she had dissolved the Wicked Witch of the West with a bucketful of water: "You liquidated her; very re-sourceful" (*The Wizard of Oz,* film, 1939). See also ASSASSINATION; CULL; FINAL SOLU-TION, THE; and HIT.

litter. Not necessarily candy wrappers and beer cans: The New York City Transit Authority in 1986 reclassified the offense of urinating in public as "littering." See also DOG DIRT/DO/LITTER/WASTE.

little (or small) people. Midgets. Like other minorities, they have banded together, and the name of their organization is the Little People of America. See also GOOD PEOPLE, THE and VERTICALLY CHALLENGED.

living will. Will to die. The document stipulates that in certain conditions the signer wants to be allowed to die, not to be kept alive, despite the instrument's name. See also LIFE INSURANCE.

long illness. A dreaded disease, usually cancer, so feared that many people avoid mentioning it by name. "Cancer works slowly, insidiously: the standard euphemism in obituaries is that someone has died after a long illness" (Susan Sontag, *New York Review of Books,* 1/26/78). Variants include *lengthy illness, lingering illness, prolonged illness,* and *incurable illness.* When George Herman Ruth died of cancer on August 16, 1948, the *New York Times* headline read "Babe Ruth Dies After Lingering Illness." See also BRIEF ILLNESS; C, THE BIG; ILL/ILLNESS; OBITUARY; and TB.

long jump. Broad jump. The U.S. Olympics Committee popularized "long jump" in the 1950s. They had a European precedent. In French, Italian, and other Continental languages, "long jump" is the name of the event. The unstated reason for the change in nomenclature was the double meaning of "broad" in American English, however. If it were purely a question of adopting international terminology, the American "pole vault" also would have been changed to "pole jump."

loo. A toilet; a British euphemism for yet another British euphemism, WC, occasionally encountered among jet-setters in the United States, too. A peculiarity of "loo" is that no one is quite sure where the word came from. High authorities have disputed learnedly over whether it is a corruption of the French *l'eau,* water; an abbreviation of *gardyloo,* an old warning that slops are descending (probably from *gardez l'eau,* or "Watch out for the water!"), or a misbegotten descendant of *lieux d'aisance,* places or rooms of comfort—COMFORT STATIONS, in effect. It has even been argued that "loo" comes from "Waterloo," a word that has been imprinted indelibly on the British psyche. And perhaps the watery "loo" does pun on the battle, with an allusion to Napoleon going down the drain. Stranger things have happened in philology. But not many. See also TOILET.

lose/loss. Elliptical references to death, i.e., the loss of life, and to the destruction or disappearance of other precious things that may not be found again, such as *lost* airplanes and *lost* jobs.

All connotations of casual negligence to the contrary, the report that "Mabel has lost her husband," doesn't mean that she has accidentally mislaid the poor man. Generals also have been known to *lose* people, and in large numbers, too, e.g., speaking of July 1, 1916, the first day of the Battle of the Somme: "In all the British had lost about sixty thousand" (John Keegan, *The Face of*

Battle, 1976). The basic construction is quite old: "We losten alle oure housbondes at that toun" (Geoffrey Chaucer, *The Knight's Tale,* ca. 1387–1400). See also CASUALTY, LET GO, and PASS AWAY.

love. Sex. The high-minded term has been used as a euphemism for low-minded thoughts and actions for hundreds of years (from 1378, *OED*). Over time, the euphemism itself has become quite transparent. Thus, the lyrics of Cole Porter's "Love for Sale," from *The New Yorkers* (1930), were banned from the nation's airwaves for many years by the Federal Communications Commission. (It was okay to play the music alone.) The controversy even caused the show's producers to change the song's presentation for blasé Broadway audiences. When the show opened, "Love for Sale" was sung by a streetwalker, while peddling her wares, but the producers shifted it to a Cotton Club scene where it was sung by three performers as part of their act. As Stephen Citron pointed out: "Such was the prevailing morality dictated by the white majority in the early '30s. It permitted a 'coloured girl' to *sing* about sex, while a Caucasian was forbidden to do so. And a white girl could certainly not *sell* it" (*Noel & Cole, The Sophisticates,* 1992). See also LOVE NEST, MAKE LOVE, and ROMANCE.

love child. A bastard. " 'You're taking it too hard. There's no disgrace in being a love child. How many of those kids in your class do you suppose were planned for?' " (Thomas W. Duncan, *Gus the Great,* 1947). Dating to at least the early nineteenth century, "love child" probably is shorthand for "love-begotten child," which was included along with the similar "merry-begotten" by Capt. Francis Grose in *A Classical Dictio-*

nary of the Vulgar Tongue (1796). It remains the nicest of the many terms for describing the issue of unmarried parents, a.k.a. BIRTHPARENTS. The sheer number of terms suggests the frequency of bastardy. Among them: *bachelor's child, by-blow, by-child, by-scrape, by-slip, come-by-chance, doorstep child, down-the-road child, engagement child, irregular child, natural child, outside child, Sunday child,* and *yard child.* See also BASTARD, BLANKET, BORN ON THE WRONG SIDE OF; *Sinfant* in ANTICIPATING; NATURAL; NONMARITAL BIRTH; SOB; *trick baby* in TRICK; and WOOD COLT.

loved one, the. Dead person, the. "As for the Loved One, poor fellow, he wanders like a sad ghost through the funeral men's pronouncements. No provision seems to have been made for the burial of the Heartily Disliked One, although the necessity for such must arise in the course of human events" (Jessica Mitford, *The American Way of Death,* 1963). In spite of the valiant efforts of Ms. Mitford and, before her, Evelyn Waugh (in *The Loved One,* 1948), the expression lives on: "He never said 'your husband' but rather 'your loved one,' and 'when he dies' always became 'when he passes on.' No wonder there is so little reality about death. Even the people who make a living from it can't accept it" (Lynn Caine, *Widow,* 1974). See also BEREAVEMENT FARE, DECEASED, and PASS AWAY.

lovemaking. See MAKE LOVE.

love nest. A meeting place for the unmarried, a.k.a. *love nook.* "The inadequate sexual fumblings of Daddy Browning and his nymphet Peaches, a kind of premature Lolita, in their hideaway, quaintly christened a *love nest* by the press" (David W. Maurer, *American Speech,* Spring/Summer

1976). Dated to 1919 (*OED*), "love nest" later was applied also to the fancier houses of prostitution. See also LOVE and, for more about Browning's love for Peaches, NECK.

love that dare not speak its name, the. Late-Victorian homosexuality. The phrase comes from a poem, "Two Loves" (1894), by Oscar Wilde's FRIEND, Alfred Lord Douglas (also known as Bosie); it was made famous by its introduction on April 30, 1895, into Wilde's trial for violating a law, enacted just ten years previously, which made it a misdemeanor for any male to commit a "gross indecency" with another male, even in private. (Note that the Victorian law did not contemplate the possibility that women might commit gross indecencies.) Seeking to establish what today would be called Wilde's SEXUAL ORIENTATION, the prosecutor quoted the following lines to the defendant:

"Sweet youth
Tell me why, sad and sighing, dost thou rove
These pleasant realms? I pray tell me sooth,
What is thy name?" He said, "My name is Love,"
Then straight, the first did turn himself to me,
And cried, "He lieth, for his name is Shame.
But I am Love, and I was wont to be
Alone in this fair garden, till he came
Unasked by night; I am true Love, I fill
The hearts of boy and girl with mutual flame."
Then sighing said the other, "Have thy will,
I am the love that dare not speak its name."

"Is it not clear," asked the prosecutor, "that the love described relates to natural love and unnatural love?"

"No," said Wilde.

The prosecutor pressed forward. "What is the 'Love that dare not speak its name'?"

And Wilde rose, most eloquently, to the challenge:

"The Love that dare not speak its name" in this century is such a great affection of an elder man for a younger man as there was between David and Jonathan, such as Plato made the very basis of his philosophy and such as you find in the sonnets of Michelangelo and Shakespeare. It is that deep spiritual affection that is as pure as it is perfect. . . . There is nothing unnatural about it.

It was perhaps partly due to Wilde's eloquence that this trial ended in a hung jury. On retrial, however, Wilde was convicted and sentenced to two years of hard labor at Reading Gaol. (He never recovered from the imprisonment and disgrace; see OSSHOLE.)

Aside from the general reluctance of Victorians to address sexual matters directly, the nameless love of Wilde and Bosie was nameless in the 1890s partly for lack of any "good" words for it. Even the word "homosexual" was still very new (1892, *OED*). Of the words that proper Victorians could bring themselves to utter, *Uranian* love was perhaps the nicest appellation. (Urania was the muse of astronomy, and "Uranian love" was supposed to be especially heavenly or spiritual in nature.) BISEXUAL also dates to the nineteenth century. In addition, one could speak of FANCY gentlemen or, a vulgar rhyme, of a *Nancy* (a person might also be said to be "a bit nancy"). Otherwise, such discussions as took place tended to be couched in terms of *inverts* and *inversions; perverts* and *perversions; unspeakable* or *nameless acts* or *crimes; gross indecency* and *indecent assault; abominable offenses; crimes against nature; incorrect tastes in love; Le Vice* (doubly euphemistic for being Frenchified as well as nonspecific); and UNNATURAL acts.

Everything is different nowadays: The "bad" words have been shoved back into the closet, and GAY has emerged, sweeping all before it.

low-income. Poor, a.k.a. *economically marginalized.* "The Census Bureau has decided to say 'low-income' instead of 'poverty' in its official releases" (*New Republic,* 8/7&14/71). The bureau was embarrassed about an increase (the first in a decade) in the number of the nation's poor, but it had excellent authority for its choice of words: "You must not use the word 'poor.' They are described as 'the lower income group'" (Winston S. Churchill, speech, Cardiff, 2/8/50). See also AFFORDABLE HOUSING, DISADVANTAGED, and INDIGENT.

lubritorium (or lubritory). A place where cars are greased, referring both to a greasing bay and a filling station, from ca. 1930. See also EMPORIUM and SERVICE STATION.

lunch hour. Anywhere from about one-half to three hours. Publishers, for example, are notorious for indulging in long lunches. Other workers are not as fortunate, as evidenced by the notice, spotted at Vidcor, 33 East Eighteenth Street, New York City (9/26/83):

We do not receive shipments
between 1:00 pm and 1:30 pm
(lunch hour)

Also illustrating the relativity of time were the advertisements proclaiming that the Food Emporium in New York City was "open 24 hours: Mon., 6 a.m. to Sat. Midnight; Sunday 7 a.m. to Midnight" (*Quarterly Review of Doublespeak,* 10/92). See also EMPORIUM and SUMMER.

M

madam. A brothel-keeper; the honorific goes with the managerial position. "In a few moments the 'madam,' as the current word characterized this type of woman, appeared" (Theodore Dreiser, *The Financier*, 1912).

"Madam," or "my lady," corresponds etymologically to "madonna" and comes from the Old French *ma dame,* my lady, the *dame* stemming in turn from the Latin *domina,* the mistress of a *domus*, or house. Originally (from pre-1300), the proper form of address for a queen or other high-ranking woman, the title of "madam" subsequently was extended to the wives of aldermen, to nuns, and to women of less elevated social standing. It was all downhill thereafter. By the early seventeenth century, "madam" had acquired such pejorative meanings as "a kept mistress" or "whore." The "madam" as manageress probably dates from this period, and it has gradually superseded the other titles for women who run brothels, including *abbess, lady abbess* (whose husband or other male companion was called the *abbott*), and *aunt,* the last being "a title of eminence for the senior dells who serve for instructoresses, midwives, &c." (Capt. Francis Grose, *A Classical Dictionary of the Vulgar Tongue,* 1796). The gradual reduction in the status of "madam" parallels the devolution of LADY and of MISTRESS. See also HONORABLE, THE; LANDLADY; and PROSTITUTE.

Madame. The guillotine, also called during the great days of the Terror (1793–94) *la petite fênetre,* the little window; *le rasoir national,* the national razor; and *le raccourcisseur national,* the national shortener.

"Madame Guillotine," the name to the contrary, was not created solely by Dr. Joseph Ignace Guillotine. Similar though cruder devices had been used since at least the sixteenth century, and Dr. Guillotine almost certainly knew something about them when he proposed to the French National Assembly, in 1789, that this means of execution be adopted. Guillotine's objectives were not only humanitarian (the machine eliminated grisly human error) but in keeping with revolutionary ideals of social equality (previously, commoners had been hanged, while beheading was a privilege of nobility). The first "Madame" went into operation in 1792 and by the time she was retired had lopped off some 8,000 heads but not, as legend has it, Dr. Guillotine's. He died in bed in 1814, after which his children escaped the cloud that had darkened his name by officially changing theirs.

The use of "Madame" for the guillotine is the leading example of the tendency to attribute feminine qualities to deadly instruments. The immediate ancestress of "Madame" was the *maiden,* a crude guillotine used in Edinburgh and other places (it was also known as the *Halifax gibbet*). There was also the infamous *iron maiden,* used by torturers; *the duke of Exeter's daughter,* which was the name of the rack in the Tower of London (apparently so called in tribute to the duke who introduced this method of questioning during the reign of Henry VI); and *the scavenger's daughter.* This last device nicely complemented the rack by squeezing a person into a ball instead of pulling him or her apart. The name punned upon the surname of its inventor, Leonard Skeffington, or Skevington, governor of the Tower of London in the sixteenth century. See also CAPITAL PUNISHMENT and PRIEST.

made a trumpet of his ass. Farted. A poetic euphemism by a great poet, Dante Alighieri. From Canto XXI of *The Inferno* (ca. 1315), as translated by John Ciardi (1954):

> They [the demons] turned along
>   the left bank in a line;
> but before they started, all of them
>   together
> had stuck their pointed tongues
>   out as a sign
> to their Captain that they wished
>   permission to pass,
> and he made a trumpet of his
>   ass.

Ciardi adds in a note that "mention of bodily function is more likely to be more shocking in a Protestant than a Catholic culture. . . . The offensive language of Protestantism is obscenity; the offensive language of Catholicism is profanity or blasphemy. . . . Dante places the Blasphemous in Hell as the worst of the Violent against God and His Works, but he has no category for punishing those who use four-letter words. . . . Chaucer, as a man of Catholic England, took exactly Dante's view of what was and what was not shocking." See also FOUR-LETTER WORD.

It should not diminish our appreciation of Dante's metaphor to know that this was not just a figment of his poetic imagination. The phenomenon of "posterior trumpeters"—individuals who can play tunes, or airs, with their airs—has long been recognized. St. Augustine noted in *The City of God* (413–426) that some people "can break wind backwards so continuously, that you would think they sung." In the seventeenth century, a pamphlet on the subject was issued under the pseudonym Don Fartando, and a few fortunate souls may remember performances by Joseph Pujol (1857–1943), who wowed audiences at the Moulin Rouge and other *boîtes* with recitals on his peculiar instrument. Cynics contended that Pujol, who performed under the name Le Petomane, was a fraud but, if so, he was a good one, for he hoodwinked the physicians who examined him. He could mimic cannon, imitate the calls of animals, and blow out candles from several feet away. His crowning achievement generally is conceded to have been his rendition of *Clair de Lune*. See also BREAK WIND.

maid. A woman servant, a.k.a. *housemaid* or *maidservant.* "There were three females . . . and Miriam Brackett, a 'maid' so called because the preacher had hired her for the 'in door work'" (John Neal, *Brother Jonathan,* 1825). See also DOMESTIC, HELP, and SERVANT.

mail cover. Postal spying; obsolete? "Covering," or recording, the names and addresses on envelopes is legal in certain circumstances, but in the case of the CIA's *mail cover* operation in New York City some 28 million letters were screened from about 1952 to 1972—and nearly 250,000 secretly, and illegally, opened and photographed. The FBI also opened other people's mail—the *mail run,* as G-men called it. See also FAMILY JEWELS and ILLEGAL.

maintenance hatch. A politically correct manhole cover. See also PERSON.

major. An honorary rank bestowed on such functionaries as railroad conductors. It is one step below COLONEL.

make. To seduce, to engage in INTERCOURSE, or, as a noun, the person who is seduced, "an easy make" being essentially the same as "an easy lay" (see LAY). "A considerable degree of manipulativeness was condoned in the behavior of a young man who was in the process of trying to 'make' a young woman. He was almost expected to be false and seductive . . . in the interest of getting her to 'come across' and go to bed with him" (Barry McCarthy, *What You Still Don't Know About Male Sexuality*, 1977). With only a small change in wording, the seduction is further depersonalized: "The old phrase, 'Did you make her?' has been changed because 'making her' is personal, intimate, warm. The cool cats say, 'Man, don't think I didn't make it with her.' The insertion of the word 'it' cools it, depersonalizes it—and coolness is all" (*Playboy*, 2/58). See also IT.

Like "lay," "make" seems to have picked up its sexual connotations comparatively recently. Eric Partridge dated "make" in the sense of "to cöit (with a girl)" to about 1918 among Canadians, who had picked it up from their neighbors to the south (*A Dictionary of Slang and Unconventional English*, 1970). The currency of the term in the United States in this period is attested by the pun contained in "Let's eat, drink, and make merry, for tomorrow Mary may reform," a remark that Americans still considered quite witty in the 1920s. And a vaudeville joke of the era ran: "I took my girl home to Long Island last night." "Jamaica?" "No, her mother was home." (Sidney Sisk, letter, 10/21/83). Muddying the etymological waters are such related expressions as *make good, make time with, on the make*, MAKE OUT, all of which have sexual aspects, as well as the now-archaic use of "make" for simply making a good impression on a person of the opposite sex, e.g., "Look at that big stiff tryin' to make that dame!" (*American Magazine*, 6/1918).

make love. With SLEEP WITH, the most common euphemism for the great FOUR-LETTER WORD that is itself euphemized as F – – – . The interchangeability of the terms is evident from the following communication to *Playboy* (7/78), from F. H., of San Mateo, California:

> We made love in the top of an 80-foot tree on a platform tree house in the spring. We fucked in rainstorms until we steamed. We made love on the frozen surface of a river. We made love in the closet of a Unitarian church.

The relevant noun is "lovemaking," as in "Several times we were right in the middle of lovemaking when our families dropped in unexpectedly" ("Dear Abby," *Boston Herald American*, 7/14/77).

"Make love" once had a more general meaning and, in fact, seems to have evolved from a euphuism into a euphemism. As a euphuism, it was the flowery equivalent of "to pay court" or "to woo," and the oldest example of the phrase in *The Oxford English Dictionary* comes from the progenitor of all euphuisms, John Lyly, who created the character that gave the flowery style its name: "A Phrase now there is which belongeth to your Shoppe boorde, that is, to make loue" (*Euphues and His England*, 1580). This is the relatively innocent sense in which most writers employed the phrase up to the twentieth century, e.g., from *Vanity Fair* (1848): " 'Here is Emmy's little friend making love to him as hard as she can,' " by which Thackeray meant only that Becky Sharp was flirting outrageously with Joseph Sedley. Mark Twain had the same meaning in mind when recalling (1906) how one of his fellow apprentice printers had made a game many years before (ca. 1848) of "constantly and persistently and loudly and elaborately making love to [a] mulatto girl and distressing the life out of her and worrying the old mother to death" (*Mark Twain's Autobiography*, 1924).

The Oxford English Dictionary did not recognize "make love" in its euphemistic, copulative sense until publication of the 1976 supplement and then the earliest example given is from 1950. Older citations, however, are to be found by those who search for them. Thus, from the great Victorian underground autobiography, *My Secret Life:*

> I began those exquisite preliminaries with this well-made, pretty woman . . . but . . . was impatient . . . Smiling she [asked] "Shall we make love?"

This particular "make love" may date from as early as 1851, when the incident took place, though the anonymous autobiography, extensively rewritten, did not go to press until about 1890.

In fact, the specific euphemistic sense appears to have coexisted with the more general meaning for some hundreds of years. For example, Lady Mary Wortley Montagu used the phrase in the modern manner when telling her daughter, Lady Bute (letter 11/30/1753?), about her next-door neighbor in Gottolengo, Italy, a matron, age forty, who seduced a young man who had come to pay his father's rent: "Ladies that can resolve to make love thus *ex tempore* may pass unobserved, especially if they can content themselves with low life, where fear may oblige their favourites to secrecy." (This lady's frolic did not "pass unobserved" by her husband, however. Returning home unexpectedly, he found her in bed with his tenant's son. The young

man jumped out the window and ran across the fields *sans* breeches. The husband, stiletto in hand, was threatening to kill his wife, when Lady Mary, called to the scene by a chambermaid, interrupted the proceedings.)

Still earlier, Shakespeare used the expression in *Hamlet* (1601–02) in a context that suggests he may have had both meanings in mind. Thus, the prince upbraids his mother for living with his father's brother "In the rank sweat of an enseamed bed,/Stewed in corruption, honeying and making love/Over the nasty sty."

See also INTERCOURSE and LOVE.

make out. In Standard English, the phrase may mean, among other things, "to make shift" or "to get along," and these general senses are mirrored in slang, where "to make out" covers a wide range of sexual activity. Thus, on the authority of Ann Landers: "Among high school and college kids, making out can mean anything from holding hands to going the whole route" (Washington, D.C., *Daily News*, 3/4/63). The evidence suggests that the heavier, more euphemistic sense is the older. For example: "When I was young, if one 'made out,' his accomplishment was a good deal more total than was implied by either *to neck* or *to pet*, or both" (*American Speech*, 2/62). A person who is noted for *making out* may be known as a *make-out* or even a *make-out artist*. See also MAKE, NECK, PARK, PET, and SPARK.

make (or pass) water. To piss. The "water" is the euphemism, of course, although "make" occasionally is used in other ways, e.g., *make wee-wee* or, simply, *make* (the latter usually meaning to DEFECATE). "Water" has stood for "urine" for the past 600 years or so. A famous example comes from the first of the articles of impeachment against Quinbus Flestrin, a.k.a. the Man-Mountain: "Whereas, by a statute made in the reign of his Imperial Majesty Calin Deffar Plune, it is enacted, that whoever shall make water within the precincts of the royal palace, shall be liable to the pains and penalties of high treason" (Jonathan Swift, *Gulliver's Travels*, 1726). See also PEE, PUMP SHIP, URINATE/URINATION, and WATER SPORTS.

male. Homosexual, as in "Male movies," a marquee ad for films in which the female roles are played by males in drag. See also FEMALE and GAY.

mammary glands. Breasts; the reference to function almost invariably conceals a prurient interest in form. See also BOSOM and GLANDS.

man. (1) Servant or laborer, a euphemistic shortening of "manservant" or "hired man"; (2) boy, typically in such constructions as *bellman* and *houseman*; (3) God, as in, from a time when profanity was banned from the stage, "For the passion of man, hold" (Ben Jonson, *Tale of a Tub*, 1633). This method of avoiding the holy name appears in many combinations, e.g., *The Good Man, The Man Above, The (Big) Man Upstairs,* and *The Old Man.* Thus, football coach Weeb Eubank gave thanks for having had the good fortune to have Joe Namath as his quarterback, saying "The Man Upstairs was good to me" (WABC-TV, 1/23/78).

Of course, politically correct persons avoid "man" even as a euphemism. They shun the word completely, resorting to such substitutions as "faithful dog" for "man's best friend," "yeti" for "abominable snowman," and "the face in the moon" for you-know-what. See also ADONAI, GARÇON, GENTLEMAN, GOSH, SCOUTING/USA, and SERVANT.

man-root. The penis. "Hips, hip-sockets, hip-strength, inward and outward round, man-balls, man-root" (Walt Whitman, "I Sing the Body Electric," *Leaves of Grass*, 1860). Though associated most closely with Whitman, the construction also was employed by others, e.g., "I kept on frigging her with my man-root while restraining myself from coming" (Frank Harris, *My Life and Loves*, 1925). See also COME, FRIG, PENIS, and ROOT.

manure. The word originally meant "to work with the hands"; it stems from the Latin *manus,* hand, and is closely related to "maneuver." Today, of course, "manure" is one of the more common euphemisms for "shit," as in "What I liked about her, she didn't give you a lot of horse manure about what a great guy her father was" (J. D. Salinger, *The Catcher in the Rye*, 1951). See also HORSEFEATHERS.

People first began spreading manure in the sixteenth century; before that, going back to the thirteenth, they spread MUCK. See also DEFECATE/DEFECATION, FERTILIZER, HONEY, and NIGHT SOIL.

marble. Limestone, all dressed up. "The building trade uses the word 'marble' for many rocks that to a geologist are just plain old limestone, and the fancy name in the catalog may have no relation to the stone's origin: 'French gray marble' . . . is actually a limestone from northern Vermont" (*Natural History*, 9/78). Other names for *French gray marble* are *Champlain black* and *radio black.*

marital aid (or device). A vibrator or other gadget used in sexual activity. "Sex toys are known by many names: marital aids, dildos, adult novelties, etc. None of the 'trade names' are very descriptive" (ad for *The Spirit of Seventy Sex, Penthouse,* 1/77). See also CORDLESS MASSAGER and MASTURBATION.

market, go to. Slaughterhouse, go to the. From an account in the *Chicago Tribune* (2/19/92) on a campaign by the National Cattlemen's Association to project a kinder, gentler image of the beef business through copious use of euphemism: "Changes include replacing 'stockyard' with 'livestock market,' 'operation' with 'farm' or 'ranch,' 'operator' with 'cattleman' or 'cattle producer,' and 'facility' with 'barn.' Finally, never mention slaughtering cattle. Better to say 'process' or 'go to market'" (*Quarterly Review of Doublespeak,* 10/92). See also ABATTOIR and HARVEST.

marketing. Sales. "Marketing is a fashionable term. The sales manager becomes a marketing vice-president. But a gravedigger is still a gravedigger even when he is called a mortician—only the price of burial goes up" (Peter Drucker, in John J. Tarrant, *Drucker: The Man Who Invented the Corporate Society,* 1976). See also ENGINEER and MORTICIAN.

marry. An archaic exclamation of surprise, which started off as a euphemistic oath, this being short for "by the Virgin Mary." See also GEE and GOSH.

massage. To beat or to rough up; to wound or to kill; to provide a sexual service.

The first sense has been dated to the early 1930s, with most of the earliest examples in print referring to the strong arms of the law. "The thugs have been caught and massaged with rubber hoses in the back room of some

station house" (*American Mercury,* 2/37). The second sense was popularized during the Vietnam war, usually in the past tense, as in "The new guy was *massaged.*" For the third sense, refer to the next entry. See also HIT.

massage parlor. A brothel or HOUSE. The *massage parlor* that specializes in providing sexual SERVICES dates to before World War I: "Along with them go the announcements of 'massage parlors' (an all-too-obvious euphemism), free whiskies, and other agencies of public injury" (*Colliers,* 1/25/13). And Ernest Weekley, defining "stew" in 1921, had this to say: "The public hot-air baths acquired a reputation like that of our massage establishments some time ago" (*Etymological Dictionary of Modern English*).

Just as there are many different kinds of HOUSES, so the *massage parlor* has evolved into different forms. There are *nude encounter centers; rap clubs,* RAP PARLORS, and *rap studios; relaxation clubs* and *parlors; sensitivity meeting* (or *training*) *centers* that specialize in *accupressure* and *reflexology;* and *sex therapy clinics.* New York City used to have a well-stacked *library,* complete with "librarians to serve you," and Las Vegas, Nevada, has boasted *coed wrestling studios.*

Some massage parlors really provide massages and nothing else. This may result in customer complaints, as was the case in Las Vegas, possibly the only American city in which a massage parlor could be closed for *not* offering sex to customers: "After trying unsuccessfully with other legal tactics to close the two large massage parlors, the city got two linguistic experts to testify that the . . . parlors' graphic advertisements in tourist newspapers were explicitly promising sexual liaisons [see LIAISON] when, in fact, they were offering only massages" (*New York Times,* 10/4/76).

In an effort to help customers, telephone company *Yellow Pages* provide separate "Massage-Therapeutic" and "Massage" listings. The entries for "Massage-Therapeutic" in the Danbury, Conn., *Yellow Pages* for 1994–95 include chiropractors, licensed masseurs, and shiatsu centers. So far, so good. But what about the massages in the other category, which includes listings for Amber's Live Phone Mates, Bunny's Escort and Massage, Elegant Escorts (with "outcall massage" and "Discreet Credit Card Billing Welcome"), and the Roman Spa (with heart-shaped tubs)? Obviously, more research is needed.

See also ADULT, CLUB, PARLOR, and STUDIO.

master. An older athlete. The Amateur Athletic Union has a *masters* program. Swimmers, divers, and water polo players who are older than twenty-five are *masters*. Track-and-field athletes, aged thirty-five or more, are *masters*, except for distance runners, who become *masters* at forty. See also GRAND MASTER, CLASSIC, and MATURE.

masturbation. The currently dominant Latinate euphemism for what was politely described during most of the last three centuries as *onanism, self-abuse,* or *self-pollution.* "Don't knock masturbation. It's sex with someone I love" (Woody Allen in *Annie Hall*, film, 1977).

The origins of "masturbation" are obscure, etymologically. *The Oxford English Dictionary*'s earliest example of the word comes from Robert Burton's *The Anatomy of Melancholy* (1621), where it appears in the form of "mastrupation." This led Eric Partridge to suggest that the term derived from the Latin *mas*, semen, and *turbāre*, to agitate. This appears to be a false trail, however. The word probably comes from the French *masturbation* (used by Montaigne in 1570) and ultimately from the Latin *manus*, hand, plus *stuprāre*, to defile, with perhaps some influence from the aforementioned *turbāre*. The modern English spelling is dated in *The Oxford English Dictionary* only to 1766; the verb, "masturbate," doesn't appear until 1857. Both forms were popularized during the Victorian period. It seems likely, though, that noun and verb were bandied about in their present forms for many years prior to *The Oxford English Dictionary*'s earliest citations. Thus, Jonathan Swift opened *Gulliver's Travels* (1726) with references in quick succession to "Mr. James Bates," "my good master Mr. Bates," and "Mr. Bates, my master," leading to a pun—missed by generations of schoolchildren—on "master Bates."

The polite terms, such as *self-abuse* and *self-pollution,* that "masturbation" superseded are simultaneously pejorative and circumlocutory—that is, they reveal society's official attitude toward this "vice" without actually describing the action at hand. For example, *The Oxford English Dictionary* (vol. M. prepared 1904–08) defined "masturbation" as "The action or practice of self-abuse." This antique expression is still encountered occasionally, but just as a joke, e.g., "A bunch of the boys asked me to ask you about Major Houlihan. Is she better than self-abuse?" (Hawkeye to Major Burns, *M.A.S.H.*, film, 1970).

The first American dictionary to define the practice in a nonopaque manner, according to Noel Perrin's *Dr. Bowdler's Legacy* (1969), was *Webster's Unabridged*, of 1957, which managed the dull but relatively explicit "Production of an orgasm by excitation of the sexual organs as by manipulation or friction." Previously, *Webster's* definition had been "Onanism; self-pollution."

Of course, Onanism, a.k.a. the Sin of Onan, is something of a euphemism, too, being an eighteenth-century misreading of Genesis 38:9. Onan's sin was not masturbation, but early withdrawal as a means of birth control (*coitus interruptus* for those who prefer Latin): "And Onan knew that the seed should not be his; and it came to pass, when he went in unto his brother's wife, that he spilled *it* on the ground, lest that he should give seed to his brother." Victorians may have adopted the erroneous reading because they thought the biblical punishment so aptly fit the crime: The Lord slew poor Onan for the dreadful deed. (For a pre-Victorian rewrite of this passage, see PECULIAR MEMBERS.)

Slang abounds with more or less periphrastic synonyms for masturbation. "Jerk," recorded from the eighteenth century, is perhaps the most common. It appears in many combinations, e.g., *jerk off, jerk one's jelly, jerk one's juice,* and *jerk the gherkin.* (It follows from this that the PENIS is a *jerking iron.*) Some others of this type (both British and American, and many of them used by women as well as by men, though the terminology is essentially male): *beat the bishop* (or *beaver* or *dummy* or *meat), box the Jesuit, flog the bishop* (or *donkey* or *sausage), have a date with Polly palm and her four sisters, jack off, jill off, make love with Mother Thumb and her four daughters, mount a corporal and four, play with (oneself), pound the meat* (or *pork), pound (one's) pud*—possibly short for PUDENDUM, *pull (one's) pudding* (or *wire), spank the monkey, toss off, touch (oneself), wank off, waste time, whack off,* and *yank (one's) yam* (or *doodle*—it's a dandy!).

See also COITION, COME, CORDLESS MAS-SAGER, DIDDLE, DILDO, FRIG, OUTERCOURSE, SELF- (or MUTUAL) PLEASURING, SOLO (or SOLITARY) SEX, and TOUCH.

matinee. Sex in the afternoon. "The most sensible of all New York [City governmental] traditions was the setting aside of Monday and Thursday as Official Mistress Nights.... With the advent of Lindsay [Mayor John V., elected 1965] and the Reformers, the institution fell into disrepute, do-gooders preferring things like 'matinees'" (*New York Times,* 2/6/74). See also AFFAIR, ASSIGNATION, and FUNCH.

matrimonial lawyer. Divorce lawyer. "After Mrs. [Joy A.] Silverman's affair with Judge [Sol] Wachtler had begun to sour, she became involved with David Samson . . . a matrimonial lawyer from Rosedale, N.J." (caption, *New York Times,* 11/15/92). The association in the field is the American Academy of Matrimonial Lawyers. Collectively, lawyers of this stripe constitute the *matrimonial bar.* See also FAMILY LAWYER.

matron. Old woman. "The Five Fragrance Ages and Stages of Woman," according to the Fragrance Foundation, a trade association of perfume makers, are Preteen, Teen, Young Adult, Middle Age, and Matron. See also FRAGRANCE and GOLDEN AGE/YEARS.

mature. An exceedingly generalized term that blankets all ages from semiadult through old; an exception occurs in the case of advertisements for women's clothes, where a *mature* woman may be a "fat" woman. Usually, it is people who are characterized as *mature,* but there are exceptions, e.g., businesses and economies. In general, a *mature* corporation is a stagnant one; a *mature* economy is old and ailing. As for people: On the lower end of the age range, a movie or TV show for *mature* audiences is one that parents are supposed to treat as "discretionary viewing" because it includes partially unclad human bodies. On the upper end of the age scale are homes for *mature* people, which look mighty like old-age homes. And at the 1964–65 New York World's Fair, the Dynamic Maturity Pavilion had a garden and benches on which *mature* people (and others) could rest. See also ADULT; AGE, OF A CERTAIN; GOLDEN AGE/YEARS; MIDDLE AGE; and YOUNG.

meadowlands. A real estate developer's swamp. The Meadowlands Sports Complex in New Jersey is built on what used to be known as the Great New Jersey Swamp. See also GREENLAND.

meaningful dialogue. Conversation; occasionally the preliminary to a MEANINGFUL RELATIONSHIP. "The American vice is explanation. This is because there is so little conversation (known as 'meaningful dialogue' to the explainers) in the greatest country in the history of the greatest world in the Milky Way" (Gore Vidal, *New York Review of Books*, 2/9/78).

meaningful relationship. An illicit sexual relationship, longer than a one-night stand (a.k.a. *McQ*, or *Meaningful Quickie*) but frequently shorter than an AFFAIR. "I never could have a meaningful relationship with anyone who wore a polyester suit" ("Rockford Files," WNBC-TV, 1/5/79). "Meaningful" has to be one of the most overworked, least meaningful words of our time; here, it functions only as a signpost, calling attention to the sexual significance of RELATIONSHIP.

means. Wealth, riches, as in "Mr. Johnson is a man of means." See also MODEST and, for one of the many advantages of *means*, refer to MENTAL HOSPITAL.

median divider. Highway department doubletalk for the center strip of a highway, as in "Do not cross the median divider." See also IMPACT ATTENUATION DEVICE.

media specialist. A librarian. "The board rejected funding a media specialist (trained librarian) in the elementary schools" (Woodbury, Conn., *Voices*, 4/14/93). See also ENGINEER, INFORMATION SPECIALIST, and SPECIALIST.

medical center. A hospital—part of a sweeping change in nomenclature in the HEALTH business. See also EXECUTIVE.

medication. Medicine. "Bayer Aspirin has relieved more pains, aches, and flu than any other medication in history" (TV commercial, 2/10/78). "Our society, like our language, is in serious trouble when . . . nobody takes medicine but rather medication. Indian tribes soon will have medication men" (Edwin Newman, *Strictly Speaking*, 1974).

medium. One of the many labels that manufacturers use in preference to the hateful "small." "*Small* is disguised as . . . medium (the dental liquid Cue divides itself into *medium, large*, and *giant*) [sizes]" (*American Speech*, 4/42). On a more elevated plane, Tiffany advertised sterling silver Valentines in 1989. They came in two sizes: Large ($275) and Medium ($125). See also LARGE.

meeting. A duel or affair; also, somewhat more specifically but still euphemistically, a "private meeting." "A meeting took place . . . between Mr. O. Joynt and Mr. P. Mckim . . . when on the first fire, the latter was struck in the forehead" (*Annual Register*, 1812). The English euphemism imitates French practice, *rencontre* (meeting) also being used for duels across the Channel. See also AFFAIR.

megadeath. One million dead people; vintage Cold War talk. "'Fifty-five megadeaths' does not sound as bad as 55 million Americans dead" (Ralph E. Lapp, *Kill & Overkill*, 1962). "Megadeath" (and "megacorpse," a synonym that never caught the public's fancy) were spinoffs of "megaton" as in "India is reported to have exploded a five-megaton device." See also DEVICE.

member. The penis; a generalization (technically, any separable, nonthoracic part of the body qualifies as a "member"), whose true meaning usually can be determined by scrutinizing the context in which it appears. Consider Nell Gwynne's ministrations to His Majesty Charles II, as described in early 1674 by John Wilmot, second earl of Rochester, in a poem that Rochester handed to the king by mistake, thinking that he was giving him the satire on Signior DILDO:

> This you'd believe, had I but time to tell ye
> The pain it costs to poor laborious Nelly,
> Whilst she employs hands, fingers,
>   mouth, and thighs
> Eer she can raise the member she enjoys.

(Rochester fled from court when he realized his error, but Charles soon forgave this act of lese majesty.)

The euphemistic "member" is by no means obsolete, e.g., "Regard how I have willed my member: no base or material desire is connected with it, yet it resembles the so-called sexual erection" (Maxwell Kenton, a.k.a. Terry Southern, *Candy*, 1965). Somewhat confusingly, in the distant past, "member" also referred to the external sexual organs of women. Thus, Geoffrey Chaucer had both sexes in mind when he wrote, "Telle me also, to what conclusion/Were membres maad of generacion/ . . . Trusteth right wel, they were nat maad for noght" (*The Wife of Bath's Prologue*, ca. 1387–1400). Other archaic variants include *carnal member, male member, privy member, virile member,* and, in the poetic words of Robert Burns (1756–96), *dearest member.* For those who prefer to cloak their thoughts in Latin, there is always *membrum virile.* Of course, care must be taken not to mistake the penile member for Noah Webster's PECULIAR MEMBERS (the testicles) or the *unruly member* (the tongue, so called after the biblical passage: "The tongue is a little member . . . the tongue can no man tame; *it is* an unruly evil" (James 3:5–8). Finally, a chamber pot, or CHAMBER, used to be called a *member mug* (or *thunder mug,* from its resonance). See also PENIS.

memorial park. A burying place; a graveyard, cemetery, or mausoleum. The type specimen is in Glendale, California, where, in 1917, an old, run-down cemetery was reborn as Forest Lawn Memorial-Park. Other parts of the country have also been blessed with *memorial parks* and the closely related *memorial gardens,* e.g., two East Coast mausoleums, Rose Hills Memorial Park in Putnam County, New York, and "Italy's Pompeii inspired" Woodbridge Memorial Gardens, in Woodbridge, N.J. "Memorial" also takes some of the sting out of death in such allied constructions as *memorial association* (funeral society), *memorial bronze* (grave marker), *memorial chapel* (an undertaker; see CHAPEL), *memorial counselor* (cemetery plot salesman), and *memorial estate* (grave site). See also CEMETERY and ESTATE.

menstruation. Periodic bleeding from the uterus; a highly tabooed subject from ancient times to the almost-present. The Latin root of "menstruate" is *mēnsis,* meaning "month" (see MONTHLIES). The strength of the taboo against female bleeding is reflected by the number of euphemisms and circumlocutions for it. A compilation by Natalie F. Joffe (*Word,* vol. 4, 1948) contained nearly 100 such expressions, and others were included in an article by Lalia Phipps Boone (*American Speech,* 12/54). Most terms of this sort fall into six somewhat overlapping categories:

1. The idea of illness or inconvenience: *come sick, cramps, curse, curse of Eve, feeling that way, fall off the roof, female complaint* or *disorder, illness,* INDISPOSED/ INDISPOSITION, *off the sports list* (a typical excuse in girls' schools), *poorliness, problem days, sickness* ("And if a man shall lie with a woman having her sickness . . . and she hath uncovered the fountain of her blood, both of them shall be cut off from among their people," Leviticus 20:18), *stub one's toe* (see ANKLE, TO SPRAIN AN), *tummy ache, unwell, watertight.*
2. The color red: *bloody Mary, the English have landed* (a French expression, recalling traditional British military dress; Flaubert used a variant of this when advising his mistress, Louise Colet, in a letter of September 13, 1846, to try a "remedy to bring on the Redcoats"), *flag day, flagging, red devil, red light, the Red Sea's in, show.*
3. Periodicity: *bad time, calendar time, courses, flowers* (sometimes *monthly flowers,* from ca. 1400, based on the French *fleurs,* flowers, itself a corruption of the Old French *flueurs,* in turn from the Latin *fluor,* flowing), *full moon, monthly blues, Old Faithful,* PERIOD, *that time, that time of month, wrong time, wrong time of month.*
4. The idea of a visit ("visit" itself being an old code word, from 1653, *OED,* for menstruation): *Aunt Flo has come, Aunt Jody's come with her suitcase, the colonel's come to stay, entertaining the general, grandma's here from Red Creek, having a friend, little sister's here, the wife's friend* (of ambiguous meaning: Is the wife thankful for another month having gone by without her becoming pregnant or is she just thankful for a respite from conjugal duties?).
5. Sanitary measures: *covering the waterfront, having the rag on, in the saddle, in the sling, O.T.R.* (for *On The Rag*), *riding the white* (or *cotton*) *horse, rag time, wearing the rag, wearing the manhole cover.*
6. Sexual unavailability: *beno* (a contraction of "There'll be no fun"), *ice-boxed, out of this world, today I'm a lady, wallflower week.*

mental. Mad, insane (itself a euphemism for "mad"); a discreet condensation of "mentally deranged," or "mentally ill," as in, "I gather she was a little queer towards the end—a bit mental, I think you people call it" (Dorothy L. Sayers, *Unnatural Death,* 1927). "Mental" is merely one of the latest in a long string of euphemisms for "mad." As Eric Partridge pointed out: "Frequently, euphemism causes successive synonyms to be suspect, displeasing, indelicate, immoral, even blasphemous. . . .

An excellent example is afforded by *mad,* which became *crazy,* which became *insane,* which became *lunatic,* which became *mentally deranged,* which became *deranged* and, a little later and in slang, *mental"* (*Usage & Abusage*, 1973).

"Mental" also appears in various euphemistic combinations, such as *mental depression* or *mental fatigue* (which is another way of saying "depression"; see FATIGUE); *mental job,* which is slang for someone who is, or is suspected of being, mentally unwell; and *to go mental,* for becoming mentally disordered. A *nonmental,* by the laws of reverse psychology, is a sane person, as in, "The Secret Service continued today to press its investigation of what was described as a 'very serious, very large' conspiracy by 'nonmentals' to assassinate President Nixon during his visit to New Orleans yesterday" (*New York Times,* 8/22/73).

See also BALMY, NON COMPOS MENTIS, and TOUCH.

mental health consumer (or **recipient).** A mentally sick patient. "Stan Mack's September 2 strip about 'Crazyman' was in extremely bad taste. For thousands of recovering mental health consumers, it was not only an injustice but further victimized them by lowering their self-worth" (letter, New York City *Village Voice,* 9/23/86). See also HEALTH and MENTAL.

mental hospital. A present-day madhouse or insane asylum; variants include *mental health center, mental home,* and *mental institution.* "They pushed him into a Mental Home, And that is like the grave" (Rudyard Kipling, *Limits & Renewals*, 1932). "Modern madhouses are called 'mental hospitals.' If they cater to people of means (another euphemism for 'rich people') they are

called 'sanatoria,' 'rehabilitation centers,' or 'Esalen'" (Anatol Rapoport, *Semantics,* 1975). See also ASYLUM, INSTITUTE/INSTITUTION, REST HOUSE, SANATORIUM/SANITARIUM, and STATE HOSPITAL.

merde. Shit—in elegant, Anglophone society (to the French, *chierie* is a stronger term).

e. e. cummings's *The Enormous Room,* as originally published in 1922, contained the lament, "My father is dead! Shit. Oh, well. The war is over." However, the "shit" so offended John S. Summer, secretary of the New York Society for Suppression of Vice, that the publisher agreed to ink it out in every copy of the first printing. Five years later, in 1927, a second edition was released, in which cummings converted the entire passage into French: *"Mon père est mort! Merde! Eh bien! La guerre est finie."* And this time, Mr. Summer did not object, thereby demonstrating once again the enormous euphemistic power of French.

Note, too, that the step-father of the hero of Charles Dickens's autobiographical novel, *David Copperfield* (1849–50), is named Edward Murdstone.

See also CRAP, DRECK, and SHORT FRENCH EXPLETIVE, A.

mess. Excrement, usually that of a pet, e.g., from an inside-the-kennel account of a presidential dog-keeper: "The dogs constantly 'make messes.' And when they are not making messes, they 'water the tulips,' 'decorate the rug,' and 'leave a present'" (*New York Times Book Review,* 8/3/75 quoting from Traphes Bryant and Frances Spatz Leighton, *Dog Days at the White House*). See also DOG DIRT/DO/LITTER/WASTE.

message. Euphemistic shorthand for the clearer but crasser "commercial message," or advertisement, typically encountered in the form of: "We'll have more baseball and more interviews after these messages from your local station" (WNBC-TV, 7/29/78). A variant is the *message unit.* As Paul V. Higgins, senior vice-president of the Lieberman-Harrison advertising agency, has said: "I don't like to use the word 'commercial.' I prefer to call our spots 'message units'" (from *Saturday Review/Education*, 12/2/72). See also INTERMISSION and WORD FROM OUR SPONSOR, AND NOW A.

message board. A newfangled scoreboard in a baseball park. Candlestick Park, home of the San Francisco Giants, has a *message board.*

meteoric water. Rain. Thus, grappling with the language of geologists: "Meteoric water, with study, turned out to be rain. It ran downhill in consequent, subsequent, obsequent, resequent, and not a few insequent streams" (John McPhee, *Basin and Range*, 1981). See also PRECIPITATION.

meteorologist. A TV weather reporter, rarely one with any formal training in the subject. In the United Kingdom, the official weather department is called the Meteorological Office.

micturate/micturition. The commendably complete index of the underground classic, *My Secret Life* (anon., ca. 1890), translates the Latin succinctly: "Micturating frolics (See pissing)." One wonders if the Latin is always understood: "I saw this word for the first time 60 years ago in my Chicago high school swimming pool. The sign said 'DO NOT MICTURATE IN THE POOL'" (George Johnson, letter, 3/15/82). FAMILY newspa-

pers continue to rely upon the two-bit terminology, however. As Russell Baker pointed out in connection with the Supreme Court's 1978 ruling on FOUR-LETTER WORDS: "In the case of 'micturition,' 'defecation,' and 'incestuous male issue,' the use of Latin is commonly adopted to take people's minds off what is being said" (*New York Times*, 7/11/78). See also PEE and WATER SPORTS.

middle age. Post–middle age. On the authority of Burt Reynolds, the actor, then forty-four: "They call that middle age, but I don't know too many 88-year-olds" (*New York Times*, 7/24/80). See also MATURE.

middle class. White. "The underlying assumption has been all along that the [urban brownstone] renovation movement is a white thing—when you say middle-class, you mean white" (Brooklyn, N.Y., *Phoenix*, 7/15/76). See also ETHNIC and HARMONIOUS.

Middle Eastern dancing. Belly dancing. See also ABDOMEN.

military government. A junta in power.

military intelligence. "Military intelligence—a contradiction in terms" (Oswald Garrison Villard, lecture, ca. 1920, from Gen. Donald Armstrong, then a newly minted lieutenant, who was there). And to paraphrase someone or other: Military intelligence is to intelligence as military music is to music.

mincemeat. No meat here; the pie filling is made by chopping up apples, raisins, spices, and so on. See also CAPE COD TURKEY and WELSH RAREBIT.

mineral fiber. Asbestos. "We have found a company in Manhattan that still manufactures asbestos tiles, although these days, asbestos is often called 'mineral fiber'" (*Old-House Journal,* 12/80).

mininuke. A smallish nuclear bomb, with a throwaway name. "One risk of developing tactical nuclear weapons, especially those now euphemistically called 'mini-nukes,' is that they may create the illusion that a limited war can be fought" (*The Defense Monitor,* 2/75). See also DEVICE, LIMITED WAR, and TACTICAL NUCLEAR WEAPON.

minority. A traditional euphemism for African-Americans and/or Hispanics, but fading into at least temporary oblivion. "How far have minority journalists come since the sixties? White editors emphasize gains, but blacks and Hispanics complain of shell games and gestures" (subhead, *Columbia Journalism Review,* 3–4/79).

In the 1960s and 1970s, "minority" generally contrasted with ETHNIC, as noted by William Safire: "When a politician speaks of minority groups, he is mainly concerned with Negroes; when he speaks of ethnic groups, he is usually speaking of Jews, occasionally of Italian, German, or other national groups" (*Safire's Political Dictionary,* 1972). African-Americans began to oppose the label in the late 1970s because the blanket term enabled other groups— white women, veterans, homosexuals, American Indians, and Asians, among them—to compete for funds in government and corporate *minority* programs that had been designed with blacks in mind. At the same time, increasing ethnic pride has led different groups to seek recognition in their own right. Thus, reporting on a "diversity training" workshop for managers: "The word 'minorities' is out; instead use 'African-Americans,' 'Asian-Americans,' 'Pacific Islanders' or 'people of color.' Even 'yuppies' is verboten; the preferred term, it seems, is 'young adults.' But of course it's still OK to call white people 'white people'" (Max Boot, *Wall Street Journal,* 8/24/94). See also BLACK and PEOPLE OF COLOR.

misadventure. Mistake. The Military Assistance Command in Vietnam classified American deaths from American fire as *misadventures.* Physicians downplay the responsibility for malpractice in the same way when they refer to their mistakes as *therapeutic misadventures.* "A reader submits a form from the Health Department on which are listed the 'Misadventure in Diagnosis/Treatment Codes' and the 'Anesthesia Misadventures—Used Only When Reporting Files on Anesthesiologists.' Reading this form we discover that 02 is the code for 'Wrong Patient or Body Part,' 06 for 'Not Indicated or Contraindicated Treatment,' and 09 for 'Surgical Foreign Body Left in Patient After Procedure'" (*Quarterly Review of Doublespeak,* 10/86). See also FRIENDLY FIRE, IATROGENIC, and THERAPEUTIC ACCIDENT (or MISADVENTURE).

miscarriage. A spontaneous abortion. "Miscarriage" is preferred because "abortion," though perfectly correct, has overtones of the formerly illegal operation. Society's divided feelings on the issue of abortion are evidenced by the number of euphemisms that cluster around the topic. See also CRIMINAL (or ILLEGAL) OPERATION, PROCEDURE, PRO-CHOICE, and THEPAPEUTIC INTERRUPTION OF PREGNANCY.

misfit. "As the business [Moss Bros.] prospered, its stocks were augmented by 'misfits' (Saville Row suits ordered by customers who could not pay for them)" (*New York Times Magazine*, 7/12/81).

misspeak. To make a blooper; especially useful for taking back impolitic statements by politicians.

"Misspeak" was popularized during the Nixon years. "'The President,' [Ron] Ziegler said, 'misspoke himself.' He explained that the President . . . had another case in mind when assuming personal responsibility for Fitzgerald's being 'fired, or discharged, or asked to resign'" (*Harper's Magazine*, 6/73). But the tactic did not work in this instance. A. Ernest Fitzgerald, an air force cost analyst who lost his job after telling Congress about a $2 billion cost overrun by Lockheed on the C-5A supercargo plane, sued Mr. Nixon for wrongful dimissal. The public declaration of "misspeaking" was offset by a tape recording (1/31/73), in which the president was heard telling special COUNSEL Charles W. Colson: "I said get rid of that son of a bitch" —or, as *The New York Times* reported it, "'Get rid of that . . .' and here he called him a profane name" (8/14/81). Mr. Nixon eventually settled out of court, paying Mr. Fitzgerald $144,000.

See also CLARIFY, INOPERATIVE, and MIS-STATEMENT.

misstatement. A lie. "It is almost imposssible to lie at all in Washington. There are only 'misstatements.' This was the euphemism evolved by the White House during the Watergate years when spokesmen were caught in 'untruths'" (Leslie H. Gelb, *New York Times*, 3/7/85). See also ERRONEOUS REPORT and MISSPEAK.

Miss White. The toilet. Speaking of Cissy Caffrey: "When she wanted to go where you know she said she wanted to run and pay a visit to Miss White" (James Joyce, *Ulysses*, 1922). The color of the object also figures in many quaint expressions—popularized at institutions of higher learning—for the act of vomiting, such as *drive the big white* (or *porcelain*) *bus, talk to Ralph on the big white phone,* and *worship the porcelain goddess.* See also TOILET and UPCHUCK.

mistress. A kept woman; one who takes the place of a wife (though usually spared the workaday tasks of housewifery). "His Protestant mistresses gave less scandal than his Popish wife" (Thomas Babington Macauley, biography of William Pitt, *Encyclopædia Britannica*, 1859).

"Mistress," like MADAM, has come a long way down the social scale. While applied to concubines from an early date (1430–40, *OED*), the word's primary meanings revolve around the senses of a woman who has authority over servants, children, a household, a territory, or a state. (For a modern example of an authoritarian mistress, see ENGLISH GUIDANCE.) The title derives from the feminine form of the Old French *maistre,* master, in turn from the Latin *magister,* with the same meaning. Curiously, the contraction, "miss," managed to escape the sexual taint that became attached to "mistress," though this title, too, once was applied to women of questionable reputation, e.g., "She being taken to the Earle of Oxford's Misse, as at this time they began to call lewd women" (John Evelyn, *Diary*, 6/9/1662). See also KEPT, NATURAL, and PROSTITUTE.

mix (or **mixed breed**). A pedigreed euphemism for "mongrel." "For adoption

. . . black and tan Shepherd Doberman mix, female tricolor Beagle mix" (Canine Control ad, Woodbury, Conn., *Voices,* 3/13/91). "At the ASPCA, the dogs we love most are the mixed breed dogs" ("Romper Room," WOR-TV, N.Y., 2/2/78). See also BASTARD.

mixologist. A bartender. "Local tavern owners and permittees said their businesses are also cheaper to run because . . . they do not require highly trained mixologists to tend bar" (*Litchfield County,* Conn., *Times,* 8/31/84). See also BEVERAGE HOST.

mobile home. A trailer. "Mobile homes have of course an unhappy history to live down, and the industry would like to bury its past in new nomenclature. Hence, the euphemism 'mobile home' itself, instead of the old 'trailer'" (*New York Times,* 7/4/76). Of course, trailers often are more or less permanently parked, in which case "mobile" really is just doubletalk for "immobile." A group of immobile *mobile homes* may be billed as a *mobile estate.* See also HOME.

model. Alas for the reputation of legitimate models, this is also a euphemism for "whore." In England, some shopwindows are crowded with notes from *models,* advising the public of their availability, while in the United States, more or less amateur models may advertise themselves in such publications as *Ace* (undated, ca. 1976):

ATLANTA NUDE MODEL DISCREET UNINHIBITED . . . looking for sgl swinging studs that know how to turn me on and make me do my thing. 38-22-34.

See also PROSTITUTE and SWINGING.

modest. Poor; typically encountered in such phrases as *modest means, modest accomplishments,* and *modest record,* e.g., "He has a modest record for having served so long in the Senate." See also MEANS.

molest. The American term for sexual assaults, comparable to the British INTERFERE WITH, often used in the past as a euphemism for "rape." The taboo against printing "rape" has eased considerably since World War II, with the result that "molest" is used more accurately, as well as less often, than formerly. An exception, harking back to past practice came in the case of a girl who had been killed by numerous stab wounds and whose body had been partly burned: "The state police and the medical examiner declined to say whether the victim had been molested" (*New York Times,* 7/30/79).

Probably, "molest" should be relegated entirely to historical fiction, where cardboard characters do not bleed:

Shanna's eyes narrowed as she gritted, "You vulgar beggar, they should hang you for a molester of women!" His eyes gleamed like hard brittle amber, and his quip jarred her. "Madam, I believe that's what they intend." (Kathleen E. Woodiwiss, *Shanna,* 1977)

See also ASSAULT, CANOLA, and LECHERY.

monarch of the jungle. In politically correct schoolrooms, the lion, erstwhile "king" of the jungle. Out on the playground, children who have been educated in this manner play "someone on top of the hill," not "king of the hill." See also PERSON.

monitor. To eavesdrop, to spy; a practitioner of such activities. *Monitoring* may be accomplished by overhearing (with a wiretap or hidden microphone) or by overlooking (as through a one-way mirror). Electronic eavesdroppers may have very large ears. Thus, a House subcommittee learned in 1975 that American Telephone and Telegraph Co. routinely *monitored* phone conversations of its one million employees. In addition, Ma Bell conducted an outreach program in 1965–70, *monitoring* some 30 million calls of ordinary folks, and making tape recordings of all or portions of more than 1.5 million of them. On a more personal level, signs at Bloomingdale's department store in New York City in 1994 notified customers that "These dressing rooms are monitored by an inventory control checker." That inventory control checker, by the way, was checking for what is known in the trade as inventory SHRINKAGE. See also INFORMANT, PARTICIPANT MONITORING, SURVEILLANCE, TATTLING, and TECHNICAL SURVEILLANCE.

monkey-business. Sexual activity; the uninhibited conduct of monkeys gives a special spin to the general term for deceitful or mischievous behavior. "Harold Ross [founding editor of the *New Yorker*] had two favorite apothegms: 'No monkey-business with the girls in the office' . . . and 'Any editor worth a damn has to take a vow of anonymity'" (Gardner Botsford, *New Yorker*, 1/28/93–1/4/94). See also HANKY-PANKY.

monosavant. Idiot savant, i.e., a COGNITIVELY CHALLENGED person who nevertheless can perform prodigious feats in a particular area—calculating large numbers mentally, for example. See also EXCEPTIONAL.

monosyllable. For most of the eighteenth and nineteenth centuries, this was the most common slang euphemism for one of the most dreaded of the FOUR-LETTER WORDS, i.e., cunt. "Mrs. *Jewkes* took a glass and drank [a toast to] the dear monosyllable. I don't understand that word, but I believe it is baudy" (Henry Fielding, *Shamela*, 1761).

The earliest example of the euphemism in *Slang and Its Analogues* (J. S. Farmer and W. E. Henley, 1890–1904) is from a work of 1714, with which Mr. Fielding seems to have been acquainted: "perhaps a bawdy monosyllable, such as boys write upon walls" (Theophilus Lucas, *The Memoirs of Gamesters and Sharpers*). The first person to include the euphemistic "monosyllable" in a dictionary, according to Eric Partridge (*A Dictionary of Slang and Unconventional English*, 1970) was Capt. Francis Grose, who defined the term as "A woman's commodity," in the 1788 edition of *A Classical Dictionary of the Vulgar Tongue*.

In conversation, "monosyllable" ordinarily was prefaced by the article "the," which resulted in a second-order euphemism. Thus, Jon Bee noted that "of all the thousand monosyllables in our language, this *one* only is designated by the definite article; therefore do some men call it 'the article,' 'my article,' and 'her article,' as the case may be" (*Slang: A Dictionary of the Turf*, etc., 1823). Bee, by the way, was a pseudonym; his real name was John Badcock—making him a formidable rival to Grose for the honor of being the Most Aptly Named Authority on Bad Talk.

Though now obsolete in its classical, anatomical sense, "monosyllable" still crops up every once in awhile as a synonym for "four-letter word." For example, Bernard De Voto noted in a discussion of some of Mark Twain's uncensored language that "the taboo of these monosyllables remained almost though not quite absolute until 1930, when it began to relax" (*Harper's Magazine*, 12/48). See also VAGINA.

Montezuma's revenge. Diarrhea and/or dysentery; the chief Mexican version of worldwide illnesses, which almost always are called by exotic names. "The North American in Mexico has coined a number of names for the inevitable dysentery and diarrhea: 'Mexican two-step,' 'Mexican foxtrot,' 'Mexican toothache,' and less directly if more colorfully, 'Montezuma's revenge,' 'the Curse of Montezuma,' and the 'Aztec hop'" (*Western Folklore*, XXI, 1962). In other parts of the world, the same gastrointestinal complaints appear as the *Aden Gut, Basra Belly, Cairo Crud* (see CRUD), *Delhi Belly, Gyppy* (i.e., Egypt) *Tummy, Ho Chi Minh's Curse, Hong Kong Dog, Mexicali Revenge, Rangoon Runs, Saigon Quickstep, turista* (in Mexico), and *touriste* (in French Canada). Soldiers everywhere have suffered from the *GI's.*

N.B.: *Montezuma's revenge* and friends are not restricted to the poorer, "dirtier" parts of the world. In most cases, the illness probably is just the result of new microbes, or species and strains thereof, being introduced into the traveler's intestines. For this reason, visitors to the "clean" old U.S.A. have been afflicted by the *Bronxville* (New York) *Bomb,* the *L.A.* (California) *Belly,* and similar, not-so-exotic complaints. See also INDISPOSED/INDISPOSITION, and STOMACHACHE.

monthlies. An oblique reference to the cycle (or PERIOD) of menstruation. "That squinty one is delicate. Near her monthlies, I expect, makes them ticklish" (James Joyce, *Ulysses,* 1922). See also MENSTRUATION.

moon child. A person born under the sign of Cancer, and believed by astrologers to be strongly influenced by the moon. In Latin, "cancer" means "crab," the disease getting its name, according to Galen, from the crablike appearance of swollen veins around a tumor. Some modern astrologers prefer not to name the crablike constellation, however, and so emphasize the secondary characteristic. In this way, Cancereans become "moon children." See also C, THE BIG.

moonlight (or midnight) requisition. Theft in the military, typically among supply sergeants, who sometimes have to go outside official channels to obtain supplies, whether for their units or sometimes, as rumor has it, for their personal benefit. See also APPROPRIATE.

Morals Division. "Immorals Division" would be more accurate, this being the modern police department name for what used to be called the "Vice Squad."

moral victory. A defeat.

mortality experience. Death. "A physician interviewed on public radio station WHYY in Philadelphia said, 'We never use the word "death." We tell a patient that you're about to have a mortality experience'" (*Quarterly Review of Doublespeak,* 4/92). See also EXPERIENCE and EXPIRE.

mortality rate. Death rate; the "mortal" derives ultimately from the Latin *mors,* death, but does not sound nearly as harsh to Anglo-Saxon ears. See also LIFE INSURANCE and PASS AWAY.

mortician. Undertaker. Modeled after "physician," this represents one of the bolder attempts by people in the death business to trade on the prestige of the medical profession. "Mortician" was formally proposed in the February 1895 issue of *Embalmer's Monthly,* and was received enthusiastically by those sensitive souls who did not think "funeral director," the reigning alternative to "undertaker," to be sufficiently high-toned. Thus, a mere six months later, the *Columbus,* Ohio, *Dispatch* carried a notice (8/14/95): "We, Mank & Webb, are the only Morticians in the city who do not belong to the Funeral Director's Protective Association." Columbus also was site of the founding of the National Selected Morticians (9/17/17), an exclusive trade group that is still alive and kicking, thank you. On the whole, though, "mortician" is showing a lack of staying power. This may be partly because the prefix "mort," from the Latin *mors,* death, is a shade too explicit. (MORTUARY also has faded, probably for the same reason.) "Mortician" also lost a lot of professional sheen on account of all the imitations it inspired. Of these, BEAUTICIAN and COSMETICIAN/COSMETOLOGIST have lasted the longest, and probably hurt the most; others, dating from the 1920s and 1930s, included *bootblackitician, fizzician* (soda jerk), *locktician* (locksmith), *shoetrician* (cobbler), and *whooptician* (cheerleader). Whatever the exact cause, the effect is beyond dispute. The Yellow Pages' directories include "mortician," but only as a cross-reference to that old standby, FUNERAL DIRECTOR.

mortuary. A deadhouse—and a relatively newfangled one at that, with the oldest example in *The Oxford English Dictionary,* in the sense of a temporary abode for the dead, coming from 1865. Previously, a "mortuary" had been (1) a payment or gift from the estate of the dead person to the parish priest; (2) a funeral; or (3) an OBITUARY.

Mortuaries come in various sizes. Thus, there are *mortuary chapels* as well as more intimate *mortuary coolers,* such as the "2-3-Mini-Walk-In" *mortuary cooler* and the "5-7-Junior-Walk-In with Add-on Capability," advertised by Bally Case & Cooler, Inc. (*Casket & Sunnyside,* 1/80). Not that there isn't good precedent for such fancy terminology. The ancient Egyptians, whose accomplishments in this particular field have rarely been equaled, let alone surpassed, called the workshop in which their embalming was done *the beautiful house.* See also CASKET, CHAPEL, and FUNERAL HOME/PARLOR.

motel. It sounds a lot posher than "auto camp," which is what "motels" started out as. It took awhile for auto camp entrepreneurs to find a suitably elegant name for themselves, but they persisted, developing ever fancier ones, e.g., *auto court, tourist court, cottage court, motor court, motor lodge,* and *motor hotel,* until 1925, when Milestone Interstate Corp. announced a plan to build a chain of "motels" between San Diego and Seattle. Other West Coast condensations that never quite made it included *autotel* and *autel.* Meanwhile, an anchorage for boats may be known as a *boatel.*

Motels have always had a somewhat risqué reputation. Perhaps this is because of the subliminal realization that "motel" spelled backwards sounds like "lettum." But there may be more to it than that; see also ASSIGNATION and FUNCH.

mother. Euphemistic shorthand for "motherfucker," which not only has taken over the position once held by "fuck" as the most obscene of the standard obscenities, but has replaced The Great American Epithet, "son of a bitch," in most of its many applications. See also F – – – and SOB.

"Motherfucker" began as black slang and was introduced to the rest of society during World War II and the immediate postwar years, thanks largely to the leveling influence of the United States Army. As the power of "fuck" was diminished through overuse, "motherfucker" naturally came to the fore—and along with it came the requisite set of euphemisms. Thus, Gen. Alexander Haig, Jr., told White House aide John Scali in December 1972: "This man [President Nixon] is going to stand tall and resume the bombing and put those B-52 mothers in there and show'em we mean business" (from Bob Woodward and Carl Bernstein, *The Final Days*, 1976). Other euphemistic synonyms of "mother" include *mammy-jammer, mommy-hopper, mother-dangler, mother-feryer, mother-flunker, mother-grabber, mother-hugger, mother-humper, mother-jumper, mother-lover, mother-raper,* and *mother-rucker*; the slurred *mo'-fo'* and *muh-fuh*; the personified *Marilyn Farmer, Marshall Field,* and *Mister Franklin*; the fancy permutation, *triple-clutcher,* popularized during the Korean POLICE ACTION by black truck drivers in construction battalions; and such abbreviations as *HMFIC* (sometimes further euphemized as Head Military Figure In Charge), *MF, BMF* (a particularly Bad one), and *RA* (or *RE*) *MF* (in the military, a Rear-Area or Rear-Echelon *MF*). See also SNAFU.

Popularity of the euphemistic "mother" gave an extra dimension to the "mother-of-all-" construction, which proliferated in many forms following Saddam Hussein's prediction in 1990 that opposition to his conquest and annexation of Kuwait would result in the "mother of all battles." A few of the many cited in *American Speech* (Winter 1991 and Spring 1992): *mother of all briefings* (Gen. Norman Schwarzkopf's televised briefing at the end of the 1990–91 Gulf war), *mother of all devaluations* (a currency devaluation in Nicaragua), *mother of all dog battles* (a corgi fight in which the owner, Queen Elizabeth, was bitten on the hand), *mother of all report cards* (a bad one), *mother of all theories* (Einstein's unified field theory), *mother of all clichés* (the expression "mother of all battles"), and *father of the mother of all clichés* (Saddam Hussein).

P.S. "Saddam" pronounced backwards is "mad ass."

motion discomfort. Motion sickness. "I was sitting at the edge of my seat . . . pondering airline euphemisms—the bag labeled 'for motion discomfort,' the card telling me what to do in the event of 'a water landing,' the instructions for using oxygen masks 'should the occasion arise'" (*Saturday Review*, 3/4/72). Another term for that "container," sometimes known as a *comfort container,* is "barf bag." See also DISCOMFORT, ILL/ILLNESS, STOMACHACHE, UPCHUCK, and WATER LANDING.

motorized transportation module. A school bus; educationese, with a FOP Index of 4.1. See also ENTRENCHING TOOL and VERTICAL TRANSPORTATION CORPS.

mouchoir. A nosewipe; see HANDKERCHIEF.

mouth music. Commenting on the language in *The New Joy of Sex* by Alex Comfort: "What a lawyer would call fellatio or cunnilingus is 'mouth music' or a 'genital kiss'" (*New York City's Literary Supplement,*

2/11/93). Music and sex seem to go together naturally, of course, and the penis often is regarded as an instrument to be performed upon in such fellatory phrases as *play the skin flute* (or *the one-holed* or *living* or *silent flute*), *play the piccolo,* and *to play the bagpipe.* (The latter, dating from the eighteenth century, was described only as "a lascivious practice; too indecent for explanation" in *Slang and Its Analogues,* 1890, by J. S. Farmer and W. E. Henley, who did not normally wear blinkers.) See also BLOW, CUNNILINGUS, FELLATIO, and SWINGING.

muck. Most commonly encountered today in the compound "muckraking," "muck" is just an old form of MANURE, itself a euphemism for "shit." As Francis Bacon put it, when explaining why it was not good policy to allow "the Treasure and Moneyes" of a nation to be gathered into a few hands: "For otherwise, a State may haue a great Stock, and yet starue. And Money is like Muck, not good except it be spread" ("Of Seditions and Troubles," *Essays,* 1625).

The journalistic "muckraking" was popularized in 1906 by President Theodore Roosevelt, who drew the metaphor from John Bunyan's *The Pilgrim's Progress* (1684). Bunyan's figure of a man working so busily with a muck rake that he never looked up to see the celestial crown being offered to him stood for the man of the world whose heart had been carried away from God by absorption with earthly things. In TR's version, "the men with the muck rakes" were the antibusiness crusaders who were "often indispensable to the well being of society; but only if they know when to stop raking the muck, and to look upward to the celestial crown above them, to the . . . beautiful things above and round about them"

(speech, 4/14/06). Even though it hadn't been intended entirely as a compliment, Lincoln Steffens and other *muckrakers* were glad to accept the label. For another TR-ism, see VOLUNTARY.

MUF. A wonderfully euphemistic acronym, given the connotations of its sound-alike, "muff," this by-product of the atomic energy business stands for "Materials Unaccounted For." The "materials" in question are *special nuclear materials,* i.e., uranium and plutonium that have been enriched sufficiently for the making of a bomb (a.k.a. DEVICE). Processing operations inevitably result in some *MUF,* but it is also possible that thieves have been at work in the United States as well as in Russia. The United States has admitted to losing thousands of pounds of highly enriched uranium and plutonium over the years— enough for producing quite a few bombs; see SIGNIFICANT QUANTITY.

multicultural. The progression at Central Connecticut State University has been from Education of the Culturally Disadvantaged to Education of the Culturally Different to Multicultural Education (Charlotte Koskoff, personal communication, 1984).

mute. Birdshit or the act of producing it. Thus, describing a critical moment in the famous Battle of the Cowshed: "All the pigeons, to the number of thirty-five, flew to and fro over the men's heads and muted upon them from mid-air" (George Orwell, *Animal Farm,* 1945). The term, which has puzzled generations of high-school and college students, is an old one, used especially by fanciers of hawks since at least the 1400s. Orwell had wanted to say that the pigeons dropped dung on the men, but his publisher would not permit this. Hence, the "muted." See also DEFECATE/DEFECATION.

mutilate. To castrate; the general term for the loss of a limb or other organ may serve as a code word for the removal of a very particular organ. "The lively, supple Greek/And Swarthy Nubia's mutilated son" (George Gordon, Lord Byron, *Childe Harold's Pilgrimage*, 1812). See also BILATERAL ORCHIDECTOMY.

N

native. Nonwhite, usually but not necessarily BLACK. "The [Memphis, Tenn.] *Commercial Appeal*'s history of excesses reads like journalistic folklore. Under former editor Frank Ahlgren, no citizen could ever be referred to as a native of Arkansas. Natives were Africans" (*[MORE]*, 5/74). The *Commercial Appeal* was imitating traditional practice in South Africa and other portions of the former British Empire. The essentially nonwhite meaning of "native" is evident from the qualified "Pale Native," a new, postapartheid term for white inhabitants of South Africa. It also is implicit in such expressions as *to go native, the natives are restless*, and *Native American,* which has largely displaced "American Indian." (In another context, "Native American" constitutes a historic exception to the color code; the Native American Party, which tried to keep immigrant Roman Catholics from obtaining political power in the 1840s and 1850s, was composed of whites. Party members were called Know-Nothings because they were supposed to say "I know nothing" when asked about their activities.)

Inevitably, the association of "native" with darker, conquered peoples, has inspired some attempts to replace it. For example, Peace Corps terminology refers to *host country nationals,* not *natives,* and the city council people in Berkeley, California, a hotbed of political correctness, officially changed the name of Columbus Day in 1992 to *Indigenous* (not *Native*) *Americans Day.* See also DARKY.

natural. A remarkably elastic word, "natural" has enjoyed a number of euphemistic meanings over the years, standing for, among other things: (1) an illegitimate child, a so-called *natural child* or LOVE CHILD, as in "*Vanity Fair* referred to Mayakovsky's having had an illegitimate daughter with a Russian-American woman. 'I was incensed by that,' she said. 'I am his natural or biological daughter'" (*New York Times,* 3/17/92); (2) the sexual organs, as a shorthand reference to the *natural parts* and *natural places,* or GENITALS, as in "Any female . . . with the desire of fulfilling the functions of her natural"; (James Joyce, *Ulysses,* 1922); (3) a SPECIAL person, as in "She is not quite a natural, that is, not an absolute idiot" (Frances Burney, *The Early Diary,* 1777); (4) a whore or MISTRESS, as in "You . . . took a pretty woman, a gentleman's natural away by force" (Thomas Shadwell, *The Squire of Alsatia,* 1688); and (5) the not necessarily natural, especially in the food business today, where "all natural" or "natural" on a package of cereal, say, has no legal or nutritional meaning: "Many health-food products are labeled 'natural.' Though the word sounds healthy, it means nothing. A product can be labeled 'natural' and still contain additives and have no organic ingredients" (*New York Times,* 2/24/93).

near miss. Near hit or collision, as of airplanes. "Reagan's Helicopter in Near Miss/Pilot of Small Plane Is Apprehended" (headline, *Boston Globe,* 8/14/87). The "miss" helps divert attention from the disaster that might have been, but even the Federal Aviation Adminsitration agrees that it is not correct. "Near misses" of the sort involving President Reagan are classified by the FAA as "near midair collisions." See also WATER LANDING.

necessary. A privy—occasionally a rather elaborate affair, judging from *The Connois-*

seur (no. 120, 1756): "The Connoisseurs in Architecture, who build . . . necessaries according to Palladio." Before the advent of indoor plumbing, there were also *necessary houses,* as well as *necessary places, stools,* and *vaults,* e.g., from 1780: "In my Botanical Garden, next the Necessary House, was sown 3 rows of Grass-seeds" (George Washington, *Diaries . . . 1748–1799,* 1925). See also PRIVY.

neck. To engage in amorous play. Giraffes can neck; humans do so only euphemistically. "In general . . . petting that is confined to lip kissing and mild embracing is referred to as necking" (Robert A. Harper, "Petting," *Aspects of Sexuality,* Albert Ellis and Albert Abarbanel, eds., 1967). "Whoever named it necking was a poor judge of anatomy" (Groucho Marx in *Leo Rosten's Carnival of Wit,* 1994).

"Neck," "necker," and "necking" were still relatively new terms in 1927 when Damon Runyon noted in his report on the celebrated separation suit between Edward W. "Daddy" Browning, New York real estate operator who admitted to age fifty-one, and his wife, Peaches (*née* Frances Belle Heenan), age fifteen: "It seems that she made record [in her diary] of the little episodes of her girlhood such as casual 'neckings' with the flaming youth of her acquaintance. When your correspondent was a 'necker' of no mean standing back in the dim and misty past, they called it 'lally-gagging.' Times have changed" (*American Speech,* 2/62).

The origin of the expression "to neck" is shrouded in appropriate darkness. It may well be an abbreviation of "neck-sawing," an old rural term for this courting custom. Most authorities date the euphemistic sense to about 1910 and say that it became common around 1920, which fits well with

Runyon's testimony. The euphemism seems to have had a previous incarnation in English dialect, however. The 1976 supplement to *The Oxford English Dictionary* gives citations going back to 1825 for "neck" in the sense of "to clasp (a member of the opposite sex) round the neck; to fondle," and some of these suggest that there was more fondling than clasping, e.g., "I'm muckle mist'en [much mistaken] if I haena seen him neckin' wi' the said Betty" (J. Service, *Thir Notandums,* 1890). See also MAKE OUT, OUTERCOURSE, PARK, and PET.

Still earlier, going back to ca. 1600, "neck" was employed as a noun in place of "breasts." Thus, in Hamlet's confrontation with his mother at the end of act three, the prince refers to the king's "paddling your neck with his damned fingers." Here, "paddling" means "caressing," the palm of the hand being compared to the blade of a long-handled, spadelike instrument. As for the rest of the metaphor, as Joseph Addison delicately explained: "When we say a woman has a handsome neck we reckon into it many of the adjacent parts" (*Guardian,* 7/6/1713). This is the kind of "neck" (technically, an anatomical displacement, as is "pain in the neck") that Col. Arthur Wesley, the future Duke of Wellington, admired when he stopped en route to India in 1796 at Capetown and paid court to a Henrietta Smith, who had a "pretty little figure and a lovely neck" (*Memoirs of George Elers, 1777–1842,* 1903, in Elizabeth Longford, *Wellington: The Years of the Sword,* 1969). Thus, the euphemistic meaning of the noun almost certainly was still current at the time of the term's earliest recorded appearance as an amorous verb, and it would not be at all surprising if the one sense did not somehow contribute to the other. See also BOSOM.

necktie party (or **sociable).** A hanging, usually but not necessarily a lynching. "Mr. Jim Clemenston, equine abductor, was . . . made the victim of a necktie sociable" (*Harper's Magazine,* 11/1871). This is only one of a great many euphemisms for hanging that flourished in nineteenth-century America, indicating the way justice was dispensed in the Wild West. Among them: *cause to die of hempen fever, dance, dance on a rope, die in a horse's nightcap* (i.e., a halter), *do a dance in mid-air, exalt, decorate a cottonwood tree, go up a tree, have throat trouble, hoist, jerk to Jesus, give a necking, kick the clouds* (or *air* or *wind*), *legally lasso, neck, put on the hempen collar* (or *cravat, necktie, necklace,* etc.), *put in a state of suspense, run up, stretch, string up,* and *swing.* (The foregoing all class as gallows humor.)

Some of these terms are of considerable antiquity. Capt. Francis Grose included *hempen fever* in the 1796 edition of *A Classical Dictionary of the Vulgar Tongue* and other writers referred to *hempen circles, collars, cravats, snares,* and so on, all meaning the hangman's noose, going back to the early fifteenth century. "Stretch" dates to the sixteenth century in the sense of hanging (and to the thirteenth in the sense of torturing people by stretching them on the rack). Yet another older term, popular from the sixteenth through the nineteenth centuries, when hangings were public entertainment, was *turn off,* originally and in full, *to turn off the ladder,* meaning the ladder to the hangman's platform.

Similar roundabouts have been used for official executions in the twentieth century. Speaking of the death chamber at the Kansas State Penitentiary for Men: "When a man is brought here to be hanged, the prisoners say he has 'gone to The Corner,' or, alternately, 'paid a visit to the warehouse' [referring to the storage room where the gallows was kept]" (Truman Capote, *In Cold Blood,* 1965). See also CAPITAL PUNISHMENT.

needs assessment. A test. "Teachers rarely test students these days. Instead they 'implement an evaluation program,' 'conduct a needs assessessment' (or, better yet, 'implement a needs assessment strategy'), or prepare an 'analysis of readiness skills' using an 'evaluation tool (or instrument)'" (William Lutz, *Doublespeak,* 1989). See also ASSESSMENT, DEFICIENCY, and INSTRUMENT.

needs some work (or **some work needed).** In the realm of real estate, a light reference to a major renovation. See also HANDYMAN'S SPECIAL.

negative. No, with a FOP Index of 5.0. In the military, the use of "negative" has been developed into a form of high art. For example, from J. Irving's *Royal Navalese* (1946): "Orders for a Church Parade 'Dress for Officers No. 3 negative swords.'" See also AFFIRMATIVE.

"Negative" also has been used to soften many of the rough edges in civilian life, as in the following constructions:

negative advancement. Demotion, as applied to employees.
negative campaigning. Attack campaigning; see COMPARATIVE CAMPAIGNING.
negative cash-flow position. Running in the red; a loss.
negative earnings. Another loss; sometimes caused by a NONPERFORMING ASSET.
negative economic growth, period of. Hard times; a RECESSION.
negative equity. No equity, as in the case of real estate whose value has declined to less than the outstanding mortgage amount.

negative impact on profits. Still another way of down-pedaling a loss.

negative net absorption of office space. Increased office vacancy, the result of more businesses moving out than moving in.

negative net worth. A deficit; a *substantial negative net worth* may be the prelude to bankruptcy.

negative patient outcome. Death in a hospital; see also EXPIRE.

negative reinforcement. A painful experience or punishment, such as an electrical shock administered by a behavioral psychologist; see also AVERSION THERAPY.

negative tax expenditures. Elimination of tax deductions in order to increase receipts; see also REVENUE ENHANCEMENT.

It follows from all of this that "negative" really means "positive" when applied to a minus quantity, e.g., a *negative deficit,* which is a profit at a technically nonprofit institution.

negligee. A shroud. "Florence Gowns Inc. of Cleveland, Ohio, exhibited their line of 'street-wear type garments and negligees' together with something new, a line of 'hostess gowns and brunch coats,' at a recent convention of the National Funeral Directors Association" (Jessica Mitford, *The American Way of Death,* 1963). See also FUNERAL DIRECTOR and FUNERAL HOME/PARLOR.

Negro. A word that has had wildly different connotations over the past several centuries, depending on time, place, and circumstance, serving sometimes as a euphemism for "nigger" (often rendered in print as "N – – – – –" or "n – – – – r") and sometimes as a dysphemism for "black." As a euphemism: In *A Dictionary of American-*

isms (1951), a quote from *The Life of Col. David Crockett, Written by Himself* (1836) is rendered as "Negro women are knocked down by the auctioneer and knocked up by the purchaser," where the redoubtable Davy originally wrote "Nigger women," etc. As for "Negro" as a dysphemism: "Long after black Americans had indicated their preference for being called 'blacks,' for example, the *Globe* [*Democrat,* of St. Louis] insisted on calling them 'Negroes,' and Muhammed Ali was Cassius Clay in the *Globe* probably longer than any place else" (*[MORE],* 5/74). African-Americans also have used "Negro" in a disparaging manner, e.g., the New York lawyers, Alton H. Maddox, Jr., and C. Vernon Mason, who "have alienated black elected officials and civic leaders by calling them 'Uncle Tom' or —their ultimate insult—'Negro'" (*New York Times,* 6/9/88).

"Negro" has an unusual history, having twice swung in and out of fashion. In the eighteenth century, "Negro" was a common euphemism for "slave," as evidenced by Capt. Francis Grose's definition: "NEGRO. A black-a-moor: figuratively used for slave. I'll be no man's negro; I will be no man's slave" (*A Classical Dictionary of the Vulgar Tongue,* 1796). Even slave-owners showed some reluctance (guilt?) about speaking openly of the condition of the victims of their PECULIAR/INSTITUTION. Thus, "Negro quarter" is first recorded in 1734, more than a century before "slave quarter" in 1837. (Nowadays, "farm quarter" is the preferred term on signs at Monticello and other *manor houses,* as they are called by tourism promoters who wish to avoid "plantation," which conjures up images of "slaves"—*enslaved persons* in newspeak.) See also SERVANT.

As the abolitionist movement slowly made headway in the early decades of the nineteenth century, "Negro" came to be avoided because of its slave associations—particularly by those blacks who were not slaves. By the 1840s, free blacks were appending to their signature *f.m.c.* or *f.w.c.* for *free man* (or *woman*) *of color*. Other terms were floated in this period, e.g., *Africo-American* (1835), *ebony* (ca. 1850), and *Afro-American* (1853), but "colored" remained dominant for about a century. The Census Bureau, on the advice of Booker T. Washington, adopted "Negro" in 1890. However, the National Association for the Advancement of Colored People was founded in 1909, and as late as 1937, Dr. Kelly Miller, a black man, could worry over the question, "*Negroes or Colored People?*"—the title of an article by him in *Opportunity*, published by the National Urban League. While conceding that "such terms as *colored lady, colored gentleman*, and *colored society*" still sounded "more polite than the corresponding Negro equivalents," Miller plumped generally for "Negro," which had in fact reestablished itself among blacks as well as whites of the better sort. (*The New York Times* began capitalizing the "N" in "Negro" in 1930; the Government Printing Office did the same thing in 1933.) "Negro" remained ascendant until the 1960s, when a new generation in need of a new term to symbolize its revolt against the status quo opted for BLACK.

See also ASIAN, COLORED, DARKY, MINORITY, NIGRA, RACE, and TIGER.

neighborhood schools. Segregated schools. "In 1966, integrationist groups protested the [New York City] Board of Education's plan to build seven neighborhood (read segregated) schools in Brownsville, East Flatbush, Carnarsie, and East New York" (*Civil Liberties in New York*, 10/73). See also HARMONIOUS.

nervous exhaustion. Mental breakdown; variants, also placing the blame on the nerves rather than the psyche, are *nervous breakdown* and *nervous fever*. See also FATIGUE.

nether parts. The unspeakable area below the waist. "The current cover of The *Village Voice* carries a photograph of a naked woman's nether parts with a tampon string hanging down" (*New York Times*, 2/5/95).

"Nether" has a long history of use in anatomical contexts, e.g., "Lest he . . . make hym lame of his neder limmes" (John Skelton, *Why Come Ye Not to Court?*, 1522). Later generations managed even to dispense with mention of "limmes" and "legs" in this connection, referring instead to *nethers*, *nether man*, or *nether person*. The *nether parts* were covered by, naturally, *nether garments*, meaning either underwear or trousers, but usually the latter, as in "His nether garment was of yellow nankeen [Chinese cotton, from the place name, Nanking]" (James Fenimore Cooper, *The Last of the Mohicans*, 1826). See also PRIVATE PART(S), SEAT, and UNMENTIONABLES.

neutralize/neutralization. To take out of action, to render harmless, to kill; the acts thereof. "It is possible to neutralize carefully selected and planned targets, such as court judges, police and state security officials, etc. For psychological purposes, it is necessary to take extreme precautions, and it is absolutely necessary to gather together the population affected, so that they will take part in the act, and formulate accusations against the oppressor" (from a CIA manual distributed to Contra leaders in Nicaragua in 1983–84).

The methods of *neutralizing* people run the gamut from character assassination through assassination. In the case of the CIA manual, for instance, President Ronald Reagan insisted that "neutralize" just meant "remove from office." (He did not say how removals of Nicaraguan government officials were to be effected without loss of life.) Nor does it appear that E. Howard Hunt, Jr., the White House PLUMBER, was contemplating murder when he sent a memo to Charles W. Colson, special COUNSEL to President Nixon, that began: "Neutralization of [Daniel] Ellsberg . . . I am proposing a skeletal operations plan aimed at building a file on Ellsberg that will contain all available overt, covert and derogatory information. This basic tool is essential in determining how to destroy his public image and credibility" (7/28/71, in Leon Jaworski, *The Right and the Power*, 1976).

In other contexts, such as the United States–financed Phoenix counterinsurgency program in Vietnam, the sense is more violent: "Despite the fact that the law provided only for the arrest and detention of the suspects, one-third of the 'neutralized agents' were reported dead" (Frances FitzGerald, *Fire in the Lake*, 1972). Even in death, there are different kinds of *neutralization*. Thus, speaking of one of the army officers accused of covering up the My Lai massacre: "His lawyer discussed 'precise neutralization' (the killing of a villager determined to be a Communist) and 'imprecise neutralization' (the killing of a villager not quite determined to be a Communist)" (John J. O'Connor, *New York Times*, 4/7/71). See also ASSASSINATION, COVERT ACTION or OPERATION, PACIFY/PACIFICATION, and RECONNAISSANCE IN FORCE.

new age beverage. A clear drink.

newly single. Divorced. "Newly single" for "divorced" was one of the many genteel sub-stitutions—words that are "in" as opposed to "out"—listed by Phyllis Martin in *The Word Watchers Handbook* (1982). Some others: "birth name" for "maiden name," "car accident" for "car wreck," "dishcloth" for "dishrag," "domestic" for "cleaning woman," "hostess gown" for "bathrobe," "meat cutter" for "butcher," "pharmacy" for "drugstore," "single mother" for "unwed mother," "spa" for "gym," and "timepiece" for "watch." The list was much longer, but you get the idea.

niacin. Nicotinic acid; the pellagra-preventing vitamin B_3. The abbreviated "niacin" was approved by the government in 1942 after antitobacco groups spread reports that eating bread enriched with nicotinic acid would foster cigarette smoking.

night apparel. Fancy underclothes for men. "And lingerie for men, more often called 'night apparel,' is a growing industry" (*Litchfield County*, Conn., *Times*, 11/27/87). See also LINGERIE.

night soil. Human excrement. Nowadays, *night soil* usually is collected from cesspools and other depositories in the mornings, but back in the eighteenth century, when the euphemism appears to have originated, the job actually was performed under cover of night, as awkward as that might seem. As a result, the poor fellow who was saddled with the task was sometimes called the *night man*. Other titles for this functionary included *gold finder, honey-dipper, jakes farmer, lavender man*, and, a modern equivalent, *environmental hygiene worker*. See also BIOSOLIDS, ENVIRONMENTAL, FERTILIZER, HONEY, MANURE, and PRIVY.

nigra (also nigga, nigrah, and niggra). An aural euphemism for "nigger." People who say "nigra" may contend that it is a legitimate southern pronunciation of "Negro," once common among both races in that part of the country. In defense of alternate pronunciations, they also can point to the father of American dictionary-makers, Noah Webster (1757–1843), who used "neger" all his life. (He also spelled "zebra" as "zeber" until his revision of 1828.) But times have changed, the euphemism has evolved into a slur, and people who say "nigra" today usually are self-conscious enough to lower their voices when they say it. Some African-Americans, however, can get away with the term, or a close approximation of it, e.g., the rap group, NWA, who identify themselves as Niggaz Wit' Attitude, and whose lyrics are punctuated with the N-word. See also NEGRO.

no Mayday. In hospital parlance, this translates as "Do Not Resuscitate"—"DNR," as the instruction generally is abbreviated. "No Mayday" derives from the international radio-telephone distress call, "Mayday," in turn, from the French *m'aider,* help me. For fear of lawsuits, instructions to let patients die may not be put in writing; one alternative is to tell doctors and nurses to "DYF," meaning Drag Your Feet. Other ways of getting the message across are to advise hospital workers not to attempt "heroic measures" or to provide "nonaggressive treatment" or "routine nursing care [only]." All are passive approaches, compared to "pull the plug," i.e., to disconnect life-sustaining apparatus. See also EXPIRE, TENDER LOVING CARE, and TRIAGE.

nom de plume. Pen name. This fancy way of hiding a writer's identity (based on *nom de guerre,* war name) originated in England in the early nineteenth century and was only adopted later by the French themselves. However good the writer's reasons for using another name, the practice seems essentially duplicitous:

> "Who then is Porlock?" I asked.
> "Porlock, Watson, is a nom-de-plume, a mere indentification mark; but behind it lies a shifty and evasive personality." (A. Conan Doyle, *The Valley of Fear,* 1915)

non compos mentis. Mad, with a FOP Index of 4.6. The Latin expression, translating as "not master of one's mind," was popularized by lawyers (from 1607, *OED*) and is still favored by them. See also MENTAL.

nondiscernible microbionoculator. A poison dart gun developed by the CIA. Electronically operated and almost silent, it could shoot a tiny dart about 100 meters. The KGB devised a similar weapon, described in a CIA report as a "jet-propelled medicine ball." This was the means employed in 1978 to kill a Bulgarian dissident in London, Georgi Markov, poisoned by a BB-size pellet shot from an umbrella tip. See also DISPOSE and ELIMINATE/ELIMINATION.

nondisabled. Normal. In the words of the executive director of the Association for Retarded Citizens of Connecticut: "Several studies done in the 1980s showed that the primary reason why very few mentally retarded people are employed after high school had little to do with their intelligence or job skills. It was primarily because they could not relate well to nondisabled people" (*New York Times,* 5/15/94). See also DISABLED.

nondomiciled. Homeless, a.k.a., *involuntarily undomiciled* or *underhoused.* As a spokesperson for the Port Authority of New York explained in the case of a rape victim: "She was nondomiciled and known to the police as a homeless individual who frequently was seen in the [bus] terminal" (*New York Times*, 10/6/88). See also STREET-BUILDER.

nonmarital birth. Bastardy. See also BIRTH-PARENT.

nonmeeting. A meeting that is closed to the public and at which minutes are not taken; common at all levels of government, from the State Department on down to local school boards. The motive ordinarily is to keep the subject of the meeting secret, often because it is SENSITIVE.

nonpaper. An exploratory paper; diplomatese. *Nonpapers* usually are produced anonymously, allowing authors to preserve their deniability unless or until the policies they advocate are accepted. See also DRAFT.

nonpass. Fail; teacher-talk, sometimes discreetly abbreviated as *NP*. For instance, Stanford University decided to revamp its marking system in 1994 and to begin failing students for the first time since 1970, when the "F" was eliminated. Under the new system, however, the failing student would receive an *NP*, not the old, impolitically correct "F." See also DEFICIENT.

nonperforming asset (or credit or loan). A bad debt; banker-talk, usually encountered in plural form. "In past times, loans that were not repaid went sour or were in default. Now they are rolled over. Or rescheduled. Or they become problem loans. Or, best of all, they are nonperforming assets" (John Kenneth Galbraith, *New York Times*, 5/26/85).

See also CASH ADVANCE, DEFER PURCHASE, GROWTH STOCK, and PROBLEM.

nonroutine operation. A crash landing. "In case of a nonroutine operation, we would like you to be familiar with the location of the airplane exits" (notice to passengers, Trans Florida Airlines, *Quarterly Review of Doublespeak*, 10/86). This same mode of thinking leads flying instructors to offer *cram* courses, not crash courses. See also WATER LANDING.

No Outlet. On traffic signs, the upbeat version of "Dead End," euphemistically comparable to the sports announcer's SUDDEN VICTORY. See also CUL-DE-SAC and START.

no recall (or memory or recollection) of. "No recall" and its cousins are legalistic hedges for protecting witnesses from committing perjury and their appearance ordinarily should be interpreted as a sign that whoever is asking the questions is getting too warm for the witness's comfort. This is particularly so in the case of those who have been advertised previously as having steel-trap minds and photographic memories, e.g., Lt. Col. Oliver North, who dodged more than thirty questions in three hours with his inability to recall during his final day on the stand in the Iran-Contra hearings (7/14/87). Colonel North was a piker, however, compared to Adm. John M. Poindexter, the ex–National Security Advisor to President Reagan, who could "not remember" 184 times during a single day on the stand in the same hearings.

The underlying principle of this testimonial tactic was explained in a meeting on March 21, 1973, of President Richard M. Nixon and Messrs. H. R. "Bob" Haldeman and John W. Dean III. The conversation (as recorded in Leon Jaworski's *The Right and the Power,* 1976) went this way:

DEAN: You just can't have a lawyer before a grand jury.

HALDEMAN: Okay, but you do have rules of evidence. You can refuse to talk.

DEAN: You can take the Fifth Amendment.

PRESIDENT: That's right. That's right.

HALDEMAN: You can say you forgot, too, can't you?

PRESIDENT: That's right.

DEAN: But you can't . . . you're in a very high risk perjury situation.

PRESIDENT: That's right. Just be damned sure you say I don't remember. I can't recall. I can't give any honest . . . an answer that I can recall. But that's it.

Similar hedges include *no personal knowledge* and *to the best of my knowledge.* See also ECONOMICAL WITH THE TRUTH, INDICATE, PLAUSIBLE DENIAL, and WITHHOLD INFORMATION.

not at home. At home, but not to the caller. The excuse has been in use for some centuries. For example, in *Twelfth Night* (1600–02), when told that a young gentleman was asking for her, Lady Olivia replies: "Go you, Malvolio. If it be a suit from the Count, I am sick, or not at home." See also INDISPOSED/INDISPOSITION.

not doing well. Dying; a circumlocution used by nurses in hospitals when breaking the bad news to the patient's doctor. See also EXPIRE.

not right. Wrong—in various ways. Thus, in the art business, an appraiser's suggestion that a painting is "not quite right" translates as "It looks like a fake." In pub-

lishing, "not right for our list" probably is the most common excuse for rejecting manuscripts. The phrase is not pure doubletalk because some manuscripts actually aren't right for some publishers though quite right for others, since different publishers have different needs and different abilities to reach different audiences. The art of the rejection slip seems to have been perfected in modern China, however, where the editors of an economics journal are reported to decline contributions with the explanation that "We have read your manuscript with boundless delight. If we were to publish your paper it would be impossible for us to publish any work of a lower standard. As it is unthinkable that, in the next thousand years, we shall see its equal, we are, to our regret, compelled to return your divine composition, and to beg you a thousand times to overlook our short sight and timidity" (London *Times,* 7/9/82).

nude. Naked. There is more to nudity than meets the eye. A woman may pose for an artist in the "nude," but if she is seen minus her clothes by a Peeping Tom, then she is "naked." And if, as happened once in an art class I attended, the unauthorized viewing is done during the posing, then the model is simultaneously "nude" and "naked." In this instance, the woman immediately grasped the semantic point as well as her robe, and would not resume her pose until the cops had been called and the peeper chased away.

Naturally, the harsher, starker "naked" is an Anglo-Saxon word. The softer, more-refined "nude" comes from the Latin *nūdus,* with some help from the obsolete French *nud,* and is a much later, eighteenth-century addition to English. Even so liberated a thinker as Sigmund Freud used Latin to cover up nakedness, telling Wilhelm Fleiss in an 1897 letter about having once seen his mother "*nūdam.*" Peter Gay elucidates: "After the passing of half a lifetime, and in a letter to his best friend, like him a physician, Freud found it necessary to clothe his incestuous desires in the decent obscurity of a learned tongue; the Latin established a space of safety between himself and his forbidden arousal" (*The Bourgeois Experience,* 1988).

See also ALTOGETHER, AU NATUREL, BIRTHDAY SUIT, and BUFF.

nuisance. A general-purpose euphemism, often preceded by the word "commit," as in, "Dammit—Fido's committed a nuisance on the Oriental rug." See also DEED and DOG DIRT/DO/LITTER/WASTE.

number one and/or **two.** Potty talk for "piss" and "shit," dating from at least the nineteenth century and still current on the nation's airwaves, in public prints, and among consenting adults, e.g., referring to water conservation measures during a California drought: "I understand that you can now flush the toilet after going number one in Marin County" (Johnny Carson, WNBC-TV, 1/19/78). And on the grimmer side, reporting on the miseries of being a prisoner on a prison train in Russia: "Sometimes the orders came before you even started: 'All right, number one only!'" (Aleksandr I. Solzhenitsyn, *The Gulag Archipelago 1918–1956,* 1974). The euphemism here is the translator's adaptation, the equivalent Russian terms being "little" and "big" (Thomas P. Whitney, trans., and Frances Lindley, ed.). See also DEFECATE/DEFECATION and PEE.

nurse. Suck. Embarrassment over the animalistic—ugh!—act of sucking dates to

the great period of pre-Victorian prudery. For example, Noah Webster substituted "to nurse" or "to nourish" for "to give suck" when he bowdlerized the Bible in 1833. But Webster's hang-ups (see PECULIAR MEMBERS for more details) were by no means peculiar to him. Consider the lengths to which proper Englishwomen went just two decades later: "There was the unpleasant association with a ceremony frequently gone through by little babies; and so, after dessert, in orange season, Miss Jenkyns and Miss Matty used to rise up, possess themselves each of an orange in silence, and withdraw to the privacy of their own rooms, to indulge in sucking oranges" (Elizabeth C. Gaskell, *Cranford,* 1853). And a refined young man of the time, when given an orange, is said to have announced, "If you will excuse me, I think I will nurse mine."

nursing home. An old-age home, and a rare double-euphemism, the "nursing" implying a degree of loving tenderness that is seldom encountered, while the "home" conceals an institution that at best has all the hominess of a good hospital and at worst is a chamber of horrors. "'If I put a man in a room, beat him, starved him, didn't give him any water, the state would put me in jail,' Dr. [Isa] Goldman said. 'If I own a nursing home and do it, the state pays me'" (*New York Times,* 1/3/75).

"Nursing home" is a fairly new import from Britain. As recently as 1945, H. L. Mencken noted: "It would be hard to imagine any American male of the plain people using such [British] terms as *rotter, braces* (for *suspenders*), *boot-shop . . . nursing home* or *master's bedroom*" (*The American Language, Supplement I*). In that era, the standard American euphemism for "old-age home" was *private hospital.* See also ADULT, CONVALESCENT HOSPITAL, RESIDENT, and the basic HOME.

nutritional avoidance therapy. "Undergoing 'nutritional avoidance therapy' sounds more challenging than dieting" (Dublin, *Irish Times,* 9/29/90). By the same token, "nutritional shortfall" equals "hunger" (with a FOP Index of 4.1).

nuts. Euphemistic slang for the balls or TESTICLES. "Oh nuts!" is the functional equivalent of "Oh balls!" while "Nuts to you!" is an emphatic "No!" (People also *go nuts* or *act nutty* when they go crazy and sometimes they even wind up in the *nut house,* but these usages derive from "nut," singular, as slang for "head.") Because of its lower anatomical meaning, "nuts" has been euphemized as *nerts* or *nertz,* and it has also —getting to the main point of the present entry—served as a euphemism for still stronger language.

By far the most famous euphemistic "nuts" is that attributed to Brig. Gen. Anthony McAuliffe, who, as acting commander of the 101st Airborne Division, is said to have given this one-word reply to the Germans on December 22, 1944, at the height of the Battle of the Bulge. McAuliffe had been asked to surrender Bastogne, a key road junction. His troops were outnumbered four to one and completely surrounded. According to the authorized version of history, as reported in newspapers at the time and in various books afterward, McAuliffe said "Nuts!" as he dropped on the floor the German note demanding that he surrender. One of his regimental commanders then translated the reply for the enemy officers who had brought the demand: "If you don't know what 'Nuts!' means, it is the same as 'Go to hell!'"

McAuliffe always will be remembered for this brave answer, but it seems most unlikely that he ever said it. Ordinarily, the general used stronger language and people familiar with his speech patterns believe that he ran true to form on this occasion, saying something just as brave but not as printable. In the words of a well-informed infantry scout, Kurt Vonnegut, Jr. (he was captured during the Battle of the Bulge): "Can you imagine the commanding general of the 101st Airborne saying anything but 'shit' . . ." (personal communication, via Walter James Miller, 1979). In this connection, it seems highly significant that McAuliffe was known fondly to his troops as "Old Crock." Vonnegut adds that the general's remark may have been "a plagiarism"; for the source from which McAuliffe (perhaps unconsciously) stole, see SHORT FRENCH EXPLETIVE, A.

O. Orgasm, a powerful word, indeed, and thus often approached obliquely, as in *the big O,* or *to cop some Os,* meaning to engage in sexual intercourse. The latter is perhaps a spinoff of *to cop some Zs,* to catch some sleep; its sexual parallels include *cop a feel,* to fondle someone stealthily, and *cop a cherry,* to deprive a person, usually female, of virginity. See also COME, INTERCOURSE, and PREORGASMIC.

obituary. A death notice; from the Latin word for death, *obitus,* which is something of a euphemism, too, with the literal meaning of "a going down" (from *obīre: ob-,* down, plus *īre,* to go). As a record or announcement of a person's death, the short "obit" preceded "obituary" into English by a couple hundred years, "obit" dating to the mid-fifteenth century, while the long form isn't recorded until the beginning of the eighteenth. See also BRIEF (or SHORT) ILLNESS, PASS AWAY, and PREPARED BIOGRAPHY.

obscene, derogatory, and scatological. Self-censorship by the press was demonstrated starkly in case of Secretary of Agriculture Earl L. Butz, who was forced to RESIGN on October 4, 1976, for having told a bad joke that only two newspapers in the land dared print—the *Capital Times,* of Madison, Wisconsin, and the *Blade,* of Toledo, Ohio, according to a poll by the Associated Press. For the rest, euphemism and circumlocution reigned. Thus, the *New York Times,* initially informed its readers that President Gerald R. Ford was reprimanding Mr. Butz because the secretary

had told an anecdote "in which black people were referred to as 'coloreds' and described as wanting only three things. The things were listed, in order, in obscene, derogatory, and scatological terms" (10/2/76). Three days later, the good, gray *Times* managed to blurt out a slightly fuller explanation, telling readers that Butz had said something about "'coloreds'" wanting "satisfying sex, loose shoes, and a warm place for bodily functions—wishes that were listed by Mr. Butz in obscene and scatological terms." With this, the *Times* surpassed its best previous euphemistic effort (BARNYARD EPITHET). Other versions of Butz's anecdote, arranged in order of increasing clarity, included:

The Associated Press: "blacks' alleged preferences in sex, 'shoes,' and bathrooms."

United Press International: "good sex, easy shoes and a warm place to go to the bathroom."

The *Washington Post*: "Coloreds only want . . . first, a tight (woman's sexual organs); second, loose shoes; and third, a warm place to (defecate)."

The *San Francisco Sunday Examiner*: "First, a tight p – – – –, second, loose shoes, and third, a warm place to s – – –."

The dashes are an old euphemistic convention (see BLANK), and here they stand, of course, for the extra letters of "pussy" and "shit" (the former being a euphemism in its own right; see PUSSY). Mr. Butz's observation had been made during an airplane flight in an answer to a serious question from Pat Boone, the singer, who had wanted to know why the Republican party couldn't attract more black voters. To which Secretary Butz had replied, that "coloreds" were interested in only three things, etc., etc., etc. Mr. Butz knew that one of his auditors, John W. Dean III, the former White House COUNSEL, was acting as a reporter for *Rolling Stone*, but apparently thought that his little joke was unprintable. This was a serious mistake. Mr. Dean did try to protect him by attributing the remark only to a "shirt-sleeved cabinet member" in his account (10/7/76), but *New Times*, by checking the traveling schedules of all eleven cabinet secretaries, quickly fingered the guilty party.

As unedifying as Butz's remark was, the spectacle of his being forced out of office for unstated reasons was still more curious. In resorting to euphemisms, most of the newspaper editors were being not only high-minded but high-handed, taking it upon themselves to make a decision about Mr. Butz that might well have been left to their voter-readers. Robert Malone, managing editor of the *Capital Times*, put the case for printing all the news this way: "We think readers have the right to know exactly what Mr. Butz said and judge for themselves whether his remarks were obscene and racist in character; the paraphrasing we've seen doesn't carry off the same meaning as the actual words" (*Columbia Journalism Review*, 11–12/76).

This wasn't the first time Mr. Butz's sense of humor had gotten him in trouble; see GAME for the second-most-famous Butz joke.

occupy. In the seventeenth and eighteenth centuries, this was the principal euphemism for cohabitation in general and sexual INTERCOURSE in particular. Consider the following ditty, from Capt. Francis Grose's *A Classical Dictionary of the Vulgar Tongue* (1796):

All you that in your beds do lie
Turn to your wives, and occupy:
And when that you have done your best,
Turn a – se to a – se, and take your rest.

So tarred was "occupy" by its secondary, euphemistic meanings that it was virtually banned from polite English in any sense at all for almost 200 years. As early as 1597, William Shakespeare noted the phenomenon in *Henry IV, Part 2*: "A captain! God's light, these villains will make the word as odious as the word 'occupy,' which was an excellent good word before it was ill-sorted." Some years later, his contemporary, Ben Jonson, explained the reason for the taboo: "Many, out of their own obscene apprehensions, refuse proper and fit words —as *occupy, nature,* and the like; so the curious industry of some, of having all alike good, hath come nearer a vice than a virtue" (*Timber: Or Discoveries Made Upon Men and Matter,* "De Stilo," ca. 1640). During this era whorehouses became *occupying houses* and the women who lived and worked in them were, inevitably, known as *occupants.* Meanwhile, the shunning of "occupy" by polite people was so complete that *The Oxford English Dictionary* included a special comment about it: "The disuse of this verb in the 17th and most of the 18th c. is notable. Against 194 quots. for 16th c., we have for 17th only 8, outside the Bible of 1611 (where it occurs 10 times), and for 18 c. only 10, all of its last 33 years. This avoidance appears to have been due to its vulgar employment." See also F – – –.

odds bodkins. God's Little Body. The euphemistic non-oath derives from *ods bodikins,* where "od" is a shortening of "God" that first appeared around 1600. "'Oddsbodikins!' said the sergeant of police, taking off his helmet and wiping his forehead" (Kenneth Grahame, *The Wind in the Willows*, 1908). The basic "od" also produced such other euphemistic exclamations as *od rabbit it, od rat it* (which may have led to the common *drat*), *od so, odsoons* (wounds), and *odzooks* (hooks). The "odd" construction was developed to its highest point by Richard Brinsley Sheridan in *The Rivals* (1755), in which Bob Acres exclaims in moments of stress "odds frogs and tambours!" and "odds flints, pans, and triggers!" See also GADZOOKS and ZOUNDS.

off. To kill or to SCREW, the commingling of death and sex in a single word being fairly standard practice (see DIE). "The Organization had ordered him to mess up a couple of guys, but instead he offed them" (John Godey, *The Taking of Pelham One Two Three*, 1973). "You may not believe this . . . when I off a nigger bitch, I close my eyes and concentrate real hard and pretty soon I get to believing that I'm riding one of them bucking blondes" (Eldridge Cleaver, *Soul on Ice*, 1968).

Among British soldiers in World War I, "off" also was slang for "die," and before that (ca. seventeenth to twentieth centuries) "off" and "go off" already stood for going off to sleep or—to sleep's look-alike—death, e.g., "The doctors told me that he might go off any day" (Sir H. Rider Haggard, *Colonel Quaritch, V.C.*, 1888).

See also EXPIRE, HIT, and INTERCOURSE.

off-hours work. Overtime. See RELOCATION DRILL.

officer. A common title for elevating the status of various trades, e.g., *animal welfare officer* (dogcatcher), *case officer* (middle-management spy), *cleaning officer* (self-

description of an elderly woman juror at the O. J. Simpson trial in 1995), *correctional officer* (prison guard), *information officer* (press agent), *pest control officer* (a British ratcatcher), *truant officer* (pupil-catcher), and, of course, the simple police *officer*. (If those on patrol are *officers*, then what are the lieutenants and captains back at the station house—*officer officers*?) See also BATON and ENGINEER.

old man's friend, the. Pneumonia; a friendly name for an illness that was feared by the aged, prior to the discovery of penicillin. See also C, THE BIG, and TB.

oncology. Cancer, as in "Parking for Oncology Patients" (sign, New Milford Hospital, New Milford, Conn., 1994). See also C, THE BIG.

oomph. Sex appeal. "You don't learn oomph. You are born with it" (*Dance, Girl, Dance,* film, 1940). "Oomph," initially spelled "umphh," was popularized by Hollywood press agents in the 1930s. Ann Sheridan was proclaimed "oomph girl of America" in 1937 and up-and-coming starlets subsequently were heralded as *oomphlets*. The term probably is of imitative origin, a distortion either of a bull's mating bellow (Eric Partridge's guess) or the spontaneous male grunt of approval caused by a breath-taking sight. See also IT.

open marriage. Open adultery; coined by George and Nena O'Neill in the their book, *Open Marriage* (1973). "Open marriage" conveniently dispenses with the sinful connotations of the A-word while putting old-fashioned monogamists on the defensive. (The psychology of the new terminology is the same as that of PRO-CHOICE.) Precursors of "open marriage" include *plural marriage,* practiced by Mormons who had *plural wives* (a.k.a. SPIRITUALS), and *complex marriage* (a.k.a. *pantagamy*), a distinctive feature of life in the Oneida Community in the mid-nineteenth century. The Oneida leader, John Noyes, articulated his vision of *complex marriage* in divinely euphemistic terms: "When the will of God is done on earth as it is in Heaven, *there will be no marriage.* The marriage supper of the Lamb is a feast at which *every dish is free to every guest*" (*Battle-Axe,* letter, 8/20/1837). See also AFFAIR, CONSENSUAL NONMONOGAMY, EXTRAMARITAL, and, for more about Oneidan customs, *coitus reservatus* in COITION or COITUS.

open shop. Nonunion shop; another semantic victory for management. See also RIGHT-TO-WORK.

opera house. The grandiose appellation for the auditorium that once played such a vital part in small-town American life, and in which operas were seldom, if ever, performed. Discussing the typical *opera house* offerings in the 1890s: "These were the great days when *Uncle Tom's Cabin,* with 'fifty men, women, and children, a pack of genuine bloodhounds, grandest street parade ever given, and two bands,' packed the Opera House to capacity" (Robert S. and Helen Merrell Lynd, *Middletown* [Muncie, Indiana], 1929). The Muncie Opera House eventually gave way to a movie house. For a note on its offerings, see PET.

operation. A burglary or other criminal act. "I don't recall using the term 'entry' or 'enter.' However, we used the terms 'operations,' 'effort,' 'covert,' which embraced what took place" (Egil "Bud" Krogh, co-chairman of the PLUMBERS, testifying at the trial of John D. Ehrlichman, 7/3/74, about the COVERT ACTION or OPERATION at the office of a Los Angeles psychiatrist).

operations center. Back office. "I wish the [New York] city would stop using the term 'back office' to describe the kind of users they would like to attract to the downtown [Brooklyn] area, and substitute the term 'operations center.' It's a lot better word" (Tony Martin, president, Brooklyn Heights Association, Brooklyn, N.Y., *Phoenix,* 10/27/83).

operative/operator. A classy detective, INVESTIGATOR, or spy; a secret AGENT.

Domestically, the high-toned term was popularized in the latter decades of the nineteenth century by the most famous of detective agencies: "The word 'detective' became so offensive . . . that it was dropped by some agencies. The word chosen by the Pinkertons to take its place was 'operative'" (*New York Press,* 10/23/05). The reason "detective" became offensive was that many agencies had begun hiring criminals, partly on the it-takes-a-thief-to-catch-a-thief principle and partly to use as muscle in the labor wars that followed the Civil War.

option. Choice. The harder sound of the two-syllable word makes the choices themselves sound harder and suggests, by association, that the people making them have harder noses, too. The vogue for "option" began in the early 1960s as the Kennedy Administration built up conventional military forces so that the nation could wage small wars instead of having to rely exclusively on the threat of massive retaliation, e.g., "The new approach . . . was recommended by Secretary [of Defense Robert S.] McNamara as part of his build-up of options" (Theodore C. Sorensen, *Kennedy*, 1965). For more about *options* in the Pentagon, see SCENARIO.

oral (or buccal) cavity. A mouth, to a dentist. "Few dentists seem to be able to use the Anglo-Saxon word *mouth* in formal speech. Even to the patient they are likely to say 'rinse out' instead of 'rinse your mouth'; and to their peers, in proper speech or writing, it becomes 'oral cavity' or even 'buccal cavity,' and somehow a purification is implied" (Theodor Roseburg, *Life on Man*, 1969).

ordnance. The generic term, classically taken to mean cannon and their supplies, conceals such modern uglies as bombs, rockets, napalm, and other munitions. Thus, speaking of the intentionally bland reports given by American military briefers in Vietnam:

> Their language, which has no connection with everyday English, has been designed to sanitize the war. Planes do not drop bombs, they "deliver ordnance." Napalm is a forbidden word and when an American information officer is forced under direct questioning to discuss it, he calls it "soft ordnance." In the press releases and the answers to newsmen's questions, there is never any sense, not even implicit, of people being killed, homes being destroyed, thousands of refugees fleeing. (Sydney H. Schanberg, "The Saigon Follies, or Trying to Head Them Off at the Credibility Gap" *New York Times Magazine*, 11/12/72).

Other kinds of "ordnance" include *contingent ordnance*, which are extra bombs dropped on secondary targets, and *incontinent ordnance*, which are bombs or shells

that fall where they're not supposed to (e.g., on friends instead of foes). Such miss-hits also may be disguised as *accidental delivery of ordnance equipment*, perhaps due to a *navigational misdirection*. Then there were the bombs that fell into a field near military barracks during operation "Just Cause" in Panama in 1989. Military briefers said at the time that this was a ploy, intended as a distraction, but "a senior military officer" later told the *Washington Post* that "bombing a field" was a euphemism for "missing the target" (William Safire, *New York Times*, 2/1/90).

Briefers relied less on "ordnance" during the Gulf war of 1991 but their language remained as bland as ever. The devastation of the bombing campaign was downplayed by converting fighter-bombers into *fighters* and bombers into *force packages* and *weapons systems*. The *force packages* did not make bombing raids; rather, they *visited a site* or *serviced the target* in order to *degrade, neutralize*, or otherwise *suppress assets* of the enemy.

See also AIR SUPPORT, CASUALTY, DELIVER, FRIENDLY FIRE, and SELECTIVE ORDNANCE.

organ. Women have internal organs but as a rule only men have external, euphemistic *organs*, i.e., the penis (a.k.a. the *male generative organ* or the *reproductive organ*), the testicles (or *male organs*), and the collective *organs of generation* (see GENERATION). The single word usually is enough to get the message across, however. As a letter writer to *Playboy* (9/76) put it: "Some just like the visual turn-on; others say a big organ feels better in their hand." (For the musically minded, *to play the organ*, or *family organ*, is to engage in INTERCOURSE.)

The Victorians usually employed the slightly more specific *reproductive organ* and *sex organ*. As a result, Charles Dickens could use "organ" alone in a way that no modern writer would, describing a church organist's infatuation for a member of the choir in this way: "When she spoke, Tom held his breath so eagerly he listened; when she sang he sat like one entranced. She touched his organ and from that bright epoch, even it, the old companion of his happiest hours, incapable as he had thought to elevation, began a new and deified existence" (*The Life and Adventures of Martin Chuzzlewit*, 1844). See also PENIS and TESTICLES.

organized crime. The Mafia. "According to a sentencing memorandum by the prosecution, the Government possesses information that Mr. [Russell A.] Bufalino 'continued to be the head of his own organized-crime family'" (*New York Times*, 10/22/77). "Organized crime" was adopted widely in the 1970s in response to complaints by Italian-Americans about the tendency of law enforcement agencies and the media to blame most of the worst criminal activities on the Mafia and to portray most of the toughest gangsters as having Italian names and characteristics. See also FOREIGNER.

organoleptic analysis. Smelling. According to the Food and Drug Administration's magazine, *FDA Consumer*, decomposition in shellfish "is detected by organoleptic analysis," which means "smelling the product" (*New York Times*, 10/1/85).

orthographically impaired. Unable to spell well. See also HEARING IMPAIRED.

osculate. The high point of first-year Latin for many students is learning that "osculate" means "to kiss," the English word deriving from the Latin *osculum*, little mouth. Such are the unexpected advantages of a classical education. "Osculate" also has acquired other esoteric meanings. Thus, biologists say that two species, or genera, "osculate" when they are connected by common characteristics, while mathematicians use the word to describe the bringing of two curves or surfaces into close contact so that they have three or more points in common—a definition that covers all but the shyest of ninth-grade *osculators*. See also EXPECTORATE.

osshole. Asshole. "Abbie Hoffman and Jerry Rubin and the Yippie kids who hang around them can be funny at times, and brave. But basically they are ossholes" (Pete Hamill, "The Language of the New Politics," in Neil Postman, et al., eds., *Language in America*, 1969). Of course, asterisks and dashes also may be used to render the base term less offensive, as in *A**HOLE NO MORE; A Self-Help Guide for Recovering A**holes* (book title, 1992 Barnes & Noble catalog), and Shirley MacLaine's categorization of David Letterman as "an assh – – –" (*New York Magazine*, 8/16/93). Considerably cleverer, back at the start of this century, was the review of *De Profundis*, Oscar Wilde's essay-letter to Lord Alfred Douglas, which noted that "It is impossible, except very occasionally, to look upon his testament as more than a literary feat. Not so, we find ourselves saying, are souls laid bare" (*Times Literary Supplement*, 2/24/1905). See also ANUS, ARSE, and, for more about Wilde-Douglas, LOVE THAT DARE NOT SPEAK ITS NAME, THE.

other. White. "In my day, the student body [at Bronx High School of Science] was 98 percent white. . . . Today the breakdown is nearly two-fifths Asian, one-fifth black and Hispanic, and two-fifths 'other' (the euphemism for white)" (William Safire, *New York Times*, 10/20/94). See also CAUCASIAN.

other than honorable discharge. The military services maintain the discriminations of rank to the bitter end; thus, an officer will get an *other than honorable discharge* where an enlisted person will receive an undesirable discharge. See also LEAVE.

outercourse. Sexual activity short of penetration. "To teach kids about 'outercourse'—everything up to intercourse—you have to accept that adolescents have sexual feelings in the first place" (*U.S. News & World Report*, 12/16/91). See also BODILY FLUIDS, INTERCOURSE, PENETRATE/PENETRATION, and PET.

outhouse. An outdoor PRIVY; the generalization originally concealed the errand. Technically, an "outhouse" can be a barn, a toolshed, or any other "outbuilding," as in "Mr. William Dobbin retreated to a remote outhouse in the playground, where he passed a half-holiday in the bitterest sadness and woe" (William Makepeace Thackeray, *Vanity Fair*, 1848). The euphemistic sense of "outhouse" was popularized in the United States. The earliest example in *The Oxford English Dictionary* is from the diary of William Sewall, who applied the term to what today would be called a HEAD: "Near the paddles or wheels which propel the vessel forward are two outhouses, which is a very great convenience" (6/14/1819). Variant forms include *doghouse* (from "I have to go see a dog"), *go-out house, honey house,* and *hundred-yard dash house.* See also TOILET.

outplacement. Finding a job for someone who is being LET GO (the correct verb in such instances is "to outplace"). "Alan Sweetser is president of Compass Incor-

porated, a local executive outplacement counselling firm" (*Minneapolis Tribune,* 7/23/78). "Professional job-search assistance, or 'outplacement' in the trade, is being used with ever greater frequency by firms when employees are fired" (*U.S. News & World Report*, 8/1/83). Synonyms for "outplacement" include *decruitment, dehiring,* and *constructive termination.* See also CAREER; DEHIRE; TERMINATE/TERMINATION; and TRANSITION, IN.

Oval Office. The president of the United States; topographical doubletalk, whereby a person is described indirectly in terms of the physical location of the body. This kind of talk may be used to elevate the stature of job-holders (as in BENCH, THE); it also introduces an element of imprecision that can be useful in establishing a PLAUSIBLE DENIAL. For example: "In fact, Krogh had told me it [approval of the Fielding break-in] came from the Oval Office, but I was still keeping the President out of things" (John W. Dean III, *Blind Ambition*, 1976). For more about the Fielding break-in, see COVERT ACTION or OPERATION.

overapplied for. Talking about doubletalk: " 'It gets worse and worse,' said Henry Steele Commager in an interview. 'Did you hear Caspar Weinberger, the Secretary of HEW, explain that we have enough medical schools—they are just over-applied for'?" (Israel Shenker, "Zieglerrata," *New Republic*, 4/13/74). The Ziegler of Zieglerrata is, of course, Ron; see INOPERATIVE.

overflight. An illegal flight over an international boundary.

The most famous American *overflight* occurred in 1960 when a U-2 spy plane (the "U" is for "Utility," something of a euphemism in its own right) piloted by Francis Gary Powers was shot down near Sverdlovsk, almost 1,300 miles inside Russia, but it was by no means the first such mission. Referring to plans for infiltrating CIA-trained AGENTS into the Soviet Union in 1949: "The A-2 [Air Force chief of intelligence] also pointed out that the Soviet ground reaction to our overflights would provide him with the first hard intelligence on the state of Soviet ground defenses against air attack" (Harry Rositzke, *The CIA's Secret Operations*, 1977). See also COVER and INCURSION.

overqualified for. Doubletalk; used when rejecting job applicants. "You're overqual-

ified" usually translates as "I'm afraid that you'll quickly become bored and unhappy with the miserable, low-paying job for which you've applied." Occasionally, it may also mean "You are too old" (the point being that it took many years to get all those qualifications) or "I'm afraid to hire you because you're better qualified than I am." *Overqualified* women may be locked in forever as ADMINISTRATIVE ASSISTANTS.

ovular. Seminar. Speaking of the politically correct desire to avoid nasty male-related words: "A professor at Washington University objects to the word 'seminar,' and uses 'ovular' instead" (*New Yorker*, 5/20/91). See also "ovarimony" in THIGH.

P

p − − −. The 1840 edition of Byron's *Occasional Pieces* quoted the epitaph he proposed in 1821 for a famous British statesman in this form: "Posterity will ne'er survey a nobler grave than this:/ Here lie the bones of Castlereagh; stop, traveller, P − − −!" A couple centuries later, this dashed construction remains in style: "What we want to know is if [Hamilton Jordan, assistant to President Carter] is the kind of person who'd tell this same assemblage, 'This administration has to take a p − − −.' We already know the *Washington Post* is too icky poo to print the *iss.*" (*[MORE]*, 2/78). But the *Post* is by no means unique: "'Basically they have a mad scientist p − − − − − off at two other scientists there,' said a police source" (New York *Daily News*, 7/27/94). See also F − − −, PEE, PO'D, and THIGH (for another note on Robert Stewart, Viscount Castlereagh).

pacify/pacification. Gentle terms for not-so-friendly forms of persuasion: to repress, destroy, lay waste, and the acts thereof. "In czarist Russia, detachments sent to punish striking workers were called 'pacifying detachments'" (Anatol Rapoport, *Semantics*, 1975). As George Orwell explained: "Political language has to consist largely of euphemism, question-begging and sheer cloudy vagueness. Defenceless villages are bombarded from the air, the inhabitants are driven out into the countryside, the cattle machine-gunned, the huts set on fire with incendiary bullets: this is called *pacification*" ("Politics and the English Language," 1946). The phraseology and the technique remained essentially the same in Vietnam, i.e., "Under the so-called Accelerated Pacification Campaign the U.S. Ninth Division almost literally 'cleaned out' the Front-held regions of the northern Mekong Delta, bombing villages, defoliating crops, and forcing the peasants to leave their land" (Frances FitzGerald, *Fire in the Lake*, 1972). None of this is new, however. Galgacus, a leader of the Britons, is said by Tacitus to have urged his countrymen to resist the *Pax Romana* and its enforcers in these terms: "To robbery, slaughter, plunder, they give the lying name of empire; they make a desert and call it peace" (*Agricola*, 98). See also NEUTRALIZE/NEUTRALIZATION.

packing house. Slaughterhouse, the killing and packing usually are accomplished under the same roof. "I make every hog which goes through my packing-house give up more lard than the Lord gave him gross weight" (G. K. Lorimore, *Letters from a Self-Made Merchant to His Son*, 1902). "In *Meat*, we could get by simply [by] attending to the intricacies of the meat packing process (itself something of a euphemism —there's more here than packing)" (film review, *New Republic*, 12/4/76). "Packing house" (1835, *OED*) is the American counterpart of the Anglo-French ABATTOIR. See also CHEVALENE.

palace. A royal appelation for various plebeian places and accomodations. Americans have shown a remarkable fondness over the years for staying at *palace hotels* (when they could afford to travel first-class), traveling in *floating palaces* (also called *palaces on paddle wheels*) and *palace cars* (the first railroad sleepers were made by the Pullman Palace Car Company, proudly incorporated as such in 1867), buying their clothes in *dry-goods palaces*, dining in *eating palaces,* drinking in *gin palaces* (i.e., gin mills) and *rum palaces* (or rum holes), and going out to be entertained in *movie palaces* (from 1917, *OED*). And this is supposed to be an egalitarian nation. See also CATHEDRAL and PARLOR.

palpitators. Nineteenth-century American falsies, also known as *palpitating bosoms* or *patent beavers.* In the fractured English of Petroleum Vesuvius Nasby (David Ross Locke): "I am a bridegroom, wich cometh from his bride on the mornin feelin releeved ub the knowledge that she wore not palpitators, nor calves, nor nothing false, afore she was hizn" (*Swinging Round the Cirkle,* 1867). See also BOSOM, BRASSIERE, and GAY DECEIVERS.

panties. Women's underpants; the diminutive minimizes the sexual associations by casting the adult wearers in the roles of children or little girls.

When "panties" first appeared on the scene, back in the 1840s, they were men's underpants—*small trousers,* as they were also called. The men's "panties" derived from "pants," naturally, with the latter being a new and still somewhat disreputable abbreviation of "pantaloons." Liberated women in the nineteenth century also wore "pants," but when that word was used in a feminine context, the reference was to "pantalets" or "bloomers." True *panties* for women do not seem to have come into style until after the turn of the century (1908, *OED*). Probably, the great change in women's fashions that took place around the time of World War I (see BRASSIERE) had much to do with the popularization of "panties," actually as well as linguistically. The singular form also has been sighted: "Olga promises to

send you the bra or pant you wanted, free of charge" (Bloomingdale's ad, *New York Times,* 1/16/92). In addition, women wear a number of other similar euphemisms, including:

Briefs: A product of the early 1930s, whose appearance was soon protested by language purists, but to no effect: "I'm bored to tears with 'scanties'/I'm sick to death of 'briefs'" ("Too Much of Too Little," *Books of To-day,* 11/10/34). "Briefs" also was adopted in France, to the despair of middle-aged French writers, who tried to have the term banned from the dictionaries because it was not the one (i.e., *pantalon de femme*) they had learned as youths (Cecil Saint-Laurent, *A History of Ladies Underwear,* 1968). Indicative of the current feminization of men's fashions is the fact that since about 1950, men also have been wearing *briefs* (along with the older, longer "shorts" or "undershorts"). As yet, men have not taken to wearing *brevities,* but this, too, may well come to pass.

Drawers: An old (1567, *OED*) and now somewhat antiquated term. In the beginning, the term seems to have been applied to "stockings" as well as to undergarments of varying length (sometimes to the ankle), depending upon the fashion of the time. "Drawers" actually describes the way the garment is put on, i.e., drawn on, not the garment itself, giving it the same euphemistic quality as the later *pull-ons* and *step-ins.* And see also SLIP.

Knickers (or knicks): Loose, short (originally knee-length) underpants, worn by British women (and children) since the late nineteenth century. The term is an abbreviation of "knickerbockers," which are men's knee-length pants, also called "plus fours" when cut in an exceptionally baggy manner, four inches too long. (The term for the pants seems to have been popularized by the illustrations of knee breeches in Washington Irving's *History of Old New York* [1809], written under the pen name Diedrich Knickerbocker.) The acronym NORWICH, composed by some unknown but lonely British serviceman in World War II, stands for "Nickers Off Ready When I Come Home."

Scanties: "Scanty trousers" appears in *The Oxford English Dictionary* from 1874, but the pantielike *scanties* of today come from the same era as *briefs* above.

Step-ins: A common euphemism of the 1930s and 1940s, as in "She came out [of the water], pulling her soaking step-ins about so as to get a maximum of modesty" (John O'Hara, *Appointment in Samarra*, 1934). N.B.: "A step-in" is an anagram of "panties."

See also LINGERIE, UNDIES, and UNMENTIONABLES.

parallel rate. Black-market rate. In international currency trading, "parallel rate" is the preferred phrase in countries whose officials are willing to look the other way in order to obtain dollars (Jane Bryant Quinn, CBS, 4/27/83).

paramour. An illicit lover of either sex. In French, *par* plus *amour* equals "by or through love," and the early connotations were not necessarily impure. In medieval times, for instance, a knight could refer to his lady love as his "paramour," and have only high-minded thoughts. The allusion might even be religious, as in a poem from 1492, in which the Virgin Mary addresses Christ as "Myne owne dere sonne and paramoure." Nevertheless, the more sensual connotations developed quickly: "My fourthe housbonde was a revelour; This to seyn he hadde a paramour" (Geoffrey Chaucer, *Prologue to the Wife of Bath's Tale,*

ca. 1387–1400). "Paramour" has an archaic ring, but is not entirely obsolete: "The state's Welfare Inspector General, Richard V. Horan, has singled out the case of a 31-year-old Queens woman who together with her five children and 'paramour,' has managed to collect $88,268.17 in benefits over the last five and one-half years" (*New York Times*, 10/13/76). See also AMOUR and FRIEND.

paraphilia. Sexual perversion; an attempt by well-intentioned diagnosticians to avoid making moral judgments (from 1925, *OED*). "The common paraphilias that we choose to call sexual perversions today, were defined by the Greeks as being parallel to love" (E. J. Trimmer et al., *Visual Dictionary of Sex*, 1978). See also ALTERNATE SEXUAL PREFERENCE and SEXUALLY OTHERWISE.

park. To cuddle in a car. By the 1920s, if not before, thanks to the impact of Henry Ford's flivver upon the nation's courting customs, the general term for halting an automobile and temporarily leaving it somewhere became a euphemism for what often took place when the vehicle was stopped and the occupants remained inside. "A boy or girl who objects to 'parking' or 'necking' in a dance" (Philadelphia *Evening Bulletin*, 3/8/50). Today, in an age of smaller, economy-size cars, with gear shifts in awkward places, the expression has grown archaic except in such metaphoric forms as *parallel park* and *park the pink Mustang up a side street*, both of which are teen-talk for INTERCOURSE. See also MAKE OUT, NECK, and PET.

parlor. A euphemism for a business establishment. While the domestic parlor has been largely superseded by the living room, the business *parlor* (from 1884 in the commercial sense) lives on in a variety of forms, among them: *beauty parlor, betting* (or *horse*) *parlor, billiard parlor* (also called an *academy*), FUNERAL PARLOR, *ice-cream parlor,* MASSAGE PARLOR, RAP PARLOR, and *shoeshine parlor.* Barbershops used to be known as *tonsorial parlors,* the first movie houses were *movie parlors;* and some of the more expensive whorehouses were called *parlor houses.* In railroad lingo, meanwhile, a *parlor car* was either a sleeper or a caboose, and a *parlor cattle car* was a superior car for transporting steers to a PACKING HOUSE.

Before the term's adoption in the business world, a *parlor* was purely a place for conversation; the French *parler* or, in its Latin form, *parlatorium,* was a room in a monastery or nunnery in which inmates could talk to visitors. See also CATHEDRAL, CLINIC, EMPORIUM, PALACE, and SALON.

parson-in-the-pulpit. The common name of the wild arum lily, formerly known as the "cuckoo pintle" (or "pint") and "priest's pintle"—"pintle" being an old (ca. 1100) word for "penis." Many plant names have been cleaned up similarly over the years. See also CANOLA, COWSLIP, SMART WEED, STONECROP, and—a rare failure along this line—*wreathewort* in BILATERAL ORCHIDECTOMY.

parson's- (or **pope's-** or **bishop's-) nose.** The rump of a chicken or other fowl; more common in the nineteenth century than in the present ecumenical age. "An epicurean morsel—a parson's nose" (Henry Wadsworth Longfellow, *Hyperion,* 1839). The papal form may be the oldest; it was included by Capt. Francis Grose in the 1788 edition of his *Classical Dictionary of the Vulgar Tongue.* The French have a similar expression: *le bonnet d'évêque,* bishop's cap. See also DRUMSTICK.

participant monitoring. Secret taping by a reporter of an interview; a generally legal but ethically dubious practice. "Surreptitious taping—or 'participant monitoring,' as some defenders of the practice prefer to call it—is not to be confused with wiretapping, in which a third party listens to, or tapes, a telephone conversation without the knowledge of the participants. While wiretapping is clearly forbidden by federal law, in most states journalists may tape their own telephone conversations without the other party's permission" (*Columbia Journalism Review,* 7–8/84). Nor should "participant monitoring" be confused with the somewhat similar "participant observation," as in "I found myself wondering how much hanging around (or 'participant observation' as we anthropologists like to dignify it) I would have to do to make any headway in my research" (Robert E. Daniels, *Natural History,* 6/89). See also MONITOR.

partner. A person who is living with another person in an unsanctified relationship. The relationship is usually but not necessarily a RELATIONSHIP, i.e., sexual, and the partners themselves may be of either, and not necessarily the opposite, sex. The term was adopted officially by the Census Bureau for the 1980 census, with "partner, roommate" being one of the four categories to which all persons "not related to person in column 1" (the de facto head of the household) could assign themselves. Census takers had employed the term occasionally from a much earlier date, however. Thus, in the case of a turn-of-the-century lesbian couple, the literary agent Elisabeth Marbury (her clients included Oscar Wilde and George Bernard Shaw) and actress-interior decorator Elsie de

Wolfe, the 1905 New York City census listed Ms. Marbury as "head of the household" at 122 East Seventeenth Street and Ms. de Wolfe as her "partner." (Such an arrangement between women also was known as a *Boston marriage*.) Modern variations on the partnership theme include *domestic partner* (which has attained legal status in San Francisco, from 1989, and other cities), *life partner, registered partner* (since *domestic partners* must be officially registered in order to qualify for health and other benefits of conventional marriage), and *casual sex partner*, sometimes abbreviated by those who engage in such abbreviated affairs as *csp*. See also COMPANION, FRIEND, POSSLQ, ROOMMATE, and SIGNIFICANT OTHER.

parts. Sexual parts. "Her neather partes misshapen, monstruous" (Edmund Spenser, *The Fairie Queene*, 1590). See also PRIVATE PART(S).

party. The festive term covers an exceedingly wide range of behavior, from the traditional tea or cocktail party, to the teenage *petting party* (see PET), to even heavier get-togethers, featuring nonalcoholic drugs and/or group sex. "The straight call girls . . . are nothing at all compared to their society's stars, the women who run the ritzier houses, where prices start at $50 for a half-hour and can go as high as $1,000 for a 'bachelor party' or orgy" (*New York Times*, 8/9/71). All this applies to the verb, too, with the PROSTITUTE's "Wanna party?" being synonymous with WANNA GO OUT? See also CALL GIRL and HOUSE.

pass away. To die; an old euphemism, dating at least to the fourteenth century, which flowered in the fertile soil of pre-Victorian prudery, being well watered with tears of artificial sentimentality. The basic "pass" comes from the French *passer*, which the French themselves use euphemistically in place of *mourir*, to die. In early usage, it implied a spiritual destination, as in *pass to God* or *pass to heaven*, but later variants tend to stress the journey rather than its conclusion, e.g., *pass beyond, pass hence, pass in, pass on, pass out (of the picture)*, and *pass over* (frequently elaborated into such poetic figures as *pass over the river, pass over the Great Divide*, and, especially among spiritualists, *pass over to the other side*). The simple "pass" also contines to see service, as in "She passed after Art, but my father passed before him, in 1951" (jazz pianist Art Tatum's sister, speaking of their parents, *New Yorker*, 9/9/85).

The prettying up of death in the decades just before Victoria ascended the throne in 1837 was recorded for posterity in the changing styles of tombstones. As one graveyard (or CEMETERY) visitor reported:

> During the eighteenth century, according to my churchyard observations, people were allowed, quite simply to die. Towards the end of that period they begin to "depart this life." That is a fuller term, but there is no evasion about it. . . . But about the year 1830 everything goes. . . . Simplicity vanishes as well as the stately and sonorous rhythm. People no longer die, like Adam: they pass over, they go home, they are carried to rest, they fall asleep, they are removed to the divine bosom, or whisked to other celestial and possibly embarrassing niches. Anything but the plain fact of death. (Ivor Brown, *A Word in Your Ear* and *Just Another Word*, 1945)

Though we are now, supposedly, well out of the Victorian era, "pass away" and its principal variants are still commonly encountered on OBITUARY pages as well as in funeral establishments (see LOVED ONE, THE for an example). Of course, the ways of not talking about death are legion, as every good FUNERAL DIRECTOR knows. Many of the euphemisms and circumlocutions are phrased in terms of REST and SLEEP (e.g., *laid to rest* and *fell asleep*); others refer to the places to which living people like to think dead people go (see HAPPY HUNTING GROUNDS, GONE TO THE), and still others refer with varying degrees of vagueness to the act of dying (see CROSS OVER, DEMISE, EXPIRE, and GO). Special vocabularies also have been developed for different kinds of untimely death; see ASSASSINATION, BITE THE DUST, BRIEF (or SHORT) ILLNESS, CAPITAL PUNISHMENT, CULL, HIT, PUT AWAY/DOWN/TO SLEEP and PUT OUT. And these only scratch the surface: There are hundreds of other euphemistic metaphors for the untoward event. Herewith, a sampling:

answer the last muster (or *roll call*). An old soldier's death.

BALL GAME, END OF THE. One of many game-playing analogies; see the entry.

bid farewell. Grand Ayatollah Ali Araki "bade farewell to the living world" on November 29, 1994, according to the official Iranian announcement on government radio.

BUY THE FARM. Popularized by World War II pilots.

call back (also *call beyond, call home, call to God, call to one's reward*). "Called Back" (tombstone, Emily Dickinson, d. 1886, West Amherst, Mass.). "Terence Cardinal Cooke . . . was called home by

Almighty God to heaven this morning at 4:45 A.M." (official announcement of the Archdiocese of New York, 10/6/83).

change one's place of residence.

CHECK OUT. A departure from a hospital, not a hotel.

close one's eyes. Not just a blink.

CODE (OUT). More medical talk.

conk off (or *out*). Probably from "conk" as slang for the head; a person who has been conked, as by a baseball bat, is dead to the world.

CRUMP. Another of the many terms used by hospital workers to avoid referring to death.

decease. A legal term that becomes a euphemism in nonlegal contexts (see DECEASED).

depart. More precise than most similar circumlocutions, even in such a flowery setting as "John has now departed this vale of tears," but clearly a euphemism when referring to John himself as the DEPARTED or to his death as a bland *departure.*

DIET. A nonce term but nicely indicative of the taboo on "die."

fade. Probably short for *fade away* (or *out*), meaning a slow departure, as in "Aunt Hattie faded last night."

give (or *grant*) *the quietus.* An accounting term, popularized by Shakespeare (see QUIETUS).

go south. "The Dakota tribes believe that the soul, driven out of the body, journeys off to the south, and 'to go south' is, among the Sioux, the favorite euphemism for death" (*Harper's Magazine,* 2/1894).

GO WEST. Popularized in World War I, and one of the many phrases involving GO.

ground(ed) for good. Another aeronautical metaphor.

hang up one's harness or *tackle.* For the last time; cowboy talk.

hop the last rattler. A hobo's death, "rattler" being a freight train, from ca. WW I.

in the grand secret. "He or she is in the grand secret, i.e., dead" (Capt. Francis Grose, *A Classical Dictionary of the Vulgar Tongue,* 1796).

kick the bucket. From the time it appeared in the eighteenth century, the phrase was used in the general sense of "to die," not "to commit suicide," which suggests that the original reference was to the beam, also called a bucket, from which slaughtered pigs were suspended, rather than the bucket on which a suicidal farmer might stand in order to hang himself. Note FDR's use of the expression in *shuffle off* below.

lay down one's knife and fork (or, depending on one's calling in life, *one's pen, shovel, hoe,* etc.).

leave. "One of the pioneering giants of the computer industy has left us" (Richard W. Miller, president of Wang Laboratories, commenting on the death of An Wang, the company's founder, *New York Times,* 3/25/90).

make one's (final) exit. Usually reserved for actors and others with large roles upon the stage of life; informally: "It's curtains for you."

napoo. Another memento of WW I and the AEF; from the French *il n'y a plus,* there is no more.

(one's) number is up. The reference probably is to a lottery number in particular, and to chance, or fate, in general.

pay the debt of (or *to*) *nature.* From the fourteenth century in English and before that in Latin, *debitum naturae.*

pop off. From 1764 (*OED*), and "pop" in the sense of a sudden blow ("One more word out of you, and I'll pop you in the snoot"), but probably much older; see POP.

promotion to glory. For members of the Salvation Army.

RELEASE. A liberation that is not always desired.

shuffle off (or *step off*) *this mortal coil.* Thus, talking about death without really talking about it, President Franklin D. Roosevelt said to Justice Felix Frankfurter on the day of a relative's funeral in 1941, "I am likely to shuffle off long before you kick the bucket." Use of "shuffle" in this connection comes from Shakespeare: "For in that sleep of death what dreams may come, when we have shuffled off this mortal coil" (*Hamlet,* 1601). "Coil" is here used in the sense of the bustle or turmoil of life. The word's origin is unknown; it may have arisen into literary use from slang, as did "rumpus," "hubbub," and other words of similar meaning.

slip one's cable. A sailor's death; also *slip one's ropes* or simply *slip off.*

SNUFF. From the age of candlelight.

step into one's last bus. A British metaphor.

step off. As in "He has stepped off to eternity" or, less formally, "He has stepped off the deep end."

step out. To disappear as well as to die. "Ay, dead!—stepped out" (T. A. Burke, *Polly Peablossom's Wedding,* 1851).

take one's last sleep. A long snooze; see SLEEP.

take off. "When Teddy & I heard yesterday from Lily of Taffy's sad taking-off we both felt a personal regret" (Edith

Wharton, letter, 6/30/08; Taffy was a dog).

take the big jump. From cowpunching, not skydiving; in full, *take the big jump weighted down with (one's) boots.*

take the last bow. Another theatrical expression.

take the last count (or *final count* or *long count*). For ex-boxers.

thirty (or *30*). A journalist's death, from the traditional use of "30" by reporters to indicate the end of a story, in turn from the practice of telegraphers to conclude transmissions in this manner. "'30' or 'Thirty' indicates the end of a shift or a day's work, and has come to mean, also, death" (*American Speech*, 12/29). See also "Mr. Thirty" in STRIPED ONE.

translate. Originally a Biblical term for those few who were *translated* directly into heaven without dying; later extended to righteous but lesser souls, who died in the ordinary way before attaining immortality, e.g., "She was ninety years of age when the Lord translated her" (Anna Jameson, *Sacred and Legendary Art*, 1848).

turn down one's cup or *glass.* The "cup" version is the older; the inverted glass metaphor comes from the last line of the *Rubáiyát of Omar Khayyám*, "turn down an empty Glass," as rendered by Edward FitzGerald (1859).

turn up one's toes to the daisies. Informally: *pushing up daisies.* The French have a similar expression, *manger les pissenlits par la racine,* which means "eating dandelions by the root." (It would be the French, of course, who would think of death in edible terms.)

went to one's last roundup. For cowboys.

went to the races. For sporting types.

wink out. What candles do.

yield up the ghost (or *breath* or *soul* or *spirit*). Basically the same as *give up the ghost.* From the Bible: "And when Jacob had made an end of commanding his sons, he gathered up his feet into the bed, and yielded up the ghost, and was gathered unto his people" (Genesis 49:33).

passenger. Corpse. People in the death business drive PROFESSIONAL CARS with *passengers* (or *silent passengers*), not hearses with dead bodies. *Passengers* may also be launched into space some day. From an interview with Rafael Ross, founder of a New York company, Lad, Inc., which has offered to put LOVED ONES into more or less perpetual orbits: "All the 'passengers'—as he calls them, in the grand tradition of funerary euphemisms—will be sterilized with gamma rays, then hermetically sealed and vacuum packed in ultra-light, ultra-strong Torlon containers" (*New York Times*, 3/13/85). Since the orbiting of *passengers* costs about $10,000 a pound, most are likely to be reduced to ashes before boarding. At the time of the interview, Mr. Ross already had made space in his office for some CRE-MAINS, including those of an Italian woman and her cat, who were scheduled for lift-off as a single payload. See also FUNERAL HOME/PARLOR.

patellar reflex. A fancy "knee jerk"; doctor talk. Sir Ernest Gowers, best remembered for his revision of H. W. Fowler's *A Dictionary of Modern English Usage*, wrote feelingly about this one: "Some 70 years ago a promising young neurologist made a discovery that necessitated the addition of a new word to the English vocabulary. He insisted that this should be 'knee jerk,' and 'knee jerk' it has remained, in spite of the effort of 'patellar reflex' to dislodge it. He was my father; so perhaps I have inherited a prejudice in favor of homemade words" (*Plain Words; A Guide to the Use of English*, 1948). See also BILATERAL ORCHIDECTOMY.

patron. A customer. "Patron," from the Latin *pater*, father, flatters by implying that the customer is the protector of the establishment—a patron saint practically. This sense of the word is preserved in French and Spanish, where the *patron* or *padron* of an inn is the innkeeper, not the customer. In English, however, the *patron* is no longer even a regular customer, but anyone who darkens the door momentarily, as in "Notice to our patrons: The Management is not responsible for articles left in the checkroom." See also CLIENT.

pay down. Pay off. Corporations prefer to *pay down* their debts because "pay off" has bad connotations. See also COMMISSION.

pay equalization concept. Pay increase. Denying that the members of the United States Senate had voted to increase their salaries by $23,200 per annum, Ted Stevens (R., Alaska) maintained that "It is not a pay raise. It is a pay equalization concept" (*Los Angeles Times*, 7/18/91).

Peacekeeper. The MX missile, as renamed by President Ronald Reagan in 1983 in an effort to get congressional approval for building the long-range, four-stage, multiple-warhead, not fully proven ("MX" is for Missile Experimental) weapon. This was in the grand tradition of weapons nomenclature. Thus, the B-36 six-engine bomber, introduced in 1948, was called the Peacemaker, as was the Colt .45 six-shooter, first produced in 1873. (The term had been applied earlier in a general sense to pistols and other weapons, an especially unhappy precedent being the twelve-inch naval cannon, dubbed the "Peacemaker," which exploded during a demonstration aboard a vessel in the Potomac in 1844. Five people were killed, among them the secretaries of War and the Navy.)

Of the many euphemistic names for military devices—e.g., *Davy Crockett* (a mortar that fires nuclear shells), DAISY-CUTTER, *Honest John* and *Little John* (short-range missiles), and *Little Boy* and *Fat Man* (the first two atomic bombs, dropped on Hiroshima and Nagasaki, respectively)—the palm goes to *Sleeping Beauty*, code-name for a Reagan-era project for using powerful electromagnetic fields to reduce people to puddles of helplessness by scrambling their central nervous systems. Runner-up in this department is *Bambi*, an early space weapon designed to hurl steel pellets at enemy missiles. (It seems significant that both of the latter names were popularized by cutesy Walt Disney characters.) Tied for third place are *Bigeye* and *Weteye*, which are nerve gas bombs. See also ANTIPERSONNEL WEAPON; DEFENSE, DEPARTMENT OF; FLYING FORTRESS; REENTRY VEHICLE (or SYSTEM); and STRATEGIC.

peace offensive. A contradiction in terms, signifying—to paraphrase Clauswitz—the continuation of war by other means. "When we speak of man's 'war against nature,' or of a 'peace offensive,' we are accepting the limitations of a metaphor that suggests, and even proposes, violent solutions" (Wendell Berry, "In Defense of Liberty," in *A Continuous Harmony*, 1970). Variants on the theme include *charm offensive*; *violent peace* (used by the U.S. Navy), and *Waging Peace*, the title of the second volume (1965) of Dwight D. Eisenhower's memoirs. See also COERCIVE DIPLOMACY.

pecker. The penis, in American English, but something quite different in British English, where the expression, "Keep your pecker up," translates innocently as "Keep your courage up," or, more freely, as "Never say die." Both the American and British "pecker" probably derive from that barnyard pecker, the cock, a.k.a. ROOSTER.

The anatomical meaning of "pecker" has produced some curious semantic ripples as fastidious people seek to avoid articulating the loaded word. For example, in some localities the "woodpecker" is called a "woodchuck." In Tennessee in the 1920s, people went one step further, referring to the real "woodchuck" as a "groundhog" on account of "woodchuck's" association with the bird, part of whose name could not be uttered before women "without the offender being guilty of a serious and practically unpardonable social blunder" (*American Speech*, 5/52). See also PENIS and TIMBERDOODLE.

peculiar members. The balls or TESTICLES—and by all odds, the most peculiar of the many euphemisms produced by Noah Webster, when that great lexicographer turned his attention to the Bible, publishing in 1833 a new version "with Amendments of the language." Thus, Leviticus 21:19–20, "Or a man that . . . hath his stones broken" (King James Version, 1611) became, in Webster's version, "Or a man that . . . have his peculiar members broken." (See MEMBER and ROCKS.) The egregiousness of Webster's euphemism is mitigated only slightly by knowing that he was using "peculiar" not in the sense of that which is odd, strange, or

queer, but in its original primary sense, relating to personal property, possessions, or privileges.

In rewriting Holy Writ, Webster was following closely in the mincing footsteps of Thomas and Henrietta Maria Bowdler, who had already cleaned up the greatest secular works in the language, with *The Family Shakespeare* (1807, rev. ed. 1818). Webster even defined his objective in virtually the same terms as the Bowdlers (see FAMILY), explaining in a letter of 1836 that his aim had been to remove those words and phrases that "cannot be uttered in families without disturbing devotion."

The extraordinary expurgatory efforts of Webster and the Bowdlers are landmarks in the period of prudery, beginning in the mid-eighteenth century, that led up to full-fledged Victorianism. Webster's "peculiar members," along with his other "amendments" to the Bible, practically constitute a map of the proto-Victorian psyche, indicating the acts, ideas, and bodily parts whose names were subject to the greatest taboos. Among his other euphemisms, as recorded by Allen Walker Read in "Noah Webster as a Euphemist" (*Dialect Notes*, vol. VI, Part VIII, 1934):

> *Breast,* a generalization for "teat," which he consistently deleted. ("Pap" was occasionally allowed to stand.) See also BOSOM.
>
> *Harlot, lewd,* or *lewd woman* for "whore." Webster completely de-whored the Bible. "To play the whore" became "to be guilty of lewdness." In Revelation 17:1, "the great whore that sitteth upon many waters" became "the great harlot." For "whoredom," Webster substituted such expressions as *carnal*

connection, idolatries, impurities, *lewd deeds, lewdness,* and *prostitution.* See also HARLOT and PROSTITUTE.

Ill smell, ill savor, odious scent, and *putrid* were among Webster's euphemisms for "stink," another word that he invariably excised. Thus, in Exodus 7:18, "the river shall stink" was rendered as "shall be offensive in smell." (For the ultimate in "stink," see FRAGRANCE.)

Lewd deeds, lewdness, or *impurity* for FORNICATE/FORNICATION.

Male organs, used as a synonym for those peculiar *peculiar members.* See also ORGAN.

Nurse for the more vivid "suck," with "woe unto them . . . that give suck in those days!" becoming "that nurse infants in those days!" (Matthew 24:19). See also NURSE.

Secrets, for the *peculiar members* and PENIS, considered collectively, e.g., "He that is wounded in the stones, or hath his privy member cut off, shall not enter into the congregation of the Lord" (Deuteronomy 23:1), was watered down by Webster to "He that is wounded or mutilated in his secrets." See also MUTILATE and PRIVATE PART(S).

Vilest excretions, for dung and piss. Webster did not worry much about "dung," changing it only a few times. Nor was "dunghill" ever touched. "Piss" was verboten, however; he deleted it every time. For example, Webster changed 2 Kings 18:17, from "the men which sit on the wall . . . may eat their own dung, and drink their own piss" to "the men which sit on the wall . . . may feed on their vilest excretions." (In this instance the divines who produced the King James Version were more explicit than the original author, their "piss" appearing in place of a euphemistic Hebrew expression, "the water of their feet.")

Of Webster's many circumlocutions, perhaps the most opaque was his rendering of the famous passage about Onan's seed (Genesis, 38:9), wherein it is reported that when Onan "went in unto his brother's wife, that he spilled *it* on the ground . . . " In Webster's version, this became "in to his brother's wife, that he frustrated the purpose." See also MASTURBATION.

We should not be too hard on Webster, however. Modern editions of the Bible frequently lean on euphemisms, too. For example, the Revised Standard Version (1946 NT, 1952 OT), widely used in Protestant churches today, follows Webster in converting "the great whore" of Babylon in Revelation into "the great harlot." And where the King James Version quotes the sister of Lazarus, who had been dead for four days, as telling Christ that "by this time he stinketh" (John 11:39), the RSV has her say "there will be an odor." Similarly, the RSV changes the reference in Exodus about the stinking river to "the Nile shall become foul." In the case of the men on the wall, the RSV compromises between the King James and Webster versions, referring to their "dung" and "urine." This would have been acceptable to Mr. Webster, however.

pee, also **P, pea,** and **pee pee.** Potty talk for "piss," the "pee" and its variants all serving to soften the sibilant sound of a word that itself is probably of onomatopoetic origin.

Knock knock?
Who's there?
Santa.
Santa who?
Centipede on the Christmas tree.
(Grade-school humor, ca. 1954)

"Piss" was not always regarded so badly as today. It came into English about the thirteenth century (see ROOSTER for an early example), deriving from the Old French *pissier*, which also passed into other Teutonic languages—e.g., German, Swedish, and Icelandic—as, of all things, a euphemism.

In times that were franker than our own, Chaucer, Shakespeare, Dryden, and Swift were among the many writers who committed "piss" to paper. The term was even used in books for children, as in the nursery rhyme, "Piss a Bed, Piss a Bed, Barley Butt, Your Bum is so heavy, You can't get up" (*Tom Thumb's Pretty Song Book,* 1744).

The prejudice against "piss" coincides with the general increase in pre-Victorian linguistic delicacy. As early as 1735, Harvard professors lapsed into Latin when forbidding freshmen to "mingo against the College wall" (see JOHN for details). In ensuing decades, the word was dropped from polite discourse. Noah Webster edited out every "piss" when he bowdlerized the Bible in 1833 (see PECULIAR MEMBERS) and Byron's publisher blanked it out when printing his epitaph on Lord Castlereagh in 1840 (see P – – –). Significantly, *The Oxford English Dictionary,* which has many early examples of the word's use, dating to ca. 1290, includes only a single citation for all the years from 1734 to 1902.

The avoidance of "piss" inspired many euphemisms. Most quaintly, the pissant or pissmire, so-called because of its smell, metamorphosed in the Ozarks into the *antmire, antymire,* or, among the exceptionally squeamish, the *step-ant.* The White House also backed off early in the Carter administration (1977) from a changing "National Security Study Memorandum," known informally as "Nissim," to "Presidential Security Study Memorandum," when the realization dawned that this would produce "Pissim."

See also CALLS (or NEEDS) OF NATURE; CAUGHT (or TAKEN) SHORT; DUTY; ELIMINATE/ELIMINATION; GO; LEAK; MAKE (or PASS) WATER; MICTURATE/MITURITION; NUMBER ONE and/or TWO; P – – –; PIDDLE; PO'D; POWDER MY NOSE, I HAVE TO; PUMP SHIP; RELIEVE; RETIRE; SPIT; URINATE/URINATION; WATER SPORTS or GOLDEN SHOWERS; WEE-WEE; and WHIZ.

penetrate/penetration. Bland generalizations for inserting a penis into a vulva, most often encountered in police reports, sex manuals, and other impersonal accounts of the highly personal activity. Thus, recalling the perils of a DEMI-VIERGE: "No penetration, as they put it later, one [chance] in a million, but there you are: you're pregnant" (Sally Belfrage, *Un-American Activities,* 1994).

It helps in understanding the Victorian psyche to know that neither the verb nor noun was admitted to *The Oxford English Dictionary* in a copulatory sense until publication of the 1982 supplement. Then, having shucked their blinders, the editors managed to find examples of the noun going back to 1613. The verb, though dated in the *OED* supplement only to 1953, must be at least as old. Certainly, Shakespeare's pun on "penetrate" in *Cymbeline* (1609–10) is suggestive. When Cloten appears at Imogene's door, he first uses the word in the sense of affecting the heart or emotions: "I would this music would come. I am advised to give her music a-mornings; they say it will penetrate." This line is the cue for musicians to enter, and Cloten continues without a break: "Come on, tune. If you can penetrate her with your fingering, so; we'll try with tongue, too." See also INTERCOURSE and OUTERCOURSE.

penguin. A creature raised semisurreptitiously on kibbutzim in Israel, under the auspices of the Institute of Animal Research. The Israeli *penguin* is a breed apart: It has four legs, a curly tail, and says "oink, oink." These *penguins* (also sometimes called *ducks*) are served in restaurants in Israel as *white meat* or *white steak.* The doubletalk is essential since observant Jews are not even supposed to say "pig" let alone eat it. In the Talmud, the word for "pig" is *davaraher,* which translates as "another thing." In the United States Army, Jewish soldiers, if hungry enough, and if given no choice but ham, bacon, or pork, have been known to ask for helpings of *chicken.* See also FILET MIGNON, FRAGRANT MEAT, HAM EVERY SATURDAY, INTERNATIONAL DINING, and WHITE MEAT.

penis. "Children in English-speaking communities learn early that their communities regard certain words as 'dirty' and instead offer euphemisms that usually are of Latin or French derivation. Instead of *prick* the child is supposed to say *penis,* and he is expected to substitute *vagina* for *cunt*" (Peter Farb, *Word Play: What Happens When People Talk,* 1974). Of course, even "penis" was not seen very often in the press—at least not in FAMILY newspapers—until June 23, 1993, when Lorena Bobbitt, of Manassas, Virginia, cut off her husband's as he slept. (It was found on the lawn of the Paty-Kake Daycare Center, preserved, and reattached.) The reticence of the press faded quickly under the pressure of the public's need to know the details of this dastardly deed. The numbers prove it: "A computer search of the first half of 1993 revealed only a paltry twenty articles mentioning penises. But after the Bobbitt case surfaced, the P-word popped up in more than 1,000 stories" (*Columbia Journalism Review,* 3–4/94).

"Penis," like other Latin terms for sanitizing sexual matters, is a relative newcomer to English, dated in *The Oxford English Dictionary* only to 1693. In the original Latin, *penis* was not considered polite. Cicero commented on this in a letter to a friend in the first century B.C.: "Our ancestors called a tail a penis, and a paint brush is called a 'penicillus' because it is like a tail; but now 'penis' has become an indecent word" (cited by Jasper Griffin, in D. J. Enright, ed., *Fair of Speech,* 1985). It follows from all of this that "penis" and "pencil" (from the Latin word for the painter's brush) are closely related. Therefore it is not only natural, but etymologically correct, that the latter should serve as a euphemism for the former, e.g., "You shoud go out with him just to find out if he's got a pencil" (*Sliver,* film, 1993), or when conveying such gems of folk wisdom as "Oysters will put lead in your pencil." Completing the metaphorical circle is "tail," which also is an old English (circa fourteenth century) term for the "penis" as well as for its female opposite; see TAIL.

Like other key components of human anatomy (e.g., ARSE and BOSOM), the *penis* has (and has had) a wide variety of other names and sobriquets. Following is a partial listing, divided into six broad categories:

1. Personal names: DICK (sometimes euphemized as *dork*), JOHN THOMAS, PETER, ROGER (or RODGER).

2. Weaponry: The analogy of the *penis* to a pointed weapon is old. A Roman nickname for it was *gladius* (sword). Naturally, the *gladius* fitted into a VAGINA (Latin for "sheath"). The English "prick," though not a weapon per se, but something with a point that pierces, continues the thought. Then there is TOOL (in the sense of "sword"), the more-complicated *engine* (meaning a battering ram, an engine of war), *lance, machine, pole-ax* (also a battle-ax), *shaft (of love), truncheon,* and the highly generalized WEAPON. Finally, the age of gunpowder has brought forth the GUN, the *(love) pistol,* and the SHORT ARM, as well as such high-tech items as the *pink torpedo* and *heat-seeking moisture missile.* Not, strictly speaking, an offensive weapon, but definitely a military metaphor is the *purple helmeted warrior (of love).*

3. Anatomical allusions: *arm,* BONE, JOINT, *leg* (or *third leg*), MEMBER, ORGAN, *pizzle* (from an old Germanic word for "sinew"), and *pud* (see PUDENDUM).

4. Miscellaneous metaphors: *banana* (especially when referring to INTERCOURSE, as in *to get one's banana peeled), bat* (and *balls), bauble* (see SCHMO), *bishop, cock* (see ROOSTER), *dipstick* (which, continuing the thought, is used sexually *to check the oil), eel, flute* (as in *play the skin flute,* a.k.a. FELLATIO or MOUTH MUSIC), *garden hose, goober* (i.e., a peanut), *hoe handle* (see HENFIRE), HOOTER, *horn, jerking iron, ladies delight, manhood,* MAN-ROOT, PECKER, *pego* (probably from the Greek word for "spring" or "fountain," though "pegomancy," sad to say, refers only to the art of divination by examining

the way bubbles rise in a spring or fountain), *pipe* (which leads to the copulatory *to lay pipe* or *tube), poker, pole* (or *Maypole* for one of exceptional size), PRONG, *putz* (see SCHMO), *rod* (or *ramrod*), ROOT, *sausage* (with many variants, often with reference to its employment, as in *play hide the sausage, bake the steak, bury the weenie, give someone a [hot] beef injection,* or, from the 1971 film, *The French Connection:* "Want to play hide the salami with the old lady?"), *schlong* (from the Yiddish *shlang,* snake), *snake* itself (as well as such individual species as the *anaconda, cobra, python,* and *one-eyed [trouser] snake,* whence also *kill the snake,* which is to put the thing to sleep by sating its sexual appetite), *stick* (as well as *joy-stick,* predating the invention of the flying machine and joysticks to control them, and the British *creamstick* and *sugarstick*), TUBE STEAK, *wick* (usually in the operational phrases *dip* or *wet one's wick), worm* (whence *worm burping,* which is like *killing the snake*), and YARD.

5. Generalizations: AFFAIR, APPARATUS, BUSINESS, *equipment,* GADGET, INSTRUMENT, *knob, movement,* PERSON, PRIVATE PART(S), THING, THINGUMBOB, and *whang* (probably from the "whang"' that is a resounding blow or BANG, and leading to such by-play as: *Q.* "Who were the first computer programmers?" *A.* "Adam and Eve. She had an Apple. He had a Wang."), *works.*

6. Nonsense and baby talk: DING-A-LING, DONG, DOODLE, *dork* (also as a verb, *to dork someone), peenie, pintle* (see PARSON-IN-THE-PULPIT), *weenie,* WEE-WEE, and *willy* or (*willie*).

people of color. Nonwhite people; a modern revival of an eighteenth-century phrase that leads to a fine semantic distinction, i.e., to call an African-American a "colored" person today is to ask for trouble even though the plural, "people of color," is politically correct. "A new formation, 'people of color,' is making its appearance these days on the near horizon and with it a gathering storm is taking shape. 'People of color' are every hue but white and are non-European in origin. And only 'people of color' are authentically American, so we are told" (Jacob Neusner, *New York Times*, 8/31/88). The phrase originally referred to people of African descent, sometimes mulattos in particular. It may have arisen in the West Indies as a translation of the French *gens de couleur.* The earliest example of the expression in the *Dictionary of American English* comes from Maryland in 1792: "Whereas it has hitherto been a practice among the poorer class of people, and people of color, to Bury their deceased relations . . . in several of the different Streets and Allies of this town." The expression was common prior to the Civil War, used by people of all races, in such forms as *free people of color, persons of color,* and *man* or *woman of color.* See also COLORED, MINORITY, and NEGRO.

people's republic. Government of the masses by a dictator or oligarchy, with the trappings of communism or socialism; sometimes, more elaborately, a *people's democratic republic.* Since, by definition, sovereignty in a republic resides with people, "people's republic" is a redundancy, and the unnecessary duplication reminds one of the person who doth protest too loudly. The modern prototype is the People's Republic of China, where 1.2 billion people, and counting, are ruled by a few old men. See also DEMOCRACY.

people with AIDS. Victims. "A new lexicon was evolving. Under the rules of AID-Speak, for example, AIDS victims could not be called victims. Instead, they were to be called People With AIDS, or PWAs, as if contracting this uniquely brutal disease was not a victimizing experience" (Randy Shilts, *And the Band Played On*, 1987). See also BODILY FLUIDS, EXPOSE, HIGH-RISK GROUP, SEXUALLY ACTIVE, and TB.

percussionist. "Percussionist . . . that's a sophisticated way of saying 'trap drummer'" (Max Roach, WNET-TV, 9/15/83). See also ENGINEER.

performance. Preview. "In the go-go 1980's came the next step: the blurring or end of labeling previews in advertising and in the signs around the box offices, with odd locutions such as 'performances begin' substituting for the former phrase 'previews begin'" (Frank Rich, *New York Times,* 12/22/91). Broadway producers avoid "preview" because of its connotations of "tryout" and "work in progress," which might make it difficult to sell high-priced tickets to troubled shows before critics pan them, e.g., the 1991 musical *Nick and Nora,* which played to nearly 100,000 people (at $30 to $60 per seat) for seventy-one *performances,* then closed after just nine real ones. See also REAR MEZZANINE.

period. The allusion is to the "menstrual period"; probably the most common of the host of ways of referring to this natural phenomenon. See also MENSTRUATION.

permanent borrowing. Theft, as of a book from a library. "Getting enough hardbound copies to make up for the inevitable 'permanent borrowing,' as the Lincoln (Neb.)

City Libraries used to put it, would be prohibitively expensive—and I'm afraid your book, because it's so much fun to browse in, would be prey to this" (Rebecca L. Brite, letter to the author about the first edition of this book, 1/17/83). See also BORROW.

permanent flowers. Artificial flowers. See also ARTIFICIAL.

perpetual care. An obligation that is manifestly impossible to fulfill, but which CEMETERIES and *mausoleums* gladly undertake anyway in return for a surcharge of 10 to 25 percent of the price of graves or crypts. The beautiful part of *perpetual care* is that all the funds collected need not be spent right away, giving the operator a bankroll for other investments. "Perpetual care? . . . in the cemetery business, it means they mow the lawn" ("Lou Grant," WCBS-TV, 10/25/78). See also PRENEED.

person. Once a human being of either sex (from the Latin *persona,* a mask worn by an actor when impersonating someone else) but since the 1970s often a substitute for "woman" in such titles as *chairperson,* CLEANING PERSON, *committeeperson, congressperson, councilperson, selectperson,* and *spokesperson.*

"Person" has become so identified with "woman" that high-status women have been known to object when the womanly (i.e., low-status) "person" is applied to them. For instance, under the dateline, Amherst, Massachusetts: "Town meeting members have voted, 140 to 70, last night against changing the job title of selectman to selectperson. Among the defenders of the established designation were Nancy Eddy and Diana Romer, the two women members of Amherst's five-member Board

of Selectmen" (AP, 5/1/76). "Person" suffered a similar setback in Berkeley, California, where the city council made an exception to its policy of desexing job titles and other terminology when a *councilperson* objected to the preparation of bids for *personhole covers* instead of manhole covers. "'The cover on a sewer,' she said, 'is not an acceptable desexed word'" (*Playboy,* 9/76).

"Person" also has had other euphemistic uses. Thus, bus boys have been converted into *bus persons* (at New York City's Harvard Club, for instance). The term for the entire body also has been employed in lieu of the name of an unmentionable part as in (a British legalism that continued to be employed into the twentieth century): "On one or two occasions, certainly more than once, Newlove [*sic*] put his person into me" (deposition to the London police by George Alma Wright in an 1896 case involving post office telegraph boys and a brothel for men in Cleveland Street). Then there is the Lorenz Hart lyric, mischievously propagating a rumor that many of Irving Berlin's songs were written for him by an anonymous black man: "Though his clothes are sloppy, he certainly makes a good pile./All the writers copy this person in the wood pile" ("There's a Boy in Harlem" in *Fools for Scandal,* film, 1938).

Today, though, "person" has become so well entrenched that the plural form often appears in cases where "people" once would have been used, e.g., "Should programs in graduate education emphasize credentials and degree requirements, or should they seek to educate persons?" (Prometheus Books catalog, 1980). Road workers in New York State have been protected by *flag persons* instead of "flag men" since 1980 when the legislature changed the wording of the law; NASA began referring to *crewpersons* in 1983 and it dropped "manned" missions altogether in 1992 (flights now are "crewed" or "uncrewed," space stations are "inhabited" or "uninhabited"); the classified pages are full of help wanted ads for *copypersons, salad persons, sandwich persons,* and *person Fridays;* juries often are blessed with *forepersons,* and some *persons* have even changed their names to it, as did Donna Ellen Cooperman (née Donna Ellen Bloom), who won a year-long legal battle in New York in December 1977 when a State Supreme Court judge granted her request to become Donna Ellen *Cooperperson.* In *Words and Women* (1976), Casey Miller and Kate Swift point out: "*Salesperson* is a word that doesn't seem to throw anyone into a tizzy. . . . As more women serve in posts once exclusively held by males, -person compounds will come to seem more natural." They are probably right—except for *personhole* covers, of course.

For more about the great and continuing effort to neuteralize the language, see, for example, ADMINISTRATIVE ASSISTANT, AGENT, ARTIFICIAL, FIRE FIGHTER, FLIGHT ATTENDANT, FRESHPERSON, HEAD OF SCHOOL, HEARTS, HERSTORY, HOMEMAKER, HUMAN/HUMANKIND, MONARCH OF THE JUNGLE, POSSLQ, REPRESENTATIVE, SUPERVISOR, and WAITRON.

personal flotation device. A life jacket or other form of life preserver, courtesy of the United States Coast Guard. Airline FLIGHT ATTENDANTS, meantime, have been known to refer to seat cushions as *water devices.* See also CUSHION FOR FLOTATION, ENTRENCHING TOOL, and IMPACT ATTENUATION DEVICE.

personal time control center. A wristwatch. Speaking of Seiko wristwatch mod-els that feature both digital and analog (i.e., with hands) displays, a company spokesman said, "We call them Personal Time Control Centers" (*Wall Street Journal,* 1/1/83). See also ENTRENCHING TOOL.

personnel. Humans, workers. "For factory or outdoor work, report ready to work at PERSONNEL POOL, formerly LABOR POOL, 217A Albany St., Boston" (classified ad, *Boston Globe,* 7/22/80).

"Personnel" weaseled its way into English toward the beginning of the last century, coming from the French, where *le personnel* distinguished an army's human assets from its nonhuman ones, i.e., *le matériel.* Attempts were made at first to Anglicize "personnel," e.g., "The personal of the army or navy" (*Westminster Review,* 4/1833), but by midcentury, the French spelling was not only winning out but spreading to other areas as corporations adopted military terminology, converting employees into *personnel,* who were supervised by *personnel administrators, personnel managers, personnel offices,* and *vice-presidents for personnel.* "Personnel" is still the term of choice in the military, often appearing in such opaque constructions as *ambient noncombatant personnel,* who were native people displaced from their homes by *combatant personnel* during the war in Vietnam; *indigenous personnel,* who are native employees, usually KP's, at overseas bases, and *personnel reaction time (nuclear),* which is the time required to take cover after being warned of a nuclear attack. In the private sector, however, the vogue for "personnel" has waned considerably, with executives schooled in human relations now thinking of their employees as HUMAN RESOURCES. See also ANTIPERSONNEL WEAPON and TRIAGE.

perspire/perspiration. Sweat, as verb and noun.

People have been *perspiring* instead of sweating since the eighteenth century: "It is well known that for some time past, neither man, woman nor child . . . has been subject to that gross kind of exudation which was formerly known by the name of *sweat*; . . . now every mortal except carters, coalheavers and Irish Chairmen . . . merely perspires" (*Gentleman's Magazine,* LXI, 1791). "I gathered that the prevailing opinion of Huck was that he was a deceitful boy who said 'sweat' when he should have said 'perspiration'" (letter, Asa Don Dickinson to Mark Twain, 11/19/05, reporting the exclusion of *Tom Sawyer* and *Huckleberry Finn* from the children's room of the Brooklyn, N.Y., Public Library, in *Mark Twain's Autobiography,* 1924).

Twain's reply warrants a digression in view of the many efforts to censor his works. (See also H – – L.) Declaring that he had written "Tom Sawyer and Huck Finn for adults exclusively," he continued: "It always distresses me when I find that boys and girls have been allowed access to them. The mind that becomes soiled in youth can never again be washed clean; I know this by my own experience, and to this day I cherish an unappeasable bitterness against the unfaithful guardians of my young life, who not only permitted but compelled me to read an unexpurgated Bible through before I was 15 years old. None can do that and ever draw a clean sweet breath again this side of the grave" (11/21/05).

Back to "perspire" and "perspiration": They are preferred by the fastidious because they are Latinate (the root *spirare* means "to breathe"), while "sweat" positively reeks of Old English. The earliest examples in *The Oxford English Dictionary* of "perspire" and "perspiration" in the sweaty sense come from 1725 and 1626, respectively. The present meaning of "sweat," by contrast, dates to at least 1375, and before that, the word referred not to the moisture exuded through the body's pores but to the very blood of life. See also ANTIPERSPIRANT, BO, GLOW, and UNDERARM WETNESS.

pet. To kiss, hug, fondle. "Petting is necking with territorial concessions" (Frederic Morton, *The Art of Courtship,* 1957). "The techniques used in petting include almost every type of physical contact imaginable" (Robert A. Harper, "Petting," *Aspects of Sexuality,* Albert Ellis and Albert Abarbanel, eds., 1967). For the sake of clarity, sexologists and others sometimes divide the activity into *light petting* (hands above the waist) and *heavy petting,* with the latter frequently serving as a euphemism for what Alfred Kinsey called *petting to climax.*

Before they began to *pet* (ca. 1920, about when NECK also came into fashion), Americans had been known to *bundle, canoodle, court, lallygag, spark,* and *spoon.* "Pet" — again like "neck" — may have been waiting in the wings for some time, ready to be adopted by the Flapper generation. The transition from noun to verb, from a pet to petting the pet, is a natural one, and the word has a long history (from 1629, *OED*) of use in the sense of "to make a pet of," "to indulge," "to spoil," but also "to fondle." The indulgent senses were the stronger, however, or a Victorian ecclesiastic would never have gotten off the line, "A little tender petting does her a great deal of good" (Bishop Thorold, *Yoke of Christ,* 1883).

The modern, distinctly erotic meaning was new enough in the early 1920s that Sinclair Lewis felt he had to enclose the term in quotation marks: "Babbitt had heard stories of what the Atlantic Club called 'goings-on' at young parties; of girls 'parking' their corsets in the dressing-room, of 'cuddling' and 'petting,' and a presumable increase in what was known as Immorality" (*Babbitt*, 1922). These "goings-on" also resulted in *petting parties* and even, in centers of higher learning, the study of *petology*. The spirit of the age was summed up in the flaming ad copy for *Alimony*, when that film played at the old OPERA HOUSE in Muncie, Indiana, circa 1925: "Brilliant men, beautiful jazz babies, mid-night revels, petting parties in the purple dawn, all ending in one terrific smashing climax that makes you gasp" (from Robert A. and Helen Merrell Lynd, *Middletown*, 1929). See also DEMI-VIERGE, MAKE OUT, OUT-ERCOURSE, and PARK.

peter. The penis. The term is in wide-spread use but of obscure origin; it could be a euphemistic elaboration of "pee," a deformation of "penis," or—a longer reach but in keeping with the common metaphor of the penis as a GUN—a corruption of "petard," an early explosive device for blowing holes through fortress gates and walls. (The petard, whose name derives from the French *péter*, to break wind, in the sense of "to fart," and the Latin *pēdere*, with the same meaning, frequently misfired; hence, the expression "to be hoist with one's own petard," i.e., to be caught in a scheme of one's own contrivance.) What-ever the derivation, the use of "peter" for "penis" has naturally caused some people to have second thoughts about the Christ-ian name. Thus, talking about folkways in the Ozarks: "Very straight-laced old-timers seldom name a boy Peter. I recall an evan-gelist from the North who shouted some-

thing about the church being founded upon Peter, and he was puzzled by the flushed cheeks of the young women and the ill-suppressed amusement of the ungodly" (Vance Randolph and George P. Wilson, *Down in the Holler: A Gallery of Ozark Folk Speech*, 1953). If women were present, men from these parts also would say "salt" or "potash" instead of "salt-peter," and many of them hesitated to say that something had "petered out." To Groucho Marx, finally, is attributed the astute observation that both parts of actor Peter O'Toole's name mean "penis." See also BREAK WIND, PENIS, and TOOL.

pharmacy. Drugstore. Telephone company *Yellow Pages* are a practically infallible guide to pretentious diction. Thus, the entry for "drugstore" (or "druggist") typi-cally refers the user to "Pharmacies." Of course, the *pharmacies* themselves some-times adopt even more esoteric guises, such as Downing Chemists Ltd. and the Village Apothecary, both in New York City.

physical. In sports: rough, tough, often dirty. A *physical* team leaves its opponents with bruises and, possibly, assorted sprains, strains, breaks, and bites. In amorous en-counters: *to get physical* is to be sexually aggressive. See also INTERCOURSE.

physical fitness. Physical appeal. The offi-cial name of the segment of the Miss Amer-ica competition in which young women strut their stuff in swimsuits is called "Physical Fitness in Swimwear." It used to be that the winner of the overall competi-tion (*physical fitness*, believe it or not, is not the only thing that counts) enjoyed a year-long "reign"; in 1993 this was changed to a politically correct year of *service*.

physically challenged. Handicapped. "The rules committee of the Democratic Party recently decided to drop the term 'handicapped' in favor of the term 'physically challenged'" (*Quarterly Review of Doublespeak,* 10/80). "We're looking at a woman who makes it possible for physically challenged people to attend Giants and Jets football games" (Nicholas Buoniconti, HBO, 11/21/91). Originally applied to people who can get around only in wheelchairs, the meaning of "physically challenged" has been broadened over the years to include those with other impairments. Thus, the Connecticut Conference Task Force for Youth and Young Adults with Physical Challenges includes people who are blind and deaf as well as those who are wheelchair-bound.

N.B.: Many of the *physically challenged* dislike the term (as they do DIFFERING ABILITIES). "'Physically challenged' doesn't distinguish me from a woman climbing Mt. Everest" (Nancy Mairs, essayist and poet with multiple sclerosis, *Washington Post,* 8/25/91). Ms. Mairs prefers "crippled." See also CHALLENGE, COGNITIVELY CHALLENGED, VERTICALLY CHALLENGED, and VISUALLY CHALLENGED.

physically correct. Anatomically complete, as applied to dolls. Archie Bunker's grandson doll was a "physically correct male," according to the box containing it (12/77). In other words, it came with a PENIS.

physique. Body in general, but in a feminine context, almost always a reference to a person's "build," meaning "large breasts," as in "Tanya has a great physique." See also BOSOM, and STATUESQUE.

piddle. To piss; potty talk, dating to at least the eighteenth century, perhaps from the earlier use of "piddle" in the sense of "to trifle," "to dally," with reinforcement from the "P" sound. As is generally true of potty talk, the older the user, the more euphemistic the expression, e.g., "The young lady's room was opposite to mine, and . . . I could not restrain myself from listening to hear when she piddled" (anon., *My Secret Life,* ca. 1890). See also PEE and WEE-WEE.

pig's eye, in a. Pig's ass, in a. "Attorney General Edward Levi let it be known that he considered the matter 'extremely serious.' To officials of the Federal Bureau of Investigation, Levi's comment was a monumental understatement. 'Extremely serious in a pig's eye,' said one. 'It's a disaster'" (*Time,* 4/5/76). This expression of incredulity, rejection, or refusal has been dated to 1872 (*OED*), but probably is much older and of ultimately bestial origin. (It parallels "fuck a duck," also used to convey surprise and disbelief.) Variants on the porcine theme include *in a pig's ear* and *in the pig's eye.* See also ARSE.

pioneer. Farmer. "Very few people living in the Middle West have grandfathers that were *farmers*: they were *pioneers*" (Allen Walker Read, "An Obscenity Symbol," *American Speech,* 12/34).

pish/pshaw. Two effete exclamations of contempt or disgust. "She writh'd with impatience more than pain,/And utterd 'pshaws!' and 'pishes!'" (Thomas Hood, *Miss Kilmansegg and Her Precious Leg,* 1840). Samuel Johnson, defining "pish" in his great *Dictionary of the English Language* (1755), noted: "This is sometimes spoken and written *pshaw.* I know not their etymology and imagine them formed by chance." Which may be so. Nevertheless, the resemblance between "pish/pshaw" and "piss/shit" is suspicious. In practice, though, either term may be substituted for almost any stronger one. For example, speaking of an otherwise innocuous card game: "Oh Hell (called Oh Pshaw or Blackout in family journals) made its appearance in New York card clubs in the 1930s" (Albert H. Morehead and Geoffrey Mott-Smith, *Hoyle's Rules of Games*, 1963). See also HECK and SHUCKS.

planned parenthood. Birth control, a.k.a. FAMILY PLANNING. The National Birth Control League, founded in 1915, evolved into the Planned Parenthood Federation in 1942. The idea, as songwriter Johnny Mercer put it in another context, is to "Ac-Cent-Tu-Ate the Positive." See also PRO-CHOICE.

plant. To bury; an Americanism, dating to the middle of the nineteenth century. "I don't want any absurd 'literary remains' & 'unpublished letters of Mark Twain' published after I am planted" (Samuel L. Clemens, letter, 1865). See also INTERMENT and REMAINS.

plantation. A ritzy subdivision on Hilton Head island, South Carolina. "In dozens of lawsuits and countersuits, the owners of the island's largest subdivisions, known locally as 'plantations,' accused one another of elaborate land swindles and bank fraud" (*New York Times*, 3/15/87). See also ENCLAVE.

plausible denial. Official lying; official ignorance. Originally a tactic for shielding the United States government from responsibility for actions abroad, "plausible denial" evolved into a ploy for protecting the president from responsibility for unlawful acts, whether at home or abroad. Speaking of CIA practice: "The theory of

'plausible denial' . . . requires that no covert operation can be traced back to the U.S. government. . . . It means that an operation, even if it is blown, can be denied as an officially sponsored act without the government's being caught in a barefaced lie" (Harry Rositzke, *The CIA's Secret Operations*, 1977). Within the White House, "plausible denial" developed in this way: "The President, I was told . . . had scrawled my orders in the margin of his daily news summary. No one had to explain why the President's name was not used. He was always to be kept one step removed, insulated, to preserve his 'deniability'" (John W. Dean III, *Blind Ambition*, 1976).

See also ASSASSINATION, COVERT ACTION (or OPERATION), and NO RECALL (or MEMORY or RECOLLECTION) OF.

pledged. Pawned, hocked.

pluck. Guts. "He wants pluck; he is a coward!" (Capt. Francis Grose, *A Classical Dictionary of the Vulgar Tongue*, 1796). As a byword for courage, "pluck" seems to have appeared before "guts," but it arose the same way and remains as a euphemism for what is now considered to be the stronger term. In truth, "pluck" really is just another word for "viscera" (i.e., g – ts). For example: "I saw . . . five unpleasant-looking objects stuck on sticks. They were the livers and lungs, and in fact the plucks, of witch-doctors" (Mary Kingsley, *Travels in West Africa*, 1897). See also BOTTOM, FRY, and INTESTINAL FORTITUDE.

plumber. An agent of the Nixon White House, a burglar. The *plumbers* were supposed to fix leaks of classified information, particularly the gusher represented by Dr. Daniel Ellsberg's disclosure of "The Pentagon Papers" in 1971. The name comes from the sign, "The Plumbers," tacked to the door of Room 16 in the basement of the Executive Office Building where the group, formally known as the Special Investigations Unit, was headquartered. The sign was the work of David R. Young, cochairman of the unit, according to William Safire (*Safire's Political Dictionary*, 1978).

The operations of the *plumbers* involved some of the choicest euphemisms, circumlocutions, and doubletalk of the Watergate era. The unit was set up after John D. Ehrlichman and Egil "Bud" Krogh, Jr., met with President Richard M. Nixon on July 24, 1971, in the OVAL OFFICE. Four days later, E. Howard Hunt, Jr., who had been working for the White House as a CONSULTANT, wrote a memo proposing the NEUTRALIZATION (public smearing) of Ellsberg. One of Hunt's ideas was to get the files of Ellsberg's psychiatrist. On August 11, Krogh and Young recommended to Ehrlichman that this be done by means of a COVERT ACTION or OPERATION (burglary). Over the Labor Day weekend, a team of burglars under Hunt and G. Gordon Liddy broke into the psychiatrist's offices but could not find the files on Ellsberg. The failed operation (also called "Hunt-Liddy Special Project #1") became a key element in the Watergate THING after Liddy and Hunt were implicated in yet another break-in—the Watergate CAPER of June 17, 1972. Hunt's threat to spill the beans to prosecutors about his earlier jobs, unless he was given some $120,000 and the assurance of clemency (see EXPLETIVE DELETED), then became a powerful force in drawing the president himself ever deeper into the COVER-UP.

It is merely a happy coincidence that "plumber," from the Latin word for "lead," *plumbum,* also is slang for "to make a mis-

take," "to botch," as in "I tho't I plumbered it" (John O'Hara, *Pal Joey,* 1939).

plump. Overweight; sometimes, *pleasingly plump,* which has a range of meanings, from "plump in the right places" to "grossly obese." In general, "plump" is the feminine counterpart of PORTLY.

PO'd. Pissed off. The initialed euphemism, common since at least World War II, is considered so innocuous that it can be used in public, even by women, without raising eyebrows or causing editors to reach for blue pencils. "Just leave out the prejudicial adjectives. When I see them I get P.O.'d" (Ruth Pearl, letter, Woodbury, Conn., *Voices,* 2/24/93). See also PEE and TEED OFF.

poke. A paper bag; see SACK.

police action. A war; specifically, the Korean War, a.k.a. CONFLICT or *emergency.* "In this war, long called a 'police action,' the United Nations suffered casualties totaling about 74,000 killed, 250,000 wounded, and 83,000 missing and captured" (*Encyclopedia Americana,* 1965).

The war could not officially be called a war because it was never legally declared by Congress to be one. The phrase, "police action," was popularized by President Harry S. Truman, but as often turns out with such utterances, the words were put into the famous man's mouth by a lowly reporter. It happened this way:

On June 29, 1950, at his first press conference after the start of the war four days before, Truman said the United States was repelling a raid by "a bunch of bandits." A reporter then asked if "it would be correct . . . to call this a police action under the United Nations?" The president replied,

"Yes, that is exactly what it amounts to." This was all the newspapers needed to justify such headlines as "Truman Calls Intervention 'Police Action.'" In *Thunder of the Captains* (1977), David Detzer suggests that the anonymous reporter, in turn, got the phrase from a Senate speech made two days earlier by William F. Knowland (R., Calif.), who compared the role of the air force to that of the police, chasing a burglar away from the scene of a crime. Asserted Knowland: "The action this government is taking is a police action against a violator of the law of nations and the Charter of the United Nations."

Technically, the Korean *police action* was classed as a LIMITED WAR. See also ACTION and VIETNAM ERA.

polygraph interview. A lie detector test. See also FIELD INTERVIEW.

poop. (1) To fart; (2) shit, whether as noun or verb. "We used the words *poop* and *poot* with their onomatopoeic significance in regard to bodily discharges" (*American Speech*, 12/48). "You touch my gun again and I'll beat the poop out of you" (MacKinlay Kantor, *Andersonville*, 1955). This is basic potty talk, perhaps with reinforcement from the "poop" that is the rear end of a sailing vessel as well as a person. All senses are at least several hundred years old and they have been extended in various ways, e.g., *bird poop, dog poop,* and POOPER-SCOOPER. See also BREAK WIND (for an early eighteenth-century "poop"), DEFECATE/DEFECATION, DIDDLY-POO, POOPER, and WEE-WEE.

pooper. The ass, i.e., that from which comes POOP. "Supermodel Claudia Schiffer turned restless . . . someone had planted their pooper in her assigned seat" (*New York Post*, 3/7/93). See also ARSE.

pooper-scooper. A small shovel for picking up POOP, a.k.a. DOG DIRT/DO/LITTER/WASTE.

poor. Black; the honest word for the lack of money becomes a dishonest word for something else when the subject under discussion is something else. "But when white professionals busy themselves with birth control for the poor (meaning blacks) it strikes many blacks as a racist plot" (*New Republic*, 8/7&14/71). See also DISADVANTAGED.

poorly buffered precipitation. Acid rain. "It was a year in which the Environmental Protection Agency forbade its employees from using the term 'acid rain' and decreed that henceforth the term would be 'poorly buffered precipitation'" (William Lutz, speech presenting the 1982 Orwell and Doublespeak awards of the National Council of Teachers of English, 11/19/82). "Acid rain" also has been eliminated in other ways, e.g., by describing it as "atmospheric deposition of anthropogenically-derived acidic substances" (*Quarterly Review of Doublespeak*, 1/85) and "wet deposition, atmospheric precipitation, or, commonly, 'acid rain'" (*Quarterly Review of Doublespeak*, 4/92). See also CLEAN AIR and PRECIPITATION.

pop. To SCREW or to kill by shooting; another of the many terms that combine sex and violent death (see also ACTION). Using the expression in the first sense, which appears to be the newer, a friend asked Claude Brown about a possible conquest: "'Well, did you pop her?'" (*Manchild in the Promised Land*, 1965). And in the second sense, describing the 1984 shooting of a high school basketball star: "It turned out that Wilson had bumped into one of the teen-agers, who turned to his companion and said, 'He pushed me; pop him'" (*New*

York Times, 2/14/93). The explosive "pop" of a handgun, especially a revolver, also known in slang since the eighteenth century as a *pop* or *popper,* almost certainly has contributed to the modern meanings. Early examples of the term in its deathly sense suggest, however, that it stemmed originally from "pop off," meaning "to die" or PASS AWAY (in turn from "pop's" oldest senses of a sudden rap or blow). Thus, from Samuel Foote's *The Patron* (1764): "If Lady Peppercorn should happen to pop off." It seems significant, too, that before people carried *poppers* that pop bullets, they had daggers for *popping off* people, e.g., "A jolly poppere bare he in his pouche—There was no man for peril durst him touche" (Geoffrey Chaucer, *The Reeve's Tale,* 1387–1400).

pope's nose. See PARSON'S (or POPE'S or BISHOP'S) NOSE.

poppycock. The word's aboveboard interpretation is "rubbish" or "nonsense," but it actually means "soft dung," from the Dutch *pappekak.* Etymology does not seem to be the strong point of the people at Sandoz Nutrition Corp., El Paso, Texas, who market a brand of popcorn called "Poppycock." See also BS and CACKA.

pork. To do the sex act, to SCREW. "Your father deserted me so he could pork his interior decorator" (*Look Who's Talking,* film, 1989). "Pork-sword" is an older British term for the PENIS, but the modern American usage probably is based more on the resemblance in sound of two words ending in "k"; see also F – – –.

portly. Fat. "Don's a little portly now," observed New York Yankee announcer Phil Rizutto, as Don Zimmer, roundish manager of the Boston Red Sox, ambled toward the pitcher's mound (WPIX-TV, NYC, 6/14/77).

"Portly" people tend to move in a slow, dignified manner, much like ocean liners docking, and the word itself once meant "stately," "dignified," "majestic," "handsome." Thus, Christopher Marlowe did not mean "fatty" when he referred to "my queen and portly empress." The Elizabethans, however, did use "portly" both ways, with that famous fat man, Sir John Falstaff, no doubt getting a laugh when he described himself as "A goodly portly man, i' faith, and a corpulent" (William Shakespeare, *Henry IV, Part 1,* 1597). See also AMPLE, BROAD-BEAMED, BUXOM, CORPORATION, KING-SIZE, PLUMP, and STOUT.

position. A "job" in managerial guise. Where an executive is ASSOCIATED WITH a company in a particular *position* or CAPACITY, his (sic) secretary has a job, unless she (sic) is an ADMINISTRATIVE ASSISTANT, in which case she may be said to have a *position,* too. "Position" has a FOP Index of 3.3. See also CAREER.

possible. Advice to a young woman about sprucing up before going out on a date: "First, you wash down as far as possible. Then you wash up as far as possible. Then you wash possible" (old saying, from a southern woman who prefers to remain anonymous). See also GENITALS.

POSSLQ (or posslq). Person of the Opposite Sex Sharing Living Quarters; an acronym devised by the U.S. Census Bureau in 1979 for couples who formerly would be described as "living in sin" (and an "improvement" upon the Bureau's first effort along this line: "Partners of the Opposite, etc.").

In trying to defuse whatever passion exists in such unsanctified relationships, the bureaucrats managed to pervert the very meaning of the words. "The Feds, as usual, screwed it up by creating POSSLQ . . . which could refer to married couples as well as unmarried or newborn twins, or just about anybody" (*National Review*, 5/25/79). See also COHABITOR, PARTNER, PERSON, and SIGNIFICANT OTHER.

post. An autopsy, short for "post-mortem"; sometimes used as a verb, as in "The patient died last night and will be posted this morning" (*American Speech*, 5/61). See also EXPIRE.

posterior(s). The ass; an elegant Latinized euphemism, comparable in a topographical sense to the more mundane BACKSIDE or REAR. Thus, Fanny Hill described one of her coworkers: "Her posteriors, plump, smooth, and prominent, form'd luxuriant tracts of animated snow, that splendidly filled the eye" (John Cleland, *Memoirs of a Woman of Pleasure*, 1749). People have been sitting upon their *posteriors* at least since the seventeenth century. No doubt, it is merely a strange—not to say unnatural—coincidence that the oldest examples in *The Oxford English Dictionary* of "posteriors" and the related DERRIÈRE both have to do with spanking. In the case of the former, the illustration is of "A poor pedantick schoolmaster sweeping his living from the posteriors of little children" (William Drummond, of Hawthornden, *Notes of B. Jonson's Conversations with D.*, 1619). See also ARSE and CUL-DE-SAC.

post-traumatic stress disorder (PTSD). A psychiatric illness; the latest version (from Vietnam) of a military affliction known as *battle* (or *combat*) *fatigue* during the Korean POLICE ACTION and World War II, and as *shell shock* during World War I. "Post-traumatic stress disorder" was adopted officially by the medical establishment with publication of the 1980 edition of the *Diagnostic and Statistical Manual*. By whatever name, the condition seems to be relatively new. Typically, its severity is a function of the length of exposure to combat; prior to the twentieth century, however, battles rarely lasted more than two or three days—not long enough to break men down this way. See also CASUALTY and FATIGUE.

pound. A pound of caviar usually weighs fourteen ounces—sort of like a baker's dozen in reverse. See also LARGE and QUARTER-POUND.

powder my nose, I have to. Use the toilet, i.e., *powder room*—a common public excuse for a private errand involving neither powder nor nose. "Where Can One Powder One's Nose?" (Cole Porter, song title, *The New Yorkers*, 1930).

The name of the destination, and the excuse for visiting it, appear to date to the 1920s. In bygone times, when people went to powder closets or powder rooms, it was to put powder on their hair or wigs, unless they happened to be aboard a ship of war, in which case they were looking for gunpowder. "During the days of Prohibition some learned speak-easy proprietor in New York hit upon the happy device of calling his retiring room for female boozers a *powder-room*" (H. L. Mencken, *The American Language, Supplement I*, 1945).

Despite recent attempts to eliminate gender differences in language, "powder my nose" is still used almost exclusively by women. Fast women, as well as fast-talking ones, may also adopt the jocular variant, "I have to powder my puff." Men, meanwhile, have their own separate euphemisms for the same mission: Perhaps the most common is "I have to see a man about a dog." A man who wants to demonstrate his *savoir faire* may vary this, announcing that he has to "see a dog about a man." This is guaranteed to impress. (In one way or another.)

Other examples of the ingenuity of mankind (and womankind) in explaining away the CALLS (or NEEDS) OF NATURE include:

cash (or *write*) *a check*

chase a rabbit (in the era of the outdoor PRIVY)

consult Mrs. Jones

drain one's radiator (or *crankcase* or *vein*)

feed a dog

freshen up

give a Chinaman a music lesson

go feed the goldfish (see also GO)

go see a dog

go pick a daisy

go see the baby

go see how high the moon is (above the OUTHOUSE, presumably)

go to Cannes or *Deauville* (two famous watering spots) or *Egypt* or *Lulu's* (see LOO)

go to my aunt's closet (or *see my aunt*)

go to the bank

go water the lawn or *the petunias* or *the stock* (all outdoors, of course)

kill a snake

mail a letter

make a pit stop (from auto racing)

make a telephone call

pay a call

pay a visit (to the old soldiers' home)

pick a daisy (or *wildflowers*), yet other outdoor errands

PUMP SHIP

raise the level of the water (if aboard ship)

see a man about a horse

see Johnny (see JOHN)

shake hands with an old friend (or *my wife's best friend*)

shake the dew off my lily

sharpen the skates

shoot a dog (American) or *a lion* (English)

spend a penny (English)

stretch my legs

tap a kidney

visit the chamber of commerce

wash my hands

wring the rattlesnake

WHIZ

See also DEFECATE/DEFECATION, PEE, TOILET, and WASHROOM.

prairie oysters. The testicles of a bull calf when presented as a delicacy for eating. Of course, flatlanders are not the only people to enjoy such fare. Gourmets in the hills eat those of boar and sheep as well as those of bulls, but to the uplanders, these dishes are known as *mountain oysters, Rocky Mountain oysters*, or simply *mountain food.* Variations on the theme include *Chicago oysters*, which are pigs' testicles, and *Cincinnati oysters*, or pigs' feet. Meantime, *prairie strawberries* on the plains are "beans" in other parts of the country. See also CAPE COD TURKEY, FILET MIGNON, FRY, and TESTICLES.

prat. The ass. An old word, "prat" is related to "pretty"; both are of obscure origin. The Old English *praett* meant a trick, or prank, while the Old English "pretty," *praettig*, meant cunning or sly. Examples of *praett* in *The Oxford English Dictionary* go back to about the year 1000, while the oldest "prat" in the sense of "a buttocks" comes from 1567. In modern times, theater people, especially, are prone to fall on their *prats* or to take *pratfalls,* usually by intent in comedy routines. (Note the retention of the "trick" element in the word's meaning after nearly a thousand years.) See also ARSE.

precipitation. Water from the sky. The generalized "precipitation" is favored by meteorologists and TV weather PERSONS, partly because the Latin term sounds altogether more professional, more scientific, and partly as a way of hedging their bets, since general forecasts have a greater chance of being correct than such specific ones as "rain," "snow," or "hail." See also METEORIC WATER, POORLY BUFFERED PRECIPITATION, and SHOWER ACTIVITY.

precision bombing. Bombs directed at particular targets; also called *discriminate deterrence* during the Gulf war of 1991.

The deceptively precise "precision bombing" has helped Americans rationalize air bombardment of civilian populations—a distinguishing feature of World War II, as opposed to World War I, which at least had the virtue of limiting battle deaths almost exclusively to the battlefield. According to the chief of the army air force, General Henry H. "Hap" Arnold, *precision bombing* "aimed at knocking out not an entire industrial area, nor even a whole factory, but the most vital parts of Germany's war machine, such as the power plants and machine shops of particular factories" ("Air Strategy for Victory," *Flying,* 10/43). On paper, this looked fine, but in practice dropping bombs on smallish targets from high altitudes under combat conditions wasn't as easy as the general implied. In 1943, only 15 percent of the bombs dropped by the 8th Air Force hit within 1,000 feet of their aiming points; in 1945, after two years' practice, accuracy improved to 60 percent. "American preci-

sion bombing had proven [this was by the spring of 1944] to be not so precise as had been hoped. . . . Even the relatively precise bombing of industrial targets inevitably killed and maimed large numbers of civilians hitherto exempt from the most direct horrors of war" (Russell F. Weigley, *The American Way of War,* 1973). *Precision bombing,* as carried out in daylight raids by B-17 FLYING FORTRESSES, contrasted with nighttime AREA BOMBING, popularized by the British Royal Air Force. For other ways of improving bombing accuracy through the power of words, see DELIVER, SPECIFIED STRIKE ZONE, *strategic bombing* in STRATEGIC, and SURGICAL STRIKE.

preemptive strike. A surprise (i.e., sneak) attack, also called a *preemptive first strike.* The uncanny resemblance between the dispassionate war-gamer's "preemptive strike" and what Japan did to the United States on December 7, 1941, was noted by Attorney General Robert F. Kennedy, when such an attack was proposed as a quick solution to the Cuban missile crisis of October 1962. Partly paraphrasing Kennedy's words, Theodore C. Sorensen reports: "A sudden airstrike at dawn Sunday without warning, said the Attorney General, would be 'a Pearl Harbor in reverse, and it would blacken the name of the United States in the pages of history' . . . the Cuban people would not forgive us for decades; and the Soviets would entertain the very dangerous notion that the United States, as they had feared all these years, was indeed capable of launching a preemptive first strike" (*Kennedy,* 1965). See also PREVENTIVE ACTION/DETENTION/WAR, and SURGICAL STRIKE.

pregnant. Gestating—*preggers* for those who do not wish to pronounce the entire word. Now the most common term for the condition, "pregnant" has a checkered history, having been drafted into service as a genteel euphemism in the pre-Victorian era, then barred from polite discourse for much of the nineteenth and twentieth centuries. Its initial rise to fashion was noted in December 1791, in *Gentleman's Magazine*:

> All our mothers and grand-mothers used in due course of time to become *with-child,* or, as Shakespeare has it, *round-wombed* . . . but it is very well known, that no female, above the degree of chamber-maid or laundress, has been *with-child* these ten years past: every decent married woman now becomes *pregnant*; nor is she ever *brought to bed,* or *delivered,* but merely, at the end of nine months, has an *accouchment*; antecedant to which she always informs her friends that at a certain time she shall be *confined.*

The veneer wore off "pregnant" within a couple of generations, so full-fledged Victorians replaced it with completely opaque terms; see DELICATE and INTERESTING CONDITION (or SITUATION or STATE) for examples from Dickens and Thackeray, respectively. Queen Victoria herself said that she had been CAUGHT, not made pregnant. Even into the 1950s, the word was considered too fraught with sexual implications to mention on television, which is why Lucille Ball, star of "I Love Lucy," became ENCEINTE. During the long period in which "pregnant" remained under the ban, people resorted to a great many other euphemisms for the condition. See also ACCIDENT; ANKLE, TO SPRAIN AN; ANTICIPATING; BLESSED EVENT; EXPECTANT; EXPECTING; FAMILY WAY, IN THE; FRAGRANT; GRIEF; KNOCK UP; THAT WAY; WITH CHILD; and YOU-KNOW-WHAT.

preliterate. The modern anthropologist's tactful, oh-so-scientific replacement for "primitive," in turn a euphemism for "savage." If she were writing today, Ruth Benedict would be tarred and feathered for opening her acknowledgments as she did in *Patterns of Culture* (1934) with a sentence that begins: "The three primitive peoples described in this volume . . ." See also FOLK ART and UNDERDEVELOPED.

preneed. Predeath; the usual way of characterizing cemetery sales that are made while the prospective occupants of the SPACE are alive and kicking, as opposed to *at need* or *postneed*, when they aren't. The aggressive cemetery promoter focuses on *preneed* selling because the market is much larger and because it enables him to close deals before the FUNERAL DIRECTOR, with whom he increasingly competes, can get his foot in the door. (This has inspired some FUNERAL HOME operators to offer *prearrangement* counseling.) *Preneed* selling also brings in cash for monuments and PERPERTUAL CARE that doesn't have to be spent right away; such monies are put into trust funds whose size has been known to tempt some operators from the strict paths of righteousness. The advantages of *preneed* selling, or something very similar, have long been recognized. Hubert Eaton, The Dreamer, who made Forest Lawn what it is today, began work for that cemetery in 1912 as agent for "before-need" sales. See also CEMETERY, INTERMENT, and MEMORIAL PARK.

preorgasmic. Sexually unresponsive. Taking the optimistic view, the Sex Advisory and Counseling Unit of the University of

California Medical School in San Francisco classified women who have never had an orgasm as "pre-orgasmic" (*Time,* 4/1/74). The institutes for Rational Living and for Rational Emotive Therapy in New York City cast a slightly wider net, conducting a "Pre-Orgasmic Women's Group" for those "who have not experienced orgasm or who have rarely reached orgasm" (1978–79 catalog). See also COME and O.

preowned. Used; shorthand for the equally euphemistic "previously owned." Honor for popularizing the fancy phrase goes to the Cadillac people. New York's Potamkin Cadillac, among others, has advertised "preowned" as well as "previously owned" vehicles on radio and television since at least the mid-1970s. Now everyone does it: "In a less exalted part of town, the second-hand car salesman will try to 'dispose' of his stock by using epithets such as 'pre-owned', 'experienced' or 'previously distinguished'" (*Irish Times,* 9/29/90). Other more-or-less euphemistic terms for second-hand cars include *nearly new, rebuilt, reconditioned,* and *repossessed.* See also AUTOMOTIVE DISMANTLER AND RECYCLER, EXPERIENCED, PREREAD, and PREUSED.

preparatory. Remedial. The state of Florida officially eliminated "remedial" instruction when the legislature approved an education bill in 1984 that changed "remedial courses" and "remedial development and instruction" into "college preparatory adult education" and "college preparatory instruction." At the same time, "remediation" turned into "additional preparation" (*Quarterly Review of Doublespeak,* 4/86).

prepared biography. A notice of a death that has not yet occurred; a before-the-fact OBITUARY. "Richard Nixon's political obits—the

Associated Press prefers the euphemism 'prepared biography'—are set in type and are on tape and film at a dozen major news organizations, where they are freshly updated" (*New York Times,* 12/17/73). Alden Whitman, chief obituary writer of the *New York Times* for many years, employed a similar round-about, "biographical essay," when asking for interviews with people whose deaths he planned to cover. See also PROTECTIVE COVERAGE.

preplan. Plan; the addition of the unnecessary "pre" produces a FOP Index of 2.0. Used mainly in bureaucratic contexts, "preplan" appears to reflect the delight that all good bureaucrats take in attending meetings. In order to prepare themselves for "planning" meetings, these cagey types gather in advance sessions that are called—naturally—"preplanning" meetings. Of course, "preplan" is gobbledegook, as demonstrated by the fact that the plain "plan" invariably can be substituted for it with no loss in meaning, e.g., "Once the inhabitants of a preplanned target area have been adequately warned that the area has been selected as a target and given sufficient time to evacuate, the area may then be struck without further warning" (MACV Dir 525-13, 5/1/71). For more about this directive, see SPECIFIED STRIKE ZONE.

preread a.k.a. **previously read.** Used, secondhand. "Preread" is to books as PREOWNED is to cars. "In 1974, Annie Adams, mother of six and former suburban housewife, went shopping for novels in a book store that had devoted a small section of its shelf space to 'pre-read' books" (Dennis L. Foster, *The Rating Guide to Franchises,* 1988). "'Previously read' library books, hardcover bestsellers a year or more old, are on sale at cut-rate prices at a number of B. Dalton stores" (*Publishers Weekly*, 4/27/92).

preused. Used. Speaking of a $15,000 Steinway that was sold as new when it wasn't really, a spokeswoman for Horne's Department Store in Pittsburgh, Pennsylvania, said, "It was an inventory-control error. It should have been marked as pre-used" (*Wall Street Journal*, 7/27/87). See also PREOWNED.

prevaricate. A long-winded, soft-sounding, Latinized "lie." "Prevaricate" and its related nouns, *prevarication* and *prevaricator,* derive from the Latin *praevāricāri,* meaning "to walk a crooked course" and, hence, to deviate from the straight path of truth. See also FABRICATION and WHITE LIE.

preventive action/detention/war. "Preventive" whitewashes dirty business in much the same way as "protective" (e.g., PROTECTIVE CUSTODY and PROTECTIVE REACTION). Thus, *preventive action,* as practiced in the FBI's Counterintelligence Program (Cointelpro to the pros), included a wide range of criminal acts, such as burglaries (BLACK BAG JOBS), mail openings, forgery, and entrapment. Meanwhile, the motive behind *preventive detention* is to rationalize the confinement of people who might possibly commit crimes, thus perverting the traditional presumption of innocence into one of guilt. The worst case of *preventive detention* in American history is the DETENTION of Japanese-Americans at the start of World War II in what were known variously as ASSEMBLY CENTERS and RELOCATION CENTERS.

Of course, the most dangerous of the "preventives" is "war." The true nature of "preventive war" has been recognized even by generals. Thus, Henry Cabot Lodge reported that Dwight D. Eisenhower "did not believe there was such a thing as preventive war . . . [and] would not even listen seriously to anyone who talked about it" (Lodge, *As It Was,* 1976). In Ike's words: "Many thousands of persons would be dead and injured and mangled, the transportation systems destroyed, and sanitation systems all gone. That is not preventive war —that is war" (press conference, 8/16/54). Not all men in all generations have had such keen perception, e.g.: "A preventive war, grounded on a just fear of invasion, is lawful" (Thomas Fuller, *The Historie of the Holy Warre,* 1639). See also DEFENSE, DEPARTMENT OF and PREEMPTIVE STRIKE.

prides. The genitals, especially male; a rural term. See also FAMILY JEWELS.

priest. The mallet or other weapon used to administer the last rites to a fish that has been caught. The principle is the same as with the medieval *misericord* (literally: compassion, mercy), which was the dagger used by one knight when delivering the *coup de grâce* (literally: stroke of grace) to another. At one time "priest" also was a euphemism for the person who did the killing, e.g.: "Seeing the deed is meritorious/And to preserve my sovereign from his foe/Say but the word, and I will be his priest" (William Shakespeare, *Henry VI, Part 2,* 1590–91).

See also MADAME.

principal (or largest) bedroom. Master bedroom, "master" being a word that is to be avoided in all connections nowadays. Following this line of reasoning, musicians no longer create "masterpieces" and the politically corrrect critic will describe Leonardo's Mona Lisa as representing the "acme of perfection," not as a "masterwork." See also BOSS.

private part(s). The external sexual organs, the GENITALS, with many variations, e.g., *daddy parts, mommy parts, lower parts, naughty parts, nether parts, secret parts,* and *sensitive parts.* "He went to a doctor with a rash on his private parts and the doctor diagnosed syphilis. The sailor became depressed and hanged himself. Then it was discovered that he did not have syphilis after all" (Norman Moss, *The Pleasures of Deception,* 1977).

The Oxford English Dictionary dates "private parts" to 1634, but it is probably older, as Spenser, Shakespeare, and other writers employed both "privates" and "parts" in a genital sense prior to this date; see CHARMS, FAVORS, and PARTS for examples. Still earlier, going back to the thirteenth century, people had *privy limbs* (see LIMB), *privy members* (see MEMBER), and *privy parts* (see PRIVY).

privy. The general term for that which is private, intimate, concealed, and done by stealth has been used to designate an outdoor toilet (a *privehouse* or *privy house,* in full) since at least the fourteenth century. A *privy stool* was the same as a "close stool" (see STOOL). People also used to have *privy parts,* an early form of PRIVATE PARTS, while to be *privy* with another person could imply a sexual RELATIONSHIP.

"Privy" usually denotes a structure of some sort (an OUTHOUSE, in effect). Unenclosed *privies* were a menace. To wit: "A very pretty Boy of 4 years old . . . fell into a scurvy open Privy before night; of which loathsom Entertainment he died in a day or two" (*The Diary of Samuel Sewall,* 9/28/1708). See also NECESSARY and TOILET.

problem. The most common of the common denominators for converting all life's difficulties, from the most trivial to the most horrible, into a uniformly bland and boneless mush. Thus, people are afflicted with *drinking problems* (alcoholism, in which case they are known as *problem drinkers*), *medical problems* (such as cancer), *sexual problems* (impotence or frigidity, say), and *problem days* (if they are female and menstruating). *Problem banks* get that way by making *problem loans* (bad ones, i.e., NONPERFORMING ASSETS) and when New York City had its *liquidity problem,* i.e., near-bankruptcy), municipal bond dealers sagely attributed their difficulties in selling their wares to a *market psychology problem* (investors were scared out of their wits). And so it goes. No one has explained the psychology of the term better than the former COUNSEL to the president of the United States, John W. Dean III, who said of "problem": "That was the word of common currency in the Administration; a 'problem' could be anything from a typographical error to a forty-year jail sentence. The word drained the emotional content from tense discussions. It helped us maintain the even, robotlike composure we considered vital to effectiveness" (*Blind Ambition,* 1976). Or, as the former president himself explained: "South Vietnam would not have gone down the drain if I hadn't had my problem" (Richard M. Nixon, as quoted by Harry Dent, a former aide, Reuters, 8/4/75). See also SITUATION, THING, and TROUBLE/TROBLESOME.

pro bono. Free; short for *pro bono publico,* for the public good. "The six organizations [are] represented pro bono (without charge) by Jeff Glatzer of Manhattan's Bondy and Schloss law firm" (Brooklyn, N.Y., *Phoenix,* 3/15/79). The point is that true gentlemen do not like to talk about money even when they are not accepting it. See also HONORARIUM.

procedure. An operation. In the words of a doctor who didn't know his voice was being recorded but who was so eager to perform abortions that he didn't always check to be sure his patients were really pregnant: "I'm just about to give you a procedure" (WCBS-TV, 2/23/79). See also CONSUMER, INVESTIGATIVE PHASE, and MISCARRIAGE.

process. To kill; part of the Nazi lexicon. "In a secret report dated July 5, 1942, Mr. [Walter] Rauff, then a section chief in the Reich security office in Berlin, which was in charge of the mass killing of Jews, said that since December 1941 '97,000 have been processed' in the vans" (*New York Times,* 5/15/84). The *processing* in this case was accomplished, fifty at a time, by exhaust fumes in vans disguised with Red Cross emblems. Others were *processed* in blast furnaces. "So far [October 1942] I had not believed it [but] it was true: 6000 people a day are 'processed' in this furnace" (Helmuth James von Moltke, *Letters to Freya, 1939–1945,* 1990). See also FINAL SOLUTION, THE.

pro-choice. Pro-abortion. "Almost no one mentions the word abortion; one is pro-life or pro-choice" (*New York Review of Books,* 7/20/78). Thus, depending on whose terminology is being used, opponents are left with the unenviable task of seeming to argue either against "life" or against "choice." Carrying the argument one step further, *pro-* or *right-to-lifers* refer to a fetus as an *unborn* (or *preborn*) *child,* while *pro-choicers* prefer to think of a fetus that has been aborted as an *unviable tissue mass* or *product of conception.*

See also MISSCARRIAGE, PLANNED PARENTHOOD, REPRODUCTIVE RIGHTS, and, for more about loading arguments in advance, OPEN MARRIAGE, OPEN SHOP, RIGHT-TO-WORK, and SEMIAUTOMATIC RIFLE.

productivity target (or standard). Quota. The AGENTS who enforce New York City's parking regulations do not have ticket quotas, but transportation commissioners have admitted over the years to setting "productivity targets" (*New York Times,* 8/16/91) and "productivity standards" (the *Times,* 9/17/76). All this is of more than passing interest to motorists, since the meter readers have been known to ticket legally parked cars as well as nonexistent ones in order to achieve their nonexistent quotas.

professional car. A hearse. "For over one hundred years funeral directors have chosen the uncompromised excellence and value of the Hess & Eisenhardt professional car" (ad, *Casket & Sunnyside,* 1/80). Other bywords for the deathly "hearse" include *coach, casket coach, funeral car, limousine,* and *service car.* See also FUNERAL DIRECTOR and PASSENGER.

professional public manager. A bureaucrat, with a FOP Index of 2.5. See also ENGINEER.

program practices. Program censorship, a.k.a., *broadcast standards* and *standards and practices.* "Fourteen years later, after serving as everything from Paris bureau chief to vice-president for program practices (or 'censor'), he [Van Gordon Sauter] would become president of CBS News" (*Columbia Journalism Review,* 3-4/86). See also ACTION and REVIEW.

projection. The scientific version of what, if uttered by a Nostradamus or a Jeane Dixon, would be called a "prediction."

"Predictions—or projections, a distinction

made by some academics who define them as mere extrapolations of today's situation into the future; really a psychological distinction rather than a real one—invariably turn out to be wrong" (Norman Metzger, *Energy: The Continuing Crisis,* 1977). See also SCENARIO.

prong. The prick, a.k.a. *joy-prong,* as in the heading from *Flasher, The News Weekly of Meaningful Sex-Exposure* (5/21/73):

> Gain Precious Inches
> Prolong your prong
> The English way!

(Those who require additional details will have to check out the source themselves. Sorry.) See also PENIS.

prosthesis (or prosthetic device). A piece of artificial anatomy, such as a leg, arm, breast, or tooth. For example, a false tooth is, technically and fastidiously, a *dental prosthesis.* To refer to a "prosthesis" instead of an "artificial leg," say, is the verbal equivalent of averting one's gaze from the area of the amputated LIMB. See also DENTURES.

prostitute. Whore; traditionally a woman, but now used with reference to men and boys, too; sometimes further euphemized by clipping as *pross, prossie, prossy, prostie,* or *prosty.*

"Prostitute" comes from the Latin *prō* (forward) plus *statuere* (to set up or to place) and so translates as "to expose publicly" or "to offer for sale." (Note the parallel to the modern expression, PUT OUT.) The Latinate word came into English as a euphemism for the blunt English one, itself apparently a euphemism for a word so old it has been

forgotten: The Old English *hōre* is cognate with such acceptable terms as the Old Irish *caraim,* I love, the Sanskrit *kāma-s,* love, and the Latin *carus,* dear or darling (which makes "whore" a distant relative of "caress" and "charity").

"Prostitute" appears first in *The Oxford English Dictionary* as a verb in a work of 1530 that would have been of some assistance to English visitors in France: "I prostytute, as a comen woman dothe her self in a bordell house, *je prostitue*" (Jehan Palsgrave, *Lesclarcissement de la Langue Francoyse*). In the pre-Victorian period, Noah Webster changed "whoredom" to "prostitution" when he bowdlerized the Bible (1833), and in our own time The Jerusalem Bible (1966) out-bowdlered Webster, with the conversion of "the great whore" of Babylon (Revelation 17:1) into "the famous prostitute." (See PECULIAR MEMBERS for Webster's handling of this passage.) FAMILY newspapers, meanwhile, avoided the term until well into the twentieth century. For example, one of the members of the cast of *Within the Gates,* which opened in New York City in 1934, was listed simply as "The Young Whore," but the *Sun* changed this to "The Young Prostitute," the *World-Telegram* to "The Young Harlot," and the *American* to "A Young Girl Who Has Gone Astray" (Robert Benchley, *New Yorker,* 11/3/34). Over the years, John Ford's *'Tis Pity She's a Whore* (1633) also has caused difficulties for those with tender sensibilities. The *New York Times* declined to print the full title for a 1930 revival, abbreviating it to *'Tis Pity,* and as late as 1967, a theater company at Michigan State University was allowed to advertise it only as *'Tis Pity She's a W – – – –.* Even today, most people tend to steer clear of the harsher-sounding term. This includes those people who are whores: They are more likely to refer to themselves as HOOKERS or WORKING GIRLS.

There are (and have been) a tremendous number of ways of implying "whore" without actually coming out and saying the word. Herewith, a lightly annotated sampling of some of the more picturesque ones:

abandoned woman (a profligate Victorian male might be called "an abandoned man"—and see *lewd woman* below); *anonyma* (also from the nineteenth century); *aphrodisian dame* (from Aphrodite, Greek goddess of erotic love); *Aspasia* (a learned allusion to the learned woman who was mistress to Pericles in Athens in the fifth century B.C.); *Athanasian wench* (specifically, one who prostitutes herself more for the love of it than for the money, from the opening words of the Athanasian creed, *quincunque vult*, whoever desires);

bad girl (a euphemism by way of understatement); *baggage*; *bangster* and *bangtail* (see BANG); *b-girl*; *blower* (see BLOW); *bobtail*; *boom-boom girl* (from the Vietnam experience and *boom-boom* as slang for copulation: *boom-boom girls* worked in *boom-boom houses*); *brothel* (the word referred to a person—a scoundrel or good-for-nothing, if a man, and a whore, if a woman—before it came to mean a bawdy house); *buttock* (from the seventeenth century, a piece of ass, in effect; alone and in many combinations, such as *buttock-broker,* a procuress or brothel manager, and *buttock and file,* a whore who was also a pickpocket);

CALL GIRL; *cat* (see CAT HOUSE and PUSSY); *club woman*; COMFORT WOMAN; COMMODE; *commodity* (an old slang term for a woman's genitals as well as the woman herself; see VAGINA); CONVENIENCE; COURTESAN; *Cyprian* (Aphrodite was said to have been born in the sea near Cyprus and the island was a center of her worship);

demimondaine (from *demimonde,* literally, half-world, coined by Alexandre Dumas *fils,* 1824–95, for that class of woman whose loose living had caused them to lose social position: gradations of the French *demimonde* during *la belle epoque* included *les demi-castors,* women kept by wealthy lovers, foreshadowing of the modern slang sense of "beaver" to refer to female genitals and to a female generally, *castor* being the animal's name in French and Latin; *les dégrafées,* the unbuttoned, and *les grandes horizontales,* referring to those who had floated on their backs to the very top of the half-world's heap); *demi-rep* (a woman of diminished, or doubtful, reputation, e.g., "a demi-rep; that is, to say, a woman . . . whom everybody knows to be what nobody calls her," Henry Fielding, *Tom Jones,* 1749); *dulcinea* (from Don Quixote's lady love, Dulcinea del Toboso); *Dutch widow* (as contrasted with a mechanical *Dutch wife* or *Dutch husband*—machines for masturbating with);

erring sister;

FALLEN WOMAN; *fancy woman* (see FANCY); FILLE DE JOIE; *fire ship* (also, a woman infected with venereal disease); *fish* (an old term for either a woman or her genitals; hence *fish-monger* meaning a pimp or bawd and *fishmarket,* a brothel); *frail sister* (originally a high-class whore, or kept woman, as in, from 1774, "In a certain set of them . . . it was an established rule that whenever any one of their frail sisters was laid hold of for debt, for them to collect together a party of volatile young men to join them in a party, and spend the days of confinement with the individual attached," *The Prodigal Rake, Memoirs of William Hickey,* Peter Quennell, ed., 1962);

game (a collective term, late seventeenth to early nineteenth centuries, when a young whore or a girl who was well on her way to becoming one might also be called a *game pullet*—and see GAME); *gay girl* (or *bit* or *woman*; see GAY); *girl of ease; girl of the* (or *about*) *town*;

hack or *hackney* (from the hackney that is a saddle horse, especially one that is available for hire, in turn, probably, from Hackney, a section of London where horses once were raised, e.g., "The hobby-horse is but a colt, and your love perhaps a hackney," William Shakespeare, *Love's Labor's Lost*, 1588–94, where "hobby-horse" and "colt" also were Elizabethan terms for a wanton woman); HARLOT; *hetaera* (adopted in the nineteenth century for a cultivated mistress, from the ancient Greek term for a female who is a companion in the fullest sense but not a wife); *high priestess of Paphos* (Paphos is on Cyprus—another reference to Aphrodite);

HOOKER; *houri* (from the Arabic word—meaning "black-eyed" or "to be gazelle-like in the eyes"—for the beautiful virgin awarded to every deserving male Muslim upon admission to Paradise); HOOR (an aural euphemism); *hustler* (like *prostitute,* often applied to males as well as females);

impure (from the eighteenth century, pre-sumably a rough and ready sort, compared to a *pure* or *purest pure,* which see below); *incognita; industrial debutante* (one who works business conventions, as opposed to those in the *home entertainment business,* who make house [or apartment] calls);

joy sister;

Kate (an especially attractive whore, perhaps punning on the sexual senses of *cat* above);

lady of easy virtue/of the evening/of the night/of pleasure (see LADY); *lewd woman* (one of Noah Webster's favorites, as noted in PECULIAR MEMBERS, but by no means peculiar to him, e.g., Ordinance No. 8267, concerning "Lewd and Abandoned Women," adopted by the city of New Orleans on March 10, 1857, to raise revenue by licensing and taxing brothels—but allowed to lapse in 1859, after Mrs. Emma Pickett, of 25 St. John Street, sued and the law was declared unconstitutional);

MADAM; *Magdalene* (a reformed whore, from Mary Magdalene, of the Bible, so called because she hailed from Magdala, a town famous for immorality);

miss (first a mistress or courtesan and later a strumpet or whore; John Evelyn noted the euphemism's appearance in his diary on January 9, 1662, referring in passing to an actress who was "taken to be the Earle of Oxford's *Misse* [Evelyn's emphasis], as at this time they began to call lewd women"); MODEL; *moll* (a diminutive of "Mary," a catch-all for any woman, but especially a whore or other woman of relaxed morals, e.g., Moll Flanders, heroine of Daniel Defoe's picaresque novel of 1722); *moose* (American military usage in the Far

East, from the Japanese *mus,* short for *musume,* a young girl or inamorata); *mort* (any woman or any girl but also, from the sixteenth through early twentieth centuries, a loose woman or whore —see the *muff* in VAGINA);

NATURAL, *naughty pack* (from the sixteenth century, when such women might be said *to do the naughty,* i.e., to play the whore, and to work in *naughty houses*); *nymph du pave;*

occupant (meaning one who is occupied —see OCCUPY); *one of the Burlap sisters* (i.e., a bag); *one of the frail sisterhood* (Victoriana);

painted (or *scarlet*) *woman* (another reference to the great whore of Babylon, vividly described in Revelation 17:1–4: "I saw a woman sit upon a scarlet coloured beast . . . having seven heads and ten horns. And the woman was arrayed in purple and scarlet colour . . . having a golden cup in her hand full of abominations and filthiness of her fornication"); *Paphian* (alluding again to Aphrodite and her ceremonies at Paphos on Cyprus); *pagan* (probably from the cult of beauty in pagan Rome and Greece; thus Prince Hal asks about Doll Tearsheet, "What pagan may that be?" *Henry IV, Part 2,* 1596–97); *patriotute* (during World War II, one who specialized in servicemen for "patriotic" reasons); *pavement princess; perfect lady* (British for a loudmouthed whore); *piece of trade* (where "trade" refers to the oldest professsion, and "piece" is an old generic [ca. thirteenth century] for anyone, male or female, usually employed contemptuously in the case of feminine objects, as in *piece of calico, piece of goods,* and *piece of mutton*); *puella* (Latin for "girl"); *punk*

(today, sexually speaking, usually a catamite, but a conventional feminine whore from Elizabethan to Victorian times, e.g.: "At London I at first took fancy again for women in the suburbs, punks who would let me have them for half a crown." Anon., *My Secret Life,* ca. 1890); *pure* (an ordinary mistress or whore, late seventeenth to early nineteenth centuries); *purest pure* (a classy mistress or whore of the same period);

quean (see QUEEN);

red-light sister; ramp (sixteenth and seventeenth centuries); *romp* (a variant of the preceding that lasted into the nineteenth century and whose boisterous, copulative sense is reflected in the still-current *romp in the hay*);

SEX WORKER; *skivvy* (popularized in Vietnam, probably from the Japanese *sukebei,* lechery, and similar only by coincidence to the skivvy that is a maidservant and the skivvies that are underwear); *soiled dove* ("a woman who belongs to the large army of soiled doves," New Orleans *Lantern,* 2/4/1888, the dove being one of Aphrodite's symbols); SPORTING GAL/ GIRL/WOMAN); STEW (a woman as well as a brothel); STREETWALKER;

TAIL; *tart* (once a term of honest endearment, comparable to "sweetheart"); *Thaïs* (after the courtesan, mistress to Ptolemy, later king of Egypt, who is said to have encouraged Alexander the Great to set fire to Parsa, more commonly known as Persepolis, seat of the kings of Persia); *tomboy* (a woman who acts out sexually as though she were male; often, in the works of Shakespeare and other Elizabethans, a whore); *town* (short for *woman of the town*); *trading girl;* TRAMP; *trick babe* (see TRICK); *trollop* (never a very complimentary term—possibly akin to "troll," the verb, in the sense of rolling back and forth, or to "troll," the noun, meaning the fairy-tale demon); *trull* (an Elizabethan synonym of *trollop,* and of the same obscure origin); *trumpery* (an old whore, from the word's primary meaning, referring to worthless stuff, especially something of less value than meets the eye);

UNFORTUNATE;

Vestal (especially, *Drury-Lane Vestal,* an ironic reference to the virgins who attended the sacred fire in the Temple of Vesta, Roman goddess of the hearth and protectress of the state); *vice sister*; VICTORY GIRL;

wet hen ("Boys, keep away from the soiled doves and wet hens," New Orleans *Lantern,* 10/20/1886); *woman of a certain character/of a certain class/of easy virtue/of pleasure/of the town,* (among others, e.g, "When any female shall by word, gesture, or movement, insult or show contempt for any officer or soldier of the United States, she shall be regarded and held liable to be treated as a woman of the town plying her vocation," General Order No. 28, Headquarters, Department of the Gulf, New Orleans, Major General Benjamin F. Butler commanding, 5/15/1862; see also WOMAN); WORKING GIRL.

protection. Keeping a woman without marrying her. "That which used to be called 'adultery,' was now only 'living under protection'" (speech, House of Commons, 3/15/1809).

protective coverage. From the TV news business: "Sending a correspondent and camera crew to church with the president is part of what the networks euphemistically call 'protective coverage.' That means they don't want to miss the pictures if someone takes a shot at the president" (Ron Nessen, *It Sure Looks Different from the Inside,* 1978). See also IN-DEPTH TREATMENT and PREPARED BIOGRAPHY.

protective custody. Custody. The "protective" operates in the same manner as "preventive" (e.g., PREVENTIVE ACTION) and always should be looked at askance if not completely ignored. The essential slipperiness of the phrase, and its potential for abuse, are betrayed by its origin. The Nazis pioneered "protective custody" *Schutzhaft,* on February 28, 1933, in the form of a law that suspended constitutional guarantees of civil liberties. This became the legal basis for putting Jews, socialists, pacifists, and anyone else they didn't like into CONCENTRATION CAMPS. Thus, "protective custody" was one of the first steps taken in Germany toward achieving the FINAL SOLUTION. The duplicity of the legalism was recognized early on: "He is declared to have been placed under protective custody. Now this phrase is a deliberate steal from the vocabulary of Nazi Germany, its purpose being to cast a pall of dignity around the proceeding when Brown Shirts take an opponent to a Brown House for the purpose of beating him with a hose" (Baltimore, Md., *Sun,* 2/17/36). See also the *custodial detention* in DETENTION.

protective reaction. Bombing; in full flower, *routine limited duration protective reaction strike.* The "protective" ploy was popularized in 1969 to help justify renewal of U.S. air raids on North Vietnam. The attacks supposedly were limited to enemy antiaircraft positions, but investigators later discovered "that the Seventh Air Force under General John D. Lavelle adopted a very broad interpretation of 'protective reaction,' including raids on such targets as oil and truck dumps" (Russell F. Weigley, *The American Way of War,* 1973). The men who actually flew the missions were even more outspoken. As one pilot told the *New York Times* (6/15/72): "Protective reaction was just a euphemism for the F-4's to stage raids over Laos and North Vietnam and bomb the hell out of them." See also AIR SUPPORT, ARMED RECONNAISSANCE, ERRONEOUS REPORT, INCURSION, RECONNAISSANCE IN FORCE, and the basic DEFENSE, DEPARTMENT OF.

pshaw. See PISH/PSHAW.

public housing development. A project. Compilers of the politically correct *Dictionary of Cautionary Words and Phrases,* a 1989 project of the University of Missouri's School of Journalism, urged writers to steer away from the apparently offensive "project," and instead use "subsidized housing" or the still longer "public housing development" (FOP Index of 5.3). See also AFFORDABLE HOUSING.

public relations or **PR.** The general euphemism for projecting a sympathetic image for a corporation, institution, person, or product, by means of news management, propaganda, outright lies, and, when push comes to shove, silence. "President [Nixon] seemed to be willing to give the aggressive and ambitious [Kenneth W.] Clawson the inclusive sway that he wanted over every aspect of White House 'public relations,' the official euphemism for overt propaganda as distinct from what passes for information" (John Osborn, *New Republic,* 5/4/74). See also SCENARIO.

Practitioners of *public relations* (see PUBLICITOR) generally insinuate the views they wish the public to hold into the news without paying for space or airtime; in this sense *public relations* is the dark side of advertising (see MESSAGE). Somewhat unfairly, newspeople, while relying heavily upon PR people for stories, tend to look down upon them. As one newsman is said to have told a coworker, when his pal announced that he was quitting the paper for a job that paid three times as much in *public relations*: "Frankly, I'd rather see you handing out towels in a Hackensack [N.J.] whorehouse."

publicitor. One who engages in PUBLIC RELATIONS; a grandiloquent press agent. "We were startled . . . yesterday by a dispatch fresh from American League offices stating that news of the Athletics' move to Kansas City was given in an announcement by the League's 'publicitor.' We take this to mean press agent" (Birmingham, Ala., *News,* 10/14/54).

"Publicitor," formed on the same principle as REALTOR, is a particularly classy version of the basic "publicist"; other variations include *public relations counsel* (a borrowing from the legal COUNSEL, made in 1919 by Edward L. Bernays and Doris E. Fleischman); *public relations officer* (see OFFICER); *publicity engineer* (see ENGINEER); *publicity director,* and *publicity representative* (see REPRESENTATIVE). These are titles that *publicitors* (the even wilder "publicator" also has been reported) confer upon themselves; to those on the receiving end of the neverending barrage of publicity releases, they are generally known as "flacks." (Long assumed to have come from the German *flak,* a World War II compression of *fliegerabwehrkanone,* antiaircraft fire, the last term actually predates the war. Fred R. Shapiro reported in the spring 1984 issue of *American Speech,* that he had found examples of it in *Variety,* from as early as 1939. The word appears to be an eponym, after Gene Flack, a motion-picture press agent, who produced enough publicity releases to be be so remembered.)

Sometimes, one or the other of the fancy publicity titles may also serve as a cover for an entirely different occupation—selling, say, or procuring. In the first, marketing sense: "We were book [encyclopedia, door-to-door] salesmen! They didn't call us that, not at first, and they didn't tell us our pay would come by commission, either. My title in the company was Publicity Representative" (*Atlantic,* 6/74). And in the second: "The girls were found by the publicist, and there is, as a matter of fact, a touch of humor to the designation 'publicist,' because one of his main functions is to keep his client's name out of the papers. The other is, of course, to provide company"' (*New York Times,* 5/26/75). See also COMMU- NICATIONS DIRECTOR.

pudendum. The external sexual organs, converted into Latin for decency's sake. The word's literal meaning is "that of which one ought to be ashamed," and it says a great deal for the consistency of western society's attitudes toward sex that the earliest example of the term in *The Oxford English Dictionary* comes from 1398. "Pudendum" may be employed in male as well as female contexts, which probably explains the origin of such quintessentially male expressions as *pud* for PENIS as well as *pound one's pud* and *pull one's pudding* for MASTURBATION. The term usually is employed in a feminine sense, however, as in the learned *pudendum muliebre* (from *mulier,* woman), and often in what is techni-

cally a plural form, "pudenda," e.g., the nineteenth-century limerick:

> That naughty old Sappho of Greece
> Said: "What I prefer to a piece
> Is to have my pudenda
> Rubbed hard by the end a
> The little pink nose of my niece."

See also GENITALS.

pump ship. To piss, i.e., to MAKE (or PASS) WATER or, a secondary meaning, to vomit. Though obviously of nautical origin, this British expression (from 1788, *OED*), has been adopted generally by landlubbers. Thus, a very famous soldier, the duke of Wellington, when asked if he could pro- duce some motto that had served him in all his campaigns, is said to have replied, "Certainly, sir; never lose an opportunity to pump ship." A person who *pumps ship* while afloat may also be said *to raise the level of the water.* See also PEE.

pupil station. A school desk.

purchasing manager. A corporate purchas- ing agent who has acquired managerial sta- tus in name if not in fact. See also ENGINEER.

pure new wool. Virgin wool, as in "Pure New Wool" (clothing label, 12/22/80).

purify. To remove people from a given area without too fine a regard for the means used. "The biblical [Hebrew] word 'le-taher,' meaning 'to purify,' has come to describe clearing an area of the enemy. And people wonder how any weapon can be 'tohar ha- nechek,' literally, 'a purified weapon' but now used to mean a defensive weapon" (*New York Times,* 9/12/82). The *Times* was prescient. On September 16, just four days after the language lesson, Paul Eedle, a Reuters correspondent, asked an Israeli colonel why his troops were not doing anything to stop Christian militia from massacring Palestinian refugees in West Beirut, and was told by the officer "that his men were working on the basis of two principles: that the Israeli army should not get involved but that the area should be 'purified'" (*New York Times*, 9/20/82). See also CLEAN and CLEANSE.

pussy. For the many people who do not feel comfortable with the technical VAGINA (the equally technical PENIS is much more widely accepted), this is probably the most common substitute for the FOUR-LETTER WORD "cunt."

"Pussy" may be a translation of the French *chat*, cat, or *minette*, kitten or pussy, both of which carry the same slang meanings in French as in English. Or it may simply be a case of parallel evolution, based on the common comparison of the female PUDENDUM to a small furry animal, e.g., *beaver*, *bun* (see RABBIT), *monkey*, and *squirrel*. "Puss," "pussy," and "pussycat" all seem to have been used to refer to women generally (usually in a contemptuous manner), as well as to their GENITALS particularly, since at least the seventeenth century. "Cat," meanwhile, is an even older word for "whore," going back at least to the beginning of the fifteenth century (see CAT HOUSE), and it has also been used in the same way as "pussy" since the nineteenth century. As common as it is in private talk, "pussy" remains bothersome enough to be euphemized by most newspapers; see OBSCENE, DEROGATORY, and SCATOLOGICAL.

put away/down/to sleep. To kill; three different ways of not mentioning death—usually used in connection with animals whose lives have become burdensome to themselves or their owners. "The dogs had long been rounded up and put away painlessly" (Evelyn Waugh, *Black Mischief*, 1932). "Goetz refused to have the colt 'put down,' as the euphemism goes" (Red Smith, *New York Herald Tribune*, 4/16/61). "The kitten, an 8- to 10-week-old gray tabby, was put to sleep July 21 and tested positive for rabies" (*Litchfield County*, Conn., *Times*, 7/29/74).

People as well as animals may be *put away* and *put down*, though not always with lethal results. Thus, it used to be said that a husband *put away* his wife when all he did was to divorce her. Or a person may be *put away* in an institution, such as a CORRECTIONAL FACILITY or MENTAL HOSPITAL. To *put down* someone usually means only that one has publicly humiliated that person. But in the past, people occasionally *put down* themselves, with more lasting effect. For example: "Word came that Eppy Telefer had 'put down' herself over night, and was found hanging dead in her own little cottage at daybreak" (*Blackwood's Edinburgh Magazine*, XXI, 1827). See also PUT OUT and SLEEP.

put out. (1) to kill; (2) to grant sexual liberties freely.

The first sense parallels PUT AWAY, etc., but probably derives from the extinguishing of a candle or other fire; see also SNUFF. Thus, from a taped conversation between an undercover cop and a seventy-one-year-old woman, who was convicted of trying to kidnap her former husband, an eighty-two-year-old multimillionaire:

WOMAN: I have no regrets. I do wish to have my husband and the people who are controlling him should be put out, because otherwise, they'd put me out.

COP: By "out," you telling me to kill them?

WOMAN: Absolutely, if it could be done, yes. (*New York Times*, 1/24/79)

The second sense is equivalent etymologically if not financially to the Latin PROSTITUTE (literally, to place forward). "The beautiful . . . countess and her beautiful . . . daughter-in-law, both of whom would put out only for Nately, who was too shy to want them" (Joseph Heller, *Catch-22*, 1961). See also FAVORS.

Q

quaint. Small, especially in real estate listings. "Being a naive real estate shopper, I was in for a seminar in semantics: 'Quaint' and/or 'cute' mean essentially the same thing: one could never lose sight of one another within the house" (Aldo Bianchi, Brooklyn, N.Y., *Phoenix,* 7/26/79). See also HANDYMAN'S SPECIAL.

quarantine. Blockade. During the Cuban missile crisis of 1962, when the United States and Russia teetered on the brink of nuclear war, President John F. Kennedy and his advisers talked of a "blockade" as being one of their OPTIONS, but when the president told the nation in a televised address on October 22 what was happening, he used the euphemistic "quarantine" instead. "The President . . . adopted the term 'quarantine' as less belligerent and more applicable to an act of peaceful self-preservation than 'blockade'" (Theodore C. Sorensen, *Kennedy,* 1965). For other *options* that were considered, see PREEMPTIVE STRIKE and SURGICAL STRIKE.

JFK's preference for "quarantine" was influenced by Franklin D. Roosevelt's use of the term when defending the right of peace-loving nations to "quarantine" themselves from aggressors (speech, Chicago, 10/5/37). The metaphor had been suggested to FDR in a meeting with Secretary of the Interior Harold L. Ickes, who noted in his *Secret Diary* (1954):

In our discussion of the international situation I said that it was just like a case of contagious disease in a community.

I was referring, of course, to Italy, Germany, and Japan. I remarked that the neighbors had a right to quarantine themselves against a contagious disease. The President said: "That's a good line; I will write it down," which he proceeded to do.

quarter-pound. One-sixth of a pound, more or less. A sampling of fast-food hamburgers, done by Certified Analytical Group, Inc., of Corona, Queens, revealed that Roy Rogers's "quarter-pound" hamburger patties weighed in at 2.66 ounces, while Wendy's "quarter-pound" patties were 2.56 ounces (*New York Times,* 4/11/90). See also POUND.

queen. Nowadays, a male homosexual who plays the female part, but before that, as the related "quean," a bold or ill-behaved woman, specifically, a whore: "Here's to the flaunting extravagant quean. And here's to the housewife that's thrifty" (Richard Brinsley Sheridan, *School for Scandal,* 1777). Back in Sheridan's era, "quean-house" was another term for "brothel" and "queanery" equaled "harlotry" (see HARLOT). "Quean's" cognates include, aside from the royal *queen,* the Old English *cwene* (woman, wife, hussy, whore); the Chaucerian *queynte* (cunt); the Dutch *kween* (a barren cow); the Gothic *qino* (woman); and the Greek *gyne* (also "woman," and from which descend both "gynecology" and "misogynist"). Homosexual "queens," meantime, have been flourishing under that title for more than a century, but "straights" have not always understood the meaning of the term. For example, during a trial in 1890, Sir Charles Russell, the Queen's (sic) Counsel, cross-examined John Saul, a male prostitute, to this effect:

Q: Did you live with a woman known as Queen Anne in Church Street, Soho?

A: No, it is a man. Perhaps you will see him later on. (From H. Montgomery Hyde. *The Cleveland Street Scandal,* 1976)

See also GAY, a word first recorded as being used in its modern sense by the same John Saul.

queen-size. Fat; the female counterpart to KING-SIZE. "Queen-sized DWF, 58 . . . seeks tall, good-looking guy" (personal ad, Woodbury, Conn., *Voices Sunday,* 10/23/94). See also DIFFERENTLY SIZED and LARGE.

questionable. Wrong—usually in a criminal as well as a moral sense.

From the euphemistic axiom that the real meaning of a word or phrase always is worse than the apparent meaning, it follows remorselessly that the explicit acknowledgment of doubt in "questionable" is tantamount to an admission of guilt. "Questionable" pops up in many contexts, e.g., *ethically questionable, questionable act, questionable payment, questionable practice,* and *questionable reputation.* For example, A. Carl Kotchian, a former president of Lockheed Aircraft Corp., defended the company's practice of making millions of dollars of *questionable payments* by saying: "Some call it gratuities, some call them questionable payments. Some call it extortion, some call it grease. Some call it bribery. I look at these payments as necessary to sell a product" (*New York Times,* 2/16/79). See also COMMISSION and CONSULTANT.

quick entry. Entry without warning—that is, by breaking through the door. "Attorney General John Mitchell's expressed preference for the term 'quick entry' over the scorned catchword 'no-knock' provides glaring evidence of the way in which the Government currently uses words as cosmetics to delude the public and even itself" (*New York Times,* 7/27/70). Not until 1995 did the U.S. Supreme Court rule in *Wilson v. Arkansas, No. 94-5707* that police ordinarily have to knock and announce themselves before bursting into someone's home. See also SURREPTITIOUS ENTRY.

quiet room. A cell, formerly known as a padded room. "At the South Florida State Hospital, a 72-year-old woman lies. . . . Dehydrated and suffering from a compound fracture of the hip, she had been left unattended in the 'quiet room'" (*U.S. News & World Report,* 11/19/79). "When the children [at Devereux Glenholme School in Washington, Conn.] cannot control themselves, they are taken to what is called the quiet room. Miss [Susan] Ubaldi admitted some children hate the padded, windowless room, 'and learn to avoid it'" (*New York Times,* 10/10/93). See also ADJUSTMENT CENTER.

quietus. Death; originally a receipt or acquittance showing that a debt had been paid or accounts cleared, the meaning of "quietus" was extended to include the discharge of a person from the obligations of office, then from life itself, and finally, the method—a blow, say—by which the discharge may be accomplished, e.g., "When he himself might his quietus make/With a bare bodkin [i.e., dagger]" (William Shakespeare, *Hamlet,* 1602). See also PASS AWAY and TERMINATE/TERMINATION.

R

rabbit. Various meats have been billed euphemistically as "rabbit" from time to time. For example, muskrat has been dolled up in the Ozarks as *marsh rabbit* (or *hare).* Parisians took a similar tack during the 135-day siege of the city in 1870–71, when "'Rabbit' became a common euphemism for cat or kitten, often smothered in onions or served as a stew" (*Natural History,* 10/77). Curiously, "lamb" continued to be sold during the siege even as the city's dog population dropped precipitously. (For more about eating meat, see FILET MIGNON.)

On a more profound level, psychologically as well as semantically, "rabbit" also is a euphemism for "cony," a word that conjured up extremely bad thoughts in the minds of our early nineteenth-century ancestors. To begin at the beginning:

"Rabbit" originally referred only to the young of the long-eared *Lepus cunicula;* an adult of the species was a "cony" (also spelled *coney, coniq, conynq, cunning, cunny*). The distinction was maintained at least until the early seventeenth century, but was lost by the middle of the eighteenth, with Dr. Johnson using the two words interchangeably in his *Dictionary of the English Language* (1755). Thereafter, though still used by those people who were most familiar with the animal (e.g., gamekeepers, poachers, furriers, cooks), "cony" faded from general use, with "rabbit" taking over in its place. *The Oxford English Dictionary* (this part of volume C went to press in October, 1891) refers guardedly to the "obsolescence" of "cony" without attempt-

ing to explain what happened. Yet the reason is clear enough to anyone who knows how the bad meanings of words tend to drive out the good ones (Gresham's Law again) and who also knows that from the sixteenth century, if not before, "cony" was both a term of endearment for a woman and a nickname for her most PRIVATE PART. Thus, as an endearment: "He calleth me his whytyng, His nobbes and his conny" (John Skelton, *The Tunnyng of Elynor Rummyng,* ca. 1528). Meantime, the use of "cony" in the other, strictly anatomical sense was reinforced not only by the furry resemblance (as with PUSSY) but by the semantic relationship, since "cony" probably is cognate to the heavily tabooed "cunt" (or VAGINA). In fact, "cony" originally was pronounced to rhyme with "honey" or "money," e.g., "A pox on your Christian cockatrices! They cry, like poulterers' wives, 'No money, no coney,'" (Philip Massinger and Thomas Decker, *The Virgin Martir, A Tragedie,* 1622). Moreover, "cony" had other pejorative meanings: *cony* or *Tom cony* once stood for "simpleton"; to engage in *cony catching* was to live by tricking or swindling (see STREETWALKER for the book title that made the term popular for some sixty years); a *cony* (or *cunny*) *warren* was a brothel; and to make a fist with the thumb inside, as girls often do, was to be *cunny thumbed.* (At the same time, "bun," as in "bunny," also stood for "cunt." For a sailor, "to touch bun for luck" before going on a voyage was something like—but not too much like—rubbing a rabbit's foot.)

With all these circumstances combining against "cony," it is not hard to see why "rabbit" became the term of choice among polite people, who were not so polite that they didn't know what cony-pronounced-cunny sounded like. There was still an annoying difficulty, however: "Cony" appeared in the Bible. What to do when reading sacred Scripture? And with women in the congregation! Not until the start of the nineteenth century did incipient Victorians arrive at the proper solution, i.e., *change the pronunciation of "cony."* As noted in *The Oxford English Dictionary,* John Walker, whose pronouncing dictionary was published in 1791, knew only the "cunny" pronunciation, but Benjamin H. Smart, who revised Walker's opus in 1836, knew both. While admitting that the word "is familiarly pronounced *cunny,*" Smart ordained that *cony* is "proper for a solemn reading." And so it is, even unto our own day, that milady may wear a "cony" coat, but only with a long "o," and that we do not say "cunny" when we speak of visiting Coney Island (New York) or Coney Creek (Colorado).

For other animals that have had difficulties with their names, see ROOSTER.

race. Black; a general substitute for the more explicit word, popularized by record producers. "In 1923, pianist Clarence Williams was helping Frank Walker initiate Columbia's 'Race Record' series, a new venture for the company. . . . The series was inspired by the success of such labels as Okey and Paramount in capturing the vast black blues market" (Chris Albertson, "Empress of the Blues," notes for the reissue of Bessie Smith's surviving recordings, *Bessie Smith—The World's Greatest Blues Singer*). "We were afraid to advertise Negro records. So I listed them in the catalogue as 'race' records and they are still known as that" (*Colliers,* 4/30/38). Subsequently, starting in the late 1940s, "race music" was replaced by the still less explicit "rhythm-

and-blues," coined by Jerry Wexler, then a writer for *Billboard* (Wexler, with David Ritz, *Rhythm and the Blues,* 1993). "Rhythm and blues is a Negro music and it was already in full flower when the jazz fans became aware of its existence" (A. J. McCarthy, *Jazzbook,* 1955). See also NEGRO, and URBAN CONTEMPORARY.

radio personality. A disk jockey. "Radio personality" sounds a lot better than "air personality," which is just as logical but suggests "airhead."

range forward contract. An option. "'There's an old corporate adage: Nobody ever makes money trading options.' . . . So Salomon Brothers has created a new product that looks and acts like a currency option program but is called a 'range forward contract' to make it easier to sell to those with option allergies" (*New York Times,* 11/25/85). See also DEFER PURCHASE.

rap parlor. A brothel or MASSAGE PARLOR. "In the face of a crackdown on street prostitution many of the girls . . . are taking refuge in 'rap clubs'—which have replaced massage parlors in the sex-for-sale world" (*New York Post,* 6/22/73). The object of the euphemism was to evade ordinances against brothels in New York and other cities by invoking the constitutional protections of the First Amendment, which guarantees freedom of speech, a.k.a. rapping.

raspberry. A derisive sound, made by putting the tongue between the lips, and blowing forcefully; also called a Bronx cheer. If properly done, the noise sounds like a fart, which is what "raspberry" really means: it is short for "raspberry tart," nineteenth-century Cockney rhyming slang for "fart," on the same order as "elephant's trunk" for "drunk," "ham and eggs" for "legs," "plates of meat" for "feet," and "Bristol cities" for "titties." See also BOSOM and BREAK WIND.

ravage. Rape. Thus, speaking of what history knows as "The Rape of Nanking" (12/13/37): "Japanese troops wantonly slaughtered some 40,000 civilians and ravaged thousands of women" (David W. Eggenberger, *A Dictionary of Battles,* 1967). "Ravage" is not a complete misnomer in the sense that it derives from *ravir,* the French word for RAVISH. See also ASSAULT.

ravish. Rape. "Ravish" and "rape" have the same Latin root, *rapere,* to seize, but the former was considered more acceptable in print during the nineteenth and much of the twentieth centuries, e.g., speaking of Cassandra, daughter of the king of Troy: "On the capture of that city she was ravished by Ajax" (*Encyclopædia Britannica,* 11th edition, 1910). See also RAVAGE.

Realtor. A real estate agent/broker/man/ person. Employing one word in place of three is almost always commendable but "Realtor" is an exception to the rule. (PUBLICITOR is another.) It is an exception because of the motive: self-aggrandizement. In the words of George Follansbee Babbitt: "We ought to insist that folks call us 'realtors' and not 'real-estate men.' Sounds more like a reg'lar profession" (Sinclair Lewis, *Babbitt,* 1922).

"Realtor" was still a new term when Babbitt spoke, having been coined in 1915 by Charles N. Chadbourn, of Minneapolis, Minnesota, who wanted to distinguish himself and fellow members of the local Real Estate Board from those dealers in land (also called *realty-men,* from 1888), who weren't certified board members. The new handle was enthusiastically adopted by the locals and, in 1916, by the National Association of Real Estate Boards, which subsequently won a number of court battles to prevent nonboarders from using it, too. (Hence, the capital "R" awarded "Realtor" in dictionaries.) Cynics suggested that "Realtor" was compounded of two Spanish words, *real* (royal) and *toro* (bull), but the originator, Mr. Chadbourn, produced another explanation for H. L. Mencken: "*Real estate* originally meant royal grant. It is so connected with land in the public mind that *realtor* is easily understood, even at first hearing. *Or* is a suffix meaning a doer, one who performs an act, as a *grantor, executor, sponsor, administrator. Realtor*: a doer in real estate" (*The American Language: Supplement I,* 1945).

As Mencken also pointed out, the *or* ending itself has especially classy connotations, probably because it stands for the Latin *ator* or the French *eur,* whereas *er* to indicate "doer" is strictly English, Thus, *advisor* and *insuror* have better vibes than ADVISER and "insurer"; an AUTHOR is esteemed more than a "writer," and both *educator* and *professor* outrank "teacher." At various times, furniture dealers have tried to turn themselves into *furnitors,* merchants into *merchantors,* and welders into *weldors.* It is a small wonder that the world does not also have *preachors* and wild animal *trainors.*

For more about building professional images, see also ENGINEER, and for more about the good work of *Realtors,* continue with ADORABLE, DEVELOP/DEVELOPMENT, EAT-IN KITCHEN, ENCLAVE, ESTATE, HANDYMAN'S

SPECIAL, HARMONIOUS, MIDDLE CLASS, NEEDS SOME WORK (or SOME WORK NEEDED), PLANTATION, QUAINT, SOLAR POOL, and TRAVEL CENTER.

rear. The ass; another of the many discreet allusions to the piece of anatomy with which everyone is blessed but whose name is deemed too vulgar to mention. "Do you think I'm too fat? Does my rear look too big in these pants?" (Consuelo Saah Baehr, *Report from the Heart,* 1976).

"Rear" is a product of the euphemistically important pre-Victorian era. Dated in the anatomical sense to 1796 (*OED*), it actually had some shock value at first. Thus, in Jane Austen's *Mansfield Park* (1814), Mary Crawford demonstrated her lack of good breeding, and caused dinner-table conversation to take a ninety-degree turn, with a risqué remark, saying "My home at my uncle's brought me acquainted with a circle of admirals. Of *Rears* and *Vices* I saw enough, I assure you. Now, do not be suspecting me of a pun, I entreat."

Rear admirals continue to be the butt of many jokes. In hospital slang, a *rear admiral* ("admire-all") is a proctologist (also called a *comprehensive physician* because he views his patient as a [w]hole). See also ARSE.

rear mezzanine. Balcony. In theory, a seat in the "rear mezzanine" of a theater should be in the rear middle part ("mezzanine," from the Italian *mezzanino,* middle), but as Broadway ticket prices have advanced to stratospheric levels, so have *rear mezzanines.* For example, in the Ethel Barrymore Theater in 1990, a *rear mezzanine* ticket landed you four rows up in what used to be known as the balcony, with only two rows between you and the back wall of the playhouse. See also FESTIVAL SEATING and PERFORMANCE.

recession. Hard times; a small depression; an economic THING. "In the 1920s, Wesley Clair Mitchell, the great business cycle analyst who was the founder of business cycle theory, offered 'recession' as a description of a relatively mild transition from 'prosperity' to 'depression.' The word it was designed to replace was 'crisis'" (*New York Times,* 12/24/78). The new term became popular among politicians, for whom "depression" was anathema (if their party happened to be in office when one occurred), e.g., "The nation's economy ... suffered, from 1957 through 1958, the third and deepest recession since World War II. . . . By June, unemployment had climbed to 5,437,000— an unwanted pinnacle, unmatched since the days before World War II" (Emmet John Hughes, *The Ordeal of Power,* 1963).

With "recessions" of this ilk coming along so regularly, the euphemism soon began wearing thin. This led to labeling all *recessions* as "temporary," and to characterizing them, when possible, as *growth recessions* (meaning that the economy is expanding but so slowly that the unemployment rate is nevertheless increasing). Innovative minds also developed completely new euphemisms, such as *crabwise movement, downphase of the economic cycle, downturn* (and the more eloquent *mild but necessary downturn* or *meaningful downturn in aggregate output*), *economic shortfall, extended seasonal slump, negative economic growth* (if more severe, a *period of advanced negative economic growth*), *period of adjustment, rolling readjustment, slowdown* (frequently qualified as a *healthy slowdown*), *slump* (or *mini-slump*), *stagnation* (or *high-level stagnation* or *persistent stagnation*), and *temporary period of slow growth.*

The award for the most imaginative substitute goes to Alfred Kahn, chairman of the Council on Wage and Price Stability during Jimmy Carter's presidency, who was instructed by the White House not to mention the word "recession," let alone "depression." Thus chastened, he said he would use "banana" instead, and was later "heard to mutter, 'The worst banana you ever saw'" (William Safire, *On Language,* 1980).

Attempting to distinguish "recession" from "depression," economists have produced complex definitions of the former, the simplest of which is Arthur M. Okun's definition—an empirical description, really —of a "recession" as a decline in the real gross national product for two consecutive quarters. For the average person, an even more elemental definition, also empirical, is contained in the adage, "A recession is when you lose your job; a depression is when I lose mine."

For more about the dismal science of economics, see ADJUST / ADJUSTMENT / READJUSTMENT, GROWTH STOCK, STABLE GROWTH, and TECHNICAL ADJUSTMENT.

reconnaissance in force. Search and destroy; VIETNAM ERA. Other roundabouts of the period included *search and clear, search and sweep, sweep and clear* (see CLEAN), *sweeping operation, reconnaissance forces sweeping operation,* and the relatively explicit *Zippo mission.*

The basic "search and destroy" dates from 1966, when U.S. Gen. William C. Westmoreland launched six major search-and-destroy attacks. As military phrases go, this one was unusually vivid. (See CASUALTY for more on the blandness of military talk.) Not until early 1968 did the general appreciate the semantic error. In his own words: "Many Americans failed to comprehend 'search and destroy,' possibly because detractors of the war chose to distort it. . . . Many people, to my suprise, came to associate it with aimless searches in the jungle and the random destroying of villages and other property. . . . Although those who saw the war as a political issue could no doubt have twisted any term, I changed it without fanfare to 'sweeping operation' or 'reconnaissance in force.' Yet the term still stuck in the minds of many" (*A Soldier Reports,* 1976).

One reason the term "stuck" was that on March 16, 1968, about the time Westmoreland made the change, C Company of the First Battalion, 20th Infantry Brigade, Americal Division, entered the village of My Lai and WASTED some 300 to 500 women, children, and old men. Charlie Company was on a routine search-and-destroy mission at the time, and it was hard to pass off the event as a *sweeping operation, reconnaissance in force,* or what have you. See also NEUTRALIZE / NEUTRALIZATION, PROTECTIVE REACTION, and SPECIFIED STRIKE ZONE.

recycler. A junkman; an operator of a junkyard. The trade association of the junkmen is the National Association of Recycling Industries. This is only their newest, recycled name; previously, this organization was known as National Association of Secondary Material Industries and, before that, as the National Association of Waste Material Dealers. See also AUTOMOTIVE DISMANTLER AND RECYCLER, ECOLOGY, LANDFILL, RESALE SHOP, and SECONDARY FIBER.

redeployment. Retreat. "It's not really a pull-out at all. It's a redeployment to a place where you can be more effective" (Defense Secretary Caspar Weinberger, 2/8/84). Mr. Weinberger was commenting on President Reagan's order the previous day that a 1,400-man Marine peacekeeping contingent in Beirut be evacuated to ships offshore. See also STRATEGIC MOVEMENT TO THE REAR.

redundancy/redundant. Unnecessary, unneeded; the standard British rationale for dismissing employees, not for cause, but in order to reduce a company's work force; comparable to the American EXCESS and SURPLUS. "Penguin Books Ltd. . . . has announced cuts in its publishing program of 22%, staff redundancies of nearly 100 and economies in overhead" (*Publishers Weekly*, 2/8/80). "Academic Press London will become exclusively a journal publisher from next April, when all book production is drawn back to the U.S. . . . One hundred and thirty staff out of a total London workforce of 247 have been made redundant" (*Bookseller*, 12/10/83). See also LET GO.

reeducation. Forced thought reform, especially in China, Vietnam, and Laos. *Reeducation* usually is effected in a prisonlike *reeducation camp* (or *center* or *facility*), typically upon the local population, as in China's Shandong Province No. 1 Reeducation Through Labor Camp, but occasionally on foreigners, e.g., "The Chinese technique of 're-education' embraced every phase of daily life in the prison camps" (*Treatment of British P.O.W.s in Korea*, 1955). See also BRAINWASH and CONCENTRATION CAMP.

reentry vehicle (or **system).** A nuclear warhead on a missile. "The United States, by possessing the ability to put multiple independently targeted reentry vehicles on

her launchers has many more nuclear warheads than the Soviet Union" (London *Times*, 2/26/73). "We are aware that the U.S. attorney has been investigating allegations regarding mischarges in the Mark 12-A [ICBM] re-entry system" (*Philadelphia Inquirer*, 3/26/85, quoting a General Electric spokesman). See also PEACEKEEPER.

refreshment. An alcoholic drink, especially whiskey; *liquid refreshment* in full, sometimes consumed at a *liquid lunch*.

"We then visited another public place, and after a few refreshments Mrs. Battistella became ill, and I enlisted the help of others in our group to assist me in seeing her safely home" (Rep. Wilbur D. Mills, D., Ark., statement to the press, 10/10/74).

Nostalgia Department: La Battistella, better known professionally as Fanne Fox, the Argentinian Firecracker, was an ECDYSIAST. After the car in which she and Mr. Mills were traveling was stopped for reckless driving in the wee morning hours of October 7, near the Jefferson Memorial in Washington, D.C., she made waves—literally and figuratively—by leaping out of the car and into the chilly waters of the nearby Tidal Basin. For Mr. Mills, chairman of the House Ways and Means Committee, and commonly described as "One of the Most Powerful Men in Washington," this was the beginning of the end of his congressional career. See also CONVIVIAL INDULGENCE, HIGH, and LIBATION.

reformatory. An optimistic euphemism for a prison, especially one for young criminals who are theoretically reformable. The first *reformatories* were established in the 1830s. It soon became obvious that they weren't working: "Our reformatories . . .

do not check the first steps in wrong-doing" (*Harper's Magazine,* 12/1878). See also CORRECTIONAL FACILITY.

registered warrant. An IOU "With the state [California] spending $4 million a day more than it is taking in . . . officials said they had no choice but to begin issuing the i.o.u.'s, called registered warrants, instead of checks on Wednesday" (*New York Times,* 2/16/83). See also CASH ADVANCE.

regular. Another of the ways for manufacturers to avoid tagging their merchandise with the supposedly unsalable word "small." A *regular* cigarette, for example, is a small one, compared to a KING-SIZE or *super-king* cigarette. And in quite another product category: "*Small* is disguised as *regular* ('Giant, family or regular size package of White King'— handbill distributed in Los Angeles, 8 Aug. 1940)" (*American Speech,* 4/42). For other kinds of "small," see MEDIUM and LARGE, and for another kind of "regular," see IRREGULARITY.

relations. Uncles? Aunts? Cousins? Uh-uh. As with INTERCOURSE, it is the prefatory "sexual" that has been delicately omitted, e.g., "They smoked some grass and then they had relations." See also CARNAL KNOWLEDGE and SEX.

relationship. In the absence of compelling evidence to the contrary, it is always safe to assume that "relationship" is sexual. Moreover, though married and homosexual couples occasionally are said to have "relationships," the term usually implies illicit, hetero goings-on—what previous generations would have called an AFFAIR, AMOUR, or CONNECTION. "In 1942, when [Gen. Dwight D.] Eisenhower first arrived in London, he met and formed a relationship with his driver, Kay Summersby" (Anthony Cave Brown, *Bodyguard of Lies,* 1975). See also CONFIDANT.

Signposts frequently are erected in front of the bland, impersonal "relationship" just to be sure that everyone gets the message. This results in such combinations as *close, personal relationship; dating relationship* (see FRATERNIZATION); *long and deep personal relationship;* MEANINGFUL RELATIONSHIP; *private, personal relationship,* and *special relationship.* Short and long forms often appear cheek by jowl, proving their essential synonymity. Thus, on May 25, 1976, Rep. Wayne L. Hays (D., Ohio) admitted to the House of Representatives that "for an extended period of time I did have a relationship with Elizabeth Ray," and then, a minute or so later, referred to "my personal relationship with Miss Ray." And "sex," of course, was at issue, though not explicitly mentioned; see also FAVORS.

release. To liberate from life or from a job, i.e., to die or to fire. "Susy was peacefully released to-day" (cablegram, received by Mark Twain, 8/18/1896, reporting the death of his beloved daughter: "It is one of the mysteries of our nature that a man, all unprepared, can receive a thunder-stroke like that and live," *Mark Twain's Autobiography,* 1924). And in the case of the second, smaller death: "Under an executive order to reduce its staff, the [New York State arts] council is releasing nine employees" (*New York Times,* 2/16/84). See also LET GO and RESOURCE.

relieve. (1) To fire from a job, i.e., to come to someone's assistance (or *relief*) by freeing (or *relieving*) that person of the onerous obligations of showing up at the office; to

LET GO. Thus, President Ronald Reagan announced Lt. Col. Oliver North's dismissal from the National Security Council staff by saying that he had been "relieved of his duties" (press conference, 11/25/87). (2) To reduce (or *relieve*) internal bodily pressures by expelling waste matter; to EASE oneself. "James Gordon Bennett, publisher of the Paris *Herald* . . . exiled himself to France in 1877—ostracized by society for relieving himself while drunk in the fireplace [or, some say, the grand piano] of his fiancée's home" (Henry Serrano Villard, *Contact: The Story of the Early Birds,* 1968). See also PEE.

relocation center. A prison camp for Japanese-Americans during World War II, also called an ASSEMBLY CENTER. "Hearst reporters got anti-Japanese statements from Mayor Fletcher Bowron and other prominent figures in Los Angeles and played up the Dies Committee's 'exposures' of the relocation centers" (S. Menefee, *Assignment: U.S.A.,* 1943). See also CONCENTRATION CAMP.

relocation drill. "A reader reports that at her place of employment fire drills are 'relocation drills' (formerly known as 'evacuation drills') and overtime is 'off-hours' work'" (*Quarterly Review of Doublespeak,* 1/85).

remains. A dead body. The oldest "remains" in *The Oxford English Dictionary* comes from John Dryden's translation of Ovid's *Metamorphoses* (1700): "Of all the mighty man the small remains/A little urn and scarcely fill'd contains." The term is still used commonly by FUNERAL DIRECTORS and others, e.g.: "Remains Shipped Worldwide" (ad, Manhattan, New York, Yellow Pages, 1990–91). From a strictly euphemistic point of view, however, "remains" is of interest today primarily for its metamor-

phosis into one of the ickier neologisms of our time—CREMAINS (a.k.a. ashes). See also DECEASED and REPATRIATION.

remove. To kill, as in "The spy had been 'removed from circulation'" (William Stevenson, *A Man Called Intrepid,* 1976). This particular spy, or AGENT, was *removed* while crossing Broadway at Times Square: A taxi knocked him down and a follow-up car completed the *removal* by running over him. Then there was the message from a South African general, C. P. van der Westhuizen, suggesting that two particularly irksome foes of apartheid be "permanently removed from society as a matter of urgency," which they were, less than three weeks later (*New York Times,* 5/24/92). A variant is "total and complete immobilization," which was the operative phrase when the killing of General Manuel Noriega (then a lieutenant colonel in charge of Panama's military intelligence) was proposed in 1972 by staffers of the U.S. Bureau of Narcotics and Dangerous Drugs as a way of reducing the flow of drugs from that country (*New York Times,* 6/13/86). See also ASSASSINATION, RUB OUT, and the general HIT.

remuneration. A payment, usually wages, as contrasted with the HONORARIUM given to someone who is not a regular employee. The attractions of the gilt-edged "remuneration" must be exceptionally strong, considering its survival despite Shakespeare's mockery in *Love's Labor's Lost* (1588–94). Thus Costard, a peasant, who has just been given a coin as a "remuneration" by the grandiloquent Don Adriano de Armado, complains:

Remuneration? O that's the Latin word for three farthings. Three farthings — remuneration. "What's the price of this inkle [band of linen]? "One penny." "No, I'll give you a remuneration." Why, it carries it! Remuneration! Why, it is a fairer name than French crown [a coin . . . and also the baldness caused by the French disease, syphilis].

repatriation. Return of a corpse to its country of origin. "The above policy covers repatriation*" (insurance certificate for international programs conducted by Loyola Marymount University, Los Angeles, received 3/95). Some benighted people may assume blithely that *repatriation* applies just to prisoners of war, exiles, and other living persons, but the asterisk in this instance leads the student applicant to an explanation in finer print: "Repatriation is the return of body remains from foreign lands to the country of origin." See also REMAINS.

replacement worker. A scab. "Since the strike began on Oct. 25, The [*Daily*] *News*'s strategy has been to publish and deliver the paper by using a combination of nonunion employees, union members who crossed the picket line and about 800 replacement workers" (*New York Times,* 1/17/91). In an effort to scare strikers, the *News* management repeatedly characterized the scabs as "permanent replacement workers." They were dismissed after the twenty-one-week strike was settled, however. See also LABOR ORGANIZER.

repose. Originally, only a temporary rest, especially one gained from sleeping, "repose" became a euphemism by the nine-

teenth century for the rest from which there is no waking. Churches celebrated the Festival of the Repose of the Virgin and some of them had Altars of Repose. FUNERAL HOMES, meanwhile, converted their laying-out rooms into *reposing rooms* or *slumber rooms.* Herewith, a sweetly solemn advertisement of United Funeral Chapels (see CHAPEL) of New York, cited by Edwin Newman in *Strictly Speaking* (1974):

> But even Roses with all their splendor
>   and heart
> Will one day their beautiful petals fall
>   apart.
> Man too, has his season like the Rose.
> And then, one day, he also must repose.

See also REST and SLEEP.

representative. Formerly a euphemism for "man," as in *advisory marketing representative, manufacturer's representative, publicity representative, registered representative* (see EXECUTIVE), and *sales representative,* but now that so many women are in business, too, a euphemism for "person." See also PERSON and TRAIL REPRESENTATIVE.

reproductive rights. Reverse English in action: "Reproductive rights" translates as "the right not to be reproductive."

"Ms. Sims, Miss West Virginia, calls her platform 'Reproductive Rights,' which she agreed was 'a little misleading.' What she means, she explained, is a woman's right to choose an abortion" (*New York Times,* 9/12/93). By the same token, an abortion clinic in Akron, Ohio, advertised itself as a "center for reproductive health" (*Washington Post,* 12/2/82). See also PRO-CHOICE.

resale shop. A junk shop. All the goods in a *resale shop* are PREOWNED. See also COLLECTIBLE and RECYCLER.

research. (1) Plagiarism. Wilson Mizner said it best: "If you steal from one author it's plagiarism; if you steal from many it's research" (quoted by John Burke in *Rogue's Progress*, 1975). See also SAMPLING. (2) Whaling for profit. The International Whaling Commission permits *research* hunts as well as commercial hunts. Japan and Norway are the principal *researchers*, each killing about 300 whales annually in recent years in addition to those allowed under IWC commercial quotas. The *research* subjects are harpooned by the same people in the same vessels, sold for profit in the same markets (at about $300 a pound in Japan in 1994), and eaten in the same way as the whales that are taken in the commercial hunts. See also HARVEST.

resident. (1) A patient in an institution for old people, a.k.a. NURSING HOME; (2) a prisoner in an institution for bad people, a.k.a. CORRECTIONAL FACILITY.

resign. To be fired or LET GO. One of the many privileges that rank hath is that of being allowed to resign: "A cabinet minister is asked to resign; a factory worker is fired" (Anatol Rapoport, *Semantics*, 1975).

resource. A person, especially one available for exploitation; short for HUMAN RESOURCES. One of the projected benefits of the merger of Bank of America and Security Pacific included a "release of resources," meaning that up to 14,000 workers would be LET GO (*Business Week*, 1/27/92). See also HUMAN RESOURCES and RELEASE.

rest. The relaxation that is obtained through death, as in *eternal rest, called to heavenly rest, go to rest,* and *laid to rest.* A *place of rest* is a grave, or SPACE, while "RIP," for *rest in peace,* is a common epitaph on headstones. (The jocular *rest in pieces* is reserved for those who have had accidents with dynamite.) See also HAPPY HUNTING GROUNDS, GONE TO THE and PASS AWAY.

rest house. Madhouse, as contrasted with a *rest home,* or CONVALESCENT HOSPITAL. "'I knew this would end up in the nut house.' '. . . I say rest house'" (Joseph Kesselring, *Arsenic and Old Lace,* film, 1944). See also MENTAL HOSPITAL.

rest room. A public toilet. "While the carnivorous rodent was being chased about the darkened theater, it fled into the rest room" (*Lubbock,* Tex., *Morning Avalanche,* 2/23/49). "Rest room" appears to be a genuine Americanism. When the term first cropped up in print, around the turn of the twentieth century, the room may simply have been for resting, but running water was soon added. Today, "rest room" is one of the most common, as well as most discreetly generalized, of the many euphemisms for such a public FACILITY. See also TOILET.

restructure. To make smaller, without confessing failure, as a corporation does when eliminating jobs or selling off pieces of itself. From a column by Andy Rooney about the hidden meanings in company memos: "'In the past year, our company has undergone significant restructuring.' This usually means a lot of people got fired and one of the company's divisions lost so much money they got rid of it" (*Litchfield*

County, Conn., *Times,* 3/27/87). When workers are fired across the board, they usually are said to be LET GO; executives are SHED. A corporation also may be *restructured* by getting rid of middle managers, thus flattening the organizational chart. This process is known as *delayering.* See also CONSOLIDATE and RIGHTSIZE.

retain/retention. To hold back, as a pupil in a class; the act thereof, also called *nonpromotion.* "But these youngsters . . . are not necessarily what their peers may refer to as 'dummies.' They are retained (the current euphemism) for a variety of reasons" (*New York Times,* 8/27/84). "It should be noted that the disadvantaged are particularly vulnerable to retention and their retention rates are much higher than the general population" (*Danbury,* Conn., *News-Times,* 6/15/93). See also DEFICIENCY and DISADVANTAGED.

retire. An omnibus term that coyly covers a variety of unspeakable actions. For example, to say that "she has retired," may mean—depending on context—either that "she has gone to bed," or that "she has gone to the toilet" (a.k.a., RETIRING ROOM—the point being that neither "bed" nor "toilet" should be mentioned in connection with a woman). On the other hand, when soldiers *retire,* they are retreating—a movement that may also be described as a RETROGRADE MOVEMENT (or MANEUVER). Civilians also may *retire* or *be retired* from their jobs. Thus, Yankee co-owner Dan Topping told the press that manager Casey Stengel had been given the chance to "retire if he desired to do so" in 1960 (after twelve years, ten pennants, and seven World Series championships), but everyone knew that there was no question but that Mr.

Stengel had once again been DISCHARGED. See also EARLY RETIREMENT and LET GO.

retiring room. A toilet.

Demonstrating once again the remarkable flair of the British for pageantry: "It has been announced that the retiring rooms specially erected at Westminster Abbey for Coronation Day will be severally marked as follows: 'Peers,' 'Gentlemen,' 'Men,' and 'Peeresses,' 'Ladies,' 'Women'" (*New York Herald Tribune,* 5/7/37). See also REST ROOM, TOILET, and, for the other side of the social coin, the South African examples in LADIES/GENTLEMEN.

retrograde movement (or maneuver). A military retreat—an orderly one, supposedly. Referring to the decision of South Vietnamese President Thieu in the spring of 1975 to shorten his lines of defense by abandoning several central and northern provinces: "A 'retrograde' maneuver—as the experts euphemistically term such a withdrawal—requires extensive planning and a coordinated command structure" (*Time,* 4/14/75).

The antipathy of soldiers toward the word "retreat" is evident from the definition for "retrograde movement" in the *U.S. Defense Department Dictionary of Military and Associated Terms* (1979): "Any movement of a command to the rear, or away from the enemy. . . . Such movements may be classified as withdrawal, retirement, or delaying action." The concept is by no means new. Thus, even so great a commander as the Duke of Wellington had occasion to note in a dispatch in 1803 during his campaign in India that "A retrograde movement is always bad in this country" (*OED*).

Euphemisms for "retreat" probably

began coming into existence shortly after the first army made the first one; see STRATEGIC MOVEMENT TO THE REAR.

revenue enhancement. A tax increase, as proposed by the Reagan administration in the fall of 1981. "The recession is likely to swell the budget deficit for the fiscal year 1982 above the $43 billion the Administration was forecasting when it submitted its request to Congress for $13 billion in extra budget cuts and $3 billion in higher taxes, which it called 'revenue enhancements'" (*New York Times*, 10/21/81). The tortured terminology was necessary if only because the president himself had assured the nation at a press conference on September 28 that it would take "a palace coup" to get him to agree to increase taxes. Coiner of the euphemism was Lawrence A. Kudlow, then chief economist of the Office of Management and Budget. "There's no better way to sell economic theory than by the euphemistic route," he told the *Times*. Other ingenious ways of avoiding "tax increases," all of which have been used at one time or another by one political party or the other, are to present them as *loophole closings, negative tax expenditures* (see NEGATIVE), *new revenues, regulatory fees, revenue augmentation, revenue enhancers, tax base broadening, tax enhancements*, and *user fees*. Or as Rep. Charles B. Rangel (D., N.Y.) pointed out: "They don't call it a tax package nowadays. They call it an economic growth package" (WABC-TV, "Eyewitness News," 12/15/91).

The euphemistic avoidance of "taxes" is a truly ancient custom. Thus, Plutarch noted in his life of Solon (638?–559? B.C.): "The way which, the moderns say, the Athenians have of softening the badness of a thing, by ingeniously giving it some pretty and innocent appellation, calling harlots, for example, 'mistresses,' taxes 'contributions,' . . . and the prison a 'chamber,' seem originally to have been Solon's contrivance, who called cancelling debts Seisacthea, a relief, or disincumbrance."

See also SERVICE, INTERNAL REVENUE, and T-WORD.

reverse engineering. Pirating, copying without permission; specifically, in electronics, taking apart a chip, or miniature integrated circuit, in order to determine how it works. "It's difficult but possible . . . to create a functionally equivalent copy of the machine. Reverse engineering is the name of that art" (Tracy Kidder, *The Soul of the New Machine*, 1981). The Japanese (according to Americans) are notorious for copying; Americans only engage in *reverse engineering*. See also INTERPRET and SAMPLING.

review. Censorship. "This report subject to U.S. military review" (National Public Radio Broadcast, 2/12/91). During the Gulf war of 1991, Iraq was said to "censor" the news. In sharp contrast, reporters with the U.S.-led coalition forces were required by the Defense Department's "Guidelines for News Media" merely to submit stories to press officers for "security review." See also PROGRAM PRACTICES.

revolving credit. Revolving debt, as on a credit card. See also CASH ADVANCE.

reward. Ransom. "Insurance underwriters insist they do not pay 'ransoms,' only 'rewards'" (*New York Times*, 7/8/84). In the case at hand, underwriters had just paid a *reward* of $20,000 for the recovery of fifteen stolen artworks. Nations don't like to admit to paying "ransom" either. For example, after $2 to $3 million in profits from arms sales to Iran was traced to the Swiss bank account of an Iranian group that financed the kidnappers of American hostages in Lebanon, an arms dealing middleman, Manucher Ghorbanifar, characterized the money as "ransom." An anonymous American official preferred, however, to describe the transaction as "payments for services rendered" (*New York Times,* 3/18/87). See also CONTRIBUTION.

rhythm-and-blues. Race (i.e., black) music; see RACE.

RIF. The acronym for Reduction In Force. Popularized, so to speak, in the U.S. Army, where it was converted quickly (late 1950s) into a verb meaning "to dismiss" or LET GO, as in "Poor Capt. Jinks has been riffed because he was three years overage in grade," the expression has since been adopted generally by private corporations as well as other governmental bureaucracies. See also RIGHTSIZE, SELECT OUT, and SURPLUS.

right, not. In the art world, a common circumlocution that enables experts to raise suspicions without descending into specifics on which they might later be shown to be wrong. From an interview with Alan Shestack, director of the Yale Art Gallery: "'Right' . . . keeps one from having to say whether it's a forgery or a fraud or an imitation. You say, 'It doesn't look *right* to me,' and that can mean anything: that it *was* executed by the artist but on a day when he wasn't feeling well, or that it's by one of his followers or students, or even that it's a fraudulent imitation intended to deceive" (*Yale Alumni Magazine,* 2/76). See

also AUTHENTIC REPRODUCTION and SERIOUS RESERVATIONS.

rightsize. Downsize; specifically, by eliminating jobs and laying off workers. "'Restructuring' and 'right-sizing' were words used in the Zondervan news release to describe decisions that affected all divisions of the company. Layoffs are effective April 6" (*Publishers Weekly,* 3/16/92). Adopted widely within the private sector in the early 1990s, as leaner times forced many companies to engage in what they also called *repositioning, reshaping,* and *streamlining,* "rightsizing" appears to be of military origin. The term was included in a round-up of Gulf war lingo in *American Speech* (Winter 1991), where it was was defined as "Reduction in personnel (specif of the military forces." See also LET GO, CONSOLIDATE, REDUNDANCY/REDUNDANT, and RESTRUCTURE.

right-to-work. Management's fair-sounding term for what labor calls "union-busting." The *right-to-work* movement is rooted in section 14-b of the Taft-Hartley Act of 1947. This section permits states to pass laws banning "union" (or "closed," in management's lexicon) shops that employees must join, or pay dues to, if they are to work for unionized firms. See also FAIR TRADE, FREE ENTERPRISE, OPEN SHOP, and PRO-CHOICE.

rising beauties. Shapely breasts; immortalized by Erskine Caldwell's quintessential redneck, Ty Ty: "Griselda has the finest pair of rising beauties a man can ever hope to see" (*God's Little Acre,* 1933). See also BOSOM.

road car inspector. A subway car mechanic in the New York City transit system. See also ENGINEER.

rock lobster. Crayfish, commonly served up on restaurant menus as *South African Rock Lobster Tail,* which certainly has a more appetizing ring than "South African Crayfish Tail," let alone *kreef,* the freshwater crustacean's original South African name. Another undersea "rock" is the *rock salmon,* a.k.a. dogfish. See also CAPE COD TURKEY, and FILET MIGNON.

rocks. Testicles; probably inspired by the much older (from the twelfth century) *stones* and perhaps reinforced by the modern slang meaning of "rocks" as diamonds, i.e., precious stones, or FAMILY JEWELS. Thus, commenting on the surprisingly effete language of the American West: "The wives and daughters of the senators and representatives of the young states, occasionally it is true . . . gave different names to various animate and inanimate objects; such as 'little rocks' for stones, 'rooster' for gamecock" (Hugo Playfair, *The Hugo Playfair Papers, or, Brother Jonathan, the Smartest Nation in All Creation,* 1841). See also PECULIAR MEMBERS, ROOSTER, and TESTICLES.

rodent operator. An English ratcatcher.

roger (or rodger). To engage in intercourse of the sexual sort; see INTERCOURSE. "I rogered her lustily" (L. B. Wright and M. Tinling, eds., *The Secret Diary of William Byrd of Westover, 1709–1712,* 1941).

The sexual sense of "roger" appears to stem from the earlier use of the term (from the mid-seventeenth century, at least) to refer to the penis—one of the many personal names that have been bestowed upon this part of the male anatomy, e.g., DICK, JOHN THOMAS, and PETER. The penile "roger," in turn, may come from the habit of farmers in the seventeenth and eighteenth

centuries of giving this name to their bulls. At one time, the term was considered to be a strong one. Thus, James Boswell did not hesitate to utter the word in front of soldiers and whores, but putting it into writing was another matter, even in the privacy of his diary, where he rendered it as "r – g – r" when recording the events of the evening of June 4, 1763. People have fewer compunctions on this score today, e.g., "Pity you're married. They could both do with a good rogering" (*The Ebony Tower,* film, 1987).

P.S. The lusty William Byrd frequently gave his wife a "flourish" as well as a *rogering.* On one occasion, they made up a morning quarrel with an afternoon *flourish,* which, he noted, "was performed on the billiard table."

roll (or romp) in the hay. A rural metaphor for sex that survives in an urbanized age, long after most hayfields have been converted to housing tracts. The phrase may be used either in verbal form, *to have a roll* (or *romp*) *in the hay,* or with reference to she who is rolled, e.g., "I thought here's a kind of pretty girl . . . and I bet she'd be a good roll in the hay" (M. Miller, *Sure Thing,* 1949). See also INTERCOURSE.

romance. Love outside marriage or, more specifically, sex (with or without marriage). In the more general sense: "She was not difficult to love. Though I knew the guilt of a longtime family man with a loyal wife and five children, I did nothing to discourage our romance once it began" (Bobby Baker, *Wheeling and Dealing,* 1978). And more specifically: "Romance does not take as much energy as an equal amount of time spent throwing a Frisbee. True or false?" ("Hollywood Squares," WABC-TV, 9/11/78). From the undercover meanings of "romance" comes *romansion,* a portmanteau term for a highfalutin whorehouse. See also HOUSE, LOVE, and SEX.

P.S. The answer to the game-show question is "True." Throwing a Frisbee is a better way of losing weight . . . if that is what interests you.

Roman culture. Orgies, group sex, the swinging party scene; personal-ad code, often shortened to *Roman:* "Italian Lady Seeks men women cpls for fr and roman cult. Have a well endowed male friend!" (*Ace,* undated, ca. 1976). See also ENDOWED/ ENDOWMENT, FRENCH, and SWINGING.

roommate. When the collegiate term is applied to grads, the emphasis is on the "mate" part, as the dormitory is usually coed and the relationship sexual but unsanctified. "If you are planning to acquire a roommate or have one already, be warned that you are leaving yourself wide open to more legal entanglements than even a married couple faces" (*Esquire,* 9/79). See also HOUSEMATE and PARTNER.

rooster. Cock. On account of its remarkable versatility, "rooster" ranks as the greatest of all barnyard euphemisms. It is also one of the hallmarks of the period of pre-Victorian prudery, dating from about 1750.

Deriving from the Old English *hrost*— the spars or rafters of a house, a perch— "rooster" has always been more popular among Americans than the English. The oldest example of the term in *A Dictionary of American English* (1944) is from 1772. A half-century later, "rooster" was still strange enough to British readers that James Flint felt he had to explain to them that the "Rooster, or he-bird [is the] Cock,

the male of the hen" (*Letters from America,* 1822). The reason for making the change didn't have to be explained, at least not to Americans. Even the bumpkin Jonathan, the best comic creation of Royall Tyler, the first successful American playwright, was sensitive enough to language to know that he didn't like the sound of "cock" (he didn't like SERVANT either), telling how "One sailor-looking man . . . clapt me on the shoulder and said, 'You are a d——d hearty cock, smite my timbers!' I told him so I was, but I thought he need not swear so, and make use of such naughty words" (*The Contrast,* 1787).

The "naughty word" refers, of course, to what is now known politely as the PENIS. The origin of "cock" in this sense is decently lost in the mists of lexicography. The metaphor may have derived from the proud, procreative "cock" or from the "cock" that is a spout or faucet. But it also is possible that the faucet was named for the anatomical item, in which case the traditional spigot handle in the shape of a rooster or rooster's comb amounts to a visual pun. (In German, *hahn* has the same complex of meanings: rooster, faucet, penis.) The penile "cock" has been traced to 1300–25 (*OED*) in the form of the dialectical "pillicock" or, as it appears in a scrap of medieval manuscript, "Mi pilkoc pisseth on mi schone [shoe]." The modern, short form, is dated to 1618 in *The Oxford English Dictionary* but must have been common before then. For instance, William Shakespeare certainly had more than firearms in mind when he had Pistol yell at Nym: "Pistol's cock is up" (*Henry V,* 1599). More daringly, considering the rising tide of Puritanism, which resulted in the banning of profanity from the stage in

1606, Shakespeare also punned in *Hamlet* (1601–02) upon the euphemistic use of "cock" for "God" in one of Ophelia's songs in Act IV:

> Alack, and fie for shame!
> Young men will do't if they come to't
> By Cock, they are to blame.

(This latter euphemism had a run of five hundred years or so: "Cokkes bones" appears in Chaucer's *Maniciple's Prologue* and "Cock's soul" in Longfellow's *Golden Legend*.)

"Rooster" was not the only word to supplant "cock": CROWER, HE-BIDDY, *he-chicken,* and even *barn-door he-biddy* also have been reported. "Crower," for example, was especially popular in the Ozarks, where, Vance Randolph relates, "I myself have seen grown men, when women were present, blush and stammer at the mere mention of such commonplace bits of hardware as *stop-cocks* or *pet-cocks,* and avoid describing a gun as *cocked* by some clumsy circumlocution, such as *she's ready t'go* or *th' hammer's back*" (*Dialect Notes,* vol. VI, Part 1, 1928). Randolph also reports that many parents scratched out references to crowing "cocks" in their childrens' schoolbooks.

Nervousness over "cock" may be greater in the southern United States than in other areas because the word also is used in that part of the country as a euphemism of sorts for the corresponding female part. The feminine form of "cock" may not have anything to do with roosters, plumbing, or guns, but derive instead from "cockle," an old slang term for the vulva (see VAGINA). Still, it can be mildly disconcerting (to a northerner) to hear a good ole boy tell how "She kept pushing my hand away but finally I was able to get it on her cock" (personal communication; Fort Sam Houston, Texas, 1957).

The squeamishness caused by "cock" is by no means limited to the South, however —"cockeyed" was among the words banned from the Keith vaudeville circuit in 1929; see FANNY—and it is nevertheless real for sometimes being half-masked by jocularity. Consider the following:

Apricots were once apricocks or apricox.

The original emblem of the Democratic party was "the cock," but it became a *rooster* before the nineteenth century was out.

The old "cock and bull tale" became, in the Ozarks at least, a *rooster and ox story.* This is a rare, triple euphemism, since "tale," a homophone of TAIL, is being replaced as well as the sexually charged "bull."

The "cockchafer" ("chafer" does mean "teaser," but this is a kind of beetle, believe it or not) had its name shortened to *chafer.*

Children have long since given up "cockhorses" for *riding horses.* The original name lives on only in the nursery rhyme, "Ride a Cock-horse to Banbury Cross."

"Cockroaches" in the nineteenth century turned into *rooster roaches* or, as today, *roaches.*

The "cocktail" occasionally metamorphosed into the *roostertail,* and some wags suggested (to avoid "tail" again), that it be called a *rooster's shirt.*

T. C. Haliburton may have been exaggerating in *Sam Slick* (1843–44) when he had a young man tell a maiden that her brother had become a *rooster-swain* in the navy, instead of a "coxswain," but the thought is true to the time. And in real life, "coxswain" has been superseded in the U.S. Navy by *bo'sun's mate.*

"Game cocks" became *roosters,* as noted in ROCKS.

"Haycocks" are now *haystacks*; see also DOODLE.

Roostercade has been reported for "cockade."

Rooster fighting gained in popularity during the second half of the nineteenth century at the expense of "cockfighting."

The "turkey cock" was converted into the *gentleman turkey.*

"Weathercocks" today are usually known as *weathervanes,* even when shaped like *he-biddies.* (The tradition of making vanes in this shape dates from a ninth-century papal decree that churches should be topped with cocks to remind the faithful not to fall into the error of the apostle Peter, who fulfilled Christ's prophecy that "the cock shall not crow this day, before that thou shalt thrice deny that thou knowest me," Luke, 22:34).

The American "woodcock" became the TIMBERDOODLE.

The author of *Little Women, Little Men, Under the Lilacs,* etc., is Louisa May Alcott because her father, Amos Bronson, changed his last name from "Alcox." (Previously, it had been "Alcock" and, before that, probably "Allcock," which seems to reflect well on one of Louisa May's ancestors.)

For more on the richly euphemistic subject of animal names, see COW BRUTE, DONKEY, GENTLEMAN, RABBIT, SIRE, SLUT, and the *groundhog* in PECKER.

root. The penis or, as a verb, its employment in venery. The term probably goes back at least to Elizabethan times (Shakespeare puns suggestively on "root" in *The Merry Wives of Windsor* [1597], linking it up with a reference to the "focative case," where "focative" is an F-WORD and "case" is an old euphemism for the VAGINA). The oldest penile *root* in *The Oxford English Dictionary,* though coming only from the mid nineteenth century, is of particular interest for helping to date (by its modern name, at least) a common offense against public decency: "*Flash,* to sport, to expose, he flashed his root" (*The Swell's Night Guide,* 1846). "Root," in its turn, has been euphemized on occasion as *radix,* which is Latin for—guess what?—"root." See also MANROOT and PENIS.

RTFM. Read The Fucking Manual; a standard response to stupid questions on electronic bulletin boards. In *Dr. Macintosh's Guide to the On-Line Universe* (Bob LeVitus with Andy Ihnatko, 1992), this and other abbreviations were discreetly deciphered, with "RTFM" coming out as "Read the ∗∗∗ manual." Others of this ilk from the same source include:

BFD. Big ∗∗∗ deal.
ESAD. Eat Spam and die.
FYC. ∗∗∗ you Charlie!
FYCITB. ∗∗∗ you Charlie. I'm the boss.
NBFD. No big ∗∗∗ deal.
PITA. Pain in the ∗∗∗.
WTF. What the ∗∗∗.

See also SNAFU and SSDD.

rubber. A general reference to an embarrassing article, i.e., a condom, also known as a *disposable sanitary device* (in the United States) and as a *specialty* or *circular protector* (in the United Kingdom). It probably is because of the association of *rubbers* (a.k.a. *rubber goods*) with condoms that fastidious people, when preparing to go out into the rain, put on "overshoes" instead.

Condoms have been euphemized visually as well as verbally. Thus, in a Bill Mauldin cartoon ("Wisht I could stand up an' git some sleep"), one of two GI's in a foxhole at Anzio has stuck a tin can over the business end of his rifle to keep the rain out. As Mauldin pointed out on the Dick Cavett show (WNET-TV, 12/28/78), GI's usually improvised with "other objects for which there was no use at the time," but the tin can was "pictorially more acceptable." See also the *French letter* in FRENCH and SAFETY.

rub out. To kill; the expression comes not, as one might expect, from the city streets of the twentieth century, but from the American West of the nineteenth, e.g.: "If you are fortunate you will discover the Black Feet before they see you. . . . If they discover you first, they will rub you all out" (J. P. Beckwourth, *Life and Adventures*, T. D. Bonner, ed., 1856). "Rub out" parallels "erase," a byword for "murder" that seems to be more popular among literary men than HIT men. See, however, the analogous REMOVE, which is used by certain high-toned practitioners of the trade.

ruddy. Bloody. "All I've got to say, is to say you've got a ruddy good billet" (Lord Charles Beresford, *Memoirs I*, 1914).

An old and perfectly legitimate word in its own right, "ruddy" was drawn into service as a euphemism toward the end of the last century. The British aversion to "bloody," which probably derives from plain, ordinary "blood," rather than "By Our Lady" (via "b'yr lady"), "God's Blood," or any of the other exotic sources that have been proposed, is itself a relatively recent phenomenon, arising around 1750, at the outset of the euphemistically important pre-Victorian period.

Although commonly used in spoken English, especially among the uncouth classes and by practically everyone who served in the bloody-Great-War (see SHORT FRENCH EXPLETIVE, A for a famous naval example), the taboo against "bloody" in polite circles remained strong until the eve of the second bloody-Great-War. In 1913, its use in George Bernard Shaw's *Pygmalion* ("Walk!" said Eliza. "Not bloody likely. I am going in a taxi") caused such a sensation that newspapers, which had previously been rendering the term as "b – – – – y," started referring to *the Shavian adjective* (see also ADJECTIVE/ADJECTIVAL) and to the adverb, *pygmalionly*.

Besides "ruddy," the taboo spawned such other euphemisms as *bally, bleeding* (see BLEEDER), *blinking, blanking, blistering, blooming, blurry, burning, ensanguinate, flaming, roseate, rose-colored,* and *sanguinary.* The term was even euphemized in nonexclamatory contexts, e.g., "All meats served in mass should be carved in thin slices . . . carefully avoiding . . . offending the delicacy of ladies . . . by too-ensanguined pieces" (*Beeton's Manners of Polite Society*, 1876). A highlight of the ban on "bloody" was the deletion of "ruddy" from *Ruddigore*, the Gilbert and Sullivan operetta of 1887. It had opened as *Ruddygore*, but some people thought this was too risqué; hence the substitution of the "i" for the "y" after the fourth performance. See also BF.

ruderal. A weed, to a botanist. "Other plants followed this pattern of expanding into areas disturbed by human activity but were not deliberately grown. Such plants are termed ruderals, or (more judgmentally) weeds" (*Natural History*, 9/89).

S

s – – –. The four-letter *S-word*, shit; especially in FAMILY newspapers. "On Sunday, June 25, 1989, Lucille Bloch and her husband [Felix S., accused but not formally charged of spying for the Soviets] were en route to Washington from New York City, where they had just had a pleasant family visit. In the car, her husband grew sober, 'I think I am in deep s – – –,' he told her" (*Wall Street Journal*, 10/20/93). And from a small paper in mid-America, far from the canyons of Sin City's financial district: "Man reports dogs loose from chapel hill and wants the dispatcher to tell the officer they are sh – – – ing all over the lawn" (Sheriff's log for 2/16/94, *Brown County*, Ind., *Democrat*, 2/23/93). See also DEFECATE/DEFECATION and FOUR-LETTER WORD.

SA. Sex appeal. The phrase itself was popularized by Hollywood press agents; the abbreviation, from ca. 1926, has been credited to *Variety* staffer Jack Conway (see also ARAB). *SA* is not, as commonly supposed, limited to the fairer sex, e.g., "He was an intensely self-absorbed young man, yet he was attractive to women; the group admitted that he had SA, the way some homely men teachers and clergymen had, and there was something about him, a dynamic verve" (Mary McCarthy, *The Group*, 1963). See also IT.

Sabbath. Sunday. Woody Guthrie (1912–67) used to joke about his writing a column for *The Sabbath Employee* (ca. 1940), meaning *The Sunday Worker*, weekend edition of the Communist *Daily Worker*. Historically,

however, Americans have used "Sabbath" with all-too-straight faces. As James Fenimore Cooper pointed out, in a remarkable anticipation of Nancy Mitford's disquisition on U and non-U (see DENTURES): "One of the most certain evidences of a man of high breeding is his simplicity of speech. . . . He does not say, in speaking of a dance, that 'the attire of the *ladies* was exceedingly elegant and peculiarly becoming at the late assembly,' but that 'the *women* were well dressed at the last ball'; nor is he apt to remark 'that the Rev. Mr. G. – – – – – – – gave us an elegant and searching discourse the past *Sabbath*,' but that 'the parson preached a good sermon last Sunday'" (*The American Democrat*, 1838). See also LADY.

sack. A paper bag; especially in the Ozarks. "A paper bag is always called a *sack* or a *poke*, since bag means scrotum in the hill country and is too vulgar for refined ears" (Vance Randolph and George P. Wilson, *Down in the Holler*, 1953). See also TESTICLES.

sacrifice. To kill an animal in the name of science. The euphemism is the term of choice among those who examine the insides of test animals by performing autopsies, e.g.: "Sacrificing these newly hatched wild chicks, he found that they had larger brains and adrenal glands than do domesticated or hybrid turkeys" (*Science*, 3/7/80). See also CULL and, for more lab talk, BINOCULAR DEPRIVATION, STARTLE REFLEX, and STRESS-PRODUCING STIMULUS.

saddle block anesthesia. So-named in preference to mentioning that portion of the anatomy that would be in contact with a saddle if the patient (usually a woman in labor) were riding a horse. The "saddle" metaphor for the female PUDENDUM, and for a female generally, in the sense of one who is mounted, is of some antiquity, e.g., "The adulterer sleeping now was riding on his master's saddle" (Robert Burton, *The Anatomy of Melancholy*, 1621).

safety. A condom; sometimes shortened to "safe." See also RUBBER and, for a short history of "condom," refer to the *French letter* in FRENCH.

safety in the streets. Law and order, a.k.a. *domestic tranquillity*, a code phrase among liberals for whom "law and order" are dirty words. "In the strange, violent New York summer just ending, it is not surprising that the law-and-order issue (better known to some converted liberals, once scornful of what they called law-and-order types, as the safety-in-the-streets issue) was the major concern during most of the local mayoral campaign" (*New York Times*, 9/5/77). See also LAW AND ORDER.

Salisbury steak. Hamburger. When a restaurant lists *Salisbury steak* on the menu instead of "hamburger," the diner should expect to pay more for it. The expensive term comes from Dr. J. H. Salisbury (1823–1905), a food faddist who urged people to eat hamburger at least three times a day. It took World War I, however, with the attendant, patriotic attempt to expunge Germanic words from the language, to convert "Salisbury" into a full-fledged euphemism. A quarter-century later, as meat-packers prepared to fight World War II, some thought was given to changing "hamburger" to *defense steak*, but nothing came of it, "hamburger" having been thoroughly Americanized in the meantime. "Hamburger" also

has been disguised as *Bifteck à la Cuisinart, chopped steak, entrecôte haché grillé, fried steak, Golden Kazoo Burger, O.K. Corral Manhandler, onion steak, Swiss steak, trailmaster steak, Wisconsin cutlet* (cheeseburger), and *Zapata Burger*. In England, meanwhile, "Wimpyburger" is regarded as a euphemism for a real-meat hamburger by those who have sunk their teeth into the real American McCoy.

For more about the great effort to de-Germanize the language, see LIBERTY CABBAGE, and for more about the meats we eat, continue with FILET MIGNON.

salon. A Frenchified shop, as in Chez Delila's Hair Salon (Danbury, Conn., Yellow Pages, 1994–95). A "salon," back when the word came into English in the early eighteenth century, was the drawing room or reception room of a palace or great house. Thus the modern beauty *salon* is the true euphemistic equivalent of the beauty PARLOR. Alternatives in the beauty biz, just to name a few of the many variants, include BOUTIQUE, *box*, CLINIC, *court*, EMPORIUM, GALLERY, *hairport, hairtique, house, lounge, nook*, SHOPPE, and STUDIO. See also BEAUTICIAN.

saloon. A bar or tavern; a nineteenth-century euphemism that fell from grace as a result of the campaign of the Anti-Saloon League. "After going into the saloon (grogshop) to 'freshen the nip' . . . they led me into the upper tier of boxes" (*The Southern Literary Messenger*, VII, 1841).

A *saloon* originally was a drawing room or parlor, i.e., a SALON, and the term was applied to business establishments of many kinds—*beauty saloons, bowling saloons*, and *ice-cream saloons*, among them. The smell of whiskey was so strong, however, that it was generally recognized that *saloonkeepers*, *saloon-men, saloonists,* and, most poetic, *saloonatics,* were not curling hair, setting up bowling pins, or selling ice cream. Although the Noble Experiment of Prohibition (see TEMPERANCE) failed, the euphemism was so tainted in the process that when the old *saloons* reopened, they did so as *bars, cocktail lounges, taprooms, taverns,* and so forth. In some backward localities the new names were necessary because laws against using "saloon" had been left on the books. This is why actor Patrick O'Neal's restaurant in New York City had to be called O'Neals' (sic) Baloon, not Saloon. For more about drinking alcohol, a custom that has inspired far more than its share of euphemisms, see HIGH.

salvage. To take without asking, to steal, as in "Let's salvage that case of wine." "Salvage" is the First World War's equivalent of the Second World War's LIBERATE and the Civil War's APPROPRIATE.

Sam Hill. Hell. The euphemism seems to be a product of the early Victorian period, with the first example in *A Dictionary of Americanisms* (Mitford M. Mathews, ed., 1951) dating to 1839: "What in sam hill is that feller ballin' about?" (Havanna, N.Y., *Republican,* 8/21). See also HECK.

sampling. Stealing, especially in the rap-music business. "Clive Cambell, otherwise known as Kool Herc, is sometimes credited with being the first modern rapper. . . . In the early 1970s, he pioneered the art of sampling. He would play a popular dance riff over and over again, throwing in rhymes and adding sound bytes from other records to create a new kind of dance mix" (Jefferson Morely, "Rap Music as American History," in Lawrence A. Stanley, ed., *Rap: The*

Lyrics, 1992). Rappers started paying fees for *sampling* after Federal Judge Kevin Thomas Duffy ruled on December 16, 1991, that Biz Markie's taking of eight bars of "Alone Again," a song composed in 1972 by Gilbert O'Sullivan, amounted to outright theft. See also APPROPRIATE; HOMAGE, TO PAY; IMPROPERLY DEPENDENT; INTERPRET; and RESEARCH.

sanatorium/sanitarium. A cleaned-up tuberculosis clinic or a madhouse. "The fancies associated with tuberculosis and insanity have many parallels. In both diseases, there is confinement. Sufferers are put into a 'sanatorium' (the common word for a clinic for tuberculars and the most common euphemism for an insane asylum)" (Susan Sontag, *New York Review of Books,* 1/26/78).

N.B.: Medical people used to make a distinction between "sanatorium" and "sanitarium," maintaining that the former had more of the characteristics of a spa, while the latter was more like a hospital. However, the distinction was too fine for ordinary people—as well as for dictionary-makers—to comprehend, and so the two words are treated correctly as synonyms. See also EMPORIUM, MENTAL HOSPITAL, and TB.

sanitation man. Garbage man. By all odds, the cleanest thing about garbage is the language associated with it. In New York City, "garbage man" was changed officially to *sanitation man* as long ago as 1939. Today, the city's *sanitation men* generally refer to themselves as *Sanmen.* They work for the *Sanitation* Department, formerly known as the Bureau of Street Cleaning, and they belong to one of the most powerful municipal unions in the country, the Uniformed Sanitationmen's Association.

New York is by no means alone in this regard. Many other cities have *sanitation departments* and at least one, Pasadena, California, even boasted a *Table Waste Disposal Department* (H. L. Mencken, *The American Language, Supplement I,* 1945). Garbage men in other cities also have been known as *sanitary engineers* or *sanitary officers* (see also ENGINEER and OFFICER). Meanwhile, the person in charge of WASTE disposal in Montclair, N.J., is a *Senior Sanitarian* (William Safire, *New York Times Magazine,* 1/16/94). And back in the Big Apple, the city Health Department has *sanitarians,* whose duties include enforcement of the local DOG DIRT law. It is unlikely that the ultimate in this category is the Portable Sanitation Association, of Washington, D.C., but it will do until a better example comes along: The PSA, among other functions, offers rewards for the apprehension of people who damage or deface public toilets. See also ENVIRONMENTAL, GARBOLOGIST, LANDFILL, RECYCLER, TECHNICIAN, and TOILET.

sanitize. To improve appearances, especially by revising or removing particular details. "The House Un-American Activities Committee has tried to sanitize its image. It changed its name to the House Internal Security Committee in 1969" (*Time,* 10/26/70). Most often, the term appears in connection with DOCUMENTS (papers) that are *sanitized* by deleting references to the sources of information they contain as well as the information itself. The documentary sense was popularized by the Central Intelligence Agency, which is a notably efficient cleaner-upper. As noted in the House ("Pike Committee") report on the agency: "We were given heavily 'sanitized' pieces of paper. 'Sanitized' was merely a euphe-

mism for blank sheets of paper" (New York *Village Voice,* 2/11/78). See also DEEP-SIX and LAUNDER.

scenario. A plan, plot, or scheme; a possible sequence of events, whether extrapolated into the future or devised to explain the past. "As we kicked 'scenarios' around the room, a public-relations strategy emerged around two central themes: hide the facts and discredit the opposition" (John W. Dean III, *Blind Ambition,* 1976). See also PUBLIC RELATIONS.

"Scenario" has been a popular word among military planners since at least the early 1960s. Thus, discussing the Cuban missile crisis of October 1962: "The air-strike advocates in our group prepared an elaborate scenario, which provided for a Presidential announcement of the missiles' presence Saturday, calling Congress back into emergency session, and then knocking the missiles out early Sunday morning, simultaneously notifying Khrushchev of our action and recommending a summit" (Theodore C. Sorensen, *Kennedy,* 1965). Scenarios can be a lot more complicated than this, of course. For example, William P. Bundy (brother to McGeorge CAPABILITY Bundy) directed the preparation of a thirty-day-long *scenario* of political and military moves leading up to full-scale bombing of North Vietnam. This *scenario* was dated May 23, 1964, more than two months before North Vietnam attacked two destroyers in the Gulf of Tonkin (August 2), thereby handing the United States the excuse it needed for conducting the first air raids. See also OPTION and PROJECTION.

scent. A distinctive odor, originally (from the fourteenth century) a strong, rank one, as of an animal, especially with reference to tracking prey, but now usually a subtle, agreeable one, as of a perfume, especially with reference to attracting prey. Thus, the Italian film *Profumo di Donna* was entitled when originally released in English in 1974 —and again when reworked in 1992—as *Scent of a Woman*. See also FRAGRANCE.

schmo (or shmo). A schmuck (or shmuck), i.e., a PENIS or, more colloquially, a "prick." "Never utter *shmuck* lightly, or in the presence of women and children. Indeed, it was the uneasiness about *schmuck* that led to the truncated euphemism *schmo*—and any shmo knows what shmo comes from" (Leo Rosten, *The Joys of Yiddish*, 1968). The Yiddish term comes from the German *schmuck,* an ornament, jewelry. Of course, in casual use, in a conversation that is being conducted mainly in English (e.g., "Oh, what a schmuck Jerry is"), the term does not always carry the powerful meaning of the Yiddish original. In translation, Jerry may be simply a fool or a jerk.

This complex of meanings is not uncommon. For example, the Yiddish *putz,* a fool, an obnoxious fellow, and also slang for the penis, comes from the German *putz,* finery, ornament, while the English *bauble,* a showy trinket, an ornament, has been used to refer to a fool as well as to the other item, as in "I would give his wife my bauble, sir, to do her service" (William Shakespeare, *All's Well That Ends Well,* 1602–03). See also DOODLE, FAMILY JEWELS, and, if in doubt about the clown's bawdy *bauble,* SERVICE.

school. An institution for young criminals, a.k.a. STUDENTS. "Seven teen-agers, including one charged with murder, were being sought today after escaping from Long Lane School, a youth correctional center, a correction official said" (AP, report from Middletown, Conn., 11/11/89). See also STATE FARM/HOSPITAL/TRAINING SCHOOL.

scientific and literary investigation. Theft and vandalism.

After the army of Gen. William Tecumseh Sherman captured the capital of Georgia, in November 1864, the troops went on the rampage, stealing and destroying. Then, in the tactful words of *New York Herald* correspondent David Conyngham: "Colonel [William] Hawley, of the 3d Wisconsin, was appointed commandant of the post, and established his headquarters in the State House, after which all scientific and literary investigation were put a stop to" (Conyngham, *Sherman's March Through the South,* 1865). For more about theft—and about Sherman's men, too—see APPROPRIATE.

scoop. Leak, in the news business. "It is generally agreed in the Washington newspaper corps than an exclusive story is a 'scoop' when you get it, and a 'leak' when when the opposition gets it" (James Reston, *New York Times,* 11/20/85).

score. To make a sexual conquest, especially by seduction or other more-or-less artful suasion; usually said of a male with reference to a female. "The greatest achievement is, of course, to have 'scored.' The male who has scored the most frequently is apt to be envied the most by his friends" (Barry McCarthy, *What You Still Don't Know About Male Sexuality,* 1977). A woman who succumbs readily is said to be an *easy score.*

The sexual senses of "score" as verb and noun appear to be relatively new; they are included in the 1960 edition of the *Dictionary of American Slang* but not the 1953 edition of the very comprehensive *American Thesaurus of Slang*. They probably derive from the common metaphor of life as a GAME. The sexual senses are in keeping, however, with the term's underworld use to refer to a success in swindling or stealing. Among criminals, a "score" may also be a planned murder or HIT, making this yet another example of a word with a violent as well as a sexual component. See also ACTION.

Scottish play, the. *Tragedy of Macbeth, The* (1606). Actors consider it bad luck to mention the play by name because of a long list of mishaps associated with productions of it, including the deaths of performers onstage and off, injuries in the fight scenes, collapse of sets, and so on. Performers may also refer to it as the *unmentionable play* and simply as *that play*. The superstitious fear of mentioning particular names is common, of course; see ADONAI and DEVIL, THE.

Scouting/USA. The nonboyish name for what is still, legally, the Boy Scouts of America. A memo to editors about the name change explained: "The word 'boy' is objectionable to minorities, our young adult (male and female) leaders and naturally to the young women enrolled in our coed Exploring program" (*New York Times*, 2/23/77). While continuing to enroll boys, ages eight to eighteen, the new "communicative" name was designed for use on billboards, letterheads, etc. Not to be outdone, the old Campfire Girls later degirled themselves, becoming Campfire, Inc. See also MAN and PERSON.

screw. Whether in the literal sense as a verb, "to screw," or as a noun, "a screw," or

in such figurative senses as "screw around," "screw off," "screw up," and "screw you," this is essentially a softer, euphemistic, five-letter version of the FOUR-LETTER WORD, "fuck." Its usage has been sanctioned by our most conspicuously religious president: "Christ says, Don't consider yourself better than someone else because one guy screws a whole bunch of women while the other guy is loyal to his wife" (Jimmy Carter, *Playboy* interview, 11/76). Illustrating the difference in attitudes toward the literal and figurative, the *New York Times* declined to print Carter's remark in toto, substituting "sexual intercourse" in place of the operative verb (9/21/76), though it later ran the complete transcript of David Frost's TV interview (5/4/77) with Richard M. Nixon, in which the former president said of Watergate: "I screwed up terribly in what was a little thing and became a big thing." (Loosening up a little, the *Times* also admitted to its OpEd page a joke about a very proper lady who said she was "going to Boston to get scrod" [8/10/93].)

The sexual sense of "screw" seems to have arisen in the early eighteenth century (1725, *OED*) as a noun, referring to a prostitute. The term may have gained in popularity thanks to the vacuum created by the banning of "fuck." For example, while forced to resort to dashes when defining "F – – K" in *A Classical Dictionary of the Vulgar Tongue* (1796), Capt. Francis Grose felt no inhibitions when he reached "TO SCREW. To copulate. A female screw; a common prostitute." In Grose's time and later, the word also has had other nonsexual, metaphorical meanings. Among them: A *screw* may be either a skeleton key or a prison guard (the two senses may be connected via "turnkey," another term for a jailer); *to be screwed* may just mean that one is drunk (see

HIGH); and, in England, a *screw* may be a person's wages or salary, as in "I get a good weekly screw." The word's retention of these other meanings makes it one of the few exceptions to Gresham's Law as it applies to language, i.e., that "bad" meanings drive out "good" ones. See also DIDDLE, F – – –, FORNICATE/FORNICATION, FRIG, and INTERCOURSE.

sea squab. The blowfish; also called the *globefish, porcupinefish, puffer, swellfish,* or—getting back to real euphemisms—the *chicken of the sea.* The latter may even be served up as *chicken sea legs,* which do, as it happens, bear a passing resemblance to DRUMSTICKS. In fish markets, customers may also have a difficult time deciding between *sea squab* and *sea trout,* the latter being the more edible name that is given to any of several fishes, especially the weakfishes. Variations on the "sea trout" theme include *gray trout, saltwater trout, shad trout,* and *sun trout.* See also CAPE COD TURKEY.

seat. The ass, or ARSE; from 1607 (*OED*). The term was sometimes elaborated into *seat of honor, seat of dishonor, seat of shame,* and *seat of vengeance,* e.g.: "A well-ventilated [bicycle-] saddle is the best preventative for those blisters which favour the seat of honour" (*Athletic World,* 5/10/1878). See also NETHER PARTS.

seat belt. Safety belt. A subtle distinction drawn originally by airlines and seconded strongly by automobile manufacturers, the point being that the mere mention of "safety" might cause people to begin thinking about the danger of accident. It is for this reason, too, that when a FLIGHT ATTENDANT offers a small round candy with a hole in the center to a passenger, she says "Mint?" not "Life Saver?" See also WATER LANDING.

seclusion. Solitary confinement. The euphemism is used both in prisons (see ADJUSTMENT CENTER) as well as in institutions for the retarded and mentally unwell. See also MENTAL HOSPITAL.

secondary fiber. Waste paper. Philadelphia zoning board members could see baled newspapers all over the lot, but Richard Montaldo demurred: "We're not a waste-paper business. We're a secondary fiber business." The city took the position, however, that "a secondary fiber business is a waste-paper business is a junkyard" (*Philadelphia Inquirer,* 12/17/82). See also ECOLOGY, ENVIRONMENTAL, and RECYCLER.

secure facility. A jail from which escape is supposed to be difficult. "Only those considered 'seriously assaultive,' . . . are housed in the one remaining 'secure facility'" (Jessica Mitford, *Kind and Usual Punishment: The Prison Business,* 1974). *Secure facilities* contrast with *residential facilities,* from which escape is no problem. See also CORRECTIONAL FACILITY.

security. Police. Many colleges are protected nowadays by *security officers* and *campus security* instead of campus cops, while Expo '86 in Vancouver, Canada, was policed by *security hosts.* Even nightclub bouncers have latched onto the more professional sounding term. "Bouncer? We don't have bouncers. We have security," said Lou Principio ("Bouncers: 'Diplomats' With Punch," *Sun Magazine,* 3/83). See also ACCESS CONTROLLER and ENGINEER.

selection room. The sales room for coffins in a FUNERAL HOME. "Leave it to [National Selected Morticians] to come out with new names for old things. We've passed through the period of the 'backroom,' the 'show room,' the 'sales room,' the 'casket display room,' the 'casket room.' Now N. S. M. offers you the 'selection room'" (*Mortuary Management*, 1951, from Jessica Mitford, *The American Way of Death*, 1963). See also CASKET and MORTICIAN.

selective ordnance. Napalm, with a FOP Index of 3.5. "Have you heard of napalm lately? No, but you may have heard of *selective ordnance*—though how napalm is 'selective' I do not know" (Peter Klappert, "Let Them Eat Wonderbread," *Saturday Review*, 10/7/72). Other ways of not saying "napalm" include the pleasant-sounding *napthagel* and the newer, improved *incendijel* (Napalm-B), also called (in semantic corruptions that more accurately describe its effects) *incendergel* or *incinderjell*.

Napalm is perhaps the world's most awful Valentine's Day present: "On Feb. 14 [1942] we reported . . . development of two lines of gels. . . . To one I gave the name Napalm" (L. F. Fieser, *Scientific Method*, 1964). Napalm is similar in composition and effect to the Byzantine Greek Fire, also called "wildfire," whose raging action inspired Geoffrey Chaucer to write in the prologue to *The Wife of Bath's Tale* (ca. 1387–1400): "Thou liknest wommenes loue . . . to wilde fyr/The moore it brenneth the moore it hath desir." See also CRISPY CRITTER, ORDNANCE, and SOFT.

selective strike. Incomplete obliteration. "The Defense Department has significantly increased its estimates of civilian casualties that would result from a 'selective' Soviet nuclear strike against military bases on the United States" (*New York Times*, 9/17/75). The estimates were raised from a range of .8 to 3 million to 3.5 to 22 million casualties.

See also CASUALTY; DEFENSE, DEPARTMENT OF; LIMITED WAR; and SURGICAL STRIKE.

select out. To fire, to dismiss. "The Senate [Foreign Relations] panel's action stems largely from concern following the suicide last April of Charles W. Thomas, a 48-year-old Foreign Service officer who was 'selected out'—dismissed—without pension in 1969 after 18 years of service" (*New York Times*, 4/24/72). See also CULL and LET GO.

self-deliverance. Suicide. Thus, one chapter in a suicide manual, *Final Exit*, which hit the best-seller list in 1991, was entitled "Self-Deliverance Via the Plastic Bag." Popularized by a group by the name of Exit, "self-deliverance" originally was used interchangeably with "self-deliveration," as in "Taking one's own life would be more readily comprehended as responsible behavior if it were expressed as 'self-deliveration'" (M. R. Babbington in M. Kohl, *Beneficient Euthanasia*, 1975). See also FELO DE SE.

self- (or mutual) pleasuring. Masturbation, alone or cooperatively.

The "pleasuring" is another step in the long campaign by the enlightened to convince people that they should not feel guilty about indulging in the near-universal practice of what used to be called "self-abuse" or "self-pollution," e.g.: "'Self-pleasuring' or 'solitary sex' are less pejorative terms, and one physician calls it 'the thinking man's television.' . . . Masturbation is important in learning to give and receive pleasure. . . . Petting is a further step, with mutual pleasuring short of intercourse a meaningful transition to full sexual partnership" (E. James Lieberman, "Teenage Sex and Birth Control," *Journal of the American Medical Association*, 7/21/78).

Variations on the "self-" theme include *self-gratification, self-help, self-indulgence, self-love, self-sexuality,* and *self-stimulation.* Alternatives, for those retiring souls who wish to downplay the role of the self, are *automanipulation, autoeroticism, digital sex,* and SOLO (or SOLITARY) SEX. See also MASTURBATION.

semiautomatic rifle. Assault rifle. The choice of terms depends on how one feels about gun control. See also PRO-CHOICE.

senior citizen. Old person; often telegraphed as *senior.* "Mr. Downey had an inspiration to do something on behalf of what he calls, for campaign purposes, 'our senior citizens'" (*Time,* 10/14/38). As happens eventually to most euphemisms, the gold plating on "senior citizen" is wearing thin, with many *seniors* themselves objecting to it: "And what's wrong with 'older man'? Why has he got to be a 'senior citizen'? There is an unwillingness to face life and like it" (Jacques Barzun, *New York Times,* 6/17/75, upon the occasion of his retirement at age sixty-seven from the faculty of Columbia University). See also GOLDEN AGE/YEARS and KEEN AGE.

sensible. Good sense, like beauty, is in the eye of the beholder, making this a useful term for clouding issues. "The names of the despoilers' pseudo-environmentalist fronts are littered with words like 'sensible' and 'responsible,' modifying words like 'control' and 'solutions,' as if it went without saying that existing statutes are cruel and unusual" (*Harrowsmith Country Life,* 5–6/92). A case in point is Citizens for Sensible Control of Acid Rain, a lobbying group that campaigned against a bill to control acid rain. The group was funded by utilities and other polluters of the atmosphere, not, as

its name suggests, by ordinary citizens. See also CLEAN AIR, ENVIRONMENTAL, and POORLY BUFFERED PRECIPITATION.

sensitive. Secret, as in Sensitive Compartmented Information, which is secret intelligence in the CIA, as well as a common justification for concealing that which is morally wrong and/or criminal. For example, a *sensitive source* (or, for emphasis, an *extremely sensitive* or *most sensitive source*) was an illegal wiretap or bug in J. Edgar Hoover's FBI; a *sensitive gift* is the same as a QUESTIONABLE payment, and a *sensitive matter* almost surely involves HANKY-PANKY. Thus, recalling an especially tight-lipped Watergate conversation: "Bob Mardian . . . had to speak directly with the President about a matter so sensitive he couldn't tell me a thing. . . . I was impressed and bested, since I could say only that I had to speak directly with [John D.] Ehrlichman on a matter so sensitive I couldn't tell Mardian a thing" (John W. Dean III, *Blind Ambition,* 1976). As events unfolded, it turned out that Mardian's *sensitive matter* was his fear that Mr. Hoover might be able to blackmail the administration because he knew about its illegal wiretaps (by *sensitive sources*) of thirteen government employees and four newsmen. Dean's *sensitive matter* was his fear that Charles Colson was going to order the firebombing of the Brookings Institution in Washington, D.C. See also HIGHLY CONFIDENTIAL (or SENSITIVE) SOURCE, ILLEGAL, and TOP SECRET.

sensual. Sexy. From an interview with Robin Grunder, editor of *Rapture Romances* for New American Library (9/15/82):

Q: Rapture Romance is reportedly more "sensual" than the romance novel of the past. Why the move to more sensuality?

A: Well, first of all, when publishers use the gracious euphemism "more sensual" what they really mean is that the books contain more sex.

See also SEX.

separate/separation. To dismiss or fire; the act of so doing. "He would feel [sorrow] at what the official college gracefully terms the 'separation' of Billy from the University" (Charles M. Flandrau, *Harvard Episodes*, 1897). "Separate" and "separation" seem to be as American as apple pie, with the oldest example of an involuntary separation from a position in *A Dictionary of Americanisms* (Mitford M. Mathews, ed., 1951) coming from 1779 and the writings of Thomas Jefferson. See also LET GO.

separate but equal. The official euphemism in the United States for three generations for justifying racial segregation. The phrase obtained the force of law in 1896 when the Supreme Court used it in *Plessy* v. *Ferguson* to rationalize the constitutionality of a Louisiana law requiring segregated railroad facilities. "Separate but equal accommodations," according to the Court majority, did not necessarily imply that the "colored race" (see COLORED) was inferior. Reinforcing the concept of "separate but equal" were the pre-Darwinian arguments of those who believed the different races were created separately. "Was Adam the progenitor of all people or only of white people? Are blacks and Indians our brothers or merely our look-alikes? In logic, separate needn't mean unequal. . . . In fact, I know of no American 'polygenist' as advocates of separate species called themselves

—who did not assume that whites were separate and superior" (Stephen Jay Gould, *Natural History*, 6–7/78).

On May 17, 1954, the Supreme Court finally reversed itself in *Brown* v. *Board of Education of Topeka*, concluding after a study of the effects of segregation that "in the field of public education the doctrine of 'separate but equal' has no place. Separate educational facilities are inherently unequal." Though qualified in application (it affected public schools in just twenty-one of the states and the District of Columbia), this decision demolished the fiction of separate equality so thoroughly that segregationists had to retreat to other euphemisms; see also HARMONIOUS.

serious and candid. A diplomatic way of characterizing a meeting (usually between diplomats) at which there has been serious disagreement. See also FRANK.

serious reservations. Disbelief, especially in cases of possible fraud. Thus, historian Samuel Eliot Morison noted of the Vinland map, which showed the edge of North America and was dated a half-century prior to Columbus' first voyage across the Atlantic: "It may yet be proved genuine by chemical analysis of the ink, etc.; but I have 'serious reservations' about it—the polite scholarly term for saying that you suspect fakery" (*The European Discovery of America: The Northern Voyages*, 1971). And detailed analysis eventually proved Admiral Morison's *serious reservations* to be well founded. See also RIGHT, NOT.

servant. Slave; a euphemism in colonial America that went decidedly out of fashion in the early nineteenth century because white servants who weren't slaves refused to accept the same label as black *servants* who were. The euphemism was used by slave-owners as well as by the slaves themselves. Thus, speaking of William Penn (1644–1718): "He was a slaveholder but he used the less pejorative term 'servant' instead of 'slave'" (*History Book Club News*, 4/75). And referring to a slave of Penn's period: "He said he was a free Negro, . . . but upon being sent to Prison, he owned he was a servant" (*Boston News-Letter*, 7/17/1704).

So well recognized was the servant-slave equation that in the statutes of the state of Connecticut, "servant" was used in place of "slave"—"a violation of terms for which it would not perhaps be difficult to assign the motive" (E. A. Kendall, *Travels Through the Northern Part of the United States*, 1809). And by Kendall's time, of course, the euphemism was so thoroughly tainted that non-slaves would no longer accept it. As James Fenimore Cooper explained: "In consequence of the *domestic servants* of America having once been Negro slaves, a prejudice has arisen among the laboring class of the whites, who not only dislike the term *servant,* but have also rejected that of master" (*The American Democrat*, 1838). And Cooper was, if anything, understating the prejudice. Nearly half a century before, Jonathan, the comic hero of Royall Tyler's *The Contrast* (1787), bridled at the "servant" label, snapping back at Jessamy, who had called him one: "Servant! Sir, do you take me for a neger,—I'm Colonel Manley's waiter." For more about slavery, see INSTITUTE/INSTITUTION and NEGRO, and for the "servant" problem, continue with BOSS, CLEANING PERSON, DOMESTIC, HELP, HOUSEKEEPER, MAID, and MAN.

service. A sexual act or, as a verb, the performance of one. "Service" seems to have come full circle. As far back as the fourteenth century, sexual INTERCOURSE was sometimes described as "the flesh's service" or "the service of Venus," and Shakespeare used the simple "service" with bawdy intent; see SCHMO for an example. The term gradually was limited mainly to barnyard doings, except in slang where it continued to be used with reference to people, e.g., Capt. Francis Grose's definition of "stallion" as "a man kept by an old lady for secret services" (*A Classical Dictionary of the Vulgar Tongue*, 1796).

By the time the relevant section of *The Oxford English Dictionary* was ready for publication in 1912, the sexual "service" apparently was entirely obsolete in a human context, the *OED* definition being restricted to "The action of covering a female animal." Perhaps the eminent lexicographers, Victorians born and bred, missed something. Whatever, there is no question but that people have since re-adopted the word and started applying it in ways that would shock most right-thinking horses. For example: "I sincerely hope that some day soon Tom will recuperate from his sexual depression. After all, what are the four of you doing to help *him*. . . . Doesn't he want to service his own wife? . . . I can't imagine that their marriage will improve all that much if he remains just an impotent spectator" (Xaviera Hollander, *Penthouse*, 1/77). Note, too, that the modern "with-it" whore may combine sexual and nonsexual meanings by describing her business as a *social service*. See also HOUSEMATE, WORKING GIRL, and, for other specialized *services*, DELIVER and PHYSICAL FITNESS.

Service, Internal Revenue. A "service" that most taxpayers feel they could do without. Formerly known as the Bureau of Internal Revenue, it used to be headed by a "collector," a title that fairly reflected the function. Now, the top dog is the *director*. Similar changes also have been made at the state level. Thus, Connecticut is blessed with a Department of Revenue Services in place of the old State Tax Department. New York, meanwhile, has an honestly named State Department of Taxation and Finance, but hidden within it is a Revenue Opportunity Division. The investigators in *that* unit devote all their waking hours to figuring out how citizens *might* cheat on taxes—and then to how they might be caught. See also REVENUE ENHANCEMENT; SERVICE, POSTAL; and WILDLIFE SERVICES.

service invoice. A bill, as in a "service invoice" for a subscription to *Time* (mailing, postmarked 10/18/91).

service, no longer in. Disconnected; telephone-company talk. See also DIRECTORY ASSISTANCE.

Service, Postal. The Department of the Post Office was reorganized in 1970 into the Postal Service, and it has been pretty much downhill since as far as the *service* goes.

service rate. Interest rate. "Don't call it an interest rate. Call it a service rate. It's not just a credit card, it's a payment mechanism" (Kirk Willison, speaking for the American Bankers Association, in William Lutz, *Doublespeak*, 1989).

service station. A filling station, a.k.a. gas station. Obsolete? The quality of the euphemism is (was?) best appreciated when seen through a dirty windshield, darkly.

serviette. An affected table napkin. Much used by Victorians, the term has been regarded since the turn of the century as a

symptom of vulgar, lower-class, non-U speech. Some English, now that they have turned against "serviette," like to think it is an Americanism. They are wrong. *Serviettes* appeared on English tables as long ago as the fifteenth century. The term fell into disuse, only to be revived in the opening decades of the nineteenth century as a French import. For more about U and non-U, see DENTURES.

sex or **s-e-x (when children are present).** Usually, "sex" is encountered in the phrase "to have sex," which is something that everyone has all the time, if the words are to be taken at face value—which, of course, is never the euphemizer's intention. Careful analysis of the context in which the phrase appears generally reveals its true meaning. For example: "When *Screw* publisher Al Goldstein ran an ad parody . . . showing Poppin' Fresh and his friend Poppie Fresh having sex in a skillet, and appropriating the company's slogan, 'Nothing says lovin' like something from the oven . . . and Pillsbury says it best,' the folks at Pillsbury . . . slapped Goldstein with a $1.5 million suit for trademark and copyright infringement" (*[MORE]*, 6/78).

The term also can be employed on its own, e.g., "If it's true Jack Kennedy used to sex around in the afternoon in a sort of athletic mode, one would have to make some argument as to how that related to his Presidential performance" (Professor James David Barber, quoted in the *New York Times*, 8/31/89). Bertrand Russell, meanwhile, used the term as a noun when he opined that "Marriage is for women the commonest mode of livelihood, and the total amount of undesired sex endured by women is probably greater in marriage than in prostitution" (*Marriage and Morals*, "Prostitution," 1929).

"Sex" also may be used in place of the real names of the sexual organs, whether male or female. Thus, Frank Harris fondly recalled one of his youthful conquests: "The end of it was that right there on the porch I drew her to me and put my sex against hers and began the rubbing of her tickler and front part of her sex that I knew would excite her" (*My Life and Loves,* 1925). See also FOXY, INTERCOURSE, PENIS, VAGINA, and the wonderfully oblique SOCIAL AND BEHAVIORIAL ASPECTS OF FERTILITY-RELATED BEHAVIOR.

sex-providing establishment. A whorehouse; in short, a HOUSE. See SEX WORKER.

sex reassignment. Sex change, accomplished through *sexual reassignment surgery.* Thus, some professional women tennis players protested when Dr. Renée Richards (née Richard Raskind) began entering their tournaments, fearing (incorrectly, as it turned out) that despite her "sex reassignment," the 6' 2", 147-lb. Dr. Richards would be too formidable a competitor for them (*Robert MacNeil Report,* WNET-TV, 8/24/76). "Reassignment" appeals particularly to those involved, feeling as they often do that they have been cloaked in the wrong sexual guise from birth, with the result that what appears to others as a "change" is perceived by them as a "reassignment" to the proper sexual state. See also APPARATUS.

sexually active. Promiscuous. In olden days, one did not have to be very active in order to class as *sexually active,* e.g., "Among the sexually active girls, the frequency of intercourse was found to be rather low, and faithfulness to partners high" (E. James Lieberman and Ellen Peck,

Sex & Birth Control, 1973). The coming of AIDS gave the expression a new and more euphemistic meaning, however. "A new lexicon was evolving. . . . 'Promiscuous' became 'sexually active,' because gay politicians declared 'promiscuous' to be 'judgmental,' a major cuss word in AIDSpeak" (Randy Shilts, *And the Band Played On,* 1987). See also PEOPLE WITH AIDS and SEXUAL VARIETY.

sexually explicit or **oriented.** Pornographic; two positive alternatives to the pejorative term.

"Using the 'I know it when I see it' test for hard-core pornography, nearly all of *The Illustrated Report* is the real stuff. Or, if you prefer, 'sexually explicit material'" (Mary Ellen Gale, [*MORE*], 2/76). See also EROTICA.

sexually otherwise. A catchall for a variety of sexual practices that used to be categorized as "perverted." As Chip Durgom, the director of an Off-Off Broadway show, *Another Way to Love,* told *Penthouse* (1/77); "We don't like to use the term S. and M. That's offensive. That's like using the word *nigger.* Instead, we'd like it to be called 'sexually otherwise' or 'kinky sex' or 'sexual variants.' And those who are into it should be called 'sex fantasists.'" See also ALTERNATE SEXUAL PREFERENCE and SM.

sexual orientation. Homosexual orientation; the phrase was popularized by GAY activists seeking to escape the stigma attached to "homosexual." Thus, a bill of homosexual rights, proposed in New York City in 1974, waltzed around the point, defining "sexual orientation" as "the choice of sexual partner according to gender," which would mean absolutely nothing to anyone who didn't already know the intent of the legislation. See also LOVE THAT DARE NOT SPEAK ITS NAME, THE.

sexual orientation disturbance. Homosexuality, as renamed by the American Psychiatric Association in 1973. The psychiatrists could have done better, however, as the bland clinical term produced a not-so-bland acronym, SOD. See also GAY.

sexual variety. Promiscuity. Reviewing the Kinsey Institute study, *Homosexualities,* Martin Duberman pointed out that "many now affirm that 'sexual variety' (the term 'promiscuity' is itself rapidly going out of favor) contributes positively to the well-being of the individual and to the partner relationship in which he or she may be involved" (*New York Times Book Review,* 11/26/78). See also AFFAIR, SEXUALLY ACTIVE, and SWINGING.

sex worker. A whore. "Mayor Rudolph W. Giuliani's crackdown on prostitution (33 New York City sex-providing establishments were raided by the police on Aug. 4) forces me out of the closet. I am a 'john.' . . . I am guilty of a crime and subject to arrest. So are those sex workers who tend to my needs" (Hugh Loebner, letter to the *New York Times,* 8/18/94). See also JOHN and PROSTITUTE.

shack up with. To spend one or more nights with a person to whom one is not married. "Christ said, 'I tell you that anyone who looks on a woman with lust has in his heart already committed adultery.' I've looked on a lot of women with lust. I've committed adultery in my heart many times. . . . God forgives me for it. But that doesn't mean that I condemn someone who not only looks on a woman with lust but

who leaves his wife and shacks up with somebody out of wedlock" (future president Jimmy Carter, *Playboy* interview, 11/76).

"Shack up" may predate World War II slightly. Truck drivers and traveling salesmen are reported to have used the phrase circa 1940, back when most auto camps (see MOTEL) were mere collections of ricky-ticky shacks. (Hobos of the period would *jungle up* in hobo camps, or "jungles.") The phrase was popularized during the war when many servicemen set up light housekeeping with women who lived in rented quarters just off-post. (The woman in such a case was, technically speaking, a *shack job* and the fellow a *shack man* or *shack rat.*) The phrase acquired extra spin in postwar Japan, where even a poorly paid private could afford to *shack up* with his *moose* (see PROSTITUTE), and houses were exceptionally flimsy by American standards.

No one is quite certain where "shack" itself comes from: In the housing sense, it might be related to "shake," via the dialectical *shackly,* shaky, rickety, or it might come from the "shackle" of "ramshackle." Neither explanation is as appealing, however, as the suggestion that "shack" derives from the Aztec *xacalli,* wooden hut, via the Mexican-Spanish *jacal,* formerly written *xacal* and pronounced as though spelled *shacal.*

The congruence of "shack" and "shag" in many senses also is noteworthy. Thus, outfielders are sometimes said to "shack" fly balls, and sometimes to "shag" them. "Shack" and "shag" also may be used interchangeably to mean "fallen" or "refuse grain," an "idle" or "rascally fellow," and a "shaking, tossing motion," as of a horse. Finally, "shag," as a verb, has meant "to copulate" since at least the eighteenth century; hence, "gang shag" and the softer "gang shay," which are synonymous with "gang bang." See also BANG, COPULATE/COPULATION, FORNICATE/FORNICATION, and INTERCOURSE.

shank's mare, to ride. To walk; also *to ride shank's nag,* or *pony,* or, most gloriously, referring to a famous horse of medieval romances, *to ride Bayard of the ten toes.*

share. Tell. Whenever anyone says "I'd like to share this with you," what they really mean is, "I'm going to tell this to you, whether or not you want to hear it."

shareholder rights plan. Poison pill. "Shareholder rights" is the rallying cry of corporate boards that seek to erect defenses to being taken over by other firms or independent raiders, a.k.a., UNAFFILIATED CORPORATE RESTRUCTURERS. Typically, a *shareholder rights plan* allows a threatened company to issue new stock at less-than-market rates to current shareholders, thus making the takeover prohibitively expensive.

sharing. An orgy, on the high authority of Alex (the aptly surnamed) Comfort, author of *The Joy of Sex* (1974) and *More Joy of Sex* (1991). See also SWINGING.

shed. Fired. "The corporate elite is never fired or sacked; in the interest of efficiency, it is only shed" (*New York Times,* 5/12/93). See also LET GO.

shoe rebuilder. Cobbler. The professional organization in the field was (it's now inactive) the Shoe Rebuilders Association. See also ENGINEER.

shoot. In the expletive form, "Oh shoot," a euphemistic mispronunciation of "shit." "Phonological euphemisms such as 'shav-

ing cream,' 'sugar,' and 'shoot' are often employed to tiptoe around the word, but, as George Carlin says, '*shoot* is simply *shit* with two *o's*'" (Richard Christopher, "A Taboo-Boo Word Revisited," *Maledicta,* Winter 1979). See also BS and SHUCKS.

shoppe. Shop; an Old Englishification, with a FOP Index of 1.5. See also SALON.

short arm. The penis; popularized in the military (from ca. WW I), where the troops are checked for signs of VD in a ceremony known variously as *short-arm drill* or *short-arm inspection.* "After the fingerprinting routine and short-arm inspection at Pontiac . . . I got my first lesson in jailbird humor" (Mezz Mezzrow and Bernard Wolfe, *Really the Blues,* 1946). This is another example of the penis being compared to a weapon, with the "short-arm" metaphor deriving from the frequent inspections of the soldier's "long arm," or rifle. See also GUN and PENIS.

short French expletive, a. On June 18, 1815, as Napoleon's once-Grand Armée dissolved in panic on the field of Waterloo, General Pierre-Jacques-Étienne Cambronne, commander of the Old Guard (from which conservative "Old Guard" Republicans in the United States get their name), supposedly disdained an invitation to surrender, replying (according to polite historians and the monument erected to his memory in Nantes), *"La Garde meurt mais ne se rend pas!"* ("The Guard dies but never surrenders"). Discussing this "phony quotation" in the *New York Times* (4/5/76), William Safire could come no closer to the real reply than the parenthetical explanation: "(What Cambronne did say was a short French expletive later used frequently by Hemingway in his novels and to this day referred to as *le mot Cambronne.*)" And what, non-Hemingway fans may ask, does this mean? Is the columnist referring to *Zut*, which is short, French, and an expletive—and which often is used with *alors* to convey anger, scorn, or flat refusal? *Mais non!* Mr. Safire, remember, is writing for a FAMILY newspaper, and this means that he cannot always express himself with his usual precision. Actually, Cambronne, who was captured anyway, was understood at the time to have said "*Merde!*" (shit), and this is what Safire meant by "a short French expletive."

Military history often is cleaned up in this way. For example, in August 1914, as the Germans approached the Meuse, General Charles Lanrezac sent a message to Sir John French, expressing the opinion that the enemy has "merely gone to the river to piss in it," not, as many later historians had it, "to fish in it." And in 1936, twenty years after the Battle of Jutland, British newspapers were still dashing out the *B-word;* thus, Admiral Sir David Beatty, after watching two battle cruisers in his squadron sink in quick succession, said to Capt. Sir Ernle Chatfield, according to the popular press: "Chatfield, there seems to be something wrong with our b – – – – – ships today. Turn two points to port." (See also RUDDY.) Then there is the question of what Ethan Allen really said when the Green Mountain Boys surprised the British by appearing before the gate of Fort Ticonderoga on May 10, 1775. According to the received, patriotic version of history, Allen said "Open in the name of the Continental Congress and the great Jehovah." Anything is possible, but the pioneer sociologist William Graham Sumner (1840–1910) thought otherwise, suggesting in a famous lecture on the expurgation of American history that Allen actually said, "Open up here, you god-damned son of a bitch." Finally, the lofty sentiment that flowered from the MERDE of Waterloo should be compared with NUTS, supposedly uttered by an American general some 78 miles to the southeast and 129 years later.

short (or **thin**) **hairs.** Pubic hairs, a.k.a., *short and curlies,* or *curlies* for short, usually in the phrase, "to have (someone) by the short hairs," i.e., to have the other person in a helpless position—in effect, to have (someone) by the balls. "Then they'll rush in, and then we've got 'em by the short hairs!" (Rudyard Kipling, *Wee Willie Winkie,* 1888). "I was really in the dumps, but fate had me by the thin hairs and wouldn't turn me loose" (Mezz Mezzerow and Bernard Wolfe, *Really the Blues,* 1946). See also TESTICLES.

shot. "Shot" is to "executed" as KILL is to "murder." Thus, the sentencing in Russia in early 1918 of Admiral Aleksei Shchastny "To be shot within twenty-four hours" caused something of a stir among courtroom spectators, who knew that the Soviet government had abolished the death penalty just a few months previously. "Prosecutor Krylenko explained: 'What are you worrying about? Executions have been abolished. But Shchastny is not being executed; he is being shot'" (Aleksandr I. Solzhenitsyn, *The Gulag Archipelago 1919–1956,* 1974). A similar distinction is made in the National Museum of Intervention in Mexico City, where Mexican deaths in the clashes that preceded the war of 1846–48 against the United States are characterized as "exterminations" or "assassinations," while the 365 Americans who were executed after having surrendered in 1836 at what is now Goliad, Texas, are described merely as having been "shot" (*New York*

Times, 1/7/88). See also CAPITAL PUNISH-MENT and EXECUTE.

shower activity. Rain, with a FOP Index of 4.75. See also PRECIPITATION.

shrinkage. Theft from a business establishment, whether by employees or "customers"—short for *inventory shrinkage* (also known as *inventory leakage*). "According to divisional merchandise manager Richard Roth, B. Dalton has been 'looking with scrutiny at our video operations because of shrinkage'" (*Publishers Weekly,* 2/20/87). One reason that compact disks are packaged in cardboard sleeves that double their size is to reduce *shrinkage.* See also APPRO-PRIATE and MONITOR.

shucks. The interjection has been used since at least the middle of the last century as an expression of disgust, regret, or impatience, making it a euphemism for "shit" in all senses. Dictionary-makers tend to derive "shucks" from the worthless "shuck," or husk, of corn, but a hint that the word arose strictly as a euphemism is contained in the oldest example of its use in *A Dictionary of Americanisms.* It comes from Edward M. Field's *The Drama of Pokerville* (1847): "And Mr. Bagley was there . . . [to shoot] any gentleman who might say 'shucks!'" Which does seem to be excessive punishment if the word stood merely for disgust, regret, impatience. See also BUSHWA, PISH/PSHAW, and SUGAR.

shy-poke. The euphemistic version of "shitepoke," the vulgar but popular name of the green heron, so-called because of the bird's tendency to DEFECATE when flushed and taking to wing. See also ROOSTER and TIMBERDOODLE.

Sicilian Vespers. The Sicilians have a mordant wit akin to that of the Spanish (see INVINCIBLE ARMADA, THE). The "Sicilian Vespers" is the name of a massacre of the ruling French in 1282—its ferocity indicated by the simple fact that it is still remembered. The uprising began in Palermo and was repeated in other cities. The bell for the evening service—Vespers—was the signal to begin, whence the name.

sick out. A strike by public employees who are forbidden legally to go on strike; if the antiwork bug bites the police, it may be called the *blue flu.* See also JOB ACTION.

sight-deprived. Blind, with a FOP Index of 3.4. "The blind are now 'sight-deprived,' as if to refute any suspicion that they got that way voluntarily" (Gary Jennings, *Personalities of Language,* 1965). The related "partially sighted," translates as "nearly blind," the distinction being that one can retain a modicum of vision ("reduced visual acuity"), while still qualifying for such dubious benefits of legal blindness as an income tax exemption. Finally, those who are merely color-blind are said to be *color deficient.* See also INCONVENIENCED.

significant other. One-half of a long-term sexual relationship; often abbreviated *SO.* "Do you have a spouse/significant other?" (from a questionnaire distributed at Harvard Law School, fall 1980, and relayed to me by Philip E. Devine, of Scranton, Pa.). "Significant other" had a considerably broader meaning when introduced by the American psychiatrist Harry Stack Sullivan (1892–1949), who used the expression to refer to anyone—parent, spouse, employer, friend, etc.—who played an important role in shaping one's beliefs and behavior. It is still sometimes used this way, but mainly by psychiatrists. In common parlance, a *significant other* is the same as a *meaningful associate, special friend, significant other person,* or any of the many other terms that have been devised to characterize what previous generations regarded as living in sin. See also COMPANION, PARTNER, and POSSLQ.

significant quantity. The amount of enriched uranium-235 required to make an atomic bomb (a.k.a. DEVICE). "The United States Atomic Energy Commission has set five kilograms [11 pounds] as the amount at and above which the material is 'significant.' . . . The Atomic Energy Commission, now much occupied with the growth and development of the peaceful nuclear-power industry, wants the atom to make a good impression on the general public. In the frankly bellicose days of the somewhat forgotten past, the term used was not 'significant' but 'strategic.' Unofficially—around the halls and over the water cooler—five kilos is known as 'the trigger quantity'" (John McPhee, *The Curve of Binding Energy,* 1974). It is a matter of continuing concern that the officially designated *significant quantity* is just a drop in the bucket compared to the amount of *special nuclear materials* (enriched uranium and plutonium) that has been "lost" over the years; see MUF.

sign off. To approve, to agree to; the circumlocution minimizes personal responsibility in much the same way as AFFIRMATIVE waters down "yes." Thus, H. R. "Bob" Haldeman reported to President Richard M. Nixon on how it came to pass that former attorney general John N. Mitchell approved a quarter-million-dollar budget for an intelligence-gathering operation that was to include the great Watergate CAPER: "[Jeb Stuart] Magruder told Mitchell . . . that [Gordon C.] Strachan had told him to get it going on Haldeman's orders on the President's orders and Mitchell signed off on it. He said, 'OK, if they say do it, go ahead'" (3/27/73, *The White House Transcripts,* 1974).

silly. Feebleminded, from at least the sixteenth century. Among the examples in *The Oxford English Dictionary*: "The King's uncle, being rather weak in intellect, was called Silly Billy" (Goldwin Smith, *Lectures and Essays,* 1881). See also SPECIAL.

simulated. Fake, phony, especially as applied to jewlery (e.g. *simulated* pearls) and other expensive items. "In the trade, it is practically impossible to find plain words for *small, artificial,* and *second grade.* . . . *Artificial* and *imitation* appear as *simulated,* and, in jewelry, as *costume*" (*American Speech,* 4/42). See also AUTHENTIC REPRODUCTION.

single-purpose agricultural structure. A chicken coop or pig pen, for purposes of depreciation under the 1986 U.S. tax reform act. See also ENTRENCHING TOOL.

sire. One of the euphemistic alternatives available to those who believe "stud," "studhorse," or even "stallion" are too sexy. Other possibilities include *he-horse, male horse, seed horse, stable horse, stock horse, stone horse,* and *top horse.* Of these, "stone horse" is slightly on the risky (or *risqué*) side, for reasons that will become apparent after consulting ROCKS. See also COW BRUTE.

sit down. The action alludes to the purpose. "For the first day in three weeks I had a normal sit down" ("Hill Street Blues," WNBC-TV, 9/10/82). See also DEFECATE/DEFECATION.

sit-me-down-upon. The ass or ARSE. "He left the impression of his sit-me-down-upon on the cushion" (Dorothy L. Sayers, *Clouds of Witness,* 1926). Obviously, "sit-me-down-upon" and the slightly abbreviated "sit-me-down" are connected closely with *sit-down-upons, sit-upons,* and *sit-in-ems,* all of which denote breeches or trousers, a.k.a. UNMENTIONABLES.

situation. An omnibus term, equally suitable for filling verbal vacuums when the mind itself has gone blank or, more seriously, for scaling down the dimensions of catastrophe and crisis. For example, consider the studiously bland opening of the minutes of the emergency meeting of the Nuclear Regulatory Commission after a nuclear power plant outside Harrisburg, Pennsylvania, released "puffs" of radiation in the spring of 1979: "As the Three Mile Island situation developed beginning Wednesday, March 28, the commissioners met to discuss the nature of the event." (See also EVENT and INCIDENT.)

Situations come in all shapes and sizes. In the strictly mindless category, there are the *punting situations, first-down situations,* and *jump ball situations,* encountered so often in football and basketball, e.g., "He's going to call a jump ball situation" (WABC-TV, 10/2/78). Then there is the military, where, partly through mindless reflex and partly to minimize disaster, ships that go bump in the night are said to get into *collision situations.* (This can result in what the U.S. Coast Guard calls *loss of hull integrity.*) Teachers, meanwhile, do their stuff in a *learning situa-*

tion, i.e., classroom (note the flattering assumption that learning is taking place), while child psychologists examine the *play situation* (which certainly seems to be a good way of taking the fun out of play).

The nation itself has suffered through a number of *crisis situations* (aside from Three Mile Island) in which the semantically unnecessary "situation" takes the edge off the "crisis." In particular, there was the "Vietnam situation," so called by a CIA witness during the Senate Intelligence Committee hearings (9/25/75), the oft-mentioned "Watergate situation," and—an earlier and less-serious scandal—"the 1919 Chicago White Sox situation" (Ralph Kiner, WOR-TV, NYC, 4/20/80).

"Situation" may be used more or less interchangeably with another of the great omnibus terms, PROBLEM. Attempts have been made to distinguish the two, but not with notable success. Thus, when Boston Celtics center Dave Cowens decided to take a vacation from basketball, leaving the team in something of a lurch, he explained that, "the problem—no, not the problem; it's not a problem, it's a situation—has been weighing heavily on my mind for a long time" (*New York Times,* 11/13/76).

See also INVOLVEMENT, IT, and THING.

size 10. Size 12. Dress manufacturers have been flattering their customers for the past several decades by making ever roomier dresses while retaining the same old size numbers. Where a size-10 dress once had a 24.5-inch waist, the smallest *size 10* today measures 26 inches, and many *size 10*s are almost another inch larger (industry-wide standards having long since been abandoned, thanks in part to Reaganesque deregulation). All this means that Ms.

America, who wore a size 10 when she was in college, can still wear a size 10 twenty years, two babies, and twenty pounds later. See also DIFFERENTLY SIZED, LARGE, and SIZE-38 DRESS.

size-38 dress. A size that has remained constant over years (unlike SIZE 10), this being underworld doubletalk for a .38 pistol. "Thus, an investigation that began with an attempt to buy a case of 'size-38 dresses'—that is, revolvers . . . evolved into an attempt to get evidence against crooked prosecutors and investigators in the office of the Queens District Attorney" (*New Yorker*, 7/12/93). See also FULLY DRESSED.

slack fill. The positive way of saying a container is partly empty and that the customer is receiving less than meets the eye. "A good deal of creative effort goes into making packages seem bigger than they are, or seem to hold more than they do. We have no basis for accusing cereal-makers of intentional deception. But, on average, one-fifth of their boxes contained air rather than cereal. That's called 'slack fill'" (*Consumer Reports*, 2/75). For more about the wonders of packaging, see LARGE.

sleep. Death—the most common way of denying death's permanence.

This euphemistic "sleep" is encountered in many forms, perhaps most often today in the phrase PUT TO SLEEP, which is how many domestic animals meet their deaths. In CEMETERIES, their masters are still described on headstones as *Fallen Asleep, Not Dead but Sleeping,* and *Asleep in Jesus* (a common child's epitaph in the nineteenth century). The basic idea is at least a couple thousand years old. Calli-

machus, the Alexandrian librarian and poet (ca. 310–240 B.C.), expressed it this way in one of his epigrams: "Here sleeps Saon, of Acanthus, son of Dicon, a holy sleep; say not that the good die" (J. Banks, trans., *The Works of Hesiod, Callimachus, and Theognis,* 1856). And in the harder-boiled prose of Raymond Chandler (1888–1959): "What did it matter where you lay once you were dead? In a dirty sump or in a marble tower on top of a high hill. You were dead, you were sleeping the big sleep, you were not bothered by things like that" (*The Big Sleep,* 1939).

It can be argued that "sleep" is a harmless euphemism—a poetic metaphor that doesn't really fool anyone—and it would be relatively easy to accept this proposition if it were not for the example of the Reverend Jim Jones, who leaned heavily on the idea of death-as-sleep when persuading some 900 followers to commit suicide at the Peoples Temple commune of Jonestown, Guyana, in 1978. From the tape recording of his final exhortation:

> Adults, adults . . . I call on you to quit exciting your children when all they're doing is going to a quiet rest. Quit telling them they're dying. All they're doing is taking a drink they take to go to sleep. That's what death is: sleep. (*New York Times,* 3/15/79)

See also PASS AWAY, REST, and the different SLUMBER constructions.

sleeper hold. Choke hold, apparently because the hold sometimes puts people to SLEEP. "The San Diego (Calif.) police now call the 'choke hold' the 'sleeper hold'" (*Quarterly Review of Doublespeak,* 10/83). See also SMOKE.

sleep with. Along with MAKE LOVE, this is one of the two most common Standard English (as opposed to the Latinate COPULATE and FORNICATE) euphemisms for "fuck," the need for "sleep" being the last thing on the minds of the parties involved and, usually, the last thing that happens, e.g., "I slept with her, and never had a more voluptuous night" (anon., *My Secret Life,* ca. 1890). Some active people rarely get any shut-eye at all: "I realized one day that in 24 hours I had slept with three different men" (Mary McCarthy, *Intellectual* [sic] *Memoirs: New York 1936–1938,* 1992).

People who *sleep with* other people more or less indiscriminately are said to *sleep about* or *sleep around.* Ms. McCarthy admitting to *sleeping with* so many men that "I stopped counting." Other people conscientiously keep track. "Sexually promiscuous Lisa Menzies . . . slept with over 425 men in the last two years of high school" (picture caption, *Book Review Digest,* 8/77). Even those who *sleep with* others for pay use the phrase. Quoting a PROSTITUTE named Michelle: "You need someone to come home to—you sleep with 10 men in a night, you're a little bit whacky" (*New York Times,* 4/9/71).

Because of its euphemistic vagueness, "sleep with" has caused scholarly disputes. What, for example, did Walt Whitman mean in the following entry from his diary for 1862–63:

Horace Ostrander Oct. 22 '62 24 4th av. from Otsego co. 60 miles west of Albany was in the hospital to see Chas. Green about 28 y'rs of age—about 1855 went on voyage to Liverpool—his experiences as a green hand (Nov. 22 4th av.) slept with him Dec. 4 '62.

Whitman's diary tells of meetings with many young men and this entry is one of four that includes "slept with." Whitman denied that there was a homosexual element in his poetry, and he also claimed (probably falsely) that he had fathered six illegitimate children. The diary entries do make one wonder, however. While it is impossible to tell if Whitman had the euphemistic meaning in mind, he certainly should have been aware of it, since the expression was common in his time. For example, the statements of unwed mothers at the Thomas Coram Foundling Hospital in London in this period (ca. 1860–70) are replete with such admissions as "Crim. Con. [see CRIMINAL CONVERSATION] took place at a Coffee House where he took me it was with my consent we slept together there" (from Françoise Barret-Ducrocq, *Love in the Time of Victoria,* 1991). Whitman also would have been familiar with the euphemism from his reading. "Sleep" has been used to imply sexual intimacy or cohabitation since at least the ninth century A.D. Poets who have employed the term include Chaucer, Shakespeare, and, closer to Whitman's time, Percy Bysshe Shelley. From *The Cenci* (1819):

> Cristofano
> Was stabbed in error by a jealous man,
> While she he loved was sleeping with
>   his rival.

See also BED, F – – –, FRIEND, INTERCOURSE, LIE WITH, and SHACK UP.

slip. A woman's sleeveless undergarment. The action of putting on—or slipping on—the article of clothing has been given to the name of the garment itself. (This is a common euphemistic formation; see "drawers," etc. in PANTIES.) The transition has been from "smock" (ca. 1000, *OED*), to "shift" (1598, and also a verb turned into a noun), to the nineteenth-century CHEMISE and "slip," with each change in nomenclature being introduced in the name of greater delicacy. The different terms have denoted different versions of the same basic garment over the years. "Slip" is dated in *The Oxford English Dictionary* to 1761 as a sleeveless garment and to 1858 as an item of underwear. The modern, close-fitting frilly is an abbreviation of "Princess slip," itself a post–WW I replacement of the prewar "Princess petticoat." See also LINGERIE.

slow. Thick-headed, disturbed—once a common catchall euphemism term for children who, for one reason or another, do not perform as well as their peers in school. "The problem of the slow learner continues to grow involved as increased numbers flow into high school" (*High Points*, 4/38). As a by-word for mental obtuseness, "slow" is very old, with examples in *The Oxford English Dictionary* dating to the ninth century. Teachers, a.k.a. EDUCATORS, latched onto "slow" in the 1930s because it is a relatively gentle word compared to some of the others that might have been used, such as dummy or feeble-minded, and because it is essentially positive, implying that progress, however halting, is being made. ("Backward" and "retarded" also have the same subtly optimistic connotations.) But the word's underlying meaning has since caught up with it; today "slow" is considered to be too plain, too pejorative, for classroom use. Hence, *slow learners* have been replaced by *less proficient learners*, who may also be described as COGNITIVELY CHAL-

LENGED, EXCEPTIONAL, or SPECIAL.

sluice. In the American West, to shoot a sitting duck; also, the correct euphemism for shooting eagles from a helicopter. "Testifying before a Senate subcommittee, James Vogan, a balding, heavyset helicopter pilot from Murray, Utah, told how he had ferried sharpshooters and so-called 'sportsmen' over ranches in Colorado and Wyoming to 'sluice' the eagles" (*Time*, 8/16/71). The airborne marksmen were reported to have killed 770 golden and bald eagles. See also CULL and SPORTSMAN.

slumber cot/robe/room. The "slumber" is very deep, for this is the sleep of the dead. A *slumber cot* is a coffin, a *slumber robe* is a shroud, and a *slumber room* is a laying-out room in a FUNERAL HOME. The *slumber robes*, at least, are passé, having been superseded generally by street clothes and, as reported by Jessica Mitford, occasionally by brunch coats, hostess gowns, and negligees (*The American Way of Death*, 1963). See also REPOSE and SLEEP.

slut. A (canine) bitch. The term was applied to women from the start of the fifteenth century, especially to dirty, slovenly, untidy specimens. Not until the early nineteenth century was it transferred to female dogs, which then became "sluts" or "slut-pups" because polite persons no longer wanted to say "bitch," especially when ladies were present. See also SOB.

SM. Sadomasochism. It sounds less painful when abbreviated. Variants include *S.M., S-M, S/M, S and M, sm,* and the nonchalant *sadie-masie*. In cyberspace, some on-line forums are devoted to *B.D.S.M.,* meaning Bondage, Domination, Submission, and Masochism.

"Sadomasochism" is the practice of obtaining sexual pleasure through pain: The sadist gives, the masochist receives. The term honors Count (usually called "Marquis") Donatien Alphonse François de Sade (1740–1814) and Leopold von Sacher-Masoch (1836–1895), whose names became associated with sexual cruelty through their writings and the peculiarities of their personal lives. De Sade, who liked to torture people, is best remembered for *Justine, or Good Conduct Well Chastised* (1791), while Sacher-Masoch, who liked to be whipped, revealed his proclivities in such novels as *The Legacy of Cain* (1870–77) and *False Ermine* (1873). Both men died in madhouses.

The flavor of SM today is conveyed in the following classified:

DOMINATRIX, YOUNG beautiful seeking slaves for sm, bondage, humiliation and spanking. If you are not interested, dont write, (*Ace*, undated, ca. 1976)

See also BD, ENGLISH GUIDANCE, SEXUALLY OTHERWISE, and TV.

small (or smallest) room. A toilet. "Has the railway carriage got a small room to it" (letter, Queen Victoria, 2/7/1858, in Roger Fulford, *Dearest Child*, 1964). "Can I have the key to the smallest room?" (spoken request, overheard at a gas station in Damariscotta, Me., 7/24/91). See also TOILET.

smart weed. The water pepper, *Polygonum hydropiper*, was generally known as *arse-mart* or *ass-smart*, until the late eighteenth century, when prudish pre-Victorians began refining their language. "Smart weed" is dated in *The Oxford English Dictionary* to 1787, about the time, not-so-coincidentally, that the barnyard ass was being converted into a DONKEY. See also PARSON-IN-THE-PULPIT.

smile. An alcoholic drink. "Want to join me in a little smile?" asked Frank Skeffington, as he walked over to the liquor cabinet (Edwin O'Connor, *The Last Hurrah*, TV movie version, 1977). This is an American contribution to the drinker's vocabulary. The earliest example in the *Dictionary of Americanisms* comes from *Spirit of the Times*: "We all agreed to take another 'smile'" (8/24/1839). Putting the "smile" within quotes suggests that the expression was relatively new in 1839. See also LIBATION.

smoke. To shoot to death. "Two Portland [Ore.] police officers were suspended for selling T-shirts with the message: 'Don't Choke 'Em, Smoke 'Em'" (*New York Times*, 5/5/85). The shirts were being sold on the day of the funeral of a man who had died after having been subdued and held by a local policeman in a choke hold, a.k.a. SLEEPER HOLD. "Smoke" in the sense of shooting someone is underworld slang, dating from the 1920s. It almost certainly derives from the smoke of a firearm when discharged but may be reinforced by another of the word's slang senses, i.e., to be executed in a gas chamber. See also CAPITAL PUNISHMENT and HIT.

snafu. The euphemistic acronym for what is euphemistically translated as "Situation Normal: All Fouled [or Foozled] Up."

"Snafu" seems to have been invented by

some unsung genius in the British army about 1940, and it was picked up and popularized by the Americans soon after they entered the war. Since confusion is the normal state of human affairs, the expression has found wide application in nonmilitary contexts. Its use is by no means limited to lower rankers. Thus, in 1951, the tremendously urbane American secretary of state, Dean Acheson, resorted to this acronym when apologizing to the British for not having given them advance warning of the U.S. plan to bomb North Korean power plants along the Yalu River: "It is only as a result of what is known as a snafu that you were not consulted about it" (*American Speech*, 5/55).

So successful was "snafu" that it spawned a host of imitations, but none has yet shown the vitality and staying power of the original. Of them all, it is the only one to have worked its way into the language sufficiently to be commonly printed in lower-case letters. Among the imitations, all dating to World War II except where noted:

COMMFU. Complete Monumental Military Fuck Up.

FIDO. Fuck It, Drive On; in Vietnam, "when in a vehicle and trouble loomed ahead" (Linda Reinberg, *In the Field: The Language of the Vietnam War*, 1991).

FIIGMO. Fuck It, I've Got My Orders, pronounced "Fig-Mo"; an expression of profound lack of concern by someone getting ready to leave a unit (Reinberg, *op. cit.*).

FOAD. Fuck Off And Die; computer talk.

FUBAR. Fucked Up Beyond All Recognition; for emphasis, *TAFUBAR*, Things Are, etc.

FUBB. Fucked Up Beyond Belief; for emphasis, *FUBAB*, Fucked Up Beyond All Belief.

FUBIO. A linguistic memento of VJ day: Fuck You, Bub. It's Over.

FUBIS(O). A variant of the above: Fuck You, Buddy, I'm Shipping (Out); from the 1960s (*Dictionary of American Slang*).

FUMTU. Fucked Up More Than Usual.

GFU. General Fuck Up; usually said of an individual who continually made mistakes.

JANFU. Joint Army-Navy Fuck Up; variants from WW II included *JAAFU*, Joint Anglo-American Fuck Up, and *JACFU*, Joint American-Chinese Fuck Up.

MFU. British: Military Fuck Up, dated by Eric Partridge to 1939 and so, possibly, the progenitor of "snafu" rather than an imitation of it (*A Dictionary of Slang and Unconventional English*, 1970). The intensive form was *IMFU*, Imperial (or Immense) Military Fuck Up.

SAMFU. Also British: Self-Adjusting Military Fuck Up. (A cousin to the British *NABU*, Nonadjustable Balls Up; *SABU*, Self-Adjusting Balls Up; and *TABU*, Typical Army Balls Up.)

SAPFU. Surpassing All Previous Fuck Ups.

SNEFU. A British variation of the basic "snafu": Situation Normal: Everything Fucked Up.

SUSFU. Situation Unchanged: Still Fucked Up.

TARFU. Things Are Really Fucked Up.

TUIFU. The Ultimate in Fuck Ups.

In view of the plenitude of *FUs*, it is surprising the Allies won the war. For similar military abbreviations, see FNG, FTA, and the *MFs* in MOTHER. For related abbreviations, useful in the realm of electronics, see RTFM.

snowing down south, it's. Back in pre-mini, prepants-suit days, when women were ladies (see LADY), and most of them wore full skirts and a full complement of undergarments most of the time, "It's snowing down south" was the delicate way of telling a PERSON that her slip was showing. Still more anciently, the phrases were "shimmy showing" (a "shimmy" being a CHEMISE) or "petticoat peeping." These could be further disguised with initials. Thus, one *s.y.t.* (sweet young thing) might whisper to another at a mixer, "Psst SS" (or "PP")—as the case might be. Other secret signals to indicate common disarrangements of clothing include:

Charlie's dead. Your slip is showing; also *Uncle Charlie's dead* and *Charlie's showing.*
It's one o'clock at the waterworks. Your fly is open.
Jack White is out of jail. Your shirttail is out.
Johnny's out of jail. Your fly is open. (See also JOHN THOMAS.)
The hot dog stand is open. Your fly is open.
VPL. Visible panty line.
You have a case of gaposis. Your blouse and skirt—or pants and shirt—are coming apart.
Your booby trap is sprung. Your brassiere has slipped. (See BRASSIERE.)
Your barn door is open. Your fly is open, with many variants referring to what might escape, e.g., *shut the barn door or the sheep will get out, your barn door is open and the owls are coming out,* and *close your barn door before the horse gets out.*
Your Wednesday is longer than your Thursday. Your slip is showing; originally a Yiddish expression.

XYZ. Examine your zipper (courtesy John Hagemann's daughter, then age four, Vermillion, S. Dak., letter, 1/21/82).

snuff. To die, to kill; often *to snuff out,* from the traditional eulogistic circumlocution, "His [or her] candle has been snuffed out." Red Smith used the term in its original, nonmurderous sense when asked by *Writer's Digest* in 1982 how much longer he planned to continue covering sports: "Until I stop enjoying it, which I think is improbable. . . . Or till I snuff it at a typewriter, the way Grantland Rice did" (Bill Strickland, ed., *On Being a Writer,* 1982). See also HIT and PASS AWAY.

so-and-so. A euphemism for a stronger but unexpressed thought, usually "bastard" or "son of a bitch." "If that so and so [newspaper columnist Drew Pearson] ever says anything to you or Margaret's detriment, I shall give him a little Western direct action that he'll long remember" (Harry S Truman, letter to his wife, 7/25/45, in *Dear Bess,* 1983). See also SOB and, for the many terms for real as opposed to figurative bastards, LOVE CHILD.

SOB. This classes as The Great American Euphemism, assuming "son of a bitch" is The Great American Epithet, and a strong case can be made for the latter. Thus, those impartial observers, the French, heard Americans use the expression so often during World War I that they called the Yanks *les sommobiches,* just as their fifteenth-century ancestors referred to the English as the GODDAMS.

Though Americans made it their own—often using it in a friendly, almost affectionate way, as well as in contempt—the basic expression arose before the United States was a gleam in anyone's eye. "Biche-sone" crops up in a romance, *Of Arthour & Merlin*, of ca. 1330, and Shakespeare employed the phrase in much the modern manner in *King Lear* (1606–06), where the Duke of Kent blasts Goneril's steward, Oswald, as a "knave, beggar, coward, pander, and the son and heir of a mongrel bitch." In effect, the epithet is merely a long way around of saying BASTARD and is equivalent to the once popular "son of a whore" or "whoreson."

The use of initials to soften the phrase's impact appears to be an American innovation, with the earliest example in *The Oxford English Dictionary* coming from a 1918 diary entry in Howard V. O'Brien's *Wine, Women and War*: "What an S.O.B. that fellow is!" It should come as no surprise to know that the abbreviation itself was banned by the bluenoses who administrated the Hollywood motion picture production code, ca. 1930–68, though it commonly appeared in print in this period, e.g., "This Drew Pearson [no one liked him; see SO-AND-SO] is a self-appointed, self-made, cross t'd, dotted i'd, double-documented, super-superlative, revolving s.o.b." (AP, 9/23/50, quoting Sen. William Jenner, R., Ind.). A "revolving sob," by the way, is one who is an *sob,* no matter which way you look at him.

Other euphemisms that were devised for "son of a bitch" over the years include *son of a bachelor, son of a bee, son of a Beechnut Gum* (among grade-schoolers), *son of a biscuit eater, son of a buck, son of a bum, son of a seacook, son of a Dutchman, son of a female canine, son of a haystack, son of a horse thief, son of a sea cook,* and *son of a gun.* The force of the expression also may be softened by distorting it slightly into *sonuvabitch* or *sunnavabitch,* and by cropping it to *son-of-*

a, son of a b., or *son,* as in " 'Tell them by God!' McLendon said. 'Tell every one of the sons . . .' " (William Faulkner, *Dry September,* 1931).

Some of these are quite old. For example, "son of a bachelor" is dated to 1678 in *The Oxford Dictionary of Proverbs and Proverbial Phrases* and it has withstood the test of time. American sailors were familiar with it ("Aft here, ye sons of bachelors," *Moby-Dick,* 1851) and James Dean spit out a variant ("You stinking sons of Benedicts!") in the film version of *Giant* (1956).

"Son of a gun," dating from the early eighteenth century, is of especial interest for having an unusually imaginative etymology: Coming from an era when wives and other women sometimes went to sea, and occasionally gave birth while afloat, the phrase often is said to allude to the place where such deliveries were accomplished, behind a canvas screen set up on the gun deck. Thus, any child born at sea might be called "a son of a gun" and, in cases of doubtful parentage, the child might be officially designated as a "Son of a gun" in the ship's log. This story would hold up better if someone had ever discovered an entry for "Son of a gun"—or daughter of a gun, for that matter—in an old ship's log. In the absence of supporting evidence, it seems likely that the phrase never had a literal meaning, but was a euphemism from the very outset.

"Son of a bitch" also may be sanitized for public consumption by dashing out part of the expression. Henry Fielding did this in *Tom Jones* (" 'You are a son of a b – – – –,' replied the squire, 'for all your laced coat,' " 1749) and so did Byron in *Don Juan* ("Pray ask of your next neighbour,/If he found not this spawn of tax-born riches,/Like lap-dogs, the least civil sons of b – – – – s," 1823). Again, however, the classic example is of American origin, coming from Owen Wister's *The Virginian* (1902), where the dashed-out expression elicited one of literature's most celebrated replies (and showing again how much meaning depends on context):

> Trampas spoke: "Your bet, you son-of-a- – – – – – ."
> The Virginian's pistol came out, and his hand lay on the table, holding it unaimed. And with a voice as gentle as ever . . . he issued his orders to the man Trampas:—
> "When you call me that, *smile.*"

Today, when almost anything goes, "son of a bitch" is considered relatively mild and the various euphemisms for it consequently have lost much of their vitality. Even the staid *New York Times* will print the epithet, as it did (3/1/86) when carrying an AP story about President Reagan's reference to reporters as "Sons of bitches!" The president, who hadn't realized he was talking in front of an open mike, initially denied making the comment. When it was discovered that the image of Mr. Reagan mouthing the horrible words had been preserved on videotape, his spokesman, the aptly named Larry Speakes, then allowed as how Mr. Reagan might have said "It is sunny, and you're rich." Thus, presidential propriety was preserved.

See also SLUT and, for more about euphemistic dashes, F – – –.

Social and Behavioral Aspects of Fertility-Related Behavior. Sex. The genesis of a 1994 study of sex in America by the National Opinion Center of the University of Chicago was in a proposal by the federal government for a national survey of "Social and Behavioral Aspects of Fertility-Related Behavior." The government had invited proposals from sex researchers for the survey but then declined to fund it, apparently deciding that the topic was too hot to handle even under that exceptionally euphemistic title (FOP index of 25.7). See also SEX.

social disease. Venereal disease; specifically, syphilis or gonorrhea. Until the 1930s, only a few newspapers were bold enough to print the names of the venereal diseases; many even shied clear of the very word "venereal." And for good reason: The Post Office, in the person of Special Agent Anthony Comstock, secretary of the New York Society for the Suppression of Vice, might threaten to lift their mailing permits. For example, after *The Call*, a New York socialist publication, ran an article on gonorrhea, as part of a series by Margaret Sanger, entitled "What Every Girl Should Know," Comstock told the paper its mailing permit would be revoked if Sanger's installment on syphilis were printed. Thus, the left-hand column of the women's page of *The Call* on February 9, 1913, was blank except for the message: "What Every Girl Should Know. NOTHING. By order of the Post Office Department" (from Lawrence Lader, *The Margaret Sanger Story*, 1955).

Despite the best efforts of Comstock, the existence of venereal diseases could not be ignored completely, and so a host of euphemisms and circumlocutions was begat. Along with "social disease," and the abbreviated *VD* (from 1920, *OED*) they included *blood disease, blood poison* and *specific blood poison, a certain disease, communicable disease, Neisserian infection* (after Albert

L. S. Neisser, discoverer of gonococcus), *preventable disease, secret disease,* and *vice disease.* Even doctors were not immune from this sort of linguistic contamination. According to Dr. Morris Fishbein, longtime editor of the *Journal of the American Medical Association,* when one doctor told another that patient Jones had a "specific stomach" or "specific ulcer," that meant the diagnosis was "syphilis" (H. L. Mencken, *The American Language,* 1936). Most of the euphemisms were forgotten during World War II, when it became necessary to discuss venereal disease in the plainest of terms in order to be sure that servicemen got the message. The exception is "social disease," which is still encountered on occasion, both literally and figuratively, e.g., "A Social Disease Among Horses" (headline, *New York Times,* 3/19/78, referring to an outbreak of equine metritis, called "The Silver Jubilee Clap" in England, where it was first identified), and "Hey, I've got a social disease" (Stephen Sondheim, "Gee, Officer Krupke!" *West Side Story,* 1957). See also the *French disease* in FRENCH, TB, and VENUSIAN.

social engineering. Theft of services and data, as by a computer hacker or phone phreak. "Hackers sometimes place telephone calls to computer system operators at a target company and trick them into divulging information about the company's computer system. The hackers call this 'social engineering'" (*New York Times,* 11/26/88). See also APPROPRIATE.

soft. Military targets are of two kinds: hard and soft. *Hard targets* are made of brick, concrete, steel, etc. *Soft targets* are less impervious to attack, frequently being made of flesh and bone. "The conventional bombs also will still have a role in attacking dispersed 'soft' targets, such as troops in a battlefield" (*New York Times,* 3/18/74). Especially suitable for attacking soft targets are *soft bombs,* which fragment into many small bomblets, and *soft ordnance,* i.e., napalm. See also ANTIPERSONNEL WEAPON, ORDNANCE, and SELECTIVE ORDNANCE.

software documentation specialist. "A friend of mine is a software documentation specialist—by any other name, technical writer" (William C. Paxson, *Writer's Connection,* 3/88). See also ENGINEER and SPECIALIST.

soixante-neuf. Mutual oral-genitalism; a borrowing from the French, who are popularly believed to be especially attached to this form of sexual exercise. The numbers —*sixty-nine* or *69,* in translation—apparently refer to the positions assumed. The practice is not necessarily heterosexual. For example, one of the earliest examples of *soixante-neuf* on record involves two women: Flossie, the heroine of the late (undated and anonymous) Victorian novel, *Flossie, a Venus of Sixteen,* and Eva Letchford, her—ah—guardian. As Flossie tells Captain Archer: "Occasionally, too we perform the *'soixant neuf.'*"

"Soixante-neuf" replaced another French term, "gamahuche" (from *gamahucher,* which may stem from an Arabic term). In the parlor games that Flossie played with Captain Archer, she cast herself in the role of "The White Queen of the Gama Huchi Islands." (Guess what the queen's scepter was?) And in the greatest work of underground nonfiction of this period, *My Secret Life* (ca. 1890), the anonymous author devotes much space to "gamahuching" in all possible combinations, while only occasionally adopting modern terminology. (An exception occurs in volume eight: "Then again came my sudden impulse of lust. . . . 'Lay over, make me sixty-nine.'") Another popular term of this period was *minette* (French for "pussy"); the participle, as taken into English, was *minetting*. (See PUSSY.) Frank Harris used the original construction when recalling how a Parisian woman asked him, "Why not *faire minette*?" (*My Life and Loves*, 1925). See also CUNNILINGUS, FELLATIO, and FRENCH.

solar pool. An outdoor, unheated (except by the sun) swimming pool. Thus, a builder in Edison, N.J., advertised houses with "customized culinary centers," i.e., kitchens, and a "sensuous . . . solar pool" (Newark, N.J., *Star-Ledger*, 3/3/85). See also REALTOR and SWIMMING ENVIRONMENT.

soldier's disease. Opium addiction (DEPENDENCE, as it is now called). Toward the end of the nineteenth century, *soldier's disease* was an all-too-common complaint of Civil War veterans who had been given too much pain-killer for too long (courtesy of Walter James Miller, poet and professor, whose great-grandfather suffered from it).

solo (or solitary) sex. Masturbation, also referred to as *solitary licentiousness*, a *solitary sexual pursuit* and, as enshrined in a 1976 Vatican statement on "Certain Questions Concerning Sexual Ethics," *solitaria voluptas*. "Solo sex resolves sexual tensions, keeps sexual desire alive, is good physical exercise and helps to preserve sexual functioning in both men and women who have no other outlets" (Robert N. Butler and Myrna I. Lewis, *Sex After Sixty*, 1976).

"Every time Ray retreats to the bathroom to relieve his frustration by employing a time-tested solitary sexual pursuit, the family dog whines at the door" (*New Yorker*, 8/22–29/94). See also MASTURBATION and SELF- (or MUTUAL) PLEASURING.

sortie. The term conjures up the image of knights charging over a drawbridge to engage in a melee, but in the modern world (from 1918, *OED*), it means one mission by one airplane, French being the language of war (e.g. PERSONNEL) as well as diplomacy. "The air campaign against heavily defended areas costs us one pilot in every 40 sorties" ("first rough draft" of a memo from Secretary of Defense Robert S. McNamara's office to President Lyndon B. Johnson, 5/19/67, *The Pentagon Papers*, 1971). Nighttime *sorties* by B-57s over North Vietnam were called DOOM Pussy missions ("DOOM" being an acronym for Da Nang Officers Open Mess). See also the *strategic bombing* in STRATEGIC.

source of information. A spy or informer. "The CIA considered using Mr. [Thomas] Riha as a 'source of information' while he was an exchange student in 1958–59 at the University of Moscow" (*New York Times*, 9/28/76). See also AGENT and HIGHLY (or USUALLY) RELIABLE SOURCE.

space. A grave site. "The 'space and bronze deal,' as it is called by the door-to-door sales specialists, is exciting, heady work, full of the romance of a new Gold Rush and the conquest of new frontiers" (Jessica Mitford, *The American Way of Death*, 1963). "Bronze" here is short for "memorial bronze." With cemeteries running short of land, more operators are offering *companion* *spaces,* which are double-decker graves, one deeper than the other, for husbands and wives, and reserving some plots for *baby-land* (three graves in the place normally occupied by one). Other, less-formal by-words for "grave" include *deep six, dust bin, earth bath, the Great Divide, last home, long home, narrow house,* and *place of rest.* See also BUY THE FARM, CEMETERY, PASS AWAY, and REST.

space adaptation syndrome. Space sickness. One of the assignments of Dr. Norman Thagard on the seventh space shuttle flight (6/18–24/1983) was to study *space adaptation syndrome.* See also SPACE TRANSPORTATION SYSTEM and *stomach awareness* in STOMACHACHE.

Space Transportation System. Space shuttle. NASA numbers shuttle flights as STS-1, STS-2, etc. Dr. Thagard was aboard STS-7. See also ENTRENCHING TOOL and SPACE ADAPTATION SYNDROME.

spank. To beat up. "I hope there is enough units to set up a powwow around the susp so he can get a good spanking and nobody c it" (unnamed Los Angeles police officer, ca. 11/89–3/91). This was one of many similar transmissions over the LAPD's Mobile Digital Terminal system, included in a report on July 9, 1991, by an independent commission, headed by Warren Christopher, that investigated the department as a result of the beating of a motorist, Rodney King, two months earlier. Other LAPD transmissions: "Take 1 handcuff off and slap him around"; "Sounds like monkey slapping time"; "We're hunting wabbits"; "Actually, muslim wabbits"; "I almost got me a Mexican last nite but he dropped the dam gun to quick, lots of wit." See also HIT.

spark. To court; to engage in amorous play, up to and including sexual intercourse (a range of meanings that parallels that of MAKE OUT). "She promised not to spark it with Solomon Dyer while I am gone" (Royall Tyler, *The Contrast,* 1787). "Eddy could then afford to spark the girls to the extent of 50¢" (*Time,* 12/29/47). Then there was the case of the hillbilly who was courting a girl name Esmeralda. "When his pappy heard about it he got worried and said, 'Son, I'll have to tell you I was sparkin' Esmereldy's ma about nine months before she was born.' The poor hillbilly boy just moped and mooned about it until his mother took him aside and said, 'Son, don't pay you pa no mind about Esmereldy bein' your sister cause—you ain't his'n either'" (B. A. Botkin, ed., *A Treasury of American Anecdotes,* 1957). See also INTERCOURSE.

speak at length. To filibuster; a U.S. Senate term.

special. Retarded, mentally crippled, or handicapped; formerly dull, NATURAL, SILLY, or SLOW. "But perhaps the saddest group of all were the students in the special class. They had IQ's so low that any attempt to bring them a standard education would inevitably fail" (Michael Harrington, *The Other America,* 1962). "In the Detroit school system during the fifties, classes for retarded children were called *Special A* and *Special B* in the belief that these neutral terms would not disclose the true nature of the classes" (*American Speech,* Fall-Winter, 1974). The reasons for being *special* are various. Thus, *The Special Child* by Robin White is "a comprehensive guide for the parents of children who suffer some form of brain handicap (retardation, epilepsy, cerebral palsy, autism, learning disabilities)" (Little Brown and Co., summer/fall catalog, 1978). Still, *special* people can accomplish much, as in the "Special Olympics," an athletic competition for mentally retarded people. See also DIFFERING ABILITIES and EXCEPTIONAL.

special coverage. Illegal wiretaps. "Haig request the F.B.I. (Sullivan) to destroy all special coverage" (President Richard M. Nixon, order for White House chief of staff Alexander Haig, as recorded by John D. Ehrlichman, *Atlantic Monthly*, 5/82). See also TECHNICAL SURVEILLANCE.

special investigation group. Death squad. "Mr. Herak said he had watched a Serbian unit called the 'special investigation group' machine-gunning 120 men, women, and children in a field outside Vogosca" (*New York Times*, 11/27/92). See also ETHNIC CLEANSING and SPECIAL TREATMENT.

specialist. A multipurpose title, comparable to CONSULTANT in the way it trades upon the prestige of the medical profession. For example, an *auto installation specialist* is a mechanic, a *loss prevention specialist* is a guard in a store, a *personal protection specialist* is a bodyguard, an *urban transportation specialist* is a bus or cab driver, and the simple military *specialist* is an enlisted man. Speaking of the latter: "'Specialist' . . . is a name of little substance for, though it imputes to its holder a delicate expertise, he very often possesses no more than is necessary to perform the very simple function which the continuing division of labour within armies has left him; feeding a belt of ammunition into a machine-gun, turning the dials of a wireless set, pulling the trigger of an automatic weapon. . . . It can be argued, and argued forcibly, that

the archer at Agincourt possessed a greater range of skills than the modern rifleman, and the mounted man-at-arms even more so" (John Keegan, *The Face of Battle*, 1976). See also INFORMATION SPECIALIST, MEDIA SPECIALIST, SOFTWARE DOCUMENTATION SPECIALIST, and TECHNICIAN.

special treatment. Mass murder; specifically by gassing. Discussing the destruction of European Jewry in the Holocaust: "Strict secrecy governed the death camps, with severe isolation from the outside world, garden landscaping as camouflage, and euphemisms as further concealment: Killing was 'special treatment,' gas chambers were 'bath houses'" (*New York Times*, 4/18/78). The Nazis also passed off killing as *special action*. Those charged with the task might be said to be on *special assignment*. See also FINAL SOLUTION, THE.

special village people. In Japan, the Burakumin (special village people) traditionally were known as the Eta (full of filth). The *special village people* have been discriminated against for centuries because their occupations as butchers and tanners are thought to render them unclean. The Japanese even avoid the word "slaughterhouse" because of its association with the *special village people*. See also CHILDREN OF GOD.

specified strike zone. A free fire zone in South Vietnam after May 1, 1971; also called a *precleared fire zone*. A new set of rules for use of firepower in the Republic of Vietnam that was issued on that date by the U.S. Military Assistance Command substituted "specified strike zone" for "free fire zone," a.k.a. "free strike zone," mandating that henceforth "the term 'free fire zone' will not be used under any circumstances."

See also PREPLAN, RECONNAISSANCE IN FORCE, and, for a historical parallel, CONCENTRATION CAMP.

speculate. Gamble. No one likes to think that our great free enterprise system depends on anything as chancy as gambling. Therefore, Wall Streeters are said to *speculate*. Though the literal meanings, or denotations, of the two words are the same, the connotations are so different that even the better gamblers avoid the dicier term. Thus, after an afternoon during which he had won about $200 at the Resorts International casino in Atlantic City, N.J., Howard Grossman, an expert blackjack player, declared "I don't gamble. I invest with a risk" (New York *City News*, 10/8/78). See also SPORTSMAN, SURE-THING PLAYER, and TURF ACCOUNTANT.

spirit. Ghost; paranormal talk, on the authority of the founder of the Center for Applied Anomalous Phenomena: "The words ghost and haunting are not used, replaced instead by 'spirit and inhabitance,' says Mr. [Scott] Jones, who is also a special assistant to Senator Claibrone Pell of Rhode Island" (*Litchfield County*, Conn., *Times*, 10/31/86).

spiritual. Short for "spiritual wife," meaning an extra wife, a concubine, among Mormons and Millerites in the nineteenth century.

spirulina. Pond scum; a blue-green algae, rich in nutrients, low in cholesterol, but marketed under the more palatable "spirulina" label in health-food stores.

spit. (1) Piss. "The vice presidency isn't worth a pitcher of warm spit," an observation attributed to John Nance Garner, two-term vice-president under FDR, which catches the spirit but not the exact phraseology of Cactus Jack. (2) Shit. "Ordinary people don't give a spit about positions until they've been checked out by world-class experts and presented on interactive TV" (Garry Trudeau, *New York Times*, 5/31/92). See also DEFECATE/DEFECATION, EXPECTORATE, and PEE.

sport. A genetic anomaly, a mutant or monster; short for "sport of nature." "The strange varieties [of livestock and crops] are often called 'monsters,' from a Latin word meaning 'to warn.' A less emotional term, is 'sport'" (Isaac Asimov, *The Wellsprings of Life*, 1960).

sporting gal/girl/woman. A whore. "'Of course, we called them sporting gals,' Lewis Gibson, the assistant police chief [of Fairbanks, Alaska], said. 'They weren't called prostitutes'" (*New Republic*, 11/1/75). A *sporting gal* normally resides in a *sporting house* (or *mansion*). See also HOUSE and PROSTITUTE.

sportsman. (1) A gambler, especially one who plunges heavily; (2) a hunter, especially one who takes no chances. The first sense was included by John Russell Bartlett in his *Dictionary of Americanisms* (1848) and *sportsmen* of this stripe are still sighted occasionally, as in "A Chicago gambler named Monte Tennes, whose bets were high enough to qualify him as a 'sportsman'" (Red Smith, *New York Times*, 11/2/75). As for the second kind of "sportsman," see SLUICE.

SSDD. A standard, shorthand response to such questions as "How are you?" or

"How's it going?" The abbreviated reply, "SSDD," heard commonly in the mid-1990s in Washington, Conn., but surely not limited to this small town, stands for "Same shit, different day." See also RTFM.

stable growth. Slow growth. When Hamilton B. Mitchell, chairman of the board of Dun & Bradstreet Companies, Inc., was asked at a meeting of The Investment Analysts Society of Chicago, 11/1/73, "What percentage of your revenues are in the slow growth and what are in the fast growth areas?" he replied, "Well, it used to be that 75 percent were in the slow growth or we might say the stable growth, if you permit me to use that word instead of slow growth."

"Stable" has a FOP Index of 1.75 compared to "slow." See also ADJUST/ADJUSTMENT/READJUSTMENT.

standards. Ethics. The word "ethics" is such a loaded one that when the behavior of a member of the U.S. House of Representatives becomes so outrageous that fellow delegates can no longer ignore it, the matter is referred not to an ethics committee but to the Committee on Standards of Official Conduct. Senators also have been known to camouflage ethics issues. For example, in the course of watering down the Foreign Corrupt Practices Act in 1981 (it prohibits American companies from paying bribes, a.k.a. COMMISSIONS, to foreign officials), the Senate also voted to change its name to the Business Practices and Records Act.

start. Stop. Riders of buses operated by the Bi-State Development Agency in St. Louis, Mo., used to wait at positive-sounding "bus starts," but after eighteen months the

agency caved in and began calling them, "bus stops" again (New York *Daily News*, 8/16/86). See also NO OUTLET.

startle reflex. A flinch, as from pain. Speaking of experiments on animals, and the language of those who do the experimenting: "Animals . . . are not given electric shocks, but respond to aversive electrical stimulation. They don't flinch, but display the startle reflex" (Toronto *Globe and Mail*, 2/2/92). See also SACRIFICE.

state farm/hospital/training school. The "state" is a signpost word, indicating that a euphemism follows. For "state farm," read "prison," as in the Cummins State Farm, in Arkansas, where, it was rumored, some 200 prisoners had been murdered, and where, on January 29, 1968, three decapitated skeletons were found in shallow graves in the mule pasture. (For taking the pains to search out the *state farm*'s unsavory past, the SUPERINTENDENT, Thomas O. Murton, was dismissed by Governor Winthrop Rockefeller, while a local grand jury considered indicting him for "grave robbing.") As for "state hospital," read "mental hospital," and for "state training school," read "reformatory" or "children's prison," or "institution for retarded people who may or may not be trainable."

This set of euphemisms is wearing thin, and new terms are coming to the fore as replacements. Thus, in New York State, the name of Matteawan State Hospital (for the criminally insane) was changed to the even blander "Correction Center for Medical Services," while the *training school* at Goshen, which features barbed wire on top of the fence around the playground for STUDENTS, steel-mesh screen over the windows, and heavy, locked doors, goes by the name of the Goshen Center for Boys. See also COR-RECTIONAL FACILITY, MENTAL HOSPITAL, and SCHOOL.

statesman. Politician, especially one who is no longer around to make deals. In the words of Rep. Thomas Reed (R., Me.), speaker of the House in the 1890s (Tsar Reed, as he was known): "A statesman is a successful politician who is dead" (in Edward Boykin, ed., *The Wit and Wisdom of Congress*, 1961).

statuesque. Large breasts. Recalling life as a police reporter on the Baltimore *Sun* in the late 1940s and the criteria that separated routine stories from "good" ones: "Any number of things could elevate a 'little murder' into a 'good murder.' Was the victim 'a prominent Baltimorean' or 'a member of an old Maryland family'? If so, 'good murder.' Could the rewrite man justifiably describe the victim as 'statuesque,' the universally understood code word meaning 'big breasts'? If so, 'good murder'" (Russell Baker, *The Good Times*, 1989). See also BOSOM, FULL-FIGURED, and PHYSIQUE.

statutory offense. The standard euphemism for "sodomy" in the newspapers through the middle of the twentieth century. "Women were never raped in news reports; they were criminally assaulted. Men were never guilty of sodomy, they were convicted of a statutory offense" (*Columbia Journalism Review*, 5–6/78). See also ASSAULT.

sterile. Homosexual, *obs.* Speaking of public reaction to Tennessee Williams following the successes of *The Glass Menagerie* (1945) and *A Streetcar Named Desire* (1947): "At the beginning, Williams was acclaimed by pretty much everyone; only *Time* magazine was consistently hostile, suspecting that Williams might be 'basically negative' and 'sterile,' code words of the day for fag" (Gore Vidal, *New York Review of Books*, 6/13/85). See also GAY.

stew. A brothel, circa thirteenth to nineteenth centuries; also, a woman who worked in one. "Stew," as brothel, derives from "stew," meaning a "heated room," or "bath," in which people "stewed" themselves in hot air or steam. The extension of the word's meaning to include "brothel" was the natural result of the frequent misuse of the public bathhouses of medieval London and other cities for immoral purposes. Public baths, it seems, have gained a bad reputation wherever established. Other forms of "brothel" in the seventeenth and eighteenth centuries included the *bagnio* (from the Italian *bagno*, bath) and the *hummums* (from the Arabic *hammam*, a hot bath). From an early date, there were also GAY *stews*. In 1530, William Tyndale noted the existence in Rome of "a stues not of women onely, but of the male kynde also agaynst nature" (*An Answer Vnto Sir Thomas Mores Dialoge*). See also FLIGHT ATTENDANT, HORSE, HOUSE, and PROSTITUTE.

stomachache. Bellyache. People suffered "bellyaches" (from 1552) for many years before the first "stomachache" (1763) was recorded. Not surprisingly, "stomach" comes from the Old French (and ultimately from the Greek *stomachos*, gullet), while "belly" is Old English (from *belg, belig*, bag). When "bellyache" is mentioned, there is a good chance that it stands for something worse, e.g, Babe Ruth's "bellyache heard round the world," which caused him to miss the first couple months of the 1925

season, and which some newspapermen who followed the Yankees suspected was due to a bad case of gonorrhea rather than his gorging out on hot dogs. What they thought was beside the point, however, since VD couldn't be mentioned in newspapers of that era, as noted in SOCIAL DISEASE.

Today, the more refined "stomach" also is the preferred prefix when referring to other internal disturbances, e.g., *stomach awareness* and *stomach distress,* for the queasy realization that one is about to lose one's cookies, and *stomach disorder,* for the actual event. For example, reporting on one of the Skylab missions: "In the voluminous interior of the space station . . . Carr, and particularly Pogue, were having more serious symptoms of what the flight surgeons referred to as 'stomach awareness.' Looking at Pogue, Gibson remarked, 'Ole sweaty-palm time there.' Pogue threw up" (Henry S. F. Cooper, Jr., *A House in Space,* 1976).

"Stomach" itself has gone in and out of fashion over time. Banned for many years from polite discourse in England, it serves as one of the markers of the pre-Victorian linguistic revolution. Thus, a writer complained in the *Spectator* (11/8/1711) of his "misfortune to be in love with a young creature who is daily committing faults. . . . After our return from a walk the other day, she . . . professed before a large company, that she was all over in a sweat. She told me this afternoon that her stomach ached; and was complaining yesterday at dinner of something that stuck in her teeth." When Dr. Johnson's friend, Mrs. Thrale, read this passage, toward the end of the century, to her daughters, aged eleven and twelve, their reaction moved her to comment on "the great change" that had taken place in "Female Manners within these few years in England." One of the girls actually

"burst out o'laughing at the idea of *a Lady* saying her Stomach ach'd, or that something stuck between her Teeth" (diary, 11/4/1782).

See also ABDOMEN, MOTION DISCOMFORT, SPACE ADAPTATION SYNDROME, TUMMY, and UPCHUCK.

stonecrop. An old (pre-1000) name for a family of mosslike herbs, especially *Sedum acre,* having thick, narrow, sharply pointed leaves, and once commonly known as "prick-madam" or "prick-my-dame." "Prick madam, or stone crop. . . . It is termed also Trick Madam" (Randle Holme, *The Academy of Armory,* 1688). See also PARSON-IN-THE-PULPIT.

stonewall. To obstruct (justice), to say little or nothing, to COVER-UP.

As President Nixon told his men on March 22, 1973, in a segment of the conversation that was *not* included when the White House transcripts were made public on April 30, 1974, but which was preserved for posterity by the House Judiciary Committee: "I don't give a shit what happens. I want you all to stonewall it, let them plead the Fifth Amendment, cover up, or anything else, if it'll save it—save the whole plan."

This use of "stonewall" probably is a tribute to Confederate General Thomas Jonathan Jackson, who became "Stonewall" Jackson after conducting a resolute defense at the first Battle of Bull Run in 1861. "Stonewall" also has an obstructionist meaning in politics in Australia and New Zealand, where it is a parliamentary stalling tactic involving long speeches (akin to a filibuster) and other delaying actions. This usage apparently derives from cricket, where a batsman who plays purely defensively is said "to stonewall."

stool. Either the seat or the fecal matter expelled while sitting upon it; originally a *close stool, privy stool,* or *stool of ease,* and later the action ("to be at stool") as well as the result. The basic stool-that-is-a-seat is of some venerability, dating to at least the fifteenth century. *The Oxford English Dictionary* includes such classic examples as "I send them by his advice to sit upon the stool and strain" (Milton, *Colasterion,* 1645). See also EASE, PRIVY, and TOILET.

story. A lie, from at least the seventeenth century. "'Mr. Easy,' replied the lieutenant, 'I never quarrel with anyone except (I won't tell a story) with my wife'" (Capt. Frederick Marryat, *Mr. Midshipman Easy,* 1836). Continuing the thought, the person who tells the false tale is known as a "storyteller" or, especially among English children, simply "a story," as in "You story, you!" Slangy variations include *bedtime story, cock-and-bull story, fairy story, ghost story,* and *tall story,* as well as such specific stories (or "yarns") as the *barroom story, bunkroom story,* and *fish story* (a.k.a. *piscatorial prevarication*). See also COVER and WHITE LIE.

stout. Fat; sometimes, *stylishly stout.* Speaking of Louis Armstrong in the early 1930s: "He was kind of stout then—that was many years before Hollywood made him reduce for that picture with Bing Crosby" (Mezz Mezzerow and Bernard Wolfe, *Really the Blues,* 1946). The original senses of "stout," from ca. 1300, involved fierceness, strength, and bravery, as in stouthearted man or the stout that is strong beer. The employment of the word as a euphemism for corpulence, from ca. 1800, has affected its meaning for the worse. See also KING-SIZE and PORTLY.

strategic. An overarching word for justifying whatever means are necessary to obtain a particular end.

The combinations in which "strategic" appears are awesome to behold. For example, there is *strategic bombing,* which in World War II meant the bombing of cities, and which later was developed into the idea of *strategic nuclear war,* also called an *all-out strategic exchange* (see EXCHANGE). A war of this sort, as contemplated by those who specialized in thinking the UNTHINKABLE, would have been waged by the Strategic Air Force (whose motto is "Peace Is Our Profession"); by *strategic submarines,* such as the *Poseidon;* by long-range *strategic nuclear weapons,* such as the PEACEKEEPER missile, which differ less in killing power than one might think from the supposedly smaller TACTICAL NUCLEAR WEAPONS; and, if it had been built, the various elements of the Strategic Defense Initiative, better known as Star Wars. The amount of fissionable material required to construct a *strategic warhead* is known, naturally, as the *strategic quantity* (for a watered-down version of this, see SIGNIFICANT QUANTITY). On a smaller scale, one of the centerpieces of the war in Vietnam was the Strategic Hamlet Program. (These "hamlets," which bore an uncanny resemblance to fortified refugee camps, were advertised as "New Life Hamlets.") And for those who want to understand the CIA, it is worth remembering that its bureaucratic predecessor was the Office of Strategic Services (derided by some as Oh So Social, Oh So Secret, and Oh So Silly).

An especially fine example of a "strategic" whose shortcomings have been swept under history's rug is *strategic bombing.* Before airplanes were invented, attacks on unfortified positions, such as cities, were considered immoral by soldiers of the better sort as well as by civilians on the receiving end. Following the carnage on the battlefields of World War I, however, far-sighted military men in Europe and America began looking for ways to shorten the next war. The flyers came up with *strategic bombing,* with General William (Billy) Mitchell and others arguing that no nation would stand up for long against air attacks on its cities ("vital centers," as Mitchell termed them). "A few gas bombs," according to Mitchell, would paralyze a city, and after completely destroying or paralyzing a few cities, the enemy would surrender.

The real meaning of *strategic bombing* was recognized by the public early in World War II, e.g., "Bombing of cities . . . is a true example of strategic bombing" (*Nineteenth Century,* 9/41). And the meaning became even clearer as the war progressed: "Consequently, any plan of strategic bombing to destroy Japan's capacity to make war . . . must include the destruction of these thousands of family factories" (*Reader's Digest,* 5/45).

In the end, it is debatable whether *strategic bombing* shortened the war or lengthened it. John Kenneth Galbraith makes a good case in *A Journey Through Economic Time* (1994) for the proposition that bombing of economic targets in order to destroy morale always achieves just the opposite results. Be that as it may, *strategic bombing* in World War II certainly didn't live up to its advance billing by producing a quick, bloodless (for our side) victory.

Nevertheless, all the arguments for *strategic bombing* were trotted out again during the Korean POLICE ACTION and the Vietnam CONFLICT, even though both Korea and Vietnam had rudimentary transportation networks, not susceptible to disruption by bombing, and few other targets worth hitting. Only after a great many tons of bombs were dropped in Vietnam did some of the war's managers begin to realize that the policy wasn't working, e.g., "It is strategic bombing that seems unproductive and unwise. . . . (The lights have not stayed off in Haiphong, and even if they had, electric lights are in no sense essential to the Communist war effort.) And against this distinctly marginal impact we have to weigh the fact that strategic bombing does tend to divide the U.S. . . . and to accentuate the unease and distemper which surround the war in Vietnam, both at home and abroad" (McGeorge Bundy, special assistant to the president for National Security Affairs, memo to Lyndon B. Johnson, president, ca. 5/4/67, *The Pentagon Papers,* 1971). Again, *strategic bombing* did not accomplish the desired objective.

Still, cold warriors managed to contemplate *strategic bombing's* lineal descendant, *strategic nuclear war,* in excruciating detail. We can only thank our lucky stars that it has not come about and hope that the advice of former secretary of defense Robert S. McNamara on this score will be remembered: "My personal opinion is . . . we cannot win a nuclear war, a strategic nuclear war, in the normal meaning of the word 'win'" (in Arthur M. Schlesinger, Jr., *A Thousand Days,* 1965).

Of course, the alternative, with which we are now blessed, is not peace but what *strategicians* call *strategic stability.*

For more about the theory and practice of *strategic bombing,* see FLYING FORTRESS and PRECISION BOMBING; for an exception to the rule that "strategic" signifies death and destruction, see STRATEGIC MOVEMENT TO THE REAR.

strategic misrepresentation. A lie, as told by an MBA.

William Safire reports that Professor Howard Raiffa, of the Harvard Graduate School of Business Administration, adopted this unusually roundabout term (FOP Index of 11.7) to help students in his course on Competitive Decision Making get over whatever qualms they might have about misleading "less scrupulous" adversaries in negotiations (*On Language,* 1980). See also WHITE LIE.

strategic movement to the rear. Retreat.

The only kind of "retreat" that proper soldiers recognize is the signal for lowering the flag at sunset. Thus, retreating armies *rearrange their lines,* make ADJUSTMENTS OF THE FRONT, or gracefully RETIRE; they engage in *mobile maneuvering* or effect *changes of base* ("change of base" was General George B. McClellan's euphemism when he began backing away from Richmond on June 26, 1862); they conduct REDEPLOYMENTS, RETRO-GRADE MOVEMENTS, or WITHDRAWALS; they BREAK OFF CONTACT WITH THE ENEMY or, if surrounded, attempt EXFILTRATION; they may even (as mainly American troops did in 1950 when Chinese VOLUNTEERS entered the Korean POLICE ACTION) resort to what GIs termed "the big bug-out." But they never—well, hardly ever—"retreat." The official *Department of Defense Dictionary of Military and Associated Terms* (1979) has more than 6,000 entries, but "retreat" is not one of them.

Since "strategy" comes from *strategos,* the ancient Greek word for "general," it is only natural that "strategic movements" are of some antiquity. Speaking of Antigonus Gonatas, king of Macedonia from 274 to 239 B.C.: "He was also probably the first man to call a retreat a 'strategic movement to the rear'" (A. R. Burn, *A Traveller's History of Greece,* 1965). Gonatas (a nickname, meaning "kneecap," from the piece of armor that covered it) was a sharp man with words and also deserves to be remembered for his reply to a poet who suggested that he might be divine, i.e., "The man who carries my chamberpot knows better." See also CHAMBER.

streetbuilder. A homeless person who constructs a shanty. "Streetbuilder" was voted the most euphemistic new word of 1993 by members of the American Dialect Society at their annual convention in Toronto that year. See also NONDOMICILED.

streetwalker. A whore, PROSTITUTE, or, in modern CB lingo, a *pavement princess.* The circumlocutory as well as circumambulatory "streetwalker"—in theory, the phrase could apply to anyone walking the street for any reason whatsoever—has been making her rounds at least since the sixteenth century. For example: "They shold see how these street walkers wil iet [to jet, in the sense of encroaching upon others] in rich garded gowns" (Robert Greene, *A Notable Discovery of Coosnage or The Art of Conny Catching,* 1592). And for more about "conny catching," which is not as bad as one might think, see RABBIT.

stress-producing stimulus. An electric shock, as administered by an accredited scientist or doctor. A *stress-producing stimulus* may be used in the course of research in a laboratory on an animal, such as a mouse, or in the course of AVERSION THERAPY in a prison on a person. In either case, the *stress-producing stimulus* may produce, in addition to stress, what is politely, and scientifically, referred to as VOCALIZATION. See also SACRIFICE.

stretch the truth. To tell what is not entirely true; to lie. "Does everyone lie about something? Well, perhaps, lie is a bit strong—let's say instead 'stretch the truth,' a description that somehow makes the whole thing sound less serious and more like a peccadillo" (Enid Nemy, *New York Times*, 1/20/91). See also EMBROIDER THE TRUTH and WHITE LIE.

"Stretch" has been used in the sense of exaggerating the truth since the seventeenth century. The relevant noun—the product of *stretching*—is a *stretcher*, and this word is just as old. Thus, from an attack on Roman Catholics: "Any story of a Cock and a Bull, will serve their turns to found a Festival upon . . . though the circumstances are never so improbable. This of removing the rock is a pretty stretcher" (1674, *OED*). Closer to our time, John Russell Bartlett defined "stretcher" as "A notorious lie" in his *Dictionary of Americanisms* (1849). Mark Twain exploited the nuances of the term in the marvelous opening paragraph of *Huckleberry Finn* (1884):

> You don't know about me without you have read a book by the name of *The Adventures of Tom Sawyer,* but that ain't no matter. That book was made by Mr. Mark Twain and he told the truth, mainly. There was some things he stretched, but mainly he told the truth. That is nothing. I never seen anybody but lied one time or another, without it was Aunt Polly or the widow, or maybe Mary. Aunt Polly— Tom's Aunt Polly, she is—and Mary and the Widow Douglas is all told

about in that book, with some stretchers as I said before.

striped one. A euphemistic circumlocution for a tiger in lands where some tigers still run wild and where cautious people do not speak the tiger's true name for fear that one might suddenly appear. "In Sumatra the tiger is mentioned as He With the Striped Coat" (Maria Leach, ed., *Funk & Wagnalls Standard Dictionary of Folklore, Mythology and Legend,* 1972). "When he came to the cave, Fear, the Hairless One, put out his hand and called him 'The Striped One that comes by night,' and the first of the Tigers was afraid of the Hairless One, and ran back to the swamps howling" (Rudyard Kipling, *The Jungle Book,* 1894). In Vietnam, American soldiers referred to the tiger as "Mr. Thirty." Linda Reinberg suggests in *In the Field: The Language of the Vietnam War* that the "Thirty" came from the tiger's habit of hunting "toward the end of the lunar month when there was little moonlight." The association of "30" with endings also is strong, however; see PASS AWAY.

Besides the tiger, many other animals in many lands rate euphemistic names. The lion, for instance, is referred to respectfully by the Algerians as "Mr. John Johnson," while to the Angolans, he is "Sir," and to the South African Botswana, he is "the boy with the beard." The wolf has gone by various names—"The Gray Shadow," "Feet in the Night," and "Curse of the Chalk," are included in Kipling's "The Knife and the Naked Chalk" (*Rewards and Fairies,* 1909). In parts of Africa and India, a snake is never called a snake. Instead, on seeing a snake, one might say "There lies a string" (or a "strap" or a "rope"). The hope is that calling it a string will make it lie still like a string; the fear is that labeling it as a snake will make it behave like a snake. In parts of South America, one never says "centipede," for fear that it will hear you and run away; instead say "There goes one with forty legs," and the other person will step on it. Observant Jews are not supposed to mention the name of the pig (see also PENGUIN). The Scotch called pigs "short-legged ones," "grunting animals," or "grunters"; in Nova Scotia, home of many people of Scottish descent, some fishermen continue to be "so frightened of this curse that they would bring their boat into the dock if anyone on board mentioned a pig" (Susan Fortunato and Giema Tsakuginow, eds., *Pigs, Piggies, and Pigelets,* 1992). Jacques Cousteau and his divers prefer to refer to sharks as "friendly visitors." And so it goes.

For more about euphemisms for animals and the reasons for them, see GRANDFATHER.

student. A young prisoner at a STATE TRAINING SCHOOL. "Of the three so-called 'training schools' for juvenile delinquent boys in the state, Goshen . . . is the only one that locks its 'students' in small individual rooms at night" (*New York Times,* 3/2/76). See also CORRECTIONAL FACILITY.

studio. An artistic word for embellishing businesses of various kinds; generally synonymous with PARLOR and SALON. "Studio" is not as popular now as in the 1920s, when the land was littered with *billiard studios, candy studios,* and *tonsorial studios* (the barbers then were *tonsorial artists*), as well as— somewhat more legitimate—*movie* and *photography studios.* However, the word still does euphemistic work in real estate ads, where *studio apartments* seldom feature

high ceilings and a north light; in the names of businesses of different kinds, such as the Above the Rest Hair Studio (a beauty shop), Ann's Studio (for massages), Cut Loose Hair Studio (a barbershop), and Monarch Studio, "for a relaxing Swedish massage in a very discreet studio" (New York, Yellow Pages, 1990–91), and, finally, in the out-and-out sex business, where a RAP STUDIO is the same as a rap parlor and a *coed wrestling studio* is an arena where the combatants rarely work up much of a sweat but the spectators do.

stuff. Shit. From a report on a freedom-of-speech case involving a sticker on a vehicle: "The [successful] appellant in the case was James Daniel Cunningham of Smyrna, Ga., who was arrested and fined $200 two years ago for displaying a decal with a vulgar variation of the phrase 'stuff happens' on the rear door of his van" (AP, 2/24/91). See also the *chicken stuffing* in CHICKEN.

subsidy publisher. A vanity publisher, i.e., one that will publish a book only at the author's expense. "There are about a dozen nationally known and advertised companies, such as Dorrance and Vantage, that actively solicit or advertise for authors. They refer to themselves as subsidy publishers, shunning the designation *vanity,* although that is the term people in the publishing industry continue to employ" (Rick Balkin, *A Writer's Guide to Book Publishing,* 1994).

substantial compliance. Noncompliance. Speaking of rules governing free mailing by congressional representatives: "[Rep. John R.] Wydler [R., N.Y.] said he had been advised it was permissible to use the picture of his son and that he was in 'substantial compliance' with the photo guidelines.

He conceded that the masthead photo was too large" (Jack Anderson, *New York Post*, 10/7/74). See also TECHNICAL VIOLATION.

sudden victory. Sudden death. The upbeat name was suggested over national TV by sportscaster Curt Gowdy for the professional football overtime period in which the first score ends the game. Novelist Jerzy Kosinski devised a similar euphemism for writers: "Deadlines—that is a bad word in English. I am self-employed. I have only myself. I must work on self-lines" (Harper & Row *Bookletter*, 11/22/76). See also INHERITANCE TAX, LIFE INSURANCE, and No OUTLET.

sugar. A sickly sweet euphemism for "shit," sometimes extended, as in "Soon the doorbell rang again. 'Oh sugarplums.' said Mrs. D'Attili, using a mild oath in hurrying upstairs" (*New York Times*, 4/3/90). See also FUDGE, SHOOT, and SHUCKS.

summer. In a not-so-subtle reform of the Gregorian calendar, Consolidated Edison Corp. of New York exacts "summer" surcharges from May 15 through October 15, thus squeezing extra money out of its customers by squeezing two extra months into the season. See also LUNCH HOUR, WEEKEND, and WEEKLY.

sunset years. Old age. "Hannibal [Missouri] was not a Sturbridge Village, reincarnated from the past, with local citizens dressed up in buckle shoes plying extinct trades. I was grateful for that—I've seen enough blacksmithing and candle dipping to last me well into my sunset years" (William Zinsser, *Smithsonian*, 10/78).

The metaphor of the setting sun of life is not new, e.g.: "Old age . . . may be called the sunne set of our dayes" (Thomas William-

son, *Goulart's Wise Vieillard*, or *Old Man*, trans. 1621). See also GO WEST and GOLDEN AGE/YEARS.

sunshine. Radiation; a euphemism that failed. "Radiation of any kind was simply not a pleasant thing, and never could be, regardless of one AEC attempt to refer to it as 'sunshine units' " (John G. Fuller, *We Almost Lost Detroit*, 1975). Similarly inspired was "Project Sunshine," the title of the official report on the investigation into the deaths of the Japanese fishermen who were caught in the fallout of an American H-bomb test in 1956 (from Justus George Lawler, "Politics and the American Language," *College English*, 4/74). For more atomic talk, begin with ABOVE CRITICAL.

superintendent. (1) The person who manages a prison or CORRECTIONAL FACILITY; formerly a warden. (2) A janitor or caretaker; see also CUSTODIAN.

supervisor. A foreman; desexualized newspeak, in which chairman becomes *chair*, draftsman becomes *drafter*, pressman becomes *press operator*, repairman becomes *repairer*, working woman (or girl) becomes *worker*, and so on. See also PERSON.

Supreme Being. Another of the many indirect ways of referring to God. Variants include *Supreme Intelligence*, *Supreme Lord*, *Supreme One*, and *Supreme Soul*. "The most tedious of all discourses are on the subject of the Supreme Being" (Ralph Waldo Emerson, *Journals*, 1836). For the general reluctance to speak God's name, see ADONAI.

sure-thing player. Crooked player, a sharper. Speaking about Mississippi riverboat gamblers prior to the Civil War: "At least ninety percent of the elegant tricksters who preyed upon the river traveler were known in the vernacular as 'sure-thing players,' which was a euphemistic way of saying they were crooked" (Herbert Asbury, *The French Quarter*, 1938). See also SPECULATE.

surgical strike. A bombing or missile attack that theoretically doesn't obliterate anything but the intended, always-strictly-military target; in extended usage, any sharp attack on any opponent, domestic as well as foreign.

The trouble with "surgical strike" in the first sense is that the strike is rarely, if ever, as clean in practice as in name. "An Israeli Army spokesman said today that Wednesday's airstrike in eastern Lebanon was a 'surgical' operation against terrorist bases . . . the International Committee of the Red Cross said that an incomplete accounting showed 40 dead and 360 wounded, most of them civilians" (AP, 1/5/84). The likelihood of such COLLATERAL DAMAGE has sometimes led planners to drop the idea instead of bombs. For example: "The idea of American planes suddenly and swiftly eliminating the missile complex [in Cuba in 1962] with conventional bombs in a matter of minutes—a so-called 'surgical' strike—had appeal to almost everyone first considering the matter, including President Kennedy" (Theodore C. Sorensen, *Kennedy*, 1965). In this case, after realizing that a *surgical strike* was bound to be messier than the name implied, the United States settled on a QUARANTINE. In the extended sense, a U.S. State Department spokesman said Russia was conducting "a surgical strike against the dissidents," after two were arrested by the Soviet government (New York *Daily News*, 7/9/78).

See also LIMITED WAR, PRECISION BOMBING, PREEMPTIVE STRIKE, and SELECTIVE STRIKE.

surplus. To get rid of; a military term that has crept into civilian life (along with the similar RIF) and at the same time been extended from things—from surplus helmets, helicopters, and so on, that are surplused—to people and other living creatures, e.g., "Executives Who Were 'Surplused'" (*New York Times* headline, 8/14/77), and the Hen Surplus Removal Fund, designed by egg producers in 1986 to keep prices up by paying bonuses to owners who killed some of their layers prematurely. See also DEPOPULATE, EXCESS, and REDUNDANCY.

surreptitious entry. A break-in, burglary, BLACK BAG JOB, or TECHNICAL TRESPASS; frequently abbreviated to the even more opaque "entry."

The usual reasons for a *surreptitious entry* are to search desks, photograph files, or install hidden microphones. The "surreptitious" implies that the "entry" is to be accomplished secretly, in contrast to the more forceful QUICK ENTRY. "*Surreptitious Entry* . . . Use of this technique is clearly illegal: it amounts to burglary. . . . However, it is also the most fruitful tool and can produce the type of intelligence which cannot be obtained in any other way" (memo, Tom Charles Huston to President Richard M. Nixon, July 1970).

Huston's plan for domestic intellience gathering was approved by the president. According to a "TOP SECRET" (see TOP SECRET) memorandum of July 15, 1970: "Restraints on the use of surreptitious entry are to be removed." Nixon later said he quickly rescinded his approval, but this was on account of FBI Director J. Edgar

Hoover's opposition, not because of any doubts about his own authority; see ILLEGAL. Hoover dragged his feet because he rightly feared that the Bureau would get a black eye if some of his men were implicated in the break-ins. Eventually this happened, leading to the following subtle distinction, made in an exchange between prosecutor and defendant at the 1980 trial of two former high-ranking FBI officials (*New York Times*, 10/6/80):

Q: Did you do a black bag job on Jennifer Dohrn's home?
A: No, I did a surreptitious entry.

surveillance. Spying, not necessarily limited to governments, e.g., from a 1976 Gimbels Brothers announcement: "Gimbels security management have evaluated their security procedures used to deter shoplifting and theft and have determined that the surveillance of fitting rooms for apprehension of shoplifters is not necessary." In other words, guards had been secretly watching customers change clothes in dressing and fitting rooms. Gimbels reevaluated its policy after a case against a woman accused of stealing a scarf was thrown out of court because the *surveillance* violated "reasonable expectations of privacy" as well as the Fourth Amendment to the United States Constitution, which protects citizens against "unreasonable searches and seizures." (But it's a different matter if a store lets customers know they are being spied on; see MONITOR.)

Surveillance comes in two main forms: physical, or eyeball, *surveillance*, and non-physical, remote *surveillance*, including wiretaps, hidden microphones, and mail watches (see MAIL COVER). Both the physical and remote types may be characterized as either *cold surveillance* or *hot surveillance*. In *cold surveillance*, the person being *surveilled* (a new verb, a typical bureaucratic back-formation, thought to have originated in the FBI) isn't supposed to know it. The Gimbels operation would class as physical, *cold surveillance*. In *hot surveillance*, the person, or TARGET, is tailed so obviously, or bugged so crudely, that he or she can't help but know it. The purpose of *hot surveillance* is to harass or intimidate as in the FBI's infamous Counterintelligence Program (Cointelpro)—for which see TECHNICAL SURVEILLANCE.

swan. Swear; an especially beautiful euphemism for those who want to avoid completely even the appearance of swearing. The basic "I swan" frequently was elaborated into *swan to goodness* and *swan to man*, both of which translate as "swear to God." The expression may derive from "I warrant," which in northern English dialects came out as *I'se warn ye* or *I'se warren*. In the oldest (1784) example of the term in *A Dictionary of Americanisms*, "I swan" is characterized as an "old saying." The expression sounds as though it should be obsolete, but it isn't, as I was asked about its origin on a radio show in 1994. See also CUSS.

sweet. All-powerful, dreadful. Discussing the shrines along the route of the annual procession conducted in ancient times from Eleusis to Athens: "Next, was the altar of Zeus Melichios, 'Sweet Zeus,' a substitution of a euphemism for a name of dread; for this was Zeus in preanthropomorphic, serpent form" (A. R. Burn, *The Lyric Age of Greece*, 1968). See also ADONAI and EUMENIDES.

sweetbread. An interior organ of a calf or other animal when it appears on the menu or dinner plate. The euphemistic value of the phrase can be gauged by trying to imagine how many people would order "pancreas" rather than *stomach sweetbread.* Or think how "thymus gland" would look on the menu of your favorite eatery: The preferred term among gourmets is *neck sweetbread* or, sweeter yet, *throat sweetbread.* It says something about our eating habits that "sweetbread" is a relatively old term, going back at least to the sixteenth century. Even older are the related "chitterlings," for small intestines, first recorded in 1280, according to *The Oxford English Dictionary,* and "tripe," for the stomach of a ruminant, also from pre-1300. (The latter dish, by the way, may have been an Islamic contribution to culinary arts, the Old French tripe, *trippe,* apparently deriving from the Arabic *tharb,* meaning "entrails" or "net.") See also FILET MIGNON, PLUCK, and VARIETY MEATS.

sweetheart. The term of endearment has also been used as a euphemism. From *The Oxford English Dictionary*: "One word alone hath troubled some, because the immodest maid soothing the young man, calls him her Prick. . . . He who cannot away with [i.e., stand for] this, instead of 'my Prick,' let him write 'my Sweetheart'" (H. M., gent., *The Colloquies or Familiar Discourses of D. Erasmus,* trans. 1671). See also PENIS.

swimming environment. Swimming pool. "My staff and I will be working in your neighborhood creating a new swimming environment" (letter, Jim Scott, received 12/1/92). Mr. Scott runs Scott Swimming Pools, Inc., of Woodbury, Conn., which has trademarked its description of itself as a builder of "Distinguished Swimming Environments since 1937." See also BALNEOLOGY and SOLAR POOL.

swinging. Promiscuity, especially when characterized by one or more of the following: mate-swapping (called "wife-swapping" in the preliberated era), group sex, and BISEXUAL activity. Frequently, the three factors conjoin:

> VERY INTERESTING MARRIED young cpl in 30s seek attr cpls versatile gals extra select males for discreet friendship and swinging fun. No fatties weirdos. (*Ace,* undated, ca. 1976; see also FUN)

Swinging is a relatively new phenomenon (by this name, that is). Perhaps helped along by Frank Sinatra's 1956 record album, "Songs for Swingin' Lovers," the sexual sense did not become popular until the 1960s. ("Swing" in the musical sense dates to before 1900, and the term was used commonly among musicians long before the big, swing bands became the rage in the mid-1930s; Benny Goodman became the "King of Swing" overnight when his fourteen-member band knocked them dead at the Palomar Ballroom in Hollywood on August 21, 1935.)

The oldest examples of sexual "swinging" and the related "swinger" in *The Oxford English Dictionary* come from the works of an exceedingly well-named couple, W. and J. Breedlove, e.g., "We will on occasion utilize 'swinger' and 'swinging' to describe the advocate of sexual partner exchange and the exercising of that practice" (*Swap Clubs,* 1964). Today, some *swingers* divide their time between partners of different sexes and so are said to *swing both ways.* When three or more *swingers* gather together, the event is known as a *swing party* (i.e., orgy). Plato's Retreat, a *swingers club* in New York City, featured twenty *miniswing* rooms, each with a carrying capacity of one to three couples. Unmarried, or single *swingers,* are known technically as *swingles* (or *mingles,* if they decide to live together in what used to be known as sin). They may also make the *swingles scene* at *swingles bars* (which are indistinguishable from "singles bars"). As far back as 1972, San Francisco was blessed with a TV show called "Swingles Scene" on Channel 20, which was described at the time by *Chronicle* critic Terrence O'Flaherty as "a kind of video auction block" for would-be daters.

"Swing," in the form of the related *swinge,* had an earlier sexual incarnation, serving in the seventeenth century as a synonym for "swive," i.e., fuck, but this meaning of the word did not flow from music. Rather, it derived from the very oldest (pre-1400) meanings of "swing," which involved rapid movement, a beating, a stroke with a sword. In the earlier phase, then, the sexual metaphor was essentially a violent one—a common conjunction. See ACTION.

The association of sex with music is nearly as strong as with violence, however. Here the leading example is "jazz." Of uncertain origin (African and Creole roots have been proposed), "jazz" almost certainly was southern black slang for sex long before the turn of the twentieth century, when it surfaced as the name of the swinging music that was played in bawdy houses and honky-tonks in New Orleans and points west. Like "swing," the sexual meaning of "jazz" included practices other

than straight COPULATION by straights. Thus, an article on "Homosexual Practices of Institutionalized Females" (Charles A. Ford, *Journal of Abnormal and Social Psychiatry,* 1–3, 1929) quoted a note from one woman prisoner to another, with the following heading:

> You can take my tie
> You can take my coller
> But I'll jazze you
> Till you holler.

"Boogie-woogie," "jelly roll" (as in "Jelly Roll Blues," by Ferdinand Joseph LaMenthe "Jelly Roll" Morton), and "juke" are other sexually charged musical terms, all originally popularized in the nineteenth century by African-Americans in the South. The first of these referred to secondary syphilis before it became the name of a dance; the second, beginning as a slang term for the vulva (and, probably, from the seventeenth century use of "jelly" for semen) gradually was extended to mean either the sex act, a loving woman, or a woman-chaser; the third, deriving from a Gullah word for something disorderly or wicked, appeared as *juke house,* a HOUSE that was a whorehouse, before becoming attached the tuneful juke box.

Still other music-related terms for sexual intercourse include *doing the bone dance* (see BONE), *doing the horizontal bop* (with "bop" also having violent overtones), *throwing a bop (into someone), bopping in the woods,* and *rock 'n' roll* (separately, "rock" and "roll" also are slang terms for COITION). Similar phrases include *doing the funky Alphonso, doing the horizontal mambo* (or *hula* or *rumble* or *twist and shout*), and *doing the tube-steak boogie.* As William Shakespeare said, though he could not have had all these connections in mind: "If music be the food of love, play on" (*Twelfth Night*, 1600–02).

See also CONSENSUAL NONMONOGAMY, INTERCOURSE, MOUTH MUSIC, and SHARING.

swipe. Steal. "I haunted the five-and-ten on Barington Street for months, picking up a flashlight, crayons, pencils, erasers, marbles. We called it *swiping*, not *stealing*" (Robert MacNeil, *Wordstruck,* 1989). Of uncertain origin (it may be a variant of "sweep"), "swipe" appears to be an Americanism, surfacing in the late nineteenth century as slang for a minor theft, as of goods from a store or, in theatrical circles,

of jokes from another performer. The psychology of the term parallels that of HOOK.

syndicate. A gang, short for "crime syndicate"; most notably, the Chicago gang of Alfonso Capone (1899–1947). "Syndicate" was popularized by newspapers following Capone's ascension as chief Chicago mobster in 1925. The professional-sounding term received the imprimatur of Scarface himself, according to an anonymous friend, who reported (*True Detective*, 6/47) that "syndicate" was "picked up by Al from the newspaper stories about him." See also GOOD FELLOW.

T

t – – –. Turd; a FOUR-LETTER WORD that was printed in full for the first seven hundred years or so of its existence (from ca. 1000), but which people began to dash out in various ways as society became more refined. Thus, according to Cotton Mather's account at the start of the euphemistically important eighteenth century, Sir William Phips told a constable who had threatened to report his conduct to Governor Simon Bradsteet that "he did not care a t – – d for the governour for he had more power than he had" (*Magnalia Christi Americana*, 1702, in Kenneth Silverman, *The Life and Times of Cotton Mather*, 1984). This reticence continued well into the twentieth century, even when conveying a common bit of folk wisdom: "'You know the old saying, the more a T – – – is stirred, the more it stinks'" (John Dickson Carr, *The Murder of Sir Edmund Godfrey*, 1936). See also DEFECATE/DEFECATION.

tactical nuclear weapon. or MININUKE. The "tactical" implies that the bomb (or DEVICE) is small, which is not necessarily the case; some short-range *tactical* weapons are more powerful than long-range STRAGETIC weapons. "Even the tactical nuclear weapons supposedly designed for 'limited' wars were not an answer. . . . Some of these 'small' weapons carried a punch five times more powerful than the bomb that destroyed Hiroshima" (Theodore C. Sorensen, *Kennedy*, 1965). "The use of 10 percent of the 7,000 U.S. tactical nuclear weapons in Europe would destroy the entire area where such massive nuclear exchanges occurred" (Center for Defense

tail. The ass, usually, but occasionally, and still more euphemistically, the genitals, whether the PENIS (which means "tail" in Latin) or the VAGINA. In the more prevalent sense: "What would become of the fraternity if all of us parked ourselves on our tails?" (Percy Marks, *The Plastic Age*, 1924).

"Tail" can be traced back to the fourteenth century in all senses, making it a leading example of the Rule of the Displaced Referent, whereby euphemisms for unmentionable parts of the body are created by naming mentionable ones in their vicinity. For example, consider the following observation of Geoffrey Chaucer, which is just as true now as it was nearly 600 years ago (ca. 1387–1400), when he wrote the prologue to *The Wife of Bath's Tale*. Herself speaks:

> And after wyn on Venus moste I thynke,
> For al so siker [just as sure] as cold
>   engendreth hayl,
> A likerous [lecherous] mouth moste
>   han a likerous tayl;
> In womman vinolent [being full of
>   wine] is no defence
> This knowen lechours by experience.

Both the male and female meanings of "tail" were encompassed in "bobtail," as defined by Capt. Francis Grose: "A lewd woman, or one that plays with her tail; also an impotent man, or an eunuch" (*A Classical Dictionary of the Vulgar Tongue*, 1796). And a century later, the anonymous author of *My Secret Life* (ca. 1890) allowed as how "every woman is immodest enough to show her tail, and feel a man's tail at times." Meanwhile, the PROSTITUTE who sold *tail* came to be called "a tail." Thus, the *Lexicon Balatronicum* ("a member of the Whip Club," 1811) illustrated its definition of "cab" in the sense of "brothel" with the following example: "Mother: how many tails have you in your cab? how many girls have you in your bawdy house?"

Finally, in a late, possibly nonce variation, the versatile "tail" was made to stand for yet another piece of nearby anatomy in the film version of *Don't Go Near the Water* (1957) when the newspaperman Gordon Ripwell stormed, "You think you've got me by the tail!"—a peculiar expression for an otherwise ballsy fellow. See also ARSE, GENITALS, and, for another early "tail" that is not an ass, the "tailis" of the "cattis," of 1401, in CAT HOUSE.

talk man. A device for forcing a prisoner of war to make a propaganda videotape by administering electric shocks via wires attached to the face; a pun on Walkman (*American Speech*, Winter 1991). See also BELL TELEPHONE HOUR.

T and A. (also **TA).** Tits and Ass, especially in the entertainment business (as opposed to the medical business, where the abbreviation stands for Tonsils and Adenoids or the psychotherapy business, where "TA" is short for Transactional Analysis). From a review of a 1990 film, *The Invisible Maniac*: "Teen spoof of *The Invisible Man,* with large amounts of T & A thrown in" (*Leonard Maltin's Movie and Video Guide*, 1995). A TV show with lots of *T and A* also may be characterized as *jiggle time.* See also A – – and BOSOM.

target. A person. When American military officials talked about bombing "leadership targets" in Iraq, what they had in mind was a form of EXECUTIVE ACTION, the principal potential *target* being Iraqi President Saddam Hussein (*New York Times, 7/28/91*). Domestically, people who refer to other people as *targets* also tend to have a bombs-away attitude. Consider Tom Charles Huston on the question of "mail coverage," i.e., opening other people's mail: "Restrictions on covert coverage should be relaxed on selected targets of priority foreign intelligence and internal security interest" (July 1970 memorandum to President Richard M. Nixon, recommending increased domestic intelligence-gathering, i.e., spying). See also MAIL COVER, SURREPTITIOUS ENTRY, and SURVEILLANCE.

tatas. Breasts. Commenting on a memoir by La Toya Jackson: "La T—a woman known more for her augmented tatas than her talent—offers a sour catalogue of beatings" (*Gentlemen's Quarterly*, 11/91). See also BOSOM.

tattling. Telling secrets; spying. "Accordingly, say those who have been both bureaucrats and White House officials, intramural spying—'tattling' or 'coordination' are words they would prefer—has become a government commonplace and will likely remain so" (*New York Times*, 7/16/75). See also SURVEILLANCE.

TB. Tuberculosis, or consumption, a killer disease that inspired a set of euphemisms comparable to those that later developed around cancer and AIDS. Attesting to the "tremendous fear [that] surrounded TB," Susan Sontag cited examples from literature and from life: "In Stendhal's *Armance* (1827), the hero's mother refuses to say 'tuberculosis' for fear that pronouncing the words will hasten the course of her son's malady"; Franz Kafka, meanwhile, wrote in April 1924 from the SANATORIUM where he was to die two months later, saying "Verbally I don't learn anything definite, since in discussing tuberculosis . . . everybody drops into a shy, evasive, glassy-eyed manner of speech" (*New York Review of Books*, 1/26/78).

Tuberculosis victims also developed a language of their own. For example, reporting on "'TB' Talk" in Arizona: "On reaching the arid southwest the patient finds that he doesn't have consumption, but has t.b. . . . Often he is referred to as a *lunger,* and sometimes as one who has *the bugs.* The newspapers will refer to him as a *health seeker,* and to enthusiastic, philanthropic ladies he is a *shut-in.* The word 'consumption' is never heard" (Anders H. Anderson, *American Speech,* 2/35). This by no means exhausted the euphemisms of patients. The SANATORIUM from which so few people returned was known to them as the *san,* and if it featured open-air cabins, it was a *cottage-san* or perhaps a *rest ranch.* To spit (or EXPECTORATE) was to *raise,* and if one was spitting blood, then one was said to *raise color.* A pulmonary hemorrhage was *spilling rubies.* And so it went.

Aside from the many abbreviations, the most popular sobriquet for tuberculosis was *the white plague* (or *the great white plague*), an appellation attributed to Oliver Wendell Holmes, Sr.: "Two diseases especially have attracted attention, above all others, with reference to their causes and prevention; cholera, the 'black death' of the nineteenth century, and consumption, the white plague of the North" (*Medical Essays* [1868], 1883).

See also C, THE BIG; PEOPLE WITH AIDS, and SOCIAL DISEASE.

teacher presence. Attendance. Far be it from teachers to apply to themselves a word that has been contaminated by students; thus, where students "attend" school, teachers reveal their "presence," as in "Teacher presence in Newark schools was normal" (WINS, 5/12/75). *Teacher presence* made news this day because of a threatened SICK OUT.

technical adjustment (also **correction, reaction, readjustment, rally).** A change in stock prices, where the "technical" ordinarily translates as "downward."

"The stock market, for example, rarely 'falls' in the words of Wall Street analysis. Instead it is discovered to be 'easing' or found to have made a 'technical correction' or 'adjustment'" (*Time,* 9/19/69). An exception to the downward rule is "technical rally," where the "technical" merely conceals the user's ignorance of true causes, as in: "Wall St. labeled the action a technical rally in the absence of any significant news development" (*New York Times,* 12/7/73). This particular *technical rally* just happened to feature what was then the sixth largest daily rise in the history of the Dow Jones industrial average.

Use of "correction" among stock marketeers is particularly mind-bending, as pointed out by Ira J. Morrow in a letter to the *New York Times Magazine*: "When the market goes up, the term 'correction' is never applied. This linguistic disparity illogically implies that it is incorrect or unnatural for the market to be high and correct for it to be low" (12/13/87). See also ADJUST/ADJUSTMENT/READJUSTMENT.

technical implementation. Implementation. Analyzing Lt. Col. Oliver North's testimony at the Iran-Contra hearings (7/20/87),

Sen. William S. Cohen (R., Maine) declared:, "I must tell you I find it troubling when you say . . . that the transfers of funds for the sale of weapons was a technical implementation, not a substantive decision. And that we did not trade arms for hostages, even though Mr. Hakim and General Secord arrived at a formula of one-and-one-half hostages for 500 TOW's." See also TECHNICAL VIOLATION.

technical surveillance. Wiretapping and bugging, FBI-ese, as distinguished from simple SURVEILLANCE (spying); also known variously as *electronic surveillance, electronic penetration,* and *trespassory microphone surveillance.* "Cartha D. Deloach, then assistant to Mr. Hoover, set up a special team of agents to conduct 'technical surveillance' (FBI jargon for wiretapping and bugging) and physical surveillance at the convention" (*New York Times,* 1/27/75). The subject, or TARGET, of *technical surveillance* in this particular instance was the Reverend Martin Luther King, Jr., whose activities were MONITORED by at least 16 different wiretaps and eight bugged rooms from 1963 to at least 1965. The *technical surveillance* of King was part of the FBI's Counterintelligence Program (Cointelpro) for harassing people, parties, and other organizations considered (by the FBI) to be threats to the state (or to the FBI).

See also AGENT, BLACK BAG JOB, HIGHLY CONFIDENTIAL (or SENSITIVE) SOURCE, and SPECIAL COVERAGE.

technical trespass. Trespass; specifically, a break-in by an employee of the U.S. government, usually an FBI AGENT. "He acknowledged that the evidence could never be introduced in court because, he said, it was 'tainted,' having been obtained through a 'technical trespass,' without obtaining search warrants or the occupants' consent" (*New York Times,* 10/6/80). This was from the trial testimony of a man who admitted to having participated in fifteen to twenty SURREPTITIOUS ENTRIES, but nevertheless insisted they were legal and constitutional. See also BLACK BAG JOB.

technical violation. Violation, as of a law or regulation; also known as a *technical breach.* "The Mondale-Ferraro campaign acknowledged yesterday that Mrs. Ferraro was in 'technical violation' of the requirement to disclose the source of her husband's earned income" (*New York Times,* 8/16/84). See also SUBSTANTIAL COMPLIANCE and TECHNICAL IMPLEMENTATION.

technician. An all-purpose label for upgrading job titles. "If you have an oil-tank cleaner, make him a petrochemical technician instead" (Jeremy Rifkin and Randy Barber, *The North Will Rise Again,* 1978). Among the many other kinds of *technician* that exist: *animal technician* (worker in an animal hospital), *auto-technician* (mechanic), *biological science technician* (an animal trapper for the federal government), *body shop technician* (car repair man), *debris disposal technician* (a garbage or SANITATION MAN), *evidence technician* (a crime-scene police investigator), *environmental technician* (a caretaker or JANITOR; see ENVIRONMENTAL), EXECUTION TECHNICIAN, *household technician* (a DOMESTIC or MAID), *nail technician* (a manicurist), and *service technician* (appliance repairman).

Besides inflating the ego of the worker, "technician" has advantages for employers, since the label replaces traditional craft titles. This fits in with "multicrafting," which is one method of avoiding unionization. Organizers come into a plant looking for plumbers or electricians to organize and all they can find are *technicians, grade one; technicians, grade two,* etc. Plant efficiency may drop somewhat, since the *technicians, grade one* have been taught only a little bit about plumbing, a little bit about electricity, a little bit about carpentry, with the result that they may not be very proficient at any one of these. But many firms find this an acceptable price to pay for maintaining an OPEN SHOP.

See also ENGINEER, INDUSTRIAL RELATIONS, and SPECIALIST.

teed (or tee'd or t'd) off. Pissed off. "You're teed off at me, aren't you?" (Dorothy Hughes, *The Expendable Man,* 1963). "Teed off" is dated in *The Oxford English Dictionary* only to 1955, with the first appearance coming from a round-up of American military slang that defined *teed off,* along with *brassed off, browned off,* and *pissed off,* as meaning "angry, indignant" (*American Speech,* 5/55). Given the inadequacy of the written record, it is impossible to say for sure, but the expression probably is a blend of the euphemistic *pee'd off* and *tee off on (someone),* in the sense of verbally assaulting another person, especially with severe criticisms. "Tee off," in turn, looks like a golfing term, but may actually derive from *tick off,* military slang again, but from World War I, for sharply reprimanding or scolding someone. And this last also resulted in *ticked off,* now used synonymously with *teed off.* See also PO'D.

temperance. Literally, "moderation," but a euphemistic stalking-horse in the nineteenth century for voluntary abstention and then involuntary prohibition. Alcohol was not the only enemy: "Tom joined the new order of Cadets of Temperance, being attracted by the showy character of their 'regalia.' He promised to abstain from smoking, chewing, and profanity as long as he remained a member" (Mark Twain, *The Adventures of Tom Sawyer,* 1876).

The first local antialcohol *temperance* societies were founded toward the start of the nineteenth century, and the term still meant moderation, in the sense of voluntary abstention from the stronger spirits, when the American Society for the Promotion of Temperance was founded in 1833. Just three years later, however, the society changed its pledge to complete abstinence from all liquors, including wine and beer. And a few years after that, as it became clear that moral suasion alone wasn't going to make the nation dry, "temperance" began to mean "prohibition." As early as 1845, New York State enacted a law banning the sale of liquor, a noble experiment that anticipated the national one of 1920–33, but that failed more quickly, New York repealing its law after only two years. A *temperance* drink is, of course, a "soft drink," as in "I'll have an orange temperance, please."

See also CLUB, HIGH, SALOON, and TRADITIONAL BEVERAGE.

tender loving care. Do not resuscitate. "'Tender loving care,' when used by British doctors, means the withdrawal of active medical care from terminally ill patients" (Dublin *Irish Times,* 9/29/90). See also NO MAYDAY.

terminate/termination. To end something, or the act of ending it, such as (1) a conversation, (2) a job, and (3) a life, either through (a) natural death, or (b) murder.

1) In the first, conversational sense, "terminate" is a relatively minor offense,

the longer word being employed in place of "end." Lawyers have an especially strong tropism toward "terminate" (FOP Index of 3.7), e.g., quoting a gentleman of the bar, "I terminated the conversation after indicating to him that I would commence work" (*New York Post*, 6/30/73).

2) In the case of jobs, "terminate" becomes a euphemism for "fire," which is what happened to a cheerleader for the Chicago Bears football team: "The Honey Bears are still performing for that club, but . . . Jackie Rohrs has been 'terminated' because the team learned that she will appear entirely out of uniform in the December issue of *Playboy*" (*New York Post*, 10/8/78). Variations on this theme include *constructive termination* (see OUTPLACEMENT) and *nonpositive termination*, which is a governmental creation: "Instead of telling the employees that they were fired in a budget-cutting move, the bureaucrats call the pink slips 'non-positive terminations'" (Jack Anderson, *Lincoln County*, Maine, *News*, 7/30/81).

3) a. Use of the same word for losing a job and losing a life is relatively common; see LET GO. Thus, Leona Helmsley's doctor said that the stress of the hotel queen's imprisonment for tax evasion and the consequent separation from her husband, "could result in a fatal termination" (*New York Observer*, 3/30/92). This fits with the use in hospitals of *terminal living* for dying and *terminal episode* for what happens when *terminal living* ceases. Of course, doctors and other hospital workers are notorious for not talking openly about death; see EXPIRE.

3) b. As a clean word for ending a life, "ter-

minate" pops up frequently in discussions of abortion, a.k.a., THERAPEUTIC INTERRUPTION OF PREGNANCY: "Thanks to the development of amniocentesis within the past few years, fetuses with chromosomal defects can be detected early enough in pregnancy to permit the gestation to be terminated" (*Natural History*, 10/78). It becomes a euphemism in a fuller sense, however, when applied to people who have been out of the womb for some years, as in "Terminate her, immediately" (*Star Wars*, film, 1977). In this instance, art (?) has merely imitated life. The murderous sense was popularized earlier by the CIA. For example: "Other reports said that the Green Berets had been advised by a CIA official in Saigon to 'terminate with extreme prejudice'—an official euphemism for murder—the suspect, and had done so with an injection of morphine, two .22 caliber pistol shots in the head, and the disposal of the weighted corpse in the sea" (*New York Times Encyclopedic Almanac*, 1970). In this connection, see also ELIMINATE/ELIMINATION.

The lethal sense of 3) b. may well have evolved within the CIA from the job-related sense of 3) a. I have it on the authority of a correspondent who studied CIA manuals of the late 1960s that the agency drew a distinction between AGENTS who were *terminated without prejudice* (meaning they were not needed at the moment but could be rehired because there was no question about their loyalty and reliability) and those who were *terminated with prejudice* (meaning that they should not be rehired, perhaps because they were suspected of being double agents but often for such mundane reasons as alcoholism or because they talked too freely to relatives). The step from "terminate with prejudice" to "terminate with *extreme* prejudice" is a small one linguistically and quite in keeping with the mindset of the spooks who financed behavior-modification experiments through a Society for the Investigation of Human Ecology and who named their in-house assassination unit the Health Alteration Committee. (See also ECOLOGY and EXECUTIVE ACTION.)

One of the dangers of using opaque, multipurpose euphemisms like "terminate" is that they may be misunderstood (as noted by the CIA inspector general in the case of the similar DISPOSE). Consider, for example, the shiver that must have gone down the spine of Manucher Ghorbanifar, an Iranian arms dealer, during a conversation with Gen. Richard Secord, as described by the general in testimony at the Iran-Contra hearings (5/6/87):

> I was having a rather acid conversation with Mr. Ghorbanifar on the telephone and I told him … that I was going to recommend that he be terminated. Now he misinterpreted that. I don't mean to be funny, but he took it the wrong way. He told Mr. [Amiram] Nir that I was trying to have him killed. I think I even said later, it's not a bad idea, but it's not what I had in mind.

terminological inexactitude. A falsehood, a lie; close kin to CATEGORICAL INACCURACY. The young Winston Churchill used the euphemism this way, when sidestepping charges that the British government was condoning slavery of Chinese laborers in South Africa: "A labour contract into which men enter voluntarily … and from which they can obtain relief … on payment of £17.10s, the cost of their passage, may not be a healthy or proper contract, but it cannot, in the opinion of His Majesty's Government, be classified as slavery in the extreme acceptance of the word, without some risk of terminological inexactitude" (speech, House of Commons 2/22/06). See also ECONOMICAL WITH THE TRUTH, LESS THAN CANDID, and WHITE LIE.

testicles. The balls. "Balls" is the word most people use informally, which is most of the time. Thus, even women may be said to be "ballsy" (see LAY for an example). When on their best behavior, however, people tend to turn to the Latinate "testicles," which, like PENIS, has entered the popular vocabulary only within the last couple of generations. As recently as the 1930s, the word in newspapers usually was GLANDS. "Testicle" is a relatively old word, however, with the first example in *The Oxford English Dictionary* coming from circa 1425. Even so, the term is not nearly as old in English as the more elemental "balls," with "ballocks" (little balls) traceable to about the year 1000. See THIGH for the curious origin of *testis* (the Latin antecedent of "testicle") as well as, for more on this general subject, the *peloné* in BALONEY, BILATERAL ORCHIDECTOMY, BOLLIXED UP, COJONES, FAMILY JEWELS, FRY, NUTS, PECULIAR MEMBERS, PRAIRIE OYSTERS, PRIDES, ROCKS, SACK, SHORT (or THIN) HAIRS, and THINGUMBOB.

thanatology. The study of death, including its effects on the dying and those around them; from *thanatos*, Greek for "death." A Center for Thanatology Research and Education is located in New York City and some schools and colleges have begun providing courses in the subject. For example, the American Academy–McAllister Institute of Funeral Service, in New York City, offers an elective in *thanatology* for those who are studying to become undertakers. A duly certified expert in the subject is correctly described as a *thanatologist*. See also FUNERAL DIRECTOR.

that way. Pregnant; the condition is discussed more openly now than once was the case, but euphemisms and circumlocutions still linger on, e.g.: "I saw she was big, but I didn't know she was that way" (resident of Damariscotta, Me., upon learning that an acquaintance was pregnant; summer of 1977). See also EXPECTANT and EXPECTING.

therapeutic accident (or misadventure). The "therapeutic" helps cover up an error by a doctor or other medical person. "In fact the patient leaves 'Admissions' with the feeling that his identification bracelet manacles him to a no-fault system in which a fatal mistake, such as the transfusion of incompatible blood, becomes a 'therapeutic accident'" (Robert Craft, *New York Review of Books*, 9/16/76). After an anesthetist turned the wrong knob and killed a woman and her unborn baby with nitrous oxide during a cesarean delivery, a spokesman for the hospital called the incident a "therapeutic misadventure" (New Orleans *Times Picayune*, 4/4/82). "A patient died because a nurse mistakenly put a wrong fluid in an intravenous feeding tube, and the coroner classified it as a 'therapeutic misadventure'" (*New York Times*, 3/25/86). See also ACCIDENT and MISADVENTURE.

therapeutic interruption of pregnancy. An abortion; also called a *pregnancy interruption* or *voluntary interrupted pregnancy*. Depending on whether one is PRO-CHOICE or not, the *therapeutic interruption* is said to take place in a *women's health center* or an "abortion mill." See also MISCARRIAGE.

thigh. The balls or testicles, biblical-style. "And the servant put his hand under the thigh of Abraham his master, and sware to him concerning the matter" (Genesis 24:9).

The ancient custom of holding one's (or as in the case of Abraham's servant, someone else's) balls when making a solemn oath is commemorated in the word "testicle," which comes from the Latin *testis*, meaning "witness." The original idea seems to be that if one swore falsely, one might be rendered impotent. From *testis*-as-witness, we also get such words as "attest," "protest," "protestant," "testament," and the "testimony," which today is offered after swearing on a Bible instead. Variants include "testilying," which is a term commonly used by New York City police officers when they talk about committing perjury in order to help ensure convictions, and "ovarimony," a feminist replacement for "testimony," suggested at the 1992 annual meeting of the Modern Language Association.

N.B. Following the Rule of the Displaced Referant, "thigh" also may be employed in place of the true names of nearby anatomical items. For example, there are the musings of Alex Haley's hero: "Kunta felt jolted even by thought of some man's *foto* [another euphemism, presumably based on a Mandingo word] entering Kizzy's thighs" (*Roots*, 1976). Then there is the case of the duel on September 21, 1809, between two famous British statesmen, George Canning and Robert Stewart, Viscount Castlereagh. Discreet historians report that Canning was shot in the "thigh" (*Encyclopædia Britannica*, 11th edition), but actually the bullet hit him in the ass—the left buttock, specifically, according to Stephen Jay Gould (*Natural History*, 5/89). Castlereagh's latest biographer was slightly more specific, according to Gould, describing the wound as being in "the fleshy part of the thigh"—a euphemistic phrase that was in vogue at the start of the twentieth century, thanks to its employment in a Boer War dispatch about Lord Methuen having been wounded in that part of his anatomy.

See also ARSE, COJONES, OVULAR (for a companion to "ovarimony'), P – – – – (for the final word on Castlereagh), and TESTICLES.

thin. Kill; animals, specifically. "Sometimes 'thinning' or 'culling' animal populations may be the only way to keep adaptable species from continuing to decimate more sensitive ones in suburban areas and elsewhere. But these are merely euphemisms for killing" (*New York Times*, 3/1/94). See also CULL.

thing. Verbal shorthand for anything one prefers not to discuss in more vivid detail; an omnibus term, with comparable carrying capacity to IT, PROBLEM, and SITUATION.

The term has been used since medieval times for the sexual parts. Geoffrey Chaucer, in *The Wife of Bath's Prologue* (1387–1400) not only used the word straight out, e.g., "Oure bothe thynges smale/Were eek [also] to knowe a femele from a male," but further euphemized it by translating it into French, as in, "If I would selle my *bele chose*/I kould walke as fressh as is a rose" (by which the good wife meant she could dress well on her earnings). After six hundred years or so, the anatomical senses are still with us. Thus, Marlene Dietrich advised her daughter about the ways of men: "They always want to put their 'thing' in—that's all they want. If you don't let them do it right away, they say you don't love them and get angry with you and leave!" (Maria Riva, *Marlene Dietrich*, 1993).

"Thing" also has been loaded down with a wide variety of nonanatomical meanings, ranging from the "economic thing," which is a "slump" or RECESSION; to "our thing," which is better known in its Italian original, i.e., Cosa Nostra; to the highly generalized "doing your own thing"; to President George Bush's equally vague "vision thing."

The White House Transcripts (1974), which form a valuable record of (among other things, so to speak) the way real people really talk in private, are replete with such opaque "things" as (all from President Nixon, as it happens) "the Segretti thing" (3/17/73, meaning dirty tricks); "the executive privilege thing" (3/22/73, meaning the COVER-UP); "the Ellsberg thing, etc.—electronically thing—you know what I mean?" (3/27/73, meaning the work of the PLUMBERS); and "the Mitchell thing" (4/14/73, meaning the effort to get former Attorney General John N. Mitchell, a.k.a., the big enchilada, to take the rap for everyone else). But the president outdid himself on March 22, 1973, when he allowed as how "we are fighting the situation thing" (meaning, apparently, the Watergate scandal), and then—most ingeniously—improved upon that, on April 16, 1973, saying to John W. Dean III:

P: It was your job to work for the President, the White House staff and they were not involved in the pre-thing. But then you thought the post-thing. . . .

Dean's reply also is instructive:

D: I thought we should cut the cancer right off because to keep this whole thing—

thingumbob. A glorified *thing*; an omnibus term for anyone or anything whose name is not known or, if known, not to be mentioned. Thus, recalling life on a New England farm (ca. 1900), where small heaps of hay were called "tumbles" and larger ones were "cocks": "One proper farmer could never bring himself to use the current name for the larger heaps but always referred to them as thingumbobs" (*American Speech*, 2/53). "Thingumbob" and its many relations (*thingum, thingamajig, thingummy*, and *thingumthangum*, among others) have been with us since at least the seventeenth century, and the euphemistic meaning of "thingumbob" was well established by the mid-eighteenth century, e.g.: "Mr. Thingumbob; a vulgar address or nomination to any person whose name is unknown. . . . Thingumbobs; testicles" (Capt. Francis Grose, *A Classical Dictionary of the Vulgar Tongue*, 1751). "Thingumbobs" also have stood for those UNMENTIONABLE articles, trousers, while "thingummy" has been a euphemism for, in Eric Partridge's discreet definition, "the penis or the pudend" (*A Dictionary of Slang and Unconventional English*, 1970). See also WHAT-YOU-MAY-CALL'EM and, for more about haycocks, ROOSTER.

three-letter man. A homosexual, the three letters in question being "f-a-g." The phrase predates the currently dominant meaning of another three-letter word: GAY. See also the four-letter man in FOUR-LETTER WORD.

thrifty. Stingy; the essential meanings of the two words are the same, but "thrifty" has much better vibes (or, as semanticists say, "connotations"). "A game said to have been invented by Bertrand Russell is called 'Conjugating Adjectives.' It is played by mentioning three adjectives having the same denotation but different connotations. Example: I am thrifty; you are tight; he is stingy" (Anatol Rapoport, *Semantics*, 1975). See also ECONOMICAL.

throne. A toilet or, before that, a chamber pot. "The door leading to the toilet room is beautiful, but the comfortable 'throne' inside is even more beautiful" (*The Pop-Up Book of Gnomes*, 1979). "Tried to fix the throne. But we could not find the shut-off valve" (note left by plumber, Boothbay, Me., 7/9/92). See also TOILET.

thunder. Hell; a popular American euphemism that emigrated to England, commonly used in such expressions as *by thunder, go to thunder*, and *what in thunder*. Apparently preceded by "thunderation," which stood for "damnation," the short form became dominant in the hellish sense by the middle of the nineteenth century. For example, after he had captured Savannah at the end of 1864, Maj. Gen. William Tecumseh Sherman quashed the suggestion that he should be promoted to equal or superior rank to Lt. Gen. Ulysses S. Grant, saying: "He stood by me when I was crazy, and I stood by him when he was drunk. And now, by thunder, we stand by each other" (from Richard Wheeler, *Sherman's March*, 1978). And on the other side of the Atlantic: " 'How in thunder came you to know anything about it?' he asked" (Sir Arthur Conan Doyle, *The Valley of Fear*, 1915). See also BOTHERATION and HECK.

tiger. Nigger—as in the sanitized version of the old counting rhyme:

> Eenie, meenie, meinie, mo,
> Catch a tiger by the toe.
> If he hollers, let him go.

During World War I, the phrase became "Catch the Kaiser by the toe," and in the next war the rhyme was again updated:

Eenie, meenie, meinie, mo,
Catch a Jap [or Hitler] by the toe.
If he hollers, make him say:
"I surrender USA."

Besides "tiger," mothers also encourage their children to use *baby, black cat, feller, rabbit,* and *rooster* in place of the offensive term. See also INDIAN and NEGRO.

timberdoodle. The American woodcock, *Philohela minor*—"doodle" being but one of many words beginning with "d" that stands for "penis" or "cock." See also DING-A-LING, PECKER, and ROOSTER.

tinkle. People as well as pianos go "tinkle, tinkle," and when they do, it is because they are talking potty talk or, to continue the metaphor, *tinkle-pot* talk; see WEE-WEE.

tissue. Paper; see BATHROOM TISSUE.

tittie. The nipple; frequently extended in meaning to include the entire breast. "Tittie" is a diminutive of "tit," an Anglo-Saxon word (from before 1000 as *titt*) that was gradually superseded among speakers of so-called Standard English by the related "teat" (from the French *tette*).

"Titty" lived on in dialect, however. The oldest example of the word in *The Oxford English Dictionary* comes from 1746, where it appears as "tetty": "Es wont ha' ma Tetties a grabbed zo" (*An Exmoor Courtship, Gentleman's Magazine,* June). "Tit," too, continued to be employed by common folk. Witness some of America's quainter place names: Wildhorse Tit, Colorado, and Two Tits, California (euphemized on some maps as *Two Teats*). And in the Ozarks, within living memory, "women of the very best families [would] *give tittie* to their babies in public, even in church, without the slightest embarrassment," but the same women would never say *"breast* in the presence of strange men" (Vance Randolph, "Verbal Modesty in the Ozarks," *Dialect Notes,* vol. VI, Part 1, 1928).

While the Ozarkians traditionally are more sensitive than most people to the nuances of language (see also PETER), they are by no means the only ones to use "tittie" where "breast" would be considered a bit too blunt. There was, for example, the high school girl who, having performed a difficult feat with the bathroom scales, is said to have announced proudly to her boyfriend upon his return home from college, "Look—four ounces of new tittie!" (personal communication, ca. 1954).

"Tit" also has had a wide variety of other meanings, most of them revolving around the idea of something young, small, or both, as a girl (especially a hussy, a "little tit" being equivalent to a "little chit"); a horse (often a filly); a kitten ("Here tit, tit," was the same as "Here puss, puss"); or a bird (e.g., titlark, titmouse, tomtit). But in the last 100 years, the anatomical sense has become so dominant that hardly anyone ever offers to give "tit for tat" anymore, even though "tit" here actually has nothing to do with "breast," being merely an alliterative conversion of "tip." The original meaning of the expression probably amounted to "blow for blow."

For more about breasts, see BOSOM.

tochus. The ass. See TUSHIE.

toilet. A place and a thing that can be discussed only in euphemistic terms for the simple reason that the English language, despite its rich vocabulary, lacks any noneuphemistic words for them.

"Toilet" is a rather recent French import. It comes from *toilette,* dressing room, which is a diminutive of *toile,* cloth. "Toilet" was used in English in various ways before it reached its present state. Thus, from the seventeenth century, the "toilet" was the process of dressing, and in the eighteenth century a "toilet call" was the formal reception of visitors by a lady of fashion while she was in the final stages of making herself fashionable. In the nineteenth century, people began to speak of "toilet articles," "toilet pails" (for slops), and "toilet paper." (Victorian women would ask men shopkeepers for "curl papers" prior to the 1880s when BATHROOM TISSUE, as it is often called today, began to be produced in perforated roll form.) The use of "toilet room" in the euphemistic sense of "bathroom" or "lavatory," as contrasted with the original sense of "dressing room," seems to have been an American innovation of the late nineteenth century. Today, the French themselves go to *les toilettes* (or *les cabinets—cabinet d'aisances,* in full) when they are not making use of the English WC. French also glories in the explicit *pissoir,* for a public urinal, but this, too, has been euphemized as the VESPASIENNE. The languages of other peoples reveal similar hang-ups. As noted by Mario Pei: "In South Africa they call it 'P.K.,' an abbreviation for the Kaffir *picanin kyah,* 'little house.' Germany has *Abort* ('away place'); . . . Spanish and Italian use words which mean 'retreat'; Russian *ubornaya* means 'adornment place'" (*The Story of Language,* 1965). And so it goes. The Dutch call it a *bestekamer* (best room), the Maori

word for it is *whare-iti* (small house), and the Melanesian islanders even have a Pidgin euphemism: *house-peck-peck.*

In the absence of any precise English word for what we now call a "toilet," euphemisms have flourished, their sheer number indicating the strength of the underlying taboo. For example, out of the pages of history, as well as from our own times, we have such picturesque expressions as:

Ajax, a pun on the older "a jakes," for a chamber pot, popularized by Sir John Harington, Rabelaisian wit and ingenious contriver, who gave his plan for a flush toilet in 1596 in *The Metamorphosis of Ajax* (the pun was used earlier by— and perhaps coined by—Shakespeare: "Your lion that holds his pole-ax sitting on a close-stool will be given to Ajax" ([*Love's Labor's Lost,* 1588–94]), where the pole-ax, or battle-ax, refers to the PENIS and a close-stool, a.k.a. STOOL, is a chamberpot); *altar room;* AMENITIES.

BATHROOM; *basement,* popularized in elementary schools, where usage ("May I please go to the basement?") reflected typical early twentieth-century school architecture; *bog house* (or *shop*) and *bogs* (from "tobog," an old word meaning "to exonerate the bowels," *OED*).

cabinet; can, perhaps originally referring to a toilet with a replaceable can beneath the seat; *Cannes,* a famous watering place and a pun on the preceding; *chaise d'aisance,* a French chamberpot (literally: chair of ease); CHAMBER; *chamber of commerce; Chick Sale,* an outhouse (after Charles "Chic" Sale, a comedian who specialized in privy humor, and wrote a much-admired book on the subject, *The Specialist,* 1929); CIRCULAR CURBSIDE

CONSTRUCTION; *cloaca,* a privy (from Cloacina, Roman goddess of disposal); CLOAKROOM; *closet* (or *seat*) *of ease* (see EASE); COMFORT STATION; COMMODE; CONVENIENCE *crap house* (with many variants: *crapper, crappery, crapping casa, crapping castle,* etc.—see CRAP).

Deauville (another famous watering place); *doniker* (or *donniker*); *dooly; dunniken* (? "dung" plus "ken," i.e., "house"); *dunny,* a diminutive of the preceding ("She bangs like a dunny door" is Australianese for "She is promiscuous").

EARTH CLOSET; *Egypt*; EUPHEMISM.

FACILITY.

gab room (for women only); *garderobe* (in medieval castles, and originally a place for keeping clothes, from *garde-r,* keep, plus *robe*); *geography* (as in "May I show you the geography of the house?"); *growler; guest relations facilities* (at Expo '86 in Montreal).

halfway house (British: when installing indoor plumbing in older houses in the nineteenth century, the simplest solution architecturally was to build an extension behind the staircase, with the result that the new room often was located off the landing, halfway between the first and second floors); HEAD; *hers/his; holy of holies; honey house* (see HONEY); *hopper; house of ease* (or *office,* and see also EASE).

intelligence center (used during the Gulf war of 1991); IT.

jacks, jakes, jane (or *Jane's* or *Aunt Jane's,* an outdoor privy); *jerry* (from Jeroboam, a large bottle and also a chamber pot), *Joe*; JOHN; *Jones' place; jordan* (another chamber pot, with an example in LEAK).

LADIES/GENTLEMEN (with many variants: *little girls'/boys' room, women/men,* etc.);

last resort; LATRINE, LAVATORY; LOO; *lounge.*

marble palace; member (or *thunder*) *mug* (see MEMBER); MISS WHITE; *Mrs. Jones; municipal relief station* (a public place, and see RELIEVE).

necessary house (or *place* or *stool,* and see NECESSARY); *no-mans-land* (for women only).

office (and *house of office*); *old soldiers' home*; OUTHOUSE.

peers/peeresses (British); *place; plumbing; poet's corner; porcelain bus* (or *god*), as in *bow to the porcelain god* or *drive the porcelain bus,* which are college English for vomiting (see UPCHUCK); *potty* (see WEE-WEE); *powder room* (see POWDER MY NOSE, I HAVE TO); *private office*; PRIVY.

REST ROOM; RETIRING ROOM; *retreat; Ruth.*

sanctuary; sanctum sanctorum; SMALL (or SMALLEST) ROOM; *smokehouse; Spice Islands* (an early nineteenth-century term for an outdoor privy); *statehouse*; STOOL.

tearoom; temple; THRONE (and *throne room*); *thunderbox.*

UTENSIL.

WALK; WASHROOM; WASTE-MANAGEMENT COMPARTMENT; WC; WHAT-YOU-MAY-CALL'EM *Widow Jones.*

YERTIZ.

tool. (1) the penis, (2) a weapon, usually (today) a gun. Both usages are old, both were originally Standard English, and both are now considered slang.

As a penis: When a crowd of people get into the palace yard toward the end of William Shakespeare's *Henry VIII* (1613), the porter wonders, "Have we some strange Indian with the great tool come to Court, the women so besiege us?" Then there are the instructions for a Japanese device for increasing a man's sexual prowess: "MORE BIG, OR RUBBER BAND. This may be used by men who have small tools in order to increase sexual pleasure which give unexplainable feeling to women" (from Shirley Green, *The Curious History of Contraception,* 1971).

"Tool" itself has been euphemized. For example, Byron used the term as a verb when challenging Douglas Kinnaird in a letter (10/26/1819): "Could any man have written it [*Don Juan*]—who has not lived in the world?—and tooled in a post-chaise? in a hackney coach? in a Gondola? against a wall? in a court carriage? in a vis à vis? on a table?—and under it?" But in Peter Quennell's *Byron: A Self-Portrait* (1950), the operative verb came out as "fooled."

The "tool" as "weapon" was originally a sword, which is what Chaucer meant in *The Nun's Priest's Tale* (ca. 1387–1400) when cataloging the virtues of a chivalric lover: "We allen desiren, if it myghte be/To han . . . no fool/Ne hym that is agast [afraid] of every tool." And in our own time, talking about pistols, the New York City Police Department's top firearms instructor explained: "We're using weapons less. We're teaching that the gun is designed as a defensive tool" (*New York Times,* 9/23/74). Developing the weapon-tool metaphor one step further was John R. Block, then Agriculture Secretary–designate, who retreated from an impolitic suggestion that food could be used as a "weapon" in United States foreign policy by saying, "Perhaps I should have said a tool for peace, an instrument for peace" ("Good Morning America," WABC-TV, 12/26/80). See also GUN, HENFIRE, INSTRUMENT, and PENIS.

top secret. A common governmental COVER-UP for that which is embarrassing or criminal. "Under our system, the American people would not tolerate censorship. Yet, we have high officials who want to protect themselves from embarrassment. So when a document arrives on their desk showing that they have mismanaged their agency, they stamp it TOP SECRET" (Jack Anderson, interview, *Book Review Digest,* 5/79). See also SENSITIVE and, for an example of a "TOP SECRET" plan that included admittedly illegal features, refer to SURREPTITIOUS ENTRY.

touch (off). To kill. From the diary of Sergeant Alvin York, the World War I hero: "There were thirty of them in continuous action, and all I could do was touch the Germans off as fast as I could. . . . In order to sight me or swing their machine guns on me, the Germans had to show their heads above the trench, and every time I saw a head I just touched it off. . . . Suddenly a German officer and five men jumped out of the trench and charged me with fixed bayonets. I changed to the old automatic and just touched them off, too. I touched off the sixth man first, then the fifth, then the fourth, then the third, and so on. I wanted them to keep coming" (Tom Skeyhill, ed., *Sergeant York, His Own Life Story and War Diary,* 1928).

The very oldest of the many meanings of "touch" involve a hit, stroke, or blow, and this may have been the original sense of the word. To "touch off" is to hit one's target exactly. See also the similarly understated HIT.

"Touch" has acquired other euphemistic meanings. For example, to say that "poor Louise is touched" or "touched in the head" is to say that she is slightly crazy—in effect, that her brains have been addled by a blow on the noggin. The generalized "touch" also has served as a euphemism for sexual contacts of different kinds, as in *to touch (oneself),* to masturbate; *to touch up,*

British slang for caressing or groping a woman, and the simple *touch,* for the act of sex, e.g., "This woman/Most wrongfully accused your substitute,/Who is as free from touch or soil with her/As she from one ungot [i.e., unbegotten]" (William Shakespeare, *Measure for Measure,* ca. 1604).

See also INTERCOURSE, MASTURBATION, and MENTAL.

toupee. A small wig or HAIRPIECE—the French (from *toupet,* a tuft of hair or forelock) helping to hide the baldness. Alexander Pope got only three out of four right when he wrote in *Art of Politicks* (1729):

Think we that modern words eternal are?
Toupet, and Tompion, Cosins, and Colmar
Hereafter will be called by some plain man
A Wig, a Watch, a Pair of Stays, a Fan.

As for those "stays," their functional equivalent today is the FOUNDATION GARMENT.

tourist. Second class—or worse; a face-saving euphemism for ticket buyers who cannot afford first class but are embarrassed to ask for second or third. "On cruises the QE2 is a one-class ship, but on trans-Atlantic crossings she has two classes—tourist and first" (*New York Times,* 12/4/77). This euphemism is by no means new. From 1895: "The *emigrant sleeping car* is now usually called a *tourist-car,* the latter being preferred by those who patronize them" (John C. Wait, *The Car-Builder's Dictionary*).

With so many carriers offering so many different plans, it is hard to be precise, but where "tourist" equals second class, the euphemism for third class usually is "coach." Another variation is "economy class," where "economy" is a euphemism for "cheap," and which may mean either second or third class in practice. Compounding confusion, the euphemism for "second class" becomes FIRST CLASS when "first class" itself is euphemized as DELUXE. If all this sounds like a plot to befuddle the public, that is probably because it is.

traffic expediter. A shipping clerk. Originally a religious term, similar to cleric or clergyman, "clerk" came to signify notarial and secretarial work during the Middle Ages when jobs of this sort were held by religious clerks, who were practically the only people who could read and write. The occupational designation was an honorable one then, since "clerk" was considered the equivalent of "scholar." Years of humble work have given the title humble connotations, however, with the result that modern clerks are glad to have new handles for themselves, such as *traffic expediter.* See also ACCESS CONTROLLER and ENGINEER.

traditional beverage. Beer. A note on campus life at the University of Richmond in Virginia: "Newspaper ads and signs announce availability of 'traditional beverage' because the word 'beer' is banned from the university publications. Students attribute these strictly enforced rules to the school's Southern Baptist backing" (*Yale Daily News* staff, *The Insider's Guide to the Colleges,* 1991). See also TEMPERANCE.

trail representative. A hired gun in the Old (ca. 1885) West. "A stray calf lost a lot of its appeal when you knew that all the big ranchers moving cattle were paying five or six hired guns, whom they called 'trail representatives' and everybody else called 'enforcers'" (Jane Kramer, *The Last Cowboy*, 1977). See also ENGINEER and REPRESENTATIVE.

tramp. A Hollywood euphemism of the 1930s and 1940s, either for a woman of low morals or a man who was a bum, a.k.a. *knight of the road*. In the first, feminine sense, "tramp" might connote either a cheap whore or a person of higher socio-economic status who gave out freebies. In the second, masculine sense, "tramp" was employed in order to avoid offending the British, who, when "bum" was mentioned, looked first to their POSTERIORS. It was for this reason that the title of Al Jolson's *Hallelujah, I'm a Bum* was changed to *Hallelujah, I'm a Tramp* when the picture was shown in England in 1938. (H. L. Mencken, *The American Language, Supplement I*, 1945).

Although bums spend a lot of time sitting down upon theirs, the vagrant "bum" and the anatomical "bum" do not seem to be connected linguistically. The vagrant "bum" probably is an abbreviation of "bummer," meaning "loafer" or "sponger," which was first recorded in 1855 (*A Dictionary of Americanisms*) and may ultimately come from the German *bummler*, an idler. The anatomical "bum," meanwhile, is a far older word, with the first example in *The Oxford English Dictionary* coming from 1387. Probably not a contraction of BOTTOM, as some have speculated, but of onomatopoetic origin, this "bum" may be related to similar-sounding words with the general meaning of "protuberance" or "swelling," such as "bumb," an old word for a pimple, and "bump." See also ARSE and PROSTITUTE.

transfer of population. Mass eviction and/or deportation. "Millions of peasants are robbed of their farms and sent trudging along roads with no more than they can carry: this is called *transfer of population* or *rectification of frontiers* (George Orwell, "Politics and the English Language," 1946). And speaking of the legacy of Rabbi Meir Kahane, founder of the Jewish Defense League, who helped change the terms of political debate in Israel after emigrating there in 1971: "The Israel he left behind was different. While many Israelis considered Rabbi Kahane an abhorrent demagogue . . . previously unthinkable ideas like the 'transfer' or removal of Arabs now had currency" (John Kifner, *New York Times*, 11/11/90). See also GENERATION.

transition, in. Out of work. "*In transition*: A many-headed euphemism, but in this case, read: unemployed. Usually reserved for executives, transitioners consider options and assess core competencies in the hope of being outplaced" (Hal Lancaster, *Wall Street Journal*, 10/18/94). See also AT LIBERTY and OUTPLACEMENT.

travel center. A truck stop, cleaned up as potential real-estate investment. "William Turchyn of E. F. Hutton Co. says partnerships investing in 'niche' properties, such as 'travel centers,' are also doing well. For those not fluent in partnership jargon, a travel center is otherwise known as a truck stop" (*Wall Street Journal*, 2/11/87). See also REALTOR.

triage. A soft word for hardhearted neglect. From the French *trier*, to pick or to cull (see CULL), the term began as a method for grading farm products, was later applied to people, and finally to entire nations.

As traditionally practiced, *triage* involves a division into thirds, according to quality. In the eighteenth and nineteenth centuries, for example, coffee beans were separated into three grades, with the lowest, composed of broken beans, being known as "triage coffee." It was during World War I that the French army (which also gave us PERSONNEL and SORTIE) popularized *triage* as a method for determining which wounded soldiers not to bother treating. As explained by John Keegan in *The Face of Battle* (1976):

> There remained, nevertheless, a brutal selectivity about military surgery which the practitioners did their best to hide from the patients but could not disguise from themselves. It was called "triage" . . . and [it] required surgeons, from the press of casualties flowing in during a battle, to send on those who could stand the journey and to choose, from the group remaining, which men were worth subjecting to serious surgery and which must be left to die; the greater the press of casualties, the larger the latter group.

Finally, in the widest, most modern sense, there is *triage* on the global scale, e.g.: "Triage—a nice clean jargon term for the rather dirty prospect of writing off whole nations who are beyond 'realistic help' and leaving them to suffer while we save the rest of the world from disaster" (John Gribbin, *Future Worlds,* ms, 1979).

See also BENIGN NEGLECT, EMERGENT, and NO MAYDAY, as well as the basic military CASUALTY.

trick. The term has many slang meanings (e.g., a crime, a jail sentence, a military enlistment), but its usual connotations today are sexual. Most commonly, a *trick* is a PROSTITUTE'S engagement, or DATE with a customer, or JOHN, or any of the sexual acts that may be performed in the course of such a transaction. Thus, describing operations in a Chicago whorehouse at the time of the First World War: "The girls explained to me that they got eighty cents a trick, one payment for each metal check—'turning a trick' was how they described one session with a john" (Mezz Mezzerow and Bernard Wolfe, *Really the Blues,* 1946). "Trick" may also refer to the customer—a *freak trick* if he demands unusual or UNNATURAL acts. The woman, meanwhile, may also use the word as a verb, e.g., "I tricked with him," or "I just tricked two johns from Nashville." She herself is sometimes known as a *trick babe,* and if she gets pregnant, the result may be a *trick baby* (once known as a whoreson or BASTARD). In extended use, among GAYS, the term also may refer to a casual sex partner or to an act of INTERCOURSE.

The various commercial senses date to at least the early twentieth century, as exemplied in *Bawdyhouse Blues,* a very old jazz song:

> Keep a-knockin' but you can't come in.
> I hear you knockin' but you can't come in.
> I got an all night trick agin,
> So keep a-knockin' but you can't come in.
>
> Keep a-knockin' but you can't come in.
> I'm busy grindin' so you can't come in.
> If you love me, you'll come back agin,
> Or come back tomorrow at half-past ten.

The basic "trick" metaphor is much older, of course. Shakespeare used it in

Measure for Measure (1604), when Claudio seeks to persuade his sister Isabella to save his life by SLEEPING WITH Angelo—a "momentary trick," in Claudio's words.

trouble/troublesome. Disaster/disastrous.

"Trouble" comes in an infinite variety of forms. Some persons have *trouble with the bottle,* in which case they are alcoholics; others *get into trouble,* in which case they probably have broken a law in some way; and still others *have a trouble* or *get in* (as opposed to *into*) *trouble,* in which case they are female-type PERSONS who have become pregnant without being married. For example, Joan Durbeyfield advised her errant daughter on no account to "say a word of your Bygone Trouble to him. . . . Many a woman—some of the Highest in the Land—have had a Trouble in their time; and why should you Trumpet yours when others don't Trumpet Theirs?" (Thomas Hardy, *Tess of the D'Urbervilles,* 1891).

"Trouble" also makes an excellent blanket for covering things up, e.g.: "A 'troubled child' may be anything from a bed-wetter to a junior grade Jack the Ripper" (Gary Jennings, *Personalities of Language,* 1965). In the plural, often as *the Troubles,* the term refers to any of the recurring periods of strife that have beset Ireland from the seventeenth through the twentieth centuries. Finally, in the *troublesome,* or disastrous, category, there was the tape recording of the conversation in which President Richard M. Nixon appeared to approve (see EXPLETIVE DELETED) the payment of hush money to E. Howard Hunt, Jr., the Watergate PLUMBER. As the president's former chief of staff reported: "Then he asked me to listen and take notes on the March 21, 1973, 'troublesome' confer-

ence with John Dean—and I ended up with a perjury charge" (H. R. Haldeman, with Joseph DiMona, *The Ends of Power,* 1978). See also PROBLEM.

TS. Tough shit; also euphemized as "tough situation." In the military during World War II, one of the standard retorts to a person whose never-ending complaints had become intolerable was "Fill out a TS slip and send it to the chaplain." Some chaplains went so far as to have TS slips printed and ready for use. See also BS.

tube steak. A frankfurter and, by analogy, a PENIS. "The food isn't bad which is mainly tube steaks (hot dogs)" (*Boston Globe,* 8/15/78). See also FILET MIGNON.

tummy a.k.a. **tum** and **tum-tum.** The belly; a nurseryism, especially beloved by manufacturers of elastic underwear, e.g.: "Hi— I'm Barbara Eden. In the blink of an eye, I made my tummy disappear" (pantyhose ad, WABC-TV, 10/6/79). Which is not to imply that only underwear-makers use it: "The hunchback . . . swiftly forced the hand across the panty sheen of her rounded tummy" (Maxwell Kenton, a.k.a. Terry Southern, *Candy,* 1965).

The strength of the desire to avoid "belly" is indicated by the euphemism's survival in the face of withering critical fire: "*Tummy* is simply disgusting when used by anyone over the age of four" (Bergen Evans and Cornelia Evans, *A Dictionary of Contemporary American Usage,* 1957). Or, as E. B. White advised: "Never call a stomach a tummy without good reason" (William Strunk, Jr., and E. B. White, *The Elements of Style,* 1959). See also ABDOMEN and INTESTINAL FORTITUDE.

tumor. Cancer. In principle: "Verbal disguise, or euphemism, is semantically self-protective. Unpleasant realities are mercifully beclouded—a *tumor* is more bearable than *cancer*" (Geoffrey Wagner, in Neil Postman, et al., eds., *Language in America*, 1969). And in practice, from an interview with a kidney specialist in Rochester, N.Y.: "You avoid words like 'cancer,'" the doctor said. "You use gentler words with the same meaning, like 'tumor'" (*New York Times*, 2/14/86). See also C, THE BIG.

turf accountant. A British gentleman's gentlemanly bookie; also called a *commission agent*. Even the basic "bookmaker" has a euphemistic quality to it since, as John Moore pointed out, "'making a book' seems politer than 'laying the odds'" (*You English Words*, 1961). See also SPECULATE.

turn. To become black; said of neighborhoods. "Although the problems of the city have touched most of the parkway only lightly, there is a distinct fear, especially among those who left racially changing areas in Borough Park and Brownsville, that the neighborhood will 'turn'" (*New York Times*, 1/20/74). Neighborhoods that are kept from *turning* may be described as HARMONIOUS.

tushie, tushy, tush. The ass. "He shakes his tushie with elegant languor" (*New York Post*, 7/23/74).

"Tushie" is a softened version of the Yiddish *tochis*, buttocks, itself anglicized variously as *tockes, tochos, tochus, tockis, tokis, tokus, tuchis,* and *tuckus*. Whatever the form, the meaning is the same. For example, consider the irate telegram from a writer to a magazine editor who had dropped his column but suggested a face-saving way for the columnist to bow out: "IF YOU WRITE THAT I HAVE GONE ON A SABBATICAL KNOWING THAT IT IS A LIE, I WILL FLOG YOUR TOKAS" (*[MORE]*, 12/76).

"Tushie/tochis, etc." have been further euphemized in the abbreviations TOT and TL. The first has been translated variously as *tochis afn tish, tochos oif'n tisch,* and *tookhus auf den tish*. The literal meaning in any case is "ass on the table," but the force of the expression amounts to "let's get down to brass tacks" or "put up or shut up." In business, a *TOT* deal is one that must be consummated in cash only. A couch, say, that is sold *TOT* has to be paid for right away. Or a *TOT* card game is one in which all losses must be paid immediately, with no credit allowed. *TL*, meanwhile, stands for *tochis lekker*, a Yiddish phrase delicately translated in *American Speech* (10/47) as "backside kisser." In turn, this has been extended into *TLer* and *TLing*.

"TL" is an example of an abbreviation whose meaning changes considerably depending on the age and ethnic extraction of the user. From one Jewish adult to another, it is, of course, a passably polite way of expressing an impolite thought. However, when one *goy* kid says to another, "I've got a TL for you," the initials stand for "trade last," by which the speaker means that he or she has a compliment to give (typically, one that originated with a third party), but that the TL user wants to hear something nice about himself or herself before passing it on. Finally, "TOT" should not be confused with another Jewish abbreviation, "MOT," which stands for "Member of Our Tribe," as in "He's an MOT," or "That's an MOT fraternity" (*American Speech*, 12/48).

See also ARSE and SCHMO.

TV. In personal ads, not "television," but "transvestite" or "transvestism": "YOUR personal fantasy is MY reality. . . . I specialize in: Bondage, Humiliation, . . . TV" (ad, *Screw*, 8/2/76). See also SM.

twin. Single, in bedding departments. From a shopping trip to Bloomingdale's in New York City: " 'So you're going beyond the twin, eh,' [the salesman] asked, scrutinizing me with interest. Even in the private world of mattresses, the word 'single' was taboo" (Susan Barron, *New York Times*, 6/6/85).

T-word. Tax. When President George Bush backed off from his oft-repeated campaign pledge, "Read my lips. No new taxes," he did so by releasing a statement on June 26, 1990, that conceded the need for "tax revenue increases."

"Discussing how the phrase was chosen, a White House official said, 'The idea was that it had to have the "T-word" in it, but it also had to be general enough that the actual decision on taxes could be left up to the budget negotiators' " (*New York Times*, 6/29/90). The hope was that the phraseology would give the president what budget director Richard G. Darman called "wiggle room," i.e., it would permit him to argue that "new tax revenues" might come from existing taxes in an expanding economy rather than from increases in established tax rates. This argument didn't cut any ice with the public, and Mr. Bush's concession to reality—he was caught between mounting deficits and the legal requirement to submit a balanced budget—became one of the main reasons for his loss to Bill Clinton in the election of 1992. Mr. Clinton then faced the same problem in much the same way. As noted in *The Wall Street Journal*: "But while the president can try to avoid the big T word, everyone knows that a government requirement to pay money is a tax" (11/10/93).

See also F-WORD and REVENUE ENHANCEMENT.

U

ugly. Ugliness, like beauty, is in the eye of the beholder, "ugly" being an old term (ca. 1900), apparently of Southern origin, for sexual intercourse, often in the phrase, *do the ugly.* "He was in [jail in Mississippi] for thirty days for throwing bricks at a woman at a church social because she wouldn't do ugly for forty cents" (*Atlantic Monthly,* 9/38). Variants, current among college-age people in a New York City suburb and, presumably, among younger and older people elsewhere, include *busting* (or *rubbing*) *uglies* and *to beat (someone) with an ugly stick* (personal communication, 8/15/90). A synonymous expression, used in the same suburban set is *doing the nasty* (said by my informant to reflect a Roman Catholic upbringing). The connection can't be documented but "ugly/nasty" look very much like spinoffs from *doing the naughty,* which dates from the 1800s as a reference to sexual intercourse. In turn, "naughty" (from "naught," a zero, something with no value), has a long sexual history, implying smuttiness or obscenity as far back as the sixteenth century. Variations on this theme included *naughty-man,* a whoremonger; *naughty-pack,* a whore, and *naughty-house,* a whorehouse, e.g., "This house, if it be not a bawd's house ... is a naughty house" (William Shakespeare, *Measure for Measure,* 1604). See also DEED, HOUSE, and INTERCOURSE.

unacceptable activities. Spying; the standard diplomatic excuse for kicking foreign diplomats out of one's country. "The [Irish] Foreign Ministry cited 'unacceptable activi-ties,' which is common diplomatic language for spying, when it announced the expulsions [of two Soviet diplomats and the wife of one of them]" (AP, 9/25/83). See also FRANK.

unaffiliated corporate restructurer. An independent raider, on the high authority of the chairman of the Federal Reserve Board: "[Alan] Greenspan calls a corporate raider an 'unaffiliated corporate restructurer' who strikes when he sees 'suboptimal asset allocation'" (*Wall Street Journal,* 2/17/89). See also SHAREHOLDER RIGHTS PLAN.

underachiever. A goof-off; educationese. "Nowadays we have a name for them: the kids with the high potential and the low grades. We call them 'under-achievers'" ("I. Ross," *Old Students Never Die,* 1962). See also ACHIEVE A DEFICIENCY.

underarm wetness. Sweat; a Madison Avenue creation and, actually, a double euphemism, the "underarm" standing for "armpit."

"Zirconium, added to some antiperspirants as an ultimate defense against—pardon the expression—underarm wetness, is suspected of causing serious lung damage" (*New Republic,* 8/29/75).

The problem of *underarm wetness* is an old one, of course. "Scent of gusset" was once the operative phrase, as in "Essence rare ... to repel, When Scent of Gousset does rebel" (Mary Evelyn, *Mundus Muliebris: Or the Ladies Dressing Room Unlock'd,* 1690). See also ANTIPERSPIRANT and PERSPIRE.

underdeveloped. Poor, backward, primitive; a second-order euphemism (for the sequence, see the third-order DEVELOPING).

"It is this concern for sensibilities that gave birth to a euphemism; for it set into motion the search for the softer word, the blunted explanation, the circumlocution aimed at mitigating the harshness of a conclusion, or an evaluation. Thus we . . . speak of 'underdeveloped' when we mean primitive . . . and of 'unaware' when we mean ignorant" (William F. Buckley, Jr., *Up from Liberalism,* 1968).

Underdeveloped lands are usually considered to be foreign ones. Occasionally, however, *underdeveloped* parts of the United States are recognized as such, e.g.: "It [the rubber-producing guayule bush] also promises to make federal research dollars flow into underdeveloped areas of the southwestern United States" (*Science,* 10/27/78). See also NATIVE, PRELITERATE, and UNDERPRIVILEGED.

underpinning. Legs, a.k.a. *underpinners,* from "pins" as slang for those LIMBS. "Do cigarette girls at work wear their dresses decollete at the bottom and show their underpinning?" (*New York Dramatic News,* 10/5/1895).

underprivileged. Poor, usually applied to individuals (especially African-Americans and Hispanics). "The university [of Washington] rejected the use of such categories as 'underprivileged' and 'disadvantaged' as being mere euphemisms for the racial classifications they were using openly" (*New York Times,* 4/12/74).

Popularized during the 1930s, when the Great Depression reduced practically everyone to poverty, "underprivileged" originally had a wider, whiter meaning than today. On occasion, though, it is employed in international contexts synonymously with UNDERDEVELOPED, e.g., "The ability to survive and even to function well with an inadequate diet can probably be attributed in part to people in underprivileged countries learning to eat certain items—including insects—considered unacceptable in richer countries" (René Dubos, *Critical Food Issues of the Eighties,* 1979). In an extended sense, "underprivileged" can even be used in fun: "My heart goes out to the underprivileged and that includes people who can't carry a tune and anyone who plays the tuba in public" (Judy Linscott, Brooklyn, N.Y., *Phoenix,* 12/7/78). See also DISADVANTAGED.

understudy. A musician in a feather bed, i.e., one who is hired only to satisfy a requirement that orchestras be of a certain size, regardless of whether all instruments are needed. "Understudy" naturally is the term the musicians use for themselves; to the people who have to hire them, they are "walkers" because the hardest part of their job is walking to the theater to get their pay.

undies. Women's underwear; the baby talk changes the frame of reference from adult to prepuberty, thereby desexualizing the subject. (PANTIES work much the same way.)

"Undies" seems to be a British invention of the the early twentieth century. *The Oxford English Dictionary*'s oldest example of "undies" comes from *Punch* (5/30/1906): "She'd blouses for Sundays, And marvelous 'undies' Concocted of ribbons and lace." Thus began a revolution in women's underwear that was largely completed by the time of World War I as the corset (euphemistically known as *stays*) was dropped and the BRASSIERE put on. *Chambers's Journal* (12/1918) retained the quotes around the term, indicating that it was still a fairly new one, but the business obviously was booming: "Manufacturing women's under-wear, or 'undies' as they are coyly called, is the greatest commercial industry here."

About the best that can be said for "undies" is that the term is not quite as gooey as another British word for the same thing, *neathies*—an abbreviation of "neathie-set." Other kinds of babyish clothes, worn by twentieth-century adult women next to their skins, include: *dainties, flimsies, frillies, fuzzy-wuzzies* (a.k.a. *woolies* for wintertime), *pretties, pretty-pretties, pullies, scanties, teddies* or *teddy bears* (a one-piece undergarment, combining CHEMISE and drawers, particularly popular in the twenties), *thesies-and-thosies,* and *under-bodies* (often abbreviated as *UBs,* as in "He walked in without knocking and saw me standing there in my UBs"). See also LINGERIE and UNMENTIONABLES.

undocumented person (or immigrant or worker). An illegal alien; one who has gained unauthorized entry into the United States. "Sometimes even euphemisms have euphemisms: *Wetbacks* (a derogation of Mexicans swimming the Rio Grande to slip into the United States) became *illegal aliens,* and are now referred to as *undocumented persons*" (William Safire, *New York Times Magazine,* 7/23/78). "'Illegal aliens' or 'undocumented immigrants.' Usage depends on whether you despise them or can muster up some memory of America's debt to the paperless" (A. M. Rosenthal, *New York Times,* 10/4/94). See also DOCUMENT and ILLEGAL.

undoubtedly. Unproved; an example of Reverse English, the word's literal meaning —"without doubt"—being bent 180 degress when writers use it to gloss over unverified statements, e.g., "They affirme undoubtedlie that the deveil plaieth Succubus to the man" (Reginald Scot, *The Discoverie of Witchcraft,* 1584). "Doubtless" often is employed in the same way and should also serve as a signal to the wary reader to begin doubting. See also VIRTUALLY.

unfortunate. A Victorian whore; a euphemistic shortening of the apparently older "unfortunate woman," a term that seems to have been devised by "fortunate" women. At least, Capt. Francis Grose defined "unfortunate women" as "Prostitutes; so termed by the compassionate and virtuous of their own sex" (*A Classical Dictionary of the Vulgar Tongue,* 1796). For more about the many words used in place of "whore," see PROSTITUTE.

unfortunate interruption/period. A war; specifically, World War II for those on the losing side. Thus, speaking of rabid Anglophiles in Hamburg, Germany: "It is not really surprising—considering the euphemistic genius of a people who can call their atomic-waste depots 'disposal parks'—that there are Hamburgers around now who refer to the Second World War as an 'unfortunate interruption' in an old relationship" (Jane Kramer, *New Yorker,* 3/20/78). On the other side of the globe, Emperor Akihito of Japan used the same turn of phrase during a visit to China when apologizing, sort of, for "an unfortunate period in which my country inflicted great suffering on the people of China" (*New York Times,* 10/24/92). See also LATE UNPLEASANTNESS.

unique replica. A more-or-less true copy or reproduction. The catalog for an exhibition of kachina dolls at the Institute for American

Indian Studies in Washington, Conn., stated that "unique replicas" of the ones on display could be purchased for $35 to $2,000 per. Probing further: "The institute's director, Albert Meloni, acknowledged that it had been difficult to find an appropriate term. The replica will be handmade by the same artist, and will vary somewhat from any other representation. But it will not be unique in the sense that the artist will then stop creating that kachina" (Woodbury, Conn., *Voices*, 2/24/93). See also AUTHENTIC REPRODUCTION.

unit. A bomb—and an uncanny, unofficial parallel to the terminology of official, government bomb-makers in Los Alamos, New Mexico.

Discussing the *modus operandi* of George Metesky, a seemingly gentle resident of Waterbury, Conn., who habitually rose early on weekday mornings, put on a business suit, and then, after his two sisters went off to their jobs, hopped into his Daimler and drove it eighty-odd feet to the family garage: "Once in the garage workshop he would change to overalls and build what he still calls his 'units.' He assembled their charges with gun powder taken from rifle bullets" (*New York Times*, 12/13/73). Metesky built an unknown number of units during the 1940s and 1950s, taking them by Daimler to New York City, then transferring to subway to spot them around town. Thirty-seven of his units went off, wounding a few people seriously but killing no one. He always gave advance warning and even halted operations during World War II out of "patriotism." Finally caught in 1957, he spent the next seventeen years in a STATE HOSPITAL. Mr. Metesky is best remembered by his sobriquet, "The Mad Bomber."

For the terminology of the sane citizens of Los Alamos, see DEVICE.

Universal Time. Greenwich Mean Time. *Universal Time* or, with all flags flying, *Coordinated Universal Time*, is reckoned from the same meridian as Greenwich Mean Time—so-called because the meridian runs through the London borough in which the Royal Observatory is located. The cosmic name is preferred by those who wish to demonstrate that their mental horizons are no longer bound by those of planet Earth, but it does seem a mite pretentious. One can't help wondering how often *UT* is used for synchronizing watches, or even cesium atomic clocks, by any *ET*s (Extra-Terrestrials) in the great Out There. It seems possible, too, that the *ET*s or, as they used to be known, the *BEM*s (Bug-Eyed Monsters), have a different idea of what constitutes an *MU* (Miss Universe). See also PERPETUAL CARE, WORLD-CLASS, and WORLD SERIES.

university. College. That the proliferation of *universities* on the American landscape diluted the term somewhat is revealed, albeit unintentionally, by the boast of a patriot of the 1870s: "There are two universities in England, four in France, ten in Prussia, and thirty-seven in Ohio" (from Arthur M. Schlesinger and Dixon Ryan Fox, eds., *A History of American Life*, 1927). The distinction between "college" and "university" began to be drawn more carefully after the founding of Johns Hopkins University in 1876. Still, some sixty years later, H. L. Mencken could note: "Euphemisms for things are almost as common in the United States as euphemisms for avocations. Dozens of forlorn little fresh-water colleges are called *universities*" (*The American Language*, 1936). See also CITY.

unlawful or **arbitrary deprivation of life.** Killing. The U.S. Department of State's annual report on the status of human rights around the world for 1983 included a section on "unlawful or arbitrary deprivation of life," where previously "killing" had been used. To give the department credit, "killing" continued to be employed in the text; it was the word's appearance in large type as a heading that caused the people in striped pants to blanche. "Unlawful, etc." has a FOP Index of 7.6. See also ABUSE OF AUTHORITY.

unmentionables. The ultimate euphemism, not merely softening the offending word but blotting it out altogether. Apparently a product of the early nineteenth century, "unmentionables" originally stood for breeches and trousers, e.g., "A blue coat . . . with a pair of blue 'unmentionables,' white fleecy stockings, and short black gaiters" (William Glascock, *Sailors and Saints; or Matrimonial Manoeuvres*, 1829). In our own century, now that it is permissible to refer publicly to men's outerwear, "unmentionables" has taken on new life as a euphemism for the underwear of children and women (a common coupling; see PANTIES and UNDIES). Because women wear so many different kinds of underclothes, it is sometimes necessary to be more precise, referring to their *lower unmentionables* and their *upper unmentionables* (see BRASSIERE). In speaking of children, the single word will do, e.g., "His little man-o'-war top and unmentionables were full of sand" (James Joyce, *Ulysses,* 1922).

"Unmentionables" is one of a long series of similar euphemisms for trousers and associated garments—not the oldest (that honor seems to go to INEXPRESSIBLES, ca. 1790), but the one that is showing the most staying power. Herewith, a list of "unmentionable's" mentionable synonyms: *indescribables, indispensables, ineffables, in-* (and *un-*) *explicables, inexpressibles, innominables, unhintables, unspeakables, untalkaboutables, unutterables,* and *unwhisperables.* It would be too much to hope that this listing is complete. In addition, there are the allied *don't-mention'ems* and *mustn't-mention'ems* (both women's underwear); *conveniences, etherials, nether continuations, nether habiliments,* and *netherlings* (all trousers); *limb shrouders* (trousers); *nether garments* (underwear as well as trousers); the marginally more specific *sit-in'ems, sit-down-upons,* and *sit-upons* (more trousers); *small clothes* (breeches); and *subtrousers* (underdrawers). Though some of these terms may have been introduced in fun, the original impulse and its many permutations are a tribute to the strength of the taboo against "leg," which is so strong that people don't even want to talk about the clothing that comes in contact with the lower EXTREMITY. See also LIMB, NETHER PARTS, and SIT-ME-DOWN-UPON.

unnatural. Homosexual—and a loaded word if there ever was one, the meaning depending entirely upon the proclivities of the user. For example, consider the parade of subjective terms in the following definition of "unnatural carnal copulation," offered in 1967 by the Louisiana Supreme Court. Opined the court: "This phrase simply means 'any and all carnal copulation or sexual joining and coition that is devious and abnormal because it is contrary to the natural traits and/or instincts intended by nature, and therefore does not conform to the order ordained by nature'" (from Jonathan Katz, *Gay American History,* 1976). Of course, it is impossible to tell from the court's definition just what all the shooting was about—a common symptom of euphemistic talk. In this case, the *unnatural* crime was "oral copulation" between two women (i.e., CUNNILINGUS). The women had been sentenced to thirty months in jail for what they did, and the state supreme court affirmed their convictions.

"Unnatural" has been used in this same, formless sense for many years. For example, from Katz's work one also learns that in 1636, the Reverend John Cotton (grandfather of Cotton Mather) wanted "unnatural filthiness" to be punishable by death in the Massachusetts Bay Colony. To a later generation, the fighting phrase was "unnatural familiarity." Here is how a committee of the Unitarian Church of Brewster, Mass., reported in 1866 on the actions of a man who was soon to win fame for his books about boys:

> That Horatio Alger, Jr., who has officiated as our Minister for about 15 months has recently been charged with gross immorality and a most heinous crime, a crime of no less magnitude than the abominable and revolting crime of unnatural familiarity with *boys*. . . . the committee sent for Alger and to him specified the charges and evidence of his guilt which he neither denied or attempted to extenuate but received it with apparent calmness of an old offender —and hastily left town on the very next train for parts unknown. (From Katz, *op. cit.*)

Of course, society's rather fuzzy definitions of what is "natural" and what isn't go back to the Bible, e.g., "Even their women did change the natural use into that which is against nature: And likewise also the men, leaving the natural use of the woman, burned in their lust one toward another" (Epistle of Paul, the Apostle, Romans 1:26–27). Society's heavy penalties for *unnatural* acts also are sanctioned by the Bible: "If a man also lie with mankind, as he lieth with a woman, both of them have committed an abomination: they shall surely be put to death; their blood *shall be* upon them" (Leviticus 20:13). See also GAY and LIE WITH.

unprintable. Anything that an editor thinks might offend the public—or his boss. For example, observing senatorial courtesy (with more punctillio than do the senators themselves): "'A pain in the unprintable', Senator Ted Stevens, Republican of Alaska, called him [Senator Howard Metzenbaum, D., Ohio]" (*New York Times*, 10/25/91). And in a more generalized sense, from an interview with the publisher of *The New Republic*: "'(Unprintable),' responds Mr. [Martin] Peretz" (*New York Times*, 4/27/92). See also ADJECTIVE/ADJECTIVAL and EXPLETIVE DELETED.

unthinkable. Unspeakable, usually with the implication that the *unthinkable* thought is unspeakable because it is immoral. Since anything the mind conceives is "thinkable," the grotesque "unthinkable" actually is an interior contradiction. If the term has any meaning at all, it is as a shorthand reference to thoughts of things that are so numerous or so nebulous that the mind is unable to grasp them fully. An old word, dating to at least the fifteenth century, it was popularized during the cold war era by Herman Kahn in *On Thermonuclear War* (1959) and *Thinking About the Unthinkable* (1962). Mr. Kahn, chief guru of the Hudson Institute (an *unthinkable* tank?), managed somehow to reach the *unthinkable* conclusion that thermonuclear war was tolerable ("people can and do rise to the occasion"). Fortunately, the people in charge of the bombs did not agree. See the opinions of John F. Kennedy in EXCHANGE and Robert S. McNamara in STRATEGIC.

untruth. A lie; one of many dodges used by careful speakers and writers for legal as well as diplomatic reasons, "lie" and "liar" being almost guaranteed to evoke libel suits. Thus, President Theodore Roosevelt spoke softly when confronted with the charge—such a rare one in American politics!—that he had agreed to trade the ambassadorship to France for campaign contributions: "A deliberate and willful untruth—by rights it should be characterized as a shorter and more ugly word" (commenting on a letter by Edward H. Harriman, written in 1904 but not published until April 2, 1907). Then there was the exceedingly fine distinction made by Bill Knapp, an aide to one of Geraldine Ferraro's opponents during a New York senatorial primary race: "I'm not calling her a liar at all. I'm saying she's not truthful" (New York *Daily News*, 9/1/92). See also WHITE LIE.

unusual occurrence. A riot. In Los Angeles, which has had more than its share of *unusual occurrences* in recent years, the police receive special "unusual occurrences training," a.k.a., riot control (National Public Radio, 3/9/93). See also CROWD MANAGEMENT.

upchuck. To puke or vomit. Back in the Roaring Twenties and Depressing Thirties, when college students swallowed large quantities of alcohol as well as goldfish, "puke" and "vomit" were considered to be coarse words, while "upchuck" was

smart. Not a lot has changed in the meantime. Synonymous expressions for the act have proliferated, among teenagers especially. This suggests that for all the public concern about substances that can be inhaled, sniffed, and so on, alcohol continues to be the most widely used drug among the people of high-school and college age. A sampling:

barf, blow (one's) cookies (or *doughnuts* or *lunch* or *groceries*)
bow to the porcelain altar (or *god*)
call (or *cry*) *Earl* (or *Hughie* or *Ruth*)
drive the porcelain bus
flash the hash
frab ("barf" backwards)
get sick
hug (or *worship*) *the throne* (or *porcelain goddess*)
liquid laugh (referring to the product as well as the act)
lose (one's) cookies (or *lunch*)
make love to the porcelain goddess
pray to the porcelain god
ralph (or *rolf*—both onomatopoetic, so to speak)
ride the porcelain bus
talk to Earl (or *Ralph*) *on* (or *into*) *the big white* (or *porcelain*) *telephone*
Technicolor yawn (both the product and the act)
toss (one's) cookies (or *groceries* or *lunch* or *tacos*)
woof (cookies)
worship the (porcelain) goddess (or *throne*)
york (more onomatapoeia)

See also MISS WHITE, MOTION DISCOMFORT, and STOMACHACHE.

urban contemporary. African-American. "By 1976 two formats were coming to dominate American music radio. One was called 'album-oriented rock' (AOR), aimed at white rock fans; the other was called 'urban contemporary,' aimed at black r&b and soul fans. . . . The very term 'urban contemporary' was designed to sell black music without calling it black" (Jefferson Morley, "Rap Music as American History," in Lawrence A. Stanley, ed., *Rap: The Lyrics,* 1992). See also BLACK and RACE.

urinate/urination. Learned Latin for "piss," popularized by physicians. "At a labor gathering in 1990, J. Bill Becker, president of the Arkansas AFL-CIO, issued a famous denunciation of the Governor [Bill Clinton] as a man who would 'pat you on the back' and then proceed to urinate on your leg" (*New York Times,* 9/28/92).

Compared to DEFECATE/DEFECATION, whose present meanings go back only to the nineteenth century, "urinate" and "urination" are relatively antique, having been employed in their modern senses at least since the sixteenth century, while doctors have been asking their patients to piss into glass vials called "urinals" since the thirteenth. Those who enjoy the sport of skin-diving may be interested to know that they were once known as "urinators," e.g.: "It is observed, that a barrell or cap . . . will not serve a Urinator or Diver for respiration" (Bishop John Wilkins, *Mathematicall Magick*

—or, *The Wonders That May Be Performed by Mechanicall Geometry,* 1648). See also PEE.

use up. To kill. "Zap that slope. Waste that gook. Use them up" (Josiah Bunting, *The Lionheads,* 1972). Characterized as "Modern; all Services" in *A Dictionary of Soldier Talk* (John R. Elting, et al., 1984), the expression had a previous incarnation. As Capt. Francis Grose defined it in *A Classical Dictionary of the Vulgar Tongue* (1796):

> USED UP. Killed: a military saying, originating from a message sent by the late General Guise, on the expedition at Carthagena, where he desired the commander in chief to order him some more grenadiers for those he had were all used up.

See also WASTE and ZAP.

utensil. A chamber pot, i.e., in full, "a chamber utensil." Thus, from Jonathan Swift's "Strephon and Chloe" (1731):

> The nymph . . .
> Steals out her hand, by nature led,
> And brings a vessel into bed;
> Fair utensil, as smooth and white
> As Chloe's skin, almost as bright.

See also CHAMBER and TOILET.

V

vagina. The most common Latin substitute for one of the most tabooed of the FOUR-LETTER WORDS, "cunt." "Vagina" means "sheath" in Latin (the Romans also referred to the PENIS as a *gladius,* or sword), and it has been in the English language for only three centuries or so. The oldest example of the term in *The Oxford English Dictionary* comes from 1682 (predating the first "penis" by two years). "Cunt," by contrast, is a legitimate (nonslang) word of the very oldest stock. It has cognates in Old Norse (*kunta*), Old Frisian (*kunte*), the Romance languages (such as the French *con*), and Latin (*cunnus,* from which CUNNILINGUS descends). It also has suspicious resemblances to *kuna* in Basque (a language that may stem from Europe's Stone Age, cave-dwelling inhabitants), to *qefen-t* in ancient Egyptian, and to *kuni,* meaning "wife" or "woman," in Nostratic, a hypothetical protolanguage spoken in the Middle East prior to 10,000 B.C. It probably is related to such innocent terms as, among others, "cunabula," a cradle or place where anything is nurtured at its beginning (and hence, also, to "incunabula"); to "cunicle," an obsolete word for an underground passage; to "coney," an old word for RABBIT, a critter that lives in "cunicular" passages or burrows; and to QUEEN.

The Romans extended the meaning of *cunnus* to include "whore," in much the same way that English-speakers have used "cunt" as a pejorative term for "woman" as well as for the anatomical part. As long ago as the first century B.C., Cicero held that *cunnus* should be avoided as obscene.

English-speakers have not always been as fastidious as the Romans—or as they themselves are today. The word shows up first in English in the names of people and places. Godwin Clawecuncte (1066), Simon Sitbithecunte (1167), and Gunoka Cuntles (1219) are among the surnames cited by James McDonald in *A Dictionary of Obscenity, Taboo and Euphemism* (1988). Gropecuntelane (with such variants as Grapecuntelane and Groppecuntelane) also was a common street name in medieval England (in London from ca. 1230), perhaps because that's where brothels were located or perhaps because they were dark, disreputable ways (Peter Fryer, *Mrs. Grundy,* 1963). The word also crept into literature. Geoffrey Chaucer used it unblushingly in his *Canterbury Tales* (ca. 1387–1400), though with a different spelling. As the lusty, much-married Wife of Bath put it in the Prologue to her tale:

> What eyleth yow to grucche thus and grone?
> Is it for ye wolde have my queynte allone?

As times became more refined, however, people came to regard the old word as vulgar and to shy away from it. Thus, street names were euphemized as Grape Lane, Gropelane, and so on, or replaced with entirely new ones. By Elizabethan times, the word could not be pronounced openly on the stage. People certainly continued using it, however, and William Shakespeare alluded to it a number of times. For example, he spelled out the "bad" word in *Twelfth Night* (1600–01), when the steward, Malvolio, upon picking up a letter, deciphers the handwriting (mistakenly, as it happens, the letter being forged) this way:

By my life, this is my lady's hand.
These be her very C's, her U's, and ['n]
her T's; and thus makes she her great P's.

This passage may well have worked at more than one level originally, since "cut" also is old slang for the female genitals, on a par with "gash," "slit," "slot." Shakespeare also punned upon the term in *Hamlet* (III:ii), with the prince's reference to "country [cunt-ree] matters" while resting his head in Ophelia's lap; in *Henry V* (III:iv), where the French princess Katharine learns that "gown," the English word for *la robe,* sounds very much like the French *con,* and in *Henry IV, Part II* (I:ii), where Falstaff berates a servant:

If thou takest leave, thou wert better
be hanged. You hunt counter. Hence!
Avaunt!

Play texts for students generally gloss "hunt counter" as meaning one who is hunting in the wrong direction, i.e., off the scent. Which may be so. But it is also a spoonerism, and it makes one suspect that Elizabethan boys must have regaled each other with such witticisms as: *Q:* "What is the difference between a goose and a snake?" *A:* "One is an asp in the grass." The modern analogue to Falstaff's "hunt counter" is: *Q:* "What is the difference between a women's track team and a group of pygmies?" *A:* "One is a bunch of cunning runts."

Shakespeare's allusions to the word represent virtually its final appearances in aboveground literature for the next 300 years. Dirty-minded boys might scrawl it on walls (see MONOSYLLABLE) and bawdy poets might employ it as in *The Royal Angler* or *Windsor,* a ditty on the subject of Charles II's Nell Gwyn, commonly though

perhaps mistakenly attributed to John Wilmot, second earl of Rochester (1647–80):

However weak and slender be the string
Bait it with Cunt, and it will hold a king.

Rochester's poems were not published in his lifetime, however. (The first edition was rushed to press surreptitiously just after he died.)

Society soon closed ranks even further. By the early eighteenth century, use of the word, previously regarded as a serious affront to public decorum when spoken, was deemed to be obscene in a legal, prosecutable sense when printed. An indictment against James Read for publishing *The Fifteen Plagues of a Maidenhead* was dismissed in 1708, but Edmund Curll was convicted in 1727—the first obscenity conviction in the English-speaking world—for reprinting *Venus in the Cloister, or the Nun in Her Smock,* a work that had first appeared in English more than forty years before, and without anyone taking (legal) offense.

As a result, authors began resorting to various typographical conventions to avoid the term while making their meaning clear. Laurence Sterne used asterisks ("My sister, I dare say, does not care to let a man come so near her ****") in *Tristram Shandy* (1759–67). Even Capt. Francis Grose, though his subject was slang, dared not print the word in full; he also employed asterisks, e.g., his definition of "biter," as "A wench whose **** is ready to bite her a – se; a lascivious, rampant wench" (*A Classical Dictionary of the Vulgar Tongue,* 1796). A similar fate befell Robert Burns: When his *Merrie Muses of Caledonia* (ca. 1790) finally was published (1911), his language was toned down for public consumption thusly:

> For ilka hair upon her c – – t,
> Was worth a royal ransom.

Capt. Sir Richard Francis Burton got away with "coynte" (and "futter") in his literal translation of the *Arabian Nights* (ten volumes, 1885, with supplemental volumes in 1886–88), but this appeared in a small edition (1,000 numbered sets) and was sold by subscription by the Kama-shastra Society of Benares. J. S. Farmer and W. E. Henley printed the entire word as it is actually spelled in the monumental *Slang and Its Analogues* (1890–1904) but this work's sale also was restricted to, as stated on the title pages of each of the seven volumes, "*SUSCRIBERS ONLY.*"

Eric Partridge, the great modern authority on slang, still was required to use dashes when annotating Grose in 1931, e.g.: "Among the soldiers in 1914–1918 the word was perhaps heard most often in some such phrase as 'you silly *or* great c – – –,' though its literal application was frequent." As late as 1959, Partridge noted in his etymological dictionary *Origins* that "c**t" was one of the two Standard English words (the other being "f**k") that could not be printed in full, unless in medical, official, or other learned papers, within the British Commonwealth.

The euphemistic asterisks and dashes might have been eliminated sooner if Sir James Murray, editor of *The Oxford English Dictionary*, had not had a failure of nerve when the C's were being prepared in 1888–93, "cunt" being one of the two (the other is "fuck," of course) most conspicuous omissions from the monumental, standard-setting *OED* (to which, curiously, other "vulgarisms," such as "cock," "prick," "twat," and even the "queynt" form of "cunt" were admitted).

As it was, the beginning of the word's return to public printability, if not respectability, can be dated to James Joyce's *Ulysses* (published in 1922 but banned from the United States until 1933), in which Leopold Bloom ruminates on, among other things, the geography of the Holy Land and the Dead Sea, or, as he thought of it, "the grey sunken cunt of the world." Of course, the taboo did not collapse because of this single breach. Even after the Second World War, which, like the First, helped loosen the restrictions on language, "cunt" (along with "prick") was excised from the manuscript of James Jones's *From Here to Eternity* (1951), though many a "fuck" and "shit" was allowed to stand (Edward Sagarin, *The Anatomy of Dirty Words*, 1962). Not until D. H. Lawrence's *Lady Chatterley's Lover* (1928) was finally cleared legally for publication in the United States (1959) and in England (1960) did it become entirely safe to print all the letters of all the words that schoolchildren know—and which the Wife of Bath used unblushingly nearly 600 years previously.

As a result of the long-standing ban on "cunt," a host of euphemisms and circumlocutions were created to fill the linguistic vacuum. Their number partly reflects the amount of gossiping that men do about sex, it being mainly the words of DWEM (Dead White European Males) that are preserved in literature. It also is a tribute to the strength of the underlying taboo. (Which has by no means gone by the boards; thus, illustrating the relative power of two highly charged words, *The New Yorker*, which had occasion to print "fucking" in a film review on May 1, 1995, delicately referred in the same article first to a word that rhymes with "blunt" and then to the "'c' word.").

Some 650 synonyms for the dread word

(about double the number for "prick") are included in the great *Slang and Its Analogues*. It seems unlikely that twentieth-century man, even with his febrile imagination, has been able to add many terms to this remarkable list. Herewith, a lightly annotated sampling of synonyms, grouped in three categories: the general, the physical, and the poetical:

1. General, more-or-less opaque references, some of which served for the PENIS, too: *article*; BUSINESS; *commodity* ("the private parts of a modest woman, and the public parts of a prostitute," Grose, *op. cit.*); GENITALS (from the Latin for "to beget"); IT (an omnibus term of many misuses); MONOSYLLABLE (the chief euphemism for most of the eighteenth and nineteenth centuries); NATURAL (another omnibus term); *novelty*; *piece*; PUDENDUM (literally "that of which one ought to be ashamed"); *quim* (seventeenth to twentieth centuries, and of uncertain origin: suggested sources include the Spanish *quemar*, to burn, and the Welsh *cwm*, valley or cleft); THING (yet another omnibus term, whose sexual possibilities were fully realized by Geoffrey Chaucer); *thingummy* (see THINGUMBOB); *toy*; *twat* (of obscure origin and sufficiently obscure meaning that Robert Browning, searching for words to lend an archaic mood to *Pippa Passes*, 1841, latched on to this one by mistake, thinking that it meant an article of clothing worn by, of all people, nuns: "The owls and bats, Cowls and twats, Monks and nuns, in a cloister's moods"); *what-do-you-call-it* (see WHAT-YOU-MAY-CALL'EM); and YOU-KNOW-WHAT.

2. Physical references, often generalized to the extent of including the adjacent pubic region: *aperture*; *basket* (also slang for the scrotum); *bearded clam; beaver; box* or *hot-box* ("He wears his honor in a box unseen," Shakespeare, *All's Well That Ends Well*, 1602–03); *bun* (see RABBIT); *bush; can; case; cauliflower* (Grose, *op. cit.*, explained the origin of the term this way: "A woman, who was giving evidence in a case wherein it was necessary to express those [private] parts, made use of the term cauliflower; for which the judge on the bench, a peevish old fellow, reproved her, saying she might as well call it an artichoke. Not so, my Lord, replied she; for an artichoke has a bottom, but a **** and a cauliflower have none"); *chamber* (see COME for a Shakespearean example); *circle; cleft; crack* (also a "whore"); *crinkum-crankum* (a variant of "crinkle-crankle," meaning "a winding way"); FANNY (an anatomical displacement); FIG (a metaphor that dates to classical times); *fish* (probably from "flesh," as in "fish and flesh," "flesh" also being old slang for the male as well as the female genitals); *fish pond; jelly roll* (see SWINGING); KEISTER (a container, also the anus); *monkey; motte* (a popular Victorian term, from the French word for "mound"); *muff* (from at least the seventeenth century, when the toast, "To the well wearing of your muff, mort," translated as "To the happy consummation of your marriage," a "mort" being any woman but also a PROSTITUTE); *nick; nock* (see KNOCK UP); *nooky* (perhaps from the "nook" that is a recess, also appearing as *nookie* or *nookey*, and also meaning COITION, a common disease on military posts

being *Lakanookie*); *notch*; *O*; *orifice*; *placket* (an extension of the term's literal meaning: a slit or pocket in a petticoat or dress); PRIVATE PARTS; PUSSY; *saddle* (see SADDLE BLOCK ANESTHESIA); *scut* (from "scut" meaning the tail of a rabbit or hare); *slit*; *slot*; *sluice*; *snatch* (perhaps from "snatch" in the sense of "snare" or "trap," but more likely from the "snatch" that is a quick grab or other act, as in, from Robert Burton's *The Anatomy of Melancholy*, of 1621: "They had rather go to the stewes, or haue now and then a snatch . . . then haue wiues of their owne"); TAIL (an extremely versatile term, used also for the PENIS and the ass, or ARSE, since the fourteenth century); THIGHS.

3. More-or-less poetical or picturesque references: *aphrodisiacal tennis court*; *bower of bliss*; *carnal trap*; *Carvel's ring* (from an old story, told in a poem by Matthew Prior, and summarized by Grose, *op. cit.*, in this way: "Hans Carvel, a jealous old doctor, being in bed with his wife, dreamed that the Devil gave him a ring, which, so long as he had it on his finger, would prevent his being made a cuckold: waking, he had got his finger the Lord knows where"); *centrique part*; *coffee house* ("To make a coffee-house of a woman's ****; to go in and out and spend nothing" Grose, *op. cit.*); *Cupid's alley* (less delicately, *cock alley* or *cock lane*); *delicate glutton*; *Eve's Custom House* ("where Adam made his first entry," Grose, *op. cit.*); *eye that weeps*; *furnace mouth*; *garden* (from Garden of Eden?); *green grocery*; *hat* ("because frequently felt," Grose, *op. cit.*); *honeypot*; *Lapland*; *living fountain*; *love's lane*; *love's paradise*; *most when most pleased*; *Mother of all Masons* (or *Saints* or *St. Patrick* or *Souls*);

pinochle ("He [a dolphin] rubs his penis along her pinochle," "Dolphins: Close Encounters," WNET-TV, 39/93); *poontang* (originally reserved for women of African descent, perhaps from *putain*, whore, by way of French-speaking New Orleans, and also used for INTERCOURSE generally, as in "It's good for the constitution to have a little poontang regularly"); *postern gate to the Elysian field*; *seminary*; *sensible part*; *temple of Venus*; *Venus's mark*; and, finally, *yum-yum*.

Which may seem like a lot but which is, really, only a sampling.

valet key. An anti-theft car key, allowing a parking attendant, a.k.a., valet, to drive the car but not to open the trunk.

variety meats. Organs or the parts of organs; the euphemistic generalization covers up such particulars as the kidneys, liver, and tongue. See also FILET MIGNON and SWEETBREAD.

venison. Deer meat; from the French (*venaison* is the modern form), and ultimately from the Latin *venari*, to hunt. *Venison* tastes much better than "deer," just as veal (from *veau*) is more palatable than the more-recognizable "calf." The term has been used in English at least since the thirteenth century. In keeping with the Latin root, "venison" originally was applied to the flesh of any animal killed in the chase—boar, hare, rabbit, as well as to deer. For more about Frenchifying the names of the animals we eat, see FILET MIGNON.

Venusian. Venereal. Reporting the results of Russian and American probes of Venus, even the best science writers produced such sentences as "An unexpectedly large amount of argon was discovered in the Venusian atmosphere," although the proper adjective for "Venus" is "Venereal." (Acceptable alternates include Venerean, Venerial, Venerian, and Venerien.) However, "Venereal" is so infected with sex that it seems certain "Venusian" will survive. A side-effect of VD: "Ruth Dunbar, educational editor of the Chicago *Sun-Times*, was known as Viola before she had to initial her news stories" (H. L. Mencken, *The American Language*, abr. and ed. by Raven I. McDavid, 1963). See also SOCIAL DISEASE.

velocity. Speed, with a FOP Index of 1.9, when applied to a baseball traveling from mound to plate. "The vocabulary of pitchers has improved. Once they would simply 'rear back and throw hard,' but now the big word is velocity, as if they were scientists testing rockets" (Dave Anderson, *New York Times*, 6/3/75).

verbalize. Talk, with a FOP Index of 2.75. The word originally meant "to talk verbosely," and its meaning has been changed by those who do.

vernacular. Low language; often ANGLO-SAXON. Thus, cleaning up the text of *The Strange Cult* (undated) by the pseudonymous George Clement: "I'm going to give you a wonderful [vernacular for coitus]. After that, if you're real nice, of course, I'm going to teach you [vernacular for fellatio]. Then I'm going to [vernacular for cunnilingus] till you [vernacular for orgasm], and after that we'll [vernacular for coitus] some more" (Eberhard and Phyllis Kronhausen, *Pornography and the Law*, 1959). See also ADJECTIVE/ADJECTIVAL. Except for "orgasm,"

which is handled under COME and O, the various Latinate terms have entries, too.

vertical insertion. A parachute drop. The invasion of Grenada, or, as it was termed by President Reagan, the "rescue mission," began with what White House and Pentagon briefers called a "predawn vertical insertion" (*New York Times*, 10/28/83). The *vertically inserted* troops were aided considerably by what are known, in Pentagonese, as AERODYNAMIC PERSONNEL DECELERATORS.

vertically challenged. Short. "The range of victims available 10 years ago—blacks, Chicanos, Indians, women, homosexuals—has now expanded to include every permutation of the halt, the blind and the short, or, to put it correctly, the vertically challenged" (*Time*, 2/3/92). It may be possible to laugh this bit of politically correct speech to death, and John Cleese has tried: "I enjoy working with people of diminished growth" ("Life of George," WNET-TV, 8/14/92). But politically correct speakers are notable for their lack of sense of humor, and the jury is still out. Also, there is the difficulty of telling where real life ends and parody begins, considering that medical doctors prefer to refer to dwarfism as "disproportionate short stature" (CNN, 9/10/91). See also LITTLE (or SMALL) PEOPLE and PHYSICALLY CHALLENGED.

Vertical Transportation Corps. For upgrading its elevator operators into a "Vertical Transportation Corps," Hahnemann Hospital in Philadelphia, Pa., received an honorable mention when the Committee on Public Doublespeak of the National Council of Teachers of English handed out its Doublespeak Awards for 1977. See also AIR SUPPORT, EGRESS, and ENGINEER.

vespasienne. A *pissoir,* or public urinal, in France. "My first request was to visit the *vespasienne*" (e. e. cummings, *The Enormous Room,* 1922). The euphemism honors the Roman emperor, Vespasian (A.D. 9–79), who not only taxed people to build public urinals but raised more money by selling the contents to launderers, who used urine for bleaching clothes. See also TOILET.

vice president. A middle-manager. "To be a vice president now is to have about as much pomp, prestige and power as a first lieutenant. A friend in a large advertising agency reports that its 1,000 employees include 150 ordinary vice presidents" (*New York Times,* 6/19/83). The same agency was said to have eleven *senior vice presidents,* plus another eleven *executive vice presidents.* And this is not just a Mad. Ave. phenomenon. Many large businesses boast multiple *chairmen, vice chairmen, presidents, chief operating officers,* and so on. Ironically, many of the people in these positions complain about the fat in the federal government, though it is blessed with only a single vice president. See also ENGINEER and EXECUTIVE.

vichyssoise. The French has a certain *je ne sais quoi* that is lacking from "cold potato soup," but during World War II the "vichy" left a bad taste in patriotic mouths. As the 1941 edition of *The Escoffier Cook Book* explained: "Vichyssoise, now called Créme Gauloise, is made by adding cream and chilling." Both names are misnomers in the sense that the dish is of domestic origin: It was devised by Louis Diat, chef at the old Ritz Carlton Hotel in New York City. See also LIBERTY CABBAGE.

Victory girl or **V-girl.** A woman with a fatal fondess for military uniforms, circa World War II; an amateur PROSTITUTE, a.k.a. *patriotute.* At the outset of the war, a "Victory girl" was a woman factory worker, but this meaning was dropped like a hot potato as the other caught on—another demonstration of the application of Gresham's Law to language. See also B-GIRL.

Vietnam era. Vietnam war, a.k.a. CONFLICT or INVOLVEMENT. The Department of Veterans Affairs listed 8,278,000 veterans of the "Vietnam era" as of July 1992 (*World Almanac and Book of Facts,* 1994). The department has to make do with "era" instead of "war" because the United States Congress never declared the war officially to be one. During this *era,* which lasted longer than any war in the nation's history, the United States suffered 210,291 CASUALTIES, nearly as many as the combined total of the Revolutionary War, the War of 1812, the Mexican War, the Spanish-American War, and the Korean War. Of course, the Korean War wasn't really a war either; see POLICE ACTION.

virtually. Not completely—a word with a built-in loophole of considerable size. "The McDonnell-Douglas Corporation said that the existing system was 'virtually foolproof' but that an extra design change was being made 'as a precautionary move'" (*New York Times,* 3/15/74). The "precautionary move" was the company's response to the apparent failure of the *virtually* foolproof system earlier that month, causing the crash of a Turkish Airlines DC-10 shortly after taking off from Paris en route to London (346 killed). See also UNDOUBTEDLY.

visually challenged. Partly blind, a.k.a., *partially sighted, sight* (or *vision*) *disadvantaged, visually handicapped,* and *visually* *impaired.* "Spunky [a lost cat] is visually challenged, with only one eye" (*Litchfield County,* Conn., *Times,* 6/3/94). "To be blind is simply to be *visually handicapped*" (Geoffrey Wagner, "The Language of Politics" in Neil Postman, et al., eds., *Language in America,* 1969). See also PHYSICALLY CHALLENGED.

vocalization. A scream, squeak, squeal, or some combination thereof. "Electric shocks were applied to the tails of mice, and if 'vocalization' did not occur after 5 minutes the animals were considered insensitive" (Louis Goldman, *When Doctors Disagree,* ms., 1976). Technically, the shock that causes *vocalization* is known as a STRESS-PRODUCING STIMULUS.

voluntary. Forced, required, involuntary. Thus, quoting a lawyer for a group seeking to increase integration in Connecticut schools: "The remedy of voluntary cooperation will simply not produce the necessary results. We believe in 'mandatory voluntary' cooperation" (John Brittain, in *Litchfield County,* Conn., *Times,* 5/5/89).

This is in the great tradition of American doubletalk, never better explained than by Theodore Roosevelt, in a speech attacking Woodrow Wilson's plan for "universal voluntary military training." This address is a landmark in the history of doubletalk, for in it Roosevelt popularized the phrase "weasel words" to describe ambiguous phraseology. In TR's words: "One of our defects as a nation is a tendency to use what has been called weasel words. When a weasel sucks eggs the meat is sucked out of the egg. If you use a weasel word after another there is nothing left of the other. You can have universal training, or you can have voluntary training, but when you use the word 'voluntary' to qual-

ify the word 'universal,' you are using a weasel word; it has sucked all the meaning out of 'universal.' The words flatly contradict one another" (speech, St. Louis, Mo., 5/31/16).

"Voluntary" also translates as "involuntary" when used to characterize national pay-price guidelines (as under President Jimmy Carter in 1978) and wage-price controls (under President Richard M. Nixon in 1971). In both instances, employees who failed to get the salary increases they expected found the *voluntary* aspect hard to appreciate. Employers, too, acted under restraints. Speaking of the 1971 controls, for example: "Voluntary compliance for the great bulk of business was the rule to be followed, with the threat of heavy fines for violations" (*The 1972 World Book*). In such cases, "voluntary"—referring to yet another contribution of TR to our political vocabulary—could be described as a lot of MUCK. And see also VOLUNTEER.

volunteer. In civilian life, "volunteer" usually is a relatively innocuous euphemism for "unpaid," as in "Matilda is doing volunteer work for the Red Cross." Principal exceptions occur in politics, where *volunteers* may be hired ("paid volunteer" is an oxymoron), as in Ross Perot's third-party run at the presidency in 1992, and in the case of students in some school districts who must perform *volunteer* community service in order to obtain diplomas —a form of servitude that is being tested in the courts.

In the military, sergeants "humorously" reverse the basic meaning of the word declaring, as they pick out men for various dirty details, "I want three volunteers for KP—you, you, and you." The same procedure seems to have been followed in the late 1940s and early 1950s when the Pentagon researched the effects of atomic bomb blasts on people, e.g., Operation Upshot-Knothole, which, according to military records, included "subjecting 12 human volunteers and 700 rabbits to the initial light flash from six atomic detonations to investigate its effect on the visual function of the human eyes and to determine burn injury processes in the dark-adapted rabbit eye" (*New York Times*, 10/12/94). It does not appear from military records that the experimenters bothered to obtain informed consent from the *volunteers.* In effect, they had about as much choice in the matter as the rabbits.

On a larger scale, but in the same manner, the Chinese sent an army of *volunteers* into Korea in 1950, e.g.: "Under the blue and white banner of the United Nations, the United States and, to a lesser extent, 15 other nations battled the North Koreans and later a force of 700,000 'volunteer' Chinese Communists for three years" (David Eggenberger, *A Dictionary of Battles*, 1967). See also POLICE ACTION and VOLUNTARY.

W

waitron. A desexed waiter or waitress. "Sandwiches are larger and reasonable. . . . The waitrons are efficient and friendly" (*Washington Post*, 11/11/83). The provenance of "waitron" is uncertain; it may be a blend of "neutron," suggestive of something neuter, with either "waiter" or "waitress." Variants include *wait, waitperson, waitri* (a plural form), and the simple *server*. "Experienced Wait Person Needed" (window sign, Mostly Magic, New York City, 8/13/92). See also PERSON.

walk. A nineteenth-century public toilet or rest room. "'Ladies' Walk, Gentlemen's Walk,' i.e., a privy. This absurd piece of squeamishness is common at hotels and at railroad-stations" (John Russell Bartlett, *Dictionary of Americanisms*, 1877). See also TOILET.

walking/walk out. To court, as in "Let's go walking," or "Let's walk out"; relics of the preindustrial, preautomobile age. In rural, nineteenth-century England, the usual progression for couples was from "speaking," to "walking out together," to "keeping company" (Françoise Barret-Ducrocq, *Love in the Time of Victoria*, 1991). See also NECK, PARK, or PET.

wanna go out? A WORKING GIRL'S way of asking a passerby if he wants to have some FUN (personal communication, frequently, Brooklyn, N.Y., 1970–80). In the nineteenth century, before inflation had reduced the value of a penny to almost nothing, the standard question of flower girls and news girls who were more interested in selling themselves than their wares was "Give me a penny, mister?" See also BED, DATE, and PROSTITUTE.

War Between the States, the. The Civil War, a.k.a. *War of Sections* and *War of Northern Aggression*."War Between the States, etc." legitimatize the great cause of States' Rights even in defeat. When a national politician adopts this terminology, it is a sure sign that he is courting the white, southern vote. The phrase may even be used out of force of habit, long after the national politician has removed himself from the possibility of ever running again for office, e.g.: "Well, what I, at root I had in mind I think was perhaps much better stated by Lincoln during the War Between the States" (Richard M. Nixon, interview with David Frost, 5/18/77). See also LATE UNPLEASANTNESS.

warrantless investigation. Illegal investigation; FBI-ese. In the words of the former head of the bureau's New York City office: "Mr. [J. Wallace] LaPrade's . . . assertion about what he described as 'warrantless investigations'—or cases in which the FBI allegedly broke into homes without search warrants and placed electronic eavesdropping devices without court approval —were made at a hastily called news conference" (*New York Times*, 4/14/78). See also BLACK BAG JOB and SURREPTITIOUS ENTRY.

wash. A preparation for tinting hair; a HAIR RINSE. "Mr. Thorne was a gentleman usually precise in his dress and prone to make the most of himself in an unpretending way. The gray hairs in his whiskers were eliminated perhaps once a month; those on his head were softened by a mixture which we will not call a dye—it was only a wash"

(Anthony Trollope, *Barchester Towers*, 1857). See also COLOR.

wash away. To kill. Talking about gangsters—trigger men, specifically—in Detroit in the 1920s: "The more guys they wash away, the more they get to feeling immortal or something" (Mezz Mezzerow and Bernard Wolfe, *Really the Blues*, 1946). See also HOSE (DOWN) and WET AFFAIR.

washlady/washerlady. Pre-Bendix niceties for "washwoman" and "washerwoman," e.g., "'Blanchisseuses,' what some folks here call 'washladies'" (Brooklyn, N.Y., *Standard Union*, 5/29/04) See also LADY.

washroom. An Americanism for "toilet," dating to the nineteenth century; the functional and euphemistic equivalent of BATHROOM and LAVATORY. The oldest "washroom" in *A Dictionary of Americanisms* comes from 1853: "Tabby came from the wash-room just then." Naturally, if anyone were to ask, Tabby would have said that she had been "washing her hands" in the *washroom*. Or, as Miss Cartwright told Julian English, after having had a couple of drinks: "I'd feel a thousand percent better if you'd let me wash my hands, my back teeth are floating" (John O'Hara, *Appointment in Samarra*, 1945). See also TOILET and POWDER MY NOSE, I HAVE TO.

waste. A euphemism, whether as a noun, in the form of bodily "waste," or as a verb, in the form of "to waste" a person—a true parallel in both senses to ELIMINATE. For example: "Dog waste is a blight" (*Park Slope*, Brooklyn, N.Y., *Civic News*, 6/78). If the *waste* is cleaned up in conformance with a canine *waste* law, it may be put into *waste management bags* (plastic trash bags) or *waste receptacles* (trash bins) for eventual processing in a *waste water treatment facility* (sewage disposal plant). See also BIOSOLIDS, DOG DIRT/DO/LITTER/WASTE, LANDFILL, and WASTE-MANAGEMENT COMPARTMENT.

The other, more obnoxious kind of "waste" seems to be a product of the VIETNAM ERA. As a byword for "kill," it began to penetrate the public consciousness about the time of the trial in 1971 of Lt. William L. Calley for his part in the murder three years before of some 300 to 500 civilian residents of the South Vietnamese village of My Lai: "Of course, the ultimate low in word—and soul—pollution was William Calley's account of 'wasting' (killing) civilians. It makes murder seem painless, like wasting unwanted food" (Grace Hechinger, *Wall Street Journal*, 10/27/71). See also RECONNAISSANCE IN FORCE.

"Waste" had other meanings before it obtained its lethal one, and the later meaning seems to be a compound of the earlier senses. For example, the only definition for the verb in Eugene Landy's *The Underground Dictionary* (1971) is "hit very hard and hurt (someone)." (See HIT in this regard.) Meanwhile, as an adjective, "wasted" was popular among drug users, meaning so loaded, wiped out, or zonked on a drug as to be nonfunctioning (i.e., "dead" to all appearances). The development of "waste" to mean "kill" may have been reinforced by the particular nature of the Vietnam war, which was perceived by many people at the time as an unusually wasteful one.

See also CASUALTY, EXPENDABLE, and USE UP.

waste-management compartment. A toilet in orbit. "[Capt. Alan L.] Bean glided into [Skylab's] bathroom. . . . The bathroom—or waste-management compartment as

NASA called it—was a small room about the size of a similar compartment on an airplane" (Henry S. F. Cooper, Jr., *A House in Space*, 1976). See also TOILET.

water cure. Water torture. "At the beginning of the new century, the systematic infliction of torture upon war prisoners, in what was politely termed the 'water cure,' by the American Army in the Philippines [helped] set the stage for the epoch we now confront, with its steadily augmenting horrors, from Buchenwald to Vietnam" (Lewis Mumford, *My Works and Days*, 1979).

There are several different kinds of water torture: The victim's head may be immersed in water until she or he is almost drowned, or water may be poured into a gauze bag in the throat, gradually forcing the gauze into the victim's stomach, or—much more sophisticated—water may be poured, ever so slowly, drop by drop by drop, on a particular spot on the victim's body. Still different was the *water cure*, used by Americans to interrogate Filipino nationalists (1899–1902). According to an account in the *New York Evening Post* (4/8/02), the victim was pinned to the ground, while up to five gallons of water were poured down his throat, making the body an "object frightful to contemplate." Since the prisoner, even if willing to talk, couldn't do so in this condition, the next step was to get the water out. This might be done by squeezing the victim or sometimes, as one young soldier told the *Post*, "We jump on them to get it out quick." After one or two doses of the *water cure*, the prisoner was either talking freely or dead. For more about this war, see CONCENTRATION CAMP.

watering hole or **place.** A jocularity for a bar or SALOON, an establishment whose stock consists principally of firewater, e.g.,

the Watering Hole Bar and Cafe in Lathrop Wells, Nev. See also HAPPY HOUR and HIGH.

water landing. Airline-ese for ditching, as in "Please use the exit over the wing in the event of a water landing." Marginally more specific was the FLIGHT ATTENDANT'S instructions on a Trump Shuttle flight from New York to Washington, D.C., about the use of life jackets "in the unlikely event that there would be a water emergency" (4/11/90).

The airline business is richer than most in euphemisms. See also BEREAVEMENT FARE, CUSHION FOR FLOTATION, DIRECT FLIGHT, EQUIPMENT, HARD LANDING, MOTION DISCOMFORT, NEAR MISS, NONROUTINE OPERATION, and SEAT BELT.

water sports or **golden showers.** Playing with urine; specifically, voiding it upon another person, who thereby obtains sexual gratification. "Truckdriver travels all 48 states. Would like to meet fem any age or race. Enjoy fr gr and all water sports" (*Ace*, ca. 1976). "Gladstone Cooley figured they were just Golden Shower Kids, and if they wanted to pay him fifty bucks an hour, he'd keep pissing in their pot of modeling clay" (Joseph Wambaugh, *The Glitter Dome*, 1981). See also MAKE WATER, MICTURATE/MICTURITION, and PEE.

WC. An English water closet or TOILET, sometimes further abbreviated as *W*. By whatever name, the expression seems so innocuous now that the mind boggles when remembering that it was NBC's editing out of "water closet" in 1960 from a joke by Jack Parr that caused one of television's greatest moments—the abrupt, on-camera resignation of Mr. Parr from the "Tonight" show. (He returned three weeks later, after which the earth began revolving again.)

"Water closets," as such, date to the mid-eighteenth century (1755, *OED*), but it was several generations before they became common. A seminal work appears to have been John Phair's, of 1814: *Observations on the Principles and Construction of Water Closets, Chimneys and Bell Hanging*—a combination that is not as odd as it seems, since bellhangers ran their wires along the perpendicular paths of *water closet* pipes. Still, nearly forty years later, the mere presence of a *water closet* could be cause for favorable comment. Thus, the anonymous author of *My Secret Life* (ca. 1890) had this to say of the appointments of a seaside lodging house which, interior evidence of his autobiography suggests, must have been built shortly before 1851: "The bedroom . . . was entered from the staircase-landing, as was the lodgers' water-closet, a convenience which few such houses had then." (A *WC* off a stairway landing often was known as a *halfway house*.) See also EARTH CLOSET and TOILET.

Wealthy One, the. Just as people have always been circumspect about speaking the names of their gods (see ADONAI), their devils (see DEVIL, THE), and other dread beings, real as well as supernatural (see GOOD PEOPLE, THE and GRANDFATHER), so they have been hesitant when referring to Death, or to the Angel of Death. In all instances, the underlying fear is that to speak the name will cause the being to appear. Thus, the ancient Greeks usually referred to Hades, lord of the underworld, as Pluto, "the Wealthy One" (hence also "plutocrat"). The euphemism alluded to the agricultural wealth that came from Hades's domain. Of course, the god of the underworld also was wealthy in souls, as suggested by another of his euphemistic names, Polydectes, "gatherer of many." Other aliases of Death include *The Arch Foe; The Destroying Angel; that fell sergeant* and *that grim ferryman* (both Shakespeare); *The Grim Reaper; The Pale Horseman* (or more poetically, *pale horse, pale rider*, from Revelation 6:8, "And I looked, and behold a pale horse: and his name that sat on him was Death"); *The Spoiler*; and *The Twin Brother of Sleep.*

weapon. In the battle of the sexes, the *weapon* is the PENIS. "And now, disengag'd from the shirt, I saw, with wonder and surprise, what? not the plaything of a boy, not the weapon of a man, but a maypole of so enormous a standard, that had proportions been observ'd, it must have belong'd to a young giant" (John Cleland, *Memoirs of a Woman of Pleasure*, 1749). The *woman* of the title is, of course, the famous Ms. Fanny Hill, who also observes that "generally speaking, it is in love as it is in war where the longest weapon carries it."

The *weapon* analogy is very old (the Romans referred to the penis as a *gladius*, or sword), and it is a key element in the complex of associations between sex, violence, and death. (See ACTION, DIE, DING, and GUN.) Cleland's work, meanwhile, is of additional interest for being not only the most famous of all dirty (a.k.a. ADULT) novels but also perhaps the most discreetly written. Not once does Ms. Hill sully her ruby lips—or the reader's eyes—with an ANGLO-SAXON WORD. For example, the *penis*, when not a "weapon" (or a "maypole"), parades in Cleland's work under a host of other names. It may be an AFFAIR, an *engine*, an INSTRUMENT, a MEMBER, a *machine*, an ORGAN, a *stake*, a *truncheon*, or even, most poetically, *love's true arrow*, but it is never, never, never a FOUR-LETTER WORD.

weekend. "Aer Lingus, the Irish airline, offers special airfares from New York to Dublin, but levies a 'weekend' surcharge of eleven dollars on Friday, Saturday, Sunday, and Monday" (*Quarterly Review of Doublespeak,* 8/82). See also SUMMER and WEEKLY.

weekly. "A reader received a notice to renew his expired subscription to *Capper's Weekly,* which is published twice a month" (*Quarterly Review of Doublespeak,* 10/86). See also SUMMER and WEEKEND.

wee-wee. Potty talk for urine, synonymous with PEE, and also, in the case of males, a euphemism for the responsible anatomical part. "Specimen of wee-wee . . . taking it to the hospital for a urinalysis" (Carson McCullers, *Reflections in a Golden Eye,* 1941).

Potty talk is the regressive language adopted by grown-ups who do not wish to use ADULT words for vital functions and organs. ("Potty" itself is something of a euphemism, being the "cute" diminutive of the "pot" in "chamber pot"; see CHAMBER.) When lapsing into potty talk, otherwise adult people announce that they are going to the *little boys' room* or *little girls' room.* When reaching their destination, they will do NUMBER ONE and/or TWO, or perhaps one or the other of the following: BM; *boom boom;* CACA; *cis cis* (or *sis sis*); DOO-DOO; PEE; PIDDLE; *poo-poo* (see DIDDLY-POO); POOP; or TINKLE.

welfare. Relief, alms, the dole; the "fare" does not allow one to live as "well" as it sounds. In general, "on welfare" equals "poor." Thus, in 1969, the U.S. Labor Department listed the criteria that had to be satisfied in order for a person to qualify as DISADVANTAGED, i.e., "A person is deemed poor if he is a member of a family that receives cash welfare payments (*The Official Associated Press Almanac,* 1973).

"Welfare," as we now know it, seems to have been invented around 1904 in Dayton, Ohio—about the same time that two citizens of that city, Wilbur and Orville Wright, were getting their act together. *Welfare* programs naturally led to *welfare* centers, child *welfare, welfare* administrators, and so forth. Today, however, the term seems to be on the way out, its "poor" connotations having caught up with it. For example, New York City's Welfare Department is now known as the Department of Social Services (it operates a string of *income maintenance* centers). By the same token, the city's old Bureau of Child Welfare is now the *Office of Direct Child Care Special Services* and Blackwell's Island, where the city prison used to be, was converted into *Welfare Island* and then *Roosevelt Island.* All this is just part of a national trend, evident on the federal as well as the local levels. Thus, the Department of Health, Education and Welfare emerged from a governmental reorganization in 1979 as the Department of Health and Human Services.

See also CORRECTIONAL FACILITY, HUMAN, and LOW-INCOME.

welfare meeting. A non-Muslim religious service in Saudi Arabia, where such meetings are officially banned. As Joseph Kraft reported in *The New Yorker* (10/20/75), an announcement at the American embassy of a forthcoming *welfare meeting* means that a religious service will be held. The person who conducts a *welfare meeting* of this sort is referred to as the *lecturer.* The faithful understand that when the *lecturer* is said to be available for *private interviews,* they will be able to make their confessions. During the Gulf war of 1991, Americans in Saudi

Arabia referred to Israel and Jerusalem as "Dixie" in order to avoid giving offense to their hosts. For yet another discreet evasion of Muslim law, see COMMISSION.

Welsh rarebit. Affected menu-ese for "Welsh rabbit." The "rabbit" form has been dated to 1725, the "rarebit" to 1785, well into the pre-Victorian period, when many of our greatest euphemisms were coming into flower. In either case, the name is a joke, the dish being a strictly meatless concoction (no rabbit, no rarebit) of melted cheese on toast or crackers.

Lacking sufficient meat for their tables, the Welsh managed to develop a taste for cheese, as noted in the eighteenth century by Capt. Francis Grose, in his definition of "Welch [sic] rabbit" or, as he also called it, "rare bit," i.e.: "The Welch are said to be so remarkably fond of cheese, that in cases of difficulty their midwives apply a piece of toasted cheese to the *janua vitae,* to attract and entice the young Taffy, who on smelling it makes most vigorous efforts to come forth" (*A Classical Dictionary of the Vulgar Tongue,* 1796). "Taffy," by the way, is a corruption of "David," patron saint of Wales. See also CAPE COD TURKEY, MINCEMEAT, and WHITE MEAT.

wet affair or **wet stuff.** A Russian intelligence operation in which blood is shed; especially, a political murder, *mokrye dela* as the Ruskies say. Thus, on the subject of the Komitet Gosurdarstvennoi Bezopasnosti (Committee for State Security): "Western analysts believe the KGB has abandoned its practice of 'wet affairs'—the Soviet euphemism for covert actions like assassinations" (*New York Times,* 6/2/75). The presumably obsolete expression parallels the American military "get wet,"

meaning to kill someone with a bayonet or knife (ca. VIETNAM ERA), and the underworld HOSE (DOWN) and WASH AWAY. See also ASSASSINATION.

whack (out). To kill; a *whack* being a severe blow, similar to a HIT. "It was probably the closest Pistone came to being unmasked and 'whacked' (killed) during the five years that he posed as Jewel Thief Donnie Brasco with the Bonanno and Columbo crime families" (*Time,* 1/18/88).

what. Shit. Quoting—more or less—Jackie Autry, executive vice president of the California Angels baseball team: "I'm perceived as a tightfisted banker who doesn't know what from Shinola" (*New York Times Magazine,* 9/18/94). Shinola is a brand of shoe polish. The expression probably is of military origin, dating to pre-1956, when the U.S. Army uniform, shoes included, was brown. See also DEFECATE/DEFECATION.

what-you-may-call'em. An omnibus term for anyone or anything a person forgets or, as a euphemism, prefers not to name; a modern (nineteenth–twentieth century) British equivalent of the American *whatchamacallit* and of the older *what-d'ye-call 'em* (or *call him, her, it,* or *um*). "'He has discovered gold under the sitting room hearth, a body under the what-you-may-call'em in the downstairs bathroom, and two wells'" (Josephine Tey, *The Singing Sands,* 1953). And going back into the pages of history: "Good evening, good Master What-ye-call-'t," which is how Touchstone delicately avoided saying "Jaques," because the name sounded like "jakes," an early form of TOILET (William Shakespeare, *As You Like It,* 1599–1600). See also ARSE, THINGUMBOB, and YOU-KNOW-WHAT.

white dielectric material. Pigeon shit—to a scientist who had to get rid of it in order to confirm one of the most remarkable astronomical discoveries of the modern era.

The *white dielectric material* became an issue in 1964 after two radio astronomers, Arnold A. Penzias and Robert W. Wilson, detected surprisingly strong radiation at the 7.35 centimeter wavelength. The radiation seemed to be of cosmic origin, but they had to check out their antenna at the Bell Telephone Laboratories site in Holmdel, N.J., just to be sure the noise was not coming from the apparatus itself. Unfortunately, a pair of pigeons had been living within the twenty-foot, horn-shaped antenna, and "in the course of their tenancy, the pigeons had coated the antenna throat with what Penzias delicately calls 'a white dielectric material,' and this material might at room temperature be a source of electrical noise" (Steven Weinberg, *The First Three Minutes*, 1977). Early in 1965, the antenna was cleaned out, but without substantially reducing the level of microwave radiation, which was soon identified as the background remnant of the primeval fireball ("The Big Bang") in which our universe apparently was created. In 1978, as deferred compensation for their struggles with the *white dielectric material,* Penzias and Wilson received Nobel Prizes.

See also DEFECATE/DEFECATION.

white lie. A lie; the addition of the extenuating "white" produces a FOP Index of 3.3. The distinction between regular lies and the supposedly small, harmless, perhaps even well-intentioned *white lies* reflects the ancient distinction between black (bad) magic and white (good) magic. People have been telling *white lies* for the past couple of centuries at the very least, with the first example of "white lie" in *The Oxford English Dictionary* coming from 1741. The essential nature of *white lies* also has long been recognized, e.g: "White lies always introduce others of a darker complexion" (William Paley, *The Principles of Moral and Political Philosophy*, 1785).

Naturally, people with forked tongues have found many ways not to use the words "lie" and "lying." See also CATEGORICAL INACCURACY, CREATIVE, ECONOMICAL WITH THE TRUTH, EMBROIDER THE TRUTH, ERRONEOUS REPORT, FABRICATION, FIB, FUNDAMENTAL TRUTH, HEAVENLY DECEPTION, INOPERATIVE, LESS THAN CANDID, MISSPEAK, MISSTATEMENT, NO RECALL OF, PREVARICATE, STORY, STRATEGIC MISREPRESENTATION, STRETCH THE TRUTH, TERMINOLOGICAL INEXACTITUTE, and WITHHOLD INFORMATION.

white meat. The breast of a fowl; a Victorian euphemism, so common today that its blushing origin has been largely forgotten. As a nineteenth-century Englishman noted of American table manners: "And some of them would scarcely hesitate to ask for the breast of a chicken, though almost all call it 'white meat,' in contradistinction to the 'dark meat,' as all ladies and gentlemen designate the legs of poultry" (Thomas C. Grattan, *Civilized America,* 1859). The English visitor may have felt especial need to translate the expression for his readers at home, who at that date would have interpreted "white meat" to mean a meatless dairy product such as milk or cheese (euphemistically comparable to WELSH RAREBIT). See also BOSOM, DRUMSTICK, LIMB, and PENGUIN.

whiz. To piss—one onomatapoetic term substituting for another. "I wish I was a gentleman/As full of wet as a watering-can/To whizz in the eye of a police-man" (D. H. Lawrence, *Pansies: Poems*, 1929).

"Must have been out taking a whiz or something" (Garry Trudeau, "Doonesbury," *Litchfield County,* Conn., *Times,* 1/15/93). See also PEE.

wildlife conservation park. See INTERNATIONAL WILDLIFE CONSERVATION PARK.

Wildlife Services. The name of the U.S. agency that controls wildlife, chiefly with posions and traps, was changed in 1993 from Animal Damage Control to Wildlife Services. See also SERVICE, INTERNAL REVENUE.

wild oats. An old metaphor for the indiscretions of youthful males, up to and including the sowing of the seeds that grow into bastards. "That wilfull and vnruly age, which lacketh rypeness and discretion, and (as wee saye) hath not sowed all theyr wyeld Oates" (Thomas Newton, *Lemnie's Touchstone of Complexions,* trans. 1565).

The *wild oat* is a tall grass with a long twisted awn. Probably similar to the wild ancestor of the cultivated oat, it frequently appears as a weed in cornfields. The metaphor alludes to the folly of sowing wild oats rather than good grain. See also LOVE CHILD.

wild thing. The act of sex; usually as *do the wild thing.* "When did you realize Santa Claus is as fake as Velveeta? . . . 'Maybe it was when I caught him and my mom doing the wild thing next to the presents'" (cartoon, *Red & Black,* University of Georgia student newspaper, 11/29/90). The expression was popularized by the refrain of Tone Lōc's rap hit, "Wild Thing" (1988). Though the song does not feature violence—the sex is all consensual—it also is the apparent source of "wilding," a violent rampage. This last term dawned on the public consciousness in April 1989, when teenage suspects in the rape and near-murder of a woman jogger in New York City's Central Park used it to describe their crime spree. See also INTERCOURSE.

with child. Pregnant—and an example of how great a difference a single letter can make, the phrase, "a woman with child," conjuring up an entirely different image than "a woman with a child." The expression is an old one, dating to ca. 1175 (*OED*). See also PREGNANT.

withdrawal. Retreat; sometimes further disguised as *phased withdrawal, strategic withdrawal,* or *tactical withdrawal.* Thus, the invasion of South Vietnamese troops into Laos in 1971, which began euphemistically as an INCURSION, ended euphemistically as a *withdrawal.* "It was not until some of the commanders on the ground threatened to take the troops out and the retreat had already begun that the order for withdrawal was formally given" (Frances FitzGerald, *Fire in the Lake,* 1972). See also STRATEGIC MOVEMENT TO THE REAR.

withhold information. To mislead; to be ECONOMICAL WITH THE TRUTH or LESS THAN CANDID; in effect, to lie. Thus, Adm. John Poindexter claimed during the Iran-Contra hearings in 1987 that it was not "fair to say that I have misinformed congress or other cabinet officers. I haven't testified to that. I've testified that I withheld information from congress." See also WHITE LIE and, for one senator's response to the admiral's hairsplitting, COVERT ACTION.

woman. A common circumlocution for "girl," whose pejorative connotations have been so greatly magnified by advocates of

Women's Liberation that it has become very risky to utter the word at all. The objections to "girl" are various, revolving around its secondary, formerly euphemistic meanings (servant, mistress, whore), but in general are much the same as those of liberated men (and women) to the contemptuous, demeaning, also formerly euphemistic BOY. As a result, it is virtually impossible to conceive of the Gibson Girl being reincarnated today, of young working women being referred to as bachelor girls, of women athletes competing in a new version of the All-American Girls Professional Baseball League (as they did from 1943 to 1954), or—another measure of how quickly the language has changed—anyone now daring to release a movie called *Les Girls,* a delightfully innocent film of 1957. Even the *Cosmopolitan* Girl, widely displayed in ads since Helen Gurley Brown's first issue as editor-in-chief in May 1965, may have her days numbered. Though she still appears in newspaper ads, *Cosmo* began describing itself in January 1993 in publications that are read by advertisers and others in the magazine trade as "the largest selling young women's magazine in the world."

"Woman" itself has a curious history, which may be of some consolation to female readers, since it shows that they are not, linguistically at least, mere derivatives of the other sex. Superficial appearance to the contrary, "woman" does not come from "man," but from the Old English "wīf-mann," where "wīf" meant "female" and "mann" meant a human being of either sex. As late as 1752, the philosopher David Hume could use "man" in the original sense, when contending that "There is in all men, both male and female, a desire and power of generation more active than is ever universally exerted." What happened as the language evolved, of course, was that males gradually arrogated the generic "mann" to themselves, while the old word for female, "wīf," was diminished into "wife," i.e., man's appendage, a.k.a. *the little woman, the old woman,* and *my woman.* Today, some men still insist that they do not intend to imply that their sex is superior when they use "man" in such constructions as "The proper study of mankind is Man" (Pope) or "Man is a tool-making animal" (credited to Ben Franklin by James Boswell), but they are fighting the tide of our time.

The word "woman" has had its share of ups and downs. In the first part of the nineteenth century, it was considered entirely too common for polite conversation; the preferred terms then were FEMALE and LADY, e.g.: "A female negro is called 'a wench,' or a 'woman'; and it is this, perhaps, which makes the term 'woman' so offensive to American ears, when applied to white females, who must all be called 'ladies'" (James A. Buckingham, *The Slave States of America,* 1842). Aside from slaves and SERVANTS, "women" of this era were most likely encountered in the form of FALLEN WOMEN or as the lower-class people served by such institutions as Philadelphia's Lying-In Charity for Attending Indigent Women in Their Homes. "Female" gradually began to acquire some of the unsavory connotations of "woman," however, while "lady," which always seemed a bit British to Americans, also demonstrated a lack of staying power. As early as 1838, James Fenimore Cooper plumped firmly for "woman" instead of "lady" in *The American Democrat* (see SABBATH for details), and in 1845, that freethinking person Margaret Fuller published *Woman in the Nineteenth Century,* without being ostracized for her choice of words. Other radicals also favored "woman," e.g., the crusaders who founded the National Woman Suffrage Association and the American Woman Suffrage Association in 1869, followed by the Woman's Christian Temperance Union in 1874. As their causes gained respectability, so did their choice of words. By the start of the next century, the *Times* of London could report (10/18/08): "The writer is a 'newspaper woman'—which is, she tells us, 'the preferred American substitute for the more polite English term "lady journalist."'"

As the twentieth century closes, "woman" continues to be the term of choice, the only threats to it coming from the more ardent proponents of feminism, or *womanism* as it is sometimes called, who would get rid of any hint of the hateful "man" by changing the spelling to "womyn" (used both as a singular and plural) and "wimmin" (plural). Both terms are making it into dictionaries, but may never be adopted widely because they are so highly charged politically. "Herstory is an excellent word in many contexts pointing out with wit and elegance that most history is precisely the story of men's lives, while wimmin might be universally applauded as a clever piece of spelling reform, had it not become associated with the unpopular 'extremism' of the women's movement" (Deborah Cameron, *Feminism and Linguistic Theory*, 1985). See also HERSTORY, HUMAN/HUMANKIND, and PERSON.

wonderful personality. "Brunnhilde has a wonderful personality" is a conventional way of saying "Brunnhilde is not good looking," i.e., she is, at best, homely.

wood colt (or woods colt). A bastard, the comparison being to a horse of unknown

paternity. "He raved, swore, called the boy a wood's colt and his instrument a thump keg" (*Saturday Evening Post*, 6/16/49). Similar rural roundabouts for illegitimacy include *bush colt, catch* (or *ketch*) *colt, grass colt, oldfield colt, stray colt,* and *wild colt.* See also LOVE CHILD.

wood up. To consume alcohol; a euphemism of the steamboat age, when stops for taking on firewood became occasions for stretching the legs and partaking REFRESHMENT. "[He] made a straight bend for Sander's 'Grocery,' and began to 'wood up'" (Jonathan F. Kelly, *The Humors of Falconbridge*, ca. 1856). See also HAPPY HOUR and HIGH.

word from our sponsor, and now a. A standard lead-in to what inevitably proves to be more than a single word, i.e., an advertisement or MESSAGE.

working girl. A whore, especially a STREETWALKER, as distinguished from a higher-class CALL GIRL or COURTESAN. "They call themselves 'working girls.' . . . Their work is a 'business,' or even . . . a 'social service.' . . . By the prostitute's code, prostitution is moral . . . 'what's immoral is giving it away free, sleeping around with anyone'" (*New York Times*, 8/9/71). See also, in the order just mentioned, BUSINESS, SERVICE, IT, and SLEEP WITH.

working to rule. A slowdown on the job; a British JOB ACTION. "'Working to rule' is what air-controllers do when they are said in the press to be 'on strike'" (*New York Review of Books*, 2/22/79). Production drops whenever employees begin *working to rule* because the rules that have been agreed upon by union and management negotiators rarely reflect the realities of the workplace. *Working to rule* is but one aspect of a general rebellion by bored and discontented employees against the nature of much of modern work. Other aspects have been labeled "voluntary inefficiency," "efficiency resistance," and "sabotage."

world-class. First class, more or less. Years ago, the claim to international quality may have had some validity, e.g., "Such is the magnetism of world class heavyweight boxers!" (*Sport,* 9/22–28/50). The term has been thoroughly debased through overuse, however, as noted in a communication to the Yale alumni magazine: "Last week, on my way home from work, I passed a new 'world-class' shopping mall, a 'world-class' linen outlet, and a 'world-class' ice cream parlor. Imagine my surprise on arriving home and reading your article 'How Fares Teaching?' to learn that Yale now requires 'world-class' scholars as senior faculty members. Please, spare us!" (Angus, K. Gillespie, '64, *Yale,* 4/88). See also FIRST CLASS, UNIVERSAL TIME, and WORLD SERIES.

World Series. The pennant winners in the American and National baseball leagues have met every year since 1903 (except for the strike year of 1994) in a "World Series" to determine the "World" championship of baseball. For most of this time, "World" translated as "United States," but in 1969, the Montreal Expos took the field, and the meaning of "World" was enlarged to "United States and Canada." It would be fitting if the moment for starting the *World Series* each year were figured in UNIVERSAL TIME.

X, Y, Z

X. The symbol for a kiss, as on the flap of an envelope, "X," or sometimes, "XXXXX," to demonstrate especial ardor. This use of *X* has been dated to 1763 (*OED*) and is probably much older.

Yah! Yah! Kill! Kill! To the members of the silent generation of the 1950s, who couldn't imagine feeling strongly enough about anything to actually fight for it, one of the more grotesque bits of basic training in the army came during bayonet instruction class when they were required to yell, just as loudly as they could, "Kill! Kill!" with each mock thrust of their weapons. Someone's mother must have complained to her congressperson because the official yell was changed during the VIETNAM ERA to "Yah! Yah!" Unofficial report even has it that the army wanted to dispense with bayonets altogether back when the M14 NATO-round rifle was being designed. It was the marines who insisted that bayonets be kept, and they were. The newer M16 takes them, too. *Yah! Yah!*

See also HIT.

yard. The penis, and not necessarily just a case of wishful thinking, since "yard" meant "stick," "staff," or "rod," before the equivalency with "three feet" or "thirty-six inches" was established. The use of "yard" for "penis" began at least as early as the fourteenth century and persisted into the nineteenth. William Shakespeare, in about the middle of this period, knew the euphemism and punned upon it in *Love's Labor's Lost* (1593):

PRINCESS OF FRANCE: Speak, brave Hector. We are much delighted.
DON ADRIANO DE ARMADO: I do adore thy sweet Grace's slipper.
BOYET [*Aside to Dumain*]: Loves her by the foot.
DUMAIN [*Aside to Boyet*]: He may not by the yard.

See also PENIS.

yentz. A low word in Yiddish, comparable to "fuck," in the sense of swindling or deceiving as well as copulating, "yentz" may be employed more freely in English contexts than Yiddish ones. "The faintness one characteristically experiences on discovering that he has been yentzed" (S. J. Perelman, *Holiday*, 3/69). "Yentz" is of additional interest for having arisen as a euphemism. It comes from the German *jenes*, meaning "that (thing)" or "the other (thing)." It is only natural that Jews should glom on to the German term because, as Leo Rosten points out, "Hebrew contains no words for the sex organs; the male member is called 'that organ' (*ever* or *gid*); the female receptacle is called 'that place' (*ossu mokum*)" (*The Joys of Yiddish*, 1968). See also INTERCOURSE.

yertiz. A toilet. Herewith, a recollection of an evening in a pub in Monmouth, on the border of Wales and England, that will benefit any readers who have occasion to travel in that vicinity: "Above an otherwise anonymous and blank door was inscribed . . . the single word YERTIZ. Only an evening's drinking revealed the true nastiness of this apparent nonsense: the word, in a phonetic reproduction of West Country speech (what actors call 'Mummerset'), means 'Here it is.' It was left to the bursting drinker to appreciate that 'it' was the pub urinal" (Jonathon Green, letter, 6/23/83). See also TOILET.

you know. A meaningless expression, traditionally associated with drug addicts, teenagers, and other vacant-minded types, e.g., "I was going down the street, you know, when I saw these two girls, you know." Even usually precise speakers have been known to suffer from the "you-know" disease. Critiquing his performance in an interview with Walter Cronkite, one of the more effective public speakers of recent times, John W. Dean III, explained the cause of the disease and the means of curing it:

"Too many 'you knows.'" These came from starting to answer before I had thought out what I was going to say. "You knows" are sound fillers. Don't answer a question until you know the answer you're prepared to give. (*Blind Ambition*, 1976)

See also AT THIS/THAT POINT IN TIME.

you-know-what. A general-purpose euphemism for anything that the writer or speaker prefers not to articulate, assuming that the audience will somehow figure out what is meant. "Mr. [Jack] Valenti recalled at an inaugural party this week that President [George] Bush laughed his head off at the off-color scene in a delicatessen in [*When Harry Met Sally*] where Meg Ryan simulates a you-know-what [orgasm], as Mr. Bush might say" (*New York Times*, 1/23/93).

Even the most distinguished semanticists have leaned on this construction. Thus, during the course of a United States Senate committee hearing on June 14, 1978, on the subject of teenage pregnancy, Sen. S.

I. Hawakawa (R., Cal.), whose nonpolitical works included a basic text, *Language in Thought and Action*, spoke with unaccustomed imprecision when he observed (more than once—he apparently liked the phrase) that "flirtation leads to you-know-what." As a euphemistic catchall, "you-know-what" compares favorably with the British WHAT-YOU-MAY-CALL'EM.

young. Middle-aged; a journalistic euphemism for *young* people in the public eye. "Anybody on the White House staff who would not be embarrassed to take an intelligence test is commonly described as 'brilliant.' Anyone under the age of 49 is 'young'" (Russell Baker, *New York Times*, 1/16/72). See also LATENCY PERIOD and MATURE.

yours truly. I—with a fine FOP Index of 13.0. "Yours truly, sir, has an eye for a fine woman and a fine horse" (Wilkie Collins, *Armadale*, 1866). Americans of the tonier sort also use the expression: "'Wish he'd stuck to [Skull and] Bones,' said Schley. 'Yours truly would feel more hopeful'" (Owen Johnson, *Stover at Yale*, 1931).

youth-oriented merchandise. Drug-taking paraphernalia, e.g., coke spoons and hash pipes, as in "Some publications specialize in ads for youth-oriented merchandise."

zap. To shoot, especially to hit and kill, with many secondary meanings, e.g. to deliver a sharp blow and, by extension, a severe criticism; to engage in sexual intercourse, whence *zap in,* an orgy (and another instance of same word serving for violence and sex); to kill a TV commercial on a recorded program by fast-forwarding through it; to cook something quickly in a microwave oven.

The oldest, lethal sense appears to have arisen in the underworld in the 1930s. It was not used widely, however, until the Vietnam war, when people were *zapped* with guns, flamethrowers, and other weapons, e.g., "They threw three grenades into your old location and zapped two men" (Frederick Downs, *The Killing Zone: My Life in the Vietnam War,* 1978). Men in unconventional warfare units also *zapped* the enemy with *zappers,* i.e., spring-steel billy clubs.

The newest, electronic uses (from the 1980s) bring the word practically full circle, the basic, onomatapoetic "zap" apparently having been coined by Philip Francis Nowlan, creator of Buck Rogers (b. 1929), as a means of expressing the sound of the comic strip star's gun for paralyzing opponents. See also HIT.

zephyr. Cancer. "As a result of several statistical surveys, the idea has arisen that there is a causal relation between zephyr and tobacco smoking, particularly cigarette smoking" (internal report, British-American Tobacco, 3/1/57, in *New York Times,* 6/16/94). See also C, THE BIG.

Zionist. An anti-Semite's euphemism for a Jew. "The Soviet Union . . . never attacks Jews, just Zionists. But, Jews over the millennia have come to know the anti-Semite without regard to the euphemisms he employs" (Edward I. Koch, letter to the *New York Times,* 1/14/74). By the same token, Muslims who prefer not to acknowledge Israel's existence refer to the Jewish state as "the Zionist entity." See also HEBREW.

zounds. The euphemistic abbreviation of "by God's wounds," circa sixteenth to nineteenth centuries. (See ODDS BODKINS for a similarly constructed phrase.) "Zounds" provides a heartfelt ending to this book, thanks to William Shakespeare's *The Life and Death of King John* (1590–91?):

Zounds! I was never so bethumped with words.